W9-BKX-318

HD
1523
.C6
1975x

Coulton, George Gordon,
1858-1947

Medieval village,manor, and
monastery

DATE DUE			

MEDIEVAL VILLAGE, MANOR, AND MONASTERY

MEDIEVAL VILLAGE, MANOR, AND MONASTERY
BY G. G. COULTON

GLOUCESTER, MASS.

PETER SMITH

1975

TO THE MEMORY OF
C. J. V.   (1897)
H. R.   (1924)
J. E. McT. (1925)

Reprinted, 1975, by Permission of
Harper and Row Publishers

ISBN: 0-8446-1910-8

AUTHOR'S PREFACE

THE substance of the present volume was delivered as a course of lectures at the invitation of the University College of Wales, Aberystwyth; and my first word must be one of grateful recognition for this privilege, and for the generous welcome which I there received.

The book itself has grown out of an original plan of three or four introductory chapters for the second volume of *Five Centuries of Religion*. It is impossible fully to understand St Francis without measuring the extent to which his gospel was a revolt against the capitalism of the older Orders. And, apart from this, we can never estimate the religion of any age or society without observing its attitude towards the poor. But this observation must be twofold; rich and poor react upon each other; to understand the monk as landlord, we must realize something of peasant life in general; and thus my preliminary sketch has grown to a size which demands separate publication. Yet it remains, in substance, an introductory essay, designed to break ground in this field and to redress an unequal balance in medieval historiography. Sooner or later, we must outgrow what may almost be called the present monopoly of constitutional theory and social theory; sooner or later, we must struggle to discover not only what men were organized to do six centuries ago, and not only what the academic publicists of that age prescribed for them to do, but what they actually did and suffered; and, by the way, what they themselves actually thought of the civil and ecclesiastical constitutions, or the social theories, under which they had to live. Not, of course, that there is any hard-and-fast line between constitutional and social history; they overlap and illustrate each other at every turn. Yet there is a real difference; each needs special study in the light of its own special records; neither has dictatorial rights over the other; and for an author to draw easy inferences from one to the other, without continual reference to actual documents, must always be hazardous and is often grossly misleading. Yet I do feel that the public has often been badly misled in this way, and that the evil is growing rather than abating. For it is the line of least resistance and of showiest results; nothing is easier than to put together a few pages of quotations and summaries from the stock philosophical books, and a few more of gild regulations, and thence to infer that these one-sided documents teach us all we need to know about medieval society. We have all learnt, by this time, how absurd it would be to describe ancient Jewish society in the bare light of the Levitical regulations and of the hortatory chapters in Isaiah. We cannot believe that, six centuries hence, any author will be foolish enough to write, or any public to buy, books which describe the University life of this present century from a mere survey of the *Statutes* and the *Student's Handbook*, or our military life from the bare *Army Regulations*. The one value of history is, that it should deal with realities; and a system which deliberately confines research to one particular fraction of the ascertainable realities—which puts concrete facts, so to speak, upon its *Index Expurgatorius*—can only lead to disaster in the long run. I am giving my readers, therefore, as many concrete facts as time and space will permit. Let others take account of the evidence here produced, adding to it and correcting it where necessary, and suggesting any working theory not irreconcilable with these facts. For no theory is put forward in these pages but as a challenge to serious future enquiry; many of the points, it is plain, need much farther special study; I only plead that they should be studied not *in vacuo*, but in the light of actual documentary evidence, which may be found by all who care to seek. Of one important conclusion, however, I do feel quite certain, since it is the more deeply confirmed by every page that I read in trustworthy books, whether old or new, and whatever be the mental or moral complexions of their authors. What is wrong with the present peasant's position must be laid at the door of all classes of society, not excluding the peasant-class itself; it must be charged to men of all creeds, from the Roman Catholic to the Agnostic. If any one class or party had consistently acted after the standard which all revile others for neglecting, then the peasant would be in a very different position today.

Much of this, I hope, will be brought out, for the English

peasant alone, by Mr H. S. Bennett, whose researches in this field are more systematic and detailed than mine can pretend to be. To him, and to Mr G. R. Potter of St John's College, I am deeply indebted for help in revision of proofs and in many other ways; and to my wife for the Index. Canon C. W. Foster, Miss A. E. Levett and Mr H. W. Saunders have generously supplied me with proofs or extracts from unpublished material. Mr C. W. Previté Orton has given me many valuable Italian references, and Mr H. G. Richardson many of equal value for English conditions, while I owe to Mr G. M. Trevelyan some very important modifications of certain seventeenth century comparisons upon which I had ventured.

Finally, I must thank Dr F. J. Allen for the photograph of Wrington which he has lent me from his vast collection of English towers and spires. My debts to previous writers are, I hope, sufficiently indicated in my references. I have found the greatest stimulus of all (in spite of the fact that our periods coincide for so short a space) in Mr Tawney's *Agrarian Revolution of the Sixteenth Century*, with its remarkable combination of research, sympathy and imagination.

A necessary eye-operation has much hampered my final revision of the proofs, especially the Appendixes; but it is to be hoped that the reader may not find much trouble in verifying my quotations and references.

G. G. C.

ST JOHN'S COLLEGE, CAMBRIDGE
June 1925

CONTENTS

CONTENTS

CONTENTS

LIST OF ILLUSTRATIONS

PLATES

TEXT-FIGURES

ABBREVIATIONS AND AUTHORITIES

ABBREVIATIONS

C.P.L.   *Calendar of Papal Letters.*
C.P.S.   *Calendar of Papal Petitions.*
C.S.   Camden Society.
E.E.T.S. Early English Text Society.
E.H.R.   *English Historical Review.*
M.G.H.   *Monumenta Germaniae Historica.*
P.L.   *Patrologia Latina.* Migne.
R.S.   Rolls Series, Chronicles and Memorials.

AUTHORITIES

IF one or two of these monographs are not found to be actually quoted in my text, this is because many passages which I had originally marked have proved superfluous in view of sufficient evidence already given from other sources.

Act. Mur.—Acta Murensis Monasterii. Spiremberg, 1618.

Adalhard.—*Les statuts d'Adalhard pour l'abbaye de Corbie*, par A. Levillain. In *Le Moyen Âge.* 1900. pp. 333 ff.

Alv. Pelag.—*Alvari Pelagii de Planctu Ecclesiae.* Lyons: Clein, 1517.

An. Normand.—Annuaire des cinq départements de la Normandie. Caen, various years.

Anton.—K. G. Anton, *Gesch. d. teutschen Landwirthschaft.* Görlitz, 1799.

Antony of Padua.—*Opera*, ed. de la Haye. Lyons, 1653.

Archbold.—W. A. J. Archbold, *The Somerset Religious Houses.* Cambridge, 1892.

Arch. Kult.—Archiv für Kulturgeschichte. Leipzig: Teubner.

Arx.—Ildefons v. Arx, *Geschichten des Kantons St-Gallen*, u.s.w. St-Gallen, 1810–13.

Aube.—Mémoires de la Société académique du département de l'Aube. Troyes, v.d.

*Bac. Past.—*J. Fr. de Pavinis, *Baculus Pastoralis.* Paris, 1508; also in *Tract. Jur.* XIV, 115 ff.

     Pavinis was Doctor of Civil and Canon Law at the University of Padua, and auditor at the Roman court. His book was dedicated to Paul II, and the Paris edition was published by Chappuis, the greatest canonist of that day.

Baildon.—Yorks. Archaeol. Soc. Record Series, vol. XVII. *Notes on the Religious and Secular Houses of Yorkshire*, by W. P. Baildon. 1895.

Barclay.—A. Barclay, *Ship of Fools*, ed. Jamieson. Edinburgh, 1874.

Brandt's *Narrenschiff*, from which Barclay translated, was published in 1494; Barclay, who was a chaplain of Ottery St Mary, translated it in 1508 in order "to redress the errors and vices of this our realm of England."

Bartels.—Adolf Bartels, *Der Bauer i. d. deutschen Vergangenheit.* Leipzig: Diederichs, 1900.

Baumann.—F. L. Baumann, *Gesch. d. Allgäus.* Kempten, 1883.

Baumont.—H. Baumont, *Étude hist. sur l'abbaye de Luxeuil.* Luxeuil, 1896.

Beaumanoir.—Philippe de Beaumanoir, *Les coutumes du Beauvoisis.* Paris, 1842.

Written about 1290.

Beevor.—Sir Hugh R. Beevor, Bart. In *Transactions of the Norfolk and Norwich Naturalists' Society*, 1924.

Belbuck.—W. Paap, *Kloster Belbuck um die Wende des 16 Jhdts.* Stettin, 1912.

Below.—Georg v. Below, *Die Ursachen der Reformation* Berlin: Oldenbourg, 1917.

Berchorius.—*Petri Berchorii* (Pierre Berchoire or Bersuire) *opera omnia.* Cologne, 1730.

The author was prior of St-Eloi at Paris and died in 1362. His voluminous works deserve more attention for social history than they have yet received.

Berlière. *Écoles claustrales.*—Dom U. Berlière, O.S.B. In *Acad. roy. de Belgique. Bulletins de la classe des lettres.* 1921. pp. 550 ff.

Berlière. *Harvengt.*—Dom U. Berlière, O.S.B., *Philippe de Harvengt.* Charleroi, 1923.

Berlière. *Honorius.*—Dom U. Berlière, O.S.B., *Honorius III et les monastères bénédictins.* In *Revue belge de Philologie et d'Histoire.* 1923.

Berlière. *Recrutement.*—Dom U. Berlière, *Le recrutement dans les monastères bénédictins,* etc. In *Mémoires de l'Acad. royale de Belgique.* 1924.

A very valuable monograph, exposing the extent to which monasteries had already become capitalistic at the end of the twelfth century.

Bernier (Abbé F.). *Essai sur le tiers-état rural, ou les paysans de Basse-Normandie, au xviiie siècle.* Paris and Lyon, 1892.

Bern. Sen.—*S. Bernardini Senensis Opera Omnia,* ed. de la Haye. Venice, 1745.

Bertin.—J. Bertin, *De la mainmorte au moyen âge.* Gray, 1896.

Bert. Regensb.—Berthold v. Regensburg, ed. F. Pfeiffer. Vienna, 1862.

Bezold.—F. v. Bezold. *Gesch. d. deutschen Reformation.* Berlin, 1890.

Blashill.—T. Blashill. *Sutton-in-Holderness.* 2nd ed. 1900.

Boissonnade.—P. Boissonnade. *Le travail dans l'Europe chrétienne au moyen âge.* Paris: Alcan, 1921.

Bonnard.—Fourier Bonnard. *Histoire de l'abbaye royale de St-Victor.* Paris, [1905] and [1907].

Bonnemère.—E. Bonnemère. *Histoire des paysans depuis la fin du moyen âge jusqu'à nos jours.* Paris, 1856.

Borderie.—A. de la Borderie. *Recueil d'actes inédits des ducs de Bretagne.* Rennes, 1888.

Bozon, N. *Contes moralisés de Nicole Bozon.* (Soc. des anciens textes français.) 1889.

Branche.—D. Branche. *L'Auvergne au moyen âge.* Clermont, 1842.

Braun.—J. W. J. Braun. *Das Minoritenkloster zu Köln.* Köln, 1862.

Bruneau.—M. Bruneau. *De Feudali condicione in baillivia bituriensi.* Bourges, 1902.

Brutails.—J. A. Brutails. *Étude sur la condition des populations rurales du Roussillon au moyen âge.* 1891.

Buonanoma.—F. Buonanoma. *Indice di documenti inediti risguardanti la badia di S. Pietro di Camajore.* Lucca, 1858.

Burrows.—Montagu Burrows. *The Cinque Ports.* 1888.

Caggese.—R. Caggese. *Classi e comuni rurali nel medio evo italiano.* Florence, 1907.

Cart. Chalon.—*Cartulaire de Hugues de Chalon* (1220–1319) avec introduction par Jules Gauthier. Lons-le-Saunier, 1904.

Cart. Rames.—*Cartularium Monasterii de Rameseia.* R.S. 1884–93.

Cart. St-Père.—*Cartulaire de l'abbaye de St-Père-de-Chartres,* ed. Guérard. Paris, 1840.

Cart. St-Trond.—C. Piot. *Cartulaire de l'abbaye de St-Trond.* Brussels, 1870 and 1874.

Charrière.—F. de Charrière. *Recherches sur le couvent de Romainmotier* (with appendix, *Cartulaire de R.*). In *Mém. et Doc. Soc. Hist. Suisse romande.* Tom. III. Lausanne, 1841.

Chassin. *Serfs.*—C. L. Chassin. *Les derniers serfs de France.* In *Journal des Économistes,* Nov. 1879—Feb. 1880. Paris: Guillaumin, 1880.

Chron. M.O.—*Antonii Bargensis Chronicon Montis Oliveti.* Florence, 1901.

Chron. Rames.—*Chronicon Abbatiae Ramesiensis.* R.S. 1886.

Clémanges.—*Nicolai de Clemangiis Opera Omnia,* ed. J. M. Lydius. Leyden, 1613.

The author was archdeacon of Bayeux, and died at an advanced age about 1440. The book, *De Corrupto Ecclesiae Statu,* commonly ascribed to him, is probably by a contemporary.

Cless.—D. F. Cless. *Versuch einer Kirchlichpolitischen Landes- und Culturgeschichte von Württemberg bis zur Reformation.* Tübingen, 1806–8.

Cod. Dun.—*Codex Dunensis,* ed. Kervyn de Lettenhove. Brussels, 1875.

Cong. Internat.—*Atti del congresso internazionale di Scienze storiche di Roma,* 1903. Loescher, 1904–6.

Couppey.—M. Couppey. *Du jury en Normandie dans le moyen âge.* Soc. roy. académique de Cherbourg. 183– .

Cullum.—J. Cullum. *History of Hawsted.* London, 1784.

Cusanus.—*Nicolai de Cusa opera*. Bâle, 1565.

Cust. Roff.—J. Thorpe. *Custumale Roffense*. London, 1788.

Davenport.—F. G. Davenport. *The Economic Development of a Norfolk Manor*. Cambridge, 1906.

Davidsohn.—R. Davidsohn. *Geschichte v. Florenz*. Bd IV, Th. i. Berlin, 1922.

Degrully (P.).—*Le droit de glanage*. Paris and Montpellier, 1912.

Delisle.—L. Delisle. *Études sur la condition de la classe agricole en Normandie au moyen âge*. Évreux, 1851.

De Pauw.—Napoléon de Pauw. *La vie intime en Flandre au moyen âge*. Brussels, 1913.

Depoin.—J. Depoin. *Livre de raison de l'abbaye de St-Martin-de-Pontoise*. Pontoise, 1900.

De Rosny.—L. de Rosny. *Hist. de l'abbaye de N.-D. de Loos*. Lille and Paris, 1837.

Desmaze.—Ch. Desmaze. *Les pénalités anciennes*. Paris: Plon, 1866.

De Smet.—*Recueil des chroniques de Flandre*, ed. J. J. de Smet. Brussels, 1837– .

Dion. Cartus.—*Dionysii Cartusiani opera omnia*. Montreuil, 1896 and following years.

Dives and Pauper.—Anonymous dialogue, probably by a friar of about 1400, printed by W. de Worde in 1496. It is not paginated, but divided into *commandments* and *chapters*.

Dubois.—Abbé Dubois. *Histoire de l'abbaye de Morimond*. Paris, 1851.

Dunod.—F. I. Dunod. *Traités de la mainmorte et des retraits*. Paris, 1760.

Durandus.—Guillaume Durand, Bp of Mende. *Tractatus de modo Generalis Concilii habendi*. Paris, 1671.

Durham Acct. Rolls.—Surtees Soc., vols. 99, 100, 103 (1898–1900), ed. by Canon Fowler.

Dutilleux-Depoin.—*L'Abbaye de Maubuisson, histoire et cartulaire*, par A. Dutilleux et J. Depoin. Pontoise, 1882.

Ébrard.—E. Ébrard. *Misère et charité dans une petite ville de France* [Bourg-en-Bresse] *de 1560 à 1862*. Bourg, 1866.

Eden.—F. M. Eden. *State of the Poor*. London, 1797.

Feillet.—A. Feillet. *La misère au temps de la Fronde et S. Vincent de Paul*. Paris, 1862.

Finke.—H. Finke. *Acta Concilii Constanciensis*, Bd I. Münster, 1896.

Firth.—C. B. Firth. *The English Church in the reign of Ed. IV*.

    Thesis accepted for the D.Litt. of London University, and deposited in the library of the University.

Fleta, ed. by J. Selden, 1647.

Fournier.—M. Fournier. *Les affranchissements*, etc. In *Rev. Historique*, tom. XXI (1883), pp. 1 ff.

Fraipont.—*Les Environs de Rouen*. 120 dessins par Fraipont, texte par MM. H. Allais, etc. Rouen: Augé, 1890.

Fyot.—*Hist. de l'église abbatiale et collégiale de St-Estienne de Dijon*, par l'abbé Fyot. Dijon, 1696.

ABBREVIATIONS AND AUTHORITIES xxv

Gaillardin.—C. Gaillardin. *Histoire de la Trappe*, 1140–1844. Paris: Comon, 1844.

Garnier.—J. Garnier. *Chartes de Communes et d'affranchissements en Bourgogne.* Dijon, 1867, etc.

Giry.—A. Giry. *Analyse et extraits d'un registre des archives municipales de Saint-Omer.* Saint-Omer, 1876.

Gladbach-Eckertz.—G. Eckertz and E. J. C. Roever. *Die Benediktiner-Abtei M. Gladbach.* Köln, 1853.

Gladbach-Stratner.—J. Stratner. *Wirthschafts- und Verwaltungsgesch. d. Abtei München-Gladbach.* M. Gladbach, 1911.

Gorce.—P. de la Gorce (de l'Académie Française). *Histoire Religieuse de la révolution française.* Tom. I. 13ᵐᵉ édition. 1917.

Grands Jours.—E. Fléchier. *Les Grands Jours d'Auvergne* (ed. Chémel, 1856).

A description, by this distinguished bishop, of the work of the extraordinary commission appointed by Louis XIV to remedy the disorders of that province.

Grappin.—Dom Grappin, O.S.B. *Dissertation sur l'origine de la mainmorte.* Besançon, 1779.

Grimm. *Rechtsalt.*—J. Grimm. *Deutsche Rechtsaltertümer.* 4ᵉ Ausgabe. Leipzig, 1899.

Grosseteste.—*Les Reules Seynt Roberd.* Rules of household management drawn up by Bishop Robert Grosseteste for the Countess of Lincoln, printed with Walter of Henley, *q.v.*

Guigne.—G. Guigne. *Les moinillons de l'abbaye de Savigny.* In *Bulletin historique et philologique du Comité des travaux historiques et scientifiques.* 1900. pp. 418 ff.

Guilhiermoz.—P. Guilhiermoz. *Enquêtes et procès.* Paris, 1892.

Guiot de Provins. *Œuvres*, ed. J. Orr. Manchester, 1915.

Habasque.—F. Habasque. *Comment Agen mangeait au temps des derniers Valois.* Agen, 1887.

Hale.—W. H. Hale. *Registrum Prioratus B.M.Wigorniensis.* (C.S.) 1865.

Haltaus.—C. G. Haltaus. *Glossarium Germanicum medii aevi.* Leipzig, 1758.

Hardt.—H. v. d. Hardt. *Magnum Oecumenicum Constantiense Concilium.* Frankfort and Leipzig, 1700 ff.

Heinemann.—O. v. Heinemann. *Gesch. v. Braunschweig und Hannover.* Gotha, 1884–6.

Helmbrecht.—Wernher der Gärtner. *Meier Helmbrecht*, ed. M. Haupt in *Zeitschrift für deutsches Alterthum*, IV, 318 ff.

Wernher was a Bavarian minstrel who wrote between 1234 and 1250. His poem is summarized in all good histories of German literature, and has been translated in Reclam's cheap *Universalbibliothek*, vol. 1188.

Hemmerlin. *Nob.*—*Felicis Malleoli, vulgo Hemmerlin, de Nobilitate et Rusticitate dialogus.* Strassburg: Prüss, [1490].

Hemmerlin. *Tract.*—*Clarissimi viri Felicis Hemmerlin Opuscula et Tractatus.* Strassburg: Prüss, [1490].

Hentsch.—A. A. Hentsch. *Littérature didactique*, etc. Cahors, 1903.

Hen. Véz.—*Visites pastorales de Maître Henri de Vézelai en* 1267 *et* 1268. In *Bib. Éc. Chartes.* 1893. pp. 457 ff.

This archdeacon was named by St Louis as one of his executors in 1270.

Höfler.—K. v. Höfler. *Geschichtschreiber d. husitischen Bewegung in Böhmen.* Vol. II. Vienna, 1865.

Hor. Sap.—*Henrici Susonis Horologium Sapientiae*, ed. J. Strange. Cologne, 1871.

Household Book.—*Northumberland Household Book*, ed. Percy. London, 1827.

Hoyer.—K. Hoyer. *Das ländliche Gastwirtsgewerbe im deutschen Mittelalter.* Oldenburg i. Gr., 1910.

Hudson-Tingey.—W. Hudson and J. C. Tingey. *Records of the City of Norwich.* Jarrold, 1906, etc.

Imbart.—P. Imbart de la Tour. *Les Origines de la Réforme.* 1905– .

Jacquin.—M. Jacquin, O.P. *Étude sur l'abbaye de Liessies.* In *Bull. com. roy. d'hist. de Belgique.* Tom. LXXI. Brussels: Kiessling, 1903.

Joubert.—A. Joubert. *Étude sur les misères de l'Anjou au xve et xvie siècles.* Angers and Paris, 1886.

Jusserand. *Épop.*—J. J. Jusserand. *L'Épopée mystique de William Langland.* Hachette, 1893.

Jusserand. *Nomade.*—J. J. Jusserand. *La vie nomade et les routes d'Angleterre au xive siècle.* Hachette, 1884.

Kirkpatrick.—J. Kirkpatrick. *History of the Religious Orders etc. of Norwich.* Yarmouth, 1845 (written about 1725).

Knapp (Th.). *Gesammelte Beiträge zur Rechts- und Wirthschaftsgeschichte.* Tübingen, 1902.

Kröss.—Kröss, A. *Die Kirche und die Sklaverei im späteren M.A.* In *Zeitschrift f. Kath. Theologie*, 1895, pp. 273 ff., 589 ff.

Lamborelle.—L. Lamborelle. *Le bon vieux temps.* 3rd ed. Brussels, 1878.

Too uncritical, but sometimes supplying useful references.

Lamprecht.—K. Lamprecht. *Deutsche Geschichte.* Berlin, 1891–9.

Lamprecht. *Beiträge.*—K. Lamprecht. *Beiträge z. Gesch. d. franz. Wirthschaftslebens*, u.s.w. Leipzig, 1878.

Lamprecht. *Wirt.*—K. Lamprecht. *Deutsches Wirthschaftsleben im Mittelalter.* Leipzig, 1885–6.

L. A. Wilson.—J. M. Wilson. *The Worcester Liber Albus.* S.P.C.K. 1920.

L. A. Worc.—*The Liber Albus*, ed. J. M. Wilson. Worcestershire Historical Society. 1919.

Leclerc-Renan.—*Hist. littéraire de la France au xive siècle*; discours de Victor Le Clerc et d'Ernest Renan. 2me édition. 1865.

Lecoy.—A. Lecoy de la Marche. *La chaire française au m. â.* 2me édition, 1886.

Le Lay (F.).—*Le Paysan et sa terre sous la seigneurie de Coetanfao*... *au xviiie siècle.* Vannes, 1911.

Lénient.—C. Lénient. *La satire en France au moyen âge*. 1859.

Leubus.—W. Thoma. *Die colonisatorische Thätigkeit d. Klosters Leubus*. Leipzig, 1894.

Lib. Guil. Major.—*Liber Guillelmi Majoris*, ed. C. Port. In *Mélanges historiques—choix de documents*. Imprim. nat. 1877.

Lipson.—E. Lipson. *Introduction to the Economic History of England*. 1915.

Lommatzsch.—E. Lommatzsch. *Gautier de Coincy als Satiriker*. Halle, 1913.

Lorain (P.). *Histoire de l'abbaye de Cluny*. Paris, 1845.

Malicorne.—J. Malicorne. *Recherches historiques sur l'agriculture dans le pays de Bray*. Rouen, 1899.

Marquiset.—Léon Marquiset. *L'abbaye St-Paul de Besançon*. Besançon, 1909.

Maury.—A. Maury. *Le socialisme au xvie siècle*. In *Revue d. Deux Mondes*, July, 1872. pp. 354 ff.

Meffret.—*Sermones Meffret de Tempore, pars aestivalis*. Munich, 1612.

Méloizes (L. des). *Le servage en Berry*. Bourges, 1907.

Merswin.—Rulman Merswin (1352). *Das Buch von den neun Felsen*, ed. C. Schmidt. Leipzig: Hirzel, 1859.

Michel.—*Histoire de la ville de Brie-Comte-Robert* (Des Origines au xve siècle), par Edmond Michel. Paris, 1902.

Mill. Cluny.—*Millénaire de Cluny*. Mâcon: Protat, 1910.

Moke.—M. Moke. *La population et la richesse de la France au xive siècle*. Memoir read before the Royal Academy of Belgium, Ap. 7, 1856. Tom. xxx.

Mon. Boic.—*Monumenta Boica*. Munich, 1763– .

A series of documents published by the Bavarian government.

Mondaye.—*Essai Historique sur l'Abbaye de Mondaye, de l'Ordre de Prémontré*, par le P. Godefroid Madelaine. Caen: F. le Blanc-Hardel, 1874.

Muratori. *Ant.*—L. A. Muratori. *Antiquitates italicae medii aevi*. Tom. I. Milan, 1738.

Noël.—E. Noël. *La campagne*. Nouvelle édition. Rouen, 1890.

Nuntiaturberichte.—*Nuntiaturberichte a. d. Schweiz seit dem Concil v. Trient*, ed. F. Steffens und H. Reinhardt. Bd I. Solothurn, 1906.

Oise.—*Mémoires de la Société Académique d'Archéologie Sciences et Arts du Département de l'Oise*. Tom. VI, 1ère partie. Beauvais, 1865.

Page.—T. W. Page. *The End of Villainage in England*. New York: Macmillan Co. 1900.

Pauw.—*See* De Pauw.

Peetz.—H. Peetz. *Die Kiemseeklöster*. Stuttgart, 1879.

Pépin. *Ninive.*—G. Pépin. *Sermones quadragesimales de destructione Ninive*. Paris: Chevallon, 1527.

Pirenne. *Soulèvement.*—H. Pirenne. *Le soulèvement de la Flandre maritime*. Brussels, 1900.

Pontissara.—*Registrum Johannes de Pontissara*. Cant. and York Soc. 1913–24.

Potg.—J. Potgiesser. *De Statu Servorum*. Lemgo, 1736.

Prevost.—G. A. Prevost. *L'Église et les campagnes au moyen âge*. Paris, 1892.

Ranke.—L. v. Ranke. *Hist. of the Reformation in Germany*, tr. Sarah Austin. 2nd ed. 1845. Vol. II.

Raulin.—Johannes Raulin. *Prima Pars Sermonum de Sanctis*. Paris: Hicquemant, 15[20].

Raulin. *Quad.*—*Sermones quadragesimales eximii....Joannis Raulin*. Venice, 1575.

Reber.—B. Reber. *Felix Hemmerlin v. Zürich*. Zürich, 1846.

Recueil.—*Recueil général des estats tenus en France*. Paris, 1651.

Reg. Grand.—*Register of John de Grandisson*, ed. Hingeston-Randolph.

Reg. Malm.—*Registrum Malmesburiense*. (R.S.) 1879–80.

Reg. Roff.—J. Thorpe. *Registrum Roffense*. 1769.

Reg. Visit. O.R.—*Regestrum Visitationum Archiepiscopi Rothomagensis* (1248–1269), ed. Th. Bonnin. Rouen, 1852.

Reg. Whet.—*Registrum Abbatiae J. Whethamstede*. (R.S.) 1872–3.

Remling.—F. X. Remling. *Urkundliche Gesch. der ehemaligen Abteien und Klöster im jetzigen Rheinbayern*. Neustadt, 1836.

Richard.—C. L. Richard. *Analysis Conciliorum*. 1778. Vol. II.

Robiou.—F. Robiou. *Les populations rurales en France de la fin des croisades à l'avénement des Valois*. In *Rev. des Quest. Historiques*. Vol. XVIII. 1875. pp. 381 ff.

Romainmotier.—*Mémoires et documens publiés par la société d'histoire de la Suisse romande*. Vol. III. Lausanne, 1841.

St-Aiglan.—A. Paillard de St-Aiglan. *Mémoire*, etc. In *Mémoires couronnés par l'académie royale de Belgique*. Tom. XVI.

Salvioli.—G. Salvioli. *Storia economica d'Italia nell' alto medio evo*. Naples: Alvano, 1913.

Sauvage, R. N. *L'abbaye de St-Martin-de-Troarn*. Caen, 1911.

Savine. *Bondmen.*—A. Savine. *Bondmen under the Tudors*. In *Trans. Roy. Hist. Soc.* Vol. XVII. 1903. pp. 235 ff.

Schannat.—J. F. Schannat. *Vindemiae Literariae*. Fulda, 1723–4.

Scheible.—J. Scheible. *Das Kloster, weltlich und geistlich*. Stuttgart, 1845. Bd 1–4.

Text of Brandt's *Narrenschiff* with Geiler's comments, and of Murner's *Schelmenzunft*.

Sée.—H. Sée. *Les classes rurales et le régime domanial en France au moyen âge*.

See review in E.H.R. XVII, 328.

Sée. *Bretagne.*—H. Sée. *Étude sur les classes rurales en Bretagne au moyen âge*. Paris and Rennes, 1896.

Review in E.H.R. XXII, 400.

Seignobos.—Ch. Seignobos. *Le régime féodal en Bourgogne jusqu'en 1360*. Paris, 1882.

Seneschaucie.—A treatise on manorial management printed with Walter of Henley, *q.v.*

Sommerlad.—Th. Sommerlad. *Die wirtschaftliche Tätigkeit d. Kirche in Deutschland*. Leipzig, 1900–5.

Star Chamber (S.S.).—I. Leadam, *Select Cases before the King's Council in the Star Chamber*. (Selden Soc.) 1902 and 1910.

Susonis Opera, ed. L. Surius. Cologne, 1588.

Tawney.—R. H. Tawney. *The Agrarian Problem in the sixteenth century*. 1912.

Thurston.—H. Thurston, S.J. *The Mediaeval Sunday*. In *Nineteenth Century*, July, 1899. pp. 36 ff.

Tir. Weis.—*Die Tirolischen Weisthümer*, ed. Zingerle and Inama-Sternegg. Vienna, 1875 and 1877.

Tosti.—Dom Luigi Tosti. *Storia della Badia di Monte-Cassino*. Naples, 1842.

Tournus.—*Nouvelle histoire de l'abbaye royale de Tournus*, par un chanoine de la même abbaye. Dijon, 1733.

Tract. Jur.—*Tractatus ex variis juris interpretibus collecti*. Lyons, 1549, 18 volumes.

Tract. Jur. Civ. Can. By John Bromyard, the author of *Summa Predicantium*.

I quote from the early printed copy in the British Museum and from MS. Royal 10 C. x, f. 123 a.

Turner and Salter.—G. J. Turner and H. E. Salter. *The Register of St Augustine's Abbey, Canterbury*. Oxford Univ. Press, 1915 and 1925.

Vale Royal.—*The Ledger Book of Vale Royal Abbey*. (Lancs. and Cheshire Record Soc.) 1914.

Val. Eccl.—*Valor Ecclesiasticus*, ed. J. Hunter. London, 1810–34.

Van Houtte.—*Essai sur la civilisation flamande au commencement du xiie siècle d'après Galbert de Bruges*, par Hubert van Houtte. Louvain, 1898.

Verriest.—L. Verriest. *Le servage dans le comté de Hainaut*. In *Acad. roy. de Belgique, mémoires, classe des lettres*. Tom. VI. 1910.

Vinogradoff. *Eng. Society.*—P. Vinogradoff. *English Society in the eleventh century*. Oxford, 1908.

Vinogradoff. *Villainage.*—P. Vinogradoff. *Villainage in England*. Oxford, 1892.

Vis. Dioc. Nor.—*Visitations of the Diocese of Norwich*, ed. A. Jessopp. (Camden Soc.) 1888.

Vogt.—W. Vogt. *Die Vorgeschichte des Bauernkriegs*. Halle, 1887.

Vreden.—B. Brons. *Gesch. d. wirtschaftlichen Verfassung u. Verwaltung d. Stiftes Vreden im Mittelalter*. Münster, 1907.

Walter of Henley. *Husbandry*, ed. Lamond and Cunningham. 1890.

Weisthümer.—J. Grimm, E. Dronke and H. Beyer. *Weisthümer*. Göttingen, 1840–78.

Wenlok.—E. H. Pearce. *Walter de Wenlok, Abbot of Westminster.* 1920.

Westlake. *Last Days.*—H. F. Westlake. *Westminster Abbey, the Last Days of the Monastery.* London, 1921.

Westlake. *Westminster.*—H. F. Westlake. *The Story of Westminster Abbey.* London, 1924.

Winter.—F. Winter, *Die Cistercienser d. n-o. Deutschlands.* Gotha, 1868–71.

Zaccaria.—F. A. Zaccaria, S.J. *Dell' antichissima badia di Leno.* Venice, 1767.

Zimmermann.—W. Zimmermann. *Gesch. d. grossen Bauernkriegs.* Stuttgart, 1856.

Zwetl.—*Liber Fundationum monasterii Zwetlensis,* ed. J. v. Frast. Vienna, 1851.

MEDIEVAL VILLAGE, MANOR, AND MONASTERY

" . . . That trust in history as a guide to truth which is happily taking possession of the more thoughtful men of England, France and Germany."

F. J. A. Hort,
in *Life*, I, 242

"You have not gone to the bottom of the difficulty. It is very easy to say 'Give facts without comment'; but in the first place, what can be so dry as mere facts? the books won't sell, nor deserve to sell. It must be ethical; but to be ethical is merely to colour a narrative with one's own mind, and to give a *tone* to it."

Letter of J. H. Newman to J. R. Hope, Nov. 6, 1843, in *Correspondence of J. H. N. with John Keble*

CHAPTER I

THE OPEN ROAD

NEARLY forty years ago, when teaching in South Wales, I often spent the summer half-holidays between noon and midnight in tracking some small tributary of the Towy to its source in the mountains; and this led me by devious ways through many solitary fields. Over and over again, when the slanting shadows were beginning to show that beautiful country-side in its most beautiful aspect—when those words of Browning's Pompilia came most inevitably home: "for never, to my mind, was evening yet but was far beautifuller than its day"—over and over again, at these moments, I found myself hailed by some lonely labourer, or by one of some small group, leaning on his hoe and crying to me across the field. It was always the same question: "What's the time of day?"—the question implicit in that verse of Job: "As a servant earnestly desireth the shadow, and as an hireling looketh for the reward of his work." The sunlight was not long enough for me on my half-holiday; it was too long for these labouring men; and the memory of those moments has often given deeper reality to that other biblical word:

Behold, the hire of the labourers who have reaped down your fields, which is of you kept back by fraud, crieth: and the cries of them which have reaped are entered into the ears of the Lord of Sabaoth....Behold, the husbandman waiteth for the precious fruit of the earth, and hath long patience for it, until he receive the early and latter rain. Be ye also patient; stablish your hearts: for the coming of the Lord draweth nigh.

No man who is concerned for the future of human society can neglect the peasant; and there is much to be said for beginning with the peasant. In him we see elementary humanity; he appeals to our deepest sympathies; we may profitably imitate his patience; his struggles may move us to that "large and liberal discontent" of which William Watson speaks, and which is the beginning of all progress in this world. And yet, the more we study him, the more we come back to that lesson of patience; for he makes us realize the great gulf that is fixed between ignorant innocence and self-controlled innocence; between the cloistered and fugitive virtue of those who are cut off from conspicuous sins, and the tried virtue of those who, amid great wealth, avoid self-indulgence, or who, wielding great power, use it rather for other men's good than for their own. During many years, the social history of the Middle Ages had made me distrust current encomiums on the Russian or the Chinese peasantry as ideal societies, and as models for our own imitation. No doubt there was once such a time in Russia, and perhaps there is still in China—a time of happy equilibrium, at which the peasant has for the moment all that he needs, and strives as yet for no more. The fifteenth century marked a time of comparative prosperity and rest for the peasantry of England and Flanders and parts of Germany. But this is a world in which things must move, sooner or later; and all movement implies friction; and the worst friction is apt to come after long periods of static peace. Under stagnant order lies always potential disorder. The peasant is often quiet only because he ignores the lessons which are learned amid more rapid social currents. We must understand the peasant; but we must understand both sides of him; if chance debars him from the rôle of Hampden and Milton, it is the same chance which forbids his wading through slaughter to a throne.

From the first, however, I must disclaim any special knowledge of two very important branches of my subject; for I have never specialized either in constitutional history or in political economy. Even with regard to our own day, my knowledge is mainly confined to what I have picked up casually from the newspapers and from ordinary books and conversation; and so also it is with the past. My impressions on those points, therefore, will be only those of a miscellaneous reader; I must try to describe things as they were seen and felt not so much by the political philosopher of the Middle Ages, as by the medieval man in the street. We have had rather too much, I think, of formal political philosophy in pre-Reformation history, and not quite enough of those miscellaneous facts, those occasional cross-lights from multitudinous angles, which help us so much to realize (in F. W. Maitland's words) our ancestors' common thoughts about common things. In a very real sense, therefore, this essay is that of a man thinking aloud on the theme first suggested by the Vale of Towy.

In the course of the years that have elapsed since those days, wandering up and down in the Middle Ages, I have constantly come across the medieval peasant, and especially the serf on monastic estates. He hails me, as of old, across the field, across the slanting sunlight, across a land that seems more beautiful as the shadows lengthen, and the glare softens into afterglow, and death lends a deeper meaning to life. "Another race hath been, and other palms are won"; but there is only slow and gradual change in the human heart; human problems remain fundamentally very much the same; the peasant who, six hundred years ago, would have cried: "Come over and help us," cries now across those centuries: "Go over and help my fellows." Therefore, though I am more conscious of ignorance than of familiarity; though there is a gulf in life and thought between me and even the modern peasant; though I could no more undertake to specify all the medieval serf's legal disabilities and abilities at law than I would undertake to act as legal adviser to his descendant of today who might be litigating with his landlord, yet I have struggled to get into closer touch with him; and it is in that spirit that I invite my readers to come with me.

We must not be afraid of ghosts or of strange fellow-travellers, nor impatient of church bells and incense; for this is a province of the *Ile Sonnante*. For good or for evil, medieval society was penetrated with religious ideas, whether by way of assent or of dissent; and medieval state law not only usually admitted the validity of church law, but often undertook to enforce church law with the help of the secular arm. It may have been absurd that the medieval socialist or communist should plead as his strongest argument a highly legendary story of Adam and Eve, and that, on the other hand, the medieval conservative should clinch the whole question with a single sentence ascribed to an illiterate Jewish fisherman; it is possible to treat this as a mere absurdity, but it is not possible to ignore it altogether without deceiving both ourselves and our readers on a point which lies at the root of all medieval history. Therefore medievalists are forced, in a sense, to write church history, and are thus exposed to all the temptations of the ecclesiastical historian. But the first step towards overcoming these besetting temptations is frankly to recognize them. When we realize that here is a subject on which every man must be more or less prejudiced (unless he be trying to get through life without any even approximately clear working theory of life in his head), then we can attach far less importance to a man's prejudices, which are more or less inevitable, than to his attempts at disguise, which are unnecessary.

We cannot fully understand the social problems of our own day without realizing how those problems presented themselves to our forefathers, and by what ways they were approached, and with what measure of success or failure. And this, again, we cannot understand without traversing ground that smoulders still with hidden fires, political or religious. But it depends only on ourselves that such a journey should diminish rather than increase our prejudices. We do indeed enter upon it with certain ideas of our own; we may quit it with even stronger convictions in the same direction, yet with more sympathy, at bottom, for the best among those who differ from us. The only real enemy which either side has to fear is mental or literary dishonesty; since this is even more formidable as a domestic than as a public foe. The greatest men of past centuries are those who, by their example, entreat us to judge their own words and actions with the most unsparing exactitude, for the guidance of all present and future efforts towards social progress. To study medieval society without thinking of present-day and future society seems to me not only impossible in fact, but even unworthy as an ideal. While we strive to see the peasant of the past as he would have appeared to open-minded observers in his own day, we must at the same time appreciate and criticize him from the wider standpoint of our later age. Aquinas and Bacon, if they had known things which the modern schoolboy knows, would have seen their contemporaries not only as they were but as they might be; therefore, if we strive to eliminate from our own minds the intellectual and moral gains of these six centuries, we gain nothing in historical focus by this limitation; we gain nothing in clearness of definition; we simply exchange our telescope for a pair of blinkers.

If this be true, then, to the modern student of village life, the main question at bottom, if not on the surface, must be a question of criticism and comparison. Were men happy six hundred years ago—happy in the full human sense, and not merely with the acquiescence of domestic animals—under conditions which would render the modern villager unhappy? And, in so far as this may be so, is it not rather deplorable? since there are certain factors of life without which no man ought to be content. Therefore the main line of enquiry, after all, is fairly simple. The documentary records of rural life in the Middle Ages are abundant. Let us face the facts which these reveal; and then, putting ourselves into the position of Plato's Er the Armenian, with one chart before us showing past conditions of existence and another showing corresponding life in our own day, let us consider which we should seriously choose.

For, in speaking of our own day, we must say "corresponding life," and not circumscribe our choice by using in both cases this word *peasant*. In Chaucer's day, probably at least 75 per cent. of the population of these islands were peasants; and, out of every hundred men we might have met, more than fifty were unfree. Therefore the analogues of Chaucer's peasants constitute three-quarters of modern society—not only our present country labourers, but a large proportion of our own wage-earning population, and even some of our professional classes, from the unskilled worker to the skilled mechanic, the clerk, the struggling tradesman, doctor, or lawyer. The writer and the reader of this present volume might easily have been born in actual serfdom five hundred years ago; the chances are more than even on that side; and which of us will feel confident that he would have fought his way upward from that serfdom into liberty, were it only the liberty of the farmer's hind or the tailor's journeyman? Therefore we must not restrict ourselves to the modern country labourer in this comparison; though, even under such restriction, it would still be difficult to regret the actual past. We must compare the medieval serf with the whole lower half of modern society; and the medieval country-folk in general with the whole of modern society except the highest stratum. From this truer standpoint, it is easier to reckon whether the centuries have brought as much improvement as might have been expected; and whether, if the modern wage-earner or his counsellors are tempted to deny that improvement, this is not because the modern proletariat has tasted the tree of the knowledge of good and evil, so that its very unrest is as true a measure of past progress as it is a true call to future efforts.

It is from this starting-point that I ask my readers to follow me in these chapters. If I emphasize the rural gloom, it is not that I am insensible to the rural glory. The sights, the sounds, the scents of English country life in the Middle Ages were all that they are pictured in William Morris's romances, and a hundred times sweeter than prose or verse will ever tell. The white spring clouds spoke to the medieval peasant as they spoke to pre-historic man. Honesty, and love, and cheerful labour worked as a rich leaven in the mass of the country-folk; the freshness of Chaucer's poetry breathes the freshness of Chaucer's England; where things went well, there was a patriarchal simplicity which must command our deepest respect. All those things are true and must never be forgotten; but not less true are the things which are too often left unsaid . Moreover, minds which search for all beauty

In sudore bultus tui besceris pane tuo
Gene. I [III]

A la sueur de ton bisaige
Tu gaigneras ta paubre bie.
Apres long trabail, et usaige,
Voicy la Mort qui te conbie.

THE PEASANT
From Holbein's *Dance of Death*

¹ J. F. Millet, the peasant-born painter of peasants, wrote to his most intimate friend: "Ce n'est jamais le côté joyeux qui m'apparaît (soit en paysages, soit en figures); je ne sais pas où il est, je ne l'ai jamais vu. Ce que je connaîs de plus gai, c'est le calme, le silence dont on jouit si délicieusement, ou dans les forêts ou dans les endroits labourés, qu'ils soient labourables ou non....Est-ce là ce travail gai, folâtre, auquel certaines gens voudraient nous faire croire? C'est cependant là que se trouve pour moi la vraie humanité, la grande poésie" (A. Sensier, *Vie de J. F. Millet*, Paris, 1881, p. 130).

everywhere will not be tempted to ignore the darker realities. The indignation of Ruskin and Morris was mainly laudable in their day; but will it not finally be seen that the highest of all artistic senses is that which, ceasing to rail at inevitable changes on the face of this universe, sets itself to make the best of them, in so far as they are inevitable? Must we not praise the mood of Samuel Butler recognizing the wonderful beauty of Fleet Street at certain moments? or of Mr J. C. Squire's *A House?*—

> And this mean edifice, which some dull architect
> Built for an ignorant earth-turning hind,
> Takes on the quality of that magnificent
> Unshakable dauntlessness of human kind.
> . . . .
> It stood there yesterday: it will to-morrow, too,
> When there is none to watch, no alien eyes
> To watch its ugliness assume a majesty
> From this great solitude of evening skies.

Ecclesiastes was right; "God hath made every thing beautiful in his time: also he hath set the world in their heart, so that no man can find out the work that God maketh from the beginning to the end."

CHAPTER II

VILLAGE DEVELOPMENT

LET us begin, then, by taking stock of the main points which differentiate medieval village life from that of today. We shall not need to reflect whether those older conditions were natural; for we shall see that, however strange to modern practice, they grew up quite naturally from the different circumstances of those times. We shall, however, ask ourselves more often whether these processes, however natural, were actually inevitable; and here, I think, we shall generally decide that they may have been avoidable in the abstract, but that we ourselves, under the same pressure of circumstances, could hardly count upon ourselves (or on our fellow-citizens as we know them), to follow any wiser and more far-seeing course than our ancestors followed. But, while acquitting the men themselves, we must weigh their institutions most critically; since easy-going indulgence to the past may spell injustice to the present and the future. We are anxious, and rightly anxious, about our wage-earning classes both in the towns and on the land; I suppose there are few who would not vote for socialism tomorrow if they could believe that socialism would not only diminish the wealth of the few but also permanently enrich the poor. We are deeply concerned with these questions; and there are some who preach a return to medieval conditions; not, of course, a direct return, but a new orientation of society which they hope would restore the medieval relation of class to class, and thus (as they believe) bring us back to a state of patriarchal prosperity and content.

This, then, brings us to a third, and very different, question; not only: Was the medieval village system natural? not only, again: Was it to all intents and purposes inevitable for the time? but, lastly, and most emphatically: Was it a model for our imitation? and, if so, to what extent? We can answer this best by looking closely into the life of the peasant six hundred years ago (say, in 1324), when he was neither at his worst nor at his best.

There is general rough agreement with Thorold Rogers's verdict that, materially speaking, the English peasant was better off from about 1450 to 1500 than in the earlier Middle Ages, and, possibly, than in the seventeenth and eighteenth centuries[1]. But in important details Rogers has been shown to be hasty or mistaken[2], especially in his assumption that there was little unemployment; and, valuable as his work was in breaking ground, the question has been thrown into wider and truer perspective by a number of later writers[3]. The peasant had a long and weary way to go before he arrived at this comparative prosperity of the fifteenth century. The break-up of the Roman Empire had been terrible for all classes, but most terrible for the poor. The barbarian invasions strengthened and accelerated a movement which had already begun before the collapse of the Empire. Both from the personal and from the financial side, small men had been driven more and more to give themselves up to the great for protection's sake. By the process called *patrocinium*, a man surrendered his person to a sort of vassalage; or, again, through the *precarium*, he made a similar half-surrender of his lands; or, thirdly, he might surrender both together to one whose protection he sought for both[4]. In certain countries and at certain times, such a richer landlord gained far more power over those who acknowledged themselves his "men" than the State itself could exercise; this is characteristic of that half-way stage between wild individualism and modern collectivism which

---

[1] Very interesting diagrams are given by Gustav F. Steffen in *The Nineteenth Century* for June 1893: but they must to some extent be discounted by the fact that they rest upon the labourer's *daily* wages—i.e. they assume continuity of employment. To take the wheat comparison only, we find that an agricultural labourer's daily wage would purchase about 9 lbs. in 1275: thence it rises fairly steadily to 31 lbs. in 1450; zigzags for the next hundred years between 16 and 26; falls in 1605 to 10½; fluctuates again for nearly two centuries between 9 and 16; thence by a rapid and steady rise to 30 in 1885. But obviously we must not generalize from bread and wages alone.

[2] E.g. by W. J. Corbett in the second volume of Traill's *Social England*, and in a *Quarterly Review* article (CLVII, 92 ff.).

[3] For foreign writers, see Preface. Bonnemère is less balanced than the others, and less scientific in his use of materials; but the picture which he gives is, on the whole, truer to the facts than that of writers like Janssen.

[4] Sée, pp. 132 ff. Seignobos sketches a clear working theory—at the present stage, no more seems possible—of the transition from Roman slavery to medieval serfdom (*Régime féodal en Bourgogne*, pp. 61 ff.).

we call the Feudal System. And the most characteristic product of that half-way stage was the serf, a person intermediate between the freeman and the slave[1]. This intermediate person was called by many different names at different places and times. I shall here call him indifferently *serf* or *villein* or *bondman*, terms which in our tongue were practically convertible in the later Middle Ages. Beaumanoir's analysis of the causes of bondage, though not historically exhaustive, is of extreme interest as a chapter in thirteenth century thought. Freedom is the original and natural state of man; but "servitude of body hath come in by divers means." First, as a punishment for those who held back when all men were summoned to do battle for their country; secondly, those who have given themselves to the church, as *donati*; thirdly, "by sale, as when a man fell into poverty, and said to some lord: 'Ye shall give me so much, and I shall become your man of my body'; or, fourthly, by their own gift, to be defended from other lords, or from certain hatreds that men had against them....By these causes above rehearsed hath the freedom of nature been corrupted"[2]. Slavery proper died out gradually during the Middle Ages, partly for philanthropic and partly for economic reasons; for slavery is almost as uneconomic, if we look to society in general, as it is unjust[3]. At the Norman Conquest, Domesday Book shows on one manor a drop from 82 slaves to 25 in twenty years. Before 1324, the slave proper had become non-existent in England, though he might still be found in other countries; *e.g.* in Italy slavery not only outlasted the Middle Ages but was a very flourishing institution even in the later sixteenth century[4].

Yet the abolition of slavery was not an unmixed gain for the lower classes as a whole. On the contrary, the lord tried,

[1] For the serf's progress, see Vinogradoff, *Villainage*, pp. 84–5, 131; for the English peasant's advantages over the German, *ibid*. p. 179. Lamprecht puts the high-water mark for Germany in general in the thirteenth and fourteenth centuries; *Wirth*. I, 1238–40. Guérard comes to much the same conclusion for France; *e.g. Irminon*, I, 305 ff., 338 ff.

[2] *Cout. Beauv*. II, 225.

[3] Beaumanoir recognizes this very clearly (II, 237); I quote the whole passage below on p. 119.

[4] Guibert of Nogent condemns the prevalence of slavery among the Greeks of about 1100 A.D. (P.L. vol. 156, col. 688): "men and women...are sold as chattels to the heathen."

naturally enough, to get out of the serf what he had previously got from the slave. The Conquest systematized serfdom[1], for a while; the strong central executive worked in the direction of extinguishing local liberties and levelling all men down to the minimum recognized by law. For instance, it was easy for a bishop of Norwich to turn the freemen of Martham into serfs, and their comparatively independent self-governing village into an episcopal manor; with the result that, while at the Conquest there were at Martham seventy-eight peasants of free condition and only seven serfs, yet, fifteen years later, sixty-five of these freemen had been reduced to servile status[2]. In the whole county of Cambridge there were, at the Conquest, 900 socmen; these sank in twenty years to 213[3]. That shows how the increase of serfdom was still more rapid than the decrease of actual slavery. Thus, by a perfectly natural process, while the slave of Anglo-Saxon days disappeared, the Anglo-Saxon freeman became frequently merged in the serf. Freemen themselves slowly but steadily grew in numbers; not only by formal manumission, but by taking advantage of many small loopholes. But the serf himself was worse off in the days of Magna Carta than he had been at the Conquest; and far more than 50 per cent. of the population were still serfs in 1324. It is very difficult to define the position of these men briefly, even at times for which documentary evidence has already become plentiful. Professor Seignobos thus sums up the position of the villager in the province which he is especially studying: "C'est qu'il n'y a pas de paysan en Bourgogne qui n'appartienne à un maître. Ces hommes ne sont même pas pour le seigneur des serviteurs personnels, mais simplement des accessoires de son domaine. Il ne se donne pas la peine de vivre avec eux ni de les gouverner, il les fait exploiter par des agents." And this was a natural consequence of the fact that "les vilains n'ont aucun droit politique....Leur rôle est purement économique"[4]. But, to a

---

[1] Cf. Vinogradoff, *Eng. Society, etc.* pp. 442, 461, 467.

[2] W. Hudson in vol. I, pp. 119, 133 of *The History Teacher's Miscellany*, a most valuable series of articles. The *H.T.M.*, published then by Mr H. W. Saunders, is now published by the Cambridge University Press.

[3] Maitland, *Domesday Book and Beyond*, p. 62. The socman was a man personally free, but holding his land under certain restrictions.

[4] pp. 37, 56, 58; see appendix 1.

certain extent, any clear-cut modern description of the manor must necessarily be untrue to medieval facts, which were anything but clear-cut and uniform. It may almost be said that no two manors had quite the same customs; and, as facts shaded off into each other by gradual differences, so also did the medieval terms used to describe those facts; the villein of England may be very different from the villein of France; or, again, the so-called serf of one moment or place may be scarcely distinguishable from the so-called freedman of another. Yet there are some general lineaments which may be seized, and some currents of development which may be traced, through all this diversity of shifting details; and I cannot but feel that there is abundant evidence, if we will but collect and sift it patiently, to justify a clear general judgement.

This multitude of men and women, at strict law, had scarcely any right against the man who was their *dominus* in both medieval senses of that word; their owner and their ruler—their landlord and their lord-and-master[1]. Such rights as the serf did gradually obtain were mainly evolved by custom. In England, the king's law did indeed protect him from actual murder or maiming, as modern law protects a horse or an ox, but on utilitarian rather than moral grounds: "the State is concerned to see that no one shall make an ill use of his property"[2]. Moreover, even here, it appears that the case had to be taken up by a third person, as in that of the modern animal; "it is not certain that the villein

[1] I speak here, of course, of the ages in which European society was most definitely feudal—let us say roughly, from 950 to 1200 A.D. The fact that a good many serfs, especially in the later Middle Ages when feudal society was breaking up, were better off than a good many freemen, and that by custom and practice (as apart from strict legal theory) they might own a good deal of property and get a hearing on civil cases in the king's courts, does not affect the general truth of this description in the text. When it is argued (*e.g.* by Prof. F. M. Powicke in *History* for Apr. 1924, p. 16) that the manorial court, in which nearly all the serf's cases were decided, "was the expression of the local society rather than of the lord's arbitrary will," these strictly true words may easily be used (as I think they are in that case) to minimize unduly the serf's actual disabilities. The modern labourer has access to courts which are practically uninfluenced by any man's arbitrary will: the medieval peasant pleaded in courts where, though custom was certainly the strongest factor, yet arbitrary will weighed very heavily indeed in a large number of cases. Compare p. 19 at the end of this Chapter.

[2] Pollock and Maitland, 2nd ed. I, 415, quoting from Bracton, f. 6, § 3; f. 155 b, § 3.

or his heir could set the law in motion by means of an 'appeal'"[1]. In strict law, the serf was incapable of possessing property; his earnings were his master's; only on sufferance could he collect and save for himself. He was bound by law to the soil. He and his "brood"—his *sequela*, as the law styled them, in contradistinction to the freeman's *liberi*—might be bought or sold, or given with the land that they tilled. And, while he might not leave the soil, yet the soil might quit him; he might be taken from it and treated as a chattel. "Countess Blanche of Champagne granted to the monks of St-Loup-de-Troyes one of her bondwomen; the monks pledged themselves to give in exchange one of their own; and, if that one be insufficient to represent the value of the bondwoman they have received, then they are to send the countess two"[2]. Though the sale of a serf apart from the land was far less common in England than on the Continent, yet even in English records such cases are not infrequent; for instance, "a villein is sold for 40 shillings...a man and his sons are sold to the chapter of St Paul's for 60 shillings, a mare, a cart and 28 sheep"[3]. Professor Sée, writing for France, says, "there is not a chartulary which does not mention many sales of serfs. Sometimes they concern single individuals, but more often a whole family, or even a group of families or all the inhabitants of a manor. The serf is a chattel who is sometimes sold, so to speak, by retail; a man grants part of a serf as he now grants a part share in a company," *e.g.* in 1252 a lady sells "the whole of Guiot the Tanner, and a half share of the children of the said Guiot" (p. 165). Such partitions were very common on the Continent; when two serfs from different manors were permitted to marry, the respective lords often covenanted that the children should be divided between them. This need not, of course, have involved any break-up

[1] *Ibid.* Towards the end of the Middle Ages, the serf had increasing chances of a hearing outside the manorial courts; but he never arrived at anything like the freeman's status before the law.

[2] H. Sée in *Rev. Hist.* LVI (1894), 235, quoting Bib. Nat. MS. lat. 5993, f. 146 a. Compare Lamprecht, *Wirth.* II, 1206, where the monks of Laach make similar bargains with several other lords.

[3] Pollock and Maitland, *Hist. Eng. Law*, I, 397. The subject is discussed in Vinogradoff, *Villainage*, p. 151. Leadam adduces more concrete evidence (*Trans. R. Hist. Soc.* VI, 195, n. 3). In Berry, des Méloizes seems to doubt whether serfs were sold apart from the land, in the later Middle Ages at any rate (pp. 7, 26, 60).

of the family life; children might live under the same roof while serving different manors; but in many cases it must have worked adversely upon family relations. Yet monks and bishops took this as a perfectly natural business proceeding. In the eleventh century, the abbey of Bèze receives, for the benefit of Sir Henry de Ferté's soul, the serf Arnulf "and one half of the sons or daughters of the aforesaid Arnulf"[1]. Again, in 1231 letters of the bishop of Paris notify that he granted "to his bondwoman Mellisande, daughter of Maugrin de Wissous," permission to marry "Noel Martin, bondman of the abbey of St-Germain-des-Prés," on condition that half of the children born of this marriage should belong to the Cathedral of Paris, and half to the abbey[2]. This kind of arrangement was normal in France and Germany; Lamprecht quotes three cases between 1231 and 1263[3]. In 1208 the nuns of Troyes sold to Sir Peter Putemonnoie two sons of a defunct bondman and a daughter, Elizabeth, on condition that "if by chance it befal that a marriage take place between my bondwomen and the bondmen of the lady abbess, I am bound and promise to give the abbess and chapter aforesaid one of my bondwomen in exchange for the said Elizabeth"[4]. Where an exception is found, this is not out of sympathy for the serf's family life, but to the economic advantage of the monks. Those of St-Denis and St-Hilaire-de-Poitiers never divided servile families, because they enjoyed, by royal charter, the right of keeping for themselves all children of mixed marriages, whoever the other lord might be[5]. So, again, at the nunnery of Frauenchiemsee in Bavaria. The custom runs for certain manors: "My lady [abbess] and her nunnery divide their bondchildren with no man; where the mother belongs to the abbess and nuns, all the children are theirs; ye shall note that well." The exception was not one of Christian charity; it was a precious commercial monopoly[6]. So far as charity went, good

---

[1] *Analecta Divionensia* (Dijon, 1875), p. 406; cf. p. 347: "Maynard, and half his children."

[2] *Arch. France Monast.* IV, 87.

[3] *Wirth.* I, 1206; for other cases see Schultz, p. 116; Coopland, pp. 111–15; des Méloizes, pp. 36, 60.

[4] *Aube*, XI (1874), 23; cf. similar bargains, pp. 8, 20.

[5] *Irminon*, I, 413.

[6] *Tir Weis*, I, 5. In other cases, both these nuns and the monks of Herrenchiemsee divided their bondchildren; see Peetz, pp. 75, 207.

churchmen saw the matter in something like the modern light. The learned monk, Regino of Prüm, in the tenth century, quotes a conciliar decree which runs: "If a bondman and bondwoman be separated by cause of sale, they must be bidden to remain thus, if we are not able to join them together." He then adds: "But Roman [civil] law certainly seems to lay down a far better precept in this matter"[1]. And he quotes the prescription of the Theodosian Codex that, when slaves are divided among heirs or other beneficiaries, families must be kept together, and some other equivalent found for the inequality thus introduced among the portions.

We must not, again, grant too unreservedly the plea that deeds of sale are not to be taken at their face value, and that what was really sold was not the man's person but his work. There is some truth in this plea; Guérard rightly notes that the low price at which a serf was sold apart from his land points to the fact that the purchaser obtained not a whole man, but half or a third or some other fraction of his weekly work. In 807, two serfs were sold for fifteen shillings each, *i.e.* the value of forty-five bushels of corn, or forty-five half-grown rams or pigs. Two generations earlier, a serf-girl had been sold for 2s. 10d., or the price of eight piglings[2]. The same implication comes out far more clearly in those continental instances where a serf is actually split into fractions, the two lords each taking a share proportionate to their landed interest. Here, for instance, are two cases from a formal document of the year 1409.

Choice hath been made by Jeannin Tixier, proctor of the lord of Chauvigny, and brother Guillaume Bachoux proctor of the abbot and convent of La Préhée...and it hath befallen that to the said lord of Chauvigny, who had the first choice, is fallen John Bernard whole and undivided, together with the fourth part of [his brother] Martin Bernard; and the other three parts of the said Martin are fallen to the abbot and his convent.

Again, in the same year, the lord got the whole of Macé Gonneau and half of his brother Simon, the abbot getting the other half[3].

[1] *De Eccl. Disc.* lib. II, c. 122 (P.L. vol. 132, col. 308).
[2] *Irminon*, I, 292, n. 16; cf. pp. 295, 703–4, and C. Leber, *Fortune privée, etc.* 1847, p. 9.
[3] Des Méloizes, p. 209.

We may fairly conclude, therefore, that the purpose of these sales or exchanges was mainly economic; yet we must not therefore ignore the personal factor altogether. Even if we assume great consideration and kindness on the lord's part, yet such a sale of the serf's labour must involve, in a very real sense, the sale of his person; especially when we remember how many rights the lord had in the bondman besides the naked claim to so many hours' work. For instance, Count Otho gave to St-Bénigne-de-Dijon, as the monastic chronicler phrases it, "many lands...together with very many bondfolk of both sexes, *and all the rents and customary services which the aforesaid bondmen and bondwomen owe*"[1]. Unless these latter words are to be treated as mere formal tautologies, the monks saw in these bondfolk something more than so many eggs and fowls and hours of labour. Moreover, quite unexceptionable witnesses from the Middle Ages explicitly forbid our ruling out the personal factor in these transactions. Peter the Venerable, abbot of Cluny, complains of the barons of his time (*i.e.* about 1130 A.D.) that their tyranny often drives the serfs to the desperate remedy of flight; and then he adds: "Nay, what is worse, the masters even fear not to sell for the vile price of money the very bodies of those bondmen whom Christ redeemed at the dear price of His own blood"[2]. Wyclif uses practically the same words. Almost equally significant is one stray sentence which has drifted down to us in a monastic chartulary. A woman, surrendering herself as bondwoman to the monastery of St-Maur, made it an express condition that she should never be sold by the monks, nor given to any man[3]. When a freeman was sold (as in the cases given by Guérard) the sale might well affect his work only; but the sale of a serf must have meant a great deal more[4].

---

[1] *Chron. de St-B.-de-D.* ed. Bougaud et Garnier (Dijon, 1875), p. 163.

[2] P.L. vol. 189, col. 146; Wyclif, *English Works* (E.E.T.S. 1880), p. 227. So also Bartholomaeus Anglicus (lib. VI, c. 12) and Petrus Berchorius (*Red. Morale*, lib. III, c. 10: "the bondwoman is not suffered to take a husband of her own will; she is bought and sold like a beast").

[3] *Irminon*, I, 428 and II, 287. For this question of the sales of serfs see also Delisle, p. 23 (who says all that can be said in favour of them); Leadam in *Trans. Roy. Hist. Soc.* VI (1892), 195, and des Méloizes, pp. 7, 26, 60. It is well summed up by Vinogradoff, *Villainage*, p. 151.

[4] *Irminon*, I, 222–3.

Just as economic interests mainly determined the lord's dealings with the serf's person, so also with his brood. If through any cause these chattels were lost to the manor, then the loss must be made good to the lord. Quite apart from the fine which the serf ordinarily paid for his daughter's marriage in any case, if she escaped from the lord by marrying into another manor, or again if the son escaped by going to school or to a monastery or by taking clerical orders, then the father was fined in order to indemnify the landlord[1]. In many places, if a freeman married a serf, the law branded him also with servile disabilities[2]. The serf originally paid his rent not in money but in labour, or in kind, under conditions which left room for constant friction and bickerings[3]. The services he had to render were not always defined with ideal clearness; at the best, their irregular incidence was wasteful of time or energy; and, as a matter of fact, a considerable part of the lord's profits came from fines for different infractions of manorial laws, or from his monopolies of mill and oven or fords or waterways; or from such casual and vexatious incidents as the lord's ransom in war, "joyous incoming," knighting of a son or marriage of a daughter; and, most exasperating of all, from the tenant's own decease, when the lord claimed, as "heriot," the dead man's best beast or best movable possession, while the priest commonly took the second best as a "mortuary." This latter custom, with the laws of tithe, mass-penny, and other similar ecclesiastical dues, arrayed the clerical interests almost as definitely against the serf as those of the lay lord. In a model manor or parish, these relations might well breathe the true patriarchal spirit and make for special intimacy; Chaucer's good priest, who was "full loth to cursen for his tithes," would stand in a position of more conspicuous spiritual advantage than the modern minister who has no such concessions to make; but we have overwhelming

[1] Originally the law refused to recognize the legitimacy of any "formariage," or marriage outside the manor; it was only by a later relaxation that these were permitted for a money fine (Sée, p. 72). As to school and orders, the first in strict law practically included the second, since even grammar-school boys were supposed to be tonsured as clerks. See A. F. Leach, *Ed. Charters, etc.* p. xii.

[2] In other cases the law went the other way, and a serf might get his liberty by marrying a freewoman, with the lord's permission, of course.

[3] See appendix 3.

testimony to the comparative rarity of these cases; the intimate history of any parish is almost always full of quarrels over tithes and dues. It must be remembered, also, that all differences between serf and lord were settled in the manor court, where the latter was too often in fact, though not in theory, both party and judge[1]. Conditions of this kind put too great a strain on human nature. Such potentialities of injustice could not long remain unrealized; the law which permits oppression invites oppression; and, though we must not too hastily assume that the serf suffered in practice all theoretical possibilities of injustice, yet it is even more dangerous to explain those wrongs away altogether. It was a medieval tenet that class-divisions were of God's making; even the best churchmen were far less often concerned with actually raising the poor than with preaching content in poverty. Both State law and Church law, if not in theory at least in practice, were unjust to the worker; and, as a natural consequence, the average employer was unjust to him[2]. This has been more clearly seen by foreign scholars,

---

[1] In theory the "dooms" were given by the peasants themselves; but the lord's officer presided, and had many chances of intimidation or downright violence. In *Piers Plowman*, the lord's steward is spoken of as the judge; it is he who "deems" in court (B. prol. 96); and his personal character may be despicable enough (C. VIII, 33). The steward's power seems to have told very heavily in Germany: see *Vreden*, p. 55. In France, also, the tenant had apparently less chance than in England. But, even in our comparatively orderly society, the appeals made to the Star Chamber from undue local influence are very significant. The Paston Letters, to go no farther, show how little chance the smaller man sometimes had against the greater even in the higher courts; and it may safely be said that every medieval moralist takes this view of his own age. It is noteworthy that Jonas of Orléans, in his chapter on the frequency of hired perjurers, specifies as one result of this false witness that "they rivet the fetters of servitude upon whomsoever they will." The French Dominican Guillaume Pépin complains that "the poor are more grievously lacerated by evil judges than by the bloodiest enemies"; he refuses to distinguish between the lay courts and the Church courts; in the presence of these evil judges, "the poor man can get no hearing if he have nothing to offer, nor do the judges merely scorn to hear them, but they even oppress them contrary to the truth"; for they are daily corrupted by bribes (Pépin, *Ninive*, Serm. 8, f. 49, cols. 2, 3; f. 54, col. 3). The poor man's disadvantages in the later French manorial courts are described with some exaggeration by G. Hanotaux, on the text of a proverb, "A lord, even though he be but of straw, can swallow a vassal of steel" (*La France en 1614*, ed. Nelson, p. 402). Cf. Durandus, *De Modo Tenendi*, etc. p. 301.

[2] There is a present-day tendency to lay what seems very undue stress upon the fact that, behind medieval legal theories, there was always an implicit or explicit appeal to natural law and equity as a safeguard against

I think, than by our own. Henri Sée, summarizing the evidence from the ninth century, writes: "Le premier effet de l'établissement du régime féodal semble avoir été d'aggraver l'exploitation domaniale et de rendre plus misérable encore la condition des paysans." Professor Imbart de la Tour, whose natural tendency is apologetic, gladly emphasizes the improvement in the peasant's condition during the second half of the fifteenth century; but he adds a sentence which damns the whole past: this improvement, "en un mot, transforme le serf en personne humaine"[1]. And medieval writers often express themselves in the same sense; they prove that potential tyranny, in their day, was not separated from actual tyranny by any moral or religious barrier which is wanting to these days of ours. To the jurist's mind, it was natural to speak of the lord's peasantry and the lord's cattle in the same breath[2]. The Dominican friar Bromyard, writing towards the end of the fourteenth century, shows that this question of mercy or cruelty towards the poor was at least as much a question of opportunity in Chaucer's day as in our own. Human cupidity (he writes), naturally leads to oppression[3].

tyranny. No doubt this was universally admitted; but so was it also universally admitted that we are all descended from Adam and Eve, and that the churl is made of the same flesh and blood as the king. Yet we know how little these latter admissions affected actual practice in medieval society; and those who emphasize the merciful effect of the appeal to natural law would do well to collect and produce evidence of its actual effect upon men's actions and upon the general progress of society. Professor Huizinga writes very truly: "The notion of equality has been borrowed by the Fathers of the Church from Cicero and Seneca. Gregory the Great, the great initiator of the Middle Ages, had given a text for coming ages in his *Omnes namque homines natura aequales sumus*. It had been repeated in all keys, but an actual social purport was not attached to it. It was a moral sentence, nothing more; to the men of the Middle Ages it meant the approaching equality of death, and was far from holding out, as a consolation for the iniquities of this world, a deceptive prospect of equality on earth" (*The Waning of the Middle Ages*, etc. tr. Hopman, Arnold, 1924, p. 53). The book is comprehensive, well-balanced and suggestive; it would be difficult to find elsewhere in the same compass an equally good description of the transition from medieval to modern conditions.

[1] *Origines de la Réforme*, t. I, p. 465.

[2] *Process. Sathan.* f. 16 a : Satan bears his torments everywhere he goes: "pain is rooted in his very bones, as a leper's leprosy, or as the moth in a moth-eaten garment, or even as the peasant or the beast of burden suffer no less pain when they bear a load of iron in the king's hall [than elsewhere]." This treatise is ascribed to the great Bartolus of Sassoferrato, but is probably by a later jurist.

[3] *Sum. Pred.* D. xii, 18 ff. All this late fourteenth century evidence is the more important since this was a time of rapid emancipation for the

For the squire is not content unless he can live as a knight; the knight would fain be a baron, the baron an earl, the earl a king; the fruit of this presumption is, that he who cannot justly spend more than twenty marks will now spend thirty or forty.... Then, to relieve their want, these men call in flattering counsellors, who say: "Your land is rich; your men (God be blessed!) are rich; you can take such and such a sum from them without hurting them." And if the lord himself, not yet hardened in cruelty, would fain deal more gently, saying: "It is better as it is," then they resist him, and say: "My lord, do you busy yourself with your delights and solace, and leave the governance of your lordship to us who are of more experience...." Hence it cometh to pass that lords have now become accustomed to say [to those peasants who complain]: "Go ye to my steward or my bailiff"; with the result that they neither know, nor wish to know, the misery of their subjects.

The peasant (adds Bromyard, echoing from Cardinal Jacques de Vitry of two centuries earlier), is foolish indeed to rejoice at the birth of a new child in his lord's family; it only means one more potential oppressor. This state of things is foreshadowed in Joel i, 4: "That which the palmerworm hath left hath the locust eaten; and that which the locust hath left hath the cankerworm eaten." For

thus, when the lord hath despoiled the common folk, that which was left and escaped from his hand is greedily picked up by the minions who follow after him.... Such folk, dwelling in a manor or a town, eat meanwhile, down to the very root, whatsoever hath been left by the great vassals aforesaid who come a few times in the year to hold courts and for suchlike affairs.

Chaucer was writing in his *Parson's Tale* as nearly as possible at this same moment,

Of covetise come these hard lordships through which men be distrained by tallages, customs, and carriages more than their duty or reason is; and eke they take of their bondmen amercements, which might more reasonably be called extortions than amercements. Of which amercements and ransoming of bondmen some lords' stewards

---

peasant, in England and France at least. What the Black Death did for England, in forcing the lords to grant better conditions to men who would otherwise risk all and run away, was done still more effectively for France by the Black Death and the ravage of war in combination. For large numbers of French peasants had a legal right of "disavowal," and lords confessed even in their charters that they must relax their claims or lose their men. This is brought out very clearly by Seignobos, pp. 54–6; cf. Davenport, p. 72

say that it is rightful, forasmuch as a churl hath no temporal thing that it is not his lord's, as they say; but certainly these lordships do wrong that bereave their bondfolk [of] things that they never gave them[1].

Another contemporary, the French monk Pierre Berchoire, writes:

The truth is, that these lords and tyrants continually steal from those who have little or nothing (to wit, peasants and diggers of the earth) and seize and take from them that little which they have.... For the poor men's goods are continually taken away, while rich men daily heap up other men's goods, as Isaiah saith (iii, 14): "The spoil of the poor is in your houses.' These [words of Matt. xiii, 12] may be applied to lords of our own day—*modernos dominos*—who in truth love no bondman or servant unless he bring gain and make for their profit[2].

Similar evidence could be produced from preachers and moralists of almost every generation in the Middle Ages. Gautier de Coincy, in the thirteenth century, reproduces the ordinary commonplaces: "The serf is poor, sad and downcast, he has little bread and an evil couch...sometimes he has little enough of rough black or brown bread." But hard as his lot is, he may scarcely be said to deserve more; true, on the one hand he works from morning to night; but, on the other, he forgets God and constantly works on Sundays or holy days, "he has no more fear of God than a sheep; nor would he give a button for the holy laws of Holy Church"; he steals from his neighbour when he can; he steals from the parson, "giving tithes not as Abel gave, but worse even than Cain did." Worst of all "many serfs hate the clergy even as Esau hated Jacob...little they love them, and still less do they believe them"[3].

With these latter characterizations of Gautier I shall have to deal later, as also with the evidence by which Johannes Janssen,

---

[1] § 750. Chaucer's words are the more remarkable that they are almost entirely his own: the French friar Lorens from whom he usually borrows writes simply "such reeves, provosts, beadles or high officials, who make the great robbings and wrongs upon the poor and buy themselves great heritages" (*Ayenbite*, p. 39). It will be noticed also that Chaucer's words coincide very closely with those of his contemporary Bromyard; the courtier-poet and the popular preacher saw here with the same eyes.

[2] *Moralitates*, lib. XXIX, c. 17.

[3] Lommatzsch, pp. 69–78, where many similar judgements are given from other thirteenth century moralists.

in his bulky and widely-read arraignment of the Reformation, seeks to prove that the peasant of Luther's day was really fortunate in his lot; meanwhile I need only quote a single witness from that day, perhaps the fullest and most competent of all, whose words became classical, and were repeated with even greater emphasis by another author writing fourteen years later[1]. Hans Beham, or Joannes Boemus, was born near Würzburg, and was chaplain to the Teutonic Knights at Ulm from about 1490 onwards. There he learned Hebrew from resident Jews, and was one of the first Germans to study the Old Testament in the original. He became a learned and laborious compiler; and his *Mores, Leges et Ritus Omnium Gentium* passed through many editions; it was translated into German, French and Italian, and, partially, into English also. It was written in 1520, at a time when, by common consent, the German peasantry were somewhere near the zenith of their medieval prosperity. In this book, after summarily describing all the countries of the world in turn, he passes on to depict his own Germany in greater detail. He writes purely for instruction, without ulterior political or satirical purpose; and his book represents the judgement of the average well-informed student of his day. We may make some allowance for his quasi-academic outlook; others, describing equally systematically, might perhaps have painted a more sympathetic picture; but, when all allowances are made, his description gives us far directer and completer evidence than any other author of the time. The passage comes in the twelfth chapter of the third book (ed. 1604, p. 253), and is headed:

The Miserable Plight of the Peasants

The [fourth and] last class [of Germans] are those who live on the land in villages and hamlets and who till that land, wherefore they are called *rustics*, or *countryfolk*. If they will believe it, their condition is very[2] wretched and hard. They live apart from the rest,

---

[1] Schultz, p. 115. It is among the most inexplicable of all Janssen's strange omissions that he completely ignores this, the most explicit and trustworthy account of the German peasantry at the time with which he deals, and perhaps also the best known and the most often quoted.

[2] "Satis misera horum et dura conditio est." I have already had occasion to note that *satis* in medieval Latin, like *assai* in Italian, has frequently this intensive force.

in lowly fashion, each with his own household and his beasts. Their cottages are of mud and timber, rising little above the ground, and covered with straw. They feed on brown bread, oatmeal porridge, or boiled peas[1]; they drink water or whey; they are clad in a linen coat, with boots of untanned leather and a dyed cap. They are ever an unquiet crew, laborious and unclean. They bring to the nearest town whatsoever each hath gained either from his field or from the produce of his flocks; and here they buy in return whatsoever each needeth; for they have few or no artificers dwelling among them. On holy-days they come all together in the morning to the church, whereof there is commonly one for each village; there they hear from their priest God's word and the sacrament [*sacra*]; then, after noon, they treat of their own affairs under a linden-tree or in some other public place. After this, the younger folk dance to the sound of the pipe, while the elders go to the tavern and drink wine. None goeth unarmed in public; each hath his sword by his side for any chance emergency. Each village chooses two or four men whom they call *Ammeister* [*rusticorum magistros*] these are umpires for disputes or contracts, and stewards of the estates; yet these have no administrative power; that resideth in the lords, or in their agents whom they appoint under the vernacular name of *bailiff* [*sculteti*]. The peasants have to work oftentimes in the year for their lord, tilling the fields, sowing and reaping and gathering into the barns, carrying wood, building, and digging ditches. There is nothing which this servile and wretched folk is not said to owe to these [lords]; nor is there aught which, if the lord bid them do it, they dare to refuse without peril; the defaulter is heavily punished. Yet there is nothing which they feel more hardly than this, that the greater part of the fields which they occupy are not their own, but belong to those lords from whom they must needs redeem them with a certain portion of their produce.

There we have a serious and responsible generalization, which we may fairly take as our text for the present. I hope to show, in my succeeding chapters, that we have here a description applicable to the English peasant also, with a few obvious changes of detail. Where the German peasant often drank wine, ours drank beer; English political conditions, bad as they sometimes were, did not compel our countryfolk to go about with swords; and, though there was a good deal of landlord tyranny with us, yet the laws and the central government kept this far more in check. There can be little doubt, I think, that the

[1] *Legumen*, possibly intended to include other vegetables also.

English serf of the Middle Ages was just about as much better off than the average continental serf, as the English peasant of the seventeenth and eighteenth centuries was than the average of his brethren in France and Germany, Italy and Spain[1].

[1] Fortescue's well-known contrast, however coloured by patriotism, is generally accepted in the main (*De Laudibus Legum Angliae*, ch. ix, printed on pp. 31 ff. of my *Social Life in Britain*).

CHAPTER III

A FEW CROSS-LIGHTS

BEFORE passing on to matters of detail, which will help us to see whether the few medieval generalizations quoted in the preceding chapter are indeed typical, and representative of what serious contemporaries really did think concerning peasant life in the Middle Ages, we must first pause to consider the very different picture which has obtained wide currency during the last quarter of a century. The writer who has produced the greatest show of evidence here, and who has most influenced even distinguished scholars who have had no leisure to verify his references and note his omissions, is Johannes Janssen in his voluminous and frequently-quoted *History of Germany at the Close of the Middle Ages*. When we look closely at that book, we find that he produces no complete and general characterization[1] from any contemporary author in support of his views. While completely ignoring Beham's unfavourable generalization, even Janssen's enormous industry—and nobody will deny to him that praise—has failed to discover any equally full and emphatic generalization in favour of peasant life. The most he can produce is the proof that the country-folk were often well fed at the exceptionally favourable time with which he is concerned—roughly, from 1450 to 1500—and that other classes satirically inveighed against the prosperity and pride of these boors. But it is evident that we cannot attach the same weight to a satirist as to a responsible and laborious student of social conditions like Beham; and, indeed, Janssen himself confesses, in a footnote, that the quotations he adduces may be partly explained by the disgust which the bourgeoisie felt for this increasing prosperity of the country-folk[2]. As a matter of fact, such jealous satirists could be quoted from much earlier dates; *e.g.* one thirteenth century bourgeois who is indignant that the peasant should ever eat a goose, he who deserves to be fed on

---

[1] For a fuller exposure of the treatment of this subject by English and German apologists, see appendix 4.
[2] I, 370, n. 3.

"straw, thistles, and thorns"; or another who would condemn the rustic to "beechmast and acorns, like the swine that he is"; or that great abbot of Tournai who cannot understand why labourers are no longer content to wear their masters' cast-off clothes[1]. It is obvious that writers of this kind must be used with considerable caution, and that their satire has probably been provoked not so much by any steady prosperity of the whole peasant class as by the exceptional prosperity and extravagance of a few. And Janssen must to some extent have realized the weakness of his own case; for, while vaguely appealing to Bensen as a favourable witness for the early fifteenth century, he avoids quoting his exact words, which put another complexion on the matter. Bensen writes:

Oppressed as the peasant was, yet there was one bright point in his yearly life, upon which he spent all his savings. This was the *Kirchweih* [village "wake"]. Then every house displayed an unwonted abundance, and neighbours flocked in from other villages to visit their kinsfolk and gossips....Not less joyous were the great bridal-feasts, when well-to-do folk gave their daughters away. All ate and drank so freely then at the cost of the young couple, that it was often long before they could recover from this expense.

Here we see Bensen carefully noting the occasional feasts as contrasting strongly with the ordinary life of those whom he characterizes as "oppressed peasantry," and his words, if they had been quoted in full, would not have suited Janssen's thesis. Indeed, we have other evidence that some peasants got enough money to use it foolishly, and that most, on special occasions, would lavish food and drink with an extravagance which crippled their resources[2]. But spasmodic outbursts of wild merriment are no evidence for steady prosperity; and all Janssen's quotations are perfectly consistent with a low general state of civilization in the German village. We have painful proof of this from

[1] Lommatzsch, p. 71; *Poésies de Gilles li Muisis*, ii, 81–3, 154. Gilles, who wrote about 1360 among what were perhaps the most prosperous peasants and artisans in Europe, attacks these for their frequent insistence on higher wages, and accuses them of wanting to live like country squires and lord it over their employers.

[2] See Vogt, p. 35. It may be apposite to refer to the evidence we get from present-day Germany. A partial case might be made out on either side by adroit selection of evidence; yet most of us are convinced that, while a minority are well-off and extravagant, the large majority are less well-off than before the war.

the Germany of the present moment. If at Cologne or Frankfort, for instance, the beer-shops and picture palaces are as full as ever, this is not because the workman is prosperous but because it is not worth his while to save money. Moreover, there are indications that medieval lords, both lay and ecclesiastical, willingly encouraged occasional extravagances of this kind. The riotous liberty enjoyed by the Roman slaves at the Saturnalia is our classical example here; and the medieval serf, like the American negro, was sometimes kept in humour by kindly indulgences which cost the giver little, but did much to reconcile those simple minds to their lot. Such indulgences were apparently more often granted, as we might expect, by great lords or by rich abbeys. We have a very interesting example from the monks of St Peter in the Black Forest. By the customs of that abbey, the peasants had to work harder than usual at vintage time, just as at harvest. They had to cart the heavy wine-casks, over those rough forest-roads, from outlying vineyards to the monks' cellar, and this more strenuous work was rewarded with proportionately liberal entertainment at the end.

And when they have unladen the wine, they shall be brought into the monastery and shall have meat and drink in abundance. A great tub shall be set there and filled with the wine that they have brought, and a stoup shall be set therein, and each shall drink for himself. And the cellarman shall lock up the cellar, and the cook his kitchen [for safety's sake]; and, if so be that the peasants wax drunken and smite the cellarman or the cook, they shall pay no fine for this deed; and they shall drink so that two of them cannot bear the third back to the waggon[1].

Other customals give us occasional glimpses of similar rough indulgences. The harvest-home is sometimes specified; and the abbot of Münster in Alsace allowed a sort of saturnalia on the day of the yearly folkmoot; play, usually forbidden, was then permitted; and assaults were not actionable, so long as they were bloodless and the injured party had sufficient life left in him to get home that evening[2]. Documents of this kind help

---

[1] *Weisthümer*, I, 357 (fifteenth century). Compare the much later descriptions of rejoicings, *ibid*. IV, 576 (seventeenth century), and Vogt, p. 12.

[2] *Weisthümer*, IV, 195. For the prohibition of skittles, ball-play, or dance on other occasions see II, 208; III, 739; V, 137.

us to understand that tractate, which we might otherwise discount heavily as a piece of medieval rhetoric, in which Nicolas de Clémanges protests against the introduction of new holy-days on the plea that those already existing were defiled with drunkenness and irreligion[1].

Of a similar type, though far less frankly indecorous, seem to have been the scot-ales on Glastonbury estates. The scot-ale was a prehistoric institution among the Anglo-Saxons; a communal feast to which each brought a money contribution to cover his share of the drink. In so far as these were connected with religious festivals, they were baptized as Christian feasts in accordance with St Gregory's well-known advice to the first missionaries from Rome to our islands, and became the church-ale of the later Middle Ages[2]. When not ecclesiastical, these feasts seem to have come naturally under the direction of the sheriff, as the chief local authority. The medieval sheriff lived under something like the same temptations as the Roman publican; here, then, was an obvious chance of making money, as at a modern raffle, by giving the people less than the total of their contributions; and we have abundant evidence that the scot-ale, in the sheriff's hand, gradually became a form of compulsory and illegitimate taxation[3]. But on the Glastonbury manors the drinking seems to have been rather at the monks' expense; the contributions may have covered the cost in the earlier days of dearer money from which we have no record;

---

[1] *De novis festivitatibus non instituendis* (*Opp.* 1613, pp. 143 ff.: a very long extract in Delisle, p. 119). There is a similar treatise by his contemporary Felix Hemmerlin, precentor of Zurich, about 1450 A.D. (*Tractatus, etc.*; Reber, p. 311). But the same complaints had been made no less emphatically, though more briefly, by Cardinal Humbert de Romans to the General Council of Lyons in 1274, "both because on feast-days there is a greater increase of sin in taverns, dances and brothels, by reason of evil idleness, and also because the working-days are scarce enough for the poor to get their livelihood." He thinks they might be allowed to work after Mass on all but the principal feast-days (Mansi, *Concilia*, t. XXIV, col. 130). Bishop Guillaume Durand emphasized the same points before the General Council of Vienne in 1311: "more evils are sometimes committed on Sundays and festivals than in all the rest of the week" (pars III, tit. 53, p. 340).

[2] For the prohibition of scot-ales in churches or under clerical direction, see Wilkins, *Concilia*, I, 474, 476, 502, 530, and *passim*: they begin at least as early as 1173 A.D. Brief sketches of the history of church-ales may be found in my *Medieval Studies*, no. 8, and in an article by E. Peacock in *Archaeol. Journ.* XL (1903), 1 ff.

[3] *E.g.* Ducange, s.v. *Scotallum*.

but in the later Middle Ages they seem hardly adequate[1]. A thirteenth century record shows that, on each Glastonbury manor, the lord abbot had the right and duty of holding three scot-ales a year; and each tenant was bound to come, with his "scot" in his hand. On the manor of Damerham, here is a typical tenant's custom, as summarized by the modern editor.

Robert Palmer, of Damerham, was entitled to attend three of these entertainments every year, and the smallness of his contribution shows that there must have been a considerable deficit for the lord of the manor to meet[2]. Each feast lasted for two days, for which Robert and his wife paid 3d. There was a further charge of ½d. if they chose to bring a man or maid, or one of their "under setles" or sub-tenants, to join the revel for one day. Robert was one of the upper tenants, and might drink ale "plenè," as much as ever he pleased; the small holders, and even the park keeper and his wife, were restrained to half-drinks and moderate draughts. There is a very full return as to the holding of the ale-clubs at Longbridge. The jury say that the lord may hold three "scot-ales" in the year after this fashion; on Saturday, the married men and youths come after dinner, and are served three times with ale; on Sunday, the husbands and wives come, with their pennies, and they can come back again the next day, if they will; the young men must pay a penny a head if they come on the Sunday, but on the Monday, they can come and drink for nothing, provided they do not sit on the bench; any one of them caught sitting down must pay his penny as before. These rights, they say, belong to the serfs born on the manor and their offspring; but a stranger who serves anyone in the manor or is abiding there, shall have no share in the right.

On the manor of Deverill the scot-ales sometimes lasted three days instead of two; these were called "full scot-ales." There were somewhat similar feasts for the peasantry after the sowing of the spring corn, after harvest, and at Christmas; but these were gratuitous.

In the Burton survey [another Glastonbury manor] there are notices of the Christmas dinner. The tenants cut and carried in the logs for a yule-fire[3]; each brought his faggot of brushwood, lest the cook should serve his portion raw, and each had his own dish and mug, and a napkin of some kind, "if he wanted to eat off a cloth."

---

[1] Somerset Record Soc. v, 244–5, 259.

[2] I should venture to question this last sentence; the contributions would be equivalent to something considerable in present coin. Robert's would pay for three gallons of weak, or six quarts of strong ale; and the servant's scot would pay for a liberal libation.

[3] For the Yule log in Normandy see Delisle, p. 373.

There was plenty of bread and broth, with two kinds of meat, and various savoury messes. At East Pennard the farmer had a right to four places at the yule-feast, and each man was entitled to have a fine white loaf and a good helping of meat, and to sit drinking after dinner in the manorial hall.

The editor of the Glastonbury *Rentalia*, from whom I have been quoting, concludes, in my opinion justly:

Many other passages might be cited to illustrate the life of the ancient peasantry, their patient struggles with fortune, and their rarely seen and somewhat dismal holidays. Enough has been said to show that the Merry England of the 13th century was a place where there was much to do, and little to get, and at any rate that the predecessors of our modern farmers had a great deal of hard work with very little in the way of amusement to lighten it[1].

Here, then, we have something tangible to start from. We have heard a few contemporary witnesses as to the status of the medieval peasant; and we have marked the cross-lights thrown upon this evidence by what Janssen and his school have collected. There seems no difficulty in reconciling these different lines of evidence, so long as we bear in mind the circumstances natural to that primitive society; and, especially, so long as we are on our guard against the delusion that, because there was comparatively little money in the Middle Ages, therefore money and money's worth had less influence in society than now[2]. Few people who know the modern French peasant will assert that money plays a less important part in his life than in that of American dollar-magnates[3]. "Medieval liberty," wrote Lord

---

[1] See appendix 5 for Christmas festivities on another monastic manor.

[2] I cannot think, for instance, that Prof. F. M. Powicke had seriously weighed both sides when he wrote: "I should be prepared to argue that to-day men are more hypnotized by wealth and power than they were in the Middle Ages" (*History*, April 1924, p. 15). The subject is of very great social importance; and, if this thesis can really be proved by medieval evidence, a scholar could hardly devote himself to a more useful task.

[3] See, for instance, P. G. Hamerton, *Round About My House* (3rd ed. 1876), pp. 213 ff., cf. pp. 110 ff., 368. This is what medieval writers tell us about their own times; they are never tired of quoting from Ecclesiastes: "All things obey money." *Freidank's Bescheidenheit* represents the proverbial philosophy of thirteenth century Germany; and this book assures us that the whole world is mainly intent upon two things, [carnal] love and gain; but, of these two, gain is the stronger impulse. Again, "nowadays, alas, men honour a rich boor before poor lords without right; a man is wretched without possessions, whatever be his knowledge or his deeds" (*Freidank*, ed. W. Grimm, pp. 55-7; ed. F. Sandvoss, Berlin, 1877, pp. 41-2).

Acton, "differs from modern in this, that it depended on property"[1]. Seignobos, again, summarizes in practically the same words, "Cette société n'estimait que l'homme indépendant et le propriétaire"[2]. And, to quote finally from another authority of the first rank, Guérard: "Ce qui forme la base de la société féodale, c'est la terre, et quiconque la possède, prêtre ou gentilhomme ou vilain, est dépositaire d'une portion plus ou moins grande de la puissance temporelle; la condition d'un individu se détermine bien moins par l'éducation, par le mérite, par la naissance même, que par la propriété"[3]. It is true that brute force was perhaps even a stronger factor than money or other property in the Dark Ages; yet money and property, except when pitted against brute force, had at least as much power then as now. I do not forget the enormous sums which were subscribed for professedly religious purposes; but we must distinguish narrowly between the purely religious and the commercial element in these transactions. When a lord who had wrung thousands from the peasantry gave a few hundreds, at his last gasp, for the privilege of burial in a monk's frock or of Masses said for his soul, we must write that down as a mainly commercial bargain[4]. One of the most parsimonious of medieval sovereigns, Louis XI of France, was most lavish in his gifts to particular shrines at particular times; but always as part of a definite business contract. When we have deducted the commercial element from these semi-religious bargains of the Middle Ages, I do not think we shall find that a greater proportion was sacrificed for purely altruistic and ideal motives than in our own day. But here we are faced with a very difficult and complicated comparison, leaving room for wide divergences of opinion. Yet no writer seriously interested in the history of the labouring classes can absolve himself from the duty of framing some con-

[1] *Letters*, ed. Figgis and Laurence (1917), p. 272. Compare F. W. Maitland on p. xx of *Select Pleas in Manorial Courts*: "In the Middle Ages liberty and property are closely-connected ideas."

[2] p. 75; cf. p. 93: "une société qui n'estime que la force et la richesse foncière." In all these brief sentences we discount, of course, the epigrammatic point of exaggeration.

[3] *Cart. St-Père*, p. cxiii.

[4] The monks of Worcester, in their earlier days, reckoned as a regular part of their income the moneys that came in from receiving dying folk *ad succurrendum* (Hale, pp. lix, 26 b, 132 a).

clusion in his own mind, however roughly, and of formulating this to his readers. At this point, therefore, I must pause to state my own conclusion in a brief and tentative form, as a guiding thread for farther detailed discussion of this subject. I should say, then, that the average medieval peasant lived a life not very dissimilar, in essence, from that of the modern French peasant-proprietor and the English village labourer of eighty years ago. Nine-tenths of the conditions, perhaps, are much the same for all these three classes, just able to maintain themselves and their families by hard and unremitting work. The serf had, perhaps, about the same chance of rising in the world as our eighteenth century labourer had; while the free medieval labourer had a little more; yet, if we take all the medieval peasants in a lump, and if we remember, on the other hand, how many of their successors have worked their way off the land altogether, it may be doubted whether there was really any appreciable advantage here on the side of the Middle Ages. As compared with the modern French peasantry, the medieval labourer had distinctly less chance of rising. And, as compared with both English and French, his want of legal freedom put him at a decided disadvantage. Therefore, even when we have made ample allowance for the quiet but enormous economic pressure of the modern world, and have reminded ourselves most emphatically that modern legal liberty need not spell actual freedom, and that the past potential tyrant was not always an actual tyrant, I cannot help concluding that there is, to put it roughly, 90 per cent. common to these three classes which we are considering, but that the 10 per cent. of difference weighs very decidedly in favour of modern times. This is not much, perhaps, as the fruit of six centuries of struggle; but, for what it is worth, it is to the good. And it seems to me that those who set the medieval peasant above his modern successors have not, at the bottom of their mind, allowed sufficient weight to the enormous contrasts of rank and power in the Middle Ages—contrasts even deeper, at bottom, than those between the modern millionaire and the proletariat upon whom he has fattened.

The medieval lord's power, we are often told, was exercised patriarchally; and it is insisted that mankind is never really happier than under wise patriarchal government. How far this

is true, we may be better able to judge in the light of documents
to which I shall come later; meanwhile, let it be noted that the
medieval peasant had this great disadvantage; the things that
most deeply concerned him were done not so much by himself
as by others for him. He may have had a great deal of liberty
in pre-Conquest times; but this he lost as an individual by that
very political progress which marked so great an advance for
the community at large—the strengthening of the central executive authority and the gradual substitution of written for
customary law. The serf to the very end, as the freeman from
the first, was a sort of juryman in the manor court; he gave the
"dooms," in accordance with the unwritten custom of the
manor[1]. However conservative the spirit may have been, these
customs themselves must have gone through considerable modifications during generations or centuries of this process; the
very diversity of detail on neighbouring or closely-allied manors
shows this. To some extent, therefore, the serf not only interpreted but made the customary law. But, when a strong lawyer-
class arose in the latter half of the twelfth century, and when
in the thirteenth all lords began systematically to reduce the
customs of their manors to writing, then these lords were not
only far more securely protected against encroachment from
the serf, but had a hundred little chances of stretching in their
own favour those brief written sentences, drafted with old-world
clumsiness, upon which their claims rested. Moreover, the
landlord had at his back the lawyers with their comparatively
clear-cut theories and aphorisms, those men who defined the
serf, for instance, as the man who "ought not to know in the
evening what work might be demanded of him tomorrow, and
is always liable to uncertain duties, and may be tallaged at the
will of his lord, more or less, and must give blood-money for
leave to give his daughter in marriage"[2]. Again, behind these
lawyers, stood a strong executive against which there was little
hope of rebellion. Though the peasant, freeman or serf, is still
doomsman in the manor court, it is now a written custom that
he has to follow, of which we may say with Wordsworth that it

---

[1] F. W. Maitland in *Select Pleas in Manorial Courts*, I, pp. lxv–lxxiii,
Pollock and Maitland, 2nd ed. I, 589, 593.
[2] Bracton, R.S. III, 376.

often lies upon him with a weight heavy as frost, and deep almost as life[1]. This lowering process could not last, of course; it was impossible permanently to keep more than half the population under this subjection in a country of steadily-growing political freedom. Therefore, in spite of the written custom, the peasant will nibble away at one corner, and buy himself a little freedom at another with hard cash; a good deal that stands clearly recorded on parchment will become obsolete in practice; and so will an even larger proportion of what the twelfth century lawyers have formulated as to the serf's disabilities. But, to the very end of the Middle Ages and beyond, there always remains this network of custom. Let us therefore roughly formulate the difference between the legal position of the modern and the medieval proletariat. The former are confronted, it may be said, by stone walls and doors of iron; a strong State with very definite laws. But they have the constitutional keys in their own hands, in so far as they can use them; by voting in a mass, the proletariat could pass freely through any legal or constitutional barrier by a strictly legal and constitutional road. And, though at present it is morally impossible for them to use this mass-force in all its fulness, yet any approach to this—any coalition of the working men which comes near to such a full combination—is so formidable that it must be taken into account; therefore the trade unions may conceivably at any given moment dictate to the executive. The medieval proletariat, on the other hand, were entangled in a sort of spider's web, from which, apart from revolution, there was no escape but by slow and patient separation of mesh from mesh. The serf's only constitutional power was this of giving dooms in accordance with custom; therefore adverse custom could be broken down only by imperceptible degrees. Yet, with patience, slow and steady progress could be made from century to century. Heavily as the scales were weighted against the serf in other ways, yet in his lord's court he had this solid ground, that the verdict must be given, formally at least, through him.

[1] Cf. Pollock and Maitland, 2nd ed. I, 376.

CHAPTER IV

A GLASTONBURY MANOR

WE may now pass from the general to the particular, and try to obtain such glimpses of actual recorded village life as shall enable us, little by little, to construct a coherent picture.

Let us take an abbey estate, as rather favourable, on the whole, to the peasant's well-being. Monastic charity was heavily counterbalanced by monastic conservatism; but the reader will probably conclude with me, if his patience will follow me to the end, that there was a slight balance of prosperity, on the whole, in favour of the peasant on Church lands; such a balance, perhaps, as there is nowadays in favour of government service. We will take, then, a great and famous English abbey like Glastonbury, with its many manors of varied soil, but more fertile than the average.

The abbot of this house was in every sense a great lord; and one of the latest of the long series, Richard Beere, drew up a terrier in 1516 which describes minutely four of his ten manor-houses and parks[1]. He may, indeed, have had more than ten; the abbot of Bury had thirteen. With this wealth at his disposal, and this baronial dignity, he could do much even in the royal courts; for instance, abbot Whethamstede of St Albans notes in his memoranda how he expended, within a few weeks, something like £300 modern upon two judges and a sheriff[2]. These English abbeys were small compared with the greatest in France, Germany and Italy: "The great monasteries of France," writes Guérard, "were real states"[3]. But Glastonbury is a good typical example; thousands of modern visitors go thither yearly, and for the past we have fairly full records; therefore it affords a good frame for our concrete picture of peasant life. It lies in a beautiful country; and its beauty is of the sort that

---

[1] Printed by T. Hearne in the appendix to *Joh. Glaston* (1726), vol. II; compare the other contemporary account printed by Archbold, p. 117. For the baronial magnificence of the abbots of Westminster see Westlake, *Last Days*, pp. 8, 44, 59, and *Westminster*, p. 55; *Wenlock*, p. 104; and for Durham, Canon Fowler in his preface to vol. III of *Durham Acct. Rolls* (Surtees Soc.).

[2] Amundesham, R.S. II, 256.

[3] *Irminon*, I, 903.

would have appealed to all men in those days with which we are concerned. A friend familiar with Welsh village life has often told me the enthusiasm with which farmers have spoken to him after their first journey over the border, to Shrewsbury or Oswestry fair: "England is a beautiful land; it is as flat as a penny!" Let us therefore repair to those rich stretches between the Mendips and the sea, dear to the farmer as to the artist, as flat as a penny, with their pastures and ploughland and woodland, and all the details described in Abbot Beere's terrier— warrens and fish ponds and natural meres, and the eminent great oaks in which the herons build, and the browsing deer below. Let us put back the clock of time by six hundred years, and imagine ourselves (if this be not too presumptuous), guests for a while of the lord abbot of Glastonbury. We have come from so far, in time if not in space, that he will not enquire too closely into our possible servile origin, but will gladly tell us what he can in exchange for the strange and moving stories that we can bring him from our own days. We shall stand with him at the oriel of his private chamber in one of these manors— let us say, at Wrington; we shall watch the peasants coming home in the autumn twilight, for all the world like the peasant of today, each with his tools on his shoulder, and with the heavy gait of a man who was in no hurry this morning, and has still less haste after the day's work, even though supper be waiting for him. We ask the great lord how these men live; what dues do they owe to the abbey? He cannot tell us off-hand, but he bids the steward fetch his terrier; and here, thanks to the diligence of Thomas Hearne the Oxford antiquary, we may look over his shoulder and read the very words[1].

Be it noted that each customary tenant [of Wrington], as often as he shall have brewed one full brew, shall give to my lord abbot 4d. under the name of *tolcestre*[2]. *Item*, each customary tenant shall give mast-money for his pigs [in the woods], as appeareth more fully in the Ancient Customal. *Item*, be it noted that the customary tenants are bound to grind their corn at my lord's mill, or to pay a yearly tribute in money, viz. each holder of a yardland 2s. 8d. [etc., down to the lowest cotter at 4d.]. Be it noted also that, when any shall die,

---

[1] *Joh. Glaston*, p. 352.
[2] See Smyth, *Lives of Berkeleys*, I, 341, for the profits from this tolcestre system.

A VILLAGE PROCESSION

WRINGTON TOWER, SOMERSET

my lord shall take his heriot, to wit his best beast. And, if there be no beast, from the holder of a yardland[1] or half a yardland he shall have one acre of corn; and from any lesser tenant, if he have so much land in cultivation, the lord shall have half an acre of his best corn. And, even though the wife die before the man, he shall give no heriot; but if she die in the holding after her husband's death, and shall have given it up to my lord or shall die in her widowhood, my lord shall have the heriot as aforesaid. And if there be no corn, then my lord shall have the best chattel found in the tenement on the day of death, etc., as appeareth in the Ancient Custumal.... Note, that whosoever shall be tenant of the customary mill, which is now held by Edmund Leneregge, is bound to provide mill-stones, so that the burden fall not upon my lord, as was found upon the copy of William Truebody, lately tenant of that house and mill.

These are quite typical customs of the later Middle Ages, but we see at once how they take for granted and omit a great deal that we might like to have explained. But let us leave this for the moment, and mount with William Truebody to the church tower, and compare the bird's eye view from that height with the same view as seen today. From Wrington tower we shall see more woodland, as in other parts of England we might see more fen, than at present; the other church towers which look across to us will be not grey, but white and new; the villages nestling under them will have somewhat fewer and smaller cottages than now, and more widely spaced, each within its little garden or toft[2]. But by far the most striking difference will be the comparative absence of hedgerows, and the curious network of long strips in the arable field. This is the web within which the medieval peasant lives and moves and has his being; we must not strictly call it a spider's web, since his own forefathers have had much to do with the spinning of it; but it is a very complicated tissue, which we must take into account before we can understand his daily life.

It seems certain that the manorial system of the Middle Ages had grown out of an earlier system in which common rights played a far greater part. At the time we are considering, private ownership was recognized, but the exercise of that ownership

[1] The yardland or virgate was usually 30 acres; sometimes it was as many as 48, at other times as few as 16.
[2] Compare, with what is said here, Tawney, pp. 401, 409, 411.

was restricted. "Medieval tillage was cooperative in character, and all the principal operations of agriculture were carried out in common"[1]. By the usual arrangement, the whole land of the manor was divided into three "fields," each of which was ploughed and sown for two years running, and left fallow for the third. There are frequent traces, however, of tillage on a "two-field" or, again, on a "four-field" system. The lord had his own land, his "demesne"; the peasants had each a small holding. A full peasant had a *virgate* or *yardland* and two oxen to plough it. The normal plough-team comprising eight oxen, four such tenants would be associated in the ploughing[2]. By the ancient laws of Wales, the land thus ploughed was divided every year among the contributors to the tillage, in order of importance; but there is no trace of this yearly redistribution in our England of 1324; each peasant has his own permanently specified lands in each of the three fields—with the exception of free labourers or landless dependents, whose status does not seem to have been sufficiently investigated[3]. Besides the arable land there was nearly always a stretch of wood and waste, in which the tenant had certain rights of taking wood to mend his house or plough, and of gathering dry sticks and fallen timber. The familiar phrase "by hook and by crook" testifies, we are sometimes told, to those cases where the man might take not only the rotten boughs within reach of his arm, but also such as he could pull down with a hooked pole. Then there were the common grazing-lands, on which each tenant had his proportionate right of pasture; lands which, though sadly shrunken, still survive in many places as the village "common" or "green"[4]. Last, there was the "Lammas-land," so called be-

[1] Lipson, p. 66; but see pp. 39–42 below.

[2] Mr H. G. Richardson, however, has given me what seem conclusive reasons to show that the plough-team of eight was never simultaneously at work; that the peasant ploughed as a rule with only four oxen at a time; therefore the full team was probably divided, four working in the morning and four in the afternoon. See appendix 40.

[3] *E.g.* the "servants" and "undersettlers" of the Glastonbury *Rentalia*, referred to above, p. 29. For French serfs who possessed servants of their own, see for instance Guilhermoz, pp. 301, 307, *Irminon*, I, 243, 307. Guérard instances a serf—*i.e.* selling to the other that freedom which he himself did not possess (*ibid.* I, 379).

[4] *E.g.* at Pentney, in Norfolk, enough of this rough pasture survives to be let for shooting and grazing rights; the rent is spent on coals for the poor.

cause it was enclosed for hay from Candlemas to Lammas—
Feb. 2 to Aug. 1. These hay meadows were very valuable,
usually much more so than the same extent of arable; and they
were not only fenced in but kept under supervision by the
hayward, who takes his name not from the hay, but from the
hedges which it was his duty to guard. There were hedges also
round the gardens and tofts—a toft was, normally, a three-acre
patch which the full yardlander had round his cottage—otherwise, all the land was open, and the holdings were in long acre
strips divided from each other only by "balks," or ridges of
unploughed turf, with "headlands" running transversely along
the tops of the strips to facilitate access.

The arable, then, was divided into three "fields," each under
a regular rotation of tillage or fallow[1]. One year, the field would
be ploughed in October and sown with wheat or rye, reaped in
August, and left in stubble. Next year it would be ploughed in
March, and sown with barley; reaped in August as before. The
third year it would lie fallow; it was ploughed up twice in June,
and rested until the fourth year, when it would again be ploughed
and sown in October. Under this custom (whether in two or
three or four fields), the individual peasant had no choice
of date or of crop; he must plough and reap with the rest,
and sow the same seed as they. As already suggested, the
ploughing and reaping were very often done on a cooperative
system[2]; but it is scarcely safe to infer this too absolutely from
the fact that any other conceivable system must have entailed
almost incredible confusion and waste. For these holdings were
mixed together in a very startling fashion. The lord's demesne
was a sort of home-farm, tilled by labour which the serfs were
bound to provide, or by free labourers whom the bailiff paid
out of moneys with which the serfs redeemed their services.
Yet demesne land frequently occurs in strips intermingled with
tenants' strips. To some extent this was advantageous for both;
the tenant, having to put in a day's ploughing for his lord, could
work at this adjoining strip instead of taking his plough and
team half-way across the manor to work. But what shall we

---

[1] At Martham, they were called respectively Westfeld, Estfeld, and
Suthfeld (W. Hudson in *Hist. Teach. Misc.* I, 98, 120).

[2] *Ibid.* pp. 98–9, 165–6; cf. Delisle, p. 135, n. 36.

say of the subdivisions and complications among the tenants themselves? The question of what became of a serf's younger sons (or elder sons, in the districts where the younger was the legal heir) needs more investigation than it has received[1], though it is much simplified by the fact that, owing to wars, pestilences, etc., population remained fairly stationary during several centuries of the Middle Ages. But there was evidently a good deal of partition among the peasant's children; this has been worked out with wonderful patience and acumen by Mr W. Hudson in

N.

Alex. de Sco.

R. Pethun, 1 acre.

(a) ———— (a) ————   R. Pethun, 1 rood.
  6 perches.   R. Pethun, 34 perches.
(b) ———— (b) ————   Alice Elsy, 1 rood.
(c) 4 perches. | Alice Elsy, 26 perches. | Agnes Elsy. 10 perches.

Agnes Elsy, 1 acre.

Common Pasture of Sea

John Longe, 1 acre.

W. Harding, 12 perches. | John Long, 28 perches.
                    W. Harding, 1 rood.
                    Ad. Harding, 1 rood.
H. de Syk, 28 perches. | A. Harding, 12 perches.

H. de Syk, 1 acre.

W. <————————————————— 40 perches (of 18 feet), or 240 yards. —————————————————> S.

(a) 3 p. Mess. of W. Blakeman.   (b) 3 p. Mess. of Thos. Else.   (c) 4 p. Mess. of Clem. Rediere.

PLAN OF BLAKEMANNESTOFTS.

the studies to which I have already referred[2]. He has succeeded in ascertaining, with mathematical exactness, the subdivisions in 1292 of two tofts—*i.e.* a block of six acres—which had once been held by Ivor Blackman, and are now divided among ten

[1] It is briefly touched upon by Vinogradoff, *Villainage*, p. 246: far more suggestive is the discussion by Tawney, p. 104; see appendix 6.

[2] *Hist. Teach. Misc.* I, 165 ff.; *Norf. Arch.* xx, 179 ff. *Trans. Roy. Hist. Soc.* 4th series, I. Miss Levett finds on the St Albans lands, in the fourteenth century, a subdivision of holdings which is perhaps even greater than this at Martham, and which leads naturally to a great complexity and irregularity of villein services. Other instances of great subdivision may be found in Delisle, p. 33, Vinogradoff, *Villainage*, pp. 231–3, and especially Seignobos, p. 365, a document almost as instructive as Mr Hudson's.

different tenants. Only one now bears the original name; he is William Blackman, and he holds only three perches, doubtless just a garden round his cottage; he was by this time super-annuated, and the main arable had gone to the younger generation. Clement Rediere, again, is in an exactly similar position. A third, Thomas Elsey, has likewise his cottage and three perches, while around him are other Elseys, doubtless his children, and some Longs, between whom and the Elseys Mr Hudson traces a connexion by marriage. Of the remaining seven tenants, four have from an acre and a half to just short of an acre, and three about a quarter of an acre each. And, although this of Blackman's tofts is the only holding which the documents have allowed Mr Hudson to map out with this absolute certainty, yet all are similarly broken up. Between Domesday and 1292 the Martham tenants had naturally increased slowly in numbers; from 63 to 107. But subdivision had gone on at an enormously greater rate of increase; there were now 935 holdings, in more than 2000 separate strips. Each tenant, that is, had on an average nearly twenty separate strips, and these might be scattered about anywhere on the manor. We possess no actual contemporary maps of a manor until after the Reformation, when the process of consolidation of holdings had already been power-fully at work; yet even those Elizabethan and Jacobean maps show a bewildering maze of tenements. There was probably, therefore, some simplification of tillage by cooperation, and Mr Hudson's conclusion will probably hold for the majority of cases.

Why did the tenants rest content with the bewildering fractions of roods and perches, and how did they distribute the produce fairly? We are not speaking of allotments which each holder can occupy with his own chosen crop. The whole 6 acres here were sown with the same crop. The divisions of tenancy were not marked. There could be but one way of distribution. The total number of sheaves of (say) barley would be divided proportionately according to the size of each tenant's holding and the due number handed to him or her. The reason why so many junior members of a family had separate portions of a holding was no doubt due to the fact that they were all expected to look after themselves even though living together. The age of maturity was entered on very early. A boy had to join a tithing at 12, which involved police responsibility, and he "came of age" at 16[1].

---

[1] *Hist. Teach. Misc.* 1, 165.

At the same time, I think we must not assume that this, which seems to us the only businesslike way of dealing with the tangle, was necessarily the way followed regularly and completely by the medieval husbandman. In fact, one passage in *Piers Plowman* seems to point clearly to a good deal of private and separate ploughing and reaping; the dishonest peasant confesses: "If I went to the plough, I pinched so narrowly that a foot-land or a furrow fetchen I would; from my next neighbour nymen [*take*] of his earth; and, if I reaped, [I would] overreach, or gave them counsel that reaped to seize to me with their sickles that which I sowed never"[1]. This evidence, I think, has not been noted; nor have I ever seen direct evidence quoted on either side from the Middle Ages[2]. On the other hand, we have very direct evidence from modern times in districts where medieval conditions of land-partition survived.

W. Thoma, on p. 91 of his monograph on the monastery of Leubus (Leipzig, 1894) quotes a terrible account of the working of the medieval field-system in 1806, just before it was abolished. The peasants declared to the commissioners

that, of some 1200 patches into which the domain was parcelled out, a very large number did not even measure half an acre; the smallest were from 20 square rods to 30; they went sometimes lengthwise, sometimes across at every conceivable angle; no man could conveniently arrange his patches for sowing, because they were often too small to plough. Those who had ill-drained land, if the autumn were wet, could not leave it unsown in winter and sow it in spring with some quick-growing crop according to circumstances; partly because, in spring, they could not get at their unsown land by reason of the other strips which had been sown in winter, and partly because even in summer, when the winter-sown crops had been reaped, they would lose the sown summer-crops for want of being able to look after them. The plots were so inextricably confused (they said),

---

[1] B. XIII, 371. Compare the presentment of a jury at East Hendred in Berkshire, "Iohn Hutchins incroachiavit aratro suo" (Lord Ernle in *Quarterly Review*, 1900, p. 35). Anton's quotations seem to show that, in the early eighteenth century, there was a good deal of separate tillage in medieval Germany (III, 213, 214).

[2] Hence the reluctance of the most careful students to give a decision. The late Dr W. Cunningham told me that he believed there must have been a great deal of communal ploughing, sowing and reaping, but that he could give no definite evidence either way. Seignobos assumes communal exploitation, but without offering evidence. Anton (III, 213) quotes an Erfurt statute which seems to bear out this evidence from *Piers Plowman*.

that nobody, even among the interested parties, could tell exactly who owned this or that parcel of land; so that one interested party had often happened to dung a piece belonging to his neighbour, while another had sown and reaped it. Some plots lay so that it was impossible to come at them except by driving lengthwise or crosswise over intermediate plots; so that a terrible amount of seed and corn was ruined, especially in seed-time and at the harvest[1].

It is probable that this confusion had grown very much with time; and Silesia was one of the backward provinces; but it must be evident that many of these difficulties were inherent in the system. In Flanders, Holland and northern Germany, where abbots and great nobles drained swamps and cleared forests on a large scale, giving out the new land in compact holdings to tenant farmers, agriculture progressed far more than under the old conservative system. On such new lands, the tiller started with a clean slate; he sometimes worked almost altogether outside the meshes of the manorial system, and could choose his own times and his own crops. The consequence was that the systematic growth of turnips and the regular rotation of crops seem to have been known in Flanders two centuries, at least, before they can be traced in England[2]. Under our open-field system, the whole stubble was thrown open after harvest to the whole cattle of the community for grazing: this rendered all experiment or innovation practically impossible. Each peasant must do as his neighbours did, and thank God it was no worse[3].

[1] For testimony as to the backwardness of medieval cultivation in a district of Burgundy, see Charrière, p. 43.

[2] H. Pirenne, *Hist. Belg.* II, 407; cf. Tawney, p. 389 and Lord Ernle, *English Farming*, etc. 2nd ed. pp. 100, 107, 111, 131-5.

[3] See appendix 7.

CHAPTER V

THE SPORTING CHANCE

THIS is only one instance of the medieval rustic's resignation to fate—or, shall we say, to a somewhat slipshod and disorderly Providence? We have seen that the customs differed in detail not only from manor to manor, but even from group to group within the same manor; so that these variations, like the rudimentary character of even the most definite arrangements, left room for endless misunderstandings and bickerings between landlord and tenant, or peasant and peasant[1].

One great difficulty, it will be seen at a glance, came from the minute and irregular subdivision of holdings. Each of these carried with it a similar subdivision of dues; as we have already seen peasants themselves divided theoretically into fractions between different lords, so the peasant's services and tributes became correspondingly fractional, even down to half a farthing and half an egg[2].

Again, the wages were often given partly in food or in kind; to the peasant who for his work-day could claim three herrings and a loaf, the age and condition of the herrings must have been very important; or again, if his wage consisted of a measure of corn, this depended greatly on the quality of the grain and the personal equation of the measurer[3]. Moreover, weights and

---

[1] E.g. two extracts from the records of a Westphalian abbey (*Gladbach*, pp. 24, 26). "The tithes of Piperlo and Mackenstein were so wasted at harvest-time in gluttony and drunkenness by the stewards' serfs that the brethren and the church got no profit from them." Again, "The rents came to us [under a former abbot of the fourteenth century] in good customary coin, full-weight; but nowadays in almost useless money, which is commonly received, and has been in these parts for some years past." Friction of this kind was inseparable from the unsettled state of society in general.

[2] "Godfrey of Boyton, and those who owe the same services as he, hold 44½ acres...and owe for reapsilver a penny and half a farthing, and render at Eastertide 44½ eggs." Manor of Ores, under St Augustine's, Canterbury, at the end of the thirteenth century (Turner and Salter, p. 109). Next page comes a holder of 3½ acres, with 3½ eggs; similar fractions come on pp. 111, 207, 278, 280; on p. 278 we come across ⅓ of a hen. Nor are these fractions in strict mathematical proportion; 8 acres pay 9 eggs, 7 acres 5 eggs; one half-acre holding pays, as we should expect, half an egg, while a three-perch holding pays a whole egg; so also does another half-acre (*ibid.* pp. 109–11).

[3] See Walter of Henley (ed. Lamond and Cunningham, 1890), p. 16.

measures differed sometimes to an almost incredible extent from district to district, or even within the bounds of the same manor. At Martham, a perch of the tenants' land measured only 18 feet; but a perch of the lord prior's land measured 18½. As Delisle points out: "the same manor had sometimes its large and its small measure; in more than one parish we find men measuring oats by a measure different from that which they used for wheat and barley"[1]. In France, under the Ancien Régime, there were literally hundreds of variations in the legal measures; and, even in England, where our fourteenth century kings tried to enforce a royal standard for the most important measures, exception had to be made for these manorial variations, and the peasant was left still at the mercy of local custom[2]. In later days, when the villagers were more advanced in freedom and civilization, they doubtless felt this more keenly; a scheme of reform put forward in the name of the Franconian peasants in 1524 pleaded that "the great disadvantage under which the poor labour in buying and selling must be considered, and one standard of measures and weights must be established for the whole country"[3]. Louis XI of France, very seriously concerned in his later years for the welfare of his poor subjects, hoped to live long enough to introduce a single system of weights and measures. But it is doubtful whether the majority of medieval peasants realized their disadvantage to the full. Even today, in Southern Italy, a very appreciable part of the housewives' morning is spent in market-chaffer; no stall has its fixed prices, and it may almost be said that the customers themselves would sometimes resent any innovation which reduced their marketing to a bald and immediate and uninteresting exchange of definite money for definite goods. The personal factor and the "sporting chance" are welcomed among folk unused to standardization except in its most rudimentary forms; and the same trend of thought may be traced in the Middle Ages. Vinogradoff prints a series of customs which may fairly be quoted as typical, from

[1] p. 540.
[2] 25 Ed. III, c. 10: "Saving the rents and farms of the lords, which shall be measured by such measures as have been customary hitherto." For the unfair advantage which astute traders could take from these variations in measure see *History* for Oct. 1921, pp. 170–1.
[3] Janssen, III, 93.

Borle[y], a manor belonging to Christ Church, Canterbury, in Essex.

And let it be known that when he, the villain, with other customers shall have done cutting the hay on the meadow in Raneholm, they will receive by custom three quarters of wheat for baking bread, and one ram of the price of eighteen pence, and one pat of butter, and one piece of cheese of the second sort from the lord's dairy, and salt, and oatmeal for cooking a stew, and all the morning milk from all the cows in the dairy, and for every day a load of hay. He may also take as much grass as he is able to lift on the point of his scythe. And when the mown grass is carried away, he has a right to one cart. And he is bound to carry sheaves, and for each service of this kind he will receive one sheaf called "mene-sheaf." And whenever he is sent to carry anything with his cart, he shall have oats, as usual, so much, namely, as he can thrice take with his hand[1].

These scythe-fulls, these hand-fulls, these sheaves, must have left much room for dispute; and often the measures are far more primitive and disputable than this. Certain tenants of the abbot of Ramsey had to go and collect "one hose of moderate size full of nuts well-cleaned of their husks"[2]. The history of costume shows us that, at this date (1150–1200), such hosen came some way up the thighs, but were not yet sewn together into a pair of breeches; they resembled the modern cyclist's "overalls"; Le Roux de Lincy has recorded an old proverb to the effect that "short hosen need long straps." Part of the reeve's fee on a Glastonbury manor was "a stall full of [or a truss of?] hay as high as to a man's loins"[3]. At the abbey of Vale Royal, in the thirteenth century, part of the tenant's rent was "a reasonable pig" or "half a customary pig"[4]. The monks of Bern were bound to render yearly to the monks of St-Trond "twenty legal salmon"[5]. Certain peasants on Ramsey manors, when they had done a day's mowing, might "carry home so much grass or straw as they can bind in a single bundle and lift upon their sickle [or scythe] handle, so that the handle touch not the ground. And, if perchance the handle break, then he shall lose

---

[1] *Villainage*, p. 175.
[2] Ramsey, 1, 300; cf. p. 394.　　　　[3] *Rentalia*, p. 106.
[4] *Ledger*, pp. 30 ff., 110 ff.
[5] *St-Trond*, 1, 227 (1247 A.D.). For the intentional vagueness of some measures see Peetz, p. 86. On the Rochester manor of Southfleet, in 1320, the complicated regulations for beer-tolls must have given room for endless haggling and disputes (*Cust. Roff.* p. 2 a).

his straw or grass and be at the lord abbot's mercy, and pay a fine, coming to the best accord that he can with the abbot"[1]. At another time, he may fetch from the abbot's farmyard a bundle of as much straw as he can carry, "but, if the band break before he has passed through the yard door, he shall lose his straw and compound by a fine as best he may"[2]. A reeve may take, at the end of his year of office, "the bottom of a haystack, of such thickness as he can pierce with one stroke of his pitchfork"[3]. After certain work, the servant may bring his own pitcher and take it home full of ale, up to a gallon, "but if the pitcher be more than a gallon, he shall be at the lord abbot's mercy"[4]. At Longbridge, under the abbot of Glastonbury, where the serf had a right to take one sheaf when he had reaped a cartload and carried it to the abbot's yard, a still more complicated method was used to secure a certain standard size for this perquisite. "If any sheaf appear less than is right, it ought to be put in the mud, and the hayward should grasp his own hair above his ear, and the sheaf should be drawn midway through his arm [i.e. inside the bend of the elbow]; and if this can be done without the defiling of his garments or his hair, then it is adjudged to be less than is right; but otherwise it is judged sufficient." Or, again, when a serf is at work collecting sheaves, he must gather "fifty sheaves, each as great as he can drag under his arm while he holds the lap of his tunic in his hand." In another specification, he is allowed "to glean one handful which is called in the vulgar tongue *lashanwul*' [leaze-handful][5]. The thirty salmon which the Northlode tenants owed yearly to Glastonbury kitchen must be "as thick at the tail as a man's wrist"[6]. The *medekniche* [mid-knee], on some Glastonbury manors, was "as much hay as the hayward can lift with his middle finger as far as his knees"[7]. More primitive still are

[1] Ramsey, p. 399; cf. *Rentalia*, p. 9.
[2] Ramsey, p. 399. Medieval English haystacks were small and circular, not much wider than a millstone; *une meule de foin*, as the French still say; here in the Ramsey chartulary it is *mullio feni*.
[3] *Ibid.* p. 415. [4] *Ibid.* p. 49.
[5] *Rentalia*, pp. 135–6; cf. p. 68. [6] *Ibid.* p. 5.
[7] *Ibid.* p. 85. For the German measures see *Weisthümer*, II, 21, 174; V, 485, I, 316, 430, 483; II, 37; V, 105, 442, 531; II, 412, 179. Many more may be followed through pp. 321–2 of the index (*sinnliches Mass* to *Zeitmass*). Cf. Grimm, *Rechtsalt.* vol. I, ch. 3.

some of the German measures. Many, as in England, offered
sporting chances; everything might depend on the question
whether the load of wood could be dragged a certain distance
from the forest before attracting attention; whether the tenant
has one foot or two within the moot-hall door before the moot
has begun; whether, when he has made up his mind to flit to
another village, the steward can hold back his laden cart by
the force of his single arm, or whether the tenant's oxen are
strong enough to drag it on in the steward's despite. At Prüm,
in 1640, if a malefactor on his way to prison "can spy that one
of the lords [*i.e.* monks of that great abbey] could be found
outside the cloister; and if the said malefactor can seize the
aforesaid lord by his cowl, then shall he have six weeks and
three days of freedom; and this, as often as he can achieve the
same"[1]. It is difficult to believe that the lords themselves did
not take a sporting interest in their tenants' struggles, just as
we know that our crusading knights earned the contempt of the
dignified Muslims by setting old women to run a race for a pig[2].

Bounds of jurisdiction or of hunting-rights are marked by
the lord's cast of an axe or a hammer from the edge of a stream
or of the forest. The monks of Chiemsee had wide rights of
justice over all their lands, "and over the lake, as far as a man
can ride in his saddle from the shore"[3]. Similarly the bounds
between the shires of Cambridge and Huntingdon ran, in some
of the meres, as far as a man might reach with his barge-pole
to the shore. Another medieval measure was "as far as a tame
hen can go at a single flight, which is reckoned at 300 of a man's
paces"[4]. A prisoner is to be kept in prison until he has been there
long enough to consume two bushels of corn; a tithe-gosling
may be refused if he be not old enough to pluck grass for himself
without relapsing into an undignified sitting position; a tithe-
hen, rejected by the lord as sickly, must be accepted if, when
frightened, she can clear the garden fence or jump upon a stool;
if a reaper be suspected of incapacity or laziness, the reeve may

---

[1] *Weisthümer*, III, 833. There were other chances of asylum also, besides
the ever-present church and churchyard; see I, 412, 413.
[2] Ousâma, p. 479; Petrus Cantor (Migne, P.L. vol. 205, col. 99) alludes
to the same sport.
[3] *Weisthümer*, III, 671; years 1393–1462.
[4] Bartels, p. 36.

bid him grasp nine ears in his hand and cut the stalks with a single stroke; if the ploughman, ploughing negligently for his lord, break the wheel of the plough, he must fine with a loaf of bread as tall as the wheel. The huntsman may pursue a stag into the lake of Lorsch "as far as a red shield can be seen"; peasants are bound to follow up a hue and cry "as far as a white horse can be seen"; the miller must not let the water in his dam mount so high above the stake as to prevent a bee from standing on the top and drinking without wetting its wings; the manslayer may claim shelter for so long as it takes him to eat a penny loaf[1]. But four of these rough measures are so curious that they may be given in greater detail[2].

At Fellenden, a village under the abbess of the great Frauenkloster at Zürich, the discipline of the domestic fowl was evidently as thorny a question as it has often proved elsewhere.

No man shall dwell outside the Etter[3]; but, if any man do so, he shall stand on the ridge of his roof, shall pass his right arm under his left and grasp his hair in his right hand; then shall he take a sickle by the point in his left hand; and, as far as he can cast, so far shall his hens go; and, when they go further to other folk's harm, he shall fine with three pence for every third fowl.

At Kilchberg, under the abbot of St-Gall, in 1515, the law was very slightly modified; it was not the man thus handicapped, but the wife who mounted the roof and cast the sickle as best she might with her left hand. Elsewhere, the housewife sat on the roof, tied an egg in her veil, and threw it as far as she could[4]. Or, again, even the man might cast the egg, but without any veil to help him[5].

At Saspach, under the bishop of Strassburg, certain tenants had a right to cut in the forest under restrictions which must have left ample room for quarrel.

When he heweth with his axe, let him cry aloud upon the forester; and, when he loadeth his cart, let him wait; and, what with his crying at the axe-work and his waiting at the lading, if he can come with his cart so far from the mark where he cut his wood that the forester

---

[1] Grimm, *Rechtsalt.* I, 105, 111, 146.
[2] *Weisthümer*, I, 29 (cf. p. 206 and IV, 414), 414, 523 (cf. p. 529), 516 (cf. p. 569).
[3] "In Swabia...the houses of a village, with their adjacent gardens and tofts, were divided by a ring-fence from the open and common fields; this enclosed precinct was called Etter" (Haltaus, col. 415).
[4] Bartels, p. 50. [5] *Weisthümer*, III, 889.

may not reach the cart with [a cast of] his axe with the left hand,
then may the forester, if he will, follow after the cart, and thrust his
right hand under his girdle, and with his left hand drag from the
cart what wood he may, until he come to the man's own toft. So
far may he go; but, if he follow the man into his toft, and the peasant
then turn round and smite the forester on the head, even unto death,
then shall no judgement be passed upon him for that deed[1].

In many places, the tenants had a right to certain fetchings of
dead wood from the forest. At Schwanheim, in 1421, each had
to bring to the abbot's wood-house, at new year, "a cart-load
of wood, sour and rotten and ill-packed, so that a magpie might
fly straight through it,"—i.e. a load of fallen branches gathered
as they lay and loosely packed upon the cart. Here the definition
is in the tenant's interest; so also at Nidde, under an abbess at
Mainz, and at Born under the count of Stolberg, where the
wood may be even looser, "so that a hare could run through
with his ears erect." But at Birgel, under St Peter's, Mainz, in
1419, "each tenant has a right to fetch two carts of rotten wood;
but he shall not have more than four horses to the cart. The
wood shall be sour and rotten and evil-laden, so that seven
hounds could chase a hare through it." Here, where the definition is against the tenant, the branches must be still more loosely
packed. This seems painfully vague, but vaguer still is the
prescription on another German manor that the serf may fish
occasionally in the village waters "as truly as you can, by oath";
i.e. he was allowed to dip his net a certain number of times,
and to swear that he had done no more[2]. The last German

---

[1] The fourteenth century statutes of the town of Leobschütz definitely
express this principle of sporting adventure; if a man come to the forest
with horse and cart, and hew wood, the forester may seize man and beast
and vehicle so long as he can catch them within the forest; but, if only they can
reach the open first, then " he has nothing to do with them; for the man
has hewed openly, and set his horse and his goods upon the venture"
(Anton, III, 481).

[2] *Weisthümer*, v, 414. For similar "natural" measures, and the chances
of friction and quarrel on the manor, see also Delisle, pp. 373, 382–3, 683,
and 465. This last enumerates the very complicated perquisites of an abbey
butler. Farther light is thrown by Depoin, p. 123. There is, naturally
enough, evidence of the same kind in the Welsh *Laws of Howell the Good*;
e.g. a tenant is to render a certain number of oatcakes "so thick as not to
bend when held by the edge" (p. 207).

custom that shall here be cited, if not more primitive than any of the others, is at least more curious in its own way. Any outside bondman who wished to marry a bondwoman from a certain manor must give the lord a brass pan in compensation; and the pan must be of such capacity that the bride should be able to sit in it without undue compression[1].

These are extreme cases; yet there were many other local and customary measures which must have required quite as much give-and-take as those agreements with regard to holy-days or sickness to which we shall come later. Equally trying must have been some of the covenants for rent, full of minute complications which to us seem absurd, until we remember the scarcity of coined money at that period[2].

Such prescriptions as these give a very vivid picture of the compromise that was needed between landlord and tenant, and the continual waste of energy through friction. Taken by them-selves, they would doubtless leave an exaggerated impression; but at least they show what might easily happen at many times and in many places. And when we remember the fundamental and inevitable friction inherent in any system of forced labour, when we think how truly the peasant's heart was in his own field while he was ploughing or reaping his lord's, we shall realize the full significance of this sentence from a customal of the abbey of Ramsey, which might be supported by abundant other evidence: "Walter Algerson holds 2 virgates and 2 hides, for which he doth homage to the abbot;...and he will come personally to all the boon-days, holding his rod over the workers; and on those days he shall have his dinner [from the monks' kitchen]." At another Ramsey manor, Ringstead, "Nicholas son of the Reeve holds 11 acres...and holds his rod over the reapers for three days in harvest, and shall eat with the abbot's sergeant; and at eventide he shall have two billings[3], and cheese,

---

[1] Cless, II, i, 427: "Nahmlich dass die Braut mit ihrem Sitztheile die Peripherie derselben ausfüllte" (from Weber, *Dissertatio de servitiis feudorum ludicris*).

[2] *E.g. Select Pleas*, pp. 126 ff. At Eschweiler, in the district of Metz, if doubt arose as to the value of a coin, the disputants gave the sexton bread and cheese for his journey on foot to Metz, where he could verify it at the mint (*Weisthümer*, II, 262).

[3] Not in N.E.D.: it seems to be a kind of loaf.

and two herrings "[1]. Many German customals expressly granted
the lord a right of "moderate chastisement" over the peasant;
in the eighteenth century this was interpreted as "a few boxes
on the ear, or a tolerable whipping "[2]. Bartholomew the Englishman, in spite of his origin and his name, probably composed
his *De Proprietatibus Rerum* in Germany; writing in the middle
of the thirteenth century, he describes the bondman as one who
"suffereth many wrongs, and is beaten with rods"[3]. Even in
England, a master was amenable to no law court for beating his
serf, apart from loss of life or limb; and a great man might
easily kill one with impunity in fact, though not in law[4]. It is
among the special distinctions of a most courteous and saintly
prior at Tournai that he had never struck a servant[5]; the friar
Salimbene boasts the same among his mother's exceptional
qualities[6]. A German monastic document of the twelfth century
prescribes the size of the rod for the serf's back: "it shall be
an ell and a quarter long, and as thick as the spit whereon meat
is roasted." The offender might buy off thirty stripes for sixpence, unless his offence became frequent, in which case the
master might refuse redemption[7].

We have here a contrast difficult to explain away; at least the
overseer with the rod has disappeared for ever from our fields,
and John Ball's words are an echo of far-off times: "We be
called their bondmen; and, without we readily do them
service, we are beaten "[8].

In addition to the above-named causes of friction there were
also so-called "gifts" which, originally voluntary, had become
by custom a sort of irregular tax. At Glastonbury, a tenant "is
bound to give as a gift"—*debet dare de dono*—or, again, a whole

---

[1] Ramsey, *Chart*. R.S. I, 309 405 459, 463; so also under the monks of
Gloucester (*Chart*. R.S. III, 181). Cf. Vinogradoff, *Villainage*, p. 407.

[2] Knapp, pp. 91, 355; cf. Peetz, p. 212. For survival of this medieval
custom in later France, see Habasque, p. 102.

[3] Trevisa's translation, bk VI, ch. 12.

[4] See appendix 8.   [5] Migne, P.L. vol. 180, col. 119.

[6] *M.G.H. Scriptt.* XXXII, 55; *From St F. to Dante*, 2nd ed. p. 13.

[7] *Irminon*, I, 324.

[8] Froissart (Globe edition), p. 251. Compare Sée, *Bretagne*, p. 37. The
Franciscan Nicole Bozon, even while he commiserates the peasant,
assumes that a certain amount of corporal punishment is good for him, as
it is for children (pp. 12, 25).

community must give such a "gift" to the abbot[1]. Some of the
Ramsey peasants, on their wedding-day, were compelled by
custom "honourably to reward the servants of the Abbot's
court with bread, beer, flesh or fish, according to his [the
husband's] means[2]". Under the abbey of Romainmotier, the
detested exaction of heriot is even glossed over under the
specious name of "alms"; it is an *elemosyna* due from the
tenant to the monks[3]. At the aristocratic nunnery of Burtscheid
near Aachen, the feudal protector [*advocatus*, *Vogt*] had unlawfully burdened the peasants with "money-contributions,"
which hitherto (1226) he exacted as free gifts. There were
serious complaints, and the archbishop of Cologne appointed a
commission which arranged a compromise; "the so-called free
gifts were not to exceed three marks, since the predecessor of
this Vogt had never received more, but rather less.... In spite
of this agreement...the Vogt did not trouble himself in the
least about keeping it"[4]. The worst of these originally voluntary,
but now oppressive taxes was "tallage," the French *taille*, which
lords could exact, sometimes according to fixed rates but often
à merci—i.e. with no limits but the lord's own conscience and
such sense of reason and public opinion as might control him[5].
After many generations, the lords naturally found that they
must bargain; in most cases, a jury was empanelled to assess
a reasonable sum for the tallage on each occasion; or even a
custom of fixed tallage grew up[6]. Yet, even after tallage had
thus become fixed by custom, it was nearly always subject to
the most arbitrary strokes of fortune. Lay lords might take heavy
toll to pay for their ransom, the knighting of a son, the marriage

[1] H. de Soliaco, p. 147 (note to p. 4); cf. Hone, p. 232.
[2] Ramsey, I, 347; cf. pp. 312, 338.
[3] *Weisthümer*, IV, 458 (1267 A.D.); cf. Borderie, pp. 103, 185.
[4] *Burtscheid*, p. 44; cf. p. 48.
[5] An interesting case of rebellion against the *taille à merci* is that of the
serfs of Esmans, told in *Arch. France Monast.* III, 228 (D. Anger), and
Guilhiermoz, *Enquêtes et procès* pp. 294, 305, etc. The serfs claimed to be
free from the abbot's *taille* in those years when the king had spent a night
in their villages, to their great financial disadvantage, of course. This tallage
at will was rarer in England, according to Professor Vinogradoff (*Vill.* p. 163);
but, in 1288 "Ralph, son of Robert Pyke de la Leye, the prior's [of Dunstable]
bondman, came into our full court at Segenhoe, and confessed himself the
prior's bondman, and tallageable at will; and he paid a fine of 20s. for having
so long absented himself from the prior's fee" (*Ann. Dunst.* R.S. p. 342).
[6] Seignobos, p. 65.

of a daughter; prelates might take it for their "housewarming," their *joyeux avènement*. At St-Paul-de-Besançon, in 1363, the abbot thus drew more than £200 tournois (the equivalent of about £50 sterling then, and something like £1000 nowadays) from his subjects; moreover (as the historian points out), if he had died, his successor had the right of raising the same tax again in the same year[1].

Dangerous also was the want of clear delimitation between the powers of the lord's bailiff and the reeve, who was supposed to represent the peasants, but who was inevitably subject, in the main, to the lord's influence in very many cases[2].

[1] Marquiset, p. 107.
[2] Compare Hemmerlin's evidence on a later page.

CHAPTER VI

BANS AND MONOPOLIES

ANOTHER great source of business uncertainties, and therefore of quarrels, was the monopoly of mill and oven. This encouraged not only such tricks as those which are described in Chaucer's *Reve's Tale* but also disputes as to the length of time during which the peasant was obliged to wait on the miller's good pleasure. Sometimes these regulations were extremely onerous; for instance, in eighteenth century Brittany, the tenants were compelled to grind at their lord's mill "if there were one within 1800 yards; at a water-mill they must wait if necessary for three days and nights, at a windmill one day and night"[1]. But they were generally fairer than this; those of Ramsey abbey in the thirteenth century may be quoted as typical[2].

All the tenants owe suit to the mill, whereunto they shall send their corn. And if they cannot, on the first day, grind as much wholemeal as may keep their household in bread for that day, the mill must grind it; and if the peasant cannot grind there that day, then he may take his corn elsewhere at his will[3]. If a man buy his corn, then he may grind it without hindrance at the next mill he comes to. From Aug. 1 to Michaelmas each man may grind where he will, if he be unable to grind at my lord abbot's mill on the day whereon he has sent the corn. Moreover, if it chance that my lord's mill be broken or his milldam burst, so that the tenant cannot grind there, then, as in the former case, he may take it elsewhere at his will. If the tenant be convicted of having failed to render suit to my lord's mill, he shall give sixpence before judgement; or, if he have gone to judgement, he shall give 12*d*.

[1] Le Lay, p. 38. I quote these post-medieval instances not as *typical* of the Middle Ages, for there is no doubt that some lords under the Ancien Régime had gradually encroached upon older custom, but as instances of what might easily happen fairly often, even in the days when custom was more favourable to the peasants, under a single oppressive lord.

[2] *Chartulary*, I, 473.

[3] At Châtelblanc, in 1303, the tenant must wait a whole day and night on the miller's pleasure; only then may he go elsewhere. On some domains, if the bailiff caught the tenant shirking the lord's mill without reasonable excuse, he might pour his corn or meal out upon the road (*Weisthümer*, I, 847; II, 12). Elsewhere he might confiscate the peasant's beast of burden (Guilhiermoz, *Enquêtes, etc.* pp. 296, 300). On one Worcester priory manor, the offender's horse was forfeited to the prior, and his grain to the steward (Hale, p. lxiii). For mill-oppressions in Brittany cf. Sée, *Bretagne*, pp. 68, 70.

There were similar regulations for the manorial oven; the working of this system is shown in some detail by a German customary of the abbey of Prüm, which, although in its present form it dates only from 1640, reproduces far older customs[1]. The citizens of Prüm, like those of Bury St Edmunds before the Dissolution, were still under many servile disabilities; and the bailiff reports:

Here is a ban-mill whereunto every citizen is bound; and if one come who hath need of bread and bringeth grain, the miller shall grind it, and if the miller have white meal between his stones, he shall put it away and grind for the citizen. If the miller be froward and will not do this, then shall the man go to the baker and tell him to turn his grain off; if he also will not do it, then may the man do it forthwith himself, that he may have bread for himself and for his children. When this is done, then shall the miller take his multure[2], a multer bowl from every two bushels of grain or of wheat, and a bowl from every bushel of unground grain.

There is also a ban-bakehouse; when a man has meal, he shall go to one of the upper bakehouse-maids and ask for a [hand-]mill; the maid shall bring him this; if it be that he have not enough to fill the oven, or no more than [what is made from] a bushel, then shall he give wood that he may have his bread baked, and the same fee for it that they take for a bushel. As soon as a man has made known his necessity, whether it be white meal or rye, then the maid shall prepare him his dough in reasonable time. At the bakehouse are a baker and two bake-maidens; from each oven-full they shall take eight loaves, each of the value of 8 halfpence, be the grain dear or cheap; two shall go to the lord abbot, two to the baker, and two each to the maids[3].

At Therfield, [in] 1323, various villeins who had secured hand-mills were fined 40d. each "because they grind their own corn and other folks', to the prejudice of the lord"[4]. The long and picturesque story of the fight between abbot and villeins at St Albans for these mill-rights is to be found in Walsingham's

---

[1] *Weisthümer*, III, 834.

[2] *Multura* was the usual term for the miller's toll; but it is sometimes called *multa*, or *moulte* in French (see Ducange, s.v. *molta*, and J. E. Decorde, *Hist. de Bures*, 1872, p. 51). This seems to explain that passage in *P. Plowman* which puzzled Skeat (B. x, 44); the miller, in his ignorance of Latin, takes *multa fecit Deus* to assert the divine right of mill-toll.

[3] The monks of Romainmotier had ten such ovens on their different manors, which seem to have brought a total profit of 80 florins a year (Charrière, p. 39).

[4] Page, p. 47.

Gesta Abbatum, I, 410 ff.; II, 149 ff., 154 ff., 159 ff., and in Froude's *Short Studies,* vol. III, no. 1 ; *Annals of an English Abbey.* The principle of these and similar regulations—when once we admit the right of monopoly—is equitable; but how was the mere peasant to defend himself against inequitable abuse in practice? At Forncett, in 1279, the lord's mill produced but little "by reason of its ricketty condition [*pro debilitate molendini*], and because hard by there are two new-built mills, and the freemen will not bring their corn to the earl's mill by reason of its disrepair"[1]. The freemen might go elsewhere, but the villeins had no choice; and the miserable thirty-six quarters of barley which the earl drew that year from his mill was wrung from these bondmen's necessities. Norwich priory possessed nine mills, which produced a gain of £21. 13s. 2d. in 1299–1300 and £11. 15s. 3d. in 1300–1, as shown by the cellarer's rolls for those years. In 1250, three ovens belonging to Mont-St-Michel brought in more than £20 a year to the abbey—the price of twenty cows or eighty sheep[2]. Even in the later Middle Ages, when the advance of civilization and freedom was beginning to wring real concessions from the lords, this ban of the mill, as it was called, remained a serious burden. The monks of St-Père-de-Chartres hit upon an intermediate provision; on three of their manors, finding themselves no longer able to prohibit free milling and baking altogether, they came to an agreement by which the tenants

might have no mill on their lands; and, if they wished to grind elsewhere than at the abbey mill, they must carry the corn on their backs—*in collo suo*—or with their own or borrowed horses and carts, but not with the horses or carts of any extra-abbatial mill. In the same way, they were not obliged to bake their bread at the abbey oven at Boisville, but none had the right to an oven of his own.

---

[1] Davenport, p. 36. On some manors, bondmen had to pay more in the lord's mill than other persons; in one case, at any rate, twice as much (Savine, *Bondmen,* p. 267).

[2] Delisle, pp. 614, 681; see also Savine, p. 127, Belbuck, p. 25, Delisle, pp. 521–4. The parson, apparently, was free from this mill-ban; the vicarage of Sturrey contained, as part of its standing furniture at the end of the thirteenth century, a hand-mill (Turner and Salter, p. 356, under the monks of St Augustine's, Canterbury).

There was evidently only one abbey mill and oven for the three manors; and later on, in 1258, the tenants bought themselves free from these modified restrictions and from all other relics of servitude by a fine of 800 livres tournois, which would be the equivalent of about £4000 sterling in pre-war currency[1].

It is not for nothing, therefore, that the miller has earned a bad name in social history; he paid a fixed rent for his mill, and had to recoup himself under the same temptations as the Roman *publicanus*. In France, up to the Revolution,

what rendered these monopolies so odious was not so much the fixed tariff or the prohibition against crushing one's own grain with a hand-mill or between two stones, and baking this meal at home, as the compulsion to carry the corn for long distances, over abominable roads, and then to wait two or even three days at the door of a mill where the pool had run dry; or, again, of accepting ill-ground meal, burned or half-baked bread, and of enduring all sorts of tricks and vexations from the millers or bakers[2].

The French adjective *banal* is a legacy from those days of the *four banal* and the *moulin banal*. The freeman might range at will; the serf, from his birth to his death, must eat *pain banal* or starve. The friction caused by all these primitive compacts, which medieval civilization had begun to outgrow from at least 1200 onwards, must have been immense. Under the Ancien Régime, it was admitted that the French peasants lost far more by these services and disabilities than the lords gained[3].

---

[1] *Cart. St-Père*, pp. cxi, cxciv, 704. The average price of a horse in these same records is £2 or £3 (p. cxc). In earlier times, the average profit brought in by mills of St-Germain-des-Près was equivalent to 68s. for a year in 1850 (*Irminon*, II, 633). One St Albans mill brought in £50 a year (*Gest. Abb*. R.S. II, 238. Bruneau emphasizes the burden of the mill-ban and oven-ban upon the French peasant down to the Revolution. He shows in detail how much more it harmed the peasant than profited the lord, even where the pecuniary receipts were considerable (pp. 89–93; cf. p. 162). The most that can truly be said in favour of these banalités may be found in Brutails, p. 230. Compare Eden, I, 21. The ninth century miller's duties are minutely described in Adalhard, p. 358.

[2] Champion, p. 142; the next three pages also should be read. He quotes from the complaint of the Commons of Rennes: "Let posterity forget, if it can, that feudal tyrants in Brittany, armed with judicial power, have not been ashamed in modern times to break hand-mills, and to sell to the wretched peasants, at a fixed annual sum, the permission of crushing a measure of barley or buckwheat between two stones." On the other hand, the peasants would sometimes try to cheat the millers; see *Court Baron*, p. 33.

[3] Champion, pp. 139, 142.

Another "ban" was that of wine. Everywhere there were considerable restrictions on sales; these were quite necessary in the landlord's interest. The peasant might not, of course, sell the holding, which in no strict sense was his own, without leave; nor again (and for similar reasons) his cattle or corn, except under definite restrictions; of all these transactions the lord took his toll. So also, by a natural process, from the trade in ale, which was generally carried on by the women; the simplest arrangement was for the lord to have a certain percentage of each brew or a toll in money; but there were sometimes very complicated dues. And, in wine-countries, the less regular supply (for wine comes only once a year, and then in very irregular quantities or qualities) gave rise to greater difficulties[1]. The usual "ban" was that the lord, at certain seasons in the year, had the monopoly of wine-sale in his village for a fortnight or so at a time. A vivid glimpse comes from the sworn evidence in a thirteenth century lawsuit between the monks of St-Germain-des-Prés and their peasants of Esmans. The commissioners called witnesses from all classes of society: these showed that the monks had certainly enforced the wine-ban in the past, but that it had lapsed of late years, probably through the stubborn passive resistance of the villagers[2]. There were those who remembered seeing "the monks and their servants selling wine *ad bannum*." A knight, Hugues de Puliers, "had seen the monks selling *ad bannum* thrice a year, for a month each time; and he himself, when the ban-wine was not good, sent to Ferric Cornebert to lend him some of his wine (for he is a taverner), and he did not dare to sell any"; this was thirty years ago. Another remembered these three ban-months sixteen years ago; "and no man dared sell in the village, except a certain knight." A third testified, however, that the authorities did not proceed to the extremity of "breaking the vessels of those who went not to the ban, and doing justice on this matter." Finally "Stephen, called the tramp—*Stephanus, dictus Trittannus*, sworn and examined concerning all the said articles, says that he knows nothing;

---

[1] An excellent description in Hoyer, pp. 13 ff.
[2] "This institution of Bannwein was, from quite early days, felt by the communites to be excessively burdensome, and they struggled to get it abolished" (Hoyer, p. 14).

but he adds that he went through the village and could get no wine, as men said to him, except at the house of the man who sold wine *ad bannum*." Yet Geoffroi el Duranz "was in the village when the monks sold ban-wine, and he entered into a certain tavern and drank of that taverner's wine; examined whether the taverner sold his wine openly, he said *No*; as to the time, he said it was eight years ago.'[1] We see here very clearly how the lord found it finally worth while to let the tenants redeem themselves from this kind of tax; but here, as in most cases, the monasteries were easy-going in some ways, painfully conservative in others. In the early fifteenth century, the Dominican abbess of St Lambrecht still had three wine-bans a year; "for one fortnight at Christmas, another at Easter and a third at Whitsuntide she was entitled to sell her wine at a penny per 'measure' dearer than the innkeepers. If nobody came to drink the wine, she had the right of bringing a half-Viertel to each house in Grevenhausen, and, if it was not paid for, to take a pledge for the price"[2]. There we have already that crowning injustice of the French *gabelle*, that the victim could not escape the tax even by denying himself the use of the article taxed. Bartels quotes a similar prescription from another manor (p. 28), and Hoyer cites five others: "If a man refused to take the prescribed quantity of Bannwein, it was poured into his cottage under the threshold or through the hen-hole; or it was put into his pig-trough." On one manor near Prüm, the customal permits itself an elephantine jest: "If the tenant have not drunk his [prescribed] two gallons [of ban-wine], then the lord shall pour a four-gallon measure over the man's roof; if the wine runs down, the tenant must pay for it; if it runs upwards, he shall pay nothing"[3].

Apart from the odium of the monopoly, there was nothing in this lordly or priestly wine-selling to scandalize the ordinary medieval mind. Strict Churchmen and Councils sometimes

---

[1] Guilhiermoz, pp. 302–10.

[2] Remling, I, 153. Remling comments: "It may be easily imagined what abuses such privileges must have introduced within these walls consecrated to quiet temperance and devotion. These abuses increased so much about the middle of the century that the bishop of Speyer found a complete reform of the convent necessary."

[3] Hoyer, p. 16, quoting from Grimm's *Weisthümer*, II, 528.

fought against it; but the attitude of the Council of Cologne in 1233 is significant; the thing is not there forbidden, but only regulated. In Italy, at the present day, you can ring at the door of a noble's house in Florence and buy from his porter a bottle of the wine made on his estates; and so it is, naturally enough, with the priest also[1]. But the large scale on which ecclesiastical wine-dealing and the wine-ban were sometimes carried out did provoke the masses who suffered from competition or monopoly; these were among the grievances put forward by the revolting peasants of Germany in 1525.

For we must not forget the patriarchal side of these medieval customs; the lord in England (where the ban-oven was rare, at any rate in the later Middle Ages) had as full control over the bakers as over the brewers; and it cannot be denied that these assizes of bread and ale operated to some extent for the public good. But it seems equally certain that we must discount this considerably by considering the friction at the best of times, and the frequent opportunities of fraudulent evasion[2]. At Norwich, as in all other places from which we have full records, the assizes were so regularly broken that the fines amounted to a sort of excise licence[3]. No doubt here, as travellers tell us

[1] At a village fair, at the end of the day, "for a moment the figure of a priest paused at the top of the [tavern] stairs, and looked down upon the feasters. He was the owner of the wine-barrels.…'It has been a splendid day for Don Michele,' remarked Dante the tinker; 'his wine is good'" (Lina Duff-Gordon, *Home Life in Italy*, 1908, p. 357).

[2] See especially *Star Chamber* (S.S.), II, p. xxxvi.

[3] Mr W. Hudson writes (Hudson-Tingey, I, p. cxxxviii): "Finally, by far the most fertile source of municipal profit [in medieval Norwich] was the amercement of those who had been guilty of breaches of the assize of ale. The assize of bread is little mentioned. Perhaps it was dealt with in some other way. The price of ale was fixed according to the price of wheat. Almost every housewife of the leading families brewed ale and sold it to her neighbours, and invariably charged more than the fixed price. The authorities evidently expected and wished this course to be taken, for these ladies were regularly presented and amerced every year for the same offence, paid their amercements and went away to go through the same process in the future as in the past. Much the same course was pursued by other trades and occupations. Fishmongers, tanners, poulterers, cooks, etc., are fined wholesale year after year for breaking every by-law that concerned their business. In short, instead of a trader (as now) taking out a licence to do his business on certain conditions which he is expected to keep, he was bound by conditions which he was expected to break and afterwards fined for the breach. The same financial result was attained or aimed at by a different method." Compare Jessopp (*The Nineteenth Century*, February 1883, p. 264): "The presentments of the beer-sellers seem to point to the existence of something

about some departments of American life, the irregularity of police action became in practice a sort of regularity, the exception became a sort of rule, which could be roughly allowed for and acted upon; the machinery worked after its own fashion, only with a certain amount of added friction. But that friction must not be left out of account in any attempt to realize the actual operation of law and custom in the medieval village, or in those urban communities where—as at Norwich, one of the greatest in the kingdom—a great deal of the daily life went on still under the old village forms, with the town authorities set in place of the lord and his bailiff. There is profound truth in the Italian proverb that hard-and-fast bargains make long friendships—*patti chiari, amicizia lunga*. Irregularities that are charmingly picturesque to the outsider are often painful to those who know them as a feature of daily life. I once remarked, to an old woman in a thatched cottage, on the cheerful sound of the cricket which lived behind her oven: she replied: "Well that dew set and holla, holla, holla till I don't know what to dew with myself." All through the Middle Ages there subsisted something, though less and less, of what Guérard, in his introduction to Irminon's *Polyptyque*, applies to the earlier and darker time: "Il y avait donc partout diversité et inégalité; et, comme nulle part rien n'était réglé, ni contenu, ni définitif, il y avait lutte et guerre." There is no greater delusion than to represent the Middle Ages as a time in which everybody knew the clear bounds of self and community, of Church and State. Almost everywhere in medieval society we find a series of confusing compromises; the main points often left purposely undefined, or defined in words which may be variously interpreted. The Reformation Settlement, with those compromises which enable one Anglican to be practically Unitarian, and another devoted to Transubstantiation, was, in one very real sense, thoroughly medieval. Just as the Frenchman needs to come to England to realize fully what the monastic churches were in the Middle

like a licensing system among the lords of manors. I know not how otherwise to explain the frequency of the fines laid upon the whole class. Thus in a court leet of the manor of Hockham held the 20th of October 1377, no less than fourteen women were fined in the aggregate 30s. 8d. who being *brassatores vendidere servisiam* (sic) *contra assisam*; one of these brewsters was fined as much as four shillings."

Ages[1], so the English genius for compromise is due to our comparative conservatism, to our fortunate insularity which has enabled us to work out our problems quietly for ourselves, and which therefore retains ancient irregularities until they begin seriously to hamper the working of the social machine. There was that same reason for sparing, during many generations of gradual progress, many strange anomalies in the Middle Ages[2].

But, it must be repeated, these anomalies, however natural in their origin, and respectable for their antiquity, were more and more felt as causes of friction, even in those distant days. The vagueness of medieval measures was typical of men's vagueness everywhere; though impossible to escape from at a bound, it was none the less severely felt at times. The ever-present question of tithes, for instance, was most horribly complicated. In some parts of pre-Revolutionary France, there were a few farms which belonged in alternate years to different parishes; this must have added enormously to the normal friction[3]. Again (to quote only one of the numberless cases which might be cited), a quarrel broke out in 1551 between the peasants and the priors of St-Martin-ès-Aires concerning certain tithes; "for a whole century, priors and peasants prosecuted each other in turn in the law-courts, secular and ecclesiastical, at Troyes and at Sens"[4].

[1] Montalembert, *Moines d'occident*, livre XVIII, c. 5: "Si l'on veut se faire une idée de la grandeur majestueuse des constructions monastiques, il faut visiter l'Angleterre. L'œuvre de dévastation y a été moins complète et moins irréparable qu'ailleurs." France built more and greater abbeys than we; but these were partly rebuilt in classical style after the Reformation by the monks themselves, and the large majority of the rest were destroyed, almost entirely, at the Revolution. Glastonbury is one of the worst sufferers among our great abbeys; but there is more left of Glastonbury than of the average French monastery.

[2] One of the greatest medievalists among living constitutional historians, Professor Charles Petit-Dutaillis, brings this out very clearly on p. 97 of his study on *Le droit de vengeance aux Pays-Bas* (Paris, 1908). He shows how long, in this field, recent law went one way while ancient custom went another, so that the customals of Douai and Lille, for instance, enunciate opposite principles almost in the same breath, and the magistrate followed whichever he found most convenient. On this he comments: "Il est curieux de constater ici, une fois de plus, combien la contradiction gênait peu les hommes d'État du Moyen Âge. A défaut de logique dans la législation, ils avaient une souplesse opportuniste, une entente des contingences, qui relèvent chez eux le sens de l'administration et ont épargné évidemment aux administrés d'alors beaucoup de déboires."

[3] Gorce, p. 22.   [4] *Aube*, XII (1875), 41.

No less were the chances of uncertainty as to a peasant's status, and even as to the all-important question whether he was bond or free. At Montréal in Burgundy the lord's accounts record:

From Perrier Jarroin and Mellot le Fontenat for the succession of Martin the Red and Benoite his wife, who died without heirs of their body in the time of the plague,... for that they said that they were free folk dwelling in a free place, whereas the castellan alleged that the said Perrier and his wife, and their forbears before them, were serfs and subject to *mainmorte*; and, since matters were doubtful on either side, therefore it was accorded that the said inheritance should stay with them and they should pay my lord 161 crowns[1].

The plague would, of course, account for some confusion; but, even so, we can see how often there must have been room for dispute, and can understand how it was a matter of controversy whether the distinguished judge William Paston was the son of a bondman and bondwoman[2]. To have introduced clear-cut definition into these essential questions would have postulated an impossibly sudden transformation of feudal, and even of ecclesiastical conditions.

And the same uncertainties, redeemed to some extent by "the sporting chance," survived and were sometimes even purposely perpetuated in all social conditions, down to the most trivial. Here, for instance, is a covenant between the nuns of St Lambrecht and the bishop of Speyer, who had undertaken to protect the nunnery in return for certain rights of hunting, fishing, and manorial fees. "The manor-customal expressly provides that, if by chance the miller should so forget himself as to send the prioress an eel caught in the Speyerbach, then the bishop's officials might come and take it even out of the frying-pan in the convent kitchen"[3].

---

[1] Seignobos, p. 402, 1356 A.D.

[2] Gairdner's introduction to the 1901 edition, p. xxxv. Many cases could be quoted for England: *e.g.* Bracton's *Note-Book*, cases 1005, 1812, 1934. See *Year-Books, 3 Ed. II* (Selden Soc.) for a particularly interesting case, in which a genealogy is produced, and relatives of the alleged villein are in court.

[3] Remling, I, 153. The date is 1414.

CHAPTER VII

THE MANOR COURT

WE have now glanced at the serf's theoretical relation in law to his lord; we have seen how this agrarian machinery worked in practice at those points where, in the nature of the case, there was most friction; let us now pass on to take a more general and at the same time more detailed view of village life in its entirety.

The self-sufficing nature of the medieval village, and the peasant's comparative isolation even from neighbouring villages, are well brought out by Dr Cunningham and Professor Ashley, Mr Tawney and Mr Lipson. The villages were small, ranging roughly from fifty to five hundred souls at most; Siméon Luce's higher estimate for Normandy can be disproved by irrefragable statistics from contemporary documents[1]. The people are few, and their ideas and words are few, the average peasant has probably never known by sight more than two or three hundred men in his whole life[2]; his vocabulary is almost certainly confined to something even less than the six hundred words which W. H. Riehl found to be the stock-in-trade of the German peasant two generations ago. His parish priest is not bound to preach to him more than four times a year; and the evidence suggests that a great many did not fulfil even this theoretical obligation[3]. But this narrow life means a great deal to him and his family; it is all the life they have, or hope to have, on this earth.

When we study this existence under the microscope, we find at once that a great many of the legal theories break down in practice. It is not only that the serfs have nibbled corners away by encroachment; but masters have often met them half-way, so that some change of custom by mutual consent has brought the peasant of earlier times one step nearer to the peasant of

[1] See appendix 9.
[2] Mr Tawney would seem to underestimate when he writes (p. 264): "an age...where most men have never seen more than a hundred separate individuals in the course of their whole lives."
[3] See my *Medieval Studies*, nos. 7 and 8.

today. The forbears of half the townsfolk, at least, had once
been under servile disabilities; there had been no constitutional
difference between *town* and *township*, between the municipal
and the rural population. Many towns bought themselves free by
charters; many others still lingered on the way, for their lords
would not sell. Jocelin of Brakelond shows very plainly how
unwilling the monks of Edmundsbury were to sell what seemed
part and parcel of their monastic dignity, though their abbot
took a more businesslike view. They clung to their right of
levying distresses from cottage to cottage down the narrow
streets, for the sake of revenues which paid little more than the
cost of collection. Some privileges became even more valueless.
The Bury cellarer had the legal right of commandeering the
townsfolk, on certain days, to go and catch eels in the waters
of Southery or Lakenheath; but these conscripted fishermen
often used to return empty-handed; therefore even the most
conservative monk must have sympathized with the commutation of this service for a *pro rata* money payment. This is only
typical of a thousand similar cases; everywhere we find similar
gaps between manorial theory and manorial practice. As late
as 1280, it was still possible for the abbot of Burton to meet his
bondmen in a court of law with the crushing retort that all their
goods and chattels were his; that the peasant had, strictly
speaking, no belongings but his belly—*nihil praeter ventrem*[1].
Yet, in fact, long before this, peasants had gradually gained the
customary right of hoarding some proportion of their earnings
and buying their freedom; though this, it is true, could only
be done by a legal fiction[2]. It was plainly to the lord's own
interest to reduce his claims to reasonable proportions. Discipline, for instance, could hardly be kept by corporal punishment
alone, however freely employed. The later system, in which
fines preponderated, was far better; but you cannot fine a bondman unless you allow him to earn and hoard money. At any

[1] Ashley, 1, 39, abbreviated from the legal proceedings published in
Staffordshire Collections (William Salt Soc.), v, 82 ff. The story should be
read in Ashley, and compared with the Vale Royal story which I give in
Chapter XI. The monks of Halesowen made the same claim in 1282 (*Hales*,
p. 203).

[2] Pollock and Maitland, 1, 410. The serf having, in theory, nothing of
his own, was obliged to give the money to a third person, who would then,
with all legal formalities, buy the man from his owner and set him free.

given point, therefore, it is hazardous to argue from manorial law to manorial facts. We have seen how the tenants of Wrington stood towards the abbot in theory; let us try to get behind this, and watch the system actually at work.

Here the evidence is plentiful; and, though we might sometimes wish that we could call up one of these bygone actors for a single moment to explain some documentary riddle, yet the general witness of these records is clear on many important points. Manorial customals and court-rolls survive in very large quantities, and a good many have found their way into print. By far the most numerous accessible survivals are monastic, as having come either into different collectors' libraries at the Dissolution, or into the muniment rooms of Oxford and Cambridge colleges at a still earlier date, or as remaining in their old homes when the prior and monks were succeeded by a dean and chapter at Westminster, Durham, Winchester and elsewhere, or as being most frequent in public collections, and therefore most accessible to the student and publisher. Of these, two valuable collections have been printed, from the great monastery of Durham and the far smaller house of Halesowen in Worcestershire[1]. I shall take the Durham Halmote Rolls here for my main text, not only on account of their intrinsic importance, but because they have been recently appealed to as principal witnesses for a theory of social life in the Middle Ages which seems to me false and mischievous[2]. Amid all the disputes as to the real state of society in those centuries, it is a great gain when writers from opposite points of view are agreed as to the capital importance of a certain series of documents, as they certainly are in this Durham case. Such agreement does at least clear this particular portion of the debatable area; it gives us a definite, if narrow, issue, uncomplicated by the frequent demurrers with which the pleaders are compelled to meet each other's assumptions wherever the discussion moves over a wide field. Let us here consider, therefore, the certainties and probabilities which emerge from these Durham records, admitted on all hands to be most illuminating; and let us take

[1] *Durham Halmote Rolls* (Surtees Soc. 1889); *Hales Manor Rolls* (Worcs. Hist. Soc. 1910–12).
[2] See appendix 10.

farther illustrations from parallel cases on Halesowen, Ramsey or other manors.

All tenants were bound to come to the lord's court, even though the summons had only reached them at midnight[1]. Unexcused absence, though frequent enough, entailed a fine of at least a day and a half's wages; and in Germany, where the rough penalties of primitive societies survived longer than with us, the lord had sometimes very strong remedies against contumacious refusal[2]. At Haslach in Alsace, in 1339, if any juror refused to attend at the lord's court, "then hath the lord power to break into his house...and to take all that is therein save only the plough and the bed; and the juror himself shall be dragged out of the house under the threshold, and tied across a horse and brought to judgement"[3].

But at Durham (as, no doubt, at Haslach except on rare occasions) the fear of fine is enough for all who cannot command at least a colourable excuse, and three-quarters of our peasants are assembled in court, both bond and free. The actual place was varied; sometimes even the parish church, if we may judge from the complaints of clerical disciplinarians that "secular courts" were held in the sacred buildings[4]; or the lord's hall, or the cellerar's chequer at an abbey, or under the most time-honoured tree in the village. Frequently, at least, the court of

[1] Vinogradoff, *l.c.* p. 366.

[2] I return to this question of punishment in Chapter XVIII and appendix 33. May I beg the reader here, and all through, to mark the dates and places of what may be called my side-illustrations? It is impossible to present even an approximately complete picture by confining ourselves to one date and place; and some critics have accused me of distorting the truth by an indiscriminate use of my material. There I think they have been unjust; for they have not, even upon challenge, specified concrete instances of confusion, and I have certainly tried to keep the different kinds of evidence apart in my own mind. Here, for instance, I do not believe that a careful reader will understand me as transferring the full roughness of the German custom to Durham. But at Durham the rule of attendance was no less strict than in Germany; and, so far from being surprised at discovering some day in the Durham rolls that the tenants were sometimes reminded roughly of their duty when they refused either to attend or to pay the usual fine, I think we should have more reason for surprise if we found evidence that no such horseplay could have been allowed.

[3] *Weisthümer*, I, 700: very interesting disciplinary prescriptions for the court at Apples, a manor of the monks of Romainmotier, may be found *ibid*. v, 10.

[4] Even as late as 1673, manorial courts for important cases such as felonies were often held in church porches or churchyards (Desmaze, p. 405).

THE LINDEN TREE

the abbot of St Albans was held "under the ash-tree in the middle court of the abbey"[1]. The German courts were very frequently held under some tree; a long list may be found in the index to Grimm's *Weisthümer* (VII, 275, s.v. *Gerichtsbaum*). The most numerous, beyond all comparison, are the lindens; there are six oaks, five hawthorns, two beeches, two hazels, one each of fir, elm, willow, walnut, pear, apple, and "the Red Tree." (Compare Bartels, p. 63.) At Eastbourne, the name of Motcombe Lane probably marks the hollow where the moots were held; in the later Middle Ages, prosperous villages like Elstow and Lavenham and Thaxted built imposing moothalls of timber.

Within the manor court itself, we catch three glimpses of actual procedure in the Paston Letters[2]. We get another still more tantalizing glimpse, from a much earlier date, in Jocelin of Brakelond[3]; how the abbot's clerk, as a capable business man, was at last set over the head of the wine-bibbing cellarer, whom he publicly mocked,

saying "I am *Bu*" (that is, the cellarer when he had exceeded the bounds of temperance in drinking).... And, seeing that this clerk oftentimes wandered about the court, and many debtors and claimants, rich and poor, followed him about as their master and chief protector, one of the officials of our abbey happening to be in the court, wept for shame at that sight.

But the reader who would pursue this matter farther should run through the records in Maitland and Baildon's *Court Baron*, a book more entertaining than a good many novels. The completest description occurs on pp. 72–6; but two other brief episodes are so characteristic of the procedure, and throw so much light on conditions to which I shall have occasion to refer later, that they may be inserted here.

Walter of the Moor, thou art attached to answer in this court wherefore by night and against the lord's peace thou didst enter the preserve of the lord and didst carry off at thy will divers manner of fish [and didst make largess of it by gift and sale]. How wilt thou

---

[1] M. Paris, *Chron. Majora*, R.S. VI, 438 (1257 A.D.).

[2] Nos. 219, 688, 817; reproduced and commented on by H. S. Bennett, *The Pastons and their England*, 1922, pp. 255 ff. Compare Delisle, p. 654, which supplies interesting sidelights, and Charrière, p. 55.

[3] C.S. p. 67; tr. Clarke, p. 118. For this *bu*, see Salimbene, p. 220, l. 26.

acquit thyself or make amends? For know this, that were anyone to prosecute thee, thou wouldst be in peril of life and member; so be advised.

Sir, by thy leave I will impart.

Then afterwards he speaks thus: Sir, for God's sake do not take it ill of me if I tell thee the truth, how I went the other evening along the bank of this pond and looked at the fish which were playing in the water, so beautiful and so bright, and for the great desire that I had for a tench I laid me down on the bank and just with my hands quite simply, and without any other device, I caught that tench and carried it off; and now I will tell you the cause of my covetousness and my desire; my dear wife had lain abed a right full month, as my neighbours who are here know, and she could never eat or drink anything to her liking, and for the great desire that she had to eat a tench I went to the bank of the pond to take just one tench; and that never other fish from the pond did I take, ready am I to do [by way of proof] whatever thou shalt award me.

W[alter], saith the steward, at least thou hast confessed in this court a tench taken and carried away in other wise than it should have been, for thou mightest have come by it in fairer fashion. Therefore we tell thee that thou art in the lord's mercy, and besides this thou must wage us a law six-handed that thou didst not take at that or any other time any other manner of fish.

As your honour pleases....

Again

And thou, John atte Water, thou art attached to answer in this court wherefore and by what hardiness and with what warrant thou without leave and without commandment tookest thy sheep out of the pound of the lord. How wilt thou amend this great trespass?

Sir, saith he, if it please thee, they were without food and drink three days and three nights, and for this sake I took them out of the pound to water them.

John, saith the steward, why were they not put back?

May it please thee, sir, this was not by my counsel.

John, in good faith tell I thee that thou shalt make full high amends.

That will I do, sir, to the best of my power.

Come them, wage us an amercement.

That will I, sir[1].

We shall not quarrel with the verdicts here; but we can see how this summary procedure might be used against the peasant in unscrupulous hands; and Professor Vinogradoff quotes a case

---

[1] *Court Baron*, pp. 54, 60; cf. the still more vivid description on p. 62.

of arbitrary judgement in the courts of the abbot of Ramsey. At the halmote of King's Ripton

The jurors of the court are called upon to decide a question of testament and succession. They say that none of them was present when the testament was made, and that they know nothing about it and will say nothing about it. "And so leaving their business undone, and in great contempt of the lord and of his bailiffs, they leave the court. And therefore it is ordered that the bailiffs do cause to be levied a sum of 40s. to the use of the lord from the property of the said jurors by distress continued from day to day." This case may stand as a good example both of the sturdy self-will which the peasantry occasionally asserted in their dealings with the lord, and of the opportunities that the lord had of asserting his superiority in a very high-handed manner[1].

The injustice of fining men for refusing to pronounce upon a point which they could not know would not have been so obvious to men accustomed to the tradition that an assembly was bound to arrive at a unanimous decision, and that the minority must finally vote with the majority or be punished—a tradition which survives to some extent in the principle of the modern jury[2]. Constitutionally, therefore, the abbot may have been within his strict rights; as Vinogradoff points out, the systematization of manorial law acted for some while adversely to the peasant's interests:

It has to be noticed that the will and influence of the lord is much more distinct and overbearing in the documents of the later 13th and of the 14th century, than in the earlier records; one more hint that the feudal conception of society took some time to push back older notions, which implied a greater liberty of the folk in regard to their rulers[3].

At the dawn of our earliest evidence, there had been much more equality in the village court; by the thirteenth century, when our documents become plentiful, the capitalistic society was beginning to develope, and with this development came marked difference between rich and poor, which made itself felt in the law-courts. One of the points which Gerson notes for fuller treatment in one of his sermons, is the fact "that the poor man's word is not believed in court"—*nota quod pauperi*

[1] *Villainage*, pp. 384–5.
[2] Cf. Rashdall, *Universities*, i, 407; Gierke-Maitland, p. 166, n. 228.
[3] *L.c.* p. 408.

non creditur in judicio[1]. So had the great Italian canon lawyer
Henry of Susa (Hostiensis) written a century and a half before
this: even in the princes' courts, "they do not keep justice for
the poor man, especially for him who hath nothing to offer;
and therefore he hath no hearing"[2]. And, not long after Gerson,
Felix Hemmerlin of Zürich tells us the same story[3]. It could
scarcely be otherwise, indeed, under a system which treated
justice as a regular, and sometimes a principal, source of income.
Magnum emolumentum est justitia was a medieval principle recognized by high and low alike; "in 1294 when the viscount of
Évreux made to the abbot of St-Taurin a formal grant of half
the fines taken at the [Whitsuntide] fair, the abbot, in order to
perpetuate the remembrance of this deed, gave two pence to
two children to buy themselves cherries"; all their life long
they would be able to bear witness to the abbot's rights[4]. This
was often done; but still more frequently the *memoria technica*
followed a diametrically opposite method, as in the famous case
of Benvenuto Cellini, his father, and the salamander[5]. Boys
were solemnly cuffed or flogged to impress the events of that
day for ever upon their memory. "At Cléville, to strike the
imagination of the inhabitants and strengthen their recollections,
Roger de Montgomery had thrown into the water his son Robert
of Bellême, clad in a fur cloak of gris, in testimony and in memorial that the lordship of the abbot [of Troarn] and his monks
extended as far as that point"[6]. Robiou, though in general he
inclines rather to the favourable view of medieval society, recognizes very fully the frequent helplessness of the French peasant
in spite of the theoretical guarantees of justice offered by the
courts (pp. 408–9); he emphasizes, again, the fact that justice
was treated as a financial business, and that the frequent sale

[1] *Opp.* vol. IV, cols. 443 f.; cf. cols. 382 f. *paupertas mater latrocinii.*
[2] *Summa Aurea* (Venice, 1570), f. 461, cols. 1 and 2.
[3] *Nob.* c. 32 (f. 128 b): justitiae suppressio tam favorabiliter frequentatur
propter infelices pauperum casus.
[4] Delisle, p. 504. For justice and money, see appendix 11.
[5] *Autobiography*, bk 1, ch. 4; cf. Bartels, p. 60, and *Weisthümer*, I, 602.
[6] Sauvage, *Troarn*, p. 256. This was in 1059. We need hardly wonder
that Robert, who grew up into a characteristic feudal tyrant, became a
frequent violator of monastic privileges, even at his father's foundation of
Troarn. A St Paul's document of 1142 records how "the schoolboys who
were present as witnesses of this purchase received 3*d.* to buy cherries"
(*Hist. MSS. Com. Rep.* IX, app. 1, p. 62 a.)

of magistracies compelled the judge to get his money's worth by oppression (pp. 409, 418–22). He points out how seldom, in fact, peasants struggled into the Court of Appeal (pp. 410 ff.), and how much they risked by doing so, since, if that court upheld the lord's judgement, the appellant was heavily fined (p. 396). Compare his judgement on the working of the lord's right of taxation (p. 414). But in England, where social order was much stronger all through the Middle Ages, there was pretty certainly less abuse of arbitrary power; and we have already seen how, side by side with the peasant's obligation to attend his lord's court, he had the right of giving his voice in that court, within the limits of the customs of that particular manor. Thus, while a tyrannous lord could sometimes encroach on his side, yet on the other side the peasantry might become prosperous and formidable enough for the lord to overlook or give way to their patient small encroachments from father to son; and we must look upon these manor courts as having gradually helped to forge, by blows and counterblows, those liberties which have broadened down in Britain from precedent to precedent. All this must be borne in mind while we take stock of the Durham and Halesowen proceedings.

CHAPTER VIII

LIFE ON A MONASTIC MANOR

THE Durham rolls range from 1296 to 1384; those of Hales-owen from 1272 to 1307. Neither series is unbroken, and the gaps are sometimes serious. But the Durham rolls are almost continuous from 1366 to 1384 inclusive; and this gives us fairly safe ground for statistical argument over that period; and, even in the most broken years, certain things come out very clearly.

There is no question, for instance, as to the enforcement of some of the heaviest burdens. Of these the worst, in the immediate and pecuniary sense, was undoubtedly the heriot with its companion the mortuary. When a serf died, the lord of the manor could claim his best beast, while the rector took his second best. For this there were definite historical reasons. The heriot (*hergeat*, or war-apparatus) had formerly been due at every tenant's death. The overlord to whom he owed military service had supplied him with the necessary weapons, which at death reverted to their original owner; the heriot was thus the resumption of a horse and armour which in legal theory had only been lent. Long before the time with which we are dealing, however, freemen had practically shaken themselves free, or rather, the system had died at the root; no horse and armour had been lent, and there was nothing to resume. But from the servile household the lord still took the best beast or, failing that, his best chattel—*melius averium* or *melius catallum*.

The rector claimed the next best beast or chattel on entirely different grounds[1]. It was held to be so improbable that a peasant had lived without having defrauded the Church of tithe

---

[1] See Lyndwood, *Provinciale* (1679), pp. 19–22, where the matter is explained at length. For parallel French and German customs see appendix 12. At Wilburton, in 1277, the monks of Ely took a heriot of thirty-two pence if the peasant possessed no beast (*Camb. Antiq. Soc. Report*, No. XXVII, 1887, p. 164). It is evident that the Bicester canons took mortuaries from the poorest; in 1315–16 they got a chest from Alice the winnowing-woman, valued at 12*d*.; in another case, three mortuaries were worth only 10*d*. in the lump. In 1386 they got one from a manservant and two from maidservants; similarly in 1408 (J. C. Blomfield, *Deanery of Bicester*, pt II, p. 192; the date is 1315–16; twenty-five mortuaries were taken in that year).

that, at his death, the Church felt secure in claiming compensation. This became a custom; and, by canon law, all customs,
so that they be laudable, acquire the strict force of law; the
peasant of our period was under strict legal compulsion to pay
what his ancestors had paid under moral compulsion. Only
Archbishop Winchelsey, in the later thirteenth century,
attempted to allay the many quarrels attendant upon the then
custom by decreeing that the rector must forgo his claim to the
second-best beast in cases where the man had left no more than
two; one beast, at least, must be left to the bereaved family.
"It would be very rigorous," comments Bishop Lyndwood,
"that no beast should be left to the wife or children of the
defunct, especially when they are poor and needy." This
restriction, however, lay upon him only as rector; in the many
cases where monks or a priest were lords of the manor, they
had their heriot in any case, and their heriot *plus* mortuary if
there were three beasts[1]. The Evesham chronicler records it
in Abbot Marlborough's honour, early in the thirteenth century,
that, "when he was sacrist [of the abbey], he first obtained the
second best animal of the dead peasants, together with their
bodies and the penny that had to be offered at the funeral-
mass"; this enabled him to endow two perpetual lamps in the
abbey church, one before the high altar and one in the Lady
Chapel[2]. Moreover, another Evesham case shows how necessary
was Archbishop Winchelsey's humane decree. In 1271, Richard
Herberd died in possession of a single cow; the Church court
adjudicated half of this animal to the monks of Evesham as
holders of the parsonage, and the other half as a heriot to the
lord of the manor[3].

The heriot, then, is a regular institution on Durham priory

[1] The three beasts need not be of the same kind; a horse, an ox and a
sheep would count as three. But the custom differed in different places; in
Venice, notes Lyndwood, the parson takes one-tenth of all the defunct's
movables; in Brittany, one-third; I think this was the custom in Wales also
though I have mislaid my reference. The parson's mortuary was taken from
all classes, and was commonly driven before the corpse to the grave; and
in the later Middle Ages, it was frequent for well-to-do folk to anticipate
this in their wills, and to leave a "foredrove," *i.e.* one or more animals to
play this part in the funeral procession. See N.E.D. s.v. *Mortuary* and
Foredrove, and E. Gepp in *Essex Review*, xxx (1921), 14.

[2] *Chron. Evesh.* R.S. p. 267.

[3] Dugdale-Caley, II, 31 b.

manors. When John, son of Matilda, dies, his son Robert has to pay for heriot the value of his best beast, viz. 15*s*., at a time when the ordinary village ox was worth 4*s*. and a cow in milk the same sum[1]. The Hales rolls, again, are full of such records; the law was strictly enforced; in 1293, when John Bedell died in such poverty that no beast was found among his belongings, the jury adjudged a thrave and a half of oats to the abbot as his mortuary perquisite[2].

The account-rolls of Durham bear frequent testimony to what was in practice another tax on the peasant—the manorial dovecote[3]. German customals seem to show the tenants often keeping doves of their own; but in France and England this was often a manorial monopoly; and, though it never seems to have borne so hardly on the English peasant as on the French under the Ancien Régime, it must yet have emphasized that difference of classes which even in the comparatively democratic *Piers Plowman* counts as a "law of holy-Church," for "lewd men to laborie, and lords to hunt" (C. x. 223). The priory of Dunstable built seven dovecotes between the years 1248 and 1273[4]. The dovecote of the monks of Pontoise produced, in 1339, four cartloads of dung for the farm; in 1491 the monks sold more than 4500 of these birds, whom they had fed partly through the winter with their own grain[5]. At Blyth priory, in 1379, the annual value of a dovecote is estimated at 10*s*., and

---

[1] p. 75. (Where there is no note to the contrary, the quotation is from Durham.) Cf. Hales, p. xciii.

[2] p. 255. The editor, probably misled by the modern use of the word, thinks that this may have meant only oat-*straw*; but the comparison of other customals shows that the whole was demanded, straw and corn together, as reaped. A thrave was a score of sheaves. Another instance of the regularity with which mortuaries were taken even from the poorer tenants may be found in the abbey of Oseney, where "in all churches appropriated to the abbey, the perpetual vicars by endowment were to have every second mortuary [after the lord of the manor had taken the first], up to the value of 6*d*., and one-half of it beyond that value" (W. Kennett, *Parochial Antiquities*, 1818, glossary s.v. *Legatum*).

[3] *Durham Acct. Rolls* (Surtees Soc. 1898), I, 8, 9, 16, 25, etc.; see index to vol. III, p. 826. The first entry (1309 A.D.) shows the monks consuming sixty doves at a time—no doubt, one each. For Normandy, see Fraipont, p. 179.

[4] *Ann. Dunst.* R.S. pp. 178, 183, 187, 258. Walter of Henley, who perhaps wrote for the monks of Canterbury, reckons the dovecote as a valuable asset (p. 7).

[5] Depoin, p. 104.

of two watermills at 20s. each[1]. The lords of Berkeley drew 2151 young pigeons from a single manor in one year; elsewhere, in 1332, "the bailiff of one estate accounts for the sale of nearly 700 pigeons"[2]. Rabbits were sometimes an even worse plague to the peasant, who might no more kill them than the doves. In 1340, we have three valuable indications of this kind from a Sussex taxation-return; the men of West Wittering allege a loss of about £150 in modern pre-war currency: "the parishioners say that the wheats in the said parish have been devoured year after year by the rabbits of the bishop of Chichester, and thereby lessened in value £7. 6s. 8d." At Ovingdean there are "100 acres arable, lying annihilated by the destruction of the rabbits of the lord Earl Warenne, valued at £1. 5s. 0d." At Findon, "the tithe of rabbits and hunting" comes to 4s.[3] The rabbit-warrens on the Durham manors come into prominence in connexion with the restriction of the peasant's dog-keeping[4].

But the lord prior had to look even more closely to preserving his servile broods than to preserving his conies. The peasant

[1] *Reports and Papers Ass. Arch. Soc.* XI (1872), 164–5.

[2] Smyth, I, 302; J. E. T. Rogers, *Six Centuries of Work and Wages* (London, 1901), p. 75; Durham, p. 179; cf. index to *Durham Acct. Rolls* (Surtees Soc. 1900). Delisle does well to caution us against exaggeration here (p. 259) but the document he prints on p. 734 shows a real grievance; cf. the demand of the Pilgrimage of Grace (Tawney, p. 336): "That no man under the degree of knight or esquire keep a dove house, except it hath been of an old ancient custom." Church towers were sometimes used as dovecotes; there is one such under Bredon Hill, and Delisle quotes cases (p. 259); cf. Skelton's poem in appendix 13. But the dovecote brought in far less than the mill; as an extreme case, the monks of Canterbury let their two mills at Bocking for £7. 1s. 8d. a year, and their dovecote for only 4d. (Vinogradoff, *Villainage*, p. 315).

[3] Blaauw in *Sussex Arch. Col.* I, 62. Rogers (*l.c.* p. 84) generalizes hastily and incorrectly here; mentions of rabbit-warrens are far more frequent than he would lead us to suppose. Here, for instance, are two significant entries in chronicles: "In that year [1292] our prior [of Dunstable] often ferreted for rabbits in Bockwood wood, as on his own common land; nor did he desist by reason of the complaints of the children of the lady [Millicent] of Eyton" (*Ann. Dunst.* R.S. p. 374). And at St Albans, in 1326, "for five years following, the citizens chased hares and rabbits in [the abbot's] warren" (*Gest. Ab. St Alb.* R.S. II, 176).

[4] We must remember, also, that the dovecotes and rabbit-warrens could not plead, as the mill and oven could, a certain utility. It had doubtless been originally a benefit that the capitalist should build what the peasants could not have built for themselves; it was only the monopoly, with its attendant abuses, which sometimes rendered the mill so great a burden that men were willing to fight hard for the right of keeping hand-mills in their own cottages.

paid for sending his son to school; in 1365 Richard, son of Thomas, was fined 3s. 4d. "because he did not recall his son from school before Michaelmas, as he was commanded at the last halmote"[1]. Marriage, again, might be an expensive luxury; Agnes, widow of William Robertson, is allowed to go on farming his land on condition that, if she marries without the prior's permission, she shall pay £4[2]. Gilbert, son of John, has allowed his sister, one of the prior's bondwomen, to marry; fine, 6s. 8d. This marriage-fine, the merchet, was one of the most odious servile disabilities. Freemen sometimes had to pay it, as an incident of their land tenure[3]; but it was generally taken as one of the most definite marks of bondage that a man had to "buy his own blood," as the lawyers sometimes phrased it. But the disability was almost universal, and in England, "even when chartering a great town, it was often thought expedient that the king should declare that the sons and daughters and widows of the burgesses should be free to marry as they pleased"[4]. Both at Durham and at Halesowen the monks raised considerable sums by this blood-tax[5]: at Durham there are 51 cases recorded, of which 46 occur in those final 19 years for which we have almost complete and continuous records.

Originally, the law had altogether voided marriages between serfs on different manors, in the lord's interest[6]. The next milder form was, that no marriages whatever between serfs might take place without the lord's consent[7], and that such

[1] These other references are to Durham, pp. 42, 59, 58; the cases of leyrwite specifically cited in my text are on pp. 13, 27, 42, 61, 74.

[2] Apparently she did marry soon afterwards, and had actually to pay 13s. 4d. This is about the usual proportion of the legal maximum which lay courts succeeded in extracting from offenders; see Mr W. Hudson's introduction to his *Leet Jurisdiction* (Selden Soc.).

[3] Vinogradoff, *Villainage*, p. 203.

[4] Pollock and Maitland, *Hist. of Eng. Law* (1895), I, 629.

[5] Page (p. 13) speaks of it as a small tax; this would seem to indicate less strictness of collection on the lay manors, many of which he has studied, than on the monastic manors with which I have been mainly concerned.

[6] Possibly not in England, where some of the most oppressive feudal burdens do not seem to have grown up, but certainly on the Continent; see Sée, p. 72.

[7] Certain serfs of Kiemsee, on entering into their holdings, "bound themselves by oath never to take wives save from among the bondfolk of the monastery" (Peetz, p. 74). As late as 1421, two Bavarian millers had their holdings under condition that, if either married a girl outside the manor, the property should at once be forfeited to the lord (Baumann, II, 632). In

consent generally entailed a fine in any case[1], while it always entailed a fine if the woman, by marrying into another manor, robbed the lord of a prospective brood; except, of course, where the lords indemnified themselves by sharing the children, as they sometimes did even in England[2]. From a business point of view, this attitude towards servile marriages was natural enough; but there is evidence of its extreme unpopularity. Not only was it bitterly resented as one more step in the approximation of human beings to chattels, but also it led to occasional abuses which have given to its French form—*le droit de marquette*—an even legendary odium. Enormously and indefensibly as some writers have exaggerated the frequency and the power of this *droit du seigneur*, the *jus primae noctis*, it is a side of medieval village life which cannot be altogether ignored[3]. And, quite apart from such occasional abuses, there were certain evils inseparable from this custom of breeding in and in. The risks from the point of view of eugenics are obvious; but the strict medieval churchman, if he had seriously studied the peasant life of his day, would have found even weightier objections than the modern scientist, since these artificial restrictions must have led in countless cases to unions which the Church condemned as incestuous. Until 1215, marriage within seven degrees of consanguinity was prohibited; and, after 1215, the prohibition still extended to the fourth degree; *i.e.* to third cousins; or, in other words, to all who had a common great-great-grandfather. Even on the largest manor, a very large proportion of the servile population must have been thus related; probably more than half; and, if the parties had been conspicuous enough to be worth attention, papal dispensations would have been needed in almost every generation of almost every village in Europe[4]. Thus, for many centuries, medieval society cherished a religious system which exaggerated the guilt of breeding-in, and, side by

France, at least, one cause of the decay of serfdom lay in the mixed marriages. Guérard traces this through the St-Germain estates; it was far more frequent for the bondman to marry a freewoman than for the bondwoman to marry above her; and by French law the children inherited the mother's rank (*Irminon*, I, 391). For other notes on the village marriage-laws see appendix 15.

[1] Cf. Hales, introd. pp. xiii, xv.

[2] See the three instances given by Mr H. W. Saunders in *Norfolk Archaeology*, XVII, 319 (about 1285 A.D.).

[3] See appendix 14.　　　　　　　　　　[4] See appendix 16.

side with this, an economic system which took heavy tribute from serfs who attempted to escape from breeding-in. No church-man of the time has ever been quoted, I believe, as condemning this anomaly, by which perhaps one churchman in every four was adding to his income. There is no sign of exceptional remission of merchet on monastic or episcopal manors; Guérard, indeed, notes how rigidly the abbeys enforced it[1].

We have next to note, on these Durham manors, a closely-allied fine which is far more frequent than even merchet, occurring 81 times in those continuous 19 years, and 101 times altogether. This is the *leyrwite*, or fine for incontinency[2]. The bondwoman is the lord's chattel; any deterioration of this, as of any other chattel, must be made good; if the offender herself could not pay, then the nearest male relative, as the person who was responsible for the chattel, must pay[3]. Preciosa, the vicar's daughter, had to pay her own leyrwite in 1332; her mother must have been a bondwoman for her to have been subject to this servile tax; unless, indeed, the prior was relying upon that ancient decree of the Council of Toledo in 655, which reduced all priests' children to servitude[4]. At Wallsend in 1360, "from

---

[1] *Irminon*, I, 414–15.

[2] Trevisa's *Higden*, R.S. II, 93: "I holde it be worthy to write here and expoune meny termes of these lawes [of Edward the Confessor]...Leyrwite, amendes for liggynge by a bondwoman." On the Hales manors, also, leyr-wite was more frequent than merchet; here we sometimes find the whole body of tenants fined because they have not reported the case (Hales, pp. 231–2, 310); just as, at Durham, a whole township is fined for having concealed a merchet due (p. 184; see pp. 231, 232, 310). For fuller discussion of this due see appendix 17.

[3] In some cases, at least, the tenant had to pay not only his daughter's but also his maidservant's leyrwite (Dugdale-Caley, III, 318 b). As a Glaston-bury record puts it, the abbot must have his fine "whenever one of the bond-girls is unchaste of her body, whereby my lord loseth the sale of her" (Vino-gradoff, *Villainage*, p. 154). Or, in the words of a St Albans register to which Miss Levett has drawn my attention, the fault is "ad huntagium domini"—to the lord's dishonour, *hontaige*. Bishop John de Pontissara of Winchester, at the end of the thirteenth century, reduced peccant maidens, on one at least of his manors, to a sort of temporary slavery, which enabled him to employ their labour gratuitously (*Register*, Cant. and York Soc. p. 674; see appendix 40). In the province of Roussillon, adultery was punished by confiscation in favour of the lord, who took all the goods of both of the guilty parties. If the husband had consented to his wife's dishonour, he also forfeited all his goods (Brutails, p. 189).

[4] In about 1080, one of the bondwomen of the abbey of Bèze was "Altrade, wife of Ulric the priest of Grenant"; a little later we find "German the priest, and his sons" (*Analecta Divionensia*, Dijon, 1875, pp. 361, 395).

Christiana, maidservant to William the Chaplain, for leyrwite with the Chaplain, 2s."; at East Merrington, in 1365, "from Christiana, the vicar's maid-servant, 6d."; in 1366, "Margaret Calvert for leyr with the chaplain [of Heselden], 12d."; the same lady, the same chaplain, and the same price, are recorded again in 1368; in each year other offenders in the batch pay only 6d. each[1].

These items of Durham priory income are merely normal; customals and deeds of donation nearly always specify the lord's right to merchet, and frequently also to leyrwite. But at Hales-owen the abbot was asserting a right, in the late thirteenth cen-tury, which we should expect to have been long extinct in England—the right of coupling his serfs. The lord, as we have seen, had always some pecuniary interest in a servile marriage; and in the case of widows he had a farther interest; he wanted not only another brood, but a strong male arm on the little holding to exploit it to the full and ensure payment of all manorial dues[2]. This, I think, must account for those forced marriages which we find on some estates. The abbot of Hales, not content with the ordinary fines which lords took for marriage within or without the manor, actually asserted a right of pre-scribing such unions at will, in spite of the parties' own *nolo maritari*[3]. In 1274, "John of Romsley and Nicholas Sewal are given until next court meeting to decide as to the widows offered to them." Three weeks later, "Nicholas Sewal is given until next Sunday"—we are now at Tuesday—"to decide as to the widow offered to him in the presence of the cellarer," who held the court as the abbot's representative. In 1279, another batch of cases is recorded: "Dec. 11. Thomas Robins of Old-bury came on summons and was commanded to take Agatha of Halesowen to wife; he said he would rather be fined; and, be-cause he could find no guarantees, it was ordered that he should be distrained. Thomas Bird of Ridgacre and Richard of Ridgacre

---

[1] It is noteworthy also that Adam del Vikers shares a tenement, in 1371, with Willelmus Bati, Vicarius (p. 106). Adam, however, may have got this name not as the son but as the servant of William.

[2] Page (p. 34) would seem here to the point.

[3] The relevant references here are to Hales, I, 55, 57, 119, 121, 124, 126. It may be pertinent to note that there were frequent disputes between this abbot and his tenants, who complained that he illegally stretched his pre-rogatives (introd. pp. xiii–xv).

were also summoned because they would neither pay the fine nor take the wife, and were distrained." On January 7, 1280, only Thomas Robins and Richard of Ridgacre "are distrained to take the wives as ordered in last court." On January 23, Robins at last paid his fine, amounting to three shillings, or about a quarter the price of an ox. Richard still remained under distraint: on February 12 he was still holding out, and his heroic resistance seems to have been rewarded, for thenceforward the rolls are silent. Miss Levett has noticed similar cases, even in the opening years of the fourteenth century, on St Albans manors: "fines were paid to remain without a wife or a husband for a year, or for life; or again for disobedience in refusing to take a particular wife selected by the cellarer"[1]. This St Albans evidence is the more significant, since it is recorded in those registers which the monks had compiled from their court-rolls in order to have legal proof at hand, at any moment, for the enforcement of their traditional rights.

Such forced marriages seem to have been much commoner in Germany. Lamprecht notes that "even as late as the tenth century, the landlords seem to have claimed the general right of marrying the daughters of their serfs to whom they chose; and it was not until the thirteenth century that Richard, King of Germany, renounced this right over the citizens of Wetzlar." His charter runs: "We have decreed this special indulgence, that none of the aforesaid citizens be compelled by us to give his daughter or niece or cousin to anyone without his full consent"[2]. The time was not yet ripe for the lady to vindicate her own right of consent. In 1423, it needed a rebellion on the part of the serfs of the monastery at Steingaden to win a verdict from the arbitration-court "that in future children shall inherit from their parents, and the monks shall compel none of their bondfolk to marry"[3]. At Liestal, near Bâle, the village customal of 1411 prescribed that "every year, before Shrove Tuesday, when folk are wont to think of holy matrimony, the bailiff shall bethink him what boys and girls are of such age that they may

[1] Compare Page, p. 37, note 2. At Brightwaltham, six widows who had come into holdings and could not render due labour were ordered "to provide themselves with husbands."

[2] *Wirthschaftsleben*, I, 1203.

[3] Bezold, pp. 45–6.

reasonably take wife or husband, so that he may then allot to each his mate, as husband or wife"[1]. This was in 1411, and may be compared with a story told by the Dominican Nider, writing at Bâle about 1430 A.D. There was a freeborn girl whom the lord of the manor gave "against her will and knowledge," to one of his bondmen. She ran away; he chased her with horse and hound; she was brought back, forced to church, and there "in face of the Church, this unreal marriage was blessed by a foolish priest." Yet she refused to cohabit with her so-called husband, and Nider knew her at Bâle in her fifties, "a servant in the house of a certain honourable matron." He goes on to speculate how it would have been if the girl had been bond and not free. Without actually denying the lord's right to force a marriage under those conditions, he insists on the girl's right of refusing cohabitation if (as in this case) she had made up her mind to a life of chastity[2].

The monopoly of the lord's mill (and, though far less universally, of the bread-oven), was as strictly enforced by monks as by layfolk. Abbot Samson of St Edmundsbury was blamed by some of his monks for a lack of strong conservative principle in such matters; yet here is what Jocelin tells us of an "adulterine" mill (p. 75; C.S. p. 43):

Herbert the dean erected the windmill upon Haberdon. When the abbot heard of this, his anger was so kindled that he would scarcely eat or utter a single word. On the morrow, after hearing Mass, he commanded the sacrist that without delay he should send his carpenters thither and overturn it altogether, and carefully put by the wooden materials in safe keeping. The dean hearing this came to him saying that he was able in law to do this upon his own frank fee, and that the benefit of the wind ought not to be denied to anyone. He further said that he only wanted to grind his own corn there, and no one else's, lest it should be imagined that he did this to the damage of the neighbouring mills. The abbot, his anger not yet appeased, answered, "I give you as many thanks as if you had cut off both my feet. By the mouth of God I will not eat bread until that building be plucked down. You are an old man, and you should have known that it is not lawful even for the king or his justiciar to alter or appoint a single thing within the banlieue, without the permission of the abbot and the convent; and why have you presumed to do such a thing?

---

[1] Schultz, p. 116; *Weisthümer*, IV, 470.
[2] *Formicarius*, lib. II, c. 10 (ed. 1602, p. 161).

Nor is this without prejudice to my mills, as you assert, because the burgesses will run to you and grind their corn at their pleasure, nor can I by law turn them away, because they are free-men. Nor would I endure that the mill of our cellarer, lately set up, should stand, except that it was erected before I was abbot. Begone," he said "begone: before you have come to your house, you shall hear what has befallen your mill." But the dean, being afraid before the face of the abbot, by the counsel of his son Master Stephen, forestalled the servants of the sacrist, and without delay caused that very mill which had been erected by his own servants to be overthrown. So that when the servants of the sacrist came thither, they found nothing to be pulled down.

And the monopoly of use was kept as strictly as that of ownership. On the Durham manors, a fine of 20s.—and, in some cases, confiscation of the horse and its load also—was decreed against all who had their corn ground elsewhere[1]. On the other hand, the prior tried to keep the miller up to his duty; he heard patiently "omnes husbandos de Byllyngham et omnes husbandos de Neuton Beuleu" who complained of the deterioration in millstones, irons, and sails through neglect of the late farmers of the mill of those two manors; for the mills were commonly farmed out. Again we find that "he enjoined upon the miller [of Dalton] that he and his servants should be ready to grind tenants' grain at their mill as often as it was needed, so that none should have cause for withdrawing from the prior's mill"[2].

Brewing was another of the landlord's monopolies; his fines from breaches of the assize of ale amounted here, as on other manors, to as regular an income as any excise system ever produced. "It was enjoined to Hugh Reynoldson and his wife that they should not hold a brewhouse on any other land than the lord prior's [and so evade his monopoly] under pain of forfeit of the land which they hold from my lord." "William Carter, the reeve, and the jurors were commanded not to permit Margaret Merry to sell beer. All the tenants of the township were bidden to have a common brewer, as had been the custom from old time." Again: "It is enjoined to all tenants of the township

[1] Durham, pp. 33, 172 and *passim*; others pp. 22, 27, 58, 86, 108, 174, 169-70. There was a similar monopoly for the village smithy; cf. p. 128.
[2] There was always some sort of provision of this kind; for a typical arrangement see Ramsey, 1, 473 and Chapter VI above.

[of Dalton] that none shall buy ale that is to sell outside their township, under pain of 3s. 4d., unless it be that the brewer [of Dalton] have none to sell." At Hales, the beer-fines are perhaps still more frequent; I reckon roughly that a batch of culprits was presented at four courts out of five, or perhaps even oftener. There, also, we find the sale of a serf to another master (p. 420). The Ramsey monks were even able to sell a burgess; but this was at an early date, perhaps 1150–1200[1].

Competition for wages was forbidden; "from John son of Gilbert (*i.e.* Gibson), because he hired a certain servant to make salt at a higher wage than his other neighbours, 3s. 4d. (by grace of my lord prior) out of the prescribed penalty of £2 "[2].

The Durham rent was often, as the editor says, "in the nature of a rack-rent, and varied with the capabilities of the land or the circumstances of the tenant. It varied from 6d. to 1s. an acre. In this respect the tenants of the bishop's manors were on a more favourable footing...in both surveys they are found the same, though 200 years intervened." But when the editor of these Halmote Rolls asserts that, on these priory manors, "the ancient rent was frequently increased, *and as frequently abated*," the words I have italicized will not be found to bear serious examination. Taking three specimens of ten pages each at random (pp. 1–10, 50–59, 100–109), we find that, in the majority of cases, no change is recorded; we may assume that none took place. But the scribe records eleven cases of increased rent, the increase averaging apparently something like 25 per cent.; in one case (p. 102) the rent is actually raised from 1s. 6d. to 5s. In thirty-four cases it is definitely specified that there is no change. There is not a single case of decrease of rent pure and simple, answering to the increases pure and simple[3]. In three cases land, hitherto unexploited to its full possibilities, is let at a low rent, to increase after periods ranging from one to four years,

---

[1] *Ramsey Chartulary*, R.S. III, 244. For the ordinary sale of serfs cf. *ibid.* II, 270 ff; Sée, *l.c.* p. 162 and his article in *Rev. Hist.* LVI (1894), 235–6; and Arx, I, 52, 161.

[2] This was in 1358, when the trouble caused by the legislation against the rise of labourers' wages was almost at its worst. See B. H. Putnam, *The Enforcement of the Statutes of Labourers* (New York, 1908), pp. 198, 218, 221 for other cases where monasteries are concerned.

[3] The Kirkstall monks rack-rented their land; see *Coucher*, introd. p. xviii.

when the tenant shall have improved the soil. In another case, a similar arrangement is made for land which has evidently got into a bad state (p. 53). And yet another case (p. 54) throws so much light on the whole system that it must be quoted in full:

1366. Burdon. One messuage and three oxgangs of land, which had been Nicholas Ben's, are assigned to William Smyth, John of Heswell and Robert Dines, to have and to hold until another tenants [sic] who shall be willing to take the land and pay the old rent, viz. 40s. per annum; the payment to be given at Whitsuntide under pain of loss of all the land which they hold from my lord prior. And be it known that they shall pay, for the first three years, by his grace, thirty shillings [per annum].

It is evident that the rent is lowered here only because no higher price can be got in the market[1]; and the same must be said of the majority of cases where apparent mercy is shown in condoning (wholly or in part) the *gersuma*, or entrance-fine upon the land, or the fine for dilapidations. It may well be that the prior was here a little more merciful than other landlords; but such comparisons need proof from wide and careful statistics; allowances of this kind are constantly made even by hard business men as a necessary preliminary to a profitable bargain. An entry on the very next page of the Durham records suggests this; the jury assess dilapidations at 18d., "which is given to John of Bicheburn and wherewith he considers himself contented." With regard to the condonations of other fines, they are far less frequent or important than those in the leet-court of Norwich, for instance, where layfolk alone were concerned on both sides[2].

[1] Page (pp. 84–87) shows how frequent this stipulation had become after the Black Death; it was common form for a landlord to make an agreement for a certain lower rent pending the discovery of a tenant willing to pay more.

[2] Hudson (*Leet Jurisdiction*, p. 26) gives a page of extracts from these *condonatur* cases at Norwich in 1288–9: "Of John the Bailiff and his wife for not observing the assize of ale; of J. de Morley and his wife for the same; of L. the clerk and his wife for the same [2s. each; each paid 1s., the rest is excused]. Of R. de Dalby for the same 2s., excused. Of Beatrice de Irstead for the same and for a muck-heap 2s.; paid 6d.; rest excused at request of Master John Man out of carnal friendship. Of J. de Sibton and his wife for same 3s.; excused because he is gate-keeper. Of J. the Limner and his wife for the same 3s.; excused at request of John de Ely, clerk. Of Editha de Parys for the same 4s.; paid the whole. Of J. le Newbird and his wife for the same (excused by the bailiff) 2s. Of John de Burgh and his wife for the same (excused by the bailiff) 1s. Of Eudo the Carter and his wife for the same, 1s.; excused because the charge is not true." Of the total amercements in one court, amounting to £8. 6s., only £2. 10s. were paid.

We must not think that this implies greater hard-heartedness on the Durham prior's part; strict enforcement of the law was so unusual in medieval society that, everywhere, the men of justice struck a rough working average between what they might legally claim and what they were likely to get. And, if my lord prior bargains on his side, so do the serfs on theirs. Some may prefer to try to "better themselves" altogether; these have sometimes wandered off from the manor; we therefore find the prior's bailiff concerned to trace them and keep his legal hold on them.

Village discipline was strict; in 1366 "injunctum est omnibus husbandis quod castigant [sic] servientes suos," who had been accustomed to play at dice, even as the "husbandi" themselves played. The pound for stray cattle, the stocks or thews or cucking-stool for peasant offenders, are everywhere in evidence. Serfs, again, had often to keep their lord's prisoners, or be held responsible for their escape[1].

Very interesting, again, are the arrangements for division of loss between landlord and tenant. When a holy-day, or bad weather, or illness prevent the serf from working on the particular day on which he owes service to the lord, who is to bear the loss? Sometimes the lord, we shall find, and sometimes the serf; but scarcely ever in identical proportions on different manors, and, in the majority of customals that have come down to us, no definite provision is made either way. To this subject I come again in Chapter XVI; meanwhile it is enough to note that even the most definite provisions tested mutual forbearance; and here, as in other cases, we may see how often these primitive methods must have caused misunderstandings or facilitated oppression, even while, in the most favourable cases, they doubtless created a patriarchal bond between lord and peasant which has now disappeared. One of the complaints of the German insurgent peasants in 1525 ran: "In what statute-book has the Lord God given them [the landlords] such power that we poor fellows should, in fine weather, labour for nothing on their farms, and in rainy weather see the fruit of our sweat perish in the fields"[2]? This gives probability to the contem-

---

[1] *Ramsey Chartulary*, I, 350; *Lib. H. de Soliaco*, pp. 26–7.
[2] Janssen, IV, 200.

porary story of oppressions on the Lupfen estates, where the peasants are recorded to have complained "that on holy-days they were obliged [by the count and countess] to hunt for snails, wind yarn, gather strawberries, cherries and sloes, and do other suchlike things; they had to work for their lords and ladies in fine weather, and for themselves in the rain"[1].

[1] Ranke, II, 210. For this question of holiday work see Thurston, pp. 41–3 and the references there given. He does not note, however, that his main original authority, *Dives and Pauper*, speaks of Sundays and holy-days as commonly ill-kept (ff. 116 a, 117 a).

CHAPTER IX

FATHERLY GOVERNMENT

WE bear steadily in mind, therefore, that this government had also its happily patriarchal side. Though most of the fines in the manor courts are inflicted entirely in the lord's interest and though all of them come into the lord's coffers, yet quite a considerable proportion are also in the interest of general peace and decency. We should not expect a churchman, any more than a lay lord, to condone theft, trespass or poaching; these offences are very prominent in the rolls. My lord prior of Durham is specially vexed by this last offence; over and over again we come across such an entry as "it was enjoined to all the tenants [at Shields] that none should permit his little dogs to wander into the rabbit-warren"; "we commanded all the tenants of this [same] township that none should keep dogs to chase rabbits, under pain of 6s. 8d."[1] Thomas Rois, whose dogs devoured a peacock, is fined 18d.; the Master of the West-Spital at Heworths is presented as "a common poacher, with his servants, in the prior's warren." There is an interesting entry about pea-gleaning at Wolveston in 1378: "It was ordained by common assent that, when the hayward blew his horn, they should come to gather peas; and, when he blew his horn again, they should depart from the said peas under pain of 6d., and also that none should gather among other peas than his own, except the poor"[2]. The beer-regulations also were, to some real extent, in the public interest, as tending to regulate price and quality.

Most interesting of all are the cases concerning the public peace and the removal of nuisances. The manorial officials, evidently, were not always popular; nor did the tenants love anything which reminded them of their bondage. There was

[1] pp. 91, 185; the Wallsend folk gave similar trouble; other pp. 131, 178, 144. For peasant sportsmen in Normandy see Delisle, p. 381. Miss Davenport (p. 75) notes the frequency of poaching, among clergy as well as laity.

[2] Here, again, we have a slight indication of particular as opposed to communal cultivation, which corroborates the evidence already cited from *Piers Plowman*. Something may possibly be inferred also from *Piers Plowman*, B. VI, 68. For farther light on gleaning see appendix 18.

difficulty in getting men to undertake the invidious office of hayward[1], or pinder. This official, who had to impound stray cattle, needed higher protection; "it was enjoined upon all the tenants of the township [of mid-Merrington] that none should assault the pinder at his duty nor curse him"; again "[fine from] John Widdowson because his wife made a rescue upon the pinder of calves that he had taken within the friths of the township"; and again "it was enjoined upon all tenants of Ferry that they should not curse the common shepherd." At Hales, mutiny went still farther; Thomas le Archer was fined 4s. for having cursed the lord abbot and the convent; Thomas de Linacre, also, defamed the abbot and the brethren; on p. 254 there is a curiously involved story of a peasant who is said to have defamed the abbot by misreporting a speech of his "to a man of Rowley whose name is yet unknown to us." And the court took cognizance also of provocative words spoken against far less important personages. As early as 1364 (p. 33) we find the injunction "upon all the tenants of East Raynton and West Raynton that none of them shall call any man of either manor 'a serf of the lord prior,' under pain of 20s. upon the offender." In 1365, at Newton Beaulieu, a fine of 6s. 8d. is decreed against anyone who calls another *rusticum*[2]; at the same court, John of Bamborough was in fact presented for calling Adam of Marton "false, perjured and 'rustic,' to the damage of the said Adam." But the fine actually adjudged was only 3s. 4d.; and, finally, "of mercy," only a single shilling was taken from John (p. 40). In 1378, again, the tenants of Wolveston were threatened with a fine of 20s. for any man who "should call any serf of my lord prior *rusticum*" (p. 144). *Rusticus* was often used as a synonym of *servus* or *villanus*; and it will be noted how directly this bears upon the modern plea that the Middle Ages saw no disgrace in servitude[3].

[1] pp. 86, 89, 130, 144, 171 (cf. Hales, p. 250, where a man pays 6d. for leave to cast off his office of constable); others pp. 42, 50 and *passim*, 179; Hales, pp. 57, 66.

[2] *Rusticus* was a common synonym for *serf*; e.g. *Kirkstall Coucher*, p. 161. This fact is significant of the earlier days when the boor was nearly always a bondman.

[3] In 1404, the matter was even taken in hand by Charles VI of France, who issued a proclamation against those who insulted their neighbours "by calling them serfs, and reproaching them hatefully and revilingly with their

There were many other similar rulings in which the terms of abuse were less definitely specified[1]. But the specific cases, where we can trace them, illustrate the medieval custom of compounding, in disciplinary matters, for a very small fraction of the legal fine. A typical case is that at Billingham (p. 144): "From Agnes of Ingleby—for transgression against William Sparrow and Gillian his wife, calling the said Gillian a whore, to the damage of £2, whence they will take at their will 13s. 4d., as was found by the jury—by way of penalty and fine 3s. 4d., reduced in mercy to 6d. It is ordained by common assent that all the women of the township control their tongues without any sort of defamation."

The cucking-stool for scolds was an indispensable village institution; Shields is fined (or threatened) three times for neglecting to provide one (pp. 38, 44, 49).

The commonest presentments are for very ordinary and natural trespasses of cattle, disrepair of hedges, shirking of common works, neglect of land or of buildings, defiling the common springs, and digging pits (after the common medieval fashion) in the public highway[2]. Cognizance was very justly taken of tenants who harboured undesirable lodgers, especially lodgers who were liable to leyrwite. "Common thieves of poultry" are presented; and, in the Halesowen manors, quite a number of tenants who made a practice of stealing firewood from the hedges[3]. Others moved boundary-stones, or appropriated such waifs and strays as a stranded porpoise, a find of

servile condition" (Desmaze, p. 79). As early as 1206, we find Guiot de Provins using the adjective *vilain* in its full modern sense of social and moral reprobation; in one long passage the play is upon its literal sense as a noun and this adjectival and metaphorical signification (*Bible*, ll. 993 ff.; the editor glosses the word as *bas*, *méchant*, *triste*). The word was evidently used in a contemptuous sense in 1290 at Norwich (Selden Soc. v, 1891, pp. lxviii, 34). When Hamlet first cried "Guilty, damnèd villain!" he was addressing an audience which knew perfectly well that the literal meaning of *villain* is *serf*. I recur to this subject in Chapter XXIII.

[1] General abuse or slander pp. 128, 147, 152, 154, 155; special implications of slanderous habits among the women, pp. 131, 144, 153. Compare the customs of Apples, in Burgundy, where the fine for calling one's neighbour leprous or adulterer—*de vocatione mesel vel avoutro injuriose*—is tenpence (*Weisthümer*, v, 12). Humbert de Romans, in his *De Eruditione Praedicatorum*, lays stress on the slanderous tongues of village women (pars II, c. xcix, p. 505).

[2] The last item is interesting enough for full references: see pp. 41, 56, (92?), 149, 170 (cf. 172).

[3] Hales, pp. 319, 327, etc.

wild honey, etc.[1] Others played on holy-days; and play, in those days, was mainly bound up with gambling, quite apart from the attendant temptation of shirking Church services; therefore it is very rare to find a medieval moralist who makes any liberal allowance for sports and pastimes, especially among the lower classes[2]. The knight, of course, must have his hunting and his tennis; but the sports of the peasant were too unruly and tumultuous; as in Germany the village dance was repressed[3], so the prior of Durham was concerned to put down the games which were customary at Southwick: "quod non ludant in gard. post fest. Pur. B. Mariae, sub poena xijd"; where the gravamen seems to be that they played after Mass in the churchyard (p. 180). At Wolveston, two tenants who had played at Ragman's Roll were fined 20s. which was finally reduced to 2s.[4] At Acley "it was enjoined upon all the tenants of the township that none should play at ball" [ad pilam][5]. This same prohibition is often repeated and culminates in the injunction at East Merrington in 1382: "It was enjoined to all the tenants that none should play at ball; and that the constables of the township should not suffer any ball-play, under pain of 40s." Why should an amusement, apparently so harmless, have been forbidden to these peasants? The editor realizes that the knot cannot be cut by simply quoting royal prohibitions, from 1337 onwards, against ball-play on Sundays or holy-days, as interfering with the practice of archery. The prior would certainly not have troubled about these royal prohibitions without

---

[1] pp. 32, 38, 98, 141, 173.

[2] This lasted down into later times; see Habasque, p. 124, and appendix 19.

[3] See Haltaus, s.v. *Platzmeister*, cols. 16 and 1491. The monks of St-Gall, even as late as 1700, "forbade dancing altogether [to the villagers] in the cantons of St-Gall and Toggenburg; in the Rhine valley they allowed it only on the dedication-day of the church, and only for three dances, which might be danced at no other hour but three in the afternoon." In Toggenburg, they forbade cards, dice and skittles under pain of three days' imprisonment; even the drinking of healths was prohibited, whether in words or by signs; the taverns were closed at 9 p.m. (Arx, III, 247–9).

[4] p. 140. Ragman's Roll was a bundle of parchments, each of which had a long tag, and was inscribed with a verse or motto, generally very uncomplimentary. The player drew a tag at random and then read aloud the motto which had fallen to him. One has been printed in T. Wright's *Anecdota Literaria* p. 83; it is certainly far from an edifying document; but it seems more probable that the Wolveston tenants used the game for gambling.

[5] p. 138; cf. pp. 149, 161, 166, 168, 171, 175.

reasons of his own. The editor refers very pertinently to a previous entry on p. 171 (Southwick, 1381):

It was found that John Green, John son of Adam of Wearmouth and William son of John Reid broke the peace by an affray at South-wick and Wearmouth, through which the lord prior's tenants were threatened by those of my lord of Hilton, and in grievous peril of their bodies, as was found by the twelve [jurymen]. Wherefore these said John, John and William, of the penalty elsewhere prescribed [for this offence] 20s. From the aforesaid John, John, William and Robert the servant of Thomas Butler, because they played at ball, through which grievous contention and contumely arose between the lord prior's tenants, as was found by the twelve jurymen, of the penalty elsewhere prescribed, 20s. It was ordained that no tenants of my lord prior should seek aid from any other lord concerning things done within my lord prior's domain, nor should procure the intervention of servants of any other lord, under pain of 40s.

Here we have more than the common monastic and ecclesiastical want of sympathy for games as useless and rather mischievous, even when they did not bring gambling or quarrels in their train—a prejudice for which all will make some allowance who remember that the umpire was a functionary unknown to medieval sport, or who have watched men playing *ad pilam* with great balls of wood, or water-rounded cobbles, in the narrow streets of a modern Italian village[1]. The indications point here to football, and football of the good old sort, one village pitted *en masse* against another. There are many scattered indications which enable us to say of medieval and even post-medieval England what a distinguished French archivist proves from definite documentary evidence in his own country, that

au XIV siècle, ce jeu, qui se ressentait de la rudesse des mœurs, n'allait guère sans plaie ou bosse, et ceux qui s'y livraient devaient s'estimer heureux s'ils n'avaient ni un œil crevé, ni un bras rompu, ni une jambe cassée. C'est qu'en réalité dans beaucoup d'endroits, la soule perpétuait sous la forme d'un amusement violent, soit des haines de race et des luttes locales séculaires, soit des rivalités in-spirées par la différence d'âge et de situation sociale[2].

---

[1] Cf. the pollution of the churchyard at St Edmundsbury by bloodshed at the wrestling-matches, as described by Jocelin of Brakelond (pp. 120–1).

[2] S. Luce, *La France pendant la guerre de cent ans*, 1890, p. 111. The nine pages which he devotes to this game of *soule* are of extraordinary interest.

The puritan Philip Stubbes describes the Sunday football of his day as

rather a friendlie kind of fyghte than a play or recreation...for doth not everyone lye in waight for his adversarie seeking to overthrow him and picke him on his nose, though it be on hard stones, on ditch or dale, on valley or hill, or whatever place soever it be he careth not, so he have him downe; and he that can serve the most of this fashion he is counted the only felow, and who but he?

Still earlier, Sir Thomas Elyot had described the game as unfit for gentlemen: "Foote-balle, wherein is nothing but beastlie furie and exstreme violence, whereof proceedeth hurte, and consequently rancour and malice do remain with them that be wounded"[1]. And, carlier again, we get a precious judgement from an English hagiographer: "Football...is a game in which young men, in country sport, propel a huge ball not by throwing it into the air but by striking and rolling it along the ground, and that not with their hands but with their feet. A game, I say, abominable enough, and, in my judgment at least, more common, undignified, and worthless than any other kind of game, rarely ending but with some loss, accident, or disadvantage to the players themselves"[2].

Yet this rough sport, very naturally, afforded one of the few outlets to the peasants' animal spirits. In Germany, the main outlet seems to have been in the dance, a pastime not many degrees less rough, if we may judge from Chaucer's well-known words, from the data collected by Alwyn Schultz, and from its modern survivals in an unsophisticated peasant society like that of present-day Tyrol[3].

It was natural, therefore, that the prior of Durham should deal with football from the same point of view from which he forbade the peasants to make their dung-heaps in the street (p. 158); to defile the common spring by cooling red-hot ploughshares in it (pp. 143, 146, 151), by washing clothes (pp. 108, 160, 176), by soaking flax or hemp (p. 169), or, finally, to "make oil" in the vicinity of other houses, "seeing that all the tenants of this township [of Billingham] complain grievously

---

[1] M. Shearman, *Football* (new.ed. 1904), pp. 6, 9.
[2] *Miracles of King Henry VI*, ed. Knox and Leslie, 1923, p. 131.
[3] Schultz, pp. 120 ff., 335 ff.; W. Baillie-Grohmann, *Tyrol and the Tyrolese* (1876), pp. 65 ff. See also appendix 19.

that such a stench cometh from this sort of infusion of oil that no man may pass that way without peril"[1].

But the worst abuses, and those which most fully justified the prior's rule as beneficent, were the frequent assaults, sometimes merely wordy but more often in grim practical earnest[2]. "From John Lollis, for that he drew his knife to smite Robert Swan, 3s. 4d.; and be it known that the damages of the said Robert are adjudged by the jury at 6s. 8d." Another, who actually strikes with a knife, is fined the same. Adam Schropp, at a later court, is fined for having continued to harbour the aggressive John in spite of the prior's prohibition:

It is enjoined upon all the tenants of the township of Wolveston that they should procure the arrest of all such as revile their neighbours, or who draw knives or swords against the peace; and if these will not be arrested, let hue and cry be raised and let every man come to aid....From John Jentilman for transgression made upon Agnes of Ingleton 6d., from Agnes, for cursing John Jentilman, 6d.

Again, there are complex assaults, e.g.:

From Beton, Richard Walker's handmaid, for assault upon Jane wife of Thomas Merriman, smiting her even to effusion of blood, 3s. 4d.; from Richard Walker, Alice his wife, and Beton his maid for transgression against Jane wife of Thomas Merriman—to the damage of the said Jane of twenty shillings, as was found upon inquisition—1s. 6d.; from Thomas Merriman for beating Richard Walker's maid—whereby she lost her office for two weeks, to her damage of 3s. 4d.—6d.

Here, evidently, was a fairly general fray, but only with natural weapons. Other assaults were more dangerous: "From Thomas Milner, for that he shot two arrows by night at Laurence Hunter, as was found by the jury, 3s. 4d."[3]; "From John Smith, for drawing his knife to smite the curate, Thomas of Bicheborn, 3s. 4d."; "Of John Webster, for drawing his knife thrice, as was found by the jury, 3s. 4d. for each time." Sometimes the

[1] p. 39. It is pretty evident that this was fish-oil; the offender's name was Thomas Herynger.

[2] pp. 36–7, 45–6, 50, 55–6, 68–9, 73 (2), 92, 95, 101, 113, 122, 131–3, 143–9, 153–4, 157–9, 163, 168–9, 171 (3)–3, 174, 183–4, 186.

[3] This was in 1383; in 1456 the Oxford Chancellor's court convicted a scholar "for shooting arrows by night at the northern proctor and his attendants" and fined him 20s., at the same time impounding his bow (*Munim. Acad.* R.S. p. 666).

WANTED, AN UMPIRE

injunctions are wholesale, even as the affrays were apt to be general; in 1382, for instance, there was a fight between Wallsend and Tynemouth *ad effusionem sanguinis* (p. 172). In 1375, "It was enjoined upon all the women in the township [of Hazeldean] that they should restrain their tongues and not scold nor curse any man"; in 1383, "it was enjoined upon all tenants of Ravensflatt that no man transgress against another in word or in deed, with staves or arrows or knives, under pain of 20s." (pp. 132, 181).

The assaults at Halesowen were less frequent than in these northern parts, though still frequent enough to suggest a primitive state of society. But, perhaps because they are rarer and therefore less commonplace, they are sometimes described in more interesting detail. At the village of Romsley, in 1271, on the feast of the Exaltation of the Holy Cross, towards vespertide, Hawise came home from the alehouse—*de cerevisia*—with her two daughters, and shut her doors, shutting out her eldest daughter, who was followed by her husband. She, wishing to enter as usual, was unable, and therefore he entered through a certain window, breaking into the house and smiting Hawise his wife's mother; whence the hue and cry was raised and the neighbours ran thither. Walter came, and assaulted Nicholas and Henry Hall with drawn knife, and the said Walter was wounded, but it is not known by which of the two aforesaid; but it is thought that Nicholas smote him. Concerning Walter's chattels, the jury say that he had five oxen, worth 20s., and one bushel of corn at Henry Green's house, and one sheep at Richard Blackhog's....Of Nicholas's chattels they say that he had oats in Farnley Grange, it is not known how many; *item* five sheep at Alan Tadenhurst's house and six at John Hill's, and three oxen and a cow at Gillian Hunnington's, and twenty sheep there, and the said Gillian owes him 20s. Henry of Hunnington had 2s. at Thomas Linacre's house, with one cow and 2s. 6d.; at William Gregg's 5 sheep; at Henry Hall's 1 cow; at J. Hill's 1 bushel of oats [worth] 3d.; at Roger Marmion's, 1 cow[1].

These inventories were necessary because the wounded man might have died; then the case would have come into the

[1] Hales, p. 32. As the editor points out, Henry Hunnington was probably the same as Henry Hall. The scattered position of these possessions, apart from the question of sub-tenancy, seems to throw light upon the obscure question of communal tillage on these manors. For opposite views on this subject see Dr Coopland, pp. 120 ff. and Mr Hudson, *Norf. and Norwich Archaeol.* xx, 316. But one is writing of French and the other of English conditions.

coroner's court and the striker's chattels might have become
forfeit to the king. But the list shows that those concerned in
the fray were better-class peasants; Henry Hunnington appears
to have had tenants of his own under him (p. 33 n.). Light is
thrown on this same subject by the specification for a peasant's
cottage in 1281 (Hales, p. 165). Thomas Bird of Romsley,
succeeding his mother Agnes on her holding, undertakes to
maintain her "fully and honourably so long as she shall live."
The food which he pledges himself to give her is plentiful; she
is to have "five cart-loads of sea-coal" (for we are here on the
edge of the Black Country); and he is to build "a competent
dwelling for her to inhabit, containing 30 feet in length within
the walls, and 14 feet in breadth, with corner-posts and three

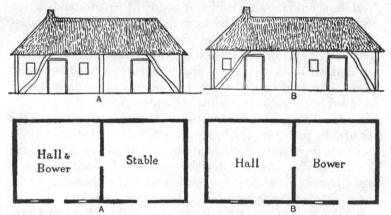

Sketch of cottage as suggested by Halesowen specifications. The more
probable form is *A* (Hall and Stable); but, if we take literally Chaucer's
division of Hall and Bower in the *Nun's Priest's Tale*, then the form would
be *B*, and the animals would share the hall, in cases where there was no
out-house.

new and competent doors and two windows." This description
seems to point clearly to one of the two types of cottage figured
here, with a partition and a door either between the widow's
"bower and hall," or between her single room and the quarters
inhabited by her sheep and fowls[1]. These Birds, again, were
evidently above the average; it is only here and there that

---

[1] Abroad, and probably in some English villages also, the cottages were
sometimes roofed with shingles or turf: *Irminon*, II, 604; Delisle, p. 286.

tenants take the trouble to make such elaborate partitions of
property and to register them in the court records. We get a
far less favourable impression from the casual notice of a
dwelling at Littleport in 1325; a cottage 24 feet by 11 feet "to
the use of Geoffrey Whitring and Mabel his wife and John their
son"[1]. Chaucer implies that his poor widow, her daughter,
and the live-stock lived on very intimate terms; St Bernardino
of Siena implies this still more definitely of the Italian peasantry[2].
The dilapidated appearance of an ordinary English village is
described, perhaps with some rhetoric, on p. 69 of *Magna
Vita S. Hugonis*: "decrepit hovels, with rotten beams and half-
ruined walls." The same passage shows how easily the ordinary
cottage could be dismantled and removed; again, at Forncett, in
Norfolk, about 1426 A.D., William Found had departed and carried
off [*abduxit*] his cottage[3]; we have similar evidence from Halesowen and from Kirkstall abbey farms; even more vivid, again,
from Italy at about the same time. For Salimbene, describing
the civil wars of 1287, names six villages in his neighbourhood
where "the men carried away their houses and rebuilt them"
on hill-tops for security against marauders; so also did peasants
in medieval Roussillon; as recorded by Brutails. Speaking of the
bonfires lighted that year by exultant victors, Salimbene writes:
"Even as the country-folk do at carnival-times, when they burn
down their cottages and hovels[4]—*domunculas suas comburunt
atque tuguria*" A vicarage-house under the abbey of Leno,
about 1160 A.D., was transferred from one district to another;
"and the present witness was one day in the village of Gote-

---

[1] *Court Baron*, p. 142.
[2] *Prediche Volgari* (Siena, 1884), II, 115, translated in *Medieval Garner*,
p. 612.
[3] Davenport, p. 104.
[4] Hales, p. 178; *Kirkstall Coucher*, p. 184; Salimbene, pp. 633, 639;
compare R. Kötzschke, *Deutsche Wirtschaftsgesch.* 1908, I, 71, "In the
Weisthümer, the house counts among movable goods." This is quite apart
from the not infrequent evidence of special dilapidation. In 1340, for
instance, thousands of acres in Sussex were waste "from the poverty of the
inhabitants and the inability to find seed"; seaboard parishes at the same
time were still more impoverished by the French raids (Blaauw in *Sussex
Archaeol. Coll.* I, 59). In the Court rolls of an Essex manor of Chaucer's
day, Dr Andrew Clark notes "the frequent mention of ruinous cottages,"
pointing to depopulation (*Essex Review*, 1904, p. 19). "In the earliest court-
roll at East Hendred (1388), no less than 7 tenements are reported to be in a
ruinous state" (*Quarterly Review*, CCXLI (1924), 35).

nengo and saw the shingles thereof laden on waggons, and climbed upon one of those waggons and was borne thereon from Gotenengo to the village of Gambara [where the house was set up afresh], for he was then a boy "[1]. A cottage at Forncett was built for £2; in the equivalent of corn and meat nowadays, less than £80[2]. Lord Ernle aptly quotes from Bishop Hall's satires in 1610, remarking that the words might apply to all the three centuries before that date:

> Of one baye's breadth, God wot! a silly cote,
> Whose thatched sparres are furr'd with sluttish soote
> A whole inch thick, shining like black-moor's brows,
> Through smok that down the head-les barrel blows:
> At his bed's-feete feeden his stalled teme;
> His swine beneath, his pullen ore the beame:
> A starved tenement, such as I gesse
> Stands stragling in the wasts of Holdernesse;
> Or such as shiver on a Peake-hill side,
> When March's lungs beate on their turfe-clad hide[3].

We get an inventory of a peasant's tools in 1301; they consist of a hoe, spade, axe, billhook, two yokes for carrying buckets, and a barrel; total estimated value 10d., or about 16s. in prewar currency[4]. A very interesting inventory of a small farmer's stock may be found in *The Archaeological Journal*, III, 65. The editor points out how large a proportion went in legacies to the Church, funeral expenses, probate, and lawyers' fees. The widow, who got most, received a cow worth 5s. by definite bequest, and 3s. 0¾d. as residuary legatee; funeral, food and drink came to 8s. 8d.; draft of will and probate to 1s. 2d.

Another court-roll entry of 1288 gives us a glimpse of the peasant's clothing. Hugh Coverer, marrying Emma Lord and taking over her father Richard's land, undertakes to "keep the said Richard in board as well as he [Hugh] keeps himself and will give him every year one garment and one pair of shirts and

---

[1] Zaccaria, p. 151.   [2] Beevor, p. 490; cf. 502. See also appendix 40.
[3] Bk v, satire 1.
[4] Hales, p. 438. On the other hand, the prosperous peasants of the Flemish seaboard had much more (Pirenne, *Soulèvement*, pp. lxvi ff.); so had well-to-do peasants in early fourteenth century Normandy (S. Luce, *Du Guesclin*, ch. III); it is, however, generally recognized now that Luce exaggerates here, and that his generalizations from a few cases are too hasty.

one pair of hose and shoes "[1]. But these folk, again, are pretty certainly above the average, or their covenant would not have come down to us.

And they are also, in all probability, distinctly superior to the contemporary standard of comfort among the peasantry of the Sister Isle. The well-known descriptions of the Irish population in Giraldus Cambrensis, equally uncomplimentary from the economic and from the religious point of view[2], may be supplemented here by the casual evidence of a business document which is far less accessible[3]. Master Laurence of Summercot, a Franciscan who had been sent to Ireland to collect papal taxes for the crusades in 1254, wrote in 1256: "When I get back to England, do with me as you please, for I am ready to go to prison rather than to be crucified again for this crusade-business in Ireland." His successor, whoever he may be,

will have to collect the legacies and other crusade-offerings from the Irish towards the end of autumn and the beginning of winter, while they have something; for, after that date, very many of them have little left. For that which they collect slenderly enough, they consume most inordinately; and, while any of their meagre substance is left, they give it away liberally—nay rather, as it mostly befalleth, they carelessly dissipate and scatter it abroad.

Yet Irish peasant-life is picturesque, and so was that of our forefathers. However primitive in themselves, those quiet cottages, glistening new or mellowed or dilapidated, clustered

[1] *Select Pleas*, p. 32. I have ventured to make my own translation here; *caligae* at this date are certainly hose, and not shoes; and the *par lineorum* might be a pair either of linen sheets or of shirts, *linen* by itself being used in either sense; see N.E.D. and Godefroy, s.v. *linge*. A parallel case in the *Durham Halmote Rolls*, p. 4, has *par pannorum lineorum*, "two pieces of linen cloth," probably for the making of two shirts, as the *unum pannum* just above would be a piece of woollen cloth for a coat. For peasants' shirts, see Luce, *l.c.* pp. 61–4.

[2] *Top. Hibern. Hist.* III, cc. 10, 19, 26, 28, 35 (R.S. v, 149, 164, 170, 173, 181).

[3] *Materials for the History of the Franciscan Province of Ireland*, by Father E. B. Fitzmaurice, O.F.M. (Manchester, 1920), p. 24. On p. 25 (1256 A.D.) we find the Bishop of Raphoe complaining to the Pope that it is only at the risk of his life that a priest can preach conversion from the Irish habits of "worshipping [heathen] idols, and taking wives from among their cousins or other prohibited degrees," a complaint which fully corroborates Giraldus's strictures.

along the hillside or nestling in the valley, would have been a delightful sight to modern eyes. With honest open-air appetites, we should occasionally relish the peasants' bread and cheese and ale as a manna from heaven. Their speech, their dress, their toil under the midday sun and the slow homeward-trudging groups silhouetted against the afterglow, might kindle us to a momentary envy of that old-world simplicity—*O fortunatos nimium, sua si bona norint!* Their very names, over all these years, come to our lips like a draught "cool'd a long age in the deep-delved earth"—no foreign Hippocrene, but, far homelier and robuster and more refreshing, the "moist and corny ale" of Chaucer's England. We may hob-nob on the Durham manors with John Jentilman, Adam Graundorge (or Barleycorn), William Littlefair, John Cherryman and John Merriman; Gilbert Uncouth and Roger Mouse; Henry Alansman, Thomas Marmaduke, Walter Mustard, John Fairjohn, Roger Litilannotson, John Stoutlook, William Teddi, Robert Punchun, Stephen Sabyne; and, most medieval of all, Robert Litany, Alan Paternoster, Robert Benedicite[1]. Could we not spend a whole tranquil lifetime tilling those dozen acres that Ralph Jolibody held of the prior? Have we not, at this distance, a soft place in our heart for Litilsteven, even though in his own day he were a *communis volator volatilium*? Who would not join in dance and sunburnt mirth with Agnes Redhead, Cicely Wilkinsdoughter, Maud Malkynsmaydin, Diote Jaksdoughter, Evote Wheelspinner, Agnes Gibbesdoughter, Alice Robinsdoughter, Emma Androwsmayden, Cicely the Pinderswoman, Cicely Dansdoughter, Alice Dobinsdoughter, Margaret Ferrywoman, Agnes Bonamy, Margaret Merry, and "Watsdoughter," so homely to the manor that the recording scribe omits her Christian name as too formal for his calendar? Yet, amid this mirth of woven paces and of waving hands, or again as we rest betweenwhiles upon the ale-house bench, let us not indiscreetly press any of these ladies to tell us what may have been her own special title to immortality in the Halmote Rolls.

[1] A prominent and prosperous serf on a manor of St-Père-de-Chartres occurs frequently under the name of Guerric Kissdevil—*Guerricus Osculans-Diabolum* (*Cart. St-Père*, p. xcvii). Dr Eileen Power sends me a tenant under the nuns of Stamford: *Robert Stoutandgay*. Mr L. F. Salzman communicated a striking list to *The Athenæum*, 1909, p. 939.

For, beneath the superficially picturesque, there run cold currents of village life which are none the less deeply poetical because they creep more silently. We shall never effectively help the man who tills our own fields, or the peasant of the future, but by tracing the real story of his forefathers, step by step, without fear or favour. Let us not plead: "These folk did indeed live from hand to mouth; it is true that they were at the mercy of the landlord's caprice; but their life had a freshness which our lives have lost." The world is eternally fresh; and, if we moderns pine and fret and grudge at it for having lost its ancient earthly Paradise, then, in that delusion, we condemn ourselves to the saddest Paradise Lost that ever was. Dante, it is to be feared, would have put us into that most ignominious of all his infernos, where the lake of black slime bubbles with the sighs of those who, while they lived, were sad under God's sunshine and are now sadder to all eternity under this foul submergence:

> —tristi fummo
> Nell' aer dolce che dal sol s'allegra,
> Portando dentro accidioso fummo;
> Or ci attristiam nella belletta negra[1].

[1] *Inferno*, VII, 121.

CHAPTER X

THE LORD'S POWER

IT has been generally acknowledged that the Durham Halmote Rolls give a typical average picture of peasant life under the three Edwards; Halesowen, Ramsey and Gloucester give similar evidence; and there is nothing of importance on any of these manors that cannot be illustrated from other medieval sources. Let us now glance at the peasant's lot in earlier times, when he had sometimes been worse off, thence let us pass to consider him in generations later than these Durham records, when he was certainly somewhat happier.

The evidence for the earlier times will be found to bear out the judgement of Dean Church, who was certainly no intemperate critic of the past. In one of his essays on St Anselm he wrote: "Feudalism, in spite of its generous maxims...soon stiffened into a hard system of customary law, interpreted and administered by those who had the stoutest arm and the fewest scruples....Our poetical notions of a gay and gentle chivalry fade away cruelly, we had almost said ludicrously, before the frightful realities of European life as drawn by the Middle Age historians "[1]. And the brute force of the Dark Ages proper must have weighed more heavily upon the peasant than upon any other. That is the one constant factor in medieval civil wars; both parties fought over the peasant's fields, forced the peasant into their ranks, and blackmailed the peasant when they had gotten the upper hand[2]. For five centuries of European history,

[1] *St Anselm and Henry I* (Routledge), p. 202.

[2] How truly this was so even in less barbarous times, we may see from the Paston Letters. When the ownership of a manor was disputed, each of the disputants tried to squeeze the manorial dues from the peasantry. It is with this important reservation in our minds that we must read Boissonnade, p. 177: "Si le vilain est sans défense contre l'arbitraire de son maître, il est du moins, le plus souvent, à l'abri des entreprises des tyranneaux voisins." The sufferings of peasants from chronic wars in Brittany are described by Sée, *Bretagne*, pp. 49–50: "Les premières victimes de tous ces troubles, ce sont toujours les paysans." He thinks (but this may be doubted) that Church tenants suffered even more heavily here, since the wealth of the Church offered special temptations to the lawless barons. Charrière (p. 150) portrays the misery of the peasants during the wars of the eleventh century in Burgundy. Caggese emphasizes the same for Italy; all through her civil wars, it was the peasant who suffered first and most continually (I, 151–2; II, 373–4).

the anarchical conditions of society discouraged saving, and pressed hardest upon the laborious middle class, who were then the better-to-do peasants. The Danegeld, raised to defend England from piratical invaders, sometimes amounted to an income-tax of seven shillings in the pound on the farmer[1].

Yet there was some reason for this, and for certain other taxes, which did sometimes stave off actual war. For many other exactions, however, there was no excuse but the interest of the stronger party; and the weakest party in the State, politically, was nearly always the peasant; more or less truly we may say of every land what Seignobos says of Burgundy: "Les vilains n'ont aucun droit politique;...leur rôle est purement économique" (pp. 56–8). The villager's ignorance and simplicity put him at a fatal disadvantage; we shall see how one of the most competent observers of the thirteenth century laid his finger exactly on the weak point; the peasant cannot combine; he lacks the necessary education and sense of social solidarity; therefore the peasant goes to the wall[2].

And we must remember that the majority of the peasants, the unfree, had scarcely the legal privileges of a human being. By an early law of the Burgundians, if two freemen fought and the serf of one helped his master, the latter paid a fine of one shilling for his serf's blow[3]. It was as if a dog had joined in the fray out of zeal for his master's cause. These half-beasts, half-men have left no records of their own; it is only here and there, among other records of these wildest times, that the veil is rent for a moment and we get a glimpse of all the wretchedness that was possible under the prevailing disabilities. Marriage re-

---

[1] Lipson, p. 14.

[2] *Bert. Regensb.* I, 478. For lords' oppressions in early Italian history see Caggese, I, 124–5. And he quotes a capitulary of 800 A.D. which shows that, in Maine, serfs were sometimes compelled to work for their masters every day in the week. Even under the monks of Brescia, five weekly days of work were exacted (*ibid.* p. 41).

[3] *Irminon*, I, 317. Compare this recorded case of the ninth century: "In the case of the man who took a serf and bade him slay his two lords in their infancy, one of 9 years and the other of 11, and who at last cast the serf, when he had slain his young masters, into a pit, it was judged that he should compound for the boy of 9 with a three-fold weregeld and the other with a double, and that he should pay three-fold for the murdered serf, and should be wholly banished from our realm" (*M.G.H. Leges*, II (*capit.* 1), 257). The *servus* of this text may be a slave in the strict sense, and not merely a serf.

strictions bore very hardly on the serf in those early days; he had scarcely a man's rights. About 830 A.D. we find the wife of the celebrated Einhard interceding for a peasant who had dared to marry not for his lord's pleasure but for his own: "A serf of yours from Mosbach, Wenilo by name, has taken a certain free-woman to himself in marriage, and now, in fear of your anger and that of his lord Albuin, has sought refuge at the shrine of Saints Marcellinus and Peter. I beg your charitable heart to deign to intercede with Albuin in my name for the man so that he may, with his favour and yours, keep the woman he has taken to wife"[1]. This was normal; the serf who married without his lord's leave was subject to heavy legal punishment; but Gregory of Tours takes us into a deeper gulf of misery. He is recounting the villainies of a certain Frankish noble; and he tells us how a bondman and bondwoman, having "loved each other, as cometh so often to pass," and having married without their master's leave, fled to a church for sanctuary. The priest would not give them up till the master had promised not to separate them; the master kept his promise by burying husband and wife alive in a single grave[2].

Things of this kind were more possible in Continental society, which suffered worse than ours from the characteristic vices of feudalism—weakness of central power, and multipli-cation of petty tyrants. With us, the building of private castles at every point of vantage, and the defiance of royalty by irre-sponsible barons, went on only during the brief reign of Stephen; but men said then that God and His saints slept[3]. In France and Germany, for many generations, God and His saints slept rather more than they waked; and the husbandman was ready for any sacrifice that would give him some sort of security. It was in these days that many freemen "com-mended" themselves to abbeys, in order to get some sort of

[1] Einhard, Ep. 37, translated by H. Preble. I shall recur to these marriage-disabilities in ch. XXIII.

[2] Bk v, ch. 3. The priest, writes Gregory, hastened to the spot and was just in time to extract the man alive; his wife was suffocated. For the barbarous practice of castrating serfs in the Dark Ages, see *Irminon*, I, 298.

[3] It has often been noted that there was no Truce of God in England, because the royal influence suppressed private war with us more effectually than the Church could suppress it on the Continent.

protection from the Church[1]. This step was taken under many different circumstances. About 965 A.D. Sicher killed a serf of Cluny; he gave the abbot his own person to servitude in compensation[2]. Half a century later, a woman recovered her sight through the prayers of St-Arnoul-de-Mouson; whereupon she put a leathern strap round her neck and gave herself up as a bondwoman to the monastery[3]. Other freemen gave themselves up to bondage because they could no longer stand by themselves; they did so not only by ones and twos, but in groups or in communities. Somewhere before 820 A.D. a group of fourteen freemen at Neauphlette gave up their lands to the abbey of St-Germain, and themselves as serfs, "because they were

---

[1] Delisle is possibly right in thinking that it was this insecurity which originated the not infrequent custom of stacking corn in the parish churches (p. 732). The advantages enjoyed by ecclesiastical serfs are not by any means referable wholly to altruism. The ancient laws exact twice or thrice the ordinary weregeld from the murderer of a royal or ecclesiastical serf; that had obvious economic advantages for the owner. On the other hand, by a capitulary of 819, no church serf might be enfranchized without the emperor's leave; here the privilege is not only mainly but wholly to the master's advantage. The same may almost be said of the ancient law that the ordinary fine imposed on any man who refused to return a runaway serf should be trebled if the fugitive belonged to a priest or a monastery (*Irminon*, 1, 342, 352, 354).

[2] AA.SS.O.S.B. v, 319; cf. *Cart. St-Père*, p. 297.

[3] *Ibid.* p. 356: cf. *Irminon*, 1, 286. Verriest emphasizes the financial profit which the Church found in these *donati* (p. 159). In a series of maps (pp. 190 ff.) he shows the great extension of the system in Hainaut and on pp. 374 ff. is a still more valuable list of cases noted, from 936 to 1390 A.D., by which time the system was dead. This table shows still more conclusively the remarkable disproportion of sexes; 206 women thus gave themselves and their property up to different religious foundations, but only 98 men. Of the numerous devotees of this kind at St-Trond, nearly all were women; and Peetz notes the same at Herrenchiemsee (p. 70). There, he adds, the charters generally express the motive: "defensionis causa" against seignorial oppression. For other material advantages enjoyed by Church serfs in the Dark Ages see K. T. Inama-Sternegg, *Deutsche Wirthschaftsgeschichte*, 1, 1879, 61, 254. Here is another specimen taken almost at random. The Emperor Otto II, in 981, granted a charter to the abbey of Leno in Italy. The document enumerates in detail the monks' possessions, their privileges, and their immunities, and guarantees inviolability to all. The monastic tenants are to be undisturbed by other lords, and even by royal officers; they are to be immune from the ordinary villagers' duties of watch and ward and forced labour for town walls or roads or bridges; and "if any man molest the abbot or monks or servants or tenants of the aforesaid abbey, or implead them in court against this right, or violate this aforesaid authority of ours, let him know that he must compound by the payment of a hundred pounds of pure fine gold, half to our treasury and half to the aforesaid abbot and his monks" (Zaccaria, p. 79: cf. 65, 70).

unable to fulfil the king's demands upon them for service in war"[1]. About 200 years later, the peasants of La Pine were in such want that they sold their cottages and gardens (a great part of their land had already been sold) to a noble who gave them to the monks of St-Père for the salvation of his own soul. The peasants themselves were deported to St-Georges, another manor belonging to St-Père[2]. The great abbey of Fulda in Germany received, in its early days, an enormous number of small holdings, under circumstances which indicate that these peasant-proprietors had given their persons with their land. In those times of anarchy, there can be no doubt that the serf had more security under the Church, and especially under the monks, than under any other lord except the king[3]. And, in those days of grievous necessity, there still survived something of the old Roman tradition that parents might sell their own children into servitude[4]; even in the late thirteenth century, we find St Bonaventura taking this axiom as his foundation for a philosophical justification of God's ways with man[5]. His contemporary, Bartholomew the Englishman, gives a description of the serf which, however exaggerated for the England of his own day, did come fairly near to the real facts of the Continental Europe in 1250, and still nearer to the conditions of earlier centuries. He writes:

A servant-woman...is fed with gross meat and simple, and is clothed with clothes and kept low under the yoke of thraldom and of servage; and if she conceive a child, it is thrall or [ever] it be born, and is taken from the mother's womb to servage....Also if a serving woman be of bond condition she is not suffered to take a husband at her own will....A bond servant-woman is bought and sold like a beast. And if a bond servant, man or woman, be made free, and afterwards be ill-behaved, he shall be called and brought again into charge of bondage and of thraldom. Also a bondservant suffereth many wrongs, and is beat with rods, and constrained and held low with divers and contrary charges and travails amongst wretchedness and woe. Scarce he is suffered to take breath[6].

---

[1] *Irminon*, I, 635; II, 31.   [2] *Cart. St-Père*, p. 119.
[3] For sales of liberty by freemen see *Irminon*, I, 223.
[4] *Ibid*. p. 286.
[5] *In Sentt*. lib. II, dist. xxxii, art. 3, q. 2. This is copied from St Anselm, *De Conceptu Virginali* (Opp. 1721, p. 106).
[6] Trevisa's *Bartholomew*, lib. VI, c. 12. I have quoted the whole passage in *Social Britain*, pp. 339 ff.

Here, again, are the words of one of the most learned, moderate, businesslike and charitable men of the twelfth century. We shall see, in Chapter XII, how Peter the Venerable defends the monks' possession of bondfolk—*servi* and *ancillae*—on the score that they treat them far more charitably than others do. He writes:

It is notorious to all men how these non-monastic masters—*seculares domini*—lord it over their peasant bondfolk. For they are not content with their due and customary services, but always unmercifully claim from themselves both their bodies and their possessions—*et res cum personis, et personas cum rebus*. Therefore, over and above the usual taxes, they plunder these poor folk thrice or four times a year, or as often as they choose, afflicting them with countless services and laying grievous and unbearable burdens upon them; whereby they oftentimes compel them to leave their native soil and to flee to strange parts; and (what is worse) their bodies themselves, which Christ redeemed at the dear price of His own blood, these masters do not shrink from selling at the vile price of mere money[1].

We must somewhat discount his blame of the lay masters, as we do his praise of the monastic lords; in each case he was tempted to some exaggeration. So, again, we have already discounted the somewhat academic description of an encyclopedist like Bartholomew the Englishman; nor must we unduly stress the fact that Petrus Berchorius, writing in Chaucer's day, can find no better description of the serf's status than to copy word for word from "that most rhetorical and Catholic writer, Bartholomaeus Anglicus"[2]. But no legitimate reservations can altogether invalidate this evidence; and certainly it is irreconcilable with the contention of Father Kröss (who produces no evidence at all), that "most masters were entirely penetrated by a sense of the greatness of their [moral] task in relation to their slaves"; so that (he argues) the question of the moral justification of the servile system became less and less pressing in the Middle Ages[3]. On p. 204 of his first volume Berchorius, writing this time without reference to Bartholomew, gives a

---

[1] *P.L.* vol. 189, col. 146. But we shall also see (Chapter XII, p. 147) that neither Cluniacs nor other monks acted consistently upon this principle laid down by Peter the Venerable.

[2] Berchorius, II, 67.

[3] *Kirche und Sklaverei*, p. 618.

very gloomy picture of the sufferings of peasants in general at the hands of their lords.

And, if we turn away from these three churchmen, we shall find almost the same evidence from the trouvère Wace, whose sympathies were with the lords, in his description of the Norman peasants' revolt under the rule of Richard le Bon:

The peasants and the villeins, the men of the forest and of the plain, I know not by what enticement nor under whose first leadership, held councils by twenties, by thirties, by hundreds...and have sworn together, that never by their own freewill shall they have lord or bailiff. The lords [they said] do them nought but harm; they can have no reason with them, nor no gain from their own work. Daily the peasants go with great grief, in pain and in toil; last year was ill, this year is worse; daily their cattle are taken for taxes or for services; there are so many pleas [in the manor-court] and quarrels, so many customs, old and new, that they cannot have an hour's peace.... They can have no warranty against their lord or his servant, who keep no covenant with the peasant; "son of a whore," they say. Wherefore then do we let them harm us; let us shake ourselves free from their domination! We, too, are men as they; limbs we have like theirs, and our bodies are as big and we can endure as much; all that we need is only a heart. Let us bind ourselves together by oath to defend ourselves and our goods; let us hold together, and then, if they will war against us, we have one or two score peasants, able to fight, against every knight of theirs.

"By these words and sayings, and others more foolish still," says Wace, "they raised that serious revolt, which was quenched in blood"[1].

The lords who had dealt thus with their native tenants in Normandy were not likely to be more merciful with their tenantry in conquered England; and here Maitland brings out the evidence supplied by Domesday. Even the holder of a small manor is now cultivating it under a French lord *graviter et miserabiliter*; "but, again, it is not on a few cases in which our record states that some man has suffered an injustice that we

---

[1] Delisle, pp. 122 ff. The oppression of the poor by the nobles is a preacher's commonplace; *e.g.* St Peter Damiani (Migne, *P.L.* vol. 144, col. 228); Bromyard, *Sum. Pred.* A. xxiv, 1; D. xii, 18–19; E. iii, 5, 7, 22, 27, 28 (but cf. 8); F. viii, 12; T. v, 30, 36; Herolt, *Serm. Disc. de Temp.* S. xcix [or civ] f.; Raulin, *Serm. de Sanctis*, f. 174, 3 a). The bailiff's reputation here was almost as bad as the lord's: a proverb of about 1300 ran: "For if the lord bid slay, the steward bids flay" (Bozon. p. 12). Cf. appendix 20.

would rely. Rather we notice that it treats it as a quite common event"[1].

From many other sources, of all kinds, we get evidence for the illegitimate aggravation of services and servitudes which, even at their best, were bad enough[2]. The arbitrary nature of tallage and forced services led to endless friction. The "angaria" or "averagium"—*i.e.* compulsion to carry loads for the lord—might take the serf not only far from his home but into perils of evil roads and highwaymen; moreover, "the villein with neither ox nor horse had himself to shoulder the load (*super dorsum*)"[3]. Guérard quotes a case where a peasant, broken down by these *angariae*, which he could fulfil only by hiring extra beasts and thus plunging into debt, attempted to extricate himself by pledging his wife and children[4]. A Dominican of the thirteenth century, outraged at the contrast between lordly ostentation and peasant squalor, takes refuge in a characteristically medieval licence of etymology: "the garments of the nobles are very properly called *robes* in the French tongue, seeing that they come from robbery"[5].

At one time, it was a step forward for the serf to obtain the right of sanctuary in Church or churchyard, like other men[6]. St Antoninus of Florence asks what is to be done with those who drag him from this asylum. The Church, he thinks, ought to refuse all offerings from such men, as she ought to refuse those of a notorious usurer; yet this would not seem a very efficient sanction, since neither the usurer nor the man who had wronged the serf might ever have the least intention of pressing offerings upon an unwilling Church[7]. Again, at the end of the Dark Ages,

---

[1] *Domesday Book and Beyond*, 1897, p. 61. For the lord's chance of exaggerating his legal control in other ways, and at a later date, see Walter of Henley, introd. p. xii.

[2] See appendix 20.

[3] Vinogradoff, *Villainage*, p. 405; Lipson, p. 34.

[4] *Irminon*, I, 799.   [5] Lecoy, p. 389.

[6] St-Aiglan points out that no monastic lawgiver dared—what, we must at once grant, would have required extreme courage—to guarantee the serf sanctuary from his master, except of course for the limited period during which a murderer also might have taken sanctuary. He remarks: "De même que les sages de l'antiquité, les moines réservèrent pour leurs frères libres la charité et la fraternité: l'esclave méprisé n'eut droit qu'à la communion de la prière" (p. 62).

[7] *Summa Major*, pars III, tit. 12, c. 11 (Lyons, 1507).

the Truce of God insisted that the plough or the wayside cross should be a sanctuary for the husbandman; but this prescription was frequently violated[1]. Delisle points out how terribly the peasantry suffered in the wars[2]; and war was almost chronic in many parts of Europe. Nicolas de Clémanges, who was archdeacon of Bayeux during the last years of the Hundred Years' War, describes the state of things in Normandy:

It is known not only to men of this kingdom, but even to foreign nations, with what burden of taxes the people of France are burdened, and with what rapine of soldiery they are afflicted. Indeed, the spoil and ravage is so general, that our unhappy peasants, for all their sweat and unceasing labour, are scarcely left—I will not say, with wheaten bread—but even with rye-bread wherewith to drag out their wretched existence. What can I say of their clothing, when their persecutors, even in mid-winter, will rob them of the very sackcloth which they ordinarily wear, unless it be too old and ragged? I say nothing of what they suffer from feudal retainers and from Church summoners and from those purveyors called *captores*, who differ only by a single letter from *raptores*, who extort from the unwilling countryfolk their wine and wheat and oats, oxen and rams and calves, and whatsoever fruits or cattle or fowls they have earned or reared for themselves, and who not only take all these things at a cheap price, but often leave a mere scrap of paper for this price, as a promise that will never be redeemed.

Why, he continues, does the Church create new holy-days, seeing that the peasant, even if he works on all the old and traditional holy-days, would still be unable to satisfy these cormorants who batten upon him?[3] One article in this arraignment, that of the purveyors whom kings and great nobles sent round to commandeer food and litter wherever they journeyed, is abundantly borne out by chroniclers and by cold-blooded documents. The Saxon chronicle tells us, under the year 1104, "wherever the king [Henry I] went, his train fell to plundering his wretched people, and withal there was much burning and manslaughter." The *Dialogus de Scaccario* tells us, of the same reign, how crowds of peasants came to court, or mobbed the king on his journeys, "offering him their [idle] ploughs in token

---

[1] Seignobos points out how the clergy themselves finally gave up the attempt to enforce this truce seriously upon the lay lords (pp. 77–79). They had good intentions here, but lacked the necessary force and persistence.

[2] *L.c.* p. 221.   [3] *Opera*, p. 153 b.

of the decay of husbandry"[1]. Yet contemporaries assure us, Henry's was an easy reign for the people compared with his two predecessors' and his successor's. Much later, the accounts of the bailiffs on different manors of Merton College, Oxford, frequently note the sums expended in buying off the royal purveyors' exactions. Here is a note from the bailiff of Cambridge in 1325: "Expenses of 6 men going about the country and to London to seek stolen oxen, for 6 days, 1s. 4d. Given to the king's servants, lest they should do greater damage, 8d." Again in 1328: "To the King's servants, that they should not carry corn away, 2s." Again in 1334, at Gamlingay near Cambridge: "To the King's bailiff, that he should not take away corn to the lord King, 3s. 4d."[2]

Delisle supplies other evidence of rural oppression, especially from an unknown poet who describes the rebellion of the serfs of Verson in Normandy about 1250 A.D.; a document all the more valuable to us because the author, like Wace, sympathized mainly with the masters[3]. And he points out how long, in France, this misery lasted (p. 646):

Le XVI siècle, avec ses guerres civiles et religieuses, ne permit, pour ainsi dire, de réaliser aucun progrès en agriculture. Même sous le règne de Henri IV, la plupart des paysans étaient plongés dans une misère, dont les plus mauvais temps du moyen âge peuvent à peine fournir un second exemple. Cependant, loin de s'améliorer, la condition du laboureur devait encore devenir plus intolérable sous Louis XIV. Sans doute, les victoires et les magnificences de ce règne en ont fait une des plus glorieuses périodes de notre histoire. Mais cette gloire fut chèrement payée par l'argent et les hommes que le monarque sacrifia pour l'acquérir. Jamais peut-être impôt ne pesa plus lourdement sur nos campagnes que les tailles de cette époque;

---

[1] Ed. Hughes, Crump and Johnson, Oxford, 1902, p. 89.

[2] J. E. T. Rogers, *Hist. Ag. and Prices*, II, 608. I have quoted others in *Social Britain*, pp. 346 ff. Cf. Jusserand, *Nomade*, p. 269, for the petition of the Commons on this subject in 1314. Even the strictly legitimate feudal incidents were sometimes very heavy; there was no doubt of the lord's right to raise a tax when he married his eldest daughter, and a stray notice shows a Farley peasant paying 6s. 8d. for this in 1291 (*ibid.* p. 609). He would have had to pay the same, or more, for the knighting of the eldest son, or for the lord's ransom. The sum, at this time, would have bought a cheap cow, or six sheep.

[3] pp. 49, 87–8, 102, 668 ff. The extent to which the peasant lost by encroachment during the Middle Ages, at the hands of lay and ecclesiastical landlords, is brought out by Boissonnade, pp. 149 ff., 152, 168, 320.

peut-être aussi les paysans ne furent-ils jamais plus impitoyablement poursuivis pour remplir les vides immenses que la mort faisait tous les jours dans les rangs de nos armées.

Part of this suffering, of course, came from material causes. Plagues were frightfully common; so were famines; Delisle's list at the end of his book, without being exhaustive, is significant enough[1]. Famines were greatly due to rude methods of tillage and to difficulties of transportation in an age where most of the roads were mere horse-tracks, and where the authorities struggled with imperfect success to prevent the nearest peasant from digging a clay-pit or any other hole that suited him in the very line of traffic[2]. Delisle points out how the archbishop of Rouen actually paid men to carry the dung from his great stables and cast it into the Seine hard by[3]; yet the prelate had his manor of Déville only a little outside the city, where the manure would have been of great value. What with these difficulties of transport, and what with oppressive tolls at almost every frequented ford or pass, it was easy for one district to starve even while its neighbours had comparative abundance. We must allow also for the very much larger extent of forest in those days, and consequent restrictions upon arable[4]. Moreover, it was not only that there was less to plough, but the beasts preyed upon the crops. The elaborate prescriptions in many manorial customals as to the amount of fencing to be done yearly by each tenant refer very often to the lord's own woods; the fence was not for keeping out the tenant's cattle, but for keeping in the wild beasts, or at any rate for preventing their wholesale egress. By ones and twos they often found means of coming out to feed upon the tillage; and the peasant, to put it mildly, fought them with one hand tied behind his back. Ralph Niger says of Henry II what might have been said even more emphatically of some of his predecessors: "To the fowls of the air, the fishes of the river, and the beasts of the field he granted immunity, and gave them the crops of the poor for their pasture"[5]. He cut off

---

[1] pp. 630 ff.; cf. Habasque, p. 12 and Alwin Schultz, *Deutsches Leben*, Appendix.

[2] See above, p. 95 and *Social Life in Britain*, p. 426.

[3] *L.c.* p. 262. Similarly, when a mill-post was needed on Forncett manor, and had to be fetched from Winfarthing (about 8 miles), eight men, two carts and sixteen horses were needed for the job (Beevor, p. 489).

[4] Delisle, pp. 242, 334, 417.   [5] Ed. Anstruther, 1851, p. 168.

poachers' hands and feet. Two German farms, in 1225, were sold "because they lay waste and were spoiled by the wild beasts, so that they brought in no profit"[1]. The États Généraux at Tours, in 1483, complain of the royal forests: "whence have come...great waste of corn by wild beasts, which men dare not touch; and the beasts have had more freedom than men"[2]. The Flemings, in 1493, besought Maximilian for some remedy against this plague of beasts; during the late civil wars,

wolves and boars had so multiplied that the countryfolk no longer dared to till their lands for fear of these beasts, who daily devoured their cows, calves, sheep, and other cattle, and did endless damage. Maximilian, in consequence, addressed the chief Huntsman of Flanders, with his officers and his clerks, bidding them help the people and chase the said boars, wolves, stags, does and other wild beasts with dogs, snares, nets, or by any other means they judge fit, for a term of six months. Apparently they did not succeed in clearing the country; for, in an autograph letter of Oct. 28, 1497, preserved in the Archives du Franc, the Chief Huntsman announces that there will be a general battue; he gives the peasants leave to drive the boars out of the fields which they ravage, and promises that none shall be prosecuted if the beasts happen to be hurt. He advises prudence; one sees that wild boars must be treated with delicacy and consideration. Yet he condescends somewhat in the boors' favour, and seems to assure them that, if they are not too rough with the swine, nobody shall be imprisoned for hurting them[3].

In 1573 the ravages of wolves round Ypres were so excessive that a very high tariff was put upon their heads. In France, this state of things lasted in some districts until the Revolution.

It is well-known what immense forests covered our land; the fields round these forests were ravaged by bands of wild beasts. Article 137 of the Ordinance of Orléans forbade the peasant to kill these beasts, even when they trespassed upon his holding; he was allowed only to drive them off with stones, *without hurting them*. In the cahiers of the États Généraux of 1789, a number of localities were still complaining that "beasts were set before men"; the lords' warrens enjoyed the same impunity and played no less havoc[4].

[1] Anton, III, 507.
[2] *Recueil*, p. 82.
[3] *État de la Campagne dans notre province*, etc. Bruges, Vandecasteele-Werbrouck, 1844, pp. 6–9.
[4] Feillet, p. 72.

Not, of course, that the medieval peasant did not poach a good deal; this was part of the "sporting chance" which, for good and for bad, plays so great a part in medieval thought and society. Moreover, his fathers handed down to him traditions of earlier days and greater freedom.

The *Sachsenspiegel* shows many traces of earlier liberties surviving among the peasants of Northern Germany during the thirteenth century; it prescribes that no man might be maimed or slain for poaching; it forbids all treading down of the growing corn by hunters; "for the corn is as it were a living thing"[1]. Yet there and elsewhere, the rich man too often enjoyed his hunting at the peasant's expense. Ideally, his skill and his privileges were given him for the protection of crops by the extermination of wild beasts. Langland here supplies our *locus classicus*[2]. In actual practice, the hunter was often at least as mischievous as his quarry:

It is a most wretched and lamentable thing that, for the sake of wild beasts which no human care has nurtured but which God has granted for the common use of mankind, the poor are despoiled by great folk and scourged and cast into prison and subjected to many other sufferings....Who can deny that this is unchristian, this infliction of so manifold injustices on so many of Christ's poor, for the sake of one man's pleasure; yet this thing is practised almost in more ways than I can rehearse.

[1] Anton, III, 497, 500.
[2] *Piers Plowman*, B. VI, 30 ff. The Ploughman addresses the Knight:
And go hunt hardily to hares and to foxes
To boars and to brockes [badgers] that breaketh a-down mine hedges,
And go affaite thee falcons, wild fowls to kill,
For such cometh to my croft and croppeth my wheat.
For the numbers of wolves in France, see Delisle, p. 114 and Malicorne, p. 78. The latter shows from documentary evidence that, in Bray, which is now one of the most fertile districts of Normandy, the peasants in 1543 had to keep watch by night and day against the wild boars of the neighbouring forest. They collected 43 dogs that October and held a battue, but killed only five; two other battues a little later produced three boars and five wolves. In 1394, Tollerast near Coutances had no inhabitants left; and in 1403, a single peasant killed five wolves (*Ann. Normand* 34e année, 1868, p. 528). But this, of course, was during the great war. For similar evidence from Germany and Italy, of wolves coming even into the cities, see Anton. III, 498, and Salimbene's chronicle, *M.G.H.* XXXII, 88, 190, 297. The dates are about 1150 and 1250 respectively: cf. *From St Francis to Dante*, 2nd ed. pp. 39, 171. The Earl of Northumberland in 1512 had 5571 deer in the north alone, excluding his possessions in Sussex and other southern counties (*Household Book*, p. 425). Cf. Delisle, p. 307.

So wrote Jonas of Orléans[1]; and Meffret, six centuries later:
"Men of military rank, whether they be nobles or vassals, seize
the goods of their poor subjects, and tread down their growing
corn with their hunting-dogs." And again, having compared
the Bride of Christ, the Church, to a human body with its
several members and their several offices, he says: "The arms of
the Bride of Christ are the knights and squires and vassals,
who in old days protected the artisans and husbandmen;...but
nowadays neither artisans nor merchants nor husbandmen are
safe from spoliation at the hands of these men"[2]. Bromyard
tells the same tale: the nobles "earn the curses of simple folk,
whose corn they destroy by riding through it with their hawks
and hounds"[3]. Geiler of Kaysersberg, preaching a century
later in Strassburg cathedral, speaks bitterly of the hunters as
ravaging the crops and throwing many other hindrances in the
way of field-work[4]. One of the primary causes which led to the
final outbreak of the German peasants in 1525 was that "huntsmen and hounds ran about without regarding the damage they
did"[5].

Yet, as we shall see, the peasant gradually won some way out
of this slough of despond; and not always without help from his
superiors. There were intelligent and humane lords, both in
Church and in State, who contributed more or less consciously
towards this transformation of the serf from an animal to a
human being, as Prof. Imbart de la Tour puts it. Albertus
Magnus, the master of St Thomas Aquinas, shows this process
in the germ. The tallages which lords lay upon their serfs (he
writes), cannot be called robbery, however grievous, nor can the
lord be held morally bound to restitution, since "the serf
possesses nothing, save in his lord's name." On the other hand,

---

[1] P.L. vol. 106, col. 215.
[2] *Temp.* pp. 455 Q and 27 V.
[3] *Sum. Pred.* N. iii, 16: cf. *Arch. Kult.* IV, 55.
[4] *Navicula Fatuorum*, turba 73 Y, Z.
[5] Ranke, II, 210; cf. the repeated complaints of the peasants in Janssen,
VI, 134, 169. In the Württemberg of 1500, any trespasser found in the ducal
forests with firearms was to have an eye put out (Bezold, p. 45). The English
statute of 1495, though far short of this, is very oppressive (ch. XVII). For
taking pheasants or partridges the fine is £10, or a country labourer's wages
for nearly two years. The same fine was decreed for all who took any hawk
or drove it from its nest; for taking hawks' eggs the penalty was imprisonment for a year and a day and a fine at the king's will.

the lord "can sin by excessive demands for forced service or by oppression of his serf, since the community is interested in the way in which a man uses his own property"[1]. Two generations after this, the matter is put still more clearly by Philippe de Beaumanoir, the great royal official and legist, about 1290:

The lord himself can only gain [by leaving more freedom of action to his bondfolk], since his serfs become readier to earn; wherefore the heriots and merchets are the greater when they fall in to him. And there is a common proverb: "He who hath once flayed his sheep loseth two or three shearings"; whence it is plain that, in the districts where the serf's earnings are taken from him from day to day, he will do no more work than he needeth for the daily sustenance of himself and his household[2].

And now, to balance the picture, let us conclude with another side of the relation between master and man. As in Roman law, so in that of the Lombards and some other Germanic races, the master was responsible for his slave; a law of Charles the Great, again, guards against the abuse by which lords sometimes abjured such responsibility, and let the undisciplined "servus" loose upon society[3]. By this time the "servus" might be either slave or serf; and this tradition of the lord's responsibility survived to some extent in far later generations, when there was no longer question of slavery in the strict sense of the word. In some countries, at least, the necessitous serf could claim maintenance from his lord; he "came upon the landlord" instead of "upon the parish." But this was carefully noted to the lord's possible advantage in the future; here, for instance, is a case of extraordinary interest at Carnières in Hainaut (1318 A.D.). Wautier le Fèvre's widow resisted the claim of heriot. Her husband had repudiated it in his lifetime; the lord one day "met the said Wautier and drew his sword upon him and said that he would have reason of him; and the said Wautier answered

---

[1] *Super Sent.* lib. III, dist. xxxvii, art. 11. We have seen that civil legists quoted this same maxim of Roman law.

[2] *Cout. Beauvoisis*, 1842, II, 237. Beaumanoir speaks here of the "more courteous" custom of Beauvoisis, in contrast to "other districts, where the lord may take from his bondfolk, living or dead, whensoever he pleaseth and as much as he pleaseth, and may constrain them to remain for ever under his rule." In Beauvoisis, the serf might live wherever he wished, so long as he duly paid his feudal services.

[3] Muratori, *Ant.* I. 796 a; Caggese, I, 125–6.

that he would give way for no evil reason, and that he was neither his serf nor any other man's." Lastly, on his deathbed, Wautier had sworn to her that he was no serf, "by God, by his own soul, by the death which was at his door and by the damnation of his soul." The lord brought witnesses to the man's servile origin.

First, Alard Barbenias of Carnières, aged 70, sworn and questioned, said upon his oath that some 25 years since he saw a woman come to Carnières called Ierembourch le Croisie, who came to the door of Goswin [lord] of Carnières and sent word to Goswin by the said Goswin's servant that he should help her, for she had not wherewith to live and, if she was utterly destitute, he would take her of his free will, since she was his bondwoman. Then the said Goswin sent for her by his servant and made them give her to eat in his house, and then Goswin sent for two échevins, to take witness who was her master; and there and then, in presence of the mayor and the échevins, the said Ierembourg acknowledged that she was the said Goswin's serf; after which the said Goswin had her brought to the hostelry at Carnières, and there she dwelt and was provided for all her life. And this witness testifieth that he was present when she lay on her deathbed; and there she acknowledged before the rector of Carnières, by the death that was at her door, that she was bond-woman to Goswin de Carnières, and that Hawise la Noire, who was her aunt and was mother to the said Wautier le Fèvre, was also bond-woman to the said Goswin. Asked whether Ierembourg's and Wautier's mother were own sisters, the witness said that they were sisters, but he knoweth not whether they were full sisters. The deponent saith also that, when the said Ierembourg died in the hostelry at Carnières, he himself, as Goswin's mayor and at Goswin's command, in the presence of échevins, made shares of the said Ierembourg's moveables; asked what portion he took, he said coats, pilches, and such things as a poor woman ought to possess[1].

[1] Verriest, pp. 75, 519 ff. A similar indication of the lord's feudal duty of protection may be found in my *Five Centuries of Religion*, I, 243; and I give a still closer parallel at the end of Chapter xv of this present book. It is possible that a similar inference may be drawn from Sergeant Keble's contention in about 1480 (Keilway, *Reports*, 1688, f. 134 a, § 116).

CHAPTER XI

EARLIER REVOLTS

THE English peasant was seldom or never so ill off as his continental brethren. There were many reasons for this; the main, no doubt, was our more orderly government and steadier growth in freedom, with which our military and police system was inseparably bound up. I have expressed elsewhere my belief that much of our prosperity in the Middle Ages was due to the fact that here, more truly than in any other great country, every man was his own soldier and his own policeman[1]. As Dr John Moore noted in the Switzerland of 1779, one cannot permanently overtax a population in which every man bears arms[1]. The "Grande Ordonnance" of Charles VII fixed upon France, for more than three centuries, the double curse of a mercenary army and irresponsible taxation. It was the king's business to keep soldiers and to raise taxes; the king's business and nobody else's. This bargain enabled Charles VII to drive out the English invader; but it left the nation helpless against despotism until 1789, while the two freest countries in Europe were Great Britain and Switzerland, each with its own national militia. While our Tudors, with a mere handful of a bodyguard, were obliged to consult the will of the nation, their French contemporaries went on from tyranny to tyranny with the support of a large standing army, and the French peasant suffered all that we have seen in Delisle's description.

But even the English peasant sometimes suffered terribly, though he had royal justice at his back in the last resort, and though there was a growing tendency among the lawyers to facilitate his emancipation[2]. He might be ejected from his holding without cause assigned:

the owner may take it away when he pleases, and alter its condition at will. The Abingdon Chronicle tells us that before the time of Abbot Faritius it was held lawful on the manors of the Abbey to

[1] *The Case for Compulsory Service* (Wessex Press, Taunton), p. 45; I quote Moore's exact words on p. 161.
[2] For the favour which law showed to emancipation, see Vinogradoff, *Villainage*, p. 179.

drive the peasants away from their tenements. The stewards and bailiffs often made free use of this right, if anybody gave them a fee out of greed, or out of spite against the holder. Nor was there any settled mode of succession, and when a man died, his wife and children were pitilessly thrown out of their home in order to make place for perfect strangers. An end was put to such a lawless condition of things by Faritius' reforms: he was very much in want of money and found it more expedient to substitute a settled custom for the disorderly rule of stewards. But he did not thereby renounce any of his manorial rights: he only regulated their application. The legal feature of base tenure—its insecurity—was not abolished on the Abingdon estates[1].

As late as 12–13 Ed. III, the judges ruled that "his [the serf's] land belongs to his lord"[2]. Nor was this mere theory; in exceptional cases it was actually enforced; even later than this, "the abbot of Eynsham takes from his peasant land which had been bought by the latter's father"; earlier in the thirteenth century, "the prior of Barnwell quotes the above-mentioned rule in support of a confiscation of a villain's land"[3].

Another source of possible injustice was the fact that freemen sometimes took up land which was burdened with villein services; they thus became tarred, so to speak, with the servile brush, and lords were tempted to claim them as bodily serfs. A Glastonbury case of this kind will be found in appendix 21. Fitzherbert wrote:

There be many freemen taken as bondmen, and their landes and goodes taken fro them, so that they shall not be able to sue for remedy, to proue them selfe fre of blode. And that is moste commonly where the free men haue the same name as the bondmen haue, or that his auncesters, of whome he is comen, was manumysed before his byrthe. In suche cases there can nat be to great a punyshment[4].

In a great many foreign manors, the land itself made bondage; all who settled there became *ipso facto* serfs[5].

---

[1] Vinogradoff, *Villainage*, p. 165.

[2] *Ibid.* pp. 45–6. In fact, this was asserted even by Elizabeth in 1575; see *Norfolk Archaeol.* XIX, 11.

[3] Vinogradoff, p. 159. Page also shows how easily injustices might be committed, pp. 14, 16, 24.

[4] Ed. 1539, ch. XIII, p. 31, quoted by Leadam in *Trans. Roy. Hist. Soc.* VI (1892), 210.

[5] Des Méloizes, p. 72 (Berry). This was perhaps still more frequent in Germany.

But perhaps the most telling documents of all are those which show how far things might go before it was possible for a villein to get even a hearing in the king's courts. In the enormous majority of cases, the lord had simply to prove that the man or the woman was his serf, and the affair was at an end; the royal judges had no further business in the matter; it must be decided in the lord's own court by doomsmen who were in the lord's own hand. Even where the royal judges had every wish to help the poor man, they could not go beyond a certain point. It will be sufficient to quote two cases, the first translated directly from the contemporary record, and the second in a modern summary.

Roger of Kirtley complains that Henry de Vere [the lord of the manor] came to his [Roger's] house at Mutford by night, on Monday in the first week of Lent, and had a lighted torch of wax carried before him, and broke the door and entered his house and asked where was Roger's daughter, whom [Roger] had often promised him; and when he could not find her in the house, he entered her chamber and sought her throughout the chamber; but her mother had got her out of the chamber-window; and when he could not find her in the chamber, he went out towards [Roger's] barn, which was full of corn, to wit, of barley,.and he found the door closed and bolted, and he broke the bolt and the door, and entered and sought her every-where; and when he could not find her, he set the torch to the corn, and burnt all the corn and the barn; and this he did wickedly and in felony and against the king's peace; and this [Roger] offers to deraign by the body of Thomas of Bradley, who has Roger's [said] daughter to wife, as [by the body of] one who himself lost property in the burning of the barn, namely, a chest with his clothes in it; and in case any mischance shall befall [Thomas] Roger offers to prove against (Henry) as the court shall consider.

And Henry comes and defends the kings peace and the felony and the burning and all of it word by word as the court shall con-sider, but desires to tell the truth. He adds that Roger is his villein, and true it is that a building was burned, but this was by mis-adventure; and the said Thomas married Roger's daughter against [Henry's] will, and whereas [Roger] could not give her in marriage without [Henry's] consent, and he [Henry] would not consent nor would he enfranchise [Roger], therefore the appeal is grounded on hate and spite; and [Henry] craves that it be allowed in his favour that [Thomas] appeals him concerning a house which is not his [Thomas's] and also that Roger, who makes this appeal, is his [Henry's] villein.

And for that Thomas appeals (Henry) of burning a house which belongs not to [Thomas], but to another, and moreover Roger confesses that on the day of the fire he [Roger], was Henry's tenant, it is considered that the appeal does not lie, but let twelve free and lawful and discreet men be summoned by whom [the truth may be known] and who are not related to Henry, nor to Roger or Thomas, and who will not for hate or love conceal the truth, to be [here] in the quindene of Hilary, to recognise whether on the said Monday Henry came by night to the house of Roger, and broke his house and burnt his barn, or no; and in the meantime, let them certify themselves as to the facts, in order that we [the king or the justices] may have no cause for betaking ourselves against them[1].

At the very best, it will be evident what delays this suitor must have suffered, how difficult it must have been to bring his witnesses for this adjourned hearing, and how little chance he and they would have against the lord.

The second case is from the year 1240.

Thos. Cusin, Hugh de Aula, and James de Ludinton came to the house of Gunilda de Stokes, carried her out into the fields, and took away all her goods. Whether Gunilda appealed to the manorial or local courts does not appear; but 4 years elapsed before her obtaining any redress. In the summer of 1244 the justices of assize came to Sherborne. What hope the unfortunate woman cherished of obtaining abstract justice at their hands is open to question. She brought her case before them, however, and Thomas was summoned. He acknowledged all her charges, and did not even seek to prove that he had any moral justification on account of her bad tenancy or default in rent, merely replying that he certainly "took her goods as of his villein, and could eject her from her tenement as from his villeinage." The case being put to the jurors they acknowledged that it was as Thomas said; and Gunilda was apparently dismissed without redress.

In a society regulated by a code of justice of which this is an instance, it is hardly surprising to find an innocent man flying from his lord for fear; it would be interesting to know more of the case of Walter Middewynter, who was presented by the jurors at the same eyre for having done so. It is at least satisfactory to know that the justices merely decided that as he had done no ill he might return if he would, but imposed no fine upon him, and gave his master no assistance towards forcing

---

[1] *Sel. Pleas of the Crown* (Selden Soc. 1887), p. 139, 1220 A.D.

him to come back[1]. These records, with those which M. Jusserand gives, exactly illustrate the well-known complaint of
Peace against *Wrong* in *Piers Plowman*[2]; and they almost justify
Michelet's bitter epigram: "the medieval peasant would have
burst, but for his hope in the Devil"[3].

Though such cases of extreme violence were doubtless exceptional at the worst of times, yet the general tone of the
medieval evidence implies that they were frequent enough to
be seriously reckoned with. But, in the later Middle Ages, the
peasant's position certainly did improve, through a variety of
causes. The influence of Christianity must be counted, acting
very slowly and fitfully, but with the gradual power of a principle
to which everybody pays lip-homage, and which, therefore,
exerts some real power when other temptations are silent.
Something was done by flat rebellion; more by the natural
dogged resistance of oppressed folk, and by flight from the
oppressor. Most influential of all, I think, were economic
causes, resting on the fortunate truth that, in the long run, it
pays better to have a few willing and capable workmen than a
great many slaves[4].

In France, the rise of "adulterine castles" gradually forced
the poor to combine, to bargain collectively with their lords, and
to form what were called *communes*, more or less free and self-
governing, except that they paid liberally for their liberties.
Conservative lords hated this movement for emancipation, which
was naturally tempted to boisterous self-assertion; "communio,
novum atque pessimum nomen," writes abbot Guibert de Nogent
of about 1100 A.D. But wiser lords even at that time were willing
to sell liberties; and within a century the majority were willing
to sell wherever the peasants could pay[5]. In England, the

---

[1] *V.C.H. Dorset*, ii, 231, quoting from *Assize R.* 201, m. 4 and m. 5 d.

[2] B. iv, 47; cf. Jusserand in *Nomade*, ch. iii *ad init.* and *Épop.* pp. 32, 117.

[3] *La Sorcière* (1862), p. 51. Compare the memorial to the États Généraux
of Tours in 1483, which I quote in ch. xxiii.

[4] Caggese gives an admirable account of the steps towards freedom in
Italy, ii, 22; cf. i, 298.

[5] For the gradual amelioration of servage in France see *Irminon*, i, 305 ff.,
338 ff.: "Their struggles for freedom multiplied from century to century,
and became more and more difficult to repress." The great step came when
Louis le Gros (1108–37) set himself to encourage the formation of small
free municipalities; from that time forward, lords found it more and more
profitable to sell such liberties to their servile communities. The gradual

movement was slower but steadier; the period of the Hundred Years' War, during which many French towns were surrendering their liberties, because they could no longer bear the corresponding duties, was the great period of expansion for English municipal life. And most towns of any importance had this privilege, that the bondman who had dwelt there for a year and a day as a recognized citizen, unclaimed by his lord, was thenceforth free for ever.

On the other hand, really serious rebellions were few and far between. As early as 821, the "conspiracies of serfs" were serious enough to embarrass the imperial government[1]. Two in Normandy, of about 1000 and 1250 A.D., have already been mentioned. The first of these was under Duke Richard II, surnamed *le Bon*; yet the peasants had little pity either from the kindly duke or from the good monk William of Jumièges, who tells us the whole story[2]. To this chronicler, Richard is "a most precious jewel of Christ," and his lieutenant was altogether laudable in his dealings with the representatives whom the peasants were sending to a general committee for the ventilation of their grievances. "He caught those delegates, with certain other peasants; he cut off their hands and feet and sent them back thus useless to their own men, that they might restrain them from like doings, and that their fate might warn the rest. The peasants, after this experience, hastily abandoned their assemblies and returned to their ploughs." The rising was put down without much difficulty, and followed by a retributive massacre[3].

A story told by John of Worcester concerning a dream of Henry I, in which he was threatened by desperate rustics and woke up in an agony of terror which disturbed his attendants, is too significant to be passed over altogether[4]. But the next actual rising of importance in European history is that of 1323, when the better-to-do peasants of the Flemish seaboard revolted. Success increased the popularity of their captains and

improvement of rural conditions in France, during the later Middle Ages, is briefly described by Imbart de la Tour, I, 464–486; but cf. p. 504.

[1] For early peasants' revolts in Italy see Caggese, I, 50, 133; for later revolts, II, 379.

[2] See above, ch. x, p. 111.

[3] A. Duchesne, *Hist. Norm. Scriptt.* 1619, p. 249.

[4] Ed. Weaver, 1908, p. 32. "They gnashed upon him with their teeth, and demanded I know not what debt from him."

the boldness of the "common folk." Vague communistic aspirations, which must long ago have taken possession of the poor, grew more definite. The peasants opposed tithe-paying and claimed to compel the abbeys to give up "the corn accruing from these said tithes, which has been gathered and stored in the monks' barns," and to distribute it in the form of "bread, among the poor folk that dwell on their lands"[1]. The rebels did in fact plunder the richest abbey of all, Dunes; and, in the full tide of success, they committed great cruelties and

HENRY I'S NIGHTMARE.
(From John of Worcester.)

preached class-war in all its nakedness; "all who did not live by handiwork were suspected"; "they would say unto a rich man: 'Thou lovest the lords more than the commonalty, through whom thou hast thy livelihood'; and, without further cause found against him, they would put him to death." The barons, on the other hand, pressed the King of France to massacre even the women and children[2]. In 1357, when the English had not only ravaged France but also extorted an enormous ransom for the king, which the dauphin was obliged to

---

[1] Pirenne, *Soulèvement*, p. xviii; cf. pp. xxv–xxvii and xxxiv for the unpopularity of the Church. "Men's lives became a burden to them," writes the monastic chronicler of Dunes.

[2] *Ibid.* xxvi, xxxi; cf. Pirenne, *Hist. de Belgique*, II, 78 ff.

wring from his subjects, the peasants rose desperately in the so-called *Jacquerie*. Here, again, in Languedoc men were murdered at sight if they could not show the horny hand of toil; the atrocities committed were even worse than in Flanders, and the reprisals bloody in proportion[1]. Next came our own revolt of 1381, which again was quenched in blood. Here, as in a series of smaller revolts which had marked the year 1327, the monasteries were a principal point of attack. Froude has told the St Albans story[2]. The prior of Bury St Edmunds had made himself unpopular by stoutly maintaining the rights of the abbey against the townsfolk; but it was his own serfs and bondmen, in 1381, who condemned him to death and cut off his head[3]. The Dunstable annalist is indignant with the ingratitude of his serfs in that year[4]; they rushed upon the abbey, which (he says) had treated them with kindness[5]. The Pilgrimage of Grace and Ket's rebellion were only agrarian in a subordinate sense, though one of Ket's demands ran: "We pray that all bondmen may be made free; for God made all men free with His precious blood shedding." The most serious and sanguinary of all these uprisings was the German Peasants' Revolt of 1524–5, the *Bauernkrieg*, partly inflamed by Luther's preaching, yet with far deeper causes behind it. But to those I must come in more detail towards the end of this book.

Those, then, are the main rebellions which have found their way into general history; but, amid the scattered documents which have drifted down to us from obscure corners of the countryside, there are many testifying to a continual ferment which must, in the long run, have done much to burst the old

---

[1] The story is told by Froissart with his usual vividness (Globe ed. p. 136).

[2] *Short Studies*, III, 80 ff.

[3] Walsingham, an. 1381, R.S. II, 1 ff.

[4] *Ann. Dunst.* R.S. 417, 419.

[5] Here, as always, we must remember that a revolt is always too blind in its fury to be just in detail; particular landlords who suffered may often have been innocent, or far less guilty than their predecessors. The peasants who rose in England may often have been as well-to-do as those who fought so desperately in West Flanders for still greater freedom. The ringleaders of the serfs who rebelled against the abbot of Meaux in Holderness (1367) had hired servants of their own. And if we are to take strictly the fact that each of the jurymen chosen to testify on this case sealed the evidence with his own seal, then either there were a good many well-to-do tenants in the manor, or the abbot had succeeded in getting a packed jury (*Chron. de Melsa*, R.S. III, 131–2).

bottles. Here and there monastic chroniclers give us vague hints of trouble with the peasantry; if as many chronicles had been kept in castles as in monasteries, we should probably have heard even more from that side. More detailed evidence comes, in a sporadic way, from more formal legal records. In 1102, on lands belonging to the monks of St-Arnoul-de-Crépy,"certain bondmen and bondwomen of the abbey broke into contradiction and rebellion against the abbey and monks; and so great waxed their numbers and the popular tumult that they utterly refused to give fines for marrying their wives and that part of their moneys which is called in the vulgar tongue *mortmain* [*i.e.* heriot]." In 1100, a small group subject to St-Michel-de-Beauvais "asserted that they might, without the assent of the abbey aforesaid, take women of any race whatsoever to their wives, and give their sisters and all the women of their race to any husbands whom they would; moreover, that they would not give at death that customary due which is called *mortmain* in the vulgar tongue"[1]. In 1189, when the abbot of Croyland impounded the cattle of the peasants who claimed certain grazing rights on the fen, the latter came "three thousand strong," armed as for battle; it was some years before the case was finally decided in the king's court and in the abbot's favour[2]. We should never have heard of these three rebellions but for the formal documents in which the monastic victories were registered in legal form, and deposited in the abbey archives.

So also with the revolt of 1220, where it needed royal intervention to compel the Chartres serfs to obey their abbot[3]; and so again with that of 1246, when the bondfolk of Esmans rebelled against the abbot of St-Germain-des-Prés[4]. They had reached a prosperity which enabled some of them to keep handmaids and servants of their own; they were free now from merchet (whether by purchase or by encroachment) and they

---

[1] *Irminon*, II, 370, 379.
[2] Neilson, p. xxxv. The whole of pp. xxv–xxxv are interesting in this connexion.
[3] *St-Père*, p. 683.
[4] The quarrel led to a government enquiry, extraordinarily interesting in the light which it throws upon medieval procedure in such cases, which is printed in full by Guilhiermoz, *Enquêtes et procès* (Paris, 1892), pp. 293 ff.

now denied the abbot's right to take heriots, to inflict tallage at will, to commandeer bedding when he chose to visit the village, to insist on the monopoly of the mill, and to hold a "ban" of wine—*i.e.* a close time during which no man might buy wine but from the monks. The depositions of the numerous witnesses show that they were very near success here; the hold of the monks had evidently relaxed, since it needed a good deal of formal testimony to convince the commissioners that the abbot had actually taken tallage from his serfs even in the years when the king also had inflicted upon them the burdensome honour of a royal visit; similarly, it had to be formally proved that he had enforced this right and the monopoly of the mill not only by moral suasion but "with violence"; that asses had been confiscated for taking corn to other mills; and that those who did not pay their tallage were distrained, as at Bury, by the monks, who "fetched serjeants from Moret to their aid and took [chattels as] pledges by force." The inquest shows clearly that these dues had become irregular—partly, perhaps, as at Bury, because the subdivision of tenancies made it sometimes hard to collect them—and that the monks, fearing to lose these villein services altogether, had recently reimposed them with unwonted strictness. Judgement, naturally, was given for the abbot, who was certainly within his legal rights; but this lengthy document shows very clearly what a hard struggle the lords must have had as soon as their tenants had reached a certain stage of self-conscious prosperity. It illustrates the familiar axiom that revolt comes not when the oppressed class has most to complain of, but when they have gained enough to give them an appetite for more.

But the most curious of these small rebellions that I have met with are English; and this is natural enough if, as is generally conceded, the English peasant was among the least unprosperous. Tallage at will was common enough abroad; in England it had become exceptional by the thirteenth century; this was one of the main grounds on which the tenants of Dunstable rebelled against the monks in 1229. They had probably no real case at civil law; certainly they were smitten with the thunderbolts of the Church; "yet they ceased not from their original fury and malice; but, confessing themselves excommunicate, they said they would rather go down to hell than be beaten in this matter of tallage"[1]. Another rebellion, on the abbey lands of Burton, is summarized at some length by Prof. Ashley[2]. In 1280, the tenants of Mickleover claimed exemption, and based their claim, quite mistakenly, on Domesday Book. They naturally lost their case, with costs; the abbot sent a small armed force and impounded the whole live-stock of the village— 800 oxen, sheep and pigs. The tenants appealed to the king; they followed him about from place to place, with their wives and children, and got a writ for the restoration of their cattle. In all, they got three royal writs. But the abbot had strict law on his side; he reminded the peasantry that they were his serfs, and therefore possessed nothing but their own bellies—*nihil extra ventrem*. They gradually submitted, one by one, and the abbot inflicted only a small fine upon all but the two ring-leaders, from whom he exacted half the corn then growing upon their land.

A still more interesting case is that of Darnall and Over, manors belonging to the Cistercians of Vale Royal in Cheshire. In 1326, we find the abbot drawing up a customal which is evidently designed to recall all his historic rights over the villeins; the inference is that they are beginning to slip from his hold, and he is consciously reacting as the abbot of St-Germain reacted at Esmans[3]. The result was inevitable; ten years later, we find the monastic scribe recording a movement so natural in its origin, so illuminating in its methods, and so typical in its results, that no mere summary of the monk's words could do it justice; I therefore give it with the omission only of formal or comparatively irrelevant sentences[4].

[1] *Ann. Dunst.* R.S. p. 122. By a final agreement, they paid £60 to the prior, who gave up his claim of tallage.

[2] *Introd. to Eng. Econom. Hist.* I (1911), 38 ff. from *Staffordshire Collections* (Henry Salt Soc.), v, 82 ff.

[3] *Vale Royal*, pp. 117 ff.; I print these customs at considerable length in appendix 22. Their position in the Ledger Book seems to point clearly to the year 1326. For similar friction through the assertion by the monks of ancient rights, or new rights claimed as ancient, see the Swaffham Prior case quoted by Vinogradoff, *Villainage*, p. 204, and the German cases to which I shall come in Chapter XXIV.

[4] *Vale Royal*, pp. 37 ff. I must here express my special gratitude to the Lancashire and Cheshire Record Society for permission to print so long an extract from this valuable volume.

Of the doings of the bond tenants of Dernehale and Overe.

Be it remembered that in the year 1336,...the villeins of Dernehale and Over conspired against their lords, the abbot and convent....
Sir Hugh de Fren, then justiciar of Chester, came to a place which is
called Harebache Crose, at which a great number of villeins had
taken refuge together, and they laid a serious complaint against the
said abbot, [declaring] that, whereas they were free and held their
lands and tenements from aforetime by charter of the Lord the King,
the aforesaid abbot, contrary to his customs hitherto observed in his
manor of Dernehale, had put them in close confinement in shackles,
as though they were villeins, and forced them to serve him in all
villein services. And when these men returned home to their houses,
by the abbot's command they were put in fetters in the house of John
Badekoc at Over, on account of their complaints aforesaid, until they
should come and acknowledge their bondage, and submit themselves
to the abbot's grace....After the said countrymen had made a fine
at the will of the abbot, and sworn upon the holy Gospels of God that
they would never again contrive any such thing against the abbot and
convent, and confessed that they were villeins, they and their sons
after them to all eternity, according to the customs always observed
in the manor of Dernehale, as you have them more in detail set forth
in this same book under the heading of Dernehale, then those
wretched men, seeing themselves thus frustrated, called together all
their neighbours of their own condition, and plotted by night to get
their liberty by rebelling against the aforesaid abbot. And they sent
some of their number on behalf of them all on a pilgrimage to
St Thomas of Hereford; and these men, contrary to their oath, came
to the King in the northern parts, and for many days were begging
his favour, which they did not deserve to find; and afterwards they
came to unforeseen misadventure, for they robbed certain people
of their goods, and were all to their great chagrin carried off to
Nottingham gaol, being wholly stripped of all their own goods that
they had with them. Afterwards, before the justices of the Lord the
King in that place, they were condemned to be hanged; but because
it was not customary by the law of the kingdom to inflict death for
theft to the amount of which they were guilty, they were set at liberty
after some time by the grace of the King, not without great expense[1]
to the other country people of Over....But they did not desist from
the matter they had undertaken, but forthwith repaired to the Lord
the King in his parliament held at Westminster, and presented a
petition to parliament setting forth that the abbot oppressed them so
greatly with injuries and contumelies and villein services, that they

---

[1] *Non sine magna effusione*; I have ventured to differ here from the editor,
who translates "great outcries."

did not dare to return to [*contingere*] their homes, their wives and their children. And by these words they so wrought upon the King that he wrote to Sir Henry de Ferrers, justiciar of Chester, that he should do ample justice to the aforesaid men of Dernehale. And therefore the justiciar, willing to satisfy the King, diligently examined into the matter aforesaid himself and through his people, by means of the charters of the Lord the King which the Abbot publicly produced, by which it plainly appeared that they were bondmen. Therefore he commanded the abbot to punish them as he pleased, as his bondmen, in such a way as to leave them no excuse for any such temerity henceforward. But, nevertheless, these country people did not desist from their evil undertaking, but presented a petition to the aforesaid justiciar, setting forth that in the manor of Dernehale there used to be ten "bondes," so called, to whom belonged and pertained all the villein services, and they besought the justiciar to compel the abbot to inquire which these now were, in order that their serfdom should never be abated. But because it was clearer than daylight to the justiciars that this was of malice and fraud on their part, they forthwith charged the abbot to punish his aforesaid bondmen so severely that they should not clamour to the King again. But when they heard this, like mad dogs [*rabicanes*], they sought out the King again at Windsor, and complained of the justiciar as well as of the abbot, saying that the abbot had spoiled them of their goods, exceeding £100 in value, with which he had so corrupted both the justiciar and all the chief people in Chester that the justice-place was not open to them. Wherefore the Lord the King wrote to Lord Edward, his eldest son, Duke of Cornwall [and] Earl of Chester, that he should in some manner assist and relieve these men, thus oppressed. Encouraged and comforted by this, the country people came in a great crowd, (for there were thirty of them or more) to the county [court] of Chester, against the abbot, who was there in person, and with the aid of some persons skilled in the law, and others, they denied they were the abbot's bondmen, and begged that the said abbot should be silenced for ever and that they themselves should be pronounced free. But as the falseness [of their claim] was obvious not only to the justiciar but also to the whole of the court then present, by the things set forth above, judgment was once more given that the abbot should punish them. And when the bondmen were informed of this, they all fled, taking with them such of their goods as they could carry, and secretly withdrew themselves by night, and went to Philippa, Queen of England, and implored her assistance, pretending that they were the men of her son, the Duke of Cornwall, of his manor of Dernehale, and that the abbot of Vale Royal, in contempt of their lord, had spoiled them of all their goods; and they besought the queen to provide some remedy for them. Moved by

these words, the Lady the Queen forthwith directed her comminatory
letters to the abbot, directing him to leave in peace the men of her son,
the Duke of Cornwall, of his said manor; and she ordered him in
courtesy to restore the goods he had taken from them, otherwise the
King, when he learnt of it, would make some other order thereupon.
Now the abbot was caught on the horns of a dilemma [*intamareto
positus fuit*[1]], so that he was almost in doubt by what way to avoid
the threatened ills; for he feared to incur the immediate anger of the
King and Queen, if he did not obey their orders; and, if he did this,
he could not by any means avoid the loss of the manor of Dernehale
and the bondmen thereof. He finally determined in his own mind
that it would be best, in a matter so complicated, to make a personal
explanation to the King and Queen; and therefore he set out, and
found them at Kyggesclive, and set before them all the premises.
Now when, by his advice, the King and Queen had examined Henry
de Ferrers, justiciar of Chester, and other people, together with a
number of charters of the kings and Earls of Chester, granting the
manor of Dernehale to the abbot of Vale Royal, and [found] that
the bondmen belonged to the said abbot by reason of the manor,
the abbot left the court in the peace of the King and Queen, and with
the greatest honour, and the said manor of Dernehale, with the bondmen and their belongings for ever, was adjudged to him, to the confusion and shame of the country people to all eternity. Now when
these things had been accomplished, the abbot was on his return to
the monastery, and a great crowd of the country people of Dernehale
came to meet him in the high way on the feast of the Nativity of
St John the Baptist, about the ninth hour, at Exton in the county of
Rutland; and they attacked him and slew his groom, William Fynche,
with an arrow.... Now Walter Walsh, the cellarer, and John Coton,
and others of the abbot's servants were about half a league behind
the abbot, having tarried for certain business; and when they saw
the fight from afar they came up at full speed, and the said armed
bondmen came up against them to assault them; but the aforesaid
cellerar (blessed be his memory), like a champion sent from God to
protect his house and father, though he was all unarmed, not without
enormous bloodshed felled those sacrilegious men to the earth, and
left all those whom he found in that place half-dead, according to the
law of the Lord[2]. But certain of them fled, and the said John Coton
followed after them and took them. Meanwhile the sound of people
running up on all sides was heard, and after all the abbot was igno-
miniously taken, with all his people, by those bestial men of Rutland,
and was brought to the city of Stamford, where the king then was,
together with his bondmen; but on the morrow, through the aid of

[1] *Sic*: apparently miswritten for *interea in arcto*: cf. I Kings xiii, 6 Vulg.
[2] *In lege domini*: the reference is probably to Ps. i, 2 or lxxvii, 10.

the Mother of Mercy, in whose cause he was acting, the abbot, with all his followers, obtained his rights, and the bondmen were left there in chains and in the greatest misery, while the abbot returned in safety to his monastery.... And when they [the bondmen] came before Geoffrey de Scrop and his colleagues, for the death of the above said William, they were set at liberty, and obtained a writ to the abbot to deliver up forthwith their lands and goods and chattels, if they had been seized by reason of the death of the aforenamed William, and not otherwise. But since the abbot had other just causes against them, they derived no advantage from that writ. And at length the bondmen, finding no other place in which they might be longer concealed, returned to the abbot their lord, submitting themselves and their goods to his grace, and the abbot put them all in fetters as his bondmen. And so it came to pass that, touching the holy gospels, they all swore they were truly the bondmen of the abbot and convent, and that they would never claim their freedom against them and their successors. And for many Sundays they stood in the choir, in the face of the convent, with bare heads and feet, and they offered wax candles in token of subjection. Some of them were still in hiding, to wit, Henry Pym, Adam Hychekyn and William del Heet, walker[1]; therefore the abbot sued forth royal writs to apprehend them and others. But one day these three came to the county [court] of Chester with their bills against the abbot, and they were taken by Henry Doun, bailiff of the abbot's liberty, near Hokenelplat; and there by the said Henry and Thomas de Rodb', who had come with him, by miry ways, were bound and taken to the stocks at Weverham. And they swore on the holy gospels, as the others had done before, and submitted themselves and all their belongings to the abbot and convent. But, because Henry Pym was the author and contriver of all these wickednesses, the abbot decreed that he should be punished more than the rest. Therefore the said Henry, so long as he should live, was to offer a wax candle to the Blessed Virgin on the feast of the Assumption in the monastery of Vale Royal, at the high mass, in the face of the convent for ever, because he had made so shameless a disturbance. And the land which, by the abbot's license, he had put to farm to the Lord the King or to a priest, he was to make no claim to, but it was to remain to the Abbot; but the land which he first had in Swanlowe, he was to have and hold in villeinage, he and his for ever. After this one of the aforesaid bondmen, William Horn, by the hands of William de Tabbele, sued forth the King's writ against the abbot, Walter Welsh the cellarer and Thomas de Rodbury because they had violently despoiled him of his goods at Exton, but they after submitted to the abbot.

---

[1] *I.e.* a fuller by trade.

The story of the serfs of the monks of Meaux in Holderness would probably have been no less interesting if we could have it in all its details; as it is, we know only half a dozen lines that the chronicler has thought it worth while to hand down to us. It was about 1360 that "our bondmen of Bedforth, Thomas of Aldwyne and John his son, who were of the stock of that Richard of Aldwyne whom Thomas, son to Walo of Dringhow, granted to us, began to rebel against us. However, being suddenly seized and taken to our grange of Waghen, and there cast into bonds, they took the due oath of serfdom to our abbot in the presence of many honest folk"[1].

The abbots of Vale Royal and Meaux had gained a legal victory, and doubtless they stood on sound law; but the story of Vale Royal, at least, shows how seriously the monks' authority was undermined. These peasants of 1336 and 1360 are men of that England which has recently shaken itself free from a tyrannous king; of the England in which Froissart reports men saying: "We have no use for a sluggish and heavy king...we would rather slay half a hundred of such, one after the other, than fail to get a king to our use and liking"; for "the King of England must needs obey his people." These men of Over and Darnhall and Meaux are the fathers and the grandfathers of those who will cry in 1381: "We are men formed in Christ's likeness, and we are kept like beasts"[2]. The Bury chronicler notes how many were the revolts of these commons "who had waxed fat" against great abbeys in or about the year 1327; not only at Bury, but "at St Albans, at Abingdon, and elsewhere"[3]. And, perhaps most important of all, the serfs are floating on the tide of a great economic revolution which must free them in the long run, apart from all political movements. It has already become plain to the wisest folk of 1336, and in half a dozen generations it will be evident to the most obtuse, that money-rents are more profitable for both parties than these ancient feudal services.

This change from feudal dues to money rent has been so often and so well described that it need not be repeated

---

[1] *Chron. de Melsa*, R.S. III, 126.
[2] Froissart, *Chroniques*, ed. Luce, pp. 214, 249, 337.
[3] *Mem. St Edmunds*, R.S. II, 329.

here[1]. Sometimes the contemporary documents expressly tell us that certain services are no longer exacted because on those occasions the lord is bound to feed his labourer, and the work is not worth the dinner[2]. Though the computation was generally made in the lord's interest, and, in its earlier forms, often against the tenant's will, yet in the long run it benefited the latter. England was ahead of other European countries in progress from a natural towards a money economy; and, with us, commutation had already gone a good way before the Black Death. That catastrophe, here as in other social fields, shook what was already tottering or decaying; and it was followed by a very rapid increase in commutation. Although this sudden movement seems to have been followed by a natural reaction, yet "the remarkable increase of free labour within thirty years after the pestilence indicates how enormous was the influence which it exercised upon the economic situation....It gave a violent shock to the ancient manorial arrangements....It is certain that the hundred years which followed witnessed the complete disintegration of the old manorial order"[3]. Labour was scarce; it was impossible fully to enforce the statutes of Labourers and to prevent villeins from fleeing either to a town, where artisans were needed, or to some other manor where the lord, in despair for a tenant, would grant his land at a cheaper rate; thus there grew up a regular system of money leases, in which the lord commonly tried to secure himself by a clause permitting him to transfer the land to a higher bidder; but higher bidders never came, and gradually the lords often let out even their own demesne to farmers who paid them a fixed rent and took all the trouble of tillage off their hands. Thus a new class of yeomen

---

[1] To name only some of the latest books, by Sée, Tawney, Lipson and Page. Delisle describes the process in Normandy (p. 51) and Guérard in France (*Irminon*, 1, 392). One other cause operated for freedom in France, though not in England; on a large number of French manors the bondman who married a freewoman became free in right of his wife: therefore, as Guérard notes, it is far more common to find the man marrying above him than below. Of course he had to buy permission from his lord.

[2] Lipson, p. 79.

[3] Lipson, p. 87. In Italy, flight assumed a wholesale character far earlier, as in almost every way the best Italian peasants were ahead of ours. Even in the Dark Ages, the peasants of the great monastery of Farfa were improving their condition by wholesale flight (Caggese, 1, 30).

farmers grew up, a real agrarian middle class[1]. There were still many causes of friction; many temptations for the lords to reassert obsolete rights or to stretch them beyond the legal point; besides the great Peasants' Revolt of 1381 there were still isolated rebellions in different manors[2]. The heriot, and a good many other servile dues, were still exacted even in a large number of cases where the rest had been commuted for money. The House of Lords, in 1537, rejected a bill for the manumission of villeins.

In 1500 there were still eight bond families on the manor of Forncett [in Suffolk]; in 1550 the number had dwindled to three, and by 1575 serfdom was here extinct....One of the bondmen on Forncett manor appears to have paid no less than £120 for manumission. ...Personal serfdom had thus survived only as an instrument of extortion. It had lost all economic significance the moment it ceased to be the basis of compulsory labour and the keystone of medieval husbandry[3].

The steps to freedom on the Continent, though neither identical nor simultaneous, were essentially similar. In France, liberation seems to have taken place partly through individual purchases of freedom by serfs, but mainly through collective bargains; a whole village would buy itself free from bodily bondage, though not from a good many of the feudal incidents of servitude[4]. Through the action of these causes, personal serfdom "had mostly disappeared before the end of the 15th century; though it survived later in certain districts, specially on some ecclesiastical or monastic estates, and was only finally abolished on that famous night of Aug. 4, 1789"[5]. In the Germany of 1500 it was mostly dead also, though not by any means so completely as Janssen asserts. Before this time, the economic forces which for some time had assisted the peasant began to turn against him. It was discovered, especially in England, that there was great profit possible in "engrossing"— *i.e.* buying out the small holder and adding strip to strip until a considerable farm had been formed, to be exploited by capitalistic methods. The most tempting of those methods was that of the sheep-run, which sent a large proportion of the

[1] W. J. Corbett in *Social England*, 1902, p. 327.
[2] See the list in Lipson, p. 109.
[3] *Ibid*. p. 112.
[4] *Ibid*. pp. 112–13.
[5] *Irminon*, 1, 393.

labourers adrift. But this tendency began to become formidable only about a century before the Reformation[1]. Until it grew strong—that is, roughly, from 1450 to 1500—the peasantry were perhaps more prosperous, in the narrowest material sense, than they have been until almost the memory of living man. They had no voice in the State; their personal services and disabilities were often such as the modern labourer would have found degrading; but it is possible to argue that a large number of them, at any rate, were better fed and had more economic security than the men whose blood saved Britain through the Napoleonic wars. The later Middle Ages saw hopeful beginnings of social emancipation. But we cannot give men freedom in the fullest sense; they must themselves use it; and the very fact that considerable numbers of peasants were then struggling upward into a stable condition of yeomanry is perfectly consistent with deterioration among the rest, sinking deeper partly with their own inert weight, partly as thrust down by the more energetic in their climb. This takes me far beyond the period which I know by its written documents; my real task here is to help the reader to judge how far these later medieval germs of social and economic emancipation were due to the efforts of the Church, and especially of the monasteries.

[1] I deal with this in Chapter XVII.

CHAPTER XII

MONKS AND SERFS

UNMITIGATED serfdom has found no defenders; its misery is admitted, if only tacitly, on all hands; we have seen Imbart de la Tour confessing that it needed the progress of the later fifteenth century to transform the bondman into a real human being. But some men suggest tentatively, and a few have asserted dogmatically, that this improvement was due to the Church, and especially to the monasteries. Yet, whether timidly whispered in our ears or boldly proclaimed from the housetops, this thesis is never supported by the documentary evidence which alone, in the long run, could reconcile thinking people to such an historical paradox. For, on the face of it, the great centuries of serfdom were the great centuries of clerical, and especially of monastic, power. Again, those two or three generations of renascence, during which the serf, the rustic and the artisan bettered their condition very sensibly, resounded with complaints from great and orthodox Catholics that Mother Church had lost her former hold upon the people, and was steering straight for a religious revolution. Again, whereas England was the first great country to break with the medieval Church, she was also one of the least favourable to servitude. The same may be said of Holland; and, whatever social evils the Reformation unsettlement may have brought in its train—whatever, again, may have been the working of that capitalist movement which had begun long before, but which was accelerated by the Reformation—there is no great country whose poor were better off than the English, on the whole, between the Middle Ages and the French Revolution. Historically, the thesis that the enslavement of the working classes began at the Reformation has not even the superficial excuse of *post hoc, ergo propter hoc*. Morally, it has on the surface a little more justification, since there is much in the Bible to discourage servitude, and medieval society was nominally governed by the Bible. But, if this is to be our direct line of argument, we must remember that the Scriptures are still more unfavourable to graven images than to slavery; yet we know how full the churches were of images; and therefore we must judge our forefathers' behaviour not according to what the Bible might have caused it to be, but according as we find it to have been in fact. All that can be justly urged in favour of the Church here, and perhaps a little more, may be found in Guérard's introduction to the *Polyptyque d'Irminon* (1, 331 ff.) and Sackur, *Die Cluniacenser* (II, 422–436).

But the wish, in many minds, is a natural father to the belief. We must make some liberal allowance for those writers who rather suggest the theory as a pious hope; but we have the right to demand stricter account from those who, professing to bring proof, are in fact mainly concerned with avoiding all inconvenient evidence, and who thus, in the long run, indirectly emphasize the historical importance of that which they take such pains to conceal.

I must begin, however, by confessing small sympathy with those who blame the cleric for not living a life altogether different from the layman's. Institutional religion is justified, on the whole, so long as it can be said that the clergy are living very much better than the average of mankind, and distinctly better even than the average educated man; and I know of no Christian age or country in which this has not been true[1] But we must not go farther than this; for we really dishonour our forefathers by bedizening them with meretricious historical finery, just as the true saint is dishonoured by tinsel and tarnished brass-leaf. A careful perusal of Janssen's or Allard's apologies shows very plainly what the medieval clergy ought to have done in order to retain their spiritual hold on the world; but, when we turn from these special pleaders to actual documentary fact, we see equally plainly that they left this *unum necessarium* undone.

In the course of this story, we have already had scattered

[1] See the able plea in A. L. Smith's *Church and State in the Middle Ages* (Oxford, 1913). If, in ch. VI, he emphasizes the positive virtues of the Church without bringing out her demerits in allowing no other institution to compete with her in teaching and well-doing, yet on pp. 135–6 he provides all non-churchmen with an admirably expressed reminder that criticism is easy, while construction on a consistent spiritual basis is the most difficult, as it is the highest, of all tasks.

opportunities of judging the Church, and especially the monasteries, as landlords. It must be remembered, of course, that the large preponderance of monastic records brings the monk into greater prominence here than the layman; and, as my object has mainly been to bring out the 10 per cent. (as I have called it) of difference between the average medieval and the average modern peasant—as I have naturally, and I hope, legitimately, paid little attention to that 90 per cent. in which their ancient and modern lives agree—therefore my story has been often sad, and the monk or churchman has frequently appeared in a light which it would be unjust to emphasize without these qualifications. Here again, therefore, let me clear the ground by trying to put my final conviction before the reader into one or two sentences. I judge the monk to have been, on the whole, a slightly better landlord than the layman. His conservatism inclined him to the harder side, since his whole economic position was fundamentally capitalistic; but his religion and his traditions of social amenity, which even at the worst kept him on a higher moral plane than the average lay lord, weighed rather more heavily in the milder scale. In the same rough and tentative way in which I reckon the modern and medieval labourers' lives to differ by about 10 per cent., I should reckon the monastic landlord to have been 4 or 5 per cent. better than his brother the layman[1]. I had reached this conclusion independently from original documents before meeting with the few lines in which Henri Sée sums up his own laborious researches[2]: "In reality, as we

[1] There is good sense in Caggese's remark that the frequency of peasant revolts against the monks in especial may point to their slightly greater material prosperity; a prosperity not sufficient, however, to render them content with the ordinary conditions of the medieval country labourer (I, 141).

[2] It is often pleaded in favour of the monks that other men's serfs, or even freemen, were glad to enter voluntarily into bondage under them. Such cases did undoubtedly occur fairly often in early days; I have already taken account of them. But, before we can give them all this weight in argument, we must have more and better vouchers for the facts themselves, e.g. Guérard seems over-hasty in assuming that a freedman, Gibuin, put himself into voluntary servitude under the monks of St-Père in 1061; I can trace nothing in the documents to prove this (Cart. St-Père, p. lvi). Secondly, even though far more evidence were produced for the actual facts, it must be borne in mind that ecclesiastical immunities protected ecclesiastical chattels, so that a monastic serf would enjoy the same comparative protection as a monastic ox. The cases of self-bondage quoted are generally from the Dark Ages, and not

have seen, the Church landlords were essentially attached to the manorial system; and they exploited their peasants no less harshly than the laity. The fact that the medieval Church exercised an undisputed sway over men's souls affords no proof whatever that the economic condition of the peasants was satisfactory "[1]. If we discount this heavily as the verdict of a French man of science who has, perhaps, little reason to love the official Church, what shall we say to the still more unfavourable judgement of one of the greatest among French cardinals in the thirteenth century? The Dominican Hugues de St-Cher was equally distinguished in learning and in Church politics. As papal commissary, he was responsible for the most delicate negotiations with great princes, and was the first really great dignitary to support the newly-invented festival of Corpus Christi, which was struggling upwards from its merely popular origins. As scholar, he was the main author of the first Bible Concordance, and the sole author of a Bible Commentary filling seven folio volumes, which was one of the standard works of the Middle Ages. In that commentary he frequently applies Old Testament prophecies to the social, and especially the monastic, conditions of his own day; as a Religious, he was mainly interested in the doings and in the status of his brethren in Religion. Commenting on Ps. lxxvii, 57 (Vulg.): "Even like

from the comparatively orderly Middle Ages proper; moreover, as has been noted, the large majority are women. Here is a quite typical case; at Fonnbach, in Bavaria, a list of similar dedications was recorded about 1170 A.D.; they include two men and nine women, one of whom devoted her two sons with herself (*Mon. Boic.* IV, 118–19). The reasons for which the peasant sought protection in the Dark Ages come out plainly in a monastic chronicle, though the protection here sought is that of a lay lord, about 1010 A.D. The Count of Altenberg got the whole district round Muri "half-justly, half-unjustly, into his power. The rest of the countryfolk of that district, who were freemen, seeing this man's power, came even of their own accord and put their farms under his protection under conditions of legal tribute. So it was that the count subjected almost the whole place, dispossessing the lawful heirs and putting his own bondfolk to dwell in their places, with their horses and cattle and all their appurtenances, even unto his death." At his death the dispossessed peasants came to fight for their farms, but were driven off, and the district, finally, became the main endowment of the abbey of Muri. The monk quiets his conscience here by noting that God's providence dealt similarly with the first possessors of Canaan, in favour of God's chosen people (*Act. Mur.* p. 4; cf. pp. 43–4, where the story is given at greater length). It will be seen later that monastic serfs sometimes attempted escape to lay lords.

[1] *L.c.* p. 539.

their fathers, they were turned aside as a crooked bow," he writes:

Religious Orders at first were princely in their poverty, for they were subject to none but God; yet now they are enslaved by reason of their riches. They were as a glowing coal in charity; they are now icy in their torpor and *accedia*. They were a garment of mercy, clothing the naked and feeding the famished; but now they oppress the poor, and flay the naked by rapine and exactions; for the clergy and Religious use their subjects and their men worse than knights or barons do....As it is written in Deuteronomy (xxxii, 15): "The beloved grew fat and kicked; he grew fat, and thick and gross."...God hath heard the evil doings of Christians, of clergy, and of Religious. ...Now there are four kinds of sins which cry properly and specially to God against those who commit them. The first is the sin of sodomy [Genesis xviii, 20]. The second is manslaughter [Genesis iv, 10]. The third is fraud against the hireling, as St James saith (v, 4): "Behold the hire of the labourers who have reaped down your fields, which by fraud has been kept back by you, crieth, and the cry of them hath entered into the ears of the Lord of sabaoth." The fourth is the oppression of the poor, as it is written in Exodus (iii, 9): "The cry of the children of Israel is come unto me, and I have seen their affliction"[1].

Whatever allowance we may make for a medieval moralist's rhetoric, those are very serious words; and we find an equally unfavourable judgement, on the verge of the Reformation, in a mandate of Bishop Longland of Lincoln to the abbot of Oseney. He speaks of avarice as having attacked "the foundations and columns of the Church, viz. abbots and priors"; "they are intent only upon money and not upon the increase of religious life; and, outside, [their monasteries] they flay their tenants worse than the secular clergy or the laity do"—*plus quam seculares aut laici suos firmarios excoriant*[2].

This cardinal and this bishop, then, orthodox contemporary witnesses, who had monks and peasants daily under their eyes, generalize in terms which, with all allowance for rhetoric, cannot suggest a more favourable picture than that which Prof. Sée

---

[1] Vol. II, p. 206, 2–4; cf. v, 81, 1–2 and 83, 2: "rapaciores et crudeliores sunt principes ecclesiastici aliquando quam principes seculi."

[2] This has not yet been printed; I owe my knowledge of its existence to Mr H. E. Salter's *Eynsham Cartulary*, II, xx, and this transcript to the kindness of Canon C. W. Foster. The date is July 21, 1526: it is in vol. xxxvi of the Lincoln registers, fol. 129 d.

has laboriously pieced together from business documents. Under the very strictest scrutiny we shall doubtless find a certain element of exaggeration in both these churchmen's verdicts, but an element natural and easily discounted. When they assert that the monks are *worse* than the laity, they mean this in the sense in which St Bernard stigmatized the priests of his day as worse than their flocks. They would probably not have maintained, in cold blood, that the serf is, on the whole, most miserable on monastic lands, but that this monastic exploitation of labour is more glaringly unchristian than that of the lay lords; they are speaking less as social students than as moralists. And Sée, again, is summing up with epigrammatic brevity; if he had been concerned to give a detailed verdict on this special side of his subject, he would probably have admitted that the Church showed certain corporate virtues side by side with the ordinary failings of a corporation. True, the totality of the secular clergy, or of the monastic community, constantly refused those humanitarian concessions which many pious individuals among them would gladly have granted; but, on the other hand, I think we can distinctly trace a certain patriarchal side to this conservatism. The monastery, in spite of its frequent and sometimes desperate financial shifts, was generally somewhat less indebted and less rapacious than the knight or squire; the cellarer had generally a little more compassion for his labourers than the lay bailiff; that same conservatism which kept the serf longer in his monastic servitude would sometimes suffer him to jog along at the same old rent, which had now become far lighter with the falling value of money. But this was often because monks could not help themselves. Brons quotes a contemporary complaint from a member of a monastic community: We are being ruined by this commutation of services for fixed rents. And he shows how vainly the nuns of Vreden struggled, in the thirteenth and fourteenth centuries, to get back to the old state of things[1]. With Religious, as with other folk, financial questions generally came first; and we find a German professor, not long before the Reformation, remonstrating with the assembled abbots of his neighbourhood; if they could no longer give the

---

[1] Vreden, pp. 57–8. For the peasant's unearned increment through these falling money-values see F. W. Maitland in E.H.R. IX, 420 ff.

alms that society expected, let them at least not thrust their tenants down into a life of misery[1].

Apart from Pecock's, mentioned in the first footnote below, the only medieval generalization known to me that can be set against Hugues and Longland is that of Peter the Venerable. This really great man, in his answer to St Bernard, asserts that, whereas lay lords treated their serfs not only without mercy but also without justice[2],

yet monks, although they own serfs, own them differently. For they use the due and lawful services of these people only for their own livelihood, vex them with no exactions, lay no unbearable burdens upon them, and, if they see them in want, even support them from their own possessions. They treat their bondmen and bondwomen not as bondmen and bondwomen but as brothers and sisters[3].

We need not doubt that, in the immediate experience of the abbot of so great and prosperous a house as Cluny, during this golden age of monasticism, there was definite proof of superior charity on the part of the monastic landlord; the monks were certainly better in 1130 than in 1260, or *a fortiori* than in 1526. But we must bear in mind that Peter is here defending his own Cluniacs against Cistercian criticisms; and that, under those

---

[1] Cless, II, i, 445, see appendix 4. Caesarius of Heisterbach complains that "some bishops nowadays impose as heavy exactions upon the common folk their subjects, as do lay lords" (I, 73). And he explicitly charges them with protecting usurers for their own profit. Two centuries later, Meffret says: "Certainly there is no such cruel beast in the world as a bad priest or monk." Yet some men, thinking to do God service, endow monasteries from the sweat of the poor man's brow; they would do better to give their money to the real poor (*Fest.* p. 296 c). The tractate *De corrupto Ecclesiae Statu*, ascribed by Tritheim to Nicolas de Clémanges, but written in 1401 by some other Paris professor, speaks of the ordinary monks as even more grasping and avaricious than the layman (Browne, *Fascic.* II, 564). Bishop Reginald Pecock, in his controversy with the Lollards, maintains that Church landlords are easier to their tenants than laymen, and spend their money more for the common benefit (*Repressor*, R.S. pp. 370 ff.). But, though we may judge that, even in the heat of controversy, a man like Pecock would not put forward notorious falsehoods, yet he says nothing which would not be satisfied by the small percentage of superiority which I have suggested in my text. We must remember too, as Archbold points out (p. 330), that mere easy-going laxity on the landlord's part does not always connote a prosperous tenantry; rather the reverse. I have already pointed out evidence for the backwardness of monastic agriculture in the later Middle Ages (ch. IV, p. 43).

[2] See p. 110 above.   [3] P.L. vol. 189, col. 146.

circumstances, even this pious and honourable man might allow himself considerable poetic licence. I have pointed out in my *Five Centuries of Religion* how Peter, when he is writing privately to his own Order, frankly admits certain important facts which are very difficult to reconcile with his defence against the Cistercian critics on those same subjects[1]. And, however the Cluniacs may have felt and acted upon their superior virtue in 1130, they certainly felt differently in 1289, when we find a mass of serfs transferred *en bloc*, as a business transaction, to a lay lord, by the prior of the great house of Romainmotier, with the express and formal consent of his superior the abbot of Cluny[2]. Thus, in so far as we take Peter's apologetic contrast literally, we are driven to one of two alternatives. Either, between 1130 and 1289, the monks as individuals had lost their superior charity towards the serf; or else their collective sense of charity was gone, and they were willing, in their corporate capacity, to abandon these bondfolk their brethren to the abominations of which Peter accuses the lay lords. Moreover, this great Order, probably the most wealthy in Europe next to the Benedictines, was no less businesslike in its treatment of the question of servile emancipation. About 1310 A.D. Abbot Henry of Cluny compiled from his predecessors' statutes a code of laws for the whole Cluniac Order. A full folio column is devoted to embezzlement:

wherefore, the better to prevent this rash and harmful presumption and this grievous and dispendious peril, by this present statute we excommunicate all and several the abbots, priors and other administrators of our Order who alienate any of the possessions of the said Order, whether movable or immovable, whether for a term or for life. [We excommunicate] those who, holding sway over serfs or

---

[1] Vol. I, pp. 329–31.

[2] *Cart. Chalon*, p. 355. The Cistercians of Meaux, even in early days, were ready to sell bondfolk to lay lords (*Chron. Mels.* R.S. I, 361, about 1220 A.D.). The Dunstable annalist writes under 1283: "In this year we sold William Pyke, our bondman, with his brood, and we received one mark from the purchaser" (*Ann. Dunst.* R.S. p. 297). So also the monks of Kempten, in 1358, before that abbey had earned its unenviable reputation for exceptional harshness (Baumann, II, 623). The Benedictines of St-Gallen not only sold serfs but, at times of pecuniary embarrassment, pawned them to other people (Arx, II, 171–2; fourteenth century). Even as late as 1481, "an abbot grants a villein of his monastery to a person for a term of years" (Savine, *Bondmen*, p. 263).

bondmen, bondwomen or women of [servile] condition pertaining
to the monasteries of our Order, grant to such persons letters and
privileges of manumission and freedom; or who grant monastic
pensions or corrodies, to the damage of their house, whether for life
or for a time, to any persons without special licence from Us or from
Our successors.

In the next redaction of the statutes (1458 A.D.) this is put still
more emphatically:

Item, those Abbots, Priors, Deans and other administrators of the
Order, who have serfs and bondmen, must come to the supervisor
of their province, within one month of their entering into the office
conferred upon them, and, with their hand in his (as standing in
the Abbot's stead) must swear expressly that they will not manumit
such serfs, or their possessions; otherwise, *ipso facto*, they incur
the sentence of suspension from their office[1].

In other words, manumission of a serf is embezzlement of
conventual property.

It will be seen, therefore, how rash it is to quote from Peter's
words in about 1130 as if they were conclusive for monastic
practice in general, or even for the practice of Cluny, which was
for so many centuries above the average. To some extent they
may convince us of the superior charity of the monks, especially
in the most favourable times and places; but we have to go only
a very little way beyond the bare text of Peter's apology in
order to see the danger of generalizing from his claims. It
is impossible to read widely in monastic chartularies and in
the records of the royal courts without coming across continual
evidence of friction between the monk and his tenants; not infrequently, the evidence points plainly to oppression. I shall
give other cases in a later chapter; one may be recorded here.
The "poor tenants" of Winkfield, in 1394, sought the king's
justice against the abbot of Abingdon, alleging that, whereas an
inquest had proved them to be tenants of the king, the abbot
had imprisoned their three leaders and tried to compel them to
seal a confession that they were his serfs[2]. The actual words of
the royal inquisition are recorded, and show the seven to have

---

[1] *Bib. Clun.* cols. 1564 b and 1606 b. As Lorain, usually so indulgent to
his own Church, observes, these statutes expressly prohibited the enfranchisement of serfs (*Hist. de Cluny*, p. 192).

[2] Selden Soc. vol. 35 (1918), pp. 83–5.

been in the right. It is quite possible that this case, which must
have caused a good deal of scandal in the neighbourhood, lies
at the back of the famous prophecy in *Piers Plowman* (B. x,
317 ff.):

> But there shall come a king, and confess you Religious,
> And beat you, as the Bible telleth, for breaking of your Rule,...
> And then shall the abbot of Abingdon, and all his issue for ever
> Have a knock of a king, and incurable the wound.

Much evidence of this kind is scattered in every direction;
meanwhile I know of no book in which any serious and consistent
attempt is made to marshal the evidence as to monastic dealings
with the peasants. Three-quarters of readers and later writers,
probably, take their ideas on this subject from Montalembert,
who is as untrustworthy here as on every other crucial point.
Not only are his references so scanty as to mock the serious
enquirer, but they are sometimes given in a form which makes
one doubt whether Montalembert had himself seen the words
to which he appeals. Moreover, after a few pages of empty
rhetoric, he finally refers his readers to Hurter, whose "in-
comparable erudition and rare perspicacity...we could only
copy: we therefore prefer to send our readers to his book." The
reader who refers to Hurter will find little to bring real conviction on the most important points[1]. Hurter is, indeed, far
superior to Montalembert in real scholarship; but in the few
pages he consecrates to this subject he scarcely ever brings more
than a single reference to support even his most sweeping
generalizations; nor is this single reference always correct.
After all, Hurter makes no pretence of special research on this
subject; his theme is Pope Innocent III, and he would have had
great reason for surprise if, nearly forty years later, he had found
his few pages of *obiter dicta* treated as an excuse for non-
production of further evidence by a celebrated author who was
devoting six volumes to this special subject of monasticism.
Yet Montalembert's book has ranked as a classic, even among
Anglicans, for another forty years, mainly owing to the silence

---

[1] *Geschichte Papst Inn. III*, bk xxi, c. 7 (ed. 1838, iii, 427 ff.). The French
translation, which Montalembert recommends to us, is bad; it exaggerates
in the text where Hurter has carefully guarded his assertions, and it omits
large numbers of important references.

of those few who, like Lord Acton, realized the scientific weakness which underlies its rhetorical strength[1]. Hurter's *obiter dicta* are valuable as those of a scholar in whom enthusiasm for his subject had not destroyed all sense of proportion; he is, on the whole, among those who have treated this question, the ablest advocate on the monastic side[2]. But nobody who wants to get at the truth can content himself, in the face of explicit complaints from contemporaries, with the scanty and inconclusive evidence produced by a writer who has evidently never read those complaints, and who makes no profession of specialist research in this field.

[1] For Montalembert and Hurter see appendix 4.
[2] Janssen does not profess to deal with any but the latest generations of the Middle Ages. Cless's monograph is more thorough and impartial than either, and gives more detailed information as to the relations of monk and peasant; but it is restricted to Württemberg.

CHAPTER XIII

THE CHANCES OF LIBERATION

L ET us begin with the question of manumission; for this is perhaps the most significant line of enquiry; that on which the fullest evidence can be found, and which has been treated in greatest detail by advocates on both sides. There is much in the Bible, there is much in the medieval creed, to favour the enfranchisement of bondfolk; in the realm of mere theory, the question might seem simple; but how far were Biblical texts and medieval churchmen practically operative in this direction[1]? Here, again, modern writers are commonly content to echo Montalembert, or at best to quote the monograph in which Paul Allard has embroidered upon his master, or Kröss's reply to Brecht[2]. Allard's main thesis is that of the Church's liberating rôle[3]. He quotes from Montalembert a passage which, taken at its face-value, might seem to carry great weight (p. 207):

As Montalembert has justly remarked, it might be said that [Gregory the Great] signed the death-warrant of slavery in advance, in this following preamble to a deed of enfranchisement: "Seeing that the Redeemer and Creator of the world vouchsafed to take man's flesh in order by the grace of freedom to break the chain of our servitude and to restore us to our first liberty, therefore we act well and wholesomely in restoring the blessing of original liberty to men whom nature hath made free, and whom human laws have bowed under the yoke of servitude. Wherefore we declare you, Montanus and Thomas, servants of the Holy Roman Church which we also serve by God's help, free from henceforth and Roman citizens; and we leave unto you all your savings [*peculium*]."

[1] Even Guérard seems to have been dominated on this point rather by theory than by observed practice. He treats it only incidentally; but the single concrete example he quotes is the very exceptional case of St Benedict of Aniane, which I cite here below (*Irminon*, I, 304).

[2] A. Kröss, S.J., *Die Kirche u. die Sklaverei im späten M.A.* (*Zeitschrift f. Kath. Theologie*, 1895). Brecht's monograph was called *Kirche u. Sklaverei* (Barmen, 1890). For these two writers see appendix 23.

[3] *Esclaves, serfs, et mainmortables*. Though Allard published in 1884, he took no notice of the documents which Fournier had cited on the other side in the *Revue historique* for Jan. 1883. For a fuller criticism of Allard see appendix 23.

The fact that this single papal pronouncement is always quoted as a convincing argument speaks volumes for the weakness of the case[1]. To begin with, it deals with an isolated case of two serfs; yet Kröss, who, like Allard, bases his main case upon it, writes of it as though it had been a public decree to the whole Church: "Pope Gregory emphatically recommends the believers of his time to further Jesus Christ's scheme of salvation by giving to His sheep the freedom that is their due" (p. 296). Fournier (*l.c.* pp. 11–12) has shown how far we should go wrong in taking these preambles to deeds of enfranchisement as proofs of a definite and general policy[2]. Moreover, we have only to go a little beyond this isolated quotation from Gregory's own letters, to realize how little he would have cared to be taken at his word in the sense which these three modern authors attribute to him. Not only were there multitudes of unfreed serfs in the possession of ecclesiastics even a thousand years after Gregory had published this "death-warrant" to servitude, but Gregory in person possessed at least hundreds, and probably thousands, of slaves whom he did not free. Again, as pope, he was trustee for the possession of thousands more, chattels of the Roman Church; yet he initiated no general papal move-

[1] Gregory's letter is the 2nd of the 6th book in his Register.

[2] Compare the following preamble of Nov. 18, 1485 (*Cal. Pat. Rolls*, Hen. VII, 1, 41). Manumission of three nativi of king's manor of Calstok "because in the beginning nature created all men free, and afterwards the law of nations put some under the yoke of servitude, and the king believes it to be pious and meritorious towards God to make free those who are subject to him in villeinage." Riley prints a similar formula from St Albans in about 1430 (Amundesham, R.S. II, 364); but we have evidence that the St Albans monks usually, if not always, sold their manumissions. Des Méloizes prints a document of 1394 in which the lord's benevolent preamble most definitely suggests gratuitous manumission; yet we presently find that the two brothers are paying 36 crowns for their freedom. He gives a single instance of monks allowing servitude simply to lapse as a thing outworn; but this was on the verge of the French Revolution (p. 192). The archives of Troarn show us a curious parallel case. "In July 1273, Henry Marmion, esquire, in presence of the parish of Fresney-le-Puceux, declares that he abandons to the abbey, in pure and perpetual alms, for the benefit of his soul and those of his ancestors, a whole series of lands and rents. The deed is drawn up in the form of a plain and solemn donation. But a second deed, drawn up under the same conditions as the first, throws light on the true character of this 'donation'; it recites how Henry Marmion has sold, granted and remitted the aforesaid lands and rents to the abbey, and has obtained such and such things in return. It is only by chance—or rather through the nature of the price paid by the abbey for this 'donation,' that both deeds happen to be preserved for us in the archives of Troarn" (Sauvage, *Troarn*, p. 135).

ment for the liberation of Church serfs. On the contrary, ecclesiastical laws constantly opposed such a policy; wherever we find a general system of emancipation, it does not come from the Roman court but from French or German rulers of the later Middle Ages[1]. We even find Gregory, in a later letter, exerting himself for the arrest of a slave, together with his wife and child and *peculium*, and for sending them back to their master. Nor had he in this case the excuse of acting as unwilling trustee for the Roman Church; for the slave in question had escaped from Gregory's own brother, and the great pope was here striving simply for the recovery of a piece of private property in slave-flesh[2]. The churchman's general attitude did not here differ perceptibly from the layman's; for reasons which will presently become clear, we possess far more records of layfolk freeing serfs for religious motives than of ecclesiastics; and canon law, no less definitely than civil law, treated the bondman as a chattel. That was the official attitude down to the time of St Alfonso Liguori in the eighteenth century; moreover, even in the nineteenth century, when the great casuist Gury came to discuss the ethics of the nigger-trade, he could find no officially authoritative Catholic condemnation to quote[3].

Janssen, again, is no less blind than Allard to the most obvious facts. Not only does he ignore Fournier's monograph on this subject, but, even in his own specially German field, he has actually the courage to quote the *Schwabenspiegel* as evidence for the *ecclesiastical* condemnation of servitude in the Middle Ages[4]. The *Schwabenspiegel* is a book, not of ecclesiastical but of civil law; and, though its author is unknown, the particular sentiment quoted from it by Janssen is notoriously borrowed from the earlier book of civil law called *Sachsenspiegel*, which

[1] Knapp, in the course of his purely scientific study in the economical and legal position of the serf in south-west Germany, describes in detail the gradual extinction of servitude, from 1525 to about 1660. In this long list there are only five ecclesiastical emancipators, one of whom yielded "after a long struggle"; in the vast majority of cases, it was to the civil power that the serfs owed their freedom (pp. 368–70). It was the Zürich citizens who freed their bondmen "because we are all God's children, and should live as brethren"; two other lay governments alleged Christian reasons for their action; no ecclesiastical body took its stand definitely on those principles, apart from pious phrases used by individual ecclesiastics.

[2] Ep. IX, 102 (P.L. vol. 77, col. 1026 a).   [3] See appendix 23.

[4] Eng. trans. (1896), I, 311; original German, 17th ed. I, 328.

we know to have been written about 1230 by a layman, and which is often quoted to prove the high culture possible among German laity at that early date. This *Sachsenspiegel* was actually condemned by Gregory XI in 1374 for fourteen points on which it wounded papal ideas of authority[1]; and nothing but the most startling ignorance of canon law could have prompted Janssen to bring its sentiments forward as a specimen of official Church doctrine. The imperial words which he quotes to this same merciful effect are in equal conflict with the frequent utterances of canon law and of the scholastic philosophers. St Thomas Aquinas has been held up, in modern times, by Innocent VI and Leo XIII as a teacher so nearly inspired "that no man has ever fallen into error by following him, nor has any man attacked him without incurring suspicion of error." Yet Aquinas explicitly justifies slavery, as economically sound and morally defensible—apart from the Utopian conditions of Paradise, lost now for ever through Adam's fault[2]. He bases himself here mainly not on the Bible, but on Aristotle; and so do the other Schoolmen[3]. Only one well-known medieval

[1] Michael, I, p. 299.

[2] It is very misleading to say, with Prof. Savine (*Bondmen*, p. 244) that "the medieval laymen and canonists strongly disapproved of serfdom in theory." The statement is true only if we confine this word *theory* to the conditions of Paradise. So far as fallen man was concerned (that is, for the only human beings with whom canon law ever had dealt or ever would have to deal in practice) there was definite theoretical approval of serfdom. When John Smith of Nibley justifies villeinage on Aristotelian grounds, he is so far from showing himself "a real son of the Renaissance" (*l.c.*) that he here follows the example of Aquinas.

[3] Brecht, *l.c.* pp. 58–9; Aquinas, *Sum. Theol.* 1ᵃ 2ᵃᵉ, q. 94, art. 5, iii; especially his comments on Aristotle's *Politics* (*Opera*, Parma ed. XXI, 368–9, 377, 658–62, 680). He agrees with Aristotle, that the peasant has no right to full citizenship in the ideal State; that the division between a fighting caste and a working caste is natural and profitable; that agriculture is a necessary but illiberal occupation; and that "in the best State, the tillers of the soil, if they can be just as we wish, should be slaves [*servos*] robust of body, that they may well labour the earth, but deficient in understanding, lest they be inventors of wiles against their masters...poor-spirited, and not of the same tribe; for thus they will be more useful for field-work, and they will not grow insolent and plot against their lords" (*l.c.* p. 662). Cf. J. J. Baumann, *Die Staatslehre des h. T. v. Aquino* (Leipzig, 1873), pp. 155–6. Aquinas's arguments from the Bible on this whole subject, I believe, are only two. First, Adam's fall has made the majority of mankind into hereditary slaves (but why, we naturally ask, has it made a minority of Adam's descendants into hereditary profiteers?). Secondly, Christ's blood is on the head of the Jews, who are therefore born slaves to the Christian Church, which has a right to dispose of their goods as it pleases (*Sum. Theol.* 2ᵃ 2ᵃᵉ, q. 10, art. 10, c).

philosopher, I believe, takes the opposite view, and that is the heretic John Wyclif[1]. It was no ecclesiastic, again, but the author of *The Reformation of Kaiser Sigismund*, whose public pronouncement, on the verge of the Reformation, struck the full modern note:

It is an unheard-of injustice, to which all Christendom must open its eyes, that there are men who can say to their fellow-man: "Thou art my chattel." Hath Christ suffered so sore for our freedom, and to loose us from all our bonds? there is no man in Christendom so lifted above another. He hath freed all estates, whether nobles or commonalty, rich or poor, great or small; he who hath been baptized and believeth is a member of Jesus Christ.

When, a hundred years later, the German peasants rose against the landlords under the watchword "we will no more be bond; we will only be Christ's men," then, though the immediate impulse may have come greatly from Luther's spiritual revolt, they fought in essence for that idea which had long been popularly attributed to the Emperor Sigismund[2].

And in practice, no less than in theory, it was lay benevolence which had here outstripped that of the ecclesiastic. In Germany, the Church was mainly responsible for those reservations which made absolute manumission almost unknown during the Middle Ages proper; the so-called "freemen" were still retained in subjection by their ecclesiastical landlords[3]. In earlier France it was the same[4]. Allard truly emphasizes the prominent part taken by French kings and princes in softening feudal bondage[5]; some of the German princes, again, worked

---

[1] For a translation of this and other brief extracts bearing on the subject, see *Social Life in Britain*, pp. 336 ff. It is true, the *Schwabenspiegel* appeals to the Bible for support: "We have it in Scripture, that no man shall be a bondman." But, for nearly a century, (this was in 1270), lay folk had been commonly appealing to Scripture for many things which still remained far from the mind of the official Church. The fact that the author bases himself thus upon a Bible text, and not upon any text of canon law, is rather a presumption against the official ecclesiastical origin of the *Schwabenspiegel*.

[2] Vogt, *l.c.* p. 2.   [3] Lamprecht, *Wirth.* I, 1221.

[4] *Irminon*, I, 379–82.

[5] pp. 242 ff.; compare Guérard (*Irminon*, I, 363): "The Frankish kings, when a son was born, freed a large number of their serfs in sign of public rejoicing and in order to bring God's protection upon the new-born boy." Louis XVI, of his own free will, swept away all relics of serfdom on his royal domains in 1779, ten years before the dawning Revolution compelled the unwilling clergy and nobility to follow his example (S. Herbert, *Fall of Feudalism in France* (1921), p. 7). In post-Reformation Germany, lay lords

far more directly to this end than any prince of the Church ever did. For Brunswick,

in 1202 Henry I decreed that the Germans living separate from the Poles should all enjoy freedom; and in 1223 the same duke, at the suggestion of Abbot Günther, gave to the abbey of Leubus the village of Sychow, after he had removed the former inhabitants, a community of 17 persons, and at the same time freed them from their serfdom[1].

In Hanover, again, "the most far-reaching measures for raising the peasants and freeing them from the burdens that pressed upon them came from the dukes"[2]. Frederick, early in the fifteenth century, abolished heriots in parts of his dominions; and, in 1433, Duke Henry not only abolished "reliefs" altogether[3], but reduced the heriot from the best to the second best chattel, and decreed that the marriage-fine should be fixed at a certain reasonable rate, secure from the lord's arbitrary increase. "Though the oppression of peasants by landlords did not entirely cease, this land-law was of epoch-making significance for the social position of the country-folk in the principality." The dues, thus reduced and limited, were now scarcely worth insisting upon; and the lords lost all real interest in serfdom, which gradually disappeared.

Two items of primary importance may be chosen to test the claim of ecclesiastical leadership in the abolition of servitude. One is total manumission; the other, *heriot* or mortuary.

Allard lays much stress on enfranchisements *en bloc*, and quotes startling numbers from early Church history, or, more strictly speaking, from early legend (p. 130); Ste-Mélanie, he calculates, freed 4,000,000 francs' worth at a single stroke for the good of her soul. But he omits to note that, while the Church encouraged this in other people, no such wholesale

and municipal authorities seem to have busied themselves far more than ecclesiastics with wholesale manumissions (Knapp, pp. 331, 368–70); and monasteries clung long to their right of heriot (*ibid*. 349–51). While the town council of Heilbronn fixed the sum for buying freedom at $2\frac{1}{2}$ per cent. of the serf's property at the end of the eighteenth century, the Teutonic Order was demanding 10 per cent. (*ibid*. 227–8).

[1] *Leubus*, p. 93.

[2] Heinemann, II, 268; see appendix 4 for the misuse of this passage by Pastor's fragmentary quotation.

[3] The "relief" was the fine paid by any new tenant—generally by the son on succeeding to his father's holding.

manumissions are recorded on the part of any churchman, with the exception of a single vague assertion of this kind to the credit of St Benedict of Aniane. The great jurist Heineccius, long ago, summed up his researches with this pessimistic conclusion: "We see, therefore, that only layfolk freed serfs gratis and for the health of their souls; the clergy, who felt sufficiently secure of their own eternal reward, granted liberty only for hard cash"[1].

Again, Allard points out (p. 133) that the Christian imperial code was favourable to the slave. Certainly, this civil law did lay the burden of proof on the master; but unfortunately canon law, which Allard strangely forgets in this context, took the exactly opposite view; it ignored these generous precedents of civil law, and laid the burden of proof on the slave or serf[2]. Among the very numerous manumissions recorded in medieval charters, only a small proportion emanate from ecclesiastics; the monasteries possessed enormous numbers of serfs, but they freed very few[3]. Where, as at Worcester, we find them freed

---

[1] *Institutiones Juris Germanici*, III, 37, quoted by Fournier, *l.c.* p. 41. Caggese is equally emphatic as the result of his researches in Italian rural history (I, 33 ff., 135 ff.; cf. pp. 284, 288). In a deed of 1107, the lady Agnes of Montigny parts with a bondmaid "for the good of her soul." But the girl is not given to freedom; she is given as a bondmaid to the abbey; Agnes bought the monks' prayers with the gift of a serf as she might have bought them with a strip of land or a few bushels of corn (AA.SS.O.S.B. IV, i, 766).

[2] Brecht, p. 75.

[3] "The Church in spite of her constant preaching for the liberation of the lower classes, was herself by no means inclined towards their absolute manumission" (Lamprecht, *Wirthschaft*. I, 1220). In an Italian inquisition of 1195 A.D., the witnesses draw a clear distinction between the abbey tenants, who are subject to certain servile tributes, and the *liberi tenuti* of neighbouring manors (Zaccaria, pp. 185–7). Von Arx notes how long some of the most oppressive rules of serfdom lasted on abbey lands in St-Gallen (II, 176 n. a): "As late as 1282, the abbot of St-Gallen could still put his men in or out of their possessions....The same is said of Pfäfers, in the Golden Book of the abbey: 'The abbey lands [in the village of Quart] may be let by the abbot, by full right and without any contradiction, to whomever he will and at whatever price.'" Yet, long before this, the serfs on most other manors had acquired by custom continuity of tenure so long as they fulfilled their services. Mr Booth notes that on the Durham priory manors, even later than this, "the rent was in the nature of a rack-rent" (*Durham Halmote Rolls*, p. xvii). Cless balances very fairly (II, i, 420–425); he shows that the Württemberg monks dealt with their serfs primarily on strictly business principles, although they were, on the whole, rather better landlords than the laity. Pirenne (*Belgique*, I, 279) emphasizes the financial motives which underlay nearly all manumissions in Flanders. The reader who studies

almost as cheaply by the monks as by other folk[1], there is strong reason to ascribe this to the known financial embarrassment of the community at that moment. Brons, from his detailed study of the monastic accounts of Vreden, concludes: "We shall not go wrong if we find the main object of these manumissions in the frequent deficits of the monastic treasury.... The monks admit this with naïve frankness, for Reg. 323 runs (lib. cat. fol. 128): 'Because [the serfs] desired to better their condition, and their money pleaded for them.' Similarly in Reg. 219"[2]. Des Méloizes notes, from his study of the records of Berry, that the majority of manumissions were for money[3]. In fact, wherever the documents enable us to pronounce clearly on either side, monastic manumissions are almost always recorded as definite matters of business; the serf, like other monastic properties, was sold, exchanged, or embezzled[4]. It was urged against Abbot Stoke of St Albans that he must have amassed large sums of money on account of three "principal" reasons, two of which were, that "he had been all his time a very great cutter-down of woods and a superfluous and even immoderate

Knapp's footnotes will remark that, wherever the late survival of any servile custom is mentioned, the reference is nearly always to the records of some monastic estate; *e.g.* pp. 227–8, 349–50. On p. 356 he notes the long survival in Bavaria of the law which bound the peasant to the soil; and Bavaria is one of the districts in which the Church has had most uninterrupted power. In Catholic Westphalia, the theory that the serf could have no property of his own was still alive even in the eighteenth century "though certainly essentially softened in practice" (p. 349). As late as 1408, the monks of Alpirsbach "looked very unfavourably on marriages of their serfs with outsiders; but about 1752 we find them permitting such marriages for a fine of one florin" (p. 354). Compare Gladbach-Stratner, p. 24, for the long continuance of serfdom on that abbey domain. In Italy, the monks of Vallombrosa were exacting marriage-fines in 1259, long after such dues had practically disappeared from other parts of the country (Caggese, I, 122).

[1] *L. A. Worc.* p. xliv and *L. A. Wilson*, p. 251. The document given in this latter place bears out my suggestion that here, as elsewhere, we have a financial expedient of not altogether unimpeachable legality.

[2] Vreden, p. 42.   [3] p. 150.

[4] Among other illegitimate financial shifts forbidden to the nuns of Nuncoton in 1440 by Bishop Alnwick is that of "alienating or selling any bondman" (E. Power, *Nunneries*, p. 225). An interesting list of embezzlements of serfs is given in *Rentalia*, pp. 199–200: some bondmen had obtained furtive freedom through marriage with kinswomen of monks. The marginal note *falsum est* to three of these cases may mean either that the other details are found to have been misstated, or that the serfs had now been recalled to their bondage. For the monks' business precautions on this subject, see appendix 24.

manumitter of bondmen"[1]. It is evident that, at Norwich cathedral priory, the manumissions were a source of income, and officials are accused of not rendering due account of sums thus received[2]. Again, in the "acquietancia" which Abbot Wallingford of St Albans gives to a bondman "by reason of his poverty, and for charity's sake," the serf is stated to have paid £2 for his freedom, *i.e.* the price of about 25 sheep. Even if we treat this statement, in view of the introductory words, as a legal fiction, the document is still conclusive as to the usual custom of taking money for enfranchisements[3]. But I do not think we can follow Riley's suggestion and so treat it; the medieval mind would not note the contrast which Riley sees here. £2, after all, was a low price for a serf, and the man's poverty explains why no more was charged. There are few more famous passages in medieval literature than Barbour's paean in praise of liberty and in dispraise of thraldom: "Ah! freedom is a noble thing!" Yet it has been pointed out that Barbour, as archdeacon of Aberdeen, was a serf-owner and serf-dealer; he was a party in the year 1388 to letting a manor out on lease "with its hawkings, huntings and fishings, with its serfs, bondages, natives, and their issues"[4].

[1] *Reg. Whet.* I, 105, 117. The question of the truth of this accusation does not much affect the present argument; a monk stating a case before his fellow-monks would certainly not name manumission as a considerable source of income if the abbey were in the habit of manumitting gratuitously.

[2] *Vis. Norwich*, C.S. p. 265. This was in 1532. Compare *Letters and Papers of Henry VIII*, XIII, ii, 521 (1538 A.D.). The abbot of Reading "has made the chief and richest of the bondmen of [his dependent priory of] Leominster free, and taken the profit to himself." The priors of Leominster have had authority to manumit bondmen; and, if Cromwell will assist the present prior to exercise this authority, he shall have half profits. There are many bondmen belonging to the priory, and "it is a royal rich country" (cf. *ibid.* XIII, i, 108). Dr London to Cromwell: the statutes of New College prevent him from alienating land or bondmen. Compare *ibid.* XII, i, 265; ii, 214; XIII, i, 51, 465; XIX, i, 167, 175, 500; ii, 471. I owe these last references to Mr H. G. Richardson.

[3] *Reg. Whet.* II, 210. The smaller sums—3s. 4d. per head—which Riley found noted in the margin of some of these records (*ibid.* introd. p. xxxiv) can scarcely represent, as he guessed, the whole price of manumission. It is far more likely that they stand for the fee claimed by clerk or steward for his share in the transaction. Caggese, who has studied the question in Italian documents, has no doubt that the reasons for enfranchisement were mainly economic (I, 33, 135–140). He shows us monks enfranchising a whole village to relieve their own pecuniary embarrassments (p. 288).

[4] J. Robertson, *Deliciae Literariae* (1840), p. 254. For further evidence see appendix 25, *Manumissions and Money*.

Allard, therefore, while supplying practically no documentary proof here, maintains his thesis in the teeth of the actual documents. No attempt has yet been made to produce, in favour of ecclesiastics, not pious pronouncements only, but such actual sacrifices of income from manumissions of serfs as we can prove in the case of lay lords and ladies[1].

A French lord, in 1285, freed a hundred bondwomen at one single stroke for the good of his soul[2]; another followed his example a few years later[3]. De Ceuleneer gives a list of Belgian rulers who manumitted serfs in large numbers, from Jean d'Avesnes in 1190 to Margaret of Flanders in 1258. Others, as he notes, gave their serfs to the Church; but he has no ecclesiastical manumissions to quote as parallels to these (*Ann. Acad. d'Archéologie de Belgique*, Série II, tom. vii, 1871, p. 143). Prof. Michael of Innsbruck, who quotes Margaret's case (p. 40), goes on to assert that serfs were "often freed wholesale (*scharenweise*) by *ecclesiastical* and lay lords"; but his references are confined to this one concrete *non-ecclesiastical* example, which he employs in order to persuade his readers that "serfdom was essentially softened by the working of the Church." Fournier, on the other hand, gives some very instructive examples (pp. 17–18 and 27). The chartulary of Notre-Dame-de-Paris records some manumissions *en bloc*; but these were for the pecuniary consideration of 1000, 2000 or even 4000 *livres*, at a time when the purchasing power of the *livre* was more than £2 sterling in modern pre-war currency. The abbot of St-Germain-des-Prés, again, sold a whole village its "freedom" for 1400 *livres*; but, even so, he explicitly retained rights of lordship over the peasants which kept them in the position of villeins on an average English manor of later date[4]. Caggese, studying the conditions in Italy, where the peasantry outstripped most of Europe in the race for liberty,

---

[1] See, however, the case of the early bishop of Lucca (778 A.D.) which will be quoted below.

[2] Baluze-Mansi, *Miscellanea*, lib. IV, p. 383. Of these 100, 65 were named *Jeanne*; this must have been almost a generic name for bondgirls in the district, like *Puss* for a cat or *Poll* for a parrot.

[3] Raoul des Presles; see Lénient, p. 218. For farther lay and ecclesiastical manumissions see appendix 26.

[4] For incomplete manumissions see appendix 27.

has no doubt that they owed this success mainly to their own exertions:

The Catholic Church, in theory, favoured servile manumissions; but in practice (as we shall see more clearly when we come to study the numerous legal documents between peasants and churches in the tenth, eleventh and twelfth centuries) she was the most tenacious and inflexible maintainer of seignorial rights over the bondmen of the soil....Yet we may consider that religious feeling was really one of the determining causes of manumissions, because it is almost a general occurrence that every testament for a pious end is followed by a manumission. We may remember the testament of Peredeo bishop of Lucca [in 778], in which he gives liberty to all his serfs[1].

We have seen, however, that monks and cathedral chapters sometimes set whole villages free for pecuniary considerations. We may compare with these more voluntary manumissions the striking incident told by Tillemont in his *Life of St Louis* as exemplifying the justice with which his mother Blanche, devoted as she was to the Church, conducted her regency during the king's first crusade. The chapter of Notre-Dame had quarrelled with its serfs in Chatenay and some other villages; many were cast into prison and were literally in danger of death from hunger and neglect. The queen remonstrated "in all humility"; the chapter replied "that they might starve their villeins as they pleased"; and, by way of emphasis, clapped the women and children also into prison, where "several died, partly from hunger, partly from the heat and overcrowding of the dungeon." The queen raised the feudal and citizen forces of Paris, struck the first blow upon the prison gates with her own staff, and caused them to be broken open. She sequestrated the chapter revenues until the canons had made satisfaction, and had consented to free these peasants in consideration of a yearly tribute in money; "for" (adds Tillemont) "these peasants, and the whole people in general, except those who had municipal rights, were then almost slaves. M. le Maistre remarks that it was St Louis's benevolence which prompted the lords to free them; there are in fact a large number of manumissions given in his reign: but there are also some of earlier date"[2]. The cruelty here is exceptional; but the economic side of the

---

[1] Vol. I, p. 34.   [2] Ed. Société de l'Histoire de France, 1848, III, 450 ff.

incident is normal. It would, I believe, be quite impossible to produce any instance of the gratuitous emancipation of even half a dozen serfs by any ecclesiastical corporation, except in very early times; for indeed the thing was strictly forbidden in canon law. Nobody denies that serfdom lingered longest on ecclesiastical, and especially on monastic, estates. In 1789, the French Church still possessed very large numbers of bondmen; 300,000 seems a moderate computation[1]. The greatest holder was perhaps the abbey of St-Claude in the Jura, recently converted into a college of canons, which possessed 20,000[2]. The abbey of Luxeuil and the priory of Fontaine had together more than 11,000[3]. It is true that many of the medieval disabilities had been removed or softened; it was no longer possible to keep men in the France of Voltaire and Rousseau exactly as they had been kept in the eleventh century. But it is quite false to maintain, as dom Benoît struggles pathetically to prove, that the serf's condition was not to be pitied. Whatever exaggerations may have marked the revolt of the six parishes against the chapter of St-Claude in 1770 and 1789, the fact remains that the bishop himself publicly sided with these men in the main, saying in a public speech:

The lands of my diocese which are not yet divided with my chapter are afflicted by this plague—*affligées de ce fléau*. I have often regretted my inability to suppress it; but I join my prayers with those of my vassals to your Majesty that you may deign to grant them gratuitous enfranchisement of their persons and their property, trusting in the justice and the goodness of the best of kings that he will vouchsafe to indemnify my see and my chapter by incorporating a few church benefices with our incomes[4].

The clergy of Amont, in their *cahier* of 1789, proclaimed this bondage as the main cause of misery in Franche-Comté. The

[1] S. Herbert, *Fall of Feudalism in France* (1921), p. 6.

[2] Chassin, pp. 30 and 39-40; the latter passage has been noted by Lord Acton's watchful pencil. Benoît (II, 776) admits that, a good many having been enfranchised at different times by the bishop or the chapter for financial considerations, these two parties "several times went so far as to reproach each other with having granted this personal freedom to serfs"—*i.e.* with having embezzled Church property.

[3] Herbert, *l.c.* p. 7: see also p. 9 for the clear terms on which freedom was sold to these men.

[4] Benoît, II, 833 (§ 2984); his attempts to prove that the serf was merely deluded into desiring freedom will be found on pp. 773 ff.

clergy of Melun pleaded for the suppression of this "barbarous" custom, by which "these unhappy folk are exposed to be shared like cattle" among different masters when father and mother were bondfolk of different manors; and at the same time we find Arthur Young expressing similar compassion[1]. But the strongest testimony is that of the abbot-commendatory of Luxeuil, J. L. A. de Clermont-Tonnerre, in his plea to the king for the abolition of *mainmorte* on the abbey estates (1775 A.D.). He wrote:

During the last 30 years that I have held this abbey, I have seen nothing but heavy, indolent, discouraged and downcast men, fields untilled, cultivation absolutely neglected, no trade or emulation, but general apathy. On the other hand, the inhabitants of the free villages, the neighbours of these men, are lively, active and laborious; their lands are well tilled and yield abundant crops.... There is only one cause for this contrast between inhabitants of the same country. The former, reduced to a sort of slavery and a mere precarious enjoyment or usufruct of their lands, limit their labour to their present needs...while the others, who are real owners with free disposal of their fortunes, working not only for themselves but for their families, limit that work only by the needs of bodily rest. The system of *mainmorte*, therefore, is destructive of agriculture, of handiwork, and of commerce; it is revolting to humanity, it may almost be said to annihilate human existence[2].

If this wealthy prelate had been willing to act up to his strong words, he might perhaps have secured the wholesale enfranchisement of these bondfolk. As it was, the monks opposed him; nothing was done until after Louis XVI's decree of 1779; and, even then, the serfs paid a great sum for their liberty. The great enfranchiser was neither Church nor State, but the serf himself, by purchase, by encroachment, or by rebellion[3].

[1] Champion, p. 218. Here, it will be noticed, some of the clergy protested; yet "it was the higher clergy of Bigorre who ruled out of their *cahier* the following article [which had been proposed by the lower clergy]: 'That a national law be passed forbidding all Frenchmen, under pain of infamy, to traffic in negroes, whether directly or indirectly'" (Chassin, p. 215).

[2] Baumont, p. 76.

[3] Guérard, in his preface to *Irminon*, points out the enfranchising effect of the frequent French prescription that the child's serfdom or freedom followed the mother's status, and not the father's. He shows statistically how far more frequent were the marriages of freewomen to serfs than *vice versa*; and Verriest, following this indication, gives three extraordinarily illuminating pedigrees, two actual and one speculative, showing how rapidly serfdom would disappear in districts where status followed the mother's condition (pp. 77–80).

Verriest, in his very exhaustive study of the movement in the single province of Hainaut, emphasizes the danger of taking at their face-value the charitable motives sometimes alleged in the preambles to deeds of manumission. Medieval landlords, he points out, were no more untrustworthy than other men, but they seldom gave anything away, except under the pressure of circumstances[1]. Two of the strongest operative causes may be summed up in two words: *pioneer* and *commune*. The forests were very commonly cleared, and the marshes drained, by settlers invited for that purpose; these men could not be tempted except by far more liberal conditions than the ordinary peasant's. These more independent men naturally were among the first to exercise mass-pressure upon the landlord; and he found his line of least resistance in selling them communal rights which they were capable in any case of fighting for. Whole villages thus became free in a sense denied to their neighbours; the example was contagious; and others, whether in common or individually, struggled for the same rights, were willing to make similar pecuniary sacrifices, and finally gained complete or partial freedom. When once the serf had got a certain way on the road to liberty, it was very difficult to prevent the most adventurous from running away and trying their fortune elsewhere[2]. In France, it was the growing prosperity, and therefore indocility, of the peasants which gave them a corporate village feeling and a moral (though not legal) power of corporate resistance, and which therefore induced the lords to sell them wholesale charters of freedom. In England, the same causes operated more slowly, until the pestilences of the fourteenth century and the Hundred Years' War shook society to its foundations. Then:

the chief means used by the villeins to compel the lords to accept their terms seems to have been desertion.... Thus at Cranfield in 1410 the jury stated in the manorial court that at that time thirteen villeins were living off the manor. Few years passed that one or more did not run away, and in 1420 eight escaped together one night and went to Gloucester. At Shillington in 1410 twenty-one villeins had gone off; at Therfield eighteen,.... At Houghton twenty-nine were gone, at Barton twenty, including two boys that had been sent

---

[1] *L.c.* pp. 19, 75. [2] *Ibid.* pp. 33, 36, 41–4, 71 ff., 160–6.

to school without permission. It was very soon after this date that a general lightening of the predial services took place on these manors[1].

Verriest's study is not only very exhaustive, but his conclusions seem so justly balanced that they may be quoted as the best brief conspectus of this whole subject. All the cases of multiple enfranchisement which he has found are by lay lords (pp. 139–141) and, normally at least, for money (p. 65). He gives an interesting list of prices paid for freedom (pp. 153 ff.). Finally he sums up (p. 157; italics his):

It would be a mistake to attribute to the medieval lord *feelings of humanity and justice* [in these transactions], and to believe that in manumitting his bondmen he acted on principles of natural law favourable to the equality of man and man. Though the lords are perfectly well aware of the weight of bondage, though they know that liberty is a "*res favorabilis*," to which bondfolk unceasingly aspire, these considerations are powerless to *determine* a single manumission. The conception of the injustice of serfdom belonged then only to cultured minds; it did not find its way into the manor-house. Yet I do not mean that all feeling of generosity or gratitude was foreign to the landlords of the Middle Ages; I think, on the contrary, that liberty was often a reward for services rendered—far oftener than the documents actually declare. *Feelings of piety* were accentuated to the highest degree among all men in the Middle Ages, and the Church exercised an irresistible ascendency. Yet it is impossible to admit that the influence of religious ideas, by themselves, brought the lords to grant enfranchisement.

Apart from a certain conventional exaggeration of the universality of religious feeling in the Middle Ages, this summary seems balanced and just. He recognizes the large part played by immediate financial reasons, but warns against exaggeration; the main factor was that lords were faced with the alternatives of selling freedom, or seeing their manors gradually depopulated (pp. 160–6). The last serf of Hainaut bought his freedom for £16 from Philip II in 1567.

[1] Page, p. 75. Cf. pp. 12, 40 ff., 68. Vinogradoff points out that, at an earlier date, the emancipating causes were circumstantial rather than humanitarian (*Villainage*, pp. 84–5, cf. 152). In France, one great cause of growing freedom was the greater liberty of transference to an easier landlord. A deed of 1242 shows that the tenants of the monastery of St-Etienne at Dijon were transferring themselves in considerable numbers to the neighbouring village of Talant, where they were under the lordship of the duke (Fyot, p. 129 and *preuves*, p. 128).

CHAPTER XIV

LEGAL BARRIERS TO ENFRANCHISEMENT

OTHER modern writers, without denying that the serf's disabilities put him at a very serious disadvantage in comparison with the modern peasant, have tried to attenuate the part played by the Church, and especially by monasticism, in perpetuating these conditions. Great pains have been taken to divert attention from the natural—it might almost be said, the necessary—legislation which supported these ecclesiastical corporations in their tenacious adherence to prescriptive rights[1]. St Benedict of Aniane (*d.* 821) is indeed recorded to have made a practice of liberating the slaves bound to the land which was given to his monks; but, from at least 1150 onwards, the contrary principle was binding upon the whole Church; no ecclesiastic had a legal right to free a serf bound to his church, any more than he had a legal right to alienate any other part of his endowment, except at his or its full market value[2].

Even before Christianity had become the State Religion, it had been compelled to accept the social system of the day; and endowments came to it in the form not only of land, houses, and money, but also of slaves who went with the land. Therefore, from very early times, Church bondmen were extremely numerous. We have seen this in the case of Gregory the Great; later, when parishes were formed, bondmen were part of the parochial endowment. In the ninth century, the theory was that each church should be endowed, for the proper maintenance of priest and service, with about 45 acres of land

---

[1] This conservatism is traced very well, down to quite modern times, in the monograph on the Westphalian abbey of Gladbach by a Roman Catholic scholar, J. Stratner; see my List of Authorities, s.v. *Gladbach*.

[2] We must, however, reckon among the *indirect* effects of ecclesiastical influence the freeing of a certain very small proportion of serfs by entrance into Holy Orders. The Church, as her own dignity demanded, insisted that the priest, whatever his origin, should count as a free man; hence a distinct stimulus to the father to buy his son's freedom in boyhood, when it could be done cheaply, in order that he might proceed to the priesthood. This movement was so strong in the Dark Ages that Charles the Great, in one of his capitularies, strove to counteract this flooding of the priesthood with sons of bondmen. But, even if every medieval priest had once been a serf, this could have freed only a very small fraction of the whole servile population.

and not less than two serfs—the higher ideal was, that the serfs should be four[1]. In some cases, again, during the Dark Ages, we have seen how tenants gave themselves voluntarily to an abbey as serfs; in those times of general insecurity and horror, the church was the safest refuge; and the evidence seems to give a slight superiority to the churchman as landlord. These relations necessarily called for fairly frequent ecclesiastical, as well as civil, legislation; and the current of this legislation runs steadily in the direction not of least moral, but of least economic, resistance. We find that, shortly before the Peasants' Revolt, Bishop Hotham of Ely would willingly have freed an old serf on account of his faithful services, but was hindered by the fact that such freedom was not his to give. This was quite natural; the oath that restrained this charitable impulse was in consonance with the Church law of many centuries[2].

As early as the sixth century, we find Church councils exerting themselves to restrict the alienation of Church bondmen, whether by manumission or otherwise. Allard is seriously embarrassed by these decrees, and is driven to strange shifts of interpretation[3]. Moreover, when he has exhausted every other plea, and is at last brought face to face with the most explicit and authoritative of all these prohibitions, then he gives up the hopeless attempt, and simply ignores this inconvenient document altogether. For the *Decretum* of Gratian, which lies at the foundation of official canon law, incorporates one most uncompromising decision of St Isidore of Seville: "It shall not be lawful for any abbot or monk to free a slave; for he who hath no property of his own cannot give liberty to another's chattel—

---

[1] *Irminon*, II, 597.

[2] Reg. Arundell. fol. 3: "Pope Gregory to Bp of Ely. Walter, son of Nicholas Godard of Teryngton, a laic of the diocese of Norwich, has petitioned us that, although by English law a man born of a nativus of the Bishop and Church of Ely, he would have been manumitted by the late Bp Hothum on account of the faithful services of the said Nicholas and Walter to the Bp and the Church, had not the Bp felt himself deterred by his oath against alienation of property of the See. We therefore grant you licence to manumit the said Walter [his father had died just before this petition] said oath notwithstanding, *after just and fitting compensation from him to you and the Church of Ely*. 10 September 1374." A few similar indults may be found in the *Calendar of Papal Letters*, IV, 398 (bp. of Ely, 1391); VI, 23 (abp. of York, 1405) and 377 (bp. of Lincoln, 1413); VII, 79 (bp. of London, 1418, six serfs); IX, 79 (three by bp. of Hereford; the financial element comes out strongly here); and 525 (bp. of Norwich, 1445).   [3] See appendix 23.

libertatem rei alienae dare non potest. For, as even civil law
hath decreed, no chattel can be alienated but by its owner."
Therefore, from Gratian onwards (about 1140), such was now
the theory of the Roman Church, as it had been her practice
for many generations at least[1]. The Greek Theodore of Tarsus,
who became archbishop of Canterbury in 668, had noted a
contrast which would have moved Paul of Tarsus to far plainer
speech: "Greek monks keep no serfs, but Roman monks possess
them"[2]. It is not surprising, therefore, that the Jesuit Professor
Michael makes no attempt to produce concrete cases in proof
of these "wholesale emancipations" which he vaguely boasts.
Cardinal Gasquet, who does profess to supply documentary
evidence, is still more unfortunate; he has merely copied,
without acknowledgement, a blunder of the painstaking and
usually accurate Cutts, who found numerous dispensations to
illegitimate clerics in the episcopal registers, and mistook them
for manumissions of serfs[3].

Not only did canon law do much to hinder manumission,
but it actually made slaves of those whom civil law would have
left free. That same Council of Toledo, whose statutes as to
manumission Allard found it so hard to explain away, passed
another still more significant decree[4]:

Seeing that the Fathers have hitherto promulgated many decisions
concerning the incontinence of the clerical order, and it hath yet
been impossible to bring about the correction of their morals, the
guilt which they have perpetrated hath so far enlarged the sentence
of their judges that vengeance should now strike not only the authors
of these iniquities, but also the progeny of those who are condemned.
Wherefore from this time forward, whosoever from among these

---

[1] For the authority of Gratian in canon law see appendix 28.

[2] P.L. vol. 99, col. 931. Miss Rose Graham points to a legatine injunction
in a MS. visitation of the Gilbertine monasteries in 1268 "prohibiting the
manumission of servile lands and serfs by priors without consent of the Master
of the Order and of the convents" (*Trans. R. Hist. Soc.* 1904, p. 147).

[3] Gasquet, *Parish Life*, p. 73, copied almost verbally from E. L. Cutts,
Parish Priests and their People (1898), pp. 130, 278. *Defectus natalium* (the
phrase used in these episcopal registers) is the common term in canon law
for illegitimacy; but, quite apart from this technical blunder, it ought to be
obvious that a bishop could not grant a "dispensation" from serfdom. He
could, on rare occasions, *manumit* his own serf; but that is quite another
process and, as we have seen, is entered quite differently in the registers.

[4] § 10 (Labbe, VI, 455). This very important decree apparently escaped
Dr H. C. Lea's notice when he was collecting evidence on this subject.

dignitaries, from the bishop down to the subdeacon, shall have begotten children, by a detestable marriage [*connubio*] with either a bondwoman or a freewoman, those who are proved to be the parents shall be condemned to the canonical penalty; and the children of this polluted union shall not only be incapable of inheriting from their parents but shall also remain, by an eternal law, as bondfolk [*in servitutem*] of that church of whose priest or minister they are the ignominious offspring[1].

Five centuries later (1051), a Council of Rome enacted that, throughout Christendom, the wives of priests should be seized as slaves and given to serve that Church which by their marriage they had outraged. In 1089, Urban II repeated this decree, with the only variation that the victims' servitude was offered "as a bribe to the nobles who should aid thus in purifying the Church"[2]. The first Synod of Santa Fé, in 1556, published a similar decree[2]. It was probably the first of these four enactments, and not (as Lea suggests) the second, which inspired Dr Martin, one of the clerical judges who condemned Cranmer, to remind him that "his children were bondmen to the see of Canterbury"[3]. It would probably be difficult to find specific instances of the strict enforcement of these laws even in the Middle Ages; it was evidently neglected, if not generally forgotten, before 1300[4]; but Dr Martin's words show how far we shall err in ignoring them altogether.

More serious were the not infrequent papal decrees of slavery against papal enemies. Boniface VIII, in his feud against the Colonna family, held this punishment over them (1303). Clement V condemned to slavery the whole population of Venice (1309); Gregory XI, a couple of generations later, the Florentines; a generation later again, Sixtus IV and Julius II decreed the same against Florence, Bologna and Venice; and Paul III, when Henry VIII repudiated him, condemned all Englishmen to servitude who took the king's part[5].

And not only in law, but in practice, ecclesiastical policy was

---

[1] Labbe, vol. VI, col. 455, c. 10.   [2] Lea, *Celibacy*, I, 222, 289; II, 246.
[3] Strype, *Memorials of Cranmer*, bk III, ch. 27.
[4] Bishop Guillaume Durand reminded the Ecumenical Council of Vienne in 1311 that, if the Church would make a serious fight for the extinction of clerical concubinage, she had this weapon in her hands; he therefore pressed for its revival (Durand, pars III, tit. 7, p. 250; tit. 29, p. 286).
[5] Brecht, pp. 155–6, where other examples will be found.

often reactionary in this matter of servitude. The chronicler of Muri, in 1142, describes how his abbey had gradually turned a free community into one of bondfolk. He writes: "This township at first consisted almost entirely of freemen, of whose progeny a few survive even now; but, when the monks first came hither, [a little more than a century ago], they collected and got in whatever ways they could, as may be seen today"[1]. On this Hurter comments very truly: "we must at least note that the advantages accruing from the acquisition of bondfolk rendered [the monks] somewhat negligent of the means whereby they acquired them" (p. 541). The Muri monk here describes exactly what Mr Hudson has proved, by the painful piecing together of scattered evidence, in the case of Norwich priory and Martham. Maitland shows how unfavourably the Norman Conquest operated in this direction; how much was done by the new lords to bring freemen, or comparatively free men, into the meshes of serfdom; and there is no reason to suppose that ecclesiastical lords were far behind the laity in this movement, or that this Norwich case, for which we happen to have irrefragable evidence, was at all exceptional. I have Professor F. M. Stenton's authority for suggesting that the marked freedom of tenants in those districts which the Danes had occupied, as contrasted with the far larger proportion of bondmen elsewhere, was very closely connected with the clean sweep which those Danes had made of the monasteries. They thus broke down a very conservative tradition; the multitudes of Church bondmen were swept away; and land tenure started again with a clean slate[2].

Yet the necessary insistence on these points must not make us forget that moral inconsistency was no monopoly of the medieval clergy. Montesquieu had only too much truth on his side when he pointed out that the governments themselves have here been guided mainly by self-interest[3]. Where economic temptations point wholly in one direction, mankind seldom rises superior

---

[1] *Act. Mur.* p. 41. Hurter, by a misprint, refers to p. 61.

[2] *Domesday Book and Beyond*, 1897, pp. 139, 339 ff. Compare appendix 30 of this book for the comparative infrequency of serfdom in Normandy and Brittany, which is suggestive of the same cause, the invasions of Northmen.

[3] "Il y a longtemps que les princes chrétiens affranchirent tous les esclaves de leurs Etats, parce que, disoient-ils, le Christianisme rend tous les hommes égaux. Il est vrai que cet acte de religion leur étoit très-utile; ils abaissoient

to these lower motives; it is amid the conflict of selfish interests
that an ideal has the best chance of swaying our final decision.
Christianity, while it discouraged the master's content in ownership, discouraged also the slave's discontent in servitude. Those
earliest generations of Christians looked upon all worldly social
order as too transitory to deserve their more serious consideration. "The Lord is at hand"; meanwhile our duty is not to
reconstruct the general framework of society, but rather to
prepare personally and individually for the new heaven and the
new earth which will come upon us like a lightning-flash. There
was much in Christianity that was destined gradually to sap the
foundations of the slave-system; but we need scarcely wonder
that this humanizing influence was slow, fitful, and unofficial.
The official Church soon found herself a slave-owner on a very
large scale; and it is no wonder if she accepted this together
with the general framework of ancient and medieval society.
Where she was strongest, servitude sometimes flourished most[1].
The Spaniards reduced to serfdom their hardworking Muslim
and Jewish peasants. The beginnings of the modern slave-trade
date from the later Middle Ages, when it flourished chiefly in
Italy and the Mediterranean countries: "In Majorca there were
as many as 20,000 [actual slaves], and the Italian statutes show
how, in Sicily and Tuscany and Venetia and Istria, slave-
labour more than once supplied the shortage of free workmen"[1].
Nicholas IV, in his bulls of 1452 and 1454, granted the king of
Portugal the right of slavery over all heathens whom he captured;
these bulls were confirmed by two later popes. Alexander VI,
in 1493, gave the South Americans over to the Spaniards in
terms which their theologians interpreted as including slavery;
the results are well-known[2].

The legend of the monk and the churchman as pioneers of
peasant freedom will not bear serious examination. St-Aiglan,
writing in 1843, sometimes says a great deal more in favour of
the monks as civilizers than would be maintained at the present

par là les seigneurs, de la puissance desquels ils retiroient le bas peuple. Ils
ont ensuite fait des conquêtes dans les pays où ils ont vu qu'il leur étoit
avantageux d'avoir des esclaves: ils ont permis d'en acheter et d'en vendre,
oubliant ce principe de religion qui les touchoit tant. Que veux-tu que je te
dise? Vérité dans un temps, erreur dans un autre" (*Lettres Persanes*, No. 75).

[1] Boissonnade, pp. 405–6.   [2] Brecht, pp. 157 ff.

day by any first-rate historical scholar of his own communion; yet, on this point, after facing the actual evidence of monastic chartularies and canon law, he concludes (p. 63):

Que deviennent, en présence de ces textes accablants, commentés pendant des siècles par l'avidité et la mollesse, appliqués sans pitié, les déclamations de ces écrivains qui pour défendre les abus compromettant, s'il était possible, la sainte cause de la religion, attribuent aux monastères l'extinction de la servitude? Dès l'origine, ils eurent des serfs; les derniers, ils en possédèrent en France. L'émancipation se fit autour d'eux et sans eux par l'action de l'évangile, des idées germaniques, de la chevalerie surtout, et par le besoin que le maître eut de son serf. Mais ils y furent étrangers, et jusqu'au temps où la comtesse Marguerite commence ses affranchissements, et où les croisades les multiplient, les chroniques, les actes des saints, les légendes miraculeuses, ne nous parlent des serfs ecclésiastiques que pour attester avec une joie lugubre leur nombre toujours croissant. A chacun donc que sa part soit faite: aux moines, la gloire de la conversion et de la civilisation belges, l'honneur de l'émancipation à ceux qui l'ont donnée aux masses.

The general evidence, then, is not favourable to those who would credit the official Church with the abolition first of slavery and then of this half-slavery called serfdom. The organized Church, like so many other organizations of idealists after their first generations of missionary fervour, was often concerned to make the best of both worlds; and nobody who faces the historical facts need wonder that servitude lived so long. But, if the Church never dared to declare plainly and officially against the system as a whole, did she not at least condemn on principle, and repudiate in practice, its worst injustices of detail? The answer here must again be unfavourable. Not only did monasteries share a serf's brood, half and half, like other lords, but economic temptations led them to lay full stress on the no less odious heriot and mortuary. We have seen how one of the most universal burdens of the serf was that, at his death (and sometimes even at a wife's death) the lord could claim his best beast, or best movable possession, in the name of *heriot*; and, in addition to this, the rector of the parish had generally his *mortuary* of the second-best beast or chattel[1]. There was scarcely any other medieval custom equally repugnant to modern

---

[1] I dealt briefly with this some years ago in the 8th of *Medieval Studies*, "Priests and People in Medieval England."

humanitarian ideas. The death of the breadwinner is, in itself, one of the heaviest strokes of fortune; yet this was aggravated by a death-duty which, unlike those of our own day, was so calculated as to press mainly upon the poor. Here and there we may find the principle reprobated by individual moralists of the Middle Ages; yet even this is not common; it would probably be easier to find ten medieval complaints against the upstart pretentions of the wage-earners than to match the indignant complaints of cardinal Jacques de Vitry, that the lords who thus preyed on their dead tenants were like vultures that prey upon death—or more loathsome still, worms feeding upon the corpse[1]. Here and there, again, we do sometimes find a monk actually refusing to exact the mortuary in some particular case; but such records, rare in themselves, are qualified by their presentation as specially characteristic of saints or other exceptional men. Such, for instance, is the charming story which Giraldus Cambrensis tells of St Hugh of Lincoln[2]. He writes:

Hugh had such bowels of pity, and was so utterly uncovetous of earthly things, that when his servants had carried off the ox of a certain dead peasant of his lordship, (as the dead man's best possession which the custom of the land gave to the lord), and the widow had come forthwith to the bishop, beseeching with tears that he should order the restoration of that ox, which alone was left to her for the sustentation of the miserable and orphaned family, then he granted her request. Hereupon the steward of this manor said unto him: "My lord, if you remit this and other similar lawful perquisites, you will never be able to keep your land." But Hugh, hearing this, leapt straight down from his horse to the ground, which in that spot was deep in mire; and, grasping both hands full of earth, he said: "Now I hold my land, and none the less do I remit to this poor woman her ox." Then, casting away the mire and looking upwards, he added: "For I seek not to cling to earth beneath but to heaven above. This woman had but two workfellows; death hath robbed her of the better, and shall we rob her of the other? God forbid that we should be so covetous! for she doth more deserve our consolation in this moment of supreme affliction, than that we should vex her farther."

[1] Lecoy de la Marche, *Chaire française*, p. 388. But when Lecoy, after quoting these two passages from Jacques de Vitry, continues "l'Église condamne toujours avec énergie ce droit de main-morte," he seems to be writing at random. Canon law expressly secured to the Church the right of preying in her turn upon the corpse, and taking the second best beast.

[2] *Opera*, R.S. VII, 96.

Giraldus goes on to relate how he once showed equal mercy in remitting the feudal "relief" due from a knight's son. Again, it was one of the special notes of sanctity in Ulrich, prior of Steinfeld, that he refused to take a foal from a widow under similar conditions[1]; and Abbot Samson of St Edmundsbury showed his magnanimity by refusing a mortuary from a suspected usurer[2].

But all these were exceptional men; and it is as exceptions that the chroniclers have handed them down to us. The ordinary monk was so far from forgoing his heriot, that he often took not one, but two; one as lord of the manor, and another as rector, in those parishes which had been appropriated to his monastery.

And, even where the parish church was not appropriated, and the abbot inherited only as lord of the manor, the customal shows him to have made claims at least as sweeping as the most burdensome that can be found on lay manors. Here are the rights of the abbot of St-Ouen-de-Rouen in 1291:

My lord abbot of St-Ouen takes to his own share all the movable goods of each of his tenants in the parish of Quincampoist when they die, and all that may come or belong to the said dead man by law, except that he shall leave all these utensils here following, which remain quit to the heir without diminution: to wit, the bastard cart and the plough and the [barrow] and [sheaf-cart] and the [cider-crusher] and the mortar and pestle, and the winnowing-fan and the bushel-measure and the kneading-trough, and one sack for grinding his corn, and a sieve for his meal and a basket, and the worst chest in the house for his bedstead, and a spade and an axe, a fork for pitching sheaves and a dung-fork, a gridiron and a trivet, and one bed, if there be more than one, and a brass pot, if the aforesaid utensils are in his house; and all other movables go to my lord abbot[3].

---

[1] *Caes. Heist.* I, 231. I give the full story in appendix 12.

[2] Jocelin of Brakelond (Clarke), p. 119: C.S. p. 67. But the autocratic fashion in which the abbot dealt with the man's property speaks volumes for what could be done in other cases: here, the autocracy was quite disinterested, but Samson's successor could almost as easily have stretched the law in his own interest.

[3] Delisle, p. 194, n. 88. The three articles bracketed are translated more or less doubtfully, as I could not trace them in Godefroy's dictionary. Only the richest peasants, of course, would have all the articles here specified; but the list is drawn up to enable the lord to take all that is not directly needed for farm and house.

Even more grasping were the monks of Vale Royal in 1326[1]—Cistercian monks, to whom, two centuries earlier, the possession of serfs had been forbidden as a thing uncharitable and smacking of worldly covetousness[2]. I have not met with any lay manor in England or France on which the death-dues even approach these in severity. It is rash to generalize at this present stage of research; but my impression is that monastic conservatism, and the comparatively strong financial position of the monasteries, enabled them to maintain the earlier and harsher burdens from which the peasant had long bought himself free on other estates[3]. Not only do monastic accounts, which survive in great numbers, show us that the Religious exacted these death-duties as a matter of regular business-routine[4], but wholesale abolitions of the heriot, exceptional as they are in any case, occur, so far as I know, only on lay domains. The great abbey of Maria Laach actually revived the heriot system in 1449, after it had long lapsed through disuse[5]. Even of St Hugh, it is not recorded that he formally washed his hands of the whole bad system. On the other hand, in pre-conquest times, an estate was given to the abbot of Ramsey by Godric, the abbot's brother, "on condition that Aednoth, my brother, abbot of the said monastery, do quit that estate of the service called *heriot* in the English tongue, and *relevatio hereditatis* in the

[1] Printed in appendix 22.
[2] See *Five Centuries of Religion*, vol. I, ch. XXVII.
[3] Cf. Noake, *Monast. and Cath. of Worcester* (1866), p. 90: "A great riot took place at Shipston in the sixth year of Hen. VI with reference to heriots, and the question was ultimately referred to the abbot of Winchcomb, who determined that the prior and convent [of Worcester] had from early times received at the death of every tenant the best animal, while the parson of Tredington received the second best." The Templars and Hospitallers in Normandy generally took one-third of the dead man's movable property (Delisle, p. 100). On the other hand, the heriot on estates of the abbey of Battle was exceptionally light (Page, p. 27).
[4] For instances of this from Germany see appendix 12; the abbot of Limburg, in 1035, was taking two-thirds of the chattels of all dead husbands who had married a wife off the manor (*Coesfeld*, p. 57); for England, a good instance may be found in the accounts of a St Albans manor printed in Dr W. Cunningham's *Growth of English Industry and Commerce*, I (1910), 612. In the autumn of 1349, during that plague which all churchmen proclaimed as God's call to repentance and unworldliness, the monks took thirteen heriots from one small hamlet—six horned cattle, six sheep and a chest. In one of these cases, the further fine for transfer of tenancy was remitted "propter paupertatem," but not the heriot.
[5] Laach, p. 70.

Latin, which is wont to be paid unto the lord by free heirs after the death of their fathers"[1]. Here, it will be noted, the actual liberator is the layman. Again, the recently published terrier of Fleet, in Lincolnshire, has a still more explicit record of lay generosity: it dates from the early thirteenth century, and is worth quoting in full[2]:

To all sons of Holy Mother Church Richard de Flete wisheth health in Christ. The business of our present life, lest it be consumed by oblivion, is wont to be eternized by the testimony of the written word[3]. Wherefore let all present and posterity know that I, Richard de Flete, striving to gain pardon for my sins by liberal almsgiving, have released unto all the widows of Fleet, present and to come, that fine which in English is called *heriotht*, which is wont to be rendered to me by the aforesaid widows after the death of their husbands; at the prayers and counsel of my wife Juliana, for our own souls and that of our kinsfolk, I make this release in pure and perpetual alms.... Moreover I, Richard de Flete, for the better confirmation of this business, have corroborated this present page with my mark and seal. Wherefore, to all who may resist this confirmation, the following penalty is decreed by the priest in his ecclesiastical authority, that whosoever infringe this aforesaid pact of release or confirmation be smitten with an everlasting curse, and be damned to eternal death and torture, with Judas who betrayed our Lord and the devil and all his ministers. Amen.

Doubtless there were a few similar cases elsewhere in England, though no other student whom I have been able to consult has helped me here[4]. But what could be done by one lord here and there, in the face of the general acceptance of the heriot system by Church and by State? Yet we can see what might conceivably have been done throughout Christendom, when we consider that which was actually achieved in Brunswick by two successive dukes, with the result that these fortunate territories were untouched, in the dark days, by that terrible Peasants' Revolt of 1525[5].

---

[1] *Chron. Ab. Ramesciensis* (R.S. 1886, p. 111).

[2] *A Terrier of Fleet*, ed. M. Neilson, 1920, p. 18.

[3] I shall have occasion later on to call attention to this frequent formula.

[4] Lamborelle (p. 95) quotes two Flemish lords who remitted all heriots in 1230 and 1235. Delisle cites a lay lord who gave up his tallages, and a lady her *pressoir banal* for cider, apparently out of charity to the tenants (pp. 95, 469).

[5] Heinemann, II, 265 ff.; see pp. 156 here above, and appendix 4. Pirenne (*Hist. de Belgique*, I, 281–2) points out that it was not the clergy who abolished the mortuary system in Flanders.

Post-reformation society bears a heavy load of guilt for its treatment of the peasant; but the worst waste of better opportunities was in the Middle Ages, when the Church had real disciplinary power, and when a self-denying ordinance on the part of the clergy might have modified very seriously the whole character of land-tenure.

CHAPTER XV

KINDLY CONCESSIONS

THESE crucial tests of manumission and heriot, therefore, do not permit us to draw an essential distinction between the lay landlord and the ecclesiastic. To both, the main question was a business question; and, though manumission for money was often a great economic advantage to the master[1], yet it cannot be said that the monks saw this more clearly than the squires. I will ask my readers to keep in mind, all through these next chapters, that rough estimate to which I have come after some years of deliberation, that it was possibly about 5 per cent. better for the peasant, on an average, to live on a monastic than on a lay estate; except, that is, on a royal estate, where the conditions were distinctly more favourable than on the monastic. This is proved most clearly by the constant attempt of peasants to escape from monastic bondage by pleading that they were originally of "ancient demesne"—*i.e.* the king's own peasants[2]. The fact that they did this desperately, in the face of plain Domesday and other records by means of which the monks convicted them, brings out even more strongly the advantages they hoped to gain by their claim. The monks themselves sometimes realized and resented this. The abbot of Meaux in Holderness tells us scornfully how the serfs of his abbey "thought it more glorious to be called and to be the king's bondmen than to fulfil their due meed of service to the Church of God and to our monastery"[3]. It is this comparison which has prompted that severe verdict in the classic *History of English Law*:

There is plenty of evidence that of all landlords the religious houses were the most severe—not the most oppressive, but the most tenacious of their rights; they were bent on the maintenance of pure villein tenure and personal villeinage. The immortal but soulless

[1] Cf. Sée, pp. 245 ff.

[2] *E.g.* the cases of Bury, Burton, St Albans and Meaux. Sometimes we find the serfs preferring even a great baron to a monastery; in 1340, two claimed to belong to the Earl of Fife; the abbot of Dunfermline claimed them for his own, and got a verdict (*Reg. Dunferm.* p. 261).

[3] *Chron. de Melsa*, R.S. III, 128. Cf. the case I quote from Fyot on p. 165, n. 1.

corporation with her wealth of accurate records would yield no inch, would enfranchise no serf, would enfranchise no tenement. In practice the secular lord was more humane, because he was more human, because he was careless, because he wanted ready money, because he would die. Still, it is to the professed in religion that we may look for a high theory of justice; and when we find that it is against them that the peasants make their loudest complaints, we may be pretty sure that the religion of the time saw nothing very wrong in the proceedings of a lord who without any cruelty tried to get the most he could out of his villein tenements....On the other hand, as we shall soon see, there is in the king's treatment of his peasants, the men of 'the ancient demesne,' a convincing proof that the just landlord was expected to pay heed to the custom and not to break through it save for good cause[1].

The authors are here too severe upon the monks, contrasting them not with the ruck but with the pick of lay lords. But their main point is incontestable; that the monks, as great landlords, did not control but were controlled by the current traditions of medieval landlordism, and monastic kindliness was pretty nearly counterbalanced by monastic conservatism. The man of Religion might take a more fatherly interest in his peasant flock; on the other hand, he wielded the double sword of the flesh and of the Spirit. The villages subject to the nuns of Sitzenroda lived under a régime distinctly milder than that of their neighbours; but the monks of Vreden excommunicated a tenant who had fallen into arrears. The abbot of Kempten allowed himself a far more unjustifiable abuse of spiritual weapons for financial ends[2]. The abbot or prior or cellarer, whose charitable heart might well have impelled him to lavish his own private property, had no right to give away what belonged to the community. Therefore monastic economy took for granted all the incidents of serfdom; and from the monk, as from the lay lord, our peasants seldom gained ground except by their own struggles[3]. If the churchmen had really offered

---

[1] Pollock and Maitland, 2nd ed. I, 378.

[2] Sitzenroda, p. 33; Vreden, p. 19; Vogt, p. 8.

[3] It is difficult to admit Bishop Hobhouse's argument, as to the preference shown by the Glastonbury bondmen for the abbot's yoke. He pleads that they "did not care to purchase their manumission"; a fact which more probably indicates high prices demanded by the abbot than any indifference to freedom on the part of the serf. He seems quite unaware of the difficulties which specially block monastic liberations (*Rentalia*, introd. p. xxii).

their tenants more advantages than (for instance) the modern County Councils or Charity Commissioners often offer beyond a hard business landlord, then it would have been impossible for men so able, orthodox, experienced and responsible as Cardinal Hugues-de-St-Cher and Bishop Longland to write as they did. We must make great allowance for strong language in the Middle Ages; but we must not, without very strong evidence, persuade ourselves that such men were saying the very opposite of what their daily experience taught them as truth.

It is true that, as St-Aiglan goes on to say, "Il faut cependant reconnaître qu'un heureux changement s'opéra par la force des choses dans le sort des serfs ecclésiastiques." But we must now go on to consider this *force des choses* and measure how far this gradual betterment actually carried the serf during the Middle Ages. And I think that this further consideration, detail by detail, will be found to justify Boissonnade's generalization; that the serf improved fairly steadily, if slowly, during the Middle Ages proper, that the zenith of his prosperity was, roughly, about 1450–1500 A.D.; and that, already before 1500, that great cleavage was beginning between capital and labour *which the Reformation hastened, but which could never have been really avoided by artificial attempts to suppress capitalism*[1].

Here, also, we shall miss all indications of any real and consistent policy of liberalism on the part of monks in general, or of ecclesiastics in general, or even of one single pope among the hundred and fifty who succeeded each other between Gregory the Great and the end of the Middle Ages. Individual saintly monks pitied the peasant, and felt as charitable towards him as that French lord who freed one hundred with a single stroke of the pen, or that countess of Flanders who emancipated all her bondmen and bondwomen; but these were exceptions scarcely affecting the general rule. To the Evesham chronicler of about 1200, most peasants are covetous boors who are "ready to do any evil for the sake of a little gain"[2]. The monastic chronicler of Farfa speaks of "the untamable ferocity of villeins and peasants, and their cruel madness."[3] The St Albans monk,

---

[1] pp. 170 ff., 303 ff., 416 ff. The last sentence which I have italicized is not expressed by Boissonnade, but I think it will be found to follow inevitably from what he says.   [2] *Chron. Eves.* R.S. p. 42.

[3] Gregory of Catino, *Hist. Farf.* c. 33 (M.G.H. XI, 579).

Thomas Walsingham, is even more bitter against the peasants of 1381, than Gower, the Kentish squire who barely escaped from them with his life.

But, though the monk's and the churchman's general policy was naturally guided mainly by the principles natural to a capitalist, we can see some real tendency to personal benevolence[1]. We have seen, in Chapter III, how there are more indications on abbey estates of occasional feast-days for the peasantry. And, in the continental documents, we can trace certain charitable allowances for the suffering. Among the *Weisthümer*, or sets of manorial customs, printed by J. Grimm, about a dozen prescribe special consideration for pregnant bondwomen, and two or three dozen for those in childbed. The first class occur almost exclusively and the latter, I think, predominantly, on monastic or Church manors. Therefore, even when we take into account that these are only a small fraction of the thousand or more which Grimm and his helpers collected, and that these again are only a fraction of all that once existed, and that, in the nature of the case, ecclesiastical records have survived in a rather larger proportion than the rest, we must still judge the clergy to have shown special consideration in this direction[2].

To take these two subjects in order[3]. In 1562, under the abbot of Lorsch: "The men of Schönau shall keep an orchard at the monks' grange, so that, if a woman with child went that way, she might satisfy her longing, without any great harm done." At Kitburg, in 1534, the abbot of Marienstadt had "all rights of game and fishery; but, if there be pregnant women or sick folk, they may use the same in their necessity." At Zozenheim,

[1] The monastic tenants at Sitzenroda had, in the sixteenth century, a definite advantage over the neighbouring tenants of lay lords. On one of the manors (Frauwalde) they were free from all duties of forced labour, while the other villagers had to do their week's work for the lords of Börln. Instances might be found in the other direction; but I think that, on the whole, the differences would be found to weigh slightly in the monks' favour (Sitzenroda, p. 33). Another instance of very easy terms to tenants on a nunnery estate is given in *Arch. Kult.* IV (1906), 54.

[2] It has been asserted that they also showed more consideration in reduction of rents and fines. The collection of exact and exhaustive statistics would be a very laborious task; but my general impression is that it would be very difficult to prove this thesis. It will be seen that independent enquirers like Leadam have found no real evidence for it.

[3] The references in this paragraph are to *Weisthümer*, I, 463, 641 (cf. II, 453); II, 160, 231, 817; III, 831, 834, 887; IV, 467; V, 41. But it may be noted that nearly all these customs are in late records.

under the prince-bishop of Mainz, a small allowance was made for pregnant women at the lord's bakehouse. At Ehr, under the abbess of Marienberg, they had a special right to refuge in the nuns' grange in times of war; "but at their own cost except for the lodging." At Wolf on the Moselle, under the Frauenkirche [at Trèves?] "if a woman with child be picking or labouring in a vineyard, she has leave to cut a small branch with two clusters [for herself]; but she must take it openly home." At Rumersheim, under Prüm, one infringement on the abbot's game and fishing laws is permitted; "if a woman be with child, she may go and fish with one foot on land and the other in the brook": so also (834) at Prüm itself, where the husband may fish for his wife: but very likely the Rumersheim allowance was meant to be construed in the same sense. At Schontra, apparently under the canons of Würzburg, the woman might send a man to fish until he had caught something for her. Similar fishing was allowed by the bishop of Bâle; a man at his periodical bleeding-time, on these latter manors, was generally allowed the privilege of the pregnant woman.

Of allowances for childbirth, by far the commonest is that of the Shrovetide hen, which was an almost universal due payable to the lord. At Ermatingen, under the abbot of Reich-enau, it is recorded as early as the fourteenth century: "If it be that a man's wife be pregnant and lying in childbed, then my lord's bailiff [who has come to levy the Shrovetide hen] shall take the hen and cut her head off and cast the rest behind his back into the house; and he shall bring my lord the head, and the woman shall eat the hen" (1, 239). So also in 1580 at Dommershausen, under the canons of Trèves (II, 210), about 1450 for the tenants of St Peter's in the Black Forest (1, 351); at Grittenach and Ober-mennig, under the abbot of Pellingen (II, 119); at Sensweiler, under the count palatine of the Rhine (II, 129); at another village of his (p. 154); many other landlords, lay and clerical, made the same remittance; e.g. IV, 454; V, 592, 667. At Bure, under the bishop of Bâle (1360), if a villager be in his blood-letting-time, or his wife in childbed, he may go and fish in the river without making fine unto my lord (V, 41). In that same village, the peasant need not work for his lord on the day when his wife is in childbed (V, 42, 1360 A.D.); so also on two lay

manors (III, 311, 680). At Herbigheim, under the abbess of
Fraulautern (1458) "if it befall that the peasant have a wife in
childbed, he shall not go farther [when the parish is called to
follow after robbers] than he can get home again at night to his
sick wife" (II, 23). Under the bishop of Bâle, he is excused
from the general levy at such a time, unless it be at a supreme
crisis when every man is needed (v, 42). In three cases the
monks show indulgence even without this reason. At Pellingen,
Wittenach and Obermennig, under the abbey of St Matthew at
Pellingen (1545), the abbot pledges himself, if the peasant be
called upon to ride with the levy beyond the Rhine, "that my
lord abbot will then take pains, with speech and with writing,
to bring the said peasant home again." At Buix, under the
Cistercians of Lucelle, in 1392, a childbed woman might claim
a load of firewood (v, 48). In other places there was generally
an invidious distinction; for a girl she might claim one load, but
for the more useful boy-child, two (I, 79, 96, 142, etc.; cf. IV,
334). At a lay manor, in 1535, the childing bondwoman was
allowed six weeks' free pasture for her cow in the common
meadow (IV, 559). At Bubikon, under a convent of Hospitallers,
"if a bondwoman of this convent give birth to a child in
matrimony, she sends to my lord commander of the convent,
who shall bid them give her a quart of wine and four loaves"
(I, 67, 1483).

Cless gives us similar evidence from Württemberg (II, i, 438;
cf. p. 422):

At Denckendorf, each lying-in bondwoman received two measures
of wine at the christening of her child, with eight white loaves. At
Martinmas, each family had a measure of wine, and on Shrove
Tuesday each child below the age of ten received one or two little
cakes, of the thickness of a finger, baked in swine's-fat; and those who
fetched it were given a plate of soup in the guest-house. Moreover,
the servants of the monastery had their feast-days, to which every
married man might bring his wife, and the bachelor his washer-
woman, to the cloister at Esslingen, where they could claim a hearty
meal and a bath. On Shrove Tuesday, the threshers received between
them an ox's head, not too sparingly measured; to this feast their
wives invited the monks' reeve, with cakes, which they contributed
also to the conventual table. These women, in their turn, were
rewarded with wine and money.

On many manors, a woman with child might claim food and drink at an inn even during the forbidden hours of morning service on Sunday[1]. Peetz (p. 83) speaks of the duties of the cellarer of Kiemsee in visiting sick tenants; but he gives no reference, and many of his other statements of this kind are evidently incorrect or exaggerated. One very definite example of monastic generosity, however, is recorded by Cless (II, i, 422). The customal of Leidringen, under the abbey of St-Georgen in the Black Forest, prescribes:

When bondmen of the abbey are taken by death, and leave children that pertain also to the abbey, and are helpless, and possess nothing, then shall the abbey bring them up until they come of age, and shall retain their father's holding for them.... About 1550 A.D. the peasants complained that this obligation had been neglected; the abbot was able to show that, since 1534, when he had been driven out of his abbey, he had no longer been able to keep this up at St-Georgen, but he had taken several [*mehrere*] such children to other conventual manors in Austria, and brought them up there. His three predecessors, he added, had done this for several children, partly educating them at school, some of whom had become fellow-monks of his, and partly causing them to be taught some handicraft, or settled in some other way about St-Georgen.

At this point, then, let me quote what is by far the strongest case I have met of a charitable reduction of monastic rents. In most cases such reductions seem obviously due to the difficulty of collecting more, or, (as an editor notes,) to mere slackness of management in the later Middle Ages[2]. But a deed of the pious Abbot Bruno of Hirsau, about 1110 A.D., is very honourable to him and his abbey:

Be it known unto all that have been anointed with the chrism of Jesus that Abbot Bruno of Hirsau, of pious memory, moved with pity for the serfs of his monastery that dwell in the village called Hall and in the neighbourhood, hath granted them this grace, that each man who had owed a yearly tribute of 20 pence should now lay 5 pennyworth of wax on St Peter's altar, and every woman who owed 12 pence should lay 3 pennyworth, and be quit of all claim. Moreover, he decreed that they should be given away in exchange to no Church[3] and to no man except at their own request. After the death of each, let his best beast or his sword be taken from the man, and

---

[1] Hoyer, p. 58. Compare also Bartels, p. 57.   [2] Belbuck, p. 58.
[3] Including monasteries; *ecclesia* is very commonly used in this sense.

from the woman the best garment. Whosoever shall set these decrees at nought, let him be plunged with Dathan and Abiram in the depths of hell[1].

We have seen, in Chapter X, how there was often a counter-tradition answering to the tradition of servile dependence; the lord was bound to defend all his bondfolk against absolute starvation. A Dunfermline record shows that the monks of that abbey, while repudiating this prescription in law, acknowledged it in Christian charity; it is of extreme interest as showing the high-water-mark of paternàl government on the monks' part, and as suggesting the influence of Celtic clan solidarity[2]. It runs:

This is the inquisition made in the chapel of Logyn on the Tuesday after St Peter *ad vincula* (Aug. 1) 1320, by the mutual consent of the abbot and convent of Dunfermline and their men of the vale of Twedale[3], by the loyal men here written; to wit, Walter of Logyn, William Squiere of Kelso[4], Robert of Dunfermline, James of the Hall, Thomas of Logyn, John Grant, and Richard Little, burgher of Dunfermline, concerning the articles of the liberties of the afore-said dalesmen as hereafter followeth, which articles they beg the aforesaid abbot and convent to fulfil. *First*, they beg that a bailiff of their own kindred [*progenie*] be given unto them by the abbot, who shall replevy them at the court of the abbot and convent; whereunto the aforesaid jurymen answer that such a bailiff ought to be given to them, yet not in fee but in the accustomed manner. *Secondly*, they beg that, if any one of their race [*genere*] come to poverty or be broken down by age, he should have sustenance from the monastery; whereunto the jury answer, in the faith of the oath which they have taken, that they are not bound thereunto by duty but by affection, seeing that they are their men. *Thirdly*, that if any man of their race have slain a man or committed any other crime compelling him to take sanctuary, and if he be come to sanctuary at Dunfermline, then he should be maintained from the goods of the abbey so long as he remain there; whereunto they answer that they would do this for a stranger, and much more for their own man of the race aforesaid. *Fourthly*, that if any of their race have committed manslaughter and pay a fine for the slaughter, then the abbot and convent aforesaid are bound to contribute twelve marks for his fine; whereunto the jury answer that they never heard any such thing during all the days of their life.

---

[1] Printed by J. F. Schannat, *Vindemiae Literariae*, I, 181 (Fulda, 1723–4).
[2] *Reg. Dunferm.* p. 240, No. 354.
[3] The abbey had possessions in the Tweed valley; but the inquisition seems to have been taken near Dunfermline, possibly in order to give the abbey more weight on the jury.   [4] *Kylsolanum*.

But when we have taken account of all this, and reminded ourselves that there was often much more of the sort which does not appear in the formal records, we must still note how far more frequent are the indications of monastic and ecclesiastical insistence upon strict business rights. The monk (as Gower says, quoting from St Bernard) was too often a bailiff in a monk's cowl[1]. The thing is perfectly natural, and might pass without remark if it were not for the well-meaning writers who, as the Church-loving St-Aiglan complains, do religion harm by claiming an unreal otherworldliness for the actual Religious of the Middle Ages. It was for the general good of civilization that the churchman should become a land-capitalist; that the *Grossherrschaft* of the Middle Ages should be led to a great extent by men who, when all was said and done, had more moral force and a clearer and more reasonable policy than the ordinary lay magnate. But *Grossherrschaft* spells capitalism, whether the lord be cleric or layman; and, in the conflict of interests between capitalist and proletariat, it was almost inevitable that the cleric should very often forget his clergy[2]. We must pass on, therefore, from these instances of special monastic generosity to consider other cases in which the monk was landlord first, and Religious in a very secondary sense.

[1] *Mirour*, ll. 20, 974.

[2] For the general progress in civilization due to this "Grossherrschaft" of the monks and other lords—to the agrarian agglomerations on a great capitalistic scale—and, at the same time, for the decay of peasant proprietorship to which this capitalism led, see Inama-Sternegg, *Deutsche Wirthschaftsgeschichte* (Leipzig, 1897), I, 293-4. He is dealing mainly with the ninth and tenth centuries, and says: "This concentration of lordship over the productive forces of the soil resulted in a steady increase of the propertyless classes, which thus sank into some sort of dependence upon the great landlords."

CHAPTER XVI

JUSTICE

"JUSTICE is great profit"; so ran the medieval lawyers' proverb, in the sense that rights of justice over the people were very lucrative. The lord reaped a fine for almost every offence; he took a fine from litigants if they came to an agreement outside his court; he took all the chattels of the condemned felon or of the fugitive offender; he took a fee from the serf who wanted to search the court-rolls for information as to his dues and services[1]. Ecclesiastical judges throve even more, if possible, on the fines taken for offences; the bishops, writes Gower, take bribes wholesale, and the deans of Christianity "desire sin; for our dean gets far more profit from a harlot than from a nun"[2]. In the courts even of kings and princes, we have seen how the poor had little chance of a hearing, since they brought no gifts to the judges[3]; and there is no reason to surmise a higher standard in the manor courts. Or rather, there is every reason to surmise an even lower standard; the steward or bailiff has as bad a reputation in the Middle Ages as the miller[4]. The Council of Tours, in 813, complained that the country was full of false witnesses ready to testify to anything for a small bribe (§ 34); Gower, again, speaks of these professional perjurers; and there is a plain allusion to the same subject in *Piers Plowman*[5]. Nicolas de Clémanges, condemning the regular and public sale of judicial offices, remarks cynically that there was more justice in hell than in France[6]. A generation later, the États Généraux at Tours, in 1483, complained of this public sale of justice as one of the worst social sores of the time[7].

---

[1] Hales, p. 372. Miss Levett, again, points out that the St Albans records supply abundant evidence here.

[2] *Vox Clam.* ed. Macaulay, p. 117; *Mirour*, ll. 20, 589 ff. I have dealt briefly with this subject on pp. 200–201 of *Chaucer and his England*.

[3] Hostiensis, *Summa Aurea* (Venice, 1570), p. 467. Compare Roper's *Life of Sir Thos. More* (ed. Lumby, 1879, p. xxxi) and Pépin, *Ninive*, f. 54. 3.

[4] See *Rot. Parl.* II, 173, for the villein's disadvantages at law in 1347 A.D.

[5] *Political Songs*, R.S. I, 359; *Piers Plowman*, B. II, 62 and c. XXII, 372, with Skeat's note on the former passage.

[6] *Opera*, ff. 49 a, 52 b.   [7] *Recueil*, pp. 67–8.

Among modern students, Sée specially emphasizes the commercial character of seignorial justice in the Middle Ages: it means "neither a public force nor a social duty"; "what specially interests the wielder of justice is the sanction, *i.e.* the fines, which form one of his steadiest revenues." Only in the late Middle Ages did the author of the *Très Ancienne Coutume* plead that the fines ought only to pay the expenses of justice; "Justice was established for charity; for, if justice were not, poor folk could not live." But, adds Sée, such principles had to wait long for practical application, "for long ages yet, seignorial justice will be simply an instrument of seignorial exploitation"[1]. And, in cases where money played a less prominent part, we are still faced with other equally primitive conditions. The right of private vengeance was recognized by law far down into the Middle Ages. Beaumanoir, in 1290, explains that this is a class-privilege, reserved now for the nobility[2]:

War, by our custom, cannot take place between bondfolk or between citizens. Therefore, if quarrels or defiance or fightings arise among them, they must be judged according to the misdeed; for they cannot plead the right of war. If so be that one such had killed another's father, and the son, after this misdeed, killed the man who had slain his father, then he would be judged for the manslaughter.... For gentlefolk alone can wage war, as we have said above.

Yet in the more democratic Flanders it was recognized semi-officially, at least, even among the commonalty as late as the fifteenth century[3]. Again, where no fines were to be reaped, the lords were tempted to fall back upon the short cut of banishment. This, one of the commonest of medieval penalties, was also one of the most dangerous to society. To Beaumanoir, casual harm from some desperate outlaw is one of the ordinary perilous contingencies of human life[4].

[1] *Bretagne*, pp. 73–8. The prior of Dunstable, in 1285, spent 33 marks in a suit against a bondman, partly in presents to the judges (*Ann. Dunst.* R.S. p. 321). Petrus Cantor, in his notes on the society of the late twelfth century, recognizes the close connexion between justice and money (P.L. vol. 205, cols. 92 c, d, 93 a, 238 c, d).

[2] Vol. ii, pp. 355–6.

[3] C. Petit-Dutaillis, *Le droit de vengeance*, pp. 44 ff. Compare de Pauw, pp. 30–1 and Arx, ii, 601, 608, where he shows the long survival of private vengeance in the canton of St-Gall.

[4] Vol. ii, p. 18.

So justice is great profit, and great churchmen profit by it as much as others; they profit sometimes even by its dirtiest gains. At a very early date it was forbidden to clerics to shed blood even in the indirect sense of pronouncing the sentence of death; hence the later formula of the Inquisition, which handed the condemned over to the secular arm and prayed that no death might ensue, even while the utterer of that prayer would have been bound to excommunicate any secular judge who should neglect to inflict death[1]. Scrupulous consciences sometimes took this general prohibition very seriously; Petrus Cantor tells how

Master Robert of Cambrai, when he was teaching at Reims, pleaded the cause of his friend's servant, who undertook wager of battle against a forger who had given him false money, and conquered him; but Master Robert never ceased to sob for that sin of his in supporting even an innocent man in a matter of bloodshed; and thenceforward he would never meddle with a case of that kind[2].

But great clerics, even bishops and abbots in England, where there were less irregularities on the whole, acted as royal justices, and constantly pronounced the death-penalty; zealous church-men complained of it as a standing abuse, but circumstances were irresistible. And, in medieval gallows-rights, we see little difference between the monk and the lay lord. Sometimes, indeed, by a very convenient division, the monk left the execution to others, while he kept the criminal's chattels for himself. The lords of Chalon, in 1289, made an accord with the monks of Romainmotier concerning four frontier villages in which both parties had feudal rights. In it the lay barons grant:

Item, we recognize that the said villages of Waut and Chantegrue with their inhabitants, in accordance with the boundaries aforesaid, are the property of the said monks, with all manner of lordship and justice, save that, by reason of guard in the aforesaid villages, we keep for ourselves the execution of justice upon those who for their mis-deeds are judged to death by command of the said monks; and, after the malefactors have been judged by the messenger of the said monks, after their request, then the castellan of Noserey for the time

---

[1] Roman Catholic scholars have now put this beyond possibility of serious denial; *e.g.* A. Vacandard, *L'Inquisition*, pp. 233–95; A. Lépicier, *De Stabilitate et Progressu Dogmatis*, p. 203.

[2] P.L. vol. 205, col. 539.

being ought to receive the condemned person, within three days, naked at the place—*doit recevoir le jugie tot nu au leu*. And of the goods of the condemned, movable or immovable, we [lords of Chalon] have nothing. And after the three days, if the condemned escape, we can demand nothing from the said monks or their messenger [by way of fine for having allowed the escape]. And whensoever the malefactor might escape, whether before or after judgement, if the mayor of the monks will swear, with three compurgators, that the malefactor has escaped without fault of theirs, we will that they be believed on their oath, and we can constrain them to no more[1].

At Troyes, the abbess of Notre-Dame-aux-Nonnains had an even better bargain; but she was a very great lady, who could even join issues with a pope[2]. By a charter of 1189, the count of Champagne grants her that "if a thief flee within the abbey liberties," which included several streets outside the actual precincts, "or if he be caught *flagrante delicto* within the liberties, he belongs to the abbess, on these conditions, that the provost is to give the abbess twenty pence for the thief, and she hands him over quite naked—*omnino nudum*—at the court's bidding." In 1196 the abbey gets similar privileges at Charnay; the lord of St-Fiol's bailiff may take the thief and hang him, but he must "give to the abbess or her maire twenty pence, and all the thief's belongings—*spolia latronis*." At the adjoining manor of Fay, "the abbess may condemn the thief if she will; if she will not, he shall be given up to the lord of St-Fiol"[3].

But in general there was no mincing of matters; the monk's bailiff condemned and hanged the thief just as a knight's bailiff would have done; he took the gallows-wrack just as he took the

---

[1] Charrière, p. 595. As the editor notes: "The Chalons recognize the monks as holding all jurisdiction, and reserve nothing but the right of *executing* the death-sentences *pronounced by the officers of the convent*." Cf. p. 183 (1272 A.D.) where the monks again secure to themselves the possessions of a malefactor punished by the castellan of Les Clées.

[2] See the bulls of Clement IV in 1366 onwards, printed in *Aube*, 1874, pp. 120 ff. Urban IV had set his heart on founding a great collegiate church on the site of his own father's house at Troyes—the present church of St-Urbain. The nuns resented this as a trespass upon their liberties, and headed a mob which broke the doors, destroyed a marble altar, and carried off the masons' tools and scaffolds and cranes. Cf. Babeau, *St-Urbain-de-Troyes*, p. 6.

[3] *Aube*, 1874, pp. 11, 15–16. There is a similar clause securing the abbess the usual advantages in cases of judicial duels at Fay. The abbess of St-Georges-de-Tinteniac had a somewhat similar understanding with neighbouring lords (Sée, *Bretagne*, p. 74).

corpse-presents. Dugdale is full of charters in which monasteries claim this right of hanging as a far from negligible item of revenue. We may say of every district of Europe what Paap notes of Pomerania in the thirteenth century: "nearly all the great abbeys had this right"[1]. A medieval monastic poet of that date reckons it among the great deeds of his abbot that he built a gibbet[2]. The Dunstable chronicler, on the other hand, counts it among a neighbour-lord's iniquities that "he cast down our prior's gallows at Edesuthe, which from the foundation of the township of Dunstable had appertained thereunto without any dispute"[3]. An interesting case is recorded in the formal complaints of the clergy to the Council of Vienne (1311). The Seneschal of Bigorre took forcible possession of the abbey of St-Pierre, "and, having pulled down the gallows which the said Abbot had had from time immemorial, he set up new gallows in the place aforesaid, and hanged a certain man forthwith on the said gallows in order to vindicate his possession thereof." The case is recorded not as an outrage to humanity, but as an indefensible trespass upon the abbot's rights[4]. And, even where nuns were concerned, business was apt to come first. About the year 1540 "a man named Lespine was accused of having caught fish in the stew-pond of the ladies [of the nunnery of Maubuisson]; for which cause they put him to trial extraordinary by their officers and justiciars, and he was hanged and strangled on the territory of the said ladies"[5].

So, again, with trial by battle. Even nunneries exercised this right of hiring the best champion they could in the market and of spoiling the vanquished[6]. The victories or defeats of monastic champions are frequently recorded in earlier days[7]. A typical

---

[1] Belbuck, p. 24. Taking three English counties at random, in the *Placita de Quo Warranto*, we find how many lords claimed gallows-rights at the end of the thirteenth century. In Cambridge, 14 lay lords and no ecclesiastics; in Gloucester, 5 laymen and 13 ecclesiastics; in Norfolk, 3 and 4 respectively. This gives 22 lay gallows to 17 ecclesiastical.

[2] De Rosny, p. 47 (Loos in Belgium, *c.* 1290).

[3] *Annales*, R.S. p. 261 (1274); compare Charrière, pp. 123, 136, 657.

[4] ALKG. IV (1888), p. 384.

[5] Dutilleux-Depoin, p. 36.

[6] Troyes as above; the abbess of Malling in Kent (*Reg. Roff.* p. 483).

[7] *E.g. Irminon*, I, 313, 335; II, 373; Mabillon, *Annales*, V, 119 [*c.* 1080] and 438 [*c.* 1100]; AA.SS.O.S.B. V, 561 (1114). On the other hand, the monks of St-Pierre-de-Bèze, in the early eleventh century, were persuaded

example is furnished by the monks of St-Germain-des-Prés in 1152. A noble neighbour of their dependent priory of Antony, Etienne de Macy, had imprisoned an abbey serf for trespass on lands which he claimed.

After prolonged enquiries and discussions, a day was fixed to decide the case. Etienne de Macy appeared with his champion; brothers Renard and Philip, monks of St-Germain, appeared with their champion in the abbot's name.... The champions fought bravely: the St-Germain man tore out his opponent's eye, felled him to earth, and compelled him to confess defeat, in virtue whereof the rights of the abbey were proclaimed[1].

By this time enlightened churchmen fully realized the objections to this barbarous ordeal. The Cluniac poet, Bernard of Morlaix, wrote in the early twelfth century. Speaking in the name of the man in the street, he describes its effect. If, seeking what is your own at the hands of justice, you accept this ordeal, then the other party sends some Goliath into the field, twice as big as yourself; he crushes you like an egg-shell, and your cause with you[2]. Petrus Cantor, at the end of the same century, states the objections more fully and philosophically[3]; Innocent III publicly condemned this form of trial in 1215; yet Aquinas, a generation later, testifies to its survival, and finds need to argue against it; such ordeals "are unreasonable; for this is to commit oneself to fortune and God's judgement[4]; and therefore it is

by the bishop to forgo trial by duel and come to terms with their adversary (*Analecta Divionensia*, 1875, p. 298). A few years later, a neighbouring knight gave them land which he had vowed to St Peter in order to secure success in his duel (*ibid.* p. 365). For another very interesting case see Fyot, p. 82, *preuves* p. 73; the good abbé is embarrassed to excuse his fellow-churchmen in the matter.

[1] *Arch. France Monast.* IV (1907), 272. Two other similar cases were decided by judicial combat in the same village at different times (pp. 271–2). Compare P.L. vol. 156, cols. 1197–8. Ducange, under the word *Collibertus*, prints an extraordinarily interesting case of this kind, where a serf's freedom is concerned, and which bears close resemblance to the incident at St-Benoît-sur-Loire which I have translated in *Five Centuries of Religion*, I, 239. The records of the abbey of Leno contain more than one notice of wager of battle for monastic possessions, or under monastic auspices (Zaccaria, pp. 22, 174, 176–7, 205, 290). So also at Romainmotier (Charrière, pp. 101, 152, 172, 185, 248, 685).

[2] Wright, *Satirical Poets*, R.S. II (1872), 76. Yet Bernard's fellow-Cluniacs of Romainmotier had no such scruples.

[3] P.L. vol. 205, cols. 229 and 545–6.

[4] *Sic* in text: *hoc est committere se fortunae et judicio divino* (*Opp.* ed. Parma, XXI, 550). Has not a *non* slipped out after *et*?

rarely done now, since men use their reason more; and still less in great cities, where are many wise folk." But we find the monks of Tynemouth fighting a case of this kind in the time of abbot William of St Albans (1214–35), and in 1238 the duke of Brittany granted to Mont-St-Michel, among other privileges at Mont-Ronault, that "the monks shall have in the aforesaid manor both duel and thief and all rights pertaining to those two matters"[1].

I have not come across any monastic protest against this ordeal by battle earlier than Bernard of Morlaix and Aquinas; it may probably be safely asserted that there was no general revolt against it in the cloister on moral grounds. Jocelin of Brakelond shows that it was not the monks of Bury, but the townsfolk, who reprobated the barbarous old custom: "The convent was grieved by the offensive words of the burgesses, who said that if the man had only dwelt within the borough, it would not have come to the ordeal [of battle]." Even then, it was only "the abbot and the saner part of the monks" who admitted this, and then not for all the villeins[2]. And, three centuries earlier, we find even plainer evidence in the same direction. Adrevald, the first monastic historian of Fleury (about 850 A.D.), cannot contain his indignation at the "bestial" lawyer who disappointed the monks of the combat for which they had prepared a champion. Their suit was against their fellow-monks of St Denis; each abbey claimed a certain group of serfs as its own; Adrevald, of course, has no doubt that God would have granted the victory to Fleury. But this bestial judge was so dishonest and corrupt as to urge "that it was not right for witnesses to fight each other for a matter of church property, and that it would be better to divide the serfs between the contending parties....But St Benedict did not forget...for no sooner had those bondmen been divided into two companies than he, by God's just sentence, was so smitten that he could speak no more, but lost the whole use of his tongue"[3]. If Lamborelle is to be trusted (pp. 239–40) Louis le Gros, in the twelfth century, formally decreed that

[1] *Gest. Ab.* R.S. 1, 273; Borderie, p. 186.
[2] C.S. p. 74; Clarke's translation, p. 132. Compare the picturesque and pathetic Leicester incident, which I have printed on p. 513 of *Social Life in Britain*.
[3] Miracles de St-Benoît, p. 57.

monks might sustain their causes at law by offering one of their serfs to fight the matter out.

Another wide generalization, again, is supplied by the relations between abbey and town, wherever a municipality had grown up at the gates of a monastery. In all these cases, the townsfolk had undoubtedly owed much of their earlier prosperity to the monks; but the debt was mainly indirect and reciprocal. The monks, for their part, drew a far better income from the taxes of these prosperous townsfolk than they could have drawn from half a dozen villeins tilling the same area. Nor had the concessions which had so benefited the townsfolk been made gratuitously and altruistically; in practically all recorded cases we know them to have been bought for hard cash. In France, the monks were the most determined opponents of these rising municipal communities—*communio, novum ac pessimum nomen*, as Abbot Guibert writes, his indignation getting the better of his native kindliness[1]. A century later, in 1213, the Synod of Paris denounced

those synagogues which usurers and profiteers have set up in almost all the cities, towns and villages of the whole realm of France, and which are called *communes* in the vulgar tongue; associations which have established devilish customs, contrary to ecclesiastical organization and making for the almost total subversion of church jurisdiction[2].

In England,

the towns which were reckoned among ecclesiastical estates lay under the special conditions that governed those estates, where religious and supernatural influences had been forced into the service of material wealth, and the attempt was made by spiritual authority to fix fluctuating political conditions into perpetual immutability....

[1] *De Vita Sua*, l. III, c. 7 (P.L. vol. 156, col. 922). To Guibert, it is intolerable that "these bondmen should all pay the customary dues for their servitude in one yearly sum, and should atone by a legally-fixed fine for all their transgressions against the laws, being thus altogether free from the other exactions of tribute which are usually inflicted upon serfs." Compare Sée, p. 281 and Luchaire, *Communes*, pp. 235–50; "L'Église" (writes the author) "a toujours fait une guerre implacable aux communes."

[2] Mansi, *Concilia*, t. XXII, col. 851, § 8. The stress is on the fight against usurers; but the hostility to the communes is none the less apparent; and it must be remembered that, at this date, the Church was still condemning as usurious certain mercantile transactions which were practised by popes and justified by saints like Aquinas in later times. See the present writer's article in *History* for July, 1922.

A dozen generations of Nottingham burghers had been ordering their
own market, taking the rents of their butcheries and fish stalls and
storage rooms, supervising their wool traders and mercers, and
admitting new burgesses to their company by common consent,
while the men of Reading were still trying in vain every means by
which they might win like privileges from the Abbot who owned the
town. Everywhere the same story is repeated, with varying incidents
of passion and violence.... If boroughs attached to a bishopric were
in a different position, the difficulty was vastly increased in the case
of those subject to the lordship and rule of a monastery. Towns owned
by abbot or prior were like all the rest stirred by the general zeal
for emancipation, but they were practically cut off from any hope of
true liberty. The power with which they had to fight was invincible.
Against the little lay corporation was set a great ecclesiastical corporation, wealthy, influential, united, persistent, immortal. All the
elements which went to make up the strength of the town were raised
in the convent to a yet higher degree of perfection, and the struggle
was prolonged, intense, and at best remained a drawn battle, setting
nothing beyond dispute save the animosity of the combatants[1].

Three striking stories of this eternal conflict have been told
in full detail and are easily accessible; the St Albans case by
J. A. Froude[2], that of St Edmundsbury by J. R. Green[3], and
Dunstable (by Green also?) in *Cornhill* for 1862, p. 830. In all
countries of Europe, popular revolts such as that of 1381 have
struck as definitely at the monasteries as at the lay landlords[4].

For monastic conservatism saw no reason why the prosperous
townsfolk should wish to shake off those irritating burdens
which their fathers, as helpless serfs, had patiently borne, and
to which the sons were still legally liable. Jocelin of Brakelond,
quite incidentally, recounts some of the dues of the Bury tenants;
to him, they are a matter of tradition, and therefore of course,
this naturally kind-hearted man betrays no sense of compassion

[1] Mrs J. R. Green, *Town Life*, 1894, I, 277, 280, 294; cf. all chapters IX–XI;
also Sée, p. 73; Pirenne, II, 79 ff.; A. Luchaire, *Communes*, pp. 21 ff., 235 ff.
Luchaire writes: "The Church waged implacable war against the communes;
if circumstances sometimes compelled her to disarm, she still remained dis-
trustful, ill-disposed, on the watch for chances of resuming the offensive and
reconquering lost advantages.... There were exceptions to this rule, but
neither so numerous nor so cogent as has been asserted." The whole of this
chapter should be read by anyone inclined to question those opening sentences.
[2] *Short Studies*, vol. III, No. 1; see esp. pp. 80–1.
[3] *Stray Studies*, 1876, pp. 211 ff.
[4] Cf. v. Arx, II, 192.

for these poor; the old women with their distaffs trouble him not as a symptom of real suffering and injustice, but because they put the abbey in such an undignified position—*celerarius turpiter ibat per villam*, and the enemies of the Lord blasphemed. These were taxes paid by the citizens of Bury from the days when their forefathers had been serfs at the abbey-gates; taxes which, conformably to human nature though not to strict reason, they now resented as the modern farmer resents the payment of tithes. They paid similar tribute for their own cows' dung, which the abbey had originally taken, as it still took that of all the tenants' sheep, compelling the owners on that account to pen them every night in the abbot's folds; moreover, "the cellarer was used freely to take all the dunghills in the street for his own use, unless it were before the doors of those who were holding averland; for to them only was it allowable to collect dung and to keep it." But, by an iniquitous modern encroachment (writes Jocelin), "everyone in his own tenement now collects dung in a heap, and the poor sell theirs to whom and when they choose!" In the town market, the cellarer had the right of buying cheaper than the citizens, and of selling dearer; he had possessed (until these modern encroachments) a monopoly of the town bull; he might buy up all the fish brought to the town before it had been offered in open market. There was, again, that right of commandeering the townsfolk to go and catch eels at Southery or Lakenheath, to which allusion has already been made, and which caused so much friction[1]. This attitude towards the peasants struggling for communal rights was quite normal[2]. Chartres, in the twelfth century, was far outstripped in the race for municipal liberties by smaller towns in the neighbourhood; it suffered here from "the splendour and influence of that great aristocratic body, the cathedral chapter"[3].

At Cluny, where the conditions were probably among the most favourable, "des prieurs ont permis à leurs hommes de s'assembler pour fixer les redevances auxquelles ils étaient tenus

[1] Clarke, pp. 133–7.
[2] For other instances see Villeneuve and Valenton in *Irminon*, I, ii, 384; cases in Berry, Méloizes, pp. 96–7; Tournus, p. 132 (Vézelay, about 1170); Dugdale, III, 107 (Bury, 1264); Éc. des Chartes, *Positions des Thèses*, 1899, p. 54; Littré, p. 212.
[3] A. Blondel, *Inst. Munic. de Chartres* (Chartres, 1903), p. 30.

(Morteau, Montbertoud, Paray, Toulon), mais là s'est bornée cette action commune. L'abbaye ne pouvait admettre sur ses terres l'existence d'un pouvoir autonome, qui serait facilement venu en rivalité et peut-être en conflit avec les moines"[1].

In 1246, the monks of St-Germain strictly forbade any of the villagers of Antony "to establish a *commune* at Antony, or to join any other *commune*, without leave of the abbot or his successors[2].

It was not until 1288 that the bishop of Liège and the abbot of St-Trond constituted "a kind of commune" at this latter place; even then, "they stipulated that this might be abolished whensoever it seemed good to them"[3].

The inhabitants of Esbarres, in 1520 "might hold no assembly without the lord's leave, under pain of 65 sols fine"[4]. This was the rule practically everywhere[5].

I have pointed out, in appendix 18, that even so natural a charity as permission to glean was not treated as a matter of course by the monks. Far from generous, again, was the spirit in which they often dealt with all the ordinary services and dues. It is the more necessary to insist upon this, since Montalembert and Cobbett have inspired modern journalists to repeat the wildest assertions on this subject.

The editor of a Belgian chartulary writes what might be written of every other monastery: from the eighth to the thirteenth century, "the dues paid by serfs constituted one of the richest items in the revenues of the abbey of St-Trond"[6]. And, though the capricious incidence of some of the heaviest dues is not chargeable to the monks, who had simply inherited the ordinary feudal claims, yet this was small consolation to the tenant upon whom they fell. I deal elsewhere more fully with what was called in France the "joyeux avènement" of a prelate; the tax which his subjects had to pay at his accession. In 1471, the 86 tenants of Martham paid the new prior of Norwich the enormous sum of £20, which we must multiply by something like 20 to bring it into present-day terms. In 1504 they paid the same sum to Robert Catton on his election as prior. So far the actual account-rolls testify: but, on looking at Dugdale,

[1] *Mill. Cluny*, I, 239. [2] *Arch. France Monast.* IV, 273.
[3] *Cart. St-Trond*. introd. p. xxxvii. [4] Garnier, III, 504, n. 34.
[5] See *e.g.* Seignobos, pp. 56–7. [6] *Cart. St-Trond*, introd. p. xxvi.

we find that three other priors have come between, in 1480, 1488 and 1502. If the rolls for those years existed and had been searched, it is practically certain that they would show us similar entries, and leave us to conclude that the Martham tenants had paid this tax five times in a single generation, at whatsoever irregular intervals it had pleased Providence to remove their former prior[1]. For the monastery, as a business institution, took its dues with business regularity. The monk of Muri, writing in 1142, shows us how naturally the Religious expected to inherit all the privileges of any manor which they acquired, and how inevitably this feeling took precedence of merely humanitarian considerations:

The township of Bollikon belonged at first, men say, to a noble lady named Berekind, from whom the founders of our abbey acquired that which we now possess there. In those days it was called Stablecourt, because it was that great lady's stable, and the privileges of the whole township were centred there. Throughout many townships in its neighbourhood, no man but she dared to keep a bull or boar or ram [for breeding]; and, whithersoever these went in or out, through a man's garden or his corn, none dared to hurt them or impound them; and the whole township took refuge in her as in a church. But, as this was done in old days by power, it ought to be done also nowadays for hope in the goodness and holiness of St Martin [of Muri][2].

He saw no harm, therefore, in these galling immunities; and from neighbouring Württemberg, at a later date, we get the same story:

The grange of Leidringen, in the name of the monks of St Georgen, kept a parish bull and boar for the propagation of the peasants' cattle; and this is how the monastic Solon himself describes the privileges of this fourfooted representative of the lords: "The parish bull has the right to go where he will, among the seedlings, the corn, and the hay; and, wheresoever he goeth, he shall incur no fine, nor shall any man smite him or mishandle him; only each may drive him from his own land to that of his neighbour." A proper lesson in human worth and neighbourly love[3]!

[1] I owe these facts to Mr H. S. Bennett, and to Messrs W. Hudson and H. W. Saunders, who have kindly lent their excerpts from the rolls.

[2] *Act.Mur*.p.60. The passage is the more significant, because the writer shows elsewhere a real conscience about questionable acquisitions; see pp. 4, 43–6.

[3] Cless, II, i, 439. Compare the custom on some of the St-Gall manors, where the abbot's boar, bull or stallion might never be driven away from the peasant's crops except through the persuasion of "a rod of one year's growth" v. Arx, I, 447 (1441 A.D.).

The abbess of Eschau's town bull at Ruffach, in 1349, was allowed to go and spend the night in whatever citizen's yard he choose; "he must not be driven out, but harboured there; he is the abbess's bull"[1].

Take tallage, again, one of the most galling of feudal dues. In 1350, the abbot of Vale Royal claimed "to tallage his villeins high and low at will" and the royal justices allowed it[2]. The monks of St-Germain-des-Prés, as we have seen before, were struggling in 1246 to revive *taillage à merci* over their tenants, their officials, as at Bury, levied distraints everywhere, and the quarrel was important enough to call for a royal commission of enquiry[3]. And we find outsiders interfering to secure mercy for monastic tenants. In 1248, the villagers of Antony bought themselves free from merchet by undertaking a yearly payment of £100 *parisis* (£25 sterling) to the monks of St-Germain-des-Prés; the English wars so crippled them that Charles VII complained to the abbot of the public danger; the villagers threatened to migrate *en masse*; "and this would be great damage, for this desert place would be a perilous pass on the Paris road; if the abbot would relax his requirements, he would do a thing agreeable to his sovereign." We do not know the result, but the abbot probably complied[4].

Take, again, the question of rent. A statement frequently quoted, directly or indirectly, is that of a manuscript in the British Museum (Cole XII), where we read: "They [the monks] never raised any rent, or took any incomes or garsomes

[1] *Weisthümer*, v, 387.

[2] *Vale Royal*, p. 134.

[3] Guilhiermoz, pp. 294, 305. What this meant for the villein may be gathered from Page, p. 17.

[4] *Arch. France Monast.* IV, 275. In contemporary England, of course, the serf had no such right of *désaveu*; he could not legally thus go forth naked to seek his fortune elsewhere. There is a similar case among the Cluny MSS. at the Bibliothèque Nationale (Coll. de Bourgogne, 82, § 369). At the Cluniac monastery of "Monsteretum" the visitors report that "the villagers complain of the prior, saying that through his negligence they are losing the right of usage which they have hitherto had in the manorial woods, wherefrom they were formerly able to take all that they needed for fire and for building. And when the visitors departed, they cried after them with a loud voice, saying that they would flee from the village if some remedy were not applied. They say that their farms are going to ruin by reason of this defect in their buildings, and many are already fallen which cannot be restored." This was about 1300 A.D.

of their tenants, nor ever took in or improved any commons"[1]. These are the words of an anonymous writer in the year 1591, 52 years after the Dissolution, who does not pretend to relate except on hearsay; yet they are regularly repeated as trustworthy evidence in the face of notorious facts! Garsome was a fine in various senses, often for marrying daughters; the only three cases which Professor Vinogradoff quotes in illustration of this word are all taken from monastic manors. It needs only a little reading in monastic charters to realize this. The bishop-abbot of Ely regularly exacted *gersuma*; see *Camb. Antiq. Soc. Reports*, VI (1887), 164, 168, 169, 171. So did the monks of Worcester, whenever they could get it (Hale, pp. xlii, 10 b). By "incomes" the anonymous writer means "reliefs" payable by the incoming tenant; it would be difficult to find anywhere a monastic bailiff's roll which contains no record of receipts from these fines. For "rents," the only pretence of corroborative evidence which I have seen adduced is the careless word of an editor who is contradicted by the very document with which he is concerned[2]. Delisle, on p. 48, gives instances of the *champart*, or proportion of his crop paid by the French peasant in lieu of rent; by far the highest of these rents happens to be monastic; "one sheaf in six; elsewhere the champart consisted only of $\frac{1}{10}$ or $\frac{1}{11}$ of the crop." As to enclosures, we have not only the well-known evidence of More's *Utopia* and Starkey's *Dialogue*, but, as will presently be seen, the latest research has proved statistically how large a part the monks took in those enclosures which did much to break down the prosperity of the fifteenth century peasant.

Tithes were a constant source of dispute between monk and villager[3]. If there is one point, again, on which we might expect the churchman to be indulgent to his tenant, it is that of Church holy-days. Religion forbade his working then; religion should have done her best to accept the resultant pecuniary loss herself; yet in fact she often thrust it upon the peasant. On a Glaston-

---

[1] Quoted in Gasquet, *Hen. VIII and the Eng. Mons.* 2nd ed. II, 501; thence the substance of it finds its way into Chesterton's *Short History of England*, p. 92, as an independent assertion.

[2] See above, ch. VIII, p. 86.

[3] *E.g. Vale Royal*, pp. 157–8, an episcopal decree which goes far to explain the friction, and Wilkins's *Concilia, passim*.

bury manor all holy-days fall to the tenant's profit; but, on a St Paul's manor, they are divided between lord and tenant[1]. On Ramsey manors the custom varies again; on two, the holy-days are divided; on one, the abbot takes all the loss, but on another, the tenant must bear it all: "be it noted that, if a feast-day fall on any day when the tenants owe work, it shall not be allowed to them, but they shall work some other day instead"[2]. So, again, with the kindred difficulty of sickness; is the serf to bear this loss, or his lord? Here, again, the Ramsey monks had varying standards, consonant, doubtless, with the variations which they had inherited. On some manors, the sick peasant was quit of all work but ploughing—which he must persuade or pay someone to do in his stead—and sometimes a little other work. This immunity lasts for a year and a day: after that, he must find the work—*i.e.* he must satisfy the abbot or quit[3]. On one, he has only a fortnight's grace for illness; on another, three weeks[4]. In one other case, if he is ill enough to receive the Lord's Body (which, except at Easter, the peasant took only at the point of death) he was quit of all work for the next fort-night[5]. The widow, in nearly all cases, was quit of work for three weeks after the man's death. At Wilburton, in 1277, the monks acquitted some of their sick peasants for fifteen days only, others for none. At the husband's death, the wife was sometimes quit of work for thirty days. Eleven of the peasants had no relief for holy-days in harvest: "it is to be known, that no celebration of a feast shall hinder him"[6].

This question of Church feasts is extremely interesting; taken strictly in the later Middle Ages, it should have meant, roughly, a second Sunday per week. In the Dark Ages, when the feasts were fewer, the abbey serfs of Corbie were forbidden to work for themselves or their masters during 24 holy-days, which are carefully specified[7]. Yet in other cases, as here at Wilburton, if it were to the churchman's advantage, the serf might be compelled to break the rule of Sunday rest. Some of the Woodeaton

[1] Vinogradoff, *Villainage*, p. 296.
[2] *Cart. Rams*. R.S. 1, 302, 366, 486, 492.
[3] *Ibid*. pp. 301, 312, 337, 347, 359, 370, 384, 395, etc.
[4] *Ibid*. pp. 457, 464. Cf. *halgethdai* in *Rentalia*, p. 251.   [5] *Ibid*. p. 477.
[6] *Camb. Antiq. Soc. Report*, No. XXVII, 1887, pp. 168–171.
[7] Adalhard, p. 362. This was in 822.

tenants were bound by the monks of Eynsham "to do the carting [for the monastery] to Eynsham on Sundays, if need be"[1]. According to a later abbot of Loos, his predecessors of the fifteenth century "avaient le privilège apostolique de faire travailler les ouvriers le dimanche"[2]. The question of loss by bad weather was similar, and was similarly solved.

I deal more fully, in a later chapter, with the modern assertion that "things like eviction or the harsh treatment of tenants were practically unknown wherever the Church was landlord"[3]. Here I need only note that it is difficult to read far in monastic manor rolls without finding suggestive evidence on this head[4]; tenants lose their holdings for arrears in rent or work, or for decrepitude; and, apart from such individual cases, we have frequent indications of the general

THE PEASANT IN SUNSHINE

---

[1] *Cart. Eyn.* II, 19.
[2] De Rosny, p. 72.
[3] G. K. Chesterton, *A Short History of England*, p. 78.
[4] We have already seen the monks of Durham as rackrenters (ch. VIII, p. 86). Two cases of monastic evictions are incidentally recorded by Sée (*Bretagne*, p. 47).

policy at this or that monastery. Who that has once read *Past and Present* can forget Carlyle's, or rather Jocelin's, tale of the

THE PEASANT IN RAIN

distresses levied on old women at Bury for default in a fraction of their rent? And, before we come to Mr Leadam's statistical testimony let me record my own impression from a good many miscellaneous sources, that it is difficult to distinguish on these points between the Church landlord and the lay landlord, except so far as we may always assume that the individual cleric was probably, on the average, a kindlier man. Of Berard, abbot of Farfa, his own monk Gregory writes about 1105 A.D.: "He took every occasion to rob and prey upon very many of the more wealthy and prosperous of his villeins; and he was a destroyer of good customs"[1]. The German Cistercians evicted tenants wholesale from the Slavonian lands that were given over to them: this was so notorious that "when Pforte, in 1204, took over the village of Hemmingen which had already been colonized by Germans, the bishop of Naumberg made it one of the conditions that the peasants should be left there; they might not

[1] M.G.H. Scriptt. XI, 564.

be removed against their will and without full compensation "[1].
A witness in 1295 was certain that a particular district belonged
to the monks of Leno, because "I myself saw how the lord
[abbot] Lanfranc caused a certain shepherd's pots and pans and
movables to be carried off "[2]. It was complained of the prior
of Spalding in 1250 that sometimes, after impounding the
peasant's cattle, he kept them so long without food that they
died [3]. The abbess of Frauenchiemsee takes care to record her
right of changing a tenant who is unable to fulfil the services
demanded of his holding [4]. Cullum notes, with regard to a lease
granted by the abbot of Bury in 1491, "the exactness of payment, and the extent of the distraining power, denote a great
extent of harshness and severity "[5]. The Parlement of Paris,
in 1293, recognized the right of the abbot of Compiègne to
carry off the doors and windows of his tenants who had not paid
the *tailles* he had imposed [6]. The Ramsey monks seized the
chattels of defaulting tenants as a matter of course, even on a
considerable scale [7]. We have seen how the prior of Savigny,
about 1500 A.D., is careful to claim the right of seizing the door
of any house which refuses to contribute to his yearly mid-Lent
bonfire; and in 1484 "the venerable and religious abbess of the
convent of St Peter at Lyons" confiscated a citizen's door in
pursuance of her claim to tax his house. If the parson of the
parish church of St-André (except on St Andrew's day and eve)
presumed to ring for service before the abbey bells rang, "our
sacristan may climb the steeples of St-André and take the
tongue (to wit, the clapper) of one of the bells and keep it until
the parson shall redeem it by a fine for his transgression "[8].
The monastery of Honau near Strassburg had a number of
small tenants on the island, who paid an annual rent ranging
upwards from the halfpenny paid by a holding "so small that
it could scarce contain six or ten trees" to an ordinary holding
which paid $1\frac{1}{2}d.$, and special holdings which paid in proportion.
The convent custumal specifies that a tenant who is a year in
arrears with this rent may be distrained even without further

---

[1] Winter, II, 178–181.
[2] Zaccaria, p. 158.
[3] Neilson, p. xxv.
[4] Peetz, p. 222; *Weisthümer*, III, 675.
[5] p. 197.
[6] Desmaze, p. 41.
[7] Page, p. 65, cf. p. 97.
[8] *Guigne*, pp. 424, 425.

formalities of law, and the monks may "dispose of his goods, as of all his other goods, at their will, without contradiction from any man, as hath ever been kept unto the present day." It quotes two instances, one of which runs: "the goods of that Kleinlauwel the Elder, which were at last sold by the lords [*i.e.* the monks] to another, viz. to his son Kleinlauwel the younger"[1]. If a tenant of the monks of St Ulrich (Bavaria) had not paid his rent on the day on which it was due, the abbot's bailiff was to eat and drink at his expense in the village inn until the Wednesday following; then, if the second summons proved ineffectual, for another week; after this, the tenant was sold up to pay for his rent *plus* the tavern bills[2]. And, finally, the following petition to the Star Chamber is too important to be abbreviated:

To...Thomas...Archbishop of Yorke and Chaunceler of England. Humbly complayneth your poor bedewoman Margery Clerke within the countie of Cheshire, that, whereas her late husbond and his auncestours for longe yeres peasibly occupied a tenement in the parishe of St Werburge in Westchester, according to the auncyent custome in that countre used, and a yearly rent of 40*s.*, oon John, late abbot, withowght any maner of forfett or other cause resonable, abowght the 8th yere [1516/1517] of the now kyng, sent dyvers his servantes to the said tenement and put owght of the same your oratrix, her late husbond and fyve smale childerne in the coldest tyme of wynter, soo that they were compellyd of necessite to goo to their parish churche, and there contynewed by the space of three wekys for lak of a howse to lye in, untill the abbot of his farther malyce commaunded the vycare of the churche to put them owght of the same[3]. The said servantes also seized all the farme stocke,

---

[1] See Schillern's note to Jacob v. Königshofen (Strassburg, 1698), p. 1154.
[2] Baumann, II, 648, from a customal of 1387. For a similar custom in fifteenth-century Zürich, though in a different connexion, see Reber, p. 325.
[3] We may find repeated traces of an ancient tradition that the otherwise homeless may claim temporary shelter in the church porch. The Christian name Peregrine, hereditary in one English family, is said to have come from an ancestor who was born in the porch during the troubled days of the Civil Wars. And here is a case from Grantchester, near Cambridge, in about 1830: "There seems to have been a curious notion prevalent here some years ago, which was that if any of the parishioners from any cause had no home, they could take up their residence in the Church porch, in which case the parish authorities were bound to find them a house. About forty years ago a man with his wife and family adopted this plan, and on the congregation going to Church on Sunday morning they found the porch thus occupied, a curtain being hung across the entrance" (S. P. Widnall, *A History of Grantchester*, 1875, p. 91).

and all the household stuffe they founde within the said howse they cast out at the dores into a great pond of water, so that it was utterly destroyed; by reson of which troubyll her said husbond for penceffnes and thowght fell into such disease and sekenes that he schortly departyd this world. Your oratrix hath divers times heretofore compleyned unto your highnes, and your grace hath directed several commyssions to serten gentylmen to examine heer and determyne according to the tenour of their commyssions, neverthelesse the said abbot by his senestre labour hath delayed and prolonged tyme, so that the said commyssioners in no wyse cowde make any ende. And now of late the said abbot hath resynyd his abbathey, and another is theer ellect, to whom your oratrix hath made peticyon, but he refuseth redress, except he be compellyd thereunto by order of the kynges lawe, which your bedewoman is nott of abylitie nor power to persue ayenst hym, she being a poore woman and he a gret lorde in thoos parties in honor and dygnyte. Wherefore [etc., etc.][1].

This is only a single case, and we have here only one side of it; but, when we remember how difficult it must have been for any really poor person to approach the Star Chamber, and how hopeless such an appeal would have been unless there had been a very strong *prima facie* case, at the least, we must allow considerable significance even to this stray record of one family's grievance.

We must remember, too, that the monk had not only money enough to employ the best lawyers and to bring the accustomed presents to judges, but that he was often a lawyer himself, in spite of papal and conciliar prohibitions[2]. He would have been more than human if he had always resisted the enormous advantage which this gave in medieval society.

It seems clear that, during the thirteenth century, the bishop of Ely increased the services of some of his Cambridgeshire tenants. He exacted one more day's work in the week....The Placitorum Abbreviatio for the first 20 years of Ed. I's reign gives at least 20 actions of this character [in which the tenants believed and sought to prove that their lords had broken the custom and imposed new burdens upon them], in ten of which the defendant was a religious house[3].

Miss Levett, again, in the St Albans halmote registers, finds some slight reason to suppose that the tenants were right in

---

[1] *Star Chamber Lancs.* I, 74.
[2] *E.g.* Westlake, *Last Days*, pp. 51, 87.
[3] Pollock and Maitland, 2nd ed. I, 378 notes.

thinking that the abbots had gained ground on them in the century before the Black Death.

The Star Chamber records are a mine of information as to the oppression of poor and middling folk by great local lords. In them, Mr Leadam has found only one case of active sympathy displayed in favour of the peasants by an eminent ecclesiastic. This was the abbot of Croxston in 1530; but, as Mr Leadam points out, he was at the same time fighting his own battle: he "had, it must be added, a like grievance of his own." Of another case, in 1509, Leadam writes: "The whole circumstances of the case, assuming [the prior's] complaints against the defendant to be true, point to dislike on the part of the agricultural classes to the monastic landlords"[1].

The forgoing evidence is obviously fragmentary; for I can make no pretence to an exhaustive study of the subject. But I doubt whether a stronger body of evidence could be produced for evictions by lay lords, under similar circumstances, during the Middle Ages. In England, as elsewhere, men often appealed from the Church to royal or princely protection. Mr Leadam is able to point out "the assurance felt by the labouring classes, [between 1494 and 1538], that the policy of the Tudor government was favourable to their interests" in their struggle against enclosing landlords[2]. In the actual documents of the time we find the medieval churchman to have acted in general as his social position tempted him to act; there was doubtless a good deal of individual kindliness, but the main determining motive was class-solidarity and conservatism. We may say of early sixteenth century England what Hanotaux says of France a century later: "L'immensité des domaines ecclésiastiques n'en compte pas moins, avec la lourdeur des impôts royaux, et avec les dernières vexations seigneuriales, parmi les causes qui contribuent le plus à arrêter le progrès tenace du paysan français"[3].

[1] *Star Chamber* (S.S.), ii, lx, xciii.
[2] *Ibid*. lix, cf. xcii.
[3] *La France en* 1614, ed. Nelson, p. 409.

CHAPTER XVII

CLEARINGS AND ENCLOSURES

THIS brings us to an extremely important part of our subject. How much did the medieval peasant owe to the Churchman, and especially to the monk, as setting him an example of honest work, creating for him an improved agriculture; and reserving for the actual labourer his fair share in the lands won from the waste?

Manual labour is insisted upon in St Benedict's Rule. The Augustinians were no less definitely pledged here than the Benedictines, since St Augustine wrote a treatise on manual work for his disciples. The reformed Benedictines and Augustinian canons, of whom the best known are Cistercians and Praemonstratensians, made the return to labour one of the pivots of their reforms. The Franciscans sometimes began even as hewers of wood and drawers of water; they did their own housework and kitchen-work, just as the early monks had done. All this, as has been constantly pointed out, was very valuable in a society which, like medieval feudalism, still retained a great deal of the barbarian's contempt for steady work. Nobody doubts that the monk, in his earlier missionary stage, worked with his own hands, adding practical experience to superior intelligence, and that this is one of his most serious contributions to civilization. But, in post-Conquest England, and in the Europe of that time, only a very small fraction of the monastic population had remained at that missionary stage, or brought themselves back to that stage. We should all see the absurdity of applying to the modern American, without further enquiry, a great many of the activities and ideas which were, beyond all doubt, characteristic of the earliest American settlers. Yet it is scarcely less anachronistic to suppose that we may safely think off-hand of the Tudor monks, or even of St Anselm's monks, in terms of St Augustine's and St Boniface's pioneers. I hope to deal more fully with the question of monastic labour in the second volume of *Five Centuries of Religion*; here I can give only the briefest summary.

Even for the first pioneer ages, we must not exaggerate the

field-labour of the monks. Mabillon himself notes this. Non-nosus, abbot of Soracte in the sixth century, did not approve of the monks working outside their monastery even for charity's sake, "lest, in leaving their monastic precincts, they should suffer the loss of their souls"[1].

Guibert of Nogent speaks of the general neglect of labour as one main cause of monastic decay about 1050 A.D.[2] Indeed, by that time the monks contended, with some colour of justice, that even St Benedict's favourite pupil, St Maur, had made no attempt to keep up a general practice of field-labour[3]. Rupert, abbot of Deutz, in about 1100, notes expressly that there were two parties in the Order, "one, which puts manual work first according to the ordinance of St Benedict's Rule, and contends that apostolic perfection is in the labour of our hands; the other, which asserts it to be preferable to serve the altar and live by the altar." Rupert is of this latter side, and sums up: "Concerning that manual work whereby more especially men earn their livelihood, such as ploughing and sowing and felling of trees, it is plain that this is not commanded by St Benedict, but only permitted, or a counsel of patience." Moreover (contends Rupert) such regular fieldwork would be contrary to the spirit of the Rule, which prescribes that no monk shall stray beyond the precincts, "since that is altogether inexpedient for their souls" (ch. LXVI). Therefore the highest choice, the choice of Mary as opposed to Martha, is to avoid the demon of idleness by "taking a holy sabbath-rest [in contemplation] with the Word of God"[4]. A little later, Peter the Venerable uses similar arguments for his thesis that it is "indecent and impossible" for monks to earn their own livelihood by manual labour[5]. And, coming down to centuries of fuller documentary evidence and greater significance for modern social history, we

---

[1] AA.SS.O.S.B. vol. I, introd. § 113, and p. 246, from St Gregory's *Dialogue*, lib. I, c. 7.

[2] P.L. vol. 156, col. 850.

[3] Rupert of Deutz (P.L. vol. 170, col. 515) and Peter the Venerable (*ibid.* vol. 189, col. 145).

[4] "Optimum autem et otiositatem effugere, et nihilominus cum verbo Dei sancto otio sabbatizare" (P.L. vol. 170, col. 515); the other quotations are from cols. 511–14.

[5] P.L. vol. 189, cols. 144 ff. Peter certainly, and Rupert probably, is arguing against the Cistercians, who at first made a point of returning to the primitive Benedictine prescription.

may say roughly that, in England, there is scarcely any trace of serious manual labour on the monks' part after 1300 A.D. Indeed, there is very little between the Conquest and that date, except for a minority of reformed houses in a single generation of fervour—say, from 1130 to 1160. Abroad, apart from this generation of Cistercian and Praemonstratensian reform, and of a small minority of houses in Italy, Germany and France during the fifteenth century, the story is very much the same. Moreover, even in these reforms, it is difficult to trace any reality of labour beyond a single generation. All through this generalization we must except the Carthusians; but these were very few, and they seldom worked outside their own cells and gardens, which were absolutely closed to the public; their influence in this field, therefore, was almost negligible.

Again, it is noticeable that Charles the Great, a monarch of restless activity in all things that concerned the improvement of fields and roads and bridges and economic conditions generally, never really encouraged monasticism[1]. With all his generosity, he founded no single monastery, nor were more than a score founded in all Germany during his forty-three years of reign. It never occurred to him to use the monks as instruments of agricultural improvement; yet, as we shall presently see, he definitely encouraged the real backwoodsman. We do indeed get traces of labour at St Benedict's own abbey of Monte Cassino in 951, when Abbot Aligerno granted "to the many monks of the monastery who are old and infirm and cannot labour with their hands," the revenues of a manor, a vineyard and five mills for their sustentation[2]. But, at the beginning of the twelfth century, labour had practically ceased in the great and advanced Order of Cluny; and Peter the Venerable actually apologizes to his brethren for "restoring, at least to some extent, the ancient and holy practice of manual work"[3]. The Praemonstratensian Abbot Philippe de Harvengt, about 1170, gives us a clear conception of monastic evolution in this field[4]. He

---

[1] See Sommerlad, II, 145 ff.
[2] Tosti, I, 229. On the other hand, the abbot's autograph signature, which Tosti gives in facsimile, and the barbarous Latin of the whole document, do not speak well for literary culture at one of the greatest abbeys in Europe.
[3] P.L. vol. 189, cols. 1036-7.
[4] *De Continentia Clericorum* (app. 81–86) (P.L. vol. 203, cols. 774 ff.).

realizes how few of the early monks had been priests, and how rare and private their Masses had been, so that a convent might sometimes be found without a single celebrant; whereas, "in our own day, this licence [from the hierarchy to celebrate public Masses] hath so grown that you may scarce find, I say not only abbots, but even monks, who are not in Holy Orders." With this has gone the parallel evolution that "monks, contrary to their early Rule, are no longer supported by the work of their own hands." For this he finds several reasons. The demerits and insufficiency of the secular clergy have rightly diverted endowments from them to the monks. Monks, again, live no longer in wildernesses only, but in great centres of population, where they are often joined by converts of tenderer upbringing and weaker bodies than the peasants, so that "they have been quite unable to keep the ancient rigour; wherefore, slackening the rein...they have abandoned that manual labour of their forefathers, and have preferred to dwell in cloisters, hiding more remissly under the shadow of quiet and ease"; and therefore the hierarchy has allowed them to appropriate ecclesiastical revenues upon which they may live and "be more freely occupied in godly reading." This has often resulted, however, in scramble for wealth and a forgetfulness of the monk's essential poverty. Worse still, it leads on to sinful pride: "If the monks deem themselves more worthy than the secular clergy because, as aforesaid, they find themselves much richer—their churches more abundantly adorned with gold, gems and silk, their tables heaped with many and various dishes, and their temporal prosperity advancing in other ways which it would be tedious and superfluous to recount—yet doubtless this feeling meriteth reprobation, since worth should never be reckoned by the measure of mere wealth."

But still, here and there at least, some monks evidently went out sometimes into the fields; for presently we find bishops forbidding this, as being a mere pretence for a picnic or for worse indiscipline[1]. Then the friar in his turn, after his first

---

[1] Archbishop Gray of York in 1250 (*Reg. Giffard*, Surtees Soc. p. 205); Archbishop Peckham of Canterbury in 1281: the Glastonbury monks are using this as "a matter of wandering abroad; and, thus mixing with the gentiles, some of the frailer monks have learned the works of the gentiles" (*Epp.* R.S. p. 259).

generation of extraordinary enthusiasm, claimed to change manual into mental work for reasons not only of physical comfort but also of ecclesiastical dignity. To Salimbene, who had been born in the life-time of St Francis, it seemed simply preposterous that a priest-friar should be obliged to take his turn at kitchen-work in the convent with those brethren who were not in Holy Orders[1]. Gower, a century later, tells us that the friar was not one of those who earned his place in heaven by labouring like Adam; yet, in these times of scarcity of labour, it would be good for society if he would turn to the plough[2]. About the same time, in 1390, the ravages of the Hundred Years' War had so impoverished the sixteen monks who still remained at the great abbey of La Trappe that the bishop pleads they are actually earning their bread by the labours of their hands, and the pope relieves them by remitting the yearly tribute they owe him[3]. Then comes the period of anti-Lollard apologetics, when the monks and their friends, in rebutting the charge of idleness, plead their psalms and Masses and studies, but never, I believe, their manual labour. John Hus is in fact merely putting into a single sentence the gist of a whole chapter in some anti-Lollard apologetic when he writes: "[Priests and monks] say, openly, without any beating about the bush, 'If we cared to do hard work, then we should be peasants or that sort of folk, and not priests'"[4]. Surviving monastic account-rolls show that the monks not only did none of their own kitchen and house-work, but that there were often more servants than brethren in the house; the monks did not even shave themselves or mow their own cloister-garth or do their own garden-work. Finally, there was a good deal written on this subject just before the Reformation, orthodox monks arguing with their brother-monks and attempting, quite vainly, to bring the

---

[1] M.G.H. Scriptt. XXXII, 102. Story, describing the gardening operations of the Franciscans in Rome under Pius IX, notes that these were mostly concerned with superintending the actual work done by hired servants (*Roba di Roma*, 1864, p. 40).

[2] *Vox Clamantis*, lib. III, c. xx, l. 937; 955 ff.

[3] Gaillardin, I, 39: similar cases in Denifle, *Désolation des Eglises*, etc. pp. 425, 454, 585.

[4] *Johannis Hus et Hieronymi Pragensis Historia & Monumenta*, Nürnberg, 1558, fol. 385 a.

Order back to the practice of manual labour[1]. To realize the true state of things, we must mark how the problem presented itself to the learned Benedictine Haeftenus, writing in 1644. He has a whole chapter of discussion: "Whether it be lawful for a monk to work with his hands?" He decides, of course, that it is; but he then devotes seven folio pages to proving that, however lawful, it is not necessary. It was bidden in early days, because many monks were laymen, and said no Masses, or, again, because "they were compelled to labour by their lack of lands and possessions, and because they could not beg alms for so great a multitude." As to the "peculiar difficulty" that labour is expressly enjoined by the Benedictine Rule, this Haeftenus meets in the same way: Benedict prescribed it for two reasons, poverty and the avoidance of idleness: but nowadays monks are no longer poor; and, "the occasion of idleness is generally removed if their time be transferred to theological studies, writing, and commenting on the Holy Scriptures." True, St Benedict wrote: "Then are they truly monks, if they live by the labours of their hands, as our fathers and the apostles did"; but we know from Peter the Venerable that Benedict's favourite disciple, St Maur, "had already exchanged manual labour for spiritual exercises"[2]. So far Haeftenus.

When, therefore, we speak of monastic services to agriculture, it must always be with this very considerable reservation. True, the lay-brethren, of whom the twelfth century monastic reformers had many, and other monasteries sometimes a few, spent their lives mainly in manual work[3]. But these were not monks in the fullest sense of the word; they ate and drank and slept apart; even in church a screen was set up between them and the choir-monks; the Order of Grammont, very early in its existence, was almost wrecked by a rebellion of its lay-brethren, and the lay-brother system was practically dead by 1400 even among the Cistercians and Praemonstratensians. The

[1] See bk II, chs. 1–3 of Guido Iuvenalis, *Reformationis Monastice Vindicie* (Paris, 1503); most of this is fully translated in the 11th of my *Medieval Studies*, pp. 12–13.

[2] *Disquis. Monast.* pp. 836–44.

[3] Very significant are the footnotes in a cautious and learned writer like Lamprecht. He gives four quotations only, from 506 A.D., from 1035, from about 1250 (Cistercians) and from 1570, where it is not the twelve nuns themselves who work, but their three lay-sisters (1, 482).

clearings and drainings, the agricultural improvements, in so far as they are attributable to monks at all, are due almost entirely to the monastic brain and purse which set the peasant's arm to work. It may be that, in the Dark Ages, much was owing to monasteries which preserved and studied Columella and the classical writers on agriculture; but I have seen no really cogent proof of this; the facts as we know them seem to indicate very fitful monastic influence here as on many other points; the peasantry who had learnt themselves under imperial Rome might well have passed down, from father to son, some such agriculture as we find in the ninth century when our clear documentary evidence begins, and again in the thirteenth, when it is abundant. In the later Middle Ages, again, monastic conservatism seems at least to have counterbalanced other monastic virtues, and there is no evidence that the monks farmed better than layfolk[1]. "Would you like to know the modern rules for agriculture in Rome, read the *Georgics*; there is so little to alter, that it is not worth mentioning"[2]. In the Low Countries, where roots and the rotation of crops were known as early as the fourteenth century, there is far more reason to attribute this to the superior freedom of the peasants, and the economic necessities of the great towns which they fed, than to any direct monastic influence. The historian of the Belgian abbey of Liessies implies that the agricultural improvements of the later twelfth century came not from the monks, but from the peasants' own experience and industry[3]. With regard to one great English monastery, Mr H. W. Saunders permits me to print here the result of his and Mr W. Hudson's patient researches. The yet unprinted cellarers' rolls of Norwich have enabled them to compare the actual yield of these Norfolk farms, in the hands of the monks and their

[1] See, for instance, Savine, pp. 148, 190, where the evidence, such as it is, seems rather to point the other way. For the slow development of agriculture in medieval Germany generally, see Lamprecht, *Wirth*. 1, 463. For England, compare W. Cunningham, *Industry and Commerce*, etc. 5th ed. 1, 553: "The thirteenth century suggestions [as to tillage] seem to have been accepted as a sufficient guide in 1558." The facts revealed by the records of the Cluniac house of Romainmotier certainly indicate rather backward cultivation at the end of the Middle Ages (Charrière, pp. 43, 70, 132). Compare also the quotations I give in appendix 7.

[2] W. W. Story, *Roba di Roma*, 3rd ed. p. 56. For other parts of Italy, see Janet Ross and Lina Duff-Gordon *passim*.

[3] Jacquin, pp. 351, 394.

tenants, with what Walter of Henley in the same century calculated as a proper crop. Mr Saunders has taken all the records together, during a period of three years for each, round and about 1300. In the lowest case, the documents enable him to generalize from 34 cases; in the highest, from 52. The wheat is normal; 19 of the cases yielded more than Walter's average, and 17 less; but, of these 17, two yielded less than the half of what they should have done. Oats come next; seven were on the right side, but 36 were under, and four of these yielded less than half. In peas and beans, seven were on the right side, and 45 under, 30 of which were less than half. Rye shows all 45 cases below the average, and 18 less than half. Barley shows 45 again under, and 35 less than half[1]. The total yields are thus very decidedly under Walter of Henley's averages. It may well be that Walter exaggerates; his calculations are, indeed, generally taken as our best information for that time, but partly, I think, because they are so clear-cut and easy to work with; yet, with all reasonable allowance, Mr Saunders's figures are very significant.

The peasants not only saw that the monk had ceased to labour, but they also knew the monk as an "outrider," a sportsman, and perhaps one who rode over their own crops. Chaucer's picture might seem a caricature, yet Gower's contemporary satire on the sporting parish parson is even more bitter. This man feeds his dogs, but not the poor; his horse is fat and his knowledge thin; he hunts the fox, yet in himself he is fox-like, devouring the village girls as Reynard ravages the hen-roosts[2]. And the hunting monk appears frequently enough in the most unexceptionable business documents. Take, for instance, this statute of Henry, the reforming abbot of Cluny, legislating about 1310 A.D. for all that great Order (*Bibl. Clun.* col. 1567 a):

Item, seeing that it is unbecoming for God's soldiers to be entangled in worldly business, and desiring that the brethren of our Order

---

[1] These and many other statistics, compiled from nearly 500 rolls, will appear, it is hoped, in a monograph by Mr Saunders on monastic economy at the priory of Norwich. Mr P. S. Godman has carefully analyzed the yields of crops on the lay manor of Wiston in Sussex, and finds that these also fall below Walter of Henley's estimates (*Sussex Arch. Coll.* vol. LIV, 1911).

[2] *Vox Clamantis*, lib. III, c. xviii, ll. 1491 ff.

should turn away altogether from the vanities of this world, to be fervent in divine and spiritual works, therefore we do more strictly forbid that any of our Order, of whatever rank or condition he be, should have or keep hawks, falcons, or other birds of chase, or hunting dogs; yet from this we except those who, in their particular monasteries, have the right, custom and usage of hunting. In these cases, we permit them to have hunting-dogs, enjoining that they should keep within the bounds of moderation and timely decency in this exercise of theirs.

A later Cluniac code (1458 A.D.) repeats this with a most significant addition: "Neither dogs nor puppies, which defile the monasteries, and oftentimes trouble the service of God by their barking, and sometimes tear the church books" (*ibid.* col. 1604 c). Even Archbishop Winchelsey's reforming articles, in 1301, allowed twelve hunting-dogs to the abbot of Gloucester (*Cart. Gloucs.* I, lxxxvi).

At a manor belonging to Vale Royal, in the early fourteenth century, one of the bondfolk's services was to feed the abbot's puppies; and rent was sometimes paid in the form of sparrow-hawks and bows and arrows[1]. On four, at least, of the St-Gall manors, when the abbot appeared with his two greyhounds and his hawk, the peasants were bound to find a loaf for the hounds and a hen for the bird to eat[2]. The abbot of Feniers in Auvergne "obligea ses paysans de Condat de lui amener des chiens pour la chasse toutes les fois qu'il voudrait s'y livrer"[3]. The monks of Kiemsee, in mid-fourteenth century, grew restive when their abbot forbade their hunting and dancing[4]. Perhaps the strongest complaints against monastic hunters come to us on the verge of the Reformation from the Franciscan Thomas Murner, who became one of Luther's busiest adversaries. There are monasteries, he says, in which the hunting-dogs outnumber the monks[5]. Hunting monks, thinks Archbishop Peckham, defraud the founders of their abbeys, who endowed them not to enjoy themselves as worldlings but to pray and sing Masses[6]. Cloisterers, it is true, were formally forbidden by canon law to

---

[1] *Ledger*, pp. 110, 120, 125.

[2] v. Arx, I, 444; document of 1441; similar evidence for other monasteries might easily be supplied.

[3] Branche, p. 415.   [4] Peetz, p. 119.

[5] Scheible, p. 884; for full translation see appendix 29.

[6] *Epp.* R.S. p. 343.

hunt[1]; yet later visitations of monasteries give even more frequent evidence of this practice, perhaps, than in earlier days; and, at the Dissolution, the peasant knew that he had lost not a fellow-labourer in the fields, but a sort of squire[2].

The point on which monastic claims—or rather, modern claims on behalf of the medieval monks—seem most justified by facts or strong probabilities, is that of having been the main transmitters of plants and fruit-trees. There was much intercourse, and therefore material and intellectual interchange, between abbey and abbey; a monk could easily carry seeds and cuttings from one to the other; there is therefore much anterior probability in favour of the tradition that the Warden pear came from Burgundy, and was popularized in England by the monks of Warden in Bedfordshire. So, again (though Dubois, as usual, gives no authority but a seventeenth-century enco-miast) there is no anterior reason to doubt his story of the Reinette Guise apple, transported from Morimond in Burgundy to the daughter-house of Altencamp in Rhineland, and thence from abbey to abbey in Thuringia, Saxony, Silesia and Poland[3]. Yet, even in this field, the earliest and most picturesque story comes to us from a lay sovereign. Duke Richard I of Normandy (who died in 996) once outrode his suite in pursuit of a heron and was lost at nightfall in the forest. Here, in a glade, he found an apple-tree laden with fruit; he ate heartily, found his way out of the forest at last and, having returned to his palace, showed some of the apples, to the admiration of all his courtiers. They went in search of the tree, which he had done his best to mark; but it could not be found. The duke planted the pips of the apples which he had brought with him, and these

---

[1] *Clement*, lib. III, tit. x, c. 1.

[2] The Norwich visitations give frequent indications of monks hunting during the last generation of English monasticism; see pp. 21, 46, 121, 147, 213, 264, 279, 280, 281, 283. See farther in appendix 29.

[3] p. 230. Dubois gives perhaps the fullest extant description of monastic benefits to agriculture (pp. 216–50); but even Winter, who draws a good deal from this source, is moved to complain that the reader never knows when Dubois writes from documents, and when from his own imagination. In the whole of his chapter XXIV he gives only fourteen references, of which one is to a medieval document, while five are to the seventeenth century *Annales Cisterciences*, and the rest to quite modern works, or to modern facts which have no proved relation to the old. A great deal of these two chapters is certainly drawn from imagination, since it conflicts with known facts.

produced the so-called Pomme-Richard, which was famous in the twelfth and thirteenth centuries[1].

We are on far safer documentary ground when we speak of monastic clearings and drainage. In the early times of Benedictinism, and again in the first days of eleventh and twelfth century reforms, a great deal of forest, heath, and swamp was given to the monks, who improved a considerable fraction into arable or pasture. Boniface and his contemporaries were often real backwoodsmen; so were the Cistercian lay brethren, and occasionally even choir-monks. But, even here, enthusiasts have picked out and presented as typical a few cases which, for the most part, are distinctly presented by the contemporary authors as instances of exceptional sanctity; and Montalembert's claims break down under examination of his too scanty references.

Kings and lay princes, to begin with, set themselves to this work side by side with, and in some cases probably even before, the monks. One of Charles the Great's decrees bids his ministers "whenever they find capable men, give them woodland to clear"[2]. In England, King Ine set himself, at the end of the seventh century, to encourage pioneer backwoodsmen by the same systematic regulations and rewards as we find in early times on the great monastic estates of Italy[3]. Romney Marsh, again, was mainly drained by the Romans; and, though the post-Conquest archbishops of Canterbury added to this when they inherited the district, yet even then some of this seems to have been done by laymen, and no attempt has been made to show that the Canterbury monks were in any way concerned[4].

---

[1] Delisle, p. 498, from the trouvère Benoît de St-More. Medieval customals, while granting certain forest rights to the peasants, sometimes reserved the wild apples, pears and plums to the lord. It is noticeable that Charles the Great commanded his gardeners to keep a greater variety of herbs than we find in Jean de Garlande's twelfth century list, and that the mulberry is among Charles's fruits, but not among Jean's (Delisle, pp. 489, 510). A guide-book tradition ascribes to him the first vineyards of Rüdesheim; he noticed, from his palace of Oberingelheim, how the snow melted first in that sunny corner, and sent his peasants to turn the forest into vineyards.

[2] *Capit. Aquisgran*, c. 19; cf. *Cap. de Villis*, c. 36. Compare the implications of such statistics as Dr J. H. Round gives for Essex forest-clearings between 1066 and 1088 (*V.C.H. Essex*, I, 377–8).

[3] Professor Vinogradoff in *Cong. Internat.* IX, 1904, 397.

[4] M. Burrows, *Cinque Ports*, pp. 11–17.

Mr H. G. Richardson has supplied me with several cases of lay drainage: a Sussex marsh in 1260; Whitefleet Marsh near Rye about 1300; two thirteenth century cases, again, in which disputes occur concerning the "lex de mariscis," which prove the existence of a regular customary law on this subject, and in which "there is nothing to show that the churchmen took any more prominent part in draining than laymen." The only exclusively clerical case he has met with in the Record Office is "one of 1206 which shows the monks of Revesby reclaiming land in Lincolnshire, presumably for themselves"[1]. A letter of Alexander III to the bishop of Worcester in 1179 distinctly implies that considerable portions, at least, of the clearings done on lands of that See had been by pioneer peasants[2].

In Italy, the vast improvements consequent upon the canalization of the Po were mainly, if not exclusively, civic. The earlier clearings of forests seem also to have been done mainly by peasant pioneers, to whom landlords gave terms which made the process profitable to both parties. As early as the beginning of the sixth century, the government decreed that any reclaimer of waste lands should enjoy them not only in full property, but free from land-tax[3]. When, in the ninth century, ecclesiastics were in possession of enormous estates, they encouraged pioneers by terms less liberal, naturally, than those of 500 A.D., yet still remunerative; they, like lay lords, generally allowed half the lands, or half the produce, to the reclaimer[4]. Sometimes the churchman offers better terms, sometimes the lay lord; on the whole, Caggese's cases seem to show the latter as rather more liberal. From the year 1106, he quotes a most significant document:

Certain labourers, with a priest at their head, came before the archbishop of Bremen and asked him for the grant, under usual forms

---

[1] Compare also the articles on "The Drainage of the Great Level" in *Fenland Notes and Queries*, v (1901–3), 33 ff. Though the author stresses the work of the monks, the actual evidence he gives seems to imply that this was fitful, to say the least. Deeping Fen seems to have been drained by a lay lord, and the neighbouring villages followed his example. The main drainage schemes were carried out by royal commissioners, with one great exception—Morton's Dyke, made in 1478 by the future cardinal, then bishop of Ely.

[2] Hardouin, *Concilia*, xxvii (1644), 657.

[3] Caggese, I, 16.   [4] *Ibid*. 157 ff.

of precarial tenure, of a great tract of hitherto untilled marshland, "not needed by the dwellers in those parts." He accedes to their request; the ground is divided into cottage-holdings and assigned to them at a relatively low rent, considering its untilled condition. And now comes the most important part of the deed; these precarial tenants are allowed to "settle all dissensions" among themselves... and, further, they may build churches in this reclaimed district, so long as they endow each church with a piece of glebe-land[1].

Italian indications, according to Caggese, point to similar processes in that country; clearings, he concludes, were conditioned mainly by economic causes behind which it is not necessary to seek for any ecclesiastical policy (II, 217). Davidsohn had previously printed evidence in the same direction for the frequency of clearings by small people[2]. Salvioli, again, points out how much was done in this way by the Italian towns, which vied with lay and ecclesiastical lords in sending immigrant families into waste places, thus founding new communities whose very names testify to their origin—Villanuova, Villafranca, Borghetto, Castelfranco, Casale, Casalino, Casalmaggiore, Castelnuovo, Castiglione, etc. He gives as many concrete examples of this, I think, as could be furnished within the same limits of time and place for similar monastic activities[3].

In Normandy, a great deal was certainly done by secular lords. The Pays de Bray, in the north of that province, which is now so fertile, seems to have been drained mainly by governmental commissions between 1480 and 1520[4]. Delisle's evidence seems to show, on the whole, more reclamation of land by laymen than by monks, the most prominent among the latter being those of Mont St-Michel, whose geographical position especially favoured their policy[5]. The great Norman abbey of Troarn was founded in a district almost as marshy as Croyland: many pages are devoted to its economic management in R. N. Sauvage's exhaustive monograph; yet it is difficult to trace here any regular and consistent policy of drainage. In the fifteenth

---

[1] Caggese, I, 252, from Inama-Sternegg, *Deut. Wirt.* II, 12–13. For Caggese's further evidence in the same direction see I, 284; II, 216 ff.

[2] *Gesch. v. Florenz*, I, 136 and *Forschungen*, I, 36.

[3] *Storia Econom.* pp. 193–5.   [4] Malicorne, pp. 24, 37, 40–1.

[5] pp. 252, 284, 292, 295–6, 392 ff., 398 ff., 403. For monastic clearings see Sackur, I, 382 and Winter, *Cist.* pp. 94, 119, 133, 146, 150–1; II, 169, 177–9, 181–2. But some of this is taken from the untrustworthy Dubois.

century, when documents are plentiful, it is evident that the
monks of France were not only not labouring themselves here,
but not systematically directing the work of clearing which was
so urgently needed after the ravage of the Hundred Years' War:
"The renewal of village life was, above all, the work of a name-
less crowd [of peasants], who set themselves bravely to work....
These melancholy circumstances permitted the peasants to
dictate their own conditions"; landlords everywhere were only
too glad to get labourers; even Italians were imported; the
pioneer who did the work demanded decent conditions of life
for his family; thus France took one great step towards the
formation of a society of peasant proprietors[1].

In Germany[2] even more was done by the great lay lords
than in France. Here the process went on far longer than in
most other countries, being continued beyond the twelfth century
reforms by the Teutonic Order. But these Teutonic knights
were only half monks from the first, and soon became practically
a Chartered Company in the modern sense, driving out or subjecting the original Slavonic peasants and filling their places
with German immigrants who drained swamps and cleared
forests. And I have come upon one clear case of pioneer
clearing even in the most civilized districts of Rhineland. In
1261, the dean and chapter of St Gereon at Cologne com-
missioned their steward at Monheim "to cause the waste land
[on that manor]...hitherto untilled, to be brought under
tillage; and let him at once grant sixty acres of the said land to
certain tillers, on condition that each acre pays an annual rent
of two pence...and, if more be tilled, then on the same conditions. And the said tillers shall possess the land by hereditary
right, even as the concession is hereby made with them "[3]. Even
in Flanders, which is generally quoted as a strong case, the monks
were neither the first nor, apparently, the greatest drainers.
The counts attracted settlers, as settlers have been attracted
to Canada in modern times, by gifts of farms: "From the end
of the eleventh century onwards, men set resolutely to work.
The count lent active support to the inhabitants; and the Cistercian abbeys, founded in this region during the course of the

---

[1] Lavisse, *Hist. de France*, IV, ii, 127.   [2] Bartels, pp. 31, 80.
[3] Lacomblet, *Urkundenbuch*, etc. II, 1846, 284.

twelfth century, brought energetic collaboration, on their side, to the undertaking"[1]. So it was in France during the next century; St Louis undertook very considerable clearings of forest land, and "chiefly made use of monks to execute his enterprize"[2]. The monks, that is, had had much experience in directing; but we cannot give all the credit to them; we must not forget the king above, who set them to work as directors, and the workmen below who actually did the job under their direction. The royal decrees of disafforestation in England gave rise to clearings on a very large scale, not only by lords but apparently by peasants also[3].

This, perhaps, may indicate the real balance of merit; the monks were very valuable and active middlemen. They were instructed and intelligent enough to see what princes had done and were doing; active enough to set the peasantry to work, and sometimes even to set them an example. But, where the documents give us details, we nearly always find the monk calling in the adventurous peasant pioneer[4]. What was done at Cluny was done in most other places:

Comme les Clunisiens ne demandaient qu'à mettre en valeur ces terres vagues, ils se sont adressés pour ce travail à des nomades, qui ont été ainsi fixés. Double avantage pour Cluny dont les terres devenaient plus riches, et pour les vagabonds qui trouvaient là l'occasion d'une vie plus régulière. Ils restaient libres, soumis seulement à une redevance fixe, mais leur intérêt était de rester[5].

---

[1] H. Pirenne, in *Soulèvement*, p. vi.   [2] Delisle, p. 392.

[3] M. Paris, *Chron. Maj.* R.S. ann. 1225 and 1245 A.D. (III, 94–5, IV, 427). Under the monks of Ramsey, John Adamson paid 5s. yearly "for the increase [of land] which he has from his own clearings"—*pro incremento quod habet de essartis suis*. This was apparently in the twelfth century (*Cart. Rames* III, 301).

[4] For further evidence see appendix 30.

[5] *Mill. Cluny*, I, 238, 243. For the way in which German monks set Dutch and German pioneers to work see Winter, pp. 119, 150–1, 177–182. Compare the twelfth century chronicler of the monastery of Muri (*Act. Mur.* p. 47): "[Our manor of] Alchuseren was at first forest, but it was cleared by the men called Wends, and made into a manor by our provost Gottfried." The instances of clearings given by Lamprecht are mostly of this kind; permissions given to squatters or pioneers by lay or ecclesiastical lords who shared in the profits; *Wirth.* I, 107, 109₂, 117, 123₂. On pp. 128–31 he describes how these acquisitions were sometimes lost again, the land reverting to waste. Boissonnade, p. 125, describes pre-monastic associations of pioneers; he deals with clearings on pp. *152*, 174, *183*, all chapter VIII, pp. *281*, *285*, 301, *393*, *399*. The pages italicized show non-monastic cases.

Flach sums up very justly in his solid and fully-documented study[1]. Pioneers got leave to settle and clear in the woodlands, and thus "the village created itself; it was really founded by the initiative of its inhabitants....Frequent as was the intervention [of religious houses], we must note that this does not deny all spontaneity to the foundation of the village by the inhabitants themselves. The religious element is often the occasional cause, rather than the voluntary and deliberate creator [of these clearings]." And he shows how, in about 1060, a forest was uprooted and a village formed by orders of the counts of Champagne.

In the more populous districts, the stage came very early at which woodland needed protection rather than destruction. Sir Hugh Beevor has proved this for parts of Norfolk[2]; and we have strong evidence in a letter from Bishop Herbert de Losinga of Norwich to one of his monastic officials. It runs:

To William the monk. Concerning the giving of Thorpe wood to the sick I gave no commands, nor do I give nor shall I give; for I appointed thee guardian, not uprooter of that wood. To the sick I will give not wood, but money, when I come to Norwich, as I did last year. Give them this answer and no other. Meanwhile do thou guard the wood of the Holy Trinity [of Norwich] even as thou wouldst wish thyself to be guarded by the Holy Trinity, and to keep my love[3].

As the modern writer on Cluny says: "Les moines protègent dans la mesure du possible les bois qu'ils possèdent, et ne les défrichent pas trop brutalement"[4].

We may now turn to the kindred subject of enclosures. Here, perhaps more than anywhere else, the monk has been unduly extolled at the layman's expense. Among the earliest scattered notices of enclosures, we find monasteries concerned. As early as 951, we find Otto I granting to Fulda that "no man shall

---

[1] *Origines de l'ancienne France*, II, 1893, 145 ff.: cf. Verriest, pp. 20, 28. Dr Fox, quite independently, from a minute study of the map of Cambridgeshire and the configuration of the ground, has concluded that most of the clearings in that county were done very early by pioneers in the fashion described by Flach.

[2] Presidential Address, in *Reports of Norf. and Norwich Naturalists Soc.* 1924.

[3] *Epistolae H. Losingae*, No. VIII (ed. Anstruther, 1846, p. 13). The letter was written between 1094 and 1120.   [4] *Mill. Cluny, l.c.*

presume to go a-hunting in the forest, wherein formerly all the inhabitants had common hunting-rights, except by leave of the abbot"[1]. In North Germany we have seen how whole villages were "laid down" by the Cistercians[2]; and, with regard to France, this was made a general accusation against them by Guiot de Provins in 1206:

The [Cistercian] priests who used to handle the Lord's Body are now sheepshearers. In many fashions they go astray; I could tell of a thousand churches where they have their granges built; everywhere they have villages and parishes and lands and houses and wastes, far more than they had of old. There are so many sheep and wethers bleating, and oxen and cows lowing, that we have wondrous fear. In the churchyards, over men's bodies, they have built their pigstyes; and their asses lie where men were wont to chant Mass....They have set their whole mind on getting all that they can see; much fear do they give to the poor folk whom they cast away from their lands; for they drive them all forth to seek their bread [elsewhere][3].

We must make liberal allowance for Guiot's satire; but he had lived four months as a novice at Clairvaux before he settled down at Cluny; and nothing that he says about the Cistercians, whether for good or bad, clashes with our other cold-blooded evidence. In England, we find monastic enclosures long before the practice had become so common as to call for government interference:

At Chesterton, for instance, near Cambridge, enclosing had reached this point [of turning off most of the farm labourers] in 1414, much

[1] Droncke, *Cod. Dip. Fuld.* p. 688, quoted by Sommerlad, II, 245.

[2] See appendix 4. A recent book, which seems very valuable, has come into my hands only just as I go to press; but I notice that the author speaks of it as "a well-known fact that the Cistercians, in districts which were already thickly populated, made room for their great grange-farms by thrusting out the peasants, so that their appearance was not infrequently marked by the disappearance of whole villages." The author here refers specially to E. O. Schulze, *Kolonisierung*, p. 140 and K. V. Inama-Sternegg, *Salland-studien*, p. 105. He goes on to suggest, however, that the wide colonizing activities of the monks would give these dispossessed peasants "abundant opportunities of procuring another, and perhaps a better, livelihood on the abbey's new clearings" (H. Muggenthaler, *Kolonisatorische u. wirtschaftliche Tätigkeit d. deutschen Zisterzienserklosters im xii. u. xiii. Jhdt.* Munich. Hugo Schmidt, 1924, p. 105). Schultze notes that the single monastery of Pforte evicted the inhabitants of at least four villages.

[3] *Les Œuvres de G. de P.* ed. John Orr, Manchester, 1915, pp. 48–9 (*Bible*, ll. 1222 ff.). The editor's note, though philologically helpful, misses the historical point.

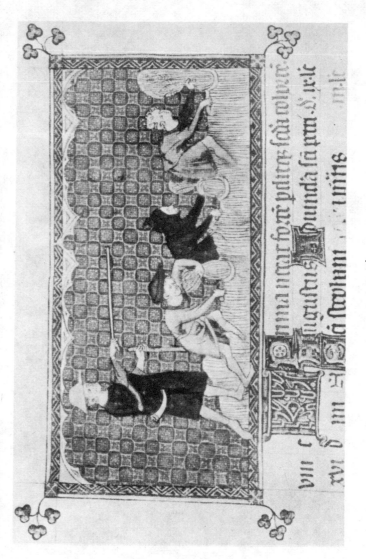

THE OVERSEER'S ROD

COTTAGE AND SKIRMISH

to the damage of the tenants, who complained that "there was great waste in the manor of Housing, that is to say, of Halles and Chambers, and of other houses of office, and none housinge left stondinge thereon but if it were a shepcote, or a berne, or a swynesty, and a few houses byside to put in be[a]stes "[1].

Then, in Tudor times, came the great temptation, leading to what has been called "the greatest revolution in English agriculture." Wool reached its maximum price between 1450 and 1550; therefore, in many cases, it became far more profitable to let the arable go to grass, and turn off three-quarters or nine-tenths of the hands employed on the farm[2]. Whole hamlets were thus destroyed sometimes; in England, as Sir Thomas More complained, sheep were eating up the men. At last, in 1489, Parliament passed an act "against pulling down of towns"— *i.e.* villages. A royal proclamation to the same effect in 1514 was evidently inoperative; for in 1515 came another act "concerning pulling down of towns." In 1517 a commission was established under Wolsey, who was determined to grapple fearlessly with the enclosures. Evidence was taken in every county as to enclosures made within the last generation; wherever they were found to be later than 1485, the authors were to be punished[3]. There is evidence that they were in fact punished about as regularly and as seriously as was possible in those days, when Sir Thomas More showed his exceptional honesty by breaking with the medieval system of judicial bribery; and the depositions before the commissioners yield evidence which, when all uncertainties are allowed for, makes it as impossible here as elsewhere to draw a hard-and-fast line between the ordinary landlord and the landlord-churchman. Mr Leadam has devoted many pages to a full analysis of the evidence; we are concerned here only with his main results.

He points out (pp. 267 ff.) that the worst monastic record is in Northamptonshire, and especially on the abbey lands of Peterborough. In Peterborough itself the abbot had enclosed

---

[1] W. J. Corbett in *Social England*, 1902, ii, 739. Compare *Reg. Malmesbury*, R.S. ii, 261–75, 284, 286, 288–9, 305, 367; also Westminster in Westlake, *Last Days*, p. 90.

[2] For most of what follows, see Leadam, *The Domesday of Inclosures*, 1897.

[3] The articles of enquiry are printed by Leadam; they were also fully transcribed for reference at the time by Bishop Bothe of Hereford (*Register*, p. 63).

much arable land for sheep-runs; in one place "he hath caused 6 cottages to be destroyed and decayed, and 24 persons are thus lost from the land" (p. 273); in another direction "12 persons have thus gone forth workless, and are seeking their work and livelihood" (p. 274); in another,

he hath enlarged his park called Meldesworth, and keepeth wild beasts now in those tenements; and by what he has taken one plough has been put down and 50 persons who were wont to dwell in the messuage and cottages aforesaid have gone forth and have been compelled to seek their dwelling elsewhere; and, what is sadder still, the aforesaid graveyard wherein the bodies of the faithful were buried and rest is now made into a pasture for wild beasts (p. 274).

They sum up that, within the vill of Peterborough alone, "eight ploughs are put down, and 100 persons who were wont to be employed in the tillage of the aforesaid lands will now be workless and are reduced to misery" (p. 275)[1]. The Hospitallers of Kirby, through their tenant John Taylor, have "converted certain lands into sheepwalks, whereby 4 ploughs are put down and withdrawn, and 30 persons who dwelt and earned their livelihood on those tillages have gone forth weeping and are reduced to worklessness and poverty" (p. 294). The prior of Daventry has destroyed a whole hamlet for the same purpose,

whereby twelve ploughs are withdrawn and laid down; moreover the parish church will go to ruin unless remedy be soon provided; for which causes 100 persons who had hitherto dwelt in the aforesaid messuages, and had been fully occupied in the tillage and care thereof until that 4th day of May of the year aforesaid, have departed in tears and have fallen into unemployment and at length, as it is supposed, have perished in utter poverty and are come thus to their last end (p. 296).

There are other cases almost as bad; and the editor writes on p. 263:

The conclusion is scarcely to be escaped that in Northants the improving ecclesiastics dealt more hardly than lay landowners with their tenants.... The abbots' inclosures, it must be said in defence, were chiefly in the north-east part of the county, in which there is still much fenland. But the rigour displayed by them, and the tone

---

[1] The editor's note, that, from the details given elsewhere, only 86 persons seem to have been evicted, seems to neglect the possibility of other details on the lost membrane. But it may be as he seems to suggest, that the summary exaggerates the actual numbers.

of the jury upon the subject, conveys to our minds one of the reasons why the dissolution of the monasteries aroused so little opposition in England.

From this worst county let us pass on to Oxfordshire. Here Leadam sums up: " Just as in the case of Berkshire and Northants, therefore, we are led to the conclusion that while the agricultural revolution was in progress in Oxfordshire the ecclesiastical landlords were more ruthless than lay landlords in their treatment of the unfortunate tillers of the soil "[1]. The more favourable evidence from other counties is very slight, and Leadam's general verdict is that ecclesiastical superiority is non-existent or non-proven.

Passing on from the matter of enclosures to compare the evidence for lay and ecclesiastical policy in other matters, Leadam gives a table of statistics for four counties for which we have the most trustworthy evidence,

which bring out the remarkable result that while the average rental values of lands in the hand of owners are considerably lower in the case of ecclesiastics than in that of lay owners, the rents of lands let by ecclesiastics are higher. It is possible that the explanation is that ecclesiastical bodies let their best land and farmed their worst, while the lay landowners more frequently engaged in farming on their own account. At any rate, the figures run counter to the tradition (probably accounted for by the rise of rents due to other causes after the Dissolution) that the religious houses were easier landlords[2].

It is true that the immediate agent, in some of these cases, was not the monk himself but the small middleman capitalist to whom he had handed over the management of his farm—in terms of modern Ireland, the "gombeen-man." But this distinction would bring no consolation to the suffering peasant, nor does it exonerate the monasteries at the bar of history. To quote Leadam again:

It must be borne in mind that the pulling down of a house and eviction of its inhabitants implied the permission of the landlord,

[1] *Domesday of Inclosures*, I, 263, 324.
[2] *L.c.* I, 65. It is relevant to quote here from *Rot. Parl.* III, 319 a (1393 A.D.). The Commons complain that monastic bondfolk get possession of lands, especially by marriage with freewomen; these lands descend to their children; then the monks finally get hold of them, and thus add to their lands in evasion of the Statute of Mortmain.

as the Returns occasionally state....What strikes us in these tables is the remarkable uniformity of results. In Bedfordshire, Leicestershire and Warwickshire the prospects of eviction were practically the same, whether the tenant held of layman or ecclesiastic. In Berkshire, Northants and Oxon he was distinctly more in danger if he was upon ecclesiastical land, in Bucks upon lay land. One result is quite clear, that, leaving out of account the question whether the evictions were the work of landlord or tenant, there was no superior security, as fancied by later generations, for the cultivators of ecclesiastical soil[1].

Moreover, these cold-blooded business records do but substantiate what we knew already, in the rough, from the most certain sources. Starkey's contemporary *Dialogue of Pole and Lupset* tells us plainly that the abbots were great offenders by enclosure; so does More's *Utopia*, in a passage of unforgettable severity: "They throw down houses, they pluck down towns, and leave nothing standing, but only the church to be made a sheep-house"[2]. The England of 1500 produced no Goldsmith; but she had her Deserted Village. Therefore, to realize the recklessness with which modern journalists are falsifying a story of which they have scarcely learned even the rudiments, let the reader contrast this unexceptionable contemporary evidence with that sentence from Cobbett which Mr Chesterton quotes as clinching the matter (*Short History of England*, p. 144): "Where monks were landlords, they did not become rackrenting landlords, and could not become absentee landlords." Even this self-taught farmer Cobbett might have realized that many monastic farms were a good deal farther distant from the monastery than Western Ireland is from London. He might then have asked himself how the landlord-monk could be other than an absentee from a large proportion of his farms. Moreover, even in Cobbett's time, all those who wanted to find the truth might have discovered that, long before the Dissolution, a large proportion of monastic farms were entirely in the hands of middlemen, the absentee monk getting his fixed rent and leaving

[1] *L.c.* 1, 48. To the instances I have elsewhere given may be added two more from documents incidentally cited by Lamprecht (*Wirth.* 1, 906; III, 7), in which monasteries insert very stringent clauses as to eviction of tenants who do not render full dues. Cf. Vinogradoff in *Cong. Internat.* IX, 1904, 397.

[2] *Utopia*, ed. Lumby (Camb. 1879), p. 32; Starkey's *Life and Letters* (E.E.T.S. extra series XXXII, pp. 96 ff.).

the middleman to deal with the peasants. Mr Tawney brings this out very plainly (p. 383); and, long before this, Mr Archbold analysed the working of a very common type of monastic demesne farm in the early sixteenth century. He remarked: "It ought, we may observe, to have had a manor house upon it, and would have had if it had been the property of a layman; this non-residence being one of the evils of the monastic system. Sometimes there was the house, but it was let, or perhaps the bailiff, a man like Stephen Stroude lived in it"[1]. We have just seen the same state of things at Chesterton, and its results for the tenants. More or less systematic rack-renting on the part of monks, and increase of the tenants' dues in proportion to his own improvements, are described by F. O. Schulte[2]. The chartulary of the Burgundian monastery of Bèze, again, shows an abbot of about 1090 taking advantage of the burning down of a village to impose harder terms of rent before he would suffer his tenants to rebuild their cottages[3]. A modern writer can scarcely make any more fatal confession of ignorance than by incautiously quoting this honest, blundering, hand-to-mouth farmer-journalist Cobbett, of a century ago, as authority for any statement of fact which lay outside the man's own immediate bucolic or political experience[4].

Yet, while insisting on facts which no man of 1150 A.D. could have denied without making himself ridiculous, let us not charge the guilt of rack-renting and eviction upon the average individual monk. This man probably bore neither more nor less responsibility than the modern citizen who may have inherited shares in some strictly-managed joint-stock company, and who keeps them still, though he knows, or might know, how the dividends are earned. He tips his own waiter generously; but he does not enquire whether this tip and this meal have been paid from the wages withheld from sweated waitresses in some restaurant which he never frequents. In matters of this kind we must not judge by bare statistics alone, any more than

[1] p. 326; cf. p. 330, where he points out that these easy methods of landlordism connoted rather a poor than a prosperous tenantry.
[2] *Kolonisierung. u. s. w.* (*Jablonowski'sche Preisschriften* Leipzig Hirzel, 1896), p. 140, n. 4.
[3] *Analecta Divionensia* (Dijon, 1875), p. 396.
[4] See appendix 4.

we can place unquestioning reliance upon such condemnations as I have quoted from St-Cher and Longland. It is true, each of these affords separately a very strong presumption; and such a presumption is very much strengthened by the width of the angle from which these two different lines of evidence start, bringing us finally to the same result. But the prelates in their hot indignation, and the statistics in their cold detachment, may easily miss one of the least ponderable factors in the problem —that of personal good-will. The monk was certainly not that incarnation of altruism and beneficence which imaginative writers have described; nor, again, did his religion teach him even theoretically to fraternize much with the peasant. But he was undoubtedly, as a rule, a man whose religion raised him above the average of that rough medieval society; and his daily habits and thoughts, even when he treated his Rule as a thing "old and somedeal strait," must have been more sympathetic to the labourer than the knight's or his vassals'. Though we may deplore the fact that idealism then, as now, commonly came in rather as an afterthought than as the first and widest basis of all conduct, yet then, as now, it was a factor which we cannot neglect without seriously falsifying the historical perspective.

CHAPTER XVIII

CHURCH ESTIMATES OF THE PEASANT

YET the churchman's personal sympathy with the peasant, in so far as we are able to judge from ecclesiastical records and writers, was at best imperfect. We find, indeed, every now and then, egalitarian utterances like that of Bishop Jonas of Orléans (821–843 A.D.). Jonas adduces a few biblical texts (Coloss. iv, 1; Gen. ix, 2; Matt. vii, 2; 1 Tim. vi, 7), and a quotation from Gregory's *Moralizations on Job*, and an eloquent passage from Augustine, who points out that the new-born noble is as indistinguishable from the new-born peasant as their bones will some day be indistinguishable in the grave. He then proceeds:

Let rich and mighty folk, taught by these sentences and those of other holy scriptures, learn that both their bondfolk and the poor are by nature their own equals. If therefore bondfolk are by nature the·equals of their lords, nay, because they are so, let not the lords think that they will suffer it with impunity that [masters,] inflamed with boiling indignation and ungovernable fury against the faults of their bondfolk, transgress against them either by scourging them with most savage stripes or by maiming them with the loss of their limbs, since they have one and the same God in heaven. Let them learn that these folk, whom they see weaklings in the world, abject in clothing and in complexion, and unequal to themselves in wealth, are by nature their peers and their equals[1].

But Guérard, who quotes this, exaggerates greatly in his comment upon it: "The dogma of an origin and a destiny common to all mortal folk, proclaimed by the powerful voice of bishops and preachers, was a continual appeal to the emancipation of the people"[2]. The passage itself is accompanied by complaints of the frequent oppressions suffered by the poor; and it would be very difficult, I think, to produce any episcopal or authoritative pronouncement from the later Middle Ages which approaches so nearly as this to modern humanitarianism; indeed, it may be suspected that Jonas himself would not have

[1] *De Inst. Laic*. l. II, c. 22 (P.L. vol. 106, p. 215).
[2] *Irminon*, I, 209.

wished his words to be taken too literally. The gist of what he says is repeated by Chaucer, who in his *Parson's Tale* (§ 760) reminds his hearers that "of such seed as churls spring, of such seed spring lords...wherefore I rede, do right so with thy churl as thou wouldest that thy lord did with thee, if thou were in his plight"[1]. Yet we know how Chaucer's aristocratic contempt for the multitude comes out in his reflections on the Griselda story:

> O stormy peple, unsad and ever untrewe!
>   Ay undiscreet and chaunging as a vane,
> Delyting ever in rumbel that is newe,...
>   Your doom is fals, your constance yvel preveth
> A ful greet fool is he that on yow leveth!

And, again, all that is most touching in that tale turns on the peasant's patience under injustice; the peasant's humility almost of a dumb animal. Griselda pleads against her husband with the helpless pathos of the sheep before his shearers:

> Naked out of my fadres hous, quod she,
>   I cam, and naked moot I turne agayn.

In *The Nun's Priest's Tale*, the real human beings are the animals; the poor widow, her daughter and the sooty cottage are just sketched in for a background.

The recognition that all were sprung from Adam was far from excluding, in the minds of the privileged class, an equally strong conviction that existing privilege is of God. The most extreme example, perhaps, of this aristocratic interpretation of the Bible story may be found in the third part of the *Book of St Albans*, ascribed to Dame Juliana Barnes, but probably translated from a French or Latin work of an earlier generation[2]. The author writes:

Insomuch that all gentleness comes of God of heaven, at heaven I will begin, where were five orders of angels, and now stand but four, in coat-armours of knowledge encrowned full high with precious stones; where[as] Lucifer with millions of angels out of

---

[1] In 1380 a bishop of Beauvais, wishing to calm a riot in Paris, cried aloud to the multitude: "Though a king were king a hundred times over, yet he reigns by the suffrage of the people" (E. Renan in *Rev. d. d. Mondes*, March 1868, p. 366).

[2] I quote from W. Blades's facsimile of the *editio princeps* of 1486, published by Eliot Stock in 1881. For the elusive Dame Juliana see the preface to that edition, and the D.N.B. The author and translator of this third part were probably men.

heaven fell unto hell and other places, and be held there in bondage, and all were created in heaven of gentle nature. A bondman or a churl will say: "All we be comen of Adam." So Lucifer with his company may say: "All we be comen of heaven." Adam, the beginning of mankind, was as a stock unsprayed and unflourished[1], and in the branches is knowledge which is rotten and which is green. Now for to divide gentlemen from churls in haste it shall be proved. There was never gentleman nor churl ordained by kind but he had father and mother. Adam and Eve had neither father nor mother; and in the sons of Adam and Eve were found both gentleman and churl. By the sons of Adam and Eve, Seth, Abel and Cain, divided was the royal blood from the ungentle. A brother to slay his brother contrary to the law, where might be more ungentleness? By that did Cain become a churl and his offspring after him, by the cursing of God and his own father Adam; and Seth was made a gentleman through his father's and mother's blessing, and of the offspring of Seth Noah came, a gentleman by kind.

The same division came after the Flood; Ham by his undutifulness earned his father's curse, with bondage for self and offspring, whereas "of the offspring of the gentleman Japhet came Abraham, Moses, Aaron and the prophets, and also the kings of the right lineage of Mary, of whom that gentleman Jesus was born, very God and man, after his manhood king of the land of Judah and of Jews, gentleman by his mother Mary, prince of coat-armour"[2]. However (the author continues on a later page) there is such a thing as "a gentleman spiritual": if a churl's son is priested, "that is a spiritual gentleman to God, and not of blood....Christ was gentleman of His Mother's behalf, and bare coat-armour of ancestors." The Evangelists and Apostles were gentlemen as descended from Judas Maccabaeus, "but that by succession of time the kindred fell to poverty after the destruction of Judas Maccabaeus, and then they fell to labours and were called no gentlemen. And the Four Doctors of Holy Church, Saints Jerome, Ambrose, Augustine and Gregory, were gentlemen of blood and of coat-armour."

It is true that Christianity did something real, if only indirectly, for the ennobling of manual labour; but the Middle Ages had here a great deal of lee-way to make up. Bishop Guillaume d'Auvergne, who by nature was no snob, writes of

[1] Without twigs or flowers.
[2] Cf. *Piers Plowman*, C. XIX, 188; XXII, 13.

servilia opera as unworthy of self-respecting men[1]. Ruskin has drawn a true contrast between the medieval noble and the Greek Laertes, pruning in his own vineyard[2]; in this matter, the baron was, as compared with the Greek or the Roman, a snob; barbarian ideas of human dignity still clung to his mind. That is why medieval writers are generally scornful of the peasant[3]; at best, they scarcely go further than to tolerate him as a necessary domestic beast.

I know of only one case where the medieval writer condescends even to quote the classic praise of rustic life[4]; and nobody, so far as I am aware, has produced any original panegyric from the vast mass of literature which was written between the wreck of the ancient world and the Reformation. To pass from such books as W. E. Heitland's *Agricola*, or Gaston Boissier's monographs, to any medieval peasant-picture except *Piers Plowman* and *Meier Helmbrecht*, is to step from the breadth and freedom of the open air into a room of little cheer. With *Piers Plowman* and *Meier Helmbrecht* we are indeed still in the open air, but we have passed from a country "of palm and orange-blossom, of olive, aloe and maize and vine" to some bleak stony upland, from which men wring a hard livelihood under inclement skies, and come out scarred by their very victories over nature. Lamprecht notes the steady depreciation of the peasant in German literature: "the rustic is best when he weeps, worst when he is merry"[5]. The very extravagance in food and drink and dress, the foolish imitation of his betters, by which he sometimes aroused the general scorn, was a very natural symptom of his

---

[1] *Opera*, Rouen, 1674, I, 354. 1. g.

[2] *Mod. Painters*, pt iv, ch. 14, § 3.

[3] Cf. Bédier, pp. 98 ff.; Vogt, 38 ff.; Sée, 555 ff.; Le Roux de Lincy, *Livre des proverbes français*, 1859, I, 78; II, 90, 104. Lamprecht, *Geschichte*, V, 86–110.

[4] Hildebert of Le Mans; see p. 238.

[5] This is repeated by Felix Hemmerlin; see appendix 31: "Rustica gens optima flens, pessima gaudens." Cf. the well-known French proverb: "Oignez vilain, il vous poindra; poignez vilain, il vous oindra"; and the similar saying quoted by v. Arx. II, 175; it was proverbial among the landowners that a certain reasonable amount of oppression is healthy for the peasant. For the Florentine citizen's scorn of the peasant, see G. Biagi, *Men and Manners of Old Florence* (London, 1909), pp. 27–8, 33. "The chroniclers [of Tuscany]," writes Davidsohn, p. 184, "considered it beneath their dignity to waste even one insignificant word on the description of the peasant's mentality and feelings."

general degradation; the white man can seldom equal the wild merriment natural to the negro at moments when he tries to forget himself. "The peasant had become the pariah of medieval society." Those words are illustrated in the bitterly satirical *Peasant Catechism* by a fifteenth century bachelor of the University of Vienna. This breathes the scorn of the clerk for the villager: a few sentences may suffice:

What part of speech is *peasant* [*rusticus*]?—A noun.—What sort of noun?—Jewish.—Wherefore?—Because he is as silly and ugly as a Jew....—What gender?—The asinine gender; for in all his deeds and works he is ever like unto an ass...the backs of all peasants are bowed like the back of an ox....The peasant grieves that the clerks make free with his wife and live on his labours.

And the *Catechism* concludes with a collect:

O God, who hast sown perpetual discord between wanton scholars [*leccatores*] and peasants, grant unto us that we may make free with their wives and daughters, and to rejoice in their death, through Antichrist, who will come riding on the ass, world without end. Amen[1].

Lamprecht, at the same time, quotes a few phrases of egalitarian rhetoric. One writer will remind us that Christ called His Father a husbandman—*Pater meus agricola* (Joh. xv, 1). Another traces even the consecrated Host to the peasant: "I till that fruit with toilsome hand, Wherefrom God springs in priestly hand"[2]. Vaguely socialistic sentiments of this kind may be found even in those scholastic philosophers who expressly justify servitude as a necessary institution since the Fall. Such, again, may be found in the poems of Gower, which, of all the sources I know, come nearest to Jonas of Orléans; but here, in Gower's case, we have some tangible evidence for the extent to which we may take him literally. Scanty and tantalizing as this is, compared with the full avowal which we might have desired, it has yet a special value to us; for Gower is typical in his faults as in his virtues, in his prejudices as in his wisdom; and he claims expressly and repeatedly to voice not so much his own private opinion as the general opinion of his place and time;

[1] P. Lehmann, *Parodistische Texte*, 1924, p. 21. From Cod. lat. 18287 of the Staatsbibliothek at Munich.
[2] *Gesch.* v, 107 ff. Other similar expressions will be found in Prévost, ch. 5 *passim* and Sée, pp. 240–1.

he claims to speak for the man in the street. In his *Vox Clamantis*, written almost immediately after that revolt of 1381 in which Gower himself had suffered much as a landlord, he writes with scant sympathy; we must discount his words very heavily indeed. But his *Mirour de l'Omme* dates from a few years before the rising—possibly only a few months before—and it shows as much sympathy with the peasants as could be expected from a man of the capitalist class. There Gower is at times even extreme in his theoretical socialism; we are all sons of Adam and Eve; not all the waters of Nile can wash away the blood that is common to the lord and the serf through that high ancestry; the serf may chance to be as comely, as strong, as intelligent as the baron (ll. 23, 389 ff.). The cry of the widow and the orphan mounts daily to heaven against their lords (ll. 23, 544; 23, 588)[1]. But, on the other hand, Gower is scandalized by the wages that labourers have taken since the Black Death, a date which marks almost as violent an economic change in the Middle Ages as the Great War marks in our own day. "The shepherd and the cowherd demand more wages now than the master-bailiff was wont to take; and, whithersoever we look, whatsoever be the work, labourers are now of such price that, when we must needs use them, where we were wont to spend two shillings we must now spend five or six." Here comes the acid test; and here Gower's sympathy fails, as even Langland's failed. The ideal labourer of *Piers Plowman* is one who would have been content to dine on yesterday's cabbage, with penny-ale and a piece of bacon; it was absurd (Langland implies) for the labourer of 1381 to demand hot fish or flesh. Gower, even before he had suffered from the Peasants' Revolt, was yet more unsympathetic; he would have set the clock still farther back; he yearned for the plain-feeding rustic of his grandfather's time; very much as, in the conservative corner of our own mind, we

---

[1] B. VI, 309; cf. D. Chadwick, *Social Life in the Days of P. Plowman*, pp. 59 ff., 81 ff. Langland does not reprobate bondage on principle; see B. XIX, 28 and XXII, 28. Compare Gower, *Vox Clamantis*, bk v, c. 10 (ed. Macaulay, p. 218). Both writers are very exactly corroborated by a presentment of a jury at Lancaster in 1350 (Putnam, p. 196*): "That William de Caburn of Lymbergh, ploughman, will not serve except by the day or the month, and will not eat salt meat but fresh; and on this account he hath departed from the township, because no man dared to hire him on those conditions in contravention of the statute of our lord the king."

ourselves regret the disappearance of the smock-frocked peasant who no longer lingers about our church porch. "Labourers of olden time," says Gower, "were not wont to eat wheaten bread; their bread was of either corn or of beans, and their drink was of the spring. Then, cheese and milk were a feast to them; rarely had they other feast than this. Their garment was of hodden grey: then was the world of such folk well ordered in its estate." Now they work little, dress and feed like their betters, and ruin stares us in the face. "Meseems that the lords [of this land] are sunk in sleep and lethargy, so that they take no heed of the madness of the common folk; thus they suffer this nettle, that is so violent in itself, to grow. He who surveyeth this time of ours may well fear that soon—if God provide no remedy—this impatient nettle will suddenly sting us before men do justice upon it." Three things (he adds) are merciless when they get the upper hand—flood, fire, and the common folk; let us forestall this by some remedy (ll. 26, 437 ff.). But this good Gower, who saw very plainly how the great lords were sitting on the safety-valve, did not realize the impossibility of maintaining even his own moderately conservative position; it would be difficult to find a clearer justification for the revolt of 1381 than by comparing his theoretical liberalism with his practical conservatism.

Elsewhere, again, Gower draws a very dark picture of village life in England; a picture which, when we have made every possible allowance for satire, could not be justly applied even to the England of Fielding and Smollett[1]. But this is characteristic; in all medieval literature, the peasant is very seldom noticed, and, even then, the notice is almost universally scornful. A feebly favourable exception may be found in the thirteenth century German tale of *Meier Helmbrecht*; a far stronger exception is supplied by *Piers Plowman*, which, so far as I know, is altogether unparalleled in medieval literature for its sympathy with peasant life. But the poet who dared to write this epic of the peasant saint dared also to question many current doctrines of his Church, to condemn the friars of his day as traitors to Christ's cause, and to write of the monks in prophetic words which, when at last the day of fulfilment came, led some men

[1] *Mirour*, ll. 20, 509 ff.

to the rash conclusion that the author must have been a Wycliff-ite[1]. This encomiast of the peasant saint cherished no blind illusions with regard to the Church of his own day.

Nor did the Church, for her part, with regard to the peasant. Delisle, who is usually so trustworthy, certainly generalizes hastily when he asserts that "medieval writers, on almost all occasions, have never failed to speak of the labourers with the most touching sympathy and the keenest solicitude"[2]. He gives only two real quotations from the Middle Ages; for his first, by Hildebert of Le Mans, is not in the strictest sense medieval; it is simply quoted verbatim from Horace and almost verbatim from Cicero's *Offices*, from which Hildebert has incorporated a good deal of other matter, after the medieval fashion, without asking himself too strictly how far it was applicable to his own age[2]. Delisle's second quotation is merely a description of the hardships endured by the medieval peasant; so, in the main, is his third, from Nicolas de Clémanges. Elsewhere, in his gloomy picture of the disorders and immoralities which commonly marked the Church festivals, Clémanges explicitly includes the peasants among the worst offenders; and these words of his must go far to qualify the testimonial which he gives them, merely by the way, in the passage cited by Delisle. In that passage, in order to heighten his picture of the barbarity with which the French peasants of 1420 were treated by nobles and by mercenary soldiers, Clémanges speaks of them as "these most innocent of men, the country-folk, among whom (in Virgil's words) 'Justice, when she quitted this earth, left her last lingering footprints'"[3]. Yet when we balance this with his other

[1] C. VI, 169 ff.

[2] Delisle, pp. 647–8; Cicero, *De Officiis*, lib. I, c. xlii, §§ 150–1. It will be evident, on reflection, that Hildebert's quotations must be far more heavily discounted, as a description of his own times, than (*e.g.*) Gower's borrowings from Nigel Wireker. Gower's social environment was almost exactly the same as Wireker's, and he adopts his predecessor's words as naturally applicable to his own time. But the rustic of Hildebert's day was quite different from the peasant-farmer of whom Roman poets and essayists wrote with an enthusiasm which is admitted to have had something artificial; and, if Hildebert quotes Cicero textually, this is because he has found the words in a classical—and therefore, to the medieval mind, almost infallible—authority. The whole context is singularly anachronistic for the twelfth century.

[3] *De Novis Festivitatibus non Instituendis*, in *Opera*, pp. 144 b, 145 b; cf. 146 a. Delisle's quotation is taken from *De Lapsu et Reparatione Justitiae*, c. IX (p. 48 .

words, and take his testimony in full, we find that he agrees pretty nearly with Gautier de Coincy of two centuries earlier[1]. The peasant has a rough life; but, on the other hand, he is himself a very rough diamond[2].

Few medieval writers were more charitable in themselves, or knew all classes of society better, than Berthold of Regensburg, the great Franciscan mission-preacher of the mid-thirteenth century, of whom Roger Bacon speaks with such unreserved admiration. In a picture which I shall presently quote more fully, he paints peasants as dishonest and untrustworthy; and, elsewhere, as given over to pagan superstitions. And, in another passage of terrible import to the medieval religious mind, he notes how few peasant saints there have been in all Christian history[3]. Scarcely a generation after this, we have the voice of Humbert de Romans, himself a great mission-preacher and writer on the art of preaching, who was General of the Dominican Order. Here, again, we might expect some special sympathy with the benighted rustic; but we expect it in vain; to Humbert even the more pious sex in the village are far from model parishioners:

Some [of these peasant-women] are so indevout towards God's word that, when they are in church where a sermon is being preached, at one moment they talk, at another they say their private prayers, at another they stand and bow and kneel before the images, at another they take holy water; and, between whiles, they can scarce be persuaded to leave their accustomed haunts and draw nigh unto the preacher[4].

Jonas of Orléans had said much the same four centuries earlier. In that same book, *On the Education of the Laity*, he has a whole chapter to prove "that, in God's Church, folk should not spend their time in idle and base speech." "There are many," he says, "who have it more at heart to spend their time in vain and obscene talk than to lend their ears to the reading of God's word"; they laugh, when they ought to bewail

---

[1] See ch. II, p. 21.

[2] This comes out even more clearly, perhaps, in the words of Bishop Rodrigo of Zamorra which space compels me to relegate to appendix 31.

[3] Schönbach, VIII, 53. Another early Franciscan preacher, Nicole Bozon, cites the rural bondman as an example of those who believe only in the present, and have no trust in the future (*Contes Moralisés*, p. 110).

[4] *Max. Bib. Pat.* xxv (1677), 506 a.

their sins; it is the devil who is at the bottom of all this. "Sometimes again, what is worse, some are kindled to fierce wrath, they fall into bitter quarrels, bring foul reproaches and accusations against each other, and clash together with fists or heels. It would have been better for such not to come to church at all." Others, again, hold lawcourts in the churches for the sake of worldly gain; and (as Bede has already said), if we rebuke all these irreverences, then the talkers or quarrellers or litigants "pursue their rebukers with obloquy or hatred or detraction, adding sin to sin"[1]. Complaints of this kind thicken as the records become more abundant: Church councils strove to enforce discipline here; but in vain. We are told that the women, in especial, indulged in unrestrained conversation during the Sunday services[2]. This gives its whole point to the well-known miracle of St Martin and St Brice. And De Caumont has published an inscription in Gothic characters from the walls of the church of Heurtereul in Normandy: "We great devils are sent speedily from hell by our grand master Lucifer, to put record on this paper of the women who chatter in this place, in order to bar them from the glory of heaven and from the fellowship of God Almighty"[3].

We see, then, that the most magnetic preachers confess themselves unable to arrest the peasant's continuous attention even by the most liberal appeals to hell-fire[4]. And we have only to read on in Humbert's treatise to realize the gulf which separated the ordinary peasant, in his inmost nature, from the established religion of his day. True, the honest labourer is doing what God sent us into this world for (Gen. iii, 19); true also that we are bidden in Ecclesiasticus (vii, 16): "Hate not laborious works, nor husbandry ordained by the Most High"; true that St Paul

---

[1] P.L. vol. 106, cols. 147–9.

[2] See the 2nd of my *Medieval Studies*, 2nd ed. p. 24, and *Med. Garner*, p. 564, from La Tour Landry (E.E.T.S. 1868), p. 41.

[3] *An. Normand.* 33ᶜ année (1867), p. 528:

> Grant diables sommes envoyés d'enfer
> Tost par nostre grant maistre Lucifer,
> Pour mettre en ce papier mémoire
> Les femmes quaquettent en ce lieu
> Pour leur empescher des cieulx la gloire
> Et l'association du grant Dieu.

[4] For full evidence here see *Five Centuries of Religion*, vol. I, appendix 2.

laboured with his hands, and in Cassian's *Collations* we find a touching story of a saintly husbandman. Of such as him, says Humbert, we may exclaim: "Fortunate are the countryfolk who lead this life or one like it; for more of these seem to come to heaven than from any other sort of lay folk"[1]. This praise will not appear excessive when we remember how cheaply the ordinary chances of salvation were accounted by medieval orthodoxy; Berthold of Regensburg reckoned the damned at 100,000 to 1, and a frequent (though of course loose) comparison is that of Noah and his small company as against the mass of submerged humanity[2]. And Humbert's faint praise must be farther discounted by Berthold's censure, far more serious to the medieval than to the modern mind, that the rustic class was almost destitute of canonized saints. A broad churchman like Langland might see below the surface, and realize the honest peasant's inward sanctity; but, even to these friars fresh from the mint of Francis and Dominic, the ordinary man who worked all day with his hands was still in most cases very far from the Kingdom of Religion. Moreover, on the coldest analysis, Berthold's verdict will be found to justify itself as fatally true. Let the reader turn to any great and orthodox collection of Saints' lives—Alban Butler's, for instance—and note in how many cases the biographer boasts his hero's noble birth; in how few cases the saint was a villager, or in any way of humble origin. Not one-tenth of those to whom the Catholic Church now prays can be claimed, with any show of probability, as coming from the less wealthy three-quarters of society[3]. We must not forget, of course, how many of the canonized saints had made themselves voluntarily poor; Berthold and Humbert themselves, let us remember, had sacrificed worldly goods. But that sacrifice had its spectacular side also; and the Church had no very quick eye for the unspectacular virtues of those who, born in poverty, had never been able to cast wealth away; and who, born under grimy conditions, went to God with their mere natural every-day grime upon them, as apart from the voluntary filth of the ascetic. Moreover, we must admit that the medieval peasant, by whatever standard we judge him, does not often seem to

[1] *Ibid.* 494 F, 495 B.   [2] *Five Centuries of Religion, l.c.*
[3] See appendix 32.

have been of the stuff that saints are made of. True, nearly all our full-length pictures of him come from churchmen; but these are too preponderantly unfavourable to be neglected. It will be sufficient to quote a few specimens here in the text.

It was about 1130 that the Cluniac monk Bernard of Morlaix wrote that poem *On the Contempt of this World* from which Neale translated the hymn *Jerusalem the Golden*. In this, one of the earliest attempts at a synthetic picture of medieval society which has come down to us, the rare and brief allusions to the peasant are such as we find down to the very end of the Middle Ages and beyond: he is a sorely oppressed creature, yet deeply guilty[1]. The knight (says Bernard) is now a wild beast to the poor; "not only does he no longer rule the peasants with the word of his mouth and protect them with his hand, but he chases and smites, burns and grinds down, those who till the fields." But the rustic, for his part, while he

eats and sows and gathers in his crops, and stuffs his barns, yet he conceals his firstfruits and picks his tithes, and in this way he spares himself....The tiller of the fields is wickedly perfidious, he walks in envy; oftentimes the ploughman will swear that his neighbour's ploughlands are his own; he swears that he may get them to himself; readily and knowingly he perjures himself; hence come frequent quarrels between man and man, frequent pleas in the courts. The peasant lays up his barley and his wheat in the barn, he makes great barns, and many capacious corn-chests; yet he will not tithe flocks or crops that God hath given him, nor doth the altar receive its sacred portion or its tenth part.

But here he only follows the example of his betters: "Money rules all things," from the Roman court down to the ordinary judge.

A century later, we find the Benedictine Gautier de Coincy drawing practically the same picture, of a creature scarcely treated as a man, yet scarce deserving of human treatment[2].

Passing over another hundred years, we come to the Cambridge canonist, John of Ayton, who commented on the legatine decrees of Otho and Ottobon. The latter has a preface lamenting the common neglect of justice in thirteenth century English society;

---

[1] *Anglo-Latin Satirical Poets*, R.S. II (1872), 53, 51, 54, 92–4, cf. 52.
[2] See ch. II, p. 21, here above.

clergy, lords and commons are alike guilty. Upon which Ayton comments:

Thirdly, the evils described in this preface are apparent in rustics and common folk, who in these days, despising agriculture and holy rusticity, swagger in disputes and in assizes, wherein they frequently commit perjury, in spite of the fact that canon law forbids a man to lie even to save another man's life....It were to be wished that some of these folk were taught to belch forth the truth even by the slitting of their tongues....Moreover, not only do they strive to steal little portions of land from their lords and from their own neighbours, but sometimes also by exacting money or gloves (to use their own word)[1] and sometimes by unjust withholding of their tithes, and by malicious miscalculation[2] they strive to defraud the churches of their dues, in contravention of many written authorities....Wherefore the Lord doth not rebuke the locusts, nor doth He remove His plagues from them[3].

Contemporary with Ayton was Alvarus Pelagius. This distinguished Franciscan was Penitentiary to the pope of his day; his *De Planctu Ecclesiae* is constantly quoted as one of our best sources for the relations of Church and State in the early fourteenth century. In that book he sets himself to characterize systematically, in turn, each class of medieval society; and at last he comes to the village folk[4]:

Let us describe the faults of rustics or labourers or tillers of the soil. They sin first of all in the matter of personal and predial tithes, which they pay not, or which they pay not wholly but with diminution, deducting from their crops the expenses and wages of the labourers, and practising other frauds[5]. Secondly, in that they pay these tardily, and of their worse grain and wine and fruits, and they bring them not to the church, as they are bound to do; and when they reap divers crops from one field they will not pay tithes but of one crop. Thirdly, they will not pay tithes of the small untithed residue, which ought to be tithed; for there is nothing so small that it should

---

[1] In modern language, "tips," in kind or in money.
[2] Text has *calcationem*, "treading under-foot"; I have translated as if it were *calculationem*.
[3] Appendix to Lyndwood's *Provinciale*, 1679, pp. 77–8.
[4] Lib. II, art. 43 (f. 147, col. 1).
[5] Tithes, unlike income-tax, were payable upon a man's gross receipts, without deduction for working expenses; moreover, they had often to be carried at the payer's and not the receiver's cost. I omit in this translation, without farther warning, the many references to canon law and similar observations with which Alvarus reinforces his remarks.

not be tithed, even as the widow, from the little that she had, put two mites into the treasury. Fourthly, rich country folk sin in not revering poor lords, or providing for them in the necessaries of life, though they ought to help all starving men; much more are they bound to do so with their lords. Fifthly, they sin by withholding their manorial rights and pleading with them and vexing them with trouble and costs, and sometimes by bribing others of greater power to protect them against their true lords, whereby their debt is not remitted but increased. Sixthly, in the matter of holy days; for they keep them not, but break and violate them, though no servile work ought to be done on such days. Seventhly, in perjuries [and] false witness, (for fear of the lords who sometimes bring them forward as witnesses,) on pretext of their poverty, whereas they ought not to obey in this matter. Eighthly, in the harm that they do to their neighbours, either through their cattle or by cutting their wood or in their vineyards or by stealing. Ninthly, they move the landmarks of their neighbours' fields. Tenthly, because they leave their own parson and go to others without his licence, for confession and hearing of Masses and making offerings and paying tithes. In the eleventh place, because on Sundays they hear not Mass fully, down to the priest's benediction, as they are bound by Church precept. Nay, rather they stay outside the church while the priest says his Mass, nor do they commonly enter but [just] to see the Lord's Body; and, even then, many enter not the church but see it from outside, where they talk of their oxen and beasts and of other base matters, like bestial folk. In the twelfth, they join themselves in lust with the beasts whom they feed and keep. In the thirteenth, they often abstain from knowing their own wives lest children should be born, fearing that they could not bring up so many, under pretext of poverty; wherein they sin most grievously and live contrary to the law of matrimony, which was principally instituted by our Lord for the procreation of children. In the fourteenth, such is the avarice of some among them that, although they be rich, for the sake of increasing their wealth—it would be otherwise if they did this for humility or for avoidance of idleness—they labour with their own hands, and cease not even when weighed down with old age, tormenting their bodies and corrupting their souls. For, even as they plough and dig the earth all day long, so they become altogether earthy; they lick the earth, they eat the earth, they speak of earth; in the earth they have reposed all their hopes, nor do they care a jot for the heavenly substance that shall remain[1]. Moreover, such

---

[1] Compare the almost contemporary words in *Piers Plowman*, B. I, 6:

> The moste partie of this people that passeth on this erthe,
> Have thei worschip in this worlde, thei willen no better;
> Of other hevene than here, holde thei no tale.

rich peasants, who will to work, are not excused from the Church fasts under pretext of their labour; let them either refrain from work on such days, or perform it through their hired men, and let them fast. In the fifteenth, they envy each other sore, especially when one harvesteth more wine or corn than another from a field of the same size; for they know not that the fruitfulness of the land standeth not in man's power, but in the goodness and liberality of the Lord. In the sixteenth, on those holy days whereon they labour not, they stand idle in the streets or in the taverns, or in game, though St Augustine saith that it is better to work [on a holyday] than to dance, and though Canon Law saith that nought else should be done on the Sunday but to spend our time with God, that no work should be done on that holy day, and that the day should be passed in nothing but psalms and hymns and spiritual songs (Gratian, *Decret*. pars III, dist. iii, c. 16). In the seventeenth, they quarrel and are on ill terms with their own priests, and murmur against them, looking to the priest's sins and not to their own. In the eighteenth, they hear the Masses knowingly (otherwise, ignorance of the law excuses them; but, after the matter is preached to them, they have no excuse) and receive the sacraments, from publicly concubinary priests, contrary to Canon Law. In the nineteenth, they are commonly inhuman to pilgrims [or travellers] and poor folk, for they are avaricious, and do not recognize God as the giver of the fruits of their fields and beasts and trees, but impute it to nature and their own labours. In the twentieth, they leave one holding and take another, against their compact and pledged faith[1]. In the twenty-first, they frequently waste [or embezzle, *intervertunt*] possessions. In the twenty-second, when they are hired at a fixed wage they do not work faithfully but deceive their lords.

There we have a Franciscan of about 1330; now let us hear a Dominican of just a century later, St Antonino, archbishop of Florence. He, like Alvarus, sets himself to characterize every class in turn, and here also, of course, the peasant comes last:

Of Husbandmen, or Labourers of the Earth. This is indeed an art and a work necessary to human life; wherefore it was said unto Adam and Eve: "In the sweat of thy brow shalt thou eat bread"; and Noah was a husbandman, in that he planted the vine after the Deluge. Husbandmen, when they work their own lands, cannot commit fraud in their work, except in selling their produce either at too

---

[1] Alvarus refers here to two decrees of Innocent III and Gregory IX, *Dilectis* (*Dec. Greg*. lib. II, tit. 28, c. 55) and *De Judaeis*, cap. ii (*ibid*. lib. v, tit. 5, c. 2). It is difficult to see any relevance at all in the first—there is perhaps a misprint—and even the second is not very directly relevant, though the gloss does something to help.

high a price or too small a measure, or in selling bad for good. But, in these days, such is the cunning and subtlety of man that they themselves are rather deceived by the buyers, who buy their produce when they are driven by necessity to sell, and who thus forestall the time of harvest, buying at a cheaper price; which partakes of the guilt of usury in the buyer. [He goes on to speak of the frauds committed sometimes by peasants themselves.] They offend also when they withhold tithes from their churches....And, when the church is vacant, the parishioners sometimes take the goods of the church or of the parson and spend and waste them in eating and drinking. Moreover they compel the priests themselves to maintain certain abuses, as that on Easter- or Christmas-Day, or other holy-days, [the priest must] give them a notable quantity of bread, and also of wine, whereof they drink even unto intoxication. In the churches themselves they sometimes dance and lead carols with women. Some, again, go to fish, which is an act not unlawful in itself, but they offend in doing this on feast-days; to wit, they catch fish and sell them, thus breaking the commandment to do no servile work on holy-days. It is different if they do this for recreation's sake, or to get a few small fish for their own eating, provided that they do not on that account neglect to hear Mass, etc. Some steal each other's fish; such are bound to restitution. Sometimes, again, they lay waste the banks of others' farms, and sometimes the fields themselves, for which damage they should render account, as I have written in my chapter on Restitution. On holy-days they spend little time on divine service or hearing of the whole Mass, but in games, or in taverns and in contentions at the church-doors. Even on holy-days, they bring their beasts laden with corn or other things to their patrons, which is a violation of the holy-day, unless they be driven to this by the greatest necessity, not being able to live otherwise. They blaspheme God and His saints on slender provocation. When angered, they curse their brute beasts. They are full of lies and perjuries; of fornication and sodomy they make no conscience[1]. Very many of them [*plurimi*] do not confess once a year, and far fewer are those who take the Communion, under the false belief that they need not communicate except when they grow old or are sick unto death. They do little to instruct their families in the manners of faithful folk. They frequently leave undone the penances enjoined on them by their confessors, and the vows they themselves have made. They use enchantments for themselves and for their beasts. Of God or of their own souls' health they think not at all. And, being commonly ignorant and caring little for their own souls or for keeping

---

[1] This was specially prevalent in Italy; see Benvenuto da Imola on Dante, *Inf.* xv, 16 ff. (I, 523), P. Toynbee, *Dante Dictionary* s.v. *Brunetto*, p. 100, *Nuntiaturberichte*, pp. 450, 504 and Bern. *Sen.*, II, 87 ff.

God's commandments, which they know not, this it is which helps to lead them along the broad way leading to destruction, to wit, their ignorance of their own vices and the carelessness and evil conscience of their parish priests, who, caring not for the flock committed unto them, but only for their wool and their milk, instruct them not through preaching and the confessional or by private admonitions, but walk in the same errors as their flocks, following their corrupt ways and not correcting them for their faults; whereby it cometh to pass that, living like beasts, they sometimes die the death of a beast[1].

Here, again, from a slightly different angle, is the judgement of St Bernardino of Siena, in sermons to town congregations:

Thou must not do as the country-folk do, who stay in the tavern drinking and filling their bellies until they hear the sacring-bell which announces the elevation of the Lord's Body; then they drink and run swiftly and, when the Lord's Body is elevated, then they go with their greasy lips, and often drunken, and kiss the altar; and then they run away and return to their wine; and in course of time mice come and nibble at the greasy altar-cloth and altar-linen[2].

But, after all, they know no better; though the sermon is really even more valuable than the Mass, yet the sermon is painfully rare:

for preachers are few, and fewer still are those who preach Christ, while there are many to sing Masses.... For there are many peasant-folk, and dwellers in the mountains and elsewhere, who would find it hard to hear sermons as they hear Mass. Yet such folk are not excused from learning, as place or time may allow, by some means or other, the things which are necessary to their salvation according to their station in life; nor are their ecclesiastical superiors excusable for not teaching them by preaching or in some other fashion; for such ignorance is no excuse in either party[3].

A generation later, the famous Denis Ryckel (Dionysius Carthusianus), though he does not share the opinion that agriculture is in itself a cursed occupation (witness the inacceptability of Cain's sacrifice), is yet willing to discuss it seriously[4].

---

[1] *Summa Major*, pars III, tit. 2, c. 4 § 13.
[2] *Opera*, ed. Delahaye, 1745, III, 265 a.
[3] *Ibid.* II, 61. Dr G. R. Owst's work on Preaching and Preachers, shortly to be published in the same series as the present volume, will show that St Bernardino might have said the same to a congregation in these islands; and French and German conditions were much the same.
[4] *Opera*, I, 122 d[2]. For farther evidence of this sort see appendix 31.

It will be noted that all the authors here quoted, and nearly all in my appendix, are monks or friars; so far is it from being true that the average monk of the Middle Ages was a missionary preaching by word and example the sanctity of manual labour. We have seen how Gower, the Kentish squire and the friend of our courtier-poet Chaucer, did at least play with the idea of his own kinship to the peasant through Adam and Eve; but Gower's younger contemporary, the monastic chronicler Walsingham, has not even lip-service for that idea. He quotes the familiar "When Adam delved and Eve span" as one of the "ravings"—*delira-menta*—of John Ball. For him, the peasants are men who "hoped to subject everything to their own folly...and to become equal to their lords, and henceforth to be constrained to no man's service." He writes fully of the matter, "in order that posterity may learn to be more happily forewarned against the deceits of the villeins"; "the perfidious, proud and upstart villeins"; "the false multitude, a perfidious folk, a treacherous crew, men of lying speech." When the villeins, pleading their own cause afterwards before the royal judges, urged accusations against St Albans abbey which were doubtless mingled with at least the usual leaven of litigants' falsehood, Walsingham tells us how "so many evil-speakers grew up against us that they disquieted almost all the friends of the abbey, even though it was publicly proclaimed that all men should be hanged who presumed to bring false accusation against the abbot, and that women should be burned"[1].

Indeed, a threat of this kind, which seems almost grotesque to the modern reader, had only too much earnest behind it in those days. It was not at all probable that the king would proceed to such extremities against the monk's adversaries, yet neither was it impossible; and, where the man was hanged, the female offender might have gone to the stake. Tanon, in his valuable studies on the ecclesiastical exercise of secular justice, shows conclusively that there was little, if anything, to choose here between the Church lord and the lay lord. The abbot or prior hanged men, and burned women or buried them alive, in as matter-of-course a fashion as the count would have done. The abbey court of St-Germain-des-Prés burned a woman for

[1] *Hist. Ang.* R.S. II, 32–3; cf. I, 453–4, II, 22, 28 ff.

child-murder; that of the abbey of Ste-Geneviève, between 1265 and 1302, buried seven women alive for thefts. In 1352, the priory court of St-Martin-des-Champs buried a woman alive "for several thefts." Kentnich, near the Rhine, was a village belonging to the abbess of St Ursula at Cologne and under the "advocacy" of the archbishop. The customal of 1447, after providing for the burning or hanging of male offenders, adds: "But if the prisoner be of the female sex, she must be examined and convicted likewise and judged by the said jury...and the aforesaid [archiepiscopal] official in Brühl, in right of the said advocacy, must then cause her to be buried alive on the land of that farm where she was caught, and thus shall he give her over finally to the supreme penalty of death; and the grave must be dug so deep that the public road in Kentnich be not infected by any stench [from the corpse]." The monks of Lorsch, higher up on the Rhine, had valuable forests; and here is their custom of 1423: "If it befall that an ashburner or any other man be caught setting fire to the forest, he shall be taken and bound in a tub, set upon a fire made of a load of wood. There shall he be set, barefooted, nine feet from the fire; and he shall be left to sit there until the soles fall from his feet"[1]. There are other terrible punishments prescribed in the German customals —disembowelling, ploughing to death, and so on[2]. These relics of wild forest life disappeared much earlier in France and Italy and England; for instance, while the penalty for moving a neighbour's landmark was sometimes ploughing to death in Germany, at Meury and Bassoncourt in Burgundy (1337 A.D.) it was only a fine of 60 sols, the same as for using false measures[3]. Yet in England women were sometimes burned for petty

---

[1] Tanon, *Justice*, c. 2 and 3; *Registre*, pp. xc–c; *Weisthümer*, II, 739 and I, 466: cf. I, 794. Under the Count of Falkenstein in 1418 "...the murderer to the wheel; the woman who slays her child to a living grave; thrust a reed into her mouth and then a stake through her heart"—*lebendig ins grab, ein rohr ins maul, ein stecken durchs herz*. In 1500, a vagrant quarrelled with the monks of Camp and burned two of their barns; in 1503 he burned two more. This time they caught him, and (writes the monastic chronicler) "he was given over to the secular judge and justice...and he was judicially adjudged to the death of incendiaries, and chained to a stake and burned at Mörse, by the public way, as a spectacle for the people as they went by" (Eckertz, *Fontes*, II, 420–2). For another woman buried alive see S. Luce, *Du Guesclin*, p. 65.

[2] See appendix 33.   [3] Garnier, II (1868), 478.

treason—*i.e.* for killing or compassing a master's death, not only through the Middle Ages but far beyond; and at Sandwich thieves were buried alive[1].

Village life, then, was rough in some places almost beyond modern realization. The following prescription from a German customal, though fortunately very exceptional, is not absolutely unique. If the lord sometimes treated the union between bondman and bondwoman rather from the economic than the moral standpoint, so also did the villagers themselves. As the lord sometimes needed to couple folk for the sake of the work and the brood, so the tenant was sometimes in absolute need of offspring, especially on those manors where the lord took everything at a childless man's death. He was then permitted to lend his wife to a neighbour, that seed might be raised up unto himself[2].

---

[1] Mrs J. R. Green, *Town Life in the Fifteenth Century*, 1894, I, 222 n.
[2] See appendix 31. The clerical author of *The Owl and the Nightingale* judges the peasant to be capable only of lust; real love is beyond him (ll. 509 ff.).

These things may be commended to the notice of those who, in personal comfort, preach the blessedness of drudgery, or

who, from their town houses, cry *Back to the land!* How much have these men really done, or their blood-ancestors or their spiritual ancestors, to fulfil the complementary condition of that same maxim by bringing the land back to the peasant? Often, in reading modern laments for the disappearance of this artist's and poet's paradise, I have been reminded of sentiment and reality as they are put before us, for one moment, by the poet of *Aucassin et Nicolete* (§ 24):

As Aucassin rode along an old grass-grown road, he raised his eyes and saw in the way a great fellow, wondrously hideous and foul to behold. He had a shock of hair blacker than coal-dust, and more than a hand-breadth between his two eyes, and thick cheeks with a huge flat nose and great wide nostrils, and blubber-

The trouvère Rutebeuf says something like that of himself; he lives from hand to mouth; he has no joys at home; a mere Grub Street poet can't afford to deal in love, which is only for rich folk; the poor man must stick to satire and buffoonery.

lips redder than roast flesh, and great hideous yellow teeth. He was clad in hosen and shoes of cowhide, bound round with linden-bast to above his knee; he was wrapped in a threadbare cloak and leaned on a great knotted staff...."Wherefore weepest thou," said he, "and makest such moan?...What! by the heart that God had in His belly! thou weepest for a stinking hound that thou hast lost?...But I have some reason for mourning and grief....I was hired to a rich peasant and drove his plough; four oxen had he. Now, these three days past, as ill luck would have it, I lost the best of my oxen—Roger, the chief of my whole team—and thus I wander in search of him. I have neither eaten nor drunken these three days, nor dared I go back to the village, for they could cast me into prison, since I have not wherewith to pay. In the whole wide world I have nought of mine own but that which thou seest on my body. A poor mother I had, who had but one poor mattress; and they have taken this from under her body, that she lieth on the bare straw; and this grieveth me more than for myself; for chattels come and go; if I have lost now, some other day I shall earn wherewith to pay for this ox; I weep not for that. And thou weepest for a filthy hound! curses on the man who shall ever prize thee more!"

The peasant, normally, is the Caliban of medieval literature. And the worst is, that he was too often no stage monster, but a reality.

CHAPTER XIX

RELIGIOUS EDUCATION

So Caliban is Caliban, and we cannot do very much with him so long as his main belief and trust rests upon Setebos. The land cannot be brought back to those who cannot master the land. St Thomas Aquinas never erred worse, perhaps, than when, following his master Aristotle, he judged the ideal state to need a peasantry strong in the arm, dull of intellect, and divided among themselves by mutual distrust[1]. His contemporary, Berthold of Regensburg, a friar like himself, but a friar who knew the poor well, did here advance one full step beyond Aquinas; he saw the social evil clearly, though he did not foresee the social remedy. He lamented (as we have seen) the lack of peasant saints; he was under no illusions as to the present state of these countryfolk who, on an average, formed half his congregation; but he did see that the root of their misery lay in their disunion. In one of his sermons, he compares different classes with different animals[2]:

These fish betoken the poor folk; for the fish is a very poor and naked beast; it is ever cold, and liveth ever in the water, and is naked and cold and bare of all graces. So are also the poor folk; they, too, are helpless. Wherefore the devils have set the bait for them that is called untruth, because they are poor and helpless; with no bait could the devil have taken so many of them as with this. Because the fishes are poor and naked, therefore they devour one another in the water; so also do poor folk; because they are helpless, therefore they have divers wiles and invent many deceits. When such a man would sell anything, he doth it untruly, lying and deceiving and stealing. But the poor naked folk that are called menservants and maidservants and that serve your needs, such will steal your salt and your bacon, your meal and your corn. But none are so false as the countryfolk among each other, who are so untrue that for envy and hatred they can scarce look upon one another. One will drive

---

[1] *Comment. in Polit.* lib. VII, lect. viii (ed. Parm, XXI, 662).
[2] *Predigten*, I, 478, translated in *Med. Garner*, pp. 348 ff. For peasant dishonesty see also *Piers Plowman*, B. XIII, l. 371 and Vinogradoff, *Villainage*, p. 234.

another's cattle to his harm and damage, and another will buy his fellow-peasant out of his farm, all from untruth.

Here, of course, we have the modern problem in an earlier and acuter form. The poor man can force his way up to something better only by combination; he can combine only in proportion as he is educated, in every sense of that word; yet how can he be educated until his hours of work are shortened? and how can his shorter hours of work pay his way from the point of view of general economics, until he is educated enough to produce in six hours what he now produces in eight or ten? Since the Great War, and to a certain extent before, modern society has recognized that this problem must be attacked in a generous spirit, by spending heavily on the manual worker and hoping for a return some day. But there was nothing that can be called an educational system in the Middle Ages: modern writers who talk of such a system have hitherto failed hopelessly to prove that good intentions ever descended from theory to practice; and even the intentions were not always good. That jealousy of primary education, which remains one of the vividest political pictures in the minds of those who remember the struggle of 1870 and the following years, must be multiplied fourfold when we think ourselves back to the Middle Ages. Quite characteristic was the petition of the Commons in 1391, that no villein should be suffered to send his sons to school, "in order to advance them by clergy," to which the king replied "Le roy s'avisera"[1].

But (it may be said) there was the Church to raise the people, with her higher ideal and her frequent services and her strict discipline. We must not forget this; even at the present day, the disappearance of the parish priest has left a sad gap in many French villages; but, on the other hand, we must not press this argument beyond what it is worth. There was a far wider gulf between religious theory and practice in the Middle Ages than in modern society; and, though the Church did much, there was far more that she failed to do. The medieval Sunday, for instance, was by law a day of strict religious observance; it is a very serious mistake, though it seems common even among professional historians, to imagine that sabbatarianism came in

---

[1] *Rot. Parl.* III, 294 a.

with the Reformation[1]. Work was strictly forbidden; the satirist Brant, in agreement with the greatest of orthodox preachers a few years before Luther's appearance, Johann Geiler, likens the Christian Sunday to the Jewish sabbath; and *sabbatizare* is a good medieval word for Sunday observance[2]. Moreover, though the peasant caught at Sundays and holy-days as propitious moments for sport and dance, the Church was, on the whole, most unfavourable here: "They who dance on Church holy-days commit mortal sin," writes Luther's adversary, Guillaume Pépin, in 1521[3]. As late as the nineteenth century, two standard theological dictionaries remind their readers that "even for the laity, the councils forbid it [dance] on Sundays and holy-days"[4]. The author of *Dives and Pauper* does, indeed, approve of dances and plays after Mass, provided they do not stir men and women to sin, "as it is right likely that they do now in our days"[5]. Otherwise no moralist, so far as I know, goes beyond Aquinas, who commends sport and relaxation in such guarded language as a Puritan like Milton might use, but who does not suggest Church holy-days as suitable times for such relaxations[6]. When Fr. Thurston writes (p. 48) that "the same strong feeling [of Sunday rest and joy] during the Middle Ages manifested itself in the encouragement of every form of innocent amusement and recreation," he flies in the face of contemporary records. It is true that folk usually did make merry after Mass; but this was to the distress of good

---

[1] Compare two writers from very different points of view: Mr B. L. Manning on pp. 123 ff. of *The People's Faith in the Time of Wyclif* and Fr. H. Thurston, S.J. in *The Nineteenth Century* for July, 1899, *The Medieval Sunday*. The former writes truly: "When modern writers adduce the 'freedom' of the old English Sunday as a proof of the easy 'liberal' attitude of the medieval Church, they are guilty of the fundamental mistake of imagining that the Church sanctioned what it was obliged—after many protests—to tolerate....Mannyng, in the early part of the [fourteenth] century, knew nothing good of that merry English Sunday which has been lovingly pictured by modern writers."

[2] Scheible, pp. 727–30; cf. my appendix 34.

[3] *Destruct. Ninive*, serm. 17: so also the author of *Luculentissimi Sermones* (Paris, 1536), serm. 132: the three "mortal sins" most common on holy-days are "fornication, drunkenness and dancing."

[4] *Dict. universel des sciences ecclés.* par M. l'abbé J.-B. Glaire (Paris, 1868, s.v. *danse*; cf. Richard et Giraud, *Bib. Sacrée* under the same heading).

[5] See his actual words in Manning and Thurston, pp. 136 and 50 respectively.

[6] *Expos. in Isaiam*, cap. 3. I deal far more fully with this subject in *Five Centuries of Religion*, vol. I, app. 23, and *Hist. Teach. Misc.* Feb. 1925.

Churchmen; "For in the Sunday reigneth more lechery, gluttony, manslaughter, robbery, backbiting, perjury and other sins, more than reigned all the week before"[1]. That was written by a simple friar; but a contemporary archbishop of Canterbury says the same in a solemn mandate to his flock: God bade us abstain from work on the seventh day, Holy Church has added other solemn days; but these reverences of earlier centuries "are now turned to blasphemy, seeing that assemblages, trading and other unlawful pursuits are specially followed upon these days; that which was prepared as a summary of devotion is made into a heap of dissipation, since upon these holy-days the tavern is rather worshipped than the Church, gluttony and drunkenness are more abundant than tears and prayers, men are busied rather with wantonness and contumely than with the leisure of contemplation"; and, though working-folk gladly claim exemption from labour on these days, yet they expect to be paid, and do not "sabbatize as they should, to the honour of God"[2].

An archbishop might fulminate in this sort of mandate; but what were he and his clergy to do? Theoretically, they might do almost anything to enforce the law of the sabbath; but in fact everything depended on the right time, the right place, and the right man. The disciplinary power of the Church was enormous wherever a dignitary could be found who had that double gift of fearlessness and moderation, rare in every age, which arms a man to fight unflinchingly against evil and evil alone. Archbishop Eudes Rigaud of Rouen, riding on St Matthew's day, 1260, from Meudon to Giset, notes in his diary that "We found ploughs working and ploughing: wherefore we caused the horses to be brought to Meulan, seeing that they presumed irreverently to labour on the day of so great a Saint." The two owners were compelled to follow to Meulan and find guarantors there for whatever fine the archbishop should decree. Later, on a Sunday in September, 1264, he met a man near Duclair with a cart and three horses loaded with timber; here again he

---

[1] *Dives and Pauper*, com. III, c. 6; cf. Myrc, *Festial*, p. 63, and the other quotations I give later.

[2] Constitution of Archbishop Simon Islip (1362 A.D.) in the second appendix to Lyndwood (1679), p. 57. For Church feasts as days of disorder see also Durandus, *De Modo Generalis Concilii habendi*, p. 340.

demanded a guarantor on the spot, and inflicted a fine of ten sous[1]. Eudes, with the prestige of his archbishopric and his knightly race and his well-known sanctity of character, could thus assert the law without counting the consequences; he himself would never be suspected of taking those ten sous for his own private enjoyment. But it needs an exceptional man to insist upon ideals of this kind; the disciplinarian's hands must be clean; if the law is to be strictly enforced from week to week in any parish, it must be by a parson after Chaucer's model. So also with the Church services, nominally so weighty and so universal. Of their actual content the ordinary peasant knew very little; and it is the priest himself who tells us so. I dealt with this, years ago, in the 7th of my *Medieval Studies*, and I am not aware that any one has impugned the accuracy of the facts there adduced. It was only heretics who possessed anything beyond the merest smatterings of Bible knowledge; our most emphatic witnesses on this point are the orthodox heresy-hunters of the thirteenth century. The peasant had scarcely the vaguest idea of the Mass service, except that, at a certain moment, the priest "made" the Body of God[2]. Berthold of Regensburg finds it necessary to explain the different stages of the service to his congregation as though they were little children. They commonly came in late, and departed before the end; as soon as the priest had held up the consecrated Host, they went clattering out (complains St Bernardino) "as if they had seen not God but the devil"[3]. The multiplication of feast-days led not to reverence so much as to irreverence; great churchmen of the later Middle Ages are unanimous on this point. And it was not peasants alone who wearied of the long Church services. Cardinal Humbert de Romans, whom in Chapter III we have seen condemning the multiplication of Church festivals, pleads also "that God's service may be so abridged that it may be recited

---

[1] *Reg. Vis.* pp. 375, 501. The whole yearly income of a curate at the same time and in the same province was about 600 sous (*ibid.* p. 345, cf. Delisle, p. 594). A labourer earned half a sou *per diem*; so that this untimely carter lost the fruit of three weeks' work (Delisle, p. 623).

[2] This phrase has recently been challenged; but it is perfectly orthodox; see the correspondence between Mgr. Moyes and Mr Hutton in *The Times* for Dec. 20 and Dec. 29, 1924.

[3] Compare also Bishop Durand of Mende in his memorial to the Council of Vienne, p. II, c. 50 (p. 162).

and heard devoutly and in its entirety"[1]. His contemporary and brother-friar, Salimbene, was even more outspoken. He tells us how they were reformed and abridged by Innocent III, and adds:

Yet even now the matter is not well ordered, as many would have it and as real truth requires. For there are many superfluities which beget rather weariness than devotion, both to hearers and to officiants; as, for instance, at Prime on Sundays, when priests have to say their Masses and the people await them, yet there is none to celebrate, for they are yet busied with Prime. So also with the recitation of the eighteen psalms at Nocturns on Sunday before the *Te Deum*. For these things beget sheer weariness, not only in summer, when we are harassed by fleas and the nights are short and the heat is intense, but in winter also. There are yet many things left in divine service which might be changed for the better. And it would be well if they were changed, for they are full of uncouth stuff, though not every man can see this[2].

Even the Ecumenical Council of Vienne had to take notice of the frequency with which the clergy themselves interrupted the services by talking and walking about. And at least one of the later popes was emphatically of Salimbene's opinion. It was among the articles objected to Pope John XXIII that, when it came to reciting vespers from his breviary, he would say to his chaplain "in his vernacular Neapolitan speech 'turn me up some saint, in a hundred devils' name, whom we can get through as quickly as possible'"[3].

The ignorance of many medieval clergy, as described, or statistically recorded, by their own superiors, is almost incredible. In 1222, out of seventeen priests serving dean and chapter livings under the cathedral of Salisbury, five were found unable to construe even the first sentence of the first collect in the Canon of the Mass[4]. Roger Bacon's scornful words as to the ignorance of the ordinary parish priest are rendered credible by the evidence of papal registers[5]. Archbishop Peckham, Bacon's younger contemporary and fellow-Franciscan, com-

---

[1] Mansi, *Concilia*, t. xxiv, col. 130. Compare the repeated efforts "to avoid tedium" implied in the treatise *De Ecclesiasticis Officiis* by Jean d'Avranches (Paris, Picard. 1923, pp. 40-1, etc.).

[2] *M.G.H. Scriptt.* xxxii, 31. [3] Hemmerlin, *Tract.* f. 42 b.

[4] *Register of St Osmund*, R.S. I, 304 ff.

[5] Berlière, *Honorius*, p. 241.

plained to the world in 1281 that "the ignorance of the priests precipitates the people into the ditch of error"; and this arraignment, substantially echoed by more than one later English bishop, was finally repeated in so many words by Wolsey in 1518. Bishop Guillaume Durand, in his memorial to the Council of Vienne in 1311, bears similar testimony; so does his colleague, Bishop Guillaume le Maire of Angers, who writes that the priesthood includes "innumerable contemptible persons of abject life, utterly unworthy in learning and morals...from whose execrable lives and pernicious ignorance infinite scandals arise, the Church sacraments are despised by the laity, and in very many districts the lay folk hold the priests as viler and more despicable than Jews"[1]. A generation later, we get the same sort of evidence from the statutes of an abbot of St Albans[2]. A century later again, Nicolas de Clémanges complains that the priests find no time to read the Bible, but only legends, so that their flocks grow up in ignorance[3]. In 1411, the University of Paris drew up an important series of articles for the consideration of the Council of Constance when it should get to work. One of these recommended the composition of elementary religious treatises, in Latin and French, for all the clergy and their parishioners. "This" (said the University) "is most expedient; nay, almost necessary; since many, and indeed almost innumerable, folk are found in very many places and dioceses who scarce understand aught of God or of the articles necessary to their own salvation"[4]. Gower, a few years before, had noted how often the English laity despised their parish priests; and he finds one great cause in their ignorance: "A foolish priest makes foolish people...a lawless clergy supposes a lawless people... it is because the unwisdom of the foolish cleric is now so manifest, that the unwise fellow's life is so much despised"[5]. Nonresidence was common among the clergy who could afford to live elsewhere and pay a curate; the episcopal registers are full of licences to non-resident rectors; and, when others absented themselves without episcopal leave, the bishop found himself powerless to deal with these men who had bought licences at

---

[1] *Lib. Guil. Major.* p. 478.   [2] *Gest. Abb.* R.S. II, 474.
[3] Clém. p. 156 a.   [4] Finke, p. 132, § 3; cf. § 36.
[5] *Vox Clamantis*, lib. III, c. xxii ll. 1681 ff.

the papal court[1]. Luchaire's description of the priests and their flocks in his *Social France at the Time of Philip Augustus* errs perhaps on the dark side, as all epigrammatic judgements must fall somewhat short of exact balance; but its substantial truth still remains unquestioned. The picture drawn by Seignobos of the ordinary parish priest in medieval Burgundy, his poverty and dependence and therefore his lack of authority in a society which judged men according to their property and their independence, is again no more exaggerated than an epigrammatic portrait must be[2]. We must remember, of course, the priest's great power at given moments over those who really believed in their hearts; but this power is too often attributed to all moments and all people, and the truth is thus as much distorted on one side as it would be on the other side if we forgot Mass and Confession and Last Unction. Lina Duff-Gordon brings this out very clearly in the case of the modern Italian peasant and his priest[3]. Seignobos emphasizes very truly, again, the helplessness of the ordinary medieval priest in face of his superiors[4]; except, of course, his last inalienable resource of passive resistance. He might steadily refuse to do his work; he might resist with great success all efforts to separate him finally from his uncanonical life-partner; or, on the other hand, a model parson like Chaucer's might do untold good in his solitary furrow; but it must be within strictly marked limits; there is far more falsehood than truth in Macaulay's oft-quoted judgement that the Roman Church has always known how to deal with healthy originality. And the priest had less help then, in the way of serious discipline from above or example from around, than in modern society. The bishop of Olmütz, replying in 1273 to the pope's request that he should note the

---

[1] *Reg. Mayew* (Hereford), pp. vii, 15–16.

[2] pp. 70, 73–5.

[3] *Home Life in Italy*, p. 231: "You must remember that the parish priest is closely linked in the minds of the people with Death, of which the Southerner has more than the usual horror. With the exception of the Easter blessing, practically the only time that a priest enters a house is when he comes to administer the last Sacraments. 'È venuto *il prete*' [the priest has come] sounds like a death-knell to the family." Compare J. R. Green, *Stray Studies*, II (1903), 252, the passage beginning: "Nothing can be more unlike an English clergyman's conception of his work than that entertained by an Italian curé."

[4] pp. 70 ff.

points which most needed reform in the Church, entered briefly into the question of parochial discipline[1]:

In the diocese of Liège and certain other parts, ruridecanal synods were wont to be held a few times yearly with lay assessors, where synodsmen chosen and sworn *ad hoc* were wont to depose and say what is done by the laity in that year against God and the Christian religion; or even those who are accused by common report, against which the accused must either prove their innocence or, if they fail, accept canonical punishment according to the custom of the land. In other dioceses, however, there has been no such custom; wherefore the transgressions of the laity remain unpunished, even though they be notorious. If, however, the priest should perchance wish to accuse such sinners in his own parish, he is oftentimes brought thereby into peril of his life.

Again, no parish registers were kept (apart from church-wardens' accounts, which begin not long before the Reformation); and, when they begin to be kept, we see how little even a rather businesslike priest in an ordinary parish may know about some of his little flock. In the Norman village of Cuy, which had about 400 souls, the curé notes in his register the death of about 60 inhabitants in the plague of 1557, adding that he has omitted to note the deaths of "many common folk—*petites gens*—whom he scarcely knew"[2]. Indeed, the moral and religious destitution of many medieval parishes is sometimes admitted by modern orthodox writers; *e.g.* by Abbé Charasson in his monograph on the mission-preacher Foulques de Neuilly[3].

Let us take two examples of religious education among the better-class poor. First, the touching lines in which Villon describes his mother's creed; the poor and unlettered woman who takes most of her ideas from the painted contrast in her parish church; from that heaven with its angel-choirs, and those damned seething in hell and, everywhere, that Blessed Virgin,

---

[1] Nearly all this document is in Raynaldus (1273 A.D.) § vi, pp. 322 ff. The medieval term *synodsman* survives in the modern *sidesman*.

[2] Malicorne, p. 47.

[3] Paris, Rudeval, 1905, pp. 23, 85, 180. Cf. Delisle on the moral state of the medieval village, pp. 187 ff. For farther documentary evidence I may be allowed to refer to my *Medieval Garner*, pp. 290 ff., 582 ff., 644 and *Social Life in Britain*, pp. 260, 263.

"exalted Goddess," who can grant the faith that will win final pardon from the Great Judge:

> Femme je suis povrette et ancienne,
> Ne riens ne sçay; oncques lettre ne leuz;
> Au moustier voy dont suis paroissienne
> Paradis painct, où sont harpes et luz,
> Et ung enfer où damnez sont boulluz:
> L'ung me faict paour, l'autre joye et liesse.
> La joye avoir fais-moy, hautte Deesse,
> A qui pecheurs doivent tous recourir,
> Comblez de foy, sans faincte ne paresse
> En ceste foy je vueil vivre et mourir[1].

Next, take Joan of Arc's as the normal religious education of a peasant-girl of the better sort, in the more civilized parts of Europe, during the later Middle Ages[2]:

She said, "I learned my Pater and Ave and Creed from my mother; nor did I learn my belief from any other than from my mother....I learned to sew linen and to spin; I fear no woman in Rouen for spinning or sewing....I confessed once a year to my own parson; and, when he was hindered, to another priest by his leave. Sometimes also, twice or thrice, I believe, I confessed to the friars at Neufchâteau; and I used to take the Sacrament of Eucharist on Easter Day." Asked whether she took the Eucharist on other days beside Easter, she told the interrogator to pass on....Asked concerning a certain tree that stands near her village, she answered: "Quite close to the village of Domremi is a tree called *The Ladies' Tree*; and others call it *The Fairies' Tree* (*des Faées* in the French tongue); and there is a fountain hard by. And I have heard say that those who are sick of fevers drink of that spring and go and fetch its water for health's sake. This I myself have seen, but I know not whether they are cured or not. Moreover, I have heard that the sick, when they are able to rise, go to that tree for a walk. And there is a great tree called Beech, whence cometh that which is called in French *le beau may*[3], and it belonged to the lord Pierre de Bourlemont. When I went walking with other girls, I made garlands at that tree for the image of St Mary at Domremi. And I heard oftentimes from old folk (but not of my own

---

[1] *Œuvres*, ed. Jannet, 1876, p. 55. Compare Hentsch, p. 160, for religious education of the poor.

[2] *Procès*, ed. Champion, vol. 1 (Paris, 1920), 34, 38, 49, cf. 172. These depositions are also fully translated in T. D. Murray, *Jeanne d'Arc* (1902), pp. 6 ff.

[3] The tree may have been an ancient hawthorn. There would be nothing very strange in Joan's calling it a beech; the historic "Linden" of the Grisons at Truns was really a maple.

family) that the Fairy Ladies haunted there. I heard say from Joan Aubrée, wife of mayor Aubrée of that village, who was one of my godmothers, that she had seen the Fairy Ladies there; but I do not know whether that was true or not. I never saw those fairies at the tree, so far as I know; I know not whether I ever saw them elsewhere, or no. I have seen girls hanging garlands on the boughs of that tree, and I have sometimes done so with them; sometimes they took the garlands away with them, and sometimes they left them....I do not know that I have danced by the tree since I came to years of discretion; but I may well have danced there with the boys [and girls][1]; and I sang there more than I danced."...Asked whether her godmother who saw the Fairy Ladies was reputed a "wise woman," she answered: "She is held and reputed a good and honest woman, and no witch or sorceress."...Asked whether she knew anything of those who go riding with the Fairies, she said: "That I never did, nor never knew. I have indeed heard that there was a ride on Thursdays, but I believe not in that which is witchcraft"[2].

She did not know her own age—she thought she might be nineteen—nor the names of all her godparents, of whom she had many.

Two things come out very clearly here. The first, the occasional nature of official Church influence. Apart from Sunday and Holy-day Mass, which she and other good girls would attend not only with bodily but with spiritual regularity, and to the real fortification of their spiritual life, there is little contact beyond the occasional ceremonies which partake rather of superstition than religion—the holy-water sprinklings and similar exorcisms which the medieval Church shared, in their outward form, with earlier paganism. Confession and communion normally only once a year; her home supplies her elementary religious education, and home and forest alike show a background of pre-Christian belief, the Good Ladies, the fairies with whom her godmother had closer points of association. We may take those two subjects in their order[3].

The irreligion of the peasant is a medieval commonplace. If all homes had been like Joan's, well and good; but we have abundant evidence to the contrary. In the Dark Ages, we may

[1] *Cum pueris.*
[2] Or possibly "I believe not that there is any witchcraft in that"—*sed in hoc non credit, imo quod est sortilegium.*
[3] Apart from the passages I shall have occasion to quote, see Lecoy, p. 424 and Bromyard A. iii *per totum.*

find religious ignorance natural; there is nothing that need shock us, perhaps, either in the evil rehearsed in the following decree attributed to Charles the Great, or in the suggested remedy:

Let all men be compelled to learn the Creed and the Lord's Prayer, or Profession of Faith. And if any man know them not now, let him either be beaten or abstain from all drink except water until he can fully repeat them; and, if he refuse compliance, let him be brought to our presence. Let women be compelled either by stripes or by fastings. Let our commissioners help the bishops to see that this be carried out; and let the counts likewise, as they would stand in our grace, help the bishops to constrain the people to learn these things[1].

That is only a single case; but here is the general verdict of Claude Fleury, a distinguished French ecclesiastic who was tutor to three princes of the blood, and whose *Histoire Ecclésiastique* is still in many ways the best history of the medieval Church in the French language. He tried to steer a middle course between the extremes of credulity and the scoffs of Protestants and Freethinkers; and his estimate of general religious education in the Dark Ages was that of most historical scholars at the present day[2]. He wrote:

The Latin was now no longer in common use; and in the French and the other vulgar languages, which were as yet but in their beginning, and unformed, nothing was written (so that as they could not understand the one, they had nothing to read in the other). But the public offices of the Church were performed in Latin, and the Scriptures were read to the people in the same language, but seldom explained....In the ninth Age we find the bishops complaining, that all the people of estate and quality had forsaken the parish churches, and earnestly pressing it upon them, that they would vouchsafe to shew themselves there at least at the solemn seasons: so they called those Feasts on which they thought all Christians obliged to communicate, which were these four, viz. *Christmas*, *Holy Thursday*, *Easter* and *Whitsuntide*. Nor were the common people better instructed than their nobility, except in some cities where they had good bishops....The priests and clergy were in too mean a capacity themselves to be able to instruct others....

---

[1] *M.G.H. leges*, II (*Capit*, vol. I), 257. The editor doubts whether this edict came from Charles himself; he finds it more characteristic of his successor, but refers to the 45th canon of the Council of Tours in 813.

[2] *An Historical Account of the Manners and Behaviour of the Christians...throughout the several Ages of the Church*. I quote from the English translation of 1698, pp. 307–13.

Under these public calamities one may easily imagine how miserably the poor were neglected. How could they be relieved by the clergy who had so much ado to live themselves?...Every one was a Christian, but in such a manner as if they had thought it a bare privilege of nature, and the Christian and the man had been the same thing: there was now no longer a distinction. Christianity was little more than a custom of the country, and scarce discovered itself in anything else than in some external formalities. As for virtues and vices, there was hardly any difference between Christians and Jews or infidels, but only in ceremonies, which have not force sufficient for the reforming men's manners. Had not the Christian Religion been the work of God, it could never have weathered out so violent a storm.

Again, in his *Histoire Ecclésiastique*, Fleury shows how difficult it was for the Church to contend with the hereditary paganism of millions whose Christianity was mainly a superficial veneer. The islanders of Rügen, in the Baltic, had been converted by monks of Corvey, who built there a church in honour of their patron saint, St Vitus. In 1168, Waldemar of Denmark conquered the island, took stock of its religion, and found that St Vitus had become a monstrous image with four heads, to which all kinds of sacrifices were offered, even human, but "only of Christian folk." So, writes Fleury, "These people having relapsed into idolatry, forgot the true God and substituted for Him this martyr, whom in their tongue they called Suantovit, making him into an idol. So dangerous is it to teach idolaters, at too early a stage, the worship of saints and their images, before thoroughly instructing them and fortifying them in the knowledge of the true God"[1].

But let us now advance a great deal farther in time and civilization, to the England of Chaucer's day. The Dominican Bromyard holds it most desirable that we should live in familiar commerce with the Holy Ghost; "but, alas! some men strive rather to resemble that shepherd of whom it is said that, when a wayfarer asked him whether he knew the Faith, he replied: 'Yes.' Asked further, whether he knew the Father, the Son, and

---

[1] Livre 71, § 54 (1168 A.D.). For the peasant's mixture of faith and pagan superstitions see Hanotaux, *La France en 1614*, ed. Nelson, p. 408. Those who believe that the simplicity of compulsory poverty connotes higher morals and a less superficial faith, should compare what we know about Russia of today with the Russia of 1913 as described by a most sympathetic writer in *The Nation* for Sept. 27, 1913, p. 956.

the Holy Ghost, he answered, 'The father and the son I know well, for I tend their sheep; but I know not that third fellow; there is none of that name in our village'"[1]. This, of course, is quoted by Bromyard as an extreme instance, though the shepherd would be, with the ploughman, among the most intelligent of the villagers. Let us therefore balance it with an opposite example from the Germany of 1450. Johann Busch, as archdeacon of Halle, put a few simple questions to a peasant who had come as synodsman from his village to the synod of the province. Busch records the questions and answers; he was astounded to find how accurately the man answered, and with what simple good sense. He made farther enquiries, and found that the priest of that parish was an exceptionally earnest man, who would not allow his taverner to sell drink to any man who could not repeat the Paternoster[2]. Here, then, was a case definitely recorded as exceptional; the ordinary peasant was more of the type which, unfortunately, has been found in all villages at all times; listlessly well-intentioned, but no more[3]. It is their pastors themselves who tell us so. A friar was expatiating in his sermon on the unrivalled excellencies of St Francis: the Saint must now be exalted over all the heavens; "and seeing that, with all his long-winded rhetoric, he could find no seat fit for him in heaven or in earth, below that of our Lord, therefore said: 'Where then shall we set him?' a certain peasant suddenly cried aloud: 'Sir! there is an empty seat here by me,' and the whole congregation laughed at the preacher's exaltation of mind"[4]. But the peasant was not always well-

---

[1] *Sum. Praed.* T. iv, 13. Compare the Italian Gentili Sermini of a generation later; in 1474 he retired to the mountains to avoid the plague in Siena; there he heard the peasants "praying after the mountain fashion, crying sometimes so loud ' donna bisoria' [for *da nobis hodie*—' give us this day'] and 'dimitte nobisse' and many other blundering words, that the priest at the altar could understand nothing, and no man could have been so melancholy as not to laugh with all his heart." (Quoted by Lommatzsch, p. 70, in illustration of the gibberish to which, according to Gautier de Coincy, the "vilain" reduced the *Ave Maria*.)

[2] Ed. Grube, p. 442.

[3] We need not here emphasize the fact that medieval children sometimes played at Church ceremonies, building their toy altars or their toy churches (Guil. Alverni, *Opp.* Paris, 1516, f. 34. 4. k; Giraldi Cambrensis, *Opp.* R.S. I, 45, translated in my *Social Life*, p. 111). There is nothing here inconsistent with what we know of their attitude towards religion in later life.

[4] Hemmerlin, *Tract.* f. 46 a.

intentioned. Just as there was a good deal of learned infidelity in the Middle Ages, so there was much unfaith at the other end of the social scale; here were folk hardly penetrable to abstractions of any kind, and confronting the refinements of medieval theology with the stubborn passive resistance of a mind already brimful with other cares. Therefore the priest, from his own professional point of view, looked with no very friendly eye on village religion as he saw it. "O hard-hearted race of peasants!" exclaims one of the monastic authors of the *Miracles de St-Benoît*, "men who look with half-pagan mind upon the cult of the spiritual law, and whose vain and frivolous and sluggish intention maketh light of the solemn institutes of the holy fathers, so that they care not a straw if one of their fellows should refuse to keep the holy-day of some saint"[1]! And this indifference was natural enough; man does not live by bread alone; but neither does faith live in mere words; and the man who lacks bread is not usually a model of religion. Far more in the Middle Ages than in our own day, the peasant was the backbone of the nation; yet the peasant mind, as a whole, was never really stirred to its depth by the Church.

For, when we seek to locate the closest spiritual contact between priest and village, we find it in the least Christian elements of medieval religion. There was a higher and a lower side to the medieval conception of the Sacraments; it was on the lower side that the two classes were most cordially agreed. The royal commissioners, at the end of the seventeenth century, found the courts of justice in Auvergne administering their most solemn oaths not on the gospels, but on a local relic, the arm of St Antony, which afforded far safer sanctions against perjury. "Le Bras de St-Antoine," they wrote home to their Government, "is held more sacred than God Almighty"[2]. The peasants of Villeneuve-St-Georges, under the monks of St-Germain, were accustomed in the Middle Ages to compel their patron saint's attention when drought or rain became intolerable; they would take St George down from his altar and plunge him in the Seine. We have not only many scattered instances elsewhere of this kind, but the fulminations of an official

[1] p. 210 (written about 1050 A.D.).
[2] Branche, p. 460.

visitor in the fifteenth century imply that the practice was common[1].

Yet these forbidden things followed only too logically, in the rustic mind, from other things which the Church permitted and practised, even when she did not actively encourage or enjoin them. The Excommunication of Caterpillars, or of other similar rural pests, forms one of the most curious chapters in the social history of the Middle Ages[2]. A modern antiquary has unearthed documentary evidence for 86 cases of animal excommunication, 26 of which date between 1120 and 1501. In 1531, the celebrated legist Chassenée dealt fully with the question in his *De Excommunicatione Animalium Insectorum*. Though, in the strictest legal sense, we cannot excommunicate that which has never communicated with the Church—not even through infant baptism—yet the term was commonly used in this connexion; indeed, it is one of the first steps in medieval social and ecclesiastical history that we should realize how loosely even the most important terms were frequently used by the people, and sometimes by priests or even by popes. Chassenée argues that, all beasts being divinely subjected to man (Gen. i, 16; Ps. viii, 6) they are therefore subject to the same canon law as man. It is merely a matter of expediency, and the expediency is plain; for we know that such excommunications are in fact effective. We know that it can destroy eels in a lake, or the sparrows that infest a church; it is well-known how a priest at Toulouse turned a white loaf black by excommunication, and white again by absolution, and how the miracle was repeated by a bishop at Troyes. Since, therefore, caterpillars and other rural pests would simply laugh at a condemnatory sentence from the civil courts, let us strike them "with the pain of anathema, which they fear more, as creatures obedient to the God who made them." But it must be done in due form of law; formal monition

---

[1] *Arch. France Monast.* III, 155. For similar outrages to saints see *Five Centuries of Religion*, I, 243 ff.; Pirenne, *Soulèvement*, p. xii; Pavinus, *De Visitatione*, Q. viii, § 40 (f. 123); this passage implies that the custom was common.

[2] I deal with this matter more fully in *The History Teachers' Miscellany* for Jan. 1925. My authority here is Gelée's paper in *Aube*, XXIX (1865), 131 ff., of which the accuracy has, I believe, never been contested. The reader will find most of the same evidence in E. Agnel, *Curiosités judiciaires*, etc. Paris, 1858, pp. 20 ff.

must precede excommunication; if possible, an advocate should be appointed to plead the insects' cause in court before their condemnation. In two recorded cases, the judge offered them pieces of waste ground to which they might retire; and in one of these (1450) we are assured that this worked successfully for some years. Gelée quotes a sentence of extraordinary interest from a monastic formulary of 1526–31, by which "caterpillars, palmer-worms, or by whatsoever other they be called," are banished from the diocese of Troyes, and all the faithful are summoned as a requisite preliminary "to join together in good works and pious prayers, and to pay their tithes without fraud and according to the custom of the district." This due payment of tithes is emphasized by Chassenée as a *sine quâ non*; at these times of common danger, tithe-payer and tithe-taker were united against the pests. It was natural, therefore, that the practice should long survive in Catholic countries. The celebrated Jesuit theologian, Th. Raynaud, wrote in 1636: "Olim frequentissimus, nec nunc prorsus abolitus [modus] intorquendi excommunicationem (sic enim nominant) in bestias frugiperdas"; and in the three years 1831–33 the grasshoppers were regularly combated in parts of Champagne by the milder weapon of ecclesiastical processions and exorcisms[1]. Gelée quotes, from Bergier's *Dictionnaire*, in modern times, a defence of those parish priests who "exorcise and adjure storms, rural pests, etc."

Priests (pleads Bergier) have several times got into trouble for refusing to give way to their parishioners' requests....It would be excellent to teach the people natural science, if they were capable of understanding it and incapable of misusing it; but they are neither one nor the other. When people learn that all natural phenomena are the natural effect of physical laws, they will draw the unbeliever's conclusion, that the world made itself and governs itself. Will the people gain much by this? If those who criticize the priests knew the people better, they would be less ready to condemn the priests[2].

[1] Compare the medieval custom of condemning and executing criminal beasts—the sow which has devoured a child, or the ox which has gored a man. Beaumanoir, with the good sense of an enlightened lay lawyer, can find neither reason nor true religion in the practice (II, 485).

[2] Compare Richard and Giraud, *Bibliothèque Sacrée* (nouv. éd. 1823), tom. x, 421. *Exorcisme*: "Elle [l'Église] exorcise aussi les chenilles, les sauterelles, les tempêtes, etc. pour les empêcher de nuire aux biens de la

Let us not condemn the medieval clergy, but let us note, with Bergier, that the Excommunication of Caterpillars was a natural and logical bye-product of the normal relation between priest and peasant. Pre-Christian ceremonies for the prosperity of agricultural operations had been adopted and baptized by the Church; there were Twelfth-Day fires, and Plough-Monday; the blessing of the corn on St Mark's Day, and of the loaf at Lammas[1]. The church bells were often inscribed with the boast that they could break the power of the storm and put demons to flight. The peasant did not stop there; the clergy themselves did not always stop there; certainly not the peasant, who in those days, as in our own, was a curious compound of patience and impatience, belief and unbelief. He was as God made him; often disconcerting to our analysis, but always as human as ourselves.

Here, as everywhere else, it was better, *ceteris paribus*, to have the priest and all the Church ceremonies on one's side; yet the villager, at need, had his own ceremonies, far more ancient than those of his priest, except where the two had a common origin. He was well able, when occasion served, to do without a priest to marry him; any old rustic could ask the couple solemnly, thrice each, whether he or she took the other to spouse; and, after the six solemn affirmatives, they were thenceforth true husband and wife not only by village law but by Church law, which here followed the ruling of pre-Christian Rome[2]. Moreover, even for the last solemn sacrament the poor man had his own substitute; a little earth was put into the dying man's mouth instead of the holy wafer, and he went into

terre. Les exorcismes ont une vertu indépendante des dispositions de l'exorciste, et ils produisent infailliblement leur effet, à moins qu'il ne s'y rencontre des obstacles du côté de l'exorciste, ou des personnes en faveur desquelles on fait les exorcismes." Compare P. G. Hamerton, *Round about my House in France*, 1876, pp. 256 ff., especially p. 262 for the peasant's attitude towards these ceremonies: "Si ça ne fait pas de bien, ça ne fera pas de mal."

[1] For these see J. Brand, *Pop. Antiquities* (Bohn's ed.), I, 31, 33, 194, 348, 506–8; E. Noël, *La Campagne* (Rouen, 1890), p. 60; P. G. Hamerton, *Round about my House in France* (3rd ed. 1876), pp. 344 ff., 356 ff., and especially the study by Dr E. Bogros of his own district in Burgundy—*A travers le Morvan* (2me éd. Château-Chinon, 1886), pp. 156 ff.

[2] *Helmbrecht*, ed. Panzer, ll. 1503 ff. It was, however, ecclesiastically irregular thus to dispense with the priest, and severely punishable if the authorities chose to prosecute the offenders.

eternity houseled as his ancestors would have houseled him before the Christian era[1].

So, also, he constantly had his own exorcisms, cheaper than the priest's exorcisms and sometimes equally efficacious. The priest might be called in at a great crisis to excommunicate the caterpillars; the church bells might be rung to drive the storm away, but at ordinary times the peasant frequently fended for himself. Even greater than the horror of the sea or the deep forest was the horror of hail and thunder; and most of all, naturally, among the hills. One of the worst of rustic sins, writes Felix Hemmerlin of Zürich[2], is this frequent habit among peasant-women of calling storms together by magic: "numberless folk of both sexes, but always peasants or common folk" have been burned for this cursed thing in the diocese of Sion in Valais.

It is but a small consolation that some, by their arts, can turn the rising storm aside, and make it burst over a barren spot. And the farther we rise from mother earth, the greater is the power of the demons.

Know that, in the diocese of Constance, on that broken mountain which is called Fracmont in common speech, and at whose foot lies the city of Lucerne with its great lake, there are three other lakes on the mountain top, one of which is round and about an acre in extent; men call it commonly *Pilate's Lake*; and this is the fashion thereof, without exception, for so long as the memory of man goeth not to the contrary, as hath been found by public experience; to wit, that, if any man approach in silence, stirring the water neither by deed nor by word, he passeth straightway unharmed. But if he utter any speech—and especially if he name Pilate—or if he cast anything into the water, however small, or if he touch or stir the water, then forthwith, however clear the sky may be, a most furious tempest ariseth in the realm of the clouds, followed by intolerable hail and snow and

---

[1] *Ibid.* ll. 1904 ff. For a picturesque list of pagan ceremonials surviving among medieval and post-medieval agricultural operations, see Bartels, pp. 48–51. [2] *Nob.* c. 32, ff. 125–6.

rain, so as to threaten the very ruin of the lands at this mountain's foot. Nay, experience hath shown how its violence, by reason of these causes aforesaid, will often overwhelm the lands and fields and meadows all around, and much of the aforesaid city. And if an ox or horse or other beast come to the lake, and go in or out, therefrom no evil ariseth. Wherefore guards are always set at the ascent of this mountain, lest the aforesaid harm fall upon the land by reason of those who come near.

For the fact of Pilate's actual burial on this mountain, Hemmerlin refers us to the Golden Legend. There is (he adds) a lake of similar properties in the Apennines, between Bologna and Pistoia[1].

And the peasant's games, being traditional, had kept many traces of heathenism. Mabillon, under the year 1077, notes the pagan character of the midsummer games[2]. Those midsummer and Christmas ceremonies in London, so picturesquely described by John Stow, were survivals from the pre-Christian village. Sabbatarianism, as we have seen, was much stricter in medieval Church theory than is generally supposed; and similar restrictions were applied to the greater holy-days[3]. But St Augustine, at the beginning of the fifth century, pleaded that it was better even to plough on the Lord's Day than to desecrate it with dance and riot[4]; and, in the fifteenth, great churchmen were still quoting Augustine, and still quoting him in vain. Bishop Grosseteste uses the saint's words to shame the country-folk of his great diocese out of their frequent irreverences and crimes committed on these holy-days, and especially out of the frequent quarrels and sometimes fatal bloodshed on those solemn festivals when all the parishes, each with its own saint's banner, went in procession to the cathedral, and jostled and fought for precedence[5]. His episcopal contemporaries in France complain: "Since the wakes which are held in churches frequently lead to many foul acts—*multa turpia*—and end very often in bloodshed, on which account it is notorious that the said churches need reconciliation, which only bishops can per-

---

[1] Compare the English Haveringmere in my *Social Life, etc.* p. 534.
[2] *Annales*, v, 115.   [3] See *e.g.* Peckham's *Register*, R.S. p. 981.
[4] *De Decem Chordis*, serm. ix, § 3.
[5] *Epp.* R.S. pp. 74–5, 162. I have already touched on this subject of holy-days and crime in ch. III.

form therefore we decree and firmly command that no wakes
be held henceforth in the aforesaid churches or cemeteries."
The Feast of the Boy Bishop was similarly forbidden on account
of the quarrels and dances in Church and other irreverences to
which it gave rise[1]. In 1311, Bishop Guillaume Durand of
Mende expressed to the pope in Ecumenical Council his scandal
at the lawcourts that were held in parish churches, and the
Church-ales "at which both clergy and layfolk swill"—*se
ingurgitant*[2]. On that same occasion, his colleague Guillaume
le Maire of Angers wrote: "On those holy-days, on which God
ought more especially to be worshipped, the Devil is worshipped;
the churches are left empty, the lawcourts and taverns and work-
shops resound with quarrels, tumults, blasphemies and perjuries, and almost all sorts of crimes are there committed. Hence
cometh it that God's law, the articles of our faith, and other
things pertaining to Christian religion and the saving of souls
are almost altogether ignored"[3]. John Gower, at the end of the
same century, says much the same[4]. The contemporary author
of *Dives and Pauper* writes: "But now...with Sunday reigneth
more lechery, gluttony, manslaughter, robbery, backbiting, perjury, and other sins, more than reigned all the week before;
and, when men come to church, they leave bedes-bidding
[*praying*] and spend their time in sinful jangling"[5]. St Bernardino of Siena, a generation later, repeats this complaint over and

---

[1] Council of the province of Cognac, 1260, §§ 1, 2.
[2] Durandus, pars II, tit. 35 (p. 133).
[3] *Lib. Guil. Major*. p. 477.
[4] *Mirour*, ll. 8, 653 ff. The poet is discussing the sin of fornication; and he
continues:

> Om fait de ce pecché les mals
> Plus commun es jours festivals
> Qu'en autre jour de labourer;
> Quant la meschine et ly vassals
> Sont deschargez de leur travals,
> Lors mettont lieu del assembler:
> Quant Robin laist le charuer
> Et Marioun le canoller,
> L'un est a l'autre parigals:
> Ja jour ne vuillont celebrer;
> Pour leur corps faire deliter
> N'ont cure de l'espiritals.

Meschine =maidservant; *charuer* =ploughing; *canoller* =spinning;
parigal =partner.

[5] Com. III, ch. 6.

over again[1]; about the same time, Hemmerlin testifies for Switzerland just as St Bernardino does for Italy and Clémanges (as we have seen) for France[2]. For Germany, Geiler of Kaysersberg complained on the verge of the Reformation that nearly all handiworkers make up for their laborious week by riot and debauchery on Sundays and holy-days[3]. The 37th of the *Hundred Grievances of the German Nation*, brought before the emperor in 1522–3 at the Diet of Nürnberg, runs:

Moreover the common layfolk are no little oppressed by so great abundance of church feasts and holy-days. And no wonder, since so many holy-days have been created that the husbandman can scarce find time, with all his efforts, to bring to the garner those fruits of the field which he has forced with such labour from the ground, sometimes endangered by floods or rain or immoderate heat, and not infrequently by hail or other tempests; which same fruits, if the holy-days did not hinder him, he could easily and securely have gathered and brought home from the field. Moreover, on feast-days, which at first were doubtless well celebrated, with good advice and to the honour of God Almighty, innumerable transgressions are now committed, with sins and crimes, rather than the worship and veneration of God. This is so notorious a fact that there is no need whatsoever of bringing [specific] testimony[4].

Nor are these the whinings of peevish puritans; we have frequent evidence from business documents. At Grünwald, near Rapperschwyl in Switzerland, the yearly dedication-day of the Church disturbed the three neighbouring convents of Béguines, who "seeing the excesses committed there, and feeling reasonably that the people, instead of casting off their sins through penances and pardons, might more probably add to their load of guilt, petitioned the bishop to transfer the dedication-feast to winter-time"[5]. Again, the customal of the abbey of Herrenchiemsee, drawn up in 1462, emphasizes its prescriptions as to the punishment of criminals by quoting a concrete case which had given great trouble in the past. "Let it be noted that, in the year 1393 after Christ's birth, sad to say, there fell a fight on St Augustine's day by reason of the Kirchweih [dedication feast] at Sankt Martin, wherein four were slain, one on the spot

---

[1] *E.g.* II, 58 b. [2] *Neb.* c. 32 (f. 128 b).
[3] *Navicula Fatuorum*, turba XCVII, xxxi, N.
[4] Browne, *Fascic.* II, 363. [5] Arx. II, 201.

and the others died later; and thus we came into great trouble with Elizabeth Torerin, who was then lady [of Sankt Martin?]." The duke sent commissioners to arbitrate, but the quarrel continued; "for Fridel Plank took to the forest, and abjured us and all ours, and took our bailiff of Wartmanning...and he burned three of our houses at Ystad, with the stuff and the people, especially a boy who perished in the fire; and at last we had to come to terms with him"[1].

Brandt in his *Narrenschiff*, and Barclay in his translation from Brandt, take only the ordinary satirist's licence in their picture of the early sixteenth century Sunday or Saint's day:

> The taverne is open before the churchë be;
> The pottis are ronge as bellys of dronkenes
> Before the churche bellys with great salemnyte;
> There here these wretches theyr Matyns and theyr masse;
> Who lysteth to take hede shall often se doutles
> The stallys of the taverne stuffyd nere echone,
> Whan in the churche stallys he shall se fewe or none[2].

All this, of course, was a violent reaction from drudgery and monotony. Clémanges gives us both sides of the shield; misery on workdays, licence on feast-days; money and leisure ill-spent by men who have had little chance to learn the best use of money and leisure; a revulsion more frequent and more extreme than the modern Bank Holiday. Most peasants are sober on workdays, says Clémanges; but then they are ignorant—*vulgus indoctum est*—and unfit to use their freedom[3].

Though ecclesiastical disciplinarians in all countries waged frequent war against the village dance, I have found no trace of this on the neutral ground of English manor customals; in Germany, however, it is frequently expressed in later days. In the two villages of Sigmundsthal and Praxmär, belonging to the monks of Wilten in Tirol, "these are the village ordinances; public dancing is abolished and done away with; drinking [late] at night is forbidden, also all play with dice or cards; yea, target-shooting also, as a recreation far too costly for the peasants, and therefore indecent and harmful to them without express

---

[1] *Weisthümer*, III, 672.
[2] *Ship of Fools* (ed. Jamieson, 1874), I, 176; Brandt in Scheible, 727–9, with Geiler's contemporary comments.   [3] Fol. 148 b.

permission of the gracious lords "—*i.e.* the monastic landlords[1]. For the villages of the Pongau district, under the archbishop of Salzburg, the customs of 1520 forbid public dance without permission of the authorities[2]. For an extraordinarily interesting account of the growth of games in a Flemish village I must refer to appendix 19.

One glance at the village inn, however, before we pass on. Here again, the main evidence is from Germany, and we cannot apply it off-hand to other countries; but probably a few rough rules were evolved elsewhere, though not so formal as what I am about to cite here[3]. These German customals are some-times very detailed as to disorder and justice at the tavern. Not only was it forbidden to bring arms in the stricter sense, but the peasant must secure society against the use of his own tools as weapons:

They must give them to the host, who was bound to keep them until the owner's departure, and not to let them out of his hands in case of quarrel. The guest, as an alternative, might sit upon his tools; no doubt men counted upon the peasant's love of ease, which would keep him from rising readily [from his drink]. If the guest had only come in for one glass, he might keep his weapon. He himself was responsible for giving it up; but the host also was bound to see that all did so, and that no man kept his arms secretly. If necessary, the host might take them by force; he might even be made responsible for the damage done by his omission. Even to draw one's weapon was punishable, unless the adversaries were reconciled without delay. From strangers the weapon must be demanded either at once or after the first glass, and they must not be given back for a quarrel.

[1] *Tit. Weis.* I, 260–1; the MS. dates from 1733; the monks had held the villages since 1140. In about 1800, no dancing was allowed at Hörtenberg without permission (*ibid.* II, 2). At Kropfsberg a similar prohibition, with exceptions for weddings and a few feast-days, existed from at least 1535 on-wards (*ibid.* II, 369).

[2] *Die Salzburger Taidinge*, ed. Siegel and Tomaschek (Vienna, 1870), p. 195. But in most German parishes, by this time, the dance seems to have been permitted under due organization; see Haltaus, cols. 16, 1492. For fuller evidence as to medieval puritanism in its relations to dance and song, see *Five Centuries of Religion*, vol. I, appendix 23, and appendix 40 here.

[3] Moreover, we shall doubtless go wrong if we take all these prescriptions too literally; like most other medieval legislation, they represent an ideal rather than a regular practice. Hoyer shows the danger of judging medieval village practice too strictly according to the theory of contemporary dis-ciplinary regulations; and it is probable that all will agree with him who take pains to compare the different lines of evidence which surviving documents supply (*l.c.* pp. 39, 43, 57–60).

If the stranger would not accede to this, nor move on, then the neighbours must earnestly ask him why he refused, and compel him to assure them that he had no evil intention. Wayfaring folk were allowed to keep their weapons.

In one village it was prescribed that, in case of quarrel, "the angry man should have a coat cast over his head, and should be hustled up and down the inn parlour until he promised to keep the peace"[1]. In every way, indeed, these German customs show anxiety to give the village a good reputation with travelling strangers. Hoyer quotes an interesting example of this (p. 54):

If a stranger came to this village and wished to play, the innkeeper was to play with him; or, if he had no time, to fetch fellow-players. If the stranger won enough to buy a horse with it, then the village had to give him a saddle and lead him in solemn procession from the village with a can of wine in his hand. "But if it so befal that the stranger lose, and begin to murmur, and to grudge, then shall they begin by giving him good words and beseech him to be appeased. Then, if good words be of no avail, the villagers who have played with him shall take a coat and cast it over his head and go with him into a corner to this man and that, and afterwards set him to table and give him to drink and ask him whether he has had justice." If he still remains angry the judge must be brought, and bring him to the assurance that he intended no harm to the village on this account.

With all this, we must still remember that though, by strict law, the rights of vendetta and private war were confined to the nobility, yet in fact the peasants and citizens often kept up the tradition among themselves[2]. The *Cavalleria Rusticana* of Sicily is a medieval survival; or rather, the Middle Ages passed it down to us from a still more primitive society.

This fragmentary chapter on religious education may close, however, on another note. The best, beyond question, of St Bernard's early biographers was Geoffrey of Auxerre, the saint's pupil and private secretary, and finally his successor as abbot. In one passage of a memorial sermon on his master,

---

[1] Hoyer, pp. 59–60, 62.
[2] See Ch. Petit-Dutaillis, *Le droit de vengeance dans les Pays-Bas au* xvᵉ *siècle* (Champion, 1908), and notably pp. 46, 103–113.

Geoffrey casts incidentally almost as much light upon the peasant as upon the saint[1]:

It is true that, comparing spiritual things with spiritual, he spake sublimely; yet did he not shrink from condescending to untaught and simple folk. But that which in him seemed the more humble was perchance more wonderful then, and is now the sweeter to our taste. For how often were we delighted then to hear, and are delighted now to recall, how he was wont to spur on those rustic men and poor simple women to duties of humanity which became their station. For he taught them that, when one of their neighbours, as often happens—*uti assolet*—lacks bread, they should cheerfully lend unto him until he could repay; or when another neighbour, perchance otherwise busied, had prepared no food, that they should charitably invite him to their own potherbs; that they should generously send him a few vegetables and share with him their scanty pulse. So also he taught them to keep the faith of lawful wedlock, nor transgress (as men ungrateful of God's gift), the bounds of wholesome indulgence. Moreover, he bade them pay their earthly dues to their earthly lords, and render faithfully their dues, or give their tithes without fraud, to Him who could more justly claim for himself nine-tenths than the husbandman could claim even one-tenth. For it was He who both made the earth and gave unto the labourer his arms and his strength; it is He also who sends His frost to lock in the seed that has been sown, His rains to water it, His vernal warmth to cherish it, and His summer suns to ripen it; so that, unless He gave the increase, the plougher would lose his labour. Moreover, he would studiously warn them to beware of magicians and their sacrilegious charms; and that, being unable to pursue with swords those who harmed them, they should not attack them with their tongues; nor should they, by cheating each other, follow after scanty gains to their own grievous destruction; but let them remember Him who, being rich, was made poor for our sakes; and let them bear in mind that the poor man is left unto Him.

It is a beautiful picture, and this may remind us, again, how St Francis's appeal was mainly to the peasantry of his native Umbria, and how that early Franciscanism which scarcely outlasted the saint's lifetime may be called predominantly a peasant religion, both in its simple strength and in its limitations.

[1] P.L. vol. 185, col. 584.

CHAPTER XX

TITHES AND FRICTION

IF then, as contemporary witnesses agree, a large proportion of the villagers lived in semi-paganism, what was responsible for this? Doubtless, in the first place, human nature; there never has been a land or an age of real faith in the Pauline sense, which implies not only acquiescence in certain formulae, but a certain effort to realize and practice that which often goes in at the ears and sometimes comes forth from the lips. It would be far less necessary to insist upon these things, if they were not daily misrepresented among us by superficial writers, and condoned by the silence of professional historians. *A priori*, nobody would expect the centuries of reconstruction after the break-up of ancient civilization to have been an age of noble and deep religion among the multitude, apart from a small minority of idealists; nor was it so in fact[1].

I have said, human nature was the first obstacle; and few men realize what a rough-hewn humanity the missionaries had to deal with at the end of the Dark Ages. Some readers will be familiar with that story in Book II of the monk of St-Gall, where he tells how noble Danes came yearly to the court of Charles the Great, seeking baptism and rebaptism for the sake of the new clothes which were distributed after the ceremony. But how many have read the life of St Liudger, who would never have been born but for his mother's marvellous escape from murder in her own family? About 750 A.D., there lived a noble in Frisia whose wife, after many years of marriage, had produced only girls; and Frisian law permitted the extinction of female children, so long as the deed was done before the new-born infant had tasted of earthly food. The latest of these girls was Liafburga; and her pagan grandmother, furious with this last and most unwelcome infant, sent a henchman to seize it before the mother had given it suck, and to drown it in a bucket. The child, with that prehensile power which modern science has

---

[1] I may refer here to the 13th of my *Medieval Studies*: "The Plain Man's Religion in the Middle Ages."

noted in new-born infants, clung to the edge of the bucket just long enough to soften the man's heart; and a woman hard by ran out and took the child while the servant went back to report what had happened. The woman then hurried with Liafburga to her own room, where she seized a pot of honey and thrust a little into the victim's mouth. A second and less merciful henchman, arriving soon after, found the little creature licking its lips over this human food. Killing would now be murder: Liafburga was spared; but it was necessary to keep her hidden so long as the pagan grandmother lived; then she was brought into the family and grew up to become St Liudger's mother[1]. In Iceland, even Christianity had to compound awhile with this heathen law of infanticide; St Olaf found the priests permitting it in the early eleventh century[2]. Such was the unredeemed north and east after the break-up of the Roman empire—Germans, Scandinavians and Slavs. These were the people who had somehow to be made into Christians, by a society in which no larger proportion of the total population were prepared to risk their lives for true religion than those who are ready to risk their lives today for one or another high ideal.

The second obstacle was that which Dante deplored, and which men had felt strongly for centuries before Dante—the riches of the clergy as a body. In the aggregate, their sympathies were necessarily capitalistic; and therefore (apart from early missionary days) neither the cleric nor the monk, as a rule, was really popular[3]. When he was rich, he naturally attracted more envy than the rich of noble birth; when (as was most frequent with those who did the real work of the parish) he was poor, and lacked the conspicuous virtues of Chaucer's model parson to counterbalance his poverty, then familiarity was apt to breed contempt.

An interesting sidelight is cast on Italian village life by the nicknames of different priests who served the parish of Gambara

[1] Mabillon, AA.SS.O.S.B. Saec. IV, p. i (1677), p. 20.
[2] P. du Chaillu, *The Viking Age*, II, 39 ff.
[3] It was unlucky to meet either priest or monk on the road; see Jacques de Vitry, *Exempla*, ed. Crane, p. 112; T. Wright, *Latin Stories*, etc. p. 77. The author of *Dives and Pauper* writes: "Some men had liever to meet with a toad or a frog in the way than with a knight or a squire or with any man of religion or of Holy Church" (Com. I, cap. 46).

between 1150 and 1190; "Bellomo" is of course complimentary (*bellus homo*); but what are we to think of those whom *vicini de Gambara vocabant Scanacaponem vel Sechafenum et Johannem Zoppum*—"Cut-the-capon's-throat" and "Dry-the-hay" and "Limping John"? Or, again, *Girardum Galinam*—"Gerard the Hen," who is apparently the same as "Gerard *Miss-hen*"—*Mancagalinam*[1].

It is sometimes asserted, but without attempt at corroborative evidence, that within the walls of the medieval church no distinction was made between rich and poor[2]. The fact is, that nobody might sit in the chancel but lords and "patrons," who were generally, in earlier days, the local squires[3]. It was one of the counts against the chaplain of Erleigh in 1224 that "he was wont indiscriminately to admit the parishioners of Sunning when he celebrated Mass in the said chapel; whereas he ought to receive none but the lord [of the manor] and his lady and their freeborn servants." The fact that the question is here, at bottom, one of Mass-offerings, does not affect its relevance to the present point[4]. As early as about 830, Jonas of Orléans complains that great folk had their private chapels, and used them as an excuse for non-attendance at the parish church[5]. In a Synod held at Pavia in 855, the bishops of the province addressed to the emperor a memorial for the reform of the more pressing abuses. One clause complains of the neglect of preaching, and adds:

Certain layfolk, and especially the rich and powerful, have chapels beside their dwellings wherein they hear divine service and are wont to come not very often [*rarius*] to the mother churches[6]. And, seeing

[1] Zaccaria, pp. 157, 161, 169.
[2] "To 'Holy Mother Church' all were the same; and within God's House the tenant, the villain and the serf stood side by side with the overlord and master" (Gasquet, *Parish Life*, p. 7; a statement dear to *The Church Times*: compare Jessopp in *The Nineteenth Century*, Jan. 1898, pp. 55 ff.). Bruneau shows how strongly rooted, even in 1789, was the privilege of a patron in the village church, and how other nobles might enjoy similar privileges. "Few rights," he says, "were more greedily sought after, by those who lacked them, than these rights of honour in the churches"; and he gives instances of bitter contests at law upon this subject (pp. 149–151).
[3] *E.g.* Bishop Quivil's decree of 1287 in Wilkins, *Concilia*, II, 140, cf. p. 184, and Grandisson's *Register*, p. 132.
[4] *Register of St Osmund*, R.S. I, 307.
[5] P.L. vol. 106, col. 144.
[6] *Majores Ecclesias*. This designation was often, but by no means always, reserved in later centuries of the Middle Ages for cathedrals.

that only the afflicted and the poor come, what else can we preach to them but that they should suffer their ills in patience? But if the rich, who are wont to do injustice to the poor, would not refuse to come, then at any rate they might be admonished to redeem their sins by alms-giving, in order that they might abstain from the flux of temporal things[1].

Very interesting, in this connexion, are the results to which P. Imbart de la Tour was led by his study of the formation of parishes in the Middle Ages. Writing of the pre-Carolingian era he concludes:

One of the distinguishing features of this society is that custom is stronger than law, and the outer shell of the institutions ill conceals the inward anarchy which threatens them. The rural clergy were already being drawn into the feudal system. The great evil from which this society suffered, the absence of security, thrust the Church, like the people, into the arms of the squirearchy [le séniorat]....The parish clergy was at last reduced to dependence upon the lords.

And again, of the middle of the eleventh century, when many priests "recommended" themselves to the local lord: "In reality, these priests became the 'men' of the lords, who imposed all sorts of obligations upon them...all the services, in one word, which a great man could exact from his vassal.... Very often, also, the lord believes himself entitled to withdraw the benefice from the priest who has broken his 'fealty'"[2].

The earliest mention known to me of privileged seats reserved for the laity in parish churches is in that inquisition taken at Gambara in 1195 which gives so many interesting glimpses of monastic and parochial life: "Moreover, the witness saith that the women of the districts of Lachexolo and Gambarella [i.e. the original core of the parish] have the first benches in the church of St Mary, and the grandmother of the present witness had a bench there, as he heard from his father." He himself could speak from a memory of "forty years and more"[3]. But, in the later Middle Ages, the reserved pew was evidently a common institution; in the early fourteenth century, Lady de

[1] Labbé, Concilia, vol. VIII (1671), col. 147.
[2] Rev. Hist. LXIII (1897), 23; LXVIII (1898), 36–7. Though the Hildebrandine reformation wrought much improvement here, yet Sir Thomas More and other writers on the verge of the Reformation complain of the large number of priests performing menial offices for the squirearchy.
[3] Zaccaria, p. 156; cf. p. 154.

Dalton found the great mystic Richard Rolle praying fervently
in her pew, and it is recorded as specially noteworthy that "of
her humility" she did not suffer her servants to expel him[1].
Two generations later, Langland speaks of the parish quarrels
engendered by this exclusiveness in church:

Among wives and widows I [Wrath] am wont to sit
Y-parked in pews: "The parson it knoweth
How little I love Lettice at the Style;
For [since] she had holy-bread ere I, mine heart began to change.
Afterward, at the meat, she and I chid."
And I, Wrath, was ware, and wrought on them both
Till either cleped other "whore!" and off with the clothes,
Till both their heads were bare, and bloody their cheeks[2].

Nor was the fight always thus fought out on unconsecrated
ground; parishioners pushed and brawled for precedence in
church, to vindicate what they considered their social consequence; Chaucer's forewords to *The Monk's Tale* might be
borne out by cold ecclesiastical records[3]. Again, the whole
parish might be kept waiting for Mass until it pleased the
knight's lady to rise and come to Church; they might even lose
their Mass because the Dame stayed beyond the lawful hour of

[1] Rolle's *English Works*, E.E.T.S. 1862, p. 42. At Norrey, in Normandy,
there was a lawsuit about the possession of a church pew which lasted at least
from 1634 to 1683 (*Norm. monumentale et pittoresque*, Havre, 1895; *Calvados*,
p. 239. Similar cases are recorded by A. Benet, *Inventaire sommaire des
archives du Calvados*, Caen, 1897, pp. 261, 285). We may here notice incidentally the *cagots* of France, once so widely spread from the Pyrenees to
Brittany. These people were kept at the back of the church, with a holy-water-
stoup of their own; the priest came down to their end only to receive their
Mass-offerings. When Leo X and Charles V, in response to their public
petition, granted them ecclesiastical equality; and again when Louis XIV, in
1683, attempted to remove their disabilities, the lower clergy often joined
with the populace in resisting these liberal decrees; even in 1784, there was
a bishop who refused to admit any of these people to Holy Orders; again, as
late as 1842, those of a Pyrenean village "were obliged to address the ecclesiastical authorities in protest against the persistent prejudice which still
confined them to separate places in church and churchyard" (*Revue des Deux
Mondes*, Jan. 1878, p. 436; *Les cagots et leurs congénères*, by L. Louis-Lande).
The superstition that these people were unhealthy and infectious, however
ill-grounded in fact, separates their case from those cited in my text. It was
calculated about 1680 that there were more than 2000 *cagots* in the single
province of Béarn.

[2] *Piers Plowman*, C. vii, 143; see also Skeat's note on the words.

[3] Compare Bozon, p. 35. It may be noted how much of the evidence on
this subject dates from before the Black Death.

noon[1]. Finally (though for this there is more excuse) burial within the church was a privilege bought with much money. A friar complains, about a century after St Francis's death, that "the world is now turned upside down; for those who would refuse to give a usurer the kiss of peace in church, would not now stick at kissing his feet...and these men, whose bodies of old time were buried in the field or the garden, are now buried in front of the high altar in church"[2]. The medieval clergy, as a whole, was a definitely capitalistic body; therefore it shared whatever odium attached to the capitalism of that day. Clerics went partners even in the usurer's unpopularity, as they were often directly or indirectly partners of his gains. Indirectly, as abettors of the usurer; for Bozon's complaint is that of many other contemporaries. Directly also, since the clergy themselves practised usury with sufficient frequency to attract the notice of Church councils, from at least as early as that of Rome in 846 to at least as late as that of Rouen in 1313[3]. It became a constant theme of the satirists from the thirteenth century onwards. In the twelfth century, a great deal of the banking business of the world was done by monasteries. Alexander III, in the Council of Tours (1163), complained of this scandal: "Many [plures] of the clergy (and, we lament to say it, even of those who by their profession, their vow and their dress have cut themselves off from this present world), while they shrink from common usury as from a thing too plainly condemned, do notwithstanding lend money to others who are in need, and take their possessions in

---

[1] The Knight of La Tour, E.E.T.S. 1868, p. 42; it is told, however, as an extreme case. Prevost alludes to "the numerous lawsuits which [in the sixteenth and seventeenth centuries] arose between lords of the manor and parish clergy on this question," i.e. whether the lord had the right "of fixing the time for divine service, and put it forward or back at his own fancy" (p. 103). He attempts to dissociate the Church from all responsibility here, and concludes optimistically, without offering evidence, that "the nobles themselves, in the Middle Ages, seem to have understood" their true place.

[2] Bozon, p. 35. Gilles de Rais, the prototype of Bluebeard, was among the worst criminals recorded in history. But, "as he was a lord, reverent justice granted him a Christian funeral, whereas the ashes of his accomplices were cast into the Loire, just as had been done a few years before with Joan of Arc," who also could claim no privilege of birth (Elie Richard, in Mercure de France, Nov. 1921, p. 594).

[3] Fleury, Hist. Eccl. an. 846, § 11. Richard, Anal. Concil. II, 320. For England see Wilkins, II, 146, § 24 and John of Worcester, ed. Weaver, 1908, p. 21.

pledge, and receive the fruits therefrom accruing beyond the principal lent"[1]. The Cistercian General Chapter of 1180 had to take notice of this abuse in the Order; and that of 1181 felt it necessary to explain and confirm the decree[2]. The Franciscan General Chapter of 1421 was compelled to legislate against friars who were not only trading, but also practising usury[3]. Robert Mannyng of Brunne, in 1303, judged that "almost all clergy" were infested with the sin of covetousness. Proceeding to inveigh against the sin of usury, he adds:

> I speak to men of richë life
> That have no chargc of child nor wife,
> Parsons, priests that have their rent,
> And others that have great extent[4].

The Dominican Guillaume Pépin, in 1524, applied to the society of his own time those words of Ps. liv, 12 Vulg.: "Usury and deceit have not departed from its streets." "Many," he says, "both among the laity and the clergy, are tainted with this vice." In another passage, he finds it natural that peasants should pay tithes unwillingly to priestly usurers[5]. And here, as in many other cases, it is possible to corroborate the preacher's indignant impeachment with colder documentary evidence from other sources. It was extremely common for Religious to buy land from small freeholders on condition of receiving a certain rent in perpetuity. Delisle, with his extraordinary diligence, has tabulated more than 200 of these rents, drawn from the accounts of three monasteries and a hospital between 1217 and 1384 A.D. He shows that the normal rent was 10 per cent. of the capital outlay—in other words, that the monks placed their money, on excellent security, at 10 per cent. True, in one case it was as low as 3·28, in another 6, and in three others less than 7 per cent.; but far more frequently these rents exceeded the normal 10; six times they actually range from 20

---

[1] Mansi, *Concilia*, vol. XXI, col. 1176.
[2] Martene, *Thesaurus*, vol. IV, coll. 1252, 1256. Compare Hoffmann in *Hist. Jahrbuch*, XXXI (1910), 710.
[3] *Ana. Fra.* II, 277. For the extent to which the Order had abandoned the rule against trading and possessing money, see H. C. Lea, *Inq. of M. Ages*, III (1901), 174 n.
[4] E.E.T.S. 1901, ll. 5, 509; 6, 065.
[5] Pépin, *Ninive*, serm. I, f. 2 b; serm. XXXIX, f. 326 a.

to 22·22 per cent.[1] In 1248 and 1250 Eudes Rigaud notes clerical usurers among his subjects[2]. Among the sinners reported by the archdeacon of Hiémois in 1268, is a clerical usurer in a Norman village[3]. "John the chaplain is an excessive usurer," reports a Norwich jury in 1290[4]. Archbishop Peckham, in 1279, reproaches the abbot of Bristol for having taken from a poor man "more than 100 per cent. of usury, which even civil law forbids to all men"[5]. The monks of Gladbach were practising usury up to about 1357, when the abbot did what he could to reform them; but the archbishop had to intervene in 1360[6].

The direct effect of usury upon the peasant will be dealt with in a later chapter; meanwhile I am concerned only to note briefly what seems to me the unquestionable fact that the poor man knew the Church to be often directly interested in the most invidious side of capitalism[7]. And this quite apart from indirect encouragement; from the fact that popes and prelates, like the lay lords, had their tame Jews and their privileged Lombards, whom they protected with one hand and squeezed with the other, thus doing much to frustrate the good intentions of scholastic philosophers, canon lawyers, and great preachers like Saints Bernardino and Antonino.

There is another chapter in the economic relations between priest and people which might afford matter for a volume, and can only be briefly indicated here. The prohibition of exacting money for the sacraments recurs with such tedious frequency

[1] Delisle, pp. 214 ff.   [2] Reg. Vis. pp. 35, 93.
[3] Hen. Véz. p. 466.
[4] Hudson-Tingey, Records of Norwich, I, 1906, 368.
[5] Epp. R.S. p. 68.
[6] Gladbach-Eckertz, pp. 116, 294. On the other hand, we find some Breton clergy, in the eighteenth century, lending to peasants at 5 per cent., without date prefixed for the repayment of the principal. This must have been a very real assistance to struggling men (Le Lay, p. 58).
[7] For the whole subject of monastic banking see R. Génestal, Du rôle des monastères comme établissements de crédit (Paris, 1901) and his article on Troarn in Vierteljahrsschrift f. Soc.- und Wirtgesch. vol. II, Heft 4 (1904), p. 616. His conclusions do not make sufficient allowance, perhaps, for the monks; see Rev. Hist. LXXVIII (1902), 347 ff., Rev. d'hist. eccl. de Louvain, VI (1905), 120, and R. N. Sauvage, L'abbaye de Troarn (Caen, 1911), p. 219. Instances are quoted also by Lamprecht, Wirth. I, pp. 678, 681, 849, 1446, 1449; II, 227–8; Delisle, pp. 195–213 (compare p. 468, which describes disguised usury, and pp. 133–4, where the monks of Fécamp are lending at 12½ per cent.); Five Centuries of Religion, I, 390; Brutails, p. 73.

in Church councils that there could be no doubt of its continual violation, even if we had not plenty of more direct evidence to the same effect. Alexander III, in the Lateran Council of 1179, deplored the horrible venality of those who, blinded by covetousness, demanded money for celebrating burials, marriages or other sacraments; he condemned them to the fate of Gehazi. But, "the Church struggled in vain to maintain the gratuitous principle....In feudal times, the sale of the sacraments was one of the regular sources of parochial income"[1]. Long before the Reformation, such exactions as Mass-penny and burial fees had become so regular as to acquire the force of customary law[2]. The transition stage is marked here by Cardinal Jacques de Vitry's anecdote of about 1200 A.D.[3]:

I have heard concerning a certain covetous priest, if so I may say, that, when the mother of a certain youth died, he would by no means give her burial until he had first gotten his money. But the youth, who was poor, knew not what to do. So, after many anxious thoughts within himself, he went at nightfall and put his mother in a sack, and bound the mouth firmly, and carried it on his back to the priest's house, saying: "Sir, I have no ready money; but I bring you a sound pledge, to wit, skeins of good yarn which my mother had spun to weave into linen"; with which words he cast down the sack and departed. Then the priest called his clerk and came joyfully to the sack, and, feeling the woman's head, he said: "Here we have a good pledge, of whatsoever sort the rest may be. This ball of yarn that I feel is very big; this is well worth the money." So he opened the sack; and it befel that the old woman's feet, which the son had bent back, smote with a mighty stroke upon the priest's breast. He therefore, in amazement and fear, seeing now the truth of the matter, was sore ashamed, and buried the corpse forthwith; and thus this covetous trickster was tricked as he deserved.

Evidence of this kind makes us understand better why Bishop Guillaume Durand, in his advice to visiting prelates, counsels them to be suspicious of "the written complaints which countryfolk often bring forward secretly against their rectors"; for, as he has reminded us a few lines above in a

---

[1] P. Imbart de la Tour in *Rev. Hist.* LXIII (1897), 31.

[2] For Jacques de Vitry's tale of the Mass-penny, see *Social Life in Britain*, p. 217, from *Alphabet of Tales*, E.E.T.S. 1904, p. 385. It is also told by Bromyard, *Sum. Praed.* D. III, 9, who makes the peasant say "Thou hast put a hard God into my mouth."

[3] *Exempla*, ed. Crane, p. 82, No. CXCVII.

sentence from canon law, "the laity are always very hostile to the clergy"[1]. That saw was already centuries old; it had recently been revived by Boniface VIII for the opening sentence of his celebrated bull *Clericis laicos*, and it was constantly repeated throughout the Middle Ages. The *Klingenberger Chronik*, though the writer is far from holding a brief for the lower classes, speaks incidentally of one notorious fact, "that ancient hatred which has subsisted between peasants and parsons"[2]. About the same time (*i.e.* about 1460) the canonist de Pavinis applies specially to the peasants that phrase from *Clericis laicos*, "the clergy have always been hated by the laity"[3]. And he, as well as his predecessor, the great canonist Hostiensis, warns visitors against listening too much to the frequent complaints of the villagers against their clergy[4]. In 1411, the University of Paris drew the attention of Western Christendom to the scandals resulting from discord between priests and people and the too hasty pronouncement of ecclesiastical sentences, "especially in causes of worldly debts," with the result that there was "an innumerable multitude of excommunicated folk" needing reconciliation to the Church[5].

This may almost be said to have been inherent in the very circumstances of medieval society. The individual ecclesiastic, we must never forget, had often a charitable mind; but, entangled in this network of immemorial custom, he was almost as powerless as his parishioners. When the great reforming Pope Benedict XII came to the throne, the king of France sent an embassy requesting his attention to 18 articles of complaint (1335). Many of these, naturally, were solely or mainly in the interests of the Crown; but one runs: "That [the Holy Father] may be pleased to abolish the evil custom and abuse whereby the parish parsons in Anjou and Maine take upon themselves to seize all movable goods of their parishioners when these die; whereby their heirs become beggars, etc."[6] No doubt many vicars, reduced to a bare living wage by the monastery or cathedral chapter which took the lion's share of

---

[1] *Speculum Juris* (Frankfurt, 1592), vol. II, f. 30 b.
[2] Bezold, p. 142. [3] *Bac. Past.* lib. I, q. 5, f. 9 b.
[4] *Tract. Jur.* vol. XIV, f. 140, §§ 97 ff. [5] Finke, p. 141, §§ 28–30.
[6] Minist. de l'instruct. publique—*Bulletin philologique et historique de l'année 1918* (Paris, 1920), p. 214.

the parochial endowments, would almost have starved unless they had enforced their customary rights. But the whole system, by this time, had become thoroughly vicious in its identification of Church interests with landlordism. Detailed evidence comes to us from every direction; even from the fragmentary records of separate country parishes. It was not only that the parson's interests were definitely on the capitalistic side in the dependence for his living upon tithes, and upon mortuaries and offerings which had been once voluntary, but which were now fixed upon the parishioner by immemorial

THE PAYMENT OF TITHES

customs which had the strict force of law. Beyond this, in proportion as a priest or a monk drew income from the glebe, he was involved in the difficulties and disputes which were implicit in all medieval ownership. At Bures, near Dieppe, for instance, "in 1340, we find a compromise to end the fresh differences which had arisen between the prior of Notre-Dame-du-Pré and the lord of Valiquerville, 'seeing that the said prior asserted that, on the days when he had his lands ploughed in Bures, none of the dwellers in the said village might plough his own, but that such an one was bound to go and help the said prior'"[1].

[1] *Hist. de Bures-en-Bray*, par l'abbé J. E. Decorde (Paris and Rouen, 1872), p. 49.

It may be pleaded that the prior was probably within his legal rights here, and that it may have been an economic necessity for him to enforce those rights, given the monastic and social conditions under which he lived. But true history is far less concerned with the rights and wrongs of individuals, even though they were emperors and popes, than with the rights and wrongs of social and religious institutions. From that point of view we can see how the villagers must have felt their prior, however strong in his legal case, to be setting an imperfect example in religion.

Innocent III, in 1204, had to deal with the frequent quarrels due "to the charity of the people growing cold" in face of "the custom reigning in certain churches, that the beds whereon the dead bodies are brought to church should become the property of that church's ministers." The clergy must be warned, he writes, not to molest the people by claiming this as a legal due; but the laity must be exhorted to keep up this "laudable custom" as a matter of piety[1]. The diocesan decree of Bishop Quivil of Exeter in 1287 is equally significant as to popular feeling on this subject (§ 50):

We have understood that the rendering of mortuaries arose from this healthy source, that, when the greater and lesser tithes and other parish dues have, through ignorance, remained unpaid, they should be rendered to the churches thus defrauded, in order that this forgetfulness, proceeding from the negligence of the man who did not pay, might at least by this [mortuary system] be excused before the face of the Stern Judge—*apud Districtum Judicem*. And, howbeit this provision were in some way fruitful for all Christians, yet some, ignoring the cause of this payment, or (which is worse) careless of their own salvation, have in wondrous wise withheld it, transmitting their wretchedness to their posterity, whereby in these times of ours—*modernis temporibus*—they would fain excuse themselves on the plea that neither they nor their forefathers ever acknowledged this due. O wretched and unhappy excuse, hatched in sin and leading the excusers to destruction![2]

This matter of medieval tithing is so often misrepresented, and is so important for any full comprehension of the peasant's mind, that I must interpose a brief quotation here, taken from what was perhaps the most popular of all late-medieval books on

---

[1] P.L. vol. 215, c. 472.   [2] Wilkins, *Concilia*, II, 158.

Church Law[1]. The parson might claim tithes from every kind of gain, excepting only illicit gains, such as the usurer's, the jongleur's, or the prostitute's[2]. No poverty excused a parishioner in strict law, however extreme; this was counterbalanced, however, by the parson's reciprocal duty of rescuing his parishioner from starvation. "Who are bound to pay tithes?" asks the author, and answers, on the authority of the great Alexander of Hales, "All; the poor as well as the rich." To which his glossator adds the following comments from the classical authorities; I omit only some of the formal references:

The poor as well, etc. Abbot Alan discusses whether he who reaps only just enough fruit to satisfy his own needs be bound to pay tithes, and concludes in the affirmative...but adds that the Church is bound to remit him enough for his bare livelihood, since she is bound to provide for him of her own revenues. The gloss on the canon *Quicunque* [*Decret Grat*. pars II, c. xvi, q. I, c. 46] says that, if a man have left his tithes unpaid so long that he could not satisfy the claim without selling all that he hath, although [on the one hand] he be bound to do this, yet [on the other] the Church is bound to allow him enough to live upon. Abbot Alan adds that, where the poverty is so great that a man cannot pay his tithe without dying of hunger, then he is not bound to pay. This solves the question whether the poor man be bound to pay tithes of the alms given unto him, seeing

---

[1] *Summa Angelica*, s.v. *Decima*, § 7. This book was compiled about 1480 by a Franciscan friar from the *Summa Theologiae* of Aquinas and from other classics of theology and canon law. Fr. Thurston, on p. 43 of the article to which I have more than once referred, bases his misleading comment upon the tithe system on a passage of *Piers Plowman* which he does not seem fully to have understood; he has apparently been misled by Skeat's inaccurate note to C. XIV, 73. I quote from the revised edition of this *Summa* published at Venice in 1669.

[2] This is the matter which has misled Skeat; compare his note with *Sum. Ang. l.c.* § 6 and Lyndwood, *Prov.* 1679, p. 195. The latter writes: "Concerning personal tithes, it is usually said that, although they be due from things unlawfully acquired, yet they must not be exacted from him who gains ill and illegally, nor received from him if he will pay....But do thou say, according to [Pope] Innocent [III], that from prostitutes and other such folk, so long as they are impenitent, tithes must not be exacted nor their alms received. But if they repent, these things should be received; for the penitent beginneth to be what he was not before....And, even though he repent not, he may pay tithes and oblations and give alms with the consent of the diocesan, and in this way also the priest may take them." Similar decisions will be found in the gloss on canon law, *Decret. Greg.* l. III, tit. xxx, c. 23, s.v. *licite*. There, the Biblical prohibitions, "Thou shalt not offer the hire of a strumpet," etc. (Deut. xxiii, 18) are countered with, "Make unto you friends of the mammon of iniquity" (Luke xvi, 9). Cf. *Dives and Pauper*, Com. VII, c. 11.

that tithes must be paid of all things lawfully acquired. We must say that he is bound, but the Church is bound to remit it to him, as above. But he says that personal tithes are not usual nowadays.

Yet in England, certainly, they were insisted on at least as late as 1425, and probably up to the Reformation. Wilkins's *Concilia* is full of episcopal complaints of tithe-friction, sometimes with special reference to this taxation of wage-earners. Bishop Lyndwood, writing about 1420, explains that it rests upon divine law, and quotes with approval "they who pay not the personal tithes are damned"[1]. Yet the law was evidently very unpopular; for in 1425 a guardian of the London friars minor, William Russell, preached publicly "that personal tithes fallen not under the commandment of God's law," and thus stirred a hornet's nest. The University of Oxford denounced him formally as "a heretic, deserving to be cut away, as a rotten limb, from the body of the Church." The archbishop of Canterbury condemned him in full Convocation; the pope condemned him on appeal; his own brethren of the London convent repudiated him, and bade people "in salvation of your souls, that ye pay truly your tithes personal"; and he was finally compelled to retract his heresy formally and publicly at Paul's Cross: "Personal tithes...be due by the commandment of the law of God, against whose commandment no custom may run without deadly sin and everlasting damnation"[2]. One thing, however, transpires from this long-drawn lawsuit: though the proctor of the English clergy maintained at Rome that personal tithes were customarily paid in England, and had been from time immemorial, yet he added that now "there are many who seek to withhold such tithes, and may have in fact withheld them, and it is reasonably to be feared that more will be withheld from the payment of such tithes, to the greatest impoverishment of incumbents, and especially of vicars, who

[1] p. 185: cf. p. 21, and *Dives and Pauper*, Com. VII, c. 14: "Tithes personals...a man shall pay." About the same time, Bishop Brumpton also takes personal tithes for granted (MS. Harl. 3760, serm. 86, f. 240 a). Bromyard clearly asserts this liability (*Sum. Pred.* D. iii, art. 4; and the *Summa Angelica*, with all its reserves about the practice, stoutly upholds the principle. Gerson has an interesting note in one of his sermons: "Nota de consuetudinibus Normanniae et Angliae, ubi persolvuntur de omni proprio decimae, praeterquam de mercimoniis (Ed. 1606, II, 439).

[2] Wilkins, *Concilia*, III, 438–459.

live only from altar-offerings and are endowed from the afore-said personal tithes." It is evident, therefore, that there was considerable resistance, and that many pleaded custom for their refusal to pay[1].

Such, then, was the minuteness with which tithes might be exacted; and we must remember that they were far more bur-densome to the peasantry than we might judge at first sight. The Remonstrance of the States General to Henri IV at Blois points out that tithe, as ordinarily exacted, was in fact often an income-tax of 20 per cent., since it was exacted from the gross proceeds of the harvest without allowance for working expenses, which the States reckon at 50 per cent. If the parson took only the twentieth instead of the tenth sheaf, it is argued, he would thus get a tenth of the peasant's actual gain[2]. And, in a large number of cases, the sheaves or corn had to be carried at the peasant's own cost in time or money; the ninth-century Statutes of Corbie show how heavily this burden was felt[3]. Again, it was exasperating to reflect how much of the proceeds went to absentees, or even to laymen. It was not only the Dissolution which gave large quantities of parochial tithes into the hands of worldly folk. On the Continent, this malversation was common at all times, down to the Revolution. In France, for instance, some of the nobles found their richest source of income in the appropriation of tithes; Bruneau names three in a single province who drew £1700, £6000 and £8000 a year respectively from this source in 1789[4]. And, at the very best, the tithe-system was vexatious in proportion to its unavoidable complications[5].

---

[1] This, however, the Church had no difficulty in refuting: "Since it is a mortal sin not to pay one's tithes, and since tithes are due in virtue of God's law, therefore no custom of non-payment can be valid at law; and this is true whether we speak of tithes of crops or of personal tithes" (Lyndwood, l.c. p. 190).

[2] Recueil, pt ii, p. 19. Compare Lyndwood, l.c. p. 188, where Archbishop Stratford rebukes the "damnable error" of those who deduct working ex-penses before paying tithe; and p. 195, where there is a very curious dis-cussion as to the working expenses of a mill.

[3] Adalhard, pp. 370 ff.

[4] p. 153. For the absorption of tithes by laymen in the Middle Ages, see P. Imbart de la Tour in Rev. Hist. LX, LXI, LXIII, LXVII, LXVIII, especially LXVIII, 33–43. During the Dark Ages, he judges that this was the case with most churches in France (p. 33).

[5] For the frequency of tithe quarrels see e.g. Peetz, p. 122, and Imbart de la Tour in Rev. Hist. LXIII (1897), 28, 34, 41 and LXVIII (1898), 21.

The monks of St Augustine's Canterbury, thought it advisable to copy into their *Black Book* that decree of Archbishop Winchelsey which complains how "many are found unwilling to give tithes," and lays down stringent rules for their exaction to the last penny[1]. All this aroused a feeling with which our own evasions of the income-tax are only remotely comparable. Even the ideal German peasant of the thirteenth century, the type of the old solid school, tells us that "I give no parson more than his bare due" in the way of tithes and offerings[2]. And, of less ideal characters, few in fact can have avoided that curse which official duty compelled even Chaucer's good parson to pronounce periodically from his pulpit. The people, writes Bishop Guillaume le Maire in 1311, have been so overdone with excommunications—"I have sometimes seen with mine own eyes three or four hundred excommunicates in a single parish, or even seven hundred"—"that they despise the Power of the Kings and utter blasphemous and scandalous words against the Church and her ministers"[3].

The Gambara inquisition of 1195 gives a lively picture of tithe-collection. In the village of Paono there were serfs, who tithed to the abbot of Leno, and free tenants who tithed to local lords, "the sons of Alberigo and Dalfino." A witness, "asked whether this fourth part [belonging to Leno] is collected with the parts of the aforesaid lords, answered: 'Yes, and I myself have collected tithes with them for the aforesaid church [of Paono]; and when all have been collected together the Church takes this fourth part.'" Another witness "says that at the gathering of tithes, which he himself collects with the monks, the church bells are rung, and the parish priest and 'consuls' of the village warn the neighbourhood of their duty of giving tithes, and send round the haywards [*camparios*] of the community from house to house to gather the tithes, and these are gathered together in the church and divided into four parts"[4].

---

[1] Turner and Salter, p. 359. Compare p. 356 for the minuteness of these exactions; a man must give the monks tithes from his little garden—*decimae de hortis pede fossis*; honey also must be tithed, and grass growing by the wayside (Lyndwood, *l.c.* p. 192). The minute details of synodal decrees upon this subject are eloquent of friction between tither and tithe-payer.

[2] *Meier Helmbrecht*, ll. 780–1.   [3] *Lib. Guil. Major*, p. 478.

[4] Zaccaria, pp. 172, 186. We shall see how commonly the nave of the parish church was used for such purposes.

CHAPTER XXI

TITHES AND FRICTION (*cont.*)

IT is true, there was another side to this question; the priest might be almost as needy as the peasant. Sometimes we get glimpses, in the Middle Ages, of that community of feeling between the peasant and the poor parson (as distinct from the numerous clerical capitalists) which was noticeable also in pre-revolutionary France. A cleric in 1394, recording the jubilee which emperor and pope concerted that year at Prag, writes "and they fleeced the innocent priests and the poor peasants and all men without exception"[1]. John Ball, "the mad priest of Kent," is another example; more than once we find a village priest in the van of some revolt[2]. But, to the ordinary peasant, such men certainly did not represent the Church; the peasant saw more squire-parsons than John Balls; and even when the parson was poor he might be obliged, by the very necessities of existence, to curse as heartily for his tithes as the richer incumbent cursed. The hunting parson (to take one species only of the genus squire) has certainly left more traces in medieval records than the parson-ringleader of revolts. And, where writers speak of the poverty of the lower priesthood, they do not represent these men as fraternizing with the peasant, but as helpless parasites upon the rich. Jonas of Orléans, in the early ninth century, speaks as bitterly as Sir Thomas More in the early sixteenth; some layfolk, says Jonas, employ priests in servile capacities, and disdain to let them even eat at the master's table[3]. More's words are even stronger: there is "such a rabble, that every man must have a priest in his house to wait upon his wife, which no man lacketh now, to the contempt of priesthood, in as vile office as his horse-keeper...and worse too, for they keep hawks and dogs"[4].

[1] Höfler, p. 64.
[2] *E.g.* John Wrawe, the priest partly responsible for the murder of the Prior of Bury in 1382 (Walsingham, *Hist. Ang.* R.S. 1, 1, 63).
[3] P.L. vol. 106, col. 209.
[4] *English Works*, 1557, p. 227.

Gower devotes a whole section of his *Vox Clamantis* to "those rectors who, though they are not non-resident, yet neglect their cure of souls and busy themselves mostly with pleasure and with hunting"[1]. In 1490, two witnesses deposed before the bishop of Hereford that his predecessor Spofford (1422–48) had substituted Sir William Hanyes as vicar of Goodrich for Sir Walter ap Gwillim, who, however, protested until William bought him out with a present of £5. One of the two witnesses, himself a priest, "added the cause why the said Sir Walter was expelled from the said vicarage, to wit, because he busied himself too much with hunting, so that on the holy-day of Good Friday he was a-hunting when he ought to have been in Church and busied with divine service"[2]. That Good Friday was evidently the last straw that broke the bishop's patience[3].

Let us try, then, to pierce this thick mist of time, shaking off as best we can all our modern ideas, whether anti-Catholic or apologetic, and see these things as the medieval peasant saw them who paid the tithes. In the case of the modern farmer, we all know how vain it is to appeal to historical origins, and how seldom we can convince him that the tithe, having existed and been taken into account from time immemorial, is fully allowed for in his rent, and therefore comes not out of his pocket but out of his landlord's. Moreover, such an appeal to history might have been a double-edged weapon in the Middle Ages, when a very large proportion of villagers saw the tithes carried off, under their eyes, by the bailiff of the monastic capitalist. A few of the better-informed at least, and perhaps the whole village in a vague sort of way, were aware that 25 per cent. of this clerical income had originally been earmarked, in ecclesiastical theory, for the parochial poor; how can they have failed, therefore, to resent that system of appropriation by which two-thirds of the tithes now left the parish (to take an average), and the vicar was fobbed off with a bare living wage which left him scarcely able, however willing, to relieve the destitute? Were these peasants much consoled to think that at the abbey,

[1] Ed. Macaulay, p. 147.
[2] *Reg. Myllyng* (Cant. and York Soc.), p. 126.
[3] For further notes on monastic huntsmen, see appendix 29.

perhaps two or three counties distant, a poor man might get bread and beer and a night's lodging? Moreover, even the monks of the later Middle Ages were often in debt, and were cutting down not only their voluntary, but even their statutory alms[1]. Only the most definite evidence could persuade us that the general laws of human nature were here suspended in favour of the medieval Church, and that her teaching and her sacraments worked a sort of transubstantiation in the peasant's heart. We all know that heart in its natural state, concentrated upon small things by the hard struggle for bare daily bread, and attributing to those small things an even exaggerated importance. We see the peasant almost ferociously tenacious of his own—for how else can he and his family live?—and we are blandly informed that, if only we grasped the real spirit of the Middle Ages, we should see how cheerfully the serf paid his tithes. Is not the real anachronism in those who fail to see that these things, so far from leaving the serf cheerfully generous, had a repulsive effect upon him which it needs an effort of imagination to conceive? The few really pious peasants might, indeed, value these sacrifices all the more, for the sake of spiritual things which would outlast all worldly goods. But the majority, in so far as they saw with different eyes to ours, would nearly always do less justice than we to those natural causes which underlay the tithe system, and to these men who carried off his sheaves, his piglings, his chickens and his milk from under his very eyes.

So, gradually, the villages learned more and more that they must shift for themselves. This is the real explanation of what happened in the later Middle Ages, when parishioners obtained a certain amount of financial control and of corporate responsibility which, limited as it was, excites the admiration of modern Roman Catholics[2]. These liberties, after all, were only such as, even at the worst of times, remained and increased in all our post-Reformation parishes. But, such as they were, they grew

[1] The Finchale Account Rolls show that, whereas the monks had received a benefaction on condition of giving £1. 6s. 8d. to the poor every Maunday Thursday, they were sometimes giving only 10s. or less of this money which belonged to them only in trust (Surtees Soc. vol. 11, 1837, pt i, p. 104, pt ii, pp. 81, 410, 413; cf. Dugdale-Caley, IV, 333).

[2] Bishop Hobhouse's description (Som. Rec. Soc. IV, xi ff.) forms the foundation for what is written in modern times on this subject; the surprise which his facts have excited in many quarters is very significant.

up in definite competition with clerical influence; the laity, who for the most part had been long since deprived of that liberal share of the tithes which ancient Church Law had tried to earmark for charitable and devotional purposes, were now themselves raising the funds for church-building and poor-relief; they paid the piper and began to call the tune. We sometimes find something almost like the modern Parish Council: by many signs, the villager is now learning to fend for himself. He puts much of this work under the wing of the Church; the Church, indeed would claim this, even if it were not voluntarily rendered; but it is not the Church which has created this self-government[1]. The villager is beginning to discover that he must organize something for his own poor, if they are to be adequately relieved at all. Norman parishes, as early as the thirteenth century, began to have their own charitable foundations, apart from the priest and the monk[2]. Pirenne emphasizes the independence of many Flemish peasants, who had drained or cleared waste land under the patronage of counts, nobles and abbeys, and therefore held it on terms very different to those of ordinary servage. "As early as the thirteenth century, at least in the *châtellenie* of Furnes, we note the appearance of associations against fire and the loss of live-stock"[3]. In Chaucer's England, the Dominican Bromyard first recites the well-known Church ideal, that the rector should keep one-quarter of the income to himself, give another to his dependent clergy, another to the church fabric and the fourth quarter to the poor; he then adds:

But, however they ought to do by law, yet in fact they divide the goods of Christ, the Church and the poor even as the wolf divideth his prey, of whom Isidore saith that, whatsoever he cannot or will not devour, he hideth it in the earth. So do these men hide in their

---

[1] The earliest gilds we know were restricted, and even forbidden, by ecclesiastical authorities, just as the communes were in the early eleventh century. When French villages, in the twelfth and thirteenth centuries, worked their way to some real form of self-government, the first and most important step was to buy off, by enormous sacrifices of money, all interference from a lord who was frequently an ecclesiastic.

[2] Delisle, p. 154. This had been the rule in very early times; all the poor were entered on the parish *matricula*; see, for example, *Rev. Hist.* LXIII, 35. There was seldom anything like a real parish council in the Middle Ages.

[3] *Soulèvement*, p. x.

chests and caskets and treasure-rooms, as though underground, whatsoever they consume not themselves, and should lawfully distribute among the poor and the lower clergy and the fabric of their church[1].

Here he says little more than a Franciscan had said a century earlier: "When a rector with two hundred pounds a year has collected two platters of broken food from his table to send to two poor men, then he weens to have done much for God, and that he may freely spend all the rest for his own use in pomp and in vanity, and, what is worse, in lechery and on his nephews"[2]. And, while we remember that the friar was commonly critical of the secular clergy, let us compare these words with those of a man who bore the burden of a great diocese. An absolutely orthodox and loyal bishop, Grandisson of Exeter, protested in 1337 to the papal nuncio who had forced an incumbent upon the people, and was forcing others like unto him. If the pope only knew how such parsons brought the Church and her services into contempt, he would apply some remedy:

For such men do no more than suck the milk and clip the fleeces of Christ's sheep and carry the spoils away [reference to Ezekiel xxxiv, 7 ff.]. For I believe that, in all this man's time, he hath not fed a single poor person in his parish from his tithes, nor intoned a

---

[1] *Sum. Pred.* O. vi, 16; cf. D. iv, 10, 11. This nominal apportionment of tithes to the poor is often described by modern writers as though it had been regularly fulfilled in fact; but we have continual evidence to the contrary. Gratian's glossator, in the thirteenth century, notes that the theory of quadripartite division had already broken down, for "nowadays the bishops take all to themselves" (on pars. ii, c. xvi, q. i c. 46 *Quicunque*). Bromyard represents "certain" parishioners as saying, in answer to this plea that the clergy ought so to divide their revenues into four parts: "If they would thus spend them, we would gladly give them [tithes]; but alas! they do not so, but some of them spend abominably upon very unlawful uses"; and again: "Those who take our tithes are either men of evil lives or absentees or men who do not do their duty to their poor parishioners; therefore we care the less to give them tithes" (*Sum. Pred.* D. iii, 9–11). The author of *Dives and Pauper* agrees with the great canonist Hostiensis; if a priest be openly lecherous or otherwise immoral, the parishioner has a right to give the tithe away from him to some higher authority, or to any Church purposes (Com. vii, c. 14 *ad fin*). This plea was, in fact, recorded two centuries earlier than that day, and was probably ancient even then. A letter of Innocent III, incorporated in canon law, complains that "some men, detesting the lives of the clergy as abominable, are bold enough to withdraw tithes from them on that account" (*Decret. Greg.* lib. iii, tit. xxx, c. 26).

[2] Bozon, p. 33. A skilled artisan of this date (1320) would be well paid at £8 a year, and a curate was generally hired for considerably less. See the valuable statistics given by H. G. Richardson in *Trans. Roy. Hist. Soc.* 1911,

single anthem in his church, nor once worn the [clerical] habit, nor restored the ruined parsonage, nor ever vouchsafed to see my face, his overlord and pastor, unworthy though I be. Wherefore I do as best I can after God's pleasure; the rest, which I cannot do by reason of those who uphold such folk, I commit to God, and lay the burden on your consciences[1].

The author of *Dives and Pauper* was of unquestioned orthodoxy; probably a friar of Chaucer's time. In this book (Com. v, ch. 8) Pauper says "also they be guilty of manslaughter that defraud servants of their hire"; he refers to Ecclus. xxxiv and James v. Dives replies:

This point of manslaughter toucheth much more of Holy Church; for, as the law saith, the tithes of holy church be tributes of them that be in need, to relieve them in their need, and all that men of Holy Church leave, it is the poor men's goods, and their houses should be common to all men at need.... But they be not bound to feed the rich folk, but ghostly, and them that have no need, with Holy Church's goods. And of the poor folk give they no tale, but to pillage them and have of them and get of them what they may by hypocrisy, by fraud, by dread and violence; and therefore God undernymeth [reproveth] them by the prophet Ezekiel and saith to them: *Ve pastoribus Israel*: woe be to the shepherds of Israel, that is to say to the prelates and curates of Holy Church, which should be shepherds of God's sheep, and of the souls that Christ bought so dear; woe be to the shepherds, for they feed themselves, and of the poor people give they no tale!... And therefore God accepteth not the prayer of such men of Holy Church, for they be without charity and full of cruelty in pillaging of the poor people.

And his indirect evidence is almost more significant, where he is dealing with parish law, and writes:

If the curate will not bury the dead body nor suffer it to be buried, but in covenant that he shall have his bed or his best clothe or some other thing, he doth simony, although it be custom to pay that he asketh. And therefore he should freely bury the dead and bless them that be needy, and so abstain him from every spice of simony, and afterward compel them to pay and keep good customs, if that they might well do it for poverty[2].... If a priest will not baptize but he have money therefore, he doth simony.

pp. 115 ff.; also Wilkins, *Concilia*, II, 147 and III, 2. The embezzlement of parish revenues by priests was dealt with by Church councils as early as 855 A.D. (Labbé, *Concilia*, vol. VIII (1671), col. 148).

[1] *Reg. Grand*, p. 297.

[2] *I.e.* "in spite of their poverty," a common M.E. use of *for*.

Another of Chaucer's contemporaries, the monk Pierre Berchoire, writes: "In these days of ours, worldly tribulations fall not upon rich or noble ecclesiastics and laymen, but upon the poor and the needy and the beggars." And again: "It is not upon the poor that church moneys are spent, but upon the cleric's own favourite nephews (*nepotuli*) and kinsfolk"[1]. Nor was it only the nearest clergy, in the parish itself, who were thus arrayed on the capitalist side in these matters; the more distant clergy, the monks, were on the same side.

With this subject I am dealing far more fully in another volume; here I will quote only a few instances taken almost at random. The Council of Vienne, in 1311, occupied itself with the scandal of monastic appropriations which killed hospitality and almsgiving in the parishes[2]. Somewhere about 1400, the Second Version of the *Lay Folks' Catechism* accuses Religious of diverting alms from the real poor to themselves[3]. The historian of the abbey of Loos brings out the contrast, in 1529, between the worldliness and creature comforts of these Cistercians, and the rigour with which they enforced the payment of tithes from the needy[4]. Therefore it was natural that, as the Middle Ages wore on, even distinguished churchmen complained more and more publicly of the gulf between rich and poor. "Money is Lord of All"—*pecuniae obediunt omnia*, writes Hemmerlin in quotation from Ecclesiastes: after which he proceeds:

And people, in derision of the clergy, quote the poet who said "I saw a man singing and celebrating Mass. It was Money who sang, and Money who chanted the responses. I saw how he wept while he preached, and how he laughed in his sleeve at the people whom he

[1] *Opera*, I, 55 c; II, 583. 13; cf. Durandus, *Tractatus*, pt ii, tit. 38 *ad fin.* His contemporary, the bishop of Angers, complains to the Council of Vienne: "The parishes are commonly so neglected or mismanaged that the poor are defrauded of the alms which should be theirs" (*Lib. Guil. Major.* p. 483).

[2] G. Durandus, *Tractatus*, pt iii, tit. 22.

[3] E.E.T.S. 1901, p. 53, 809 ff. A fifteenth century friar was said to have collected a *peculium* of 1700 gold florins (v.d. Hardt, *Mag. Conc. Const.* I, 191). At Rots, in Normandy, a collection for the poor was made in about 1630; the main owners were two great monasteries, yet the onus of collection was thrown upon two villagers (A. Benet, *Inventaire sommaire des archives du Calvados*, Caen, 1897, p. 279).

[4] De Rosny, pp. 85–6. The neighbours, at an earlier date, found the abbey so grasping that they nicknamed its head "l'abbé à qui tout faut" (*ibid.* p. 49).

was cheating." And [in canon law], possessions of any kind come under this appellation of "money"; real property and movables and all things which can be given or received[1].

Then, as now, society thought a great deal of money; and society was increasingly inclined to judge that the priest often earned his money too easily.

Men see that layfolk have heavy cares, and get their food and raiment with grievous labour, while Churchmen lead an easy and quiet life of enjoyment. They hear the common proverb: "He who would live a day in delight, let him cook a hen; for two days, a goose; for a whole week, a pig; for a whole month, an ox. If he will be happy for a whole year, let him take a wife; but if he would live in pleasure his whole life long, he must take to the priesthood"[2].

These are the words of a preacher, but of one of the ablest and most orthodox among pre-reformation preachers; and though his words are racier, the sense is not more damning than that of the official reports presented to the Council of Vienne in 1311 by two of the most efficient bishops in Christendom: Guillaume Durand of Mende and Guillaume le Maire of Angers. A few sentences from the former will show us very clearly the light in which the tithe-paying peasant too often saw these tithe-takers. He saw wealthy ecclesiastics "enjoying more delicate and richer and more varied dishes than kings and princes, contrary to ecclesiastical honesty and the clerical rule"[3]. He witnessed clerical quarrels: "there is scarce any [clerical] society wherein this sin of envy doth not make divisions, rents, and partialities...they tear the Lord's seamless and undivided robe into small pieces"[4]. He witnessed "the indiscipline and scandalous behaviour of clerics and Religious, who have the certainty that they will not be handed over to the worldly courts for these misdeeds, nor put to death"[5]. His parson was often

[1] *Tract.* f. 44 b:

> Vidi cantantem [quemdam et] missam celebrantem.
> Nummus cantabat, nummus responsa parabat.
> Vidi quod flebat dum sermonem faciebat
> Et subridebat populum quem decipiebat.

For the power of money in medieval trading towns, see F. C. Hodgson, *Venice in the 13th and 14th Centuries*, 1910, pp. 327–8.

[2] J. Geiler v. Kayserberg, *Navicula Fatuorum*, turba LXXII, xxxiii M. (Strassburg, 1513).

[3] Durandus, *Tractatus*, pt iii, tit. 36 (p. 309).   [4] *Ibid.* tit. 37.

[5] *Ibid.* tit. 38, cf. 49.

"an insufficient and illiterate youth promoted by the favour of influential and wealthy kinsfolk" who had perhaps a papal dispensation of absence from his parish, and let souls go to ruin while he only cared to collect his dues[1]. The parson sometimes sold drink on the premises[2], or stocked his corn or did his brewing within the parish church[3]; why then should not the peasant hold his markets in the churchyard or his Church-ales in the nave? Why should we wonder that "the people seems not to care for divine things [on Sundays or holy-days], but for songs and games, dancing and leaping and unhonest and foul ballads, even within the churches and their yards, haunting such vanities by day and by night"[4]. And what can be more natural than to find Charles V's ambassador writing to him from London on Dec. 13, 1529: "Nearly all the people here hate the priests"[5]?

Yet we must not so emphasize the forgoing evidence, with much more of the sort that might be brought forward, as to fall into the opposite extreme of injustice to the medieval clergy. All through the Middle Ages their civilizing influence was great; their worst faults were the faults of their time; even when the Reformation came, the clergy as a whole were decidedly above the intellectual and moral average of the laity as a whole; and, if only the Church could have suffered other modes of thought to compete fairly with her own, there would have been no sufficient excuse for revolution. With the individual clergy, again, we must sympathize; it was not one parson's own fault that he must needs insist on all his dues or starve, nor was it altogether the fault of another that he had been dumped, as a boy, into some fat living of which the current system allowed him to ignore the responsibilities. All these things had been the growth of ages; it would be absurd to judge them from any solely modern point of view; yet it is still more absurd, if

---

[1] *Ibid*. titt. 44–48.

[2] Church councils fulminate frequently against this practice. As late as 1578, the papal nuncio in Switzerland reported that the system of clerical innkeeping needed suppression, and that wine "was sold by retail in women's convents, according to the custom of wineshops" (*Nuntiaturberichte*, p. 124).

[3] *Ibid*. tit. 53: so also at St Marychurch in 1301 (*Reg. Stapeldon*, p. 337); I have collected many such instances.

[4] Durandus, *l.c.*   [5] *Cal. State Papers*, Spain, IV, 232.

possible, to ignore them as demonstrable facts. The witnesses quoted in this chapter will be found in complete agreement with that very remarkable picture of village morals and religion and rustico-clerical relations which was drawn by a French church-man in 1527, and which is so lengthy, even in summary, that I am obliged to relegate it to an appendix[1]. It is not cheerful reading; yet it would be still more melancholy to believe that the world is essentially worse now than it was four hundred years ago. In spite of all the shortcomings that can be justly charged against modern society, no man need despair who has not a party-reason for quarrelling with his own age. The worst ghosts that haunt us now are as old as the dawn of history; and medieval holy-water was less efficacious against them, when all is said and done, than the antiseptics of a modern laboratory. The legend of a lost Arcadia, so busily repeated in some quarters, is mainly a very recent growth, based upon the writings of foreign writers who often tamper with documentary evidence, and echoed by English journalists who abstain from documentary evidence. A scholar like S. R. Maitland, who is sometimes vaguely invoked, would have laughed at the exaggerations which are now spread abroad with every device of hustling advertisement. So would even Dr Jessopp, who, though in many cases his imagination and his superficial knowledge of the documents led him to idealize the Middle Ages, had read enough to realize something of the truth here. He wrote:

It is often said that the monasteries were the great supporters of the poor, and fed them in times of scarcity. It may be so, but I should like to see evidence for the statement. At present, I doubt the fact, at any rate as far as Norfolk goes. On the contrary, I am strongly impressed with the belief that 600 years ago they had no friends. The parsons were needy themselves. In too many cases one clergyman held two or three livings, took his tithes and spent them in the town, and left a chaplain with a bare subsistence to fill his place in the country. There was no parson's wife to drop in and speak a kind word—no clergyman's daughter to give a friendly nod, or teach the little ones at Sunday school—no softening influences, no sympathy, no kindliness. What could you expect from people with such dreary surroundings?—what but that which we know actually was

[1] App. 36. Compare the picture of Swiss village life immediately following it.

the condition of affairs? The records of crime and outrage in Norfolk 600 years ago are still preserved, and may be read by anyone who knows how to decipher them[1].

In another essay, it is true, he asked concerning fifteenth century England: "How was it that high and low did so dearly love going to church"[2]? This is like Charles II's famous question to the Royal Society: "Why does a dead fish weigh more than when it was alive?" We have seen that a Norfolk parson of five centuries before Dr Jessopp would have been under no illusions on this point. What deceived this modern antiquary was the size and beauty of the churches then built, and the richness of their ornaments. Even here he exaggerates, by laying undue stress on certain inventories and ignoring others which show neglect and disrepair; but, taking the facts as he states them, we shall find that his argument is quashed by the evidence of *Dives and Pauper*, where a perfectly orthodox author of the time denounces these same architectural and artistic glories as worldly pomps which vainly seek to cloak a poverty of true religion[3].

The more we study the actual contemporary evidence of village life and parish life, the less we shall be inclined, I think, to quarrel with the verdict of the great economic historian Lamprecht. He writes, concerning the last two or three generations before the Reformation:

The universal scorn, no less than the coarse and clownish luxury in which the peasant strove to set himself beside the other social strata, show with fearful clearness that he was separated from the rank of those classes which were moving forwards on an even line of progress, and that he had become the pariah of society. Who was there now that understood his upbringing, his thoughts and his feelings? They were hoarily old-fashioned; and in a thousand forms of customary law or superstitious usages they harked back to primeval ages of our nation. Over the peasant's head had swept the Latin culture of the clergy in the Carolingian and Ottonian renascence, and then the poetic culture of the Hohenstaufen chivalry, and then the development of civic spirit in the fourteenth century. All this had gone over his head. Was he to be oppressed still farther and longer? Was he to become the ignorant, suffering, despised slave of his nation? That was the question [at the dawn of the sixteenth century][4].

---

[1] "Village Life in Norfolk 600 years ago," *Nineteenth Century*, Feb. 1883, p. 265. [2] *The Nineteenth Century*, Jan. 1898, pp. 55-7.
[3] Com. 1, ch. 51 *ad fin.* Other greater writers, from St Jerome onwards, had already said the same. [4] Lamprecht, *Geschichte*, v, 89.

If Lamprecht is not concerned in this passage to balance all aspects of the truth, yet his words do at least emphasize one most important aspect which is steadily ignored by his compatriots Janssen and Pastor. The medieval peasant, like the Russian peasant of yesterday, had the solid qualities of a primitive race; but he was as yet untried in those more complicated matters which test the simple man's adaptability to higher stages of civilization. Chaucer's ploughman and the priest his brother are as real and as admirable as his knight and squire. But, to the rustic mass (as apart from this pick of the village population) the very elements of modern civilization were as yet scarcely accessible; the more struggling half of that community was even less fortunate than the more struggling half of our own.

CHAPTER XXII

POVERTY UNADORNED

HITHERTO we have generally considered the peasant in his relation to someone else. Let us try, in this chapter, to see him rather in himself and in his own home; to travel over the past centuries as Defoe takes us over the South Seas, and to visit this Robinson Crusoe in his hut with his man Friday and his dog. We have tried to sound his spiritual poverty; let us now estimate his material destitution.

We may start from Aelfric's *Colloquy*, written in 1005 by a monk of Canterbury as a text-book of conversational Latin for his pupils. In this little book, men of different occupations describe their daily manner of life, each in turn; the form is that of a dialogue between a master and his several pupils.

M. What do you say, ploughman, how do you do your work?

P. Oh, sir, I work very hard. I go out at dawn, driving the oxen to the field, and I yoke them to the plough; however hard the winter I dare not stay at home for fear of my master; but, having yoked the oxen and made the plough-share and coulter fast to the plough, every day I have to plough a whole acre or more.

M. Have you any companion?

P. I have a boy who drives the oxen with the goad, and he is even now hoarse with cold and shouting.

M. What more do you do in the day?

P. A good deal more, to be sure. I have to fill the oxen's cribs with hay, and give them water, and carry the dung outside.

M. Oh, oh, it is hard work.

P. Yes, it is hard work, because I am not a free man[1].

This is what the ploughman says of himself; let us turn now to what was expected of him by the medieval lord in search of ideal servants. The late thirteenth-century manual called *Fleta* deserves, doubtless, all the hard words that Maitland has said of it from the legal and statistical point of view[2]; but this does not

---

[1] Translated from T. Wright's *Anglo-Saxon Vocabularies*, I, 89; cf. A. F. Leach, *Ed. Charters and Doct.* pp. 40–1.

[2] *Domesday Book and Beyond*, p. 397. The ideal of a manorial servant is dealt with in bk II of *Fleta*, chs. 71–88. While the author borrows a great deal from Walter of Henley or the *Seneschaucie*, or both, he has touches which they lack: each of these authors complements the other.

detract from the value of its evidence when the writer describes the sort of peasant that the lord will love to have. We cannot afford to neglect an age's ideal any more than its actual practice[1]. If possible, then,

let your ploughman be no melancholy or wrathful man, but merry, joyful, given to song, that the oxen may take their delight in his chants and melodies.... Let him love them, and sleep with them at night; let him tickle them, curry them, rub them down, and keep them well at all points.... It is well also to rub the oxen twice daily with a wisp of straw, that they may lick themselves with more affection.

Moreover, the ploughman must be the "handy man" of the manor. Besides the care of his beasts and the mending of broken ploughs or harrows, he should be an expert sower, hedger and ditcher, thresher and drainer. The many other trades to which he turns for his own profit in leisure hours are enumerated in *Piers Plowman*. The cowherd also is to sleep every night with his cows, and the shepherd in his fold[2]. The hayward, too, "must go round early and late spying upon the woods, the farmyard, the meadows and fields and other appurtenances of the manor"; for this duty we need "a vigorous and austere man". Neither cowherd nor shepherd, nor other man in charge of the beasts, may "go to fairs or markets or wrestling-matches or taverns" without asking leave and providing efficient substitutes[3]. The ideal dairymaid is, perhaps, the most exemplary character of all; we must remember that we here have men describing what they would wish their womenfolk to be.

The dairymaid should be chaste and honest and faithful, laborious in her dairy duties, wise and neat-handed; not lavish but of a thrifty nature. For she must not suffer any man or woman to come to her in the dairy and carry aught away which might make her render the less perfect account. Now it is her work to receive the vessels proper for her office with a written indenture from the Reeve, and to restore them according to the same indenture when she leaves, and in this record it must be noted on what day she began work. She must

---

[1] *Fleta* affords here a very exact parallel to those monastic customals which describe, one by one, the ideal conventual officer. If we imagined the community actually living as the customals exhort them to live, we should go far astray; yet it is very important to study these points at which the legislators were aiming.

[2] *Seneschaucie*, pp. 113, 115.

[3] *Ibid*. pp. 98, 102; *Fleta*, p. 172. At the busiest times, if not at others, he must lie out at nights like the shepherd (*Piers Plowman*, C. VI, 16).

receive the milk by tallies, and make cheese and butter according to the tale of the gallons; she must keep ward over the poultry, and render to the Bailiff and Reeve frequent account of the profits arising therefrom; nor will some Auditors allow her to account for less than twelve pence a year for every goose and four pence for every hen. Moreover it is her duty to winnow or sift, to cover up the fire, and to do such like petty works when she can find time for them[1].

What wages then, did such a domestic treasure command? It is painful, both for her own sake and for the sake of tantalized modern employers, to record that she could be hired "at much less cost than a man," and that the dairyman himself was the cheapest of all the farm servants, receiving only five shillings a year to the bailiff's thirteen shillings and fourpence, the ploughman's ten shillings and the carter's six shillings and eightpence. Plain board and lodging were, of course, included; and the five shillings was roughly equivalent to five pounds in these days. A girl, for doing most of the dairywork in 1281, is recorded in one bailiff's accounts to have received twopence halfpenny a week, no doubt in addition to simple meals from the dairy itself. And even the dairywoman needs "auditing"; the lord ought to know how many eggs, how much milk, to expect from such and such a number of hens and cows and sheep; "there be many bailiffs and dairymaids that will say nay to this," but in that case they are wasteful or untrustworthy[2]. For, even in the thirteenth century, farm-servants are no longer what they were in the good old days. We must always be on our guard against their idleness or deceit[3]; moreover, they sometimes even show disrespect: in that case "if any of them speak back or grumble, tell them that you will be lord or lady, and that you will that all serve your will and pleasure, and whoever will not do so send away, and get others who will serve your pleasure—of whom you will find enough"[4]. There, it will be seen, the lord had a stronger position than he has now; and he had another old-world advantage in the custom of Bible-swearing: "The accountant shall swear that he will render a lawful account....The clerk shall swear that he has lawfully entered on his roll," and so forth. Yet, while trusting God, let us keep our powder dry: if your

[1] *Fleta*, p. 172; *Husbandry*, p. 74; *Seneschaucie*, p. 116.
[2] Walter of Henley, p. 53.   [3] *Ibid.* p. 11.
[4] *Grosseteste*, p. 137; cf. p. 149.

reeve is worth his salt, he will keep furtive watch—*insidiabitur*—
upon the threshers and winnowing-women, lest they "steal
some of the corn in their bosom or hosen or boots or pouches,
or in wallets or sacks hidden near the barn"[1]. For nowadays,
from the highest official on the manor to the lowest hind, there
are "many" who forget the love and respect due to their lord,
and who, so far from treating his interests as their own, "know
well that the business is another's and not theirs, and take
right and left where they judge best that their disloyalty will not
be perceived"[2]. For the peasant had discovered that simple
faith fared ill when it came into conflict with Norman blood[3].
Walter of Henley sketches the same high ideal for the lord as
for his men; but it is to be feared that the defaulters were as
numerous on one side as on the other. There is one most
significant passage in his book:

Some men replace other [sheep] for those which died of murrain.
How? I will tell you. If a sheep die suddenly they put the flesh in
water for as many hours as are between midday and three o'clock,
and then hang it up, and when the water is drained off they salt it
and then dry it. And if any sheep begin to fall ill they see if it be
because the teeth drop, and if the teeth do not fall out they cause it to
be killed and salted and dried like the others, and then they cut it up
and distribute it in the household among the servants and labourers, and
they shall then yield as much as they cost, for by this means and with
the skins they can replace as many. But I do not wish you to do this[4].

[1] *Seneschaucie*, p. 99. The *huse*, there translated *tunics*, is evidently the
word which gave its name to our Robert Courtheuse of Normandy; we have
already seen (chapter v, p. 46) how a Ramsey serf was sometimes compelled
to collect a hosefull of nuts in the woods for the monks.

[2] Walter of Henley, p. 35.

[3] Preachers, chroniclers, etc. often quote such and such a "vulgare pro-
verbium"; and these are nearly always cynical. An admirable example may
be quoted from Rolandino of Padua (about 1250): "The vulgar proverb
saith that, even though God help those who are fewer in number, yet the more
numerous party is wont to come off victorious [in war]" (*Chron.* bk v, ch. 4).

[4] *L.c.* p. 29. Tusser, in 1550, gave advice which is suggestive of a fairly
recent election-cry of our own day; he counselled the export of unsound flesh
for foreign consumption:

> Thy measeled bacon-hog, sow, or thy boar,
> Shut up for to heal, for infecting thy store;
> Or kill it for bacon, or souse it to sell
> For Fleming, that loves it so daintily well.

By medieval regulations in London, at Oxford, and in Scottish boroughs,
the meat condemned as putrid by the supervisors of the market was confiscated and given to hospitals; (see my *Chaucer and his England*, p. 132 n.).

This brings us to the very important question of the peasant's diet. Many attempts have been made to work this out statistically, by calculating what he could afford to buy and eat. For France, the golden age of the peasant was probably the early fourteenth century, and for Italy perhaps earlier. Moke's calculations for France are interesting but superficial (pp. 37–46). He reckons that the unskilled labourer's wage was roughly equivalent to that of to-day [*i.e.* 1856], but that he earned this by a work of 200 days per annum, as against his 270 in modern France. Thence Moke concludes that, in a household where both husband and wife are earning wages, the ratio is in favour of the fourteenth century as 700 francs to 660. But he does not take account of the fact that the Church claimed a personal tithe; *i.e.* theoretically at least, 70 of these 700 francs: unless, indeed, this claim had now been abandoned in France. Again, he assumes too readily that, when the royal ordinance fixed the yearly wage of a regular labourer at only 200 times the daily wage of a casual labourer, this meant that the former was bound to work only 200 days (p. 38 n. 2). Fixity of tenure would naturally reconcile a man to a somewhat lower rate of pay. It is difficult, again, to accept his argument that because, in certain years when we know corn to have gone up to four or five times its normal price, the chroniclers speak neither of famine nor of mortality, therefore "men got over these dear years almost with impunity...the mass of the population was comparatively rich." Chroniclers were often sparing of words, especially where they wrote to men whose own experience supplied the necessary deductions from very simple premises. When they wrote "This was a dear year," it would scarcely be necessary to add the words *mortality* and *famine*, except in extreme cases which called for unusual emphasis, as when they tell us here and there of cannibalism. We are on safer ground, I think, when we attempt to estimate the peasant's food according to the scattered contemporary notices.

Janssen brings evidence for a good deal of flesh-food, at times of hard work, in Tirol and those parts of Germany where the peasantry were at their best, in the later fifteenth century[1];

---

[1] Janssen, I, 370, 374 ff. (17th edition, 1897); Bartels, p. 43; Bezold, p. 43. But Sebastian Brandt, one of the contemporary witnesses, contrasts this prosperity of about 1500 with earlier and more frugal times (Bezold, *l.c.*).

Bartels and Bezold, who approach the subject from a different point of view, are here in agreement with him. Luce's description of the French peasantry before the Hundred Years' War is often quoted; but in the first place he is there, *ex professo*, describing a brief period of unusual prosperity; and, secondly, apart from the fact that his concrete instances are far from convincing, on some important points he can be shown to exaggerate; and he admits that "there are provinces in which men live mainly on gruel [*bouillie*] and rye-bread"[1]. Sir John Fortescue writes of the English population as a whole, in 1470: "They eat plentifully of all kinds of flesh and fish: they wear fine woollen cloth in all their apparel." But he is here speaking loosely of the population in general, and contrasting it with that of France, where (he says)

the people...do live in great misery, drinking water daily; neither do the inferior sort taste any other liquor, saving only at solemn feasts. Their shamewes [*slops*] are made of hemp, much like unto sack cloth.... Their women go barefoot saving on holidays; neither men nor women eat any flesh there, but only lard of bacon, with a small quantity whereof they fatten their pottage and broths. As for roasted or sodden meat of flesh they taste none, except it be of the inwards sometimes and heads of beasts, that be killed for gentlemen and merchants[2].

We must balance, therefore, between the two descriptions—each, no doubt, somewhat heightened for the sake of contrast—and it is difficult to follow the Jesuit professor Pastor in his notes to Janssen. Quoting only from Fortescue's description of food and dress in England, applying it to "the English working-folk" alone, and entirely ignoring the French side of the shield, which he contemplates only in Luce's modern picture of the specially

---

[1] *Du Guesclin*, pp. 52–3. For his exaggerations see appendix 9.

[2] *De Laudibus*, ch. 18, from Mulcaster's translation of 1573. Pastor, in his notes to Janssen, is even more unfortunate with Sismondi, whom he refers to, but without actual quotation, as corroborating Janssen's argument for the well-being of the German peasant (*Hist. des Rép. It.* ch. 91). While Sismondi draws a vague, but very favourable, picture of the Italian peasants' prosperity during the first half of the fifteenth century, in contrast with their misery under the petty tyrants of the Renaissance and later ages, he is so far from supporting Janssen that he writes: "Si on compare [le sort du paysan italien] à celui des paysans de la France, de l'Angleterre, de l'Espagne et de l'Allemagne à la memê époque, sans doute on le trouvera infiniment plus heureux."

favourable conditions of about 1300 A.D., Pastor writes: "The Christian economic system of the Middle Ages had founded there also a state of prosperity for the lower classes to which we can find no parallel in earlier or later history."

Let us therefore take as many generalizations as we can find from contemporary authors. Janssen's quotations from noble or middle-class authors who grudged at the prosperity and ostentation of the richer peasants are not quite to the point; far more trustworthy are the authors who speak in general terms of the peasant's food[1]. The most favourable I know are the two quoted by Janssen. An anonymous *Book of Fruits, Trees and Herbs* in 1478 tells us: "While the countryman works, he has also abundant food, and eats plenty of flesh of all kinds and fish, bread and fruit, and drinks wine oftentimes to excess, which is not praiseworthy. Otherwise the countryman's diet may be accounted the most wholesome." Here, let us note, reference is to all classes of agriculturists, *der Bauer* includes the well-to-do farmer as well as the serf and the day-labourer. The second case is where a writer of 1550 tells us that

even in my father's recollection, the countryfolk ate far better than now. Every day there was flesh and food in superfluity; and at church wakes or other feasts the tables broke down under the loads that they had to bear; then, men drank wine as though it were water, they ate and filled themselves to their heart's content; for there were riches and superfluity. Now, things are very different. The times have been very dear and costly for many years past; and the food of the best countryfolk, it may almost be said, is far worse than that of journeymen and hinds in the olden time.

It is notorious, of course, that old writers are least to be trusted when they describe their fathers' days in contrast to their own; but a passage like this cannot be ruled out altogether. We must compare it with what other witnesses tell us, generalizing from their different points of view. And, first of all, with that distinguished writer on social conditions who was contemporary with our anonymous writer of 1478, whose book was published not, like the Unknown's, in one single edition, now unprocurable,

[1] Alwin Schultz preserves this necessary distinction. While quoting complaints of satirists that the lower classes in Austria were beginning to demand fish and olive-oil like their betters, he finds evidence, on the whole, for a much plainer diet (*Höfisches Leben*, 2nd ed. 1, 382, 439, 440).

but in many editions and at least four languages; yet whom Janssen, with his annotator Pastor, so inexplicably ignores altogether. This Hans Beham, as we have already seen, describes the German peasants thus: "They feed on brown bread, oatmeal porridge, or boiled peas; they drink water or whey; they are clad in a linen coat, with boots of untanned leather and a dyed cap"[1].

The other witnesses may be taken in chronological order. Etienne de Fougères, bishop of Rennes, wrote about 1170 that the bondman "is very glad when he can get black bread and milk and butter"[2]. The Benedictine Gautier de Coincy, about 1220, tells us that the "vilains" of his day "gnaw and browse upon their bread in great sweat of their brow, in great travail"; they have "little bread and an evil couch"; "sometimes they have little enough of rough black or brown bread"[3]. A few years later, *Meier Helmbrecht* seems to make it quite plain that flesh and fowls were very exceptional on the table even of one of the richest peasants in thirteenth-century Bavaria; the ordinary food is very clearly specified; pork-cheese as a special treat, but mainly porridge of millet or oatmeal, with black bread; amid all the extravagant cheer with which the father honours his son who has come home from court, he has no wine, and the young man must drink water for a week. The women had to labour as they labour on the Continent at the present day[4]. The Flemish *Kerelslied*, speaking of the peasant rebels of 1323–8, calls them "eaters of curds and whey and milk cheese, who, with their long beards and tattered garments, are as proud as a count, and imagine that the whole world belongs to them, both towns and countryside"[5]. Chaucer's poor widow in the *Nun's Priest's Tale* fed on "milk and brown bread, singed bacon, and sometimes an egg or two." Three times the author of *Piers Plowman* comes to this subject of food. There are, indeed, labourers who take

[1] See above, ch. II, p. 23.

[2] Lommatzsch, p. 71. Compare the implications of St Bernard's words which we have seen at the end of Chapter XIX.

[3] *Ibid.* pp. 70–76. He uses the verbs he would use of an animal: "leur pain rungent et broustent." Cf. Bert. v. Regensburg in app. 1 (p. 398).

[4] *Helmbrecht*, ll. 439 ff., 890 ff., 1115 ff., 1353 ff. When Bartels quotes Freidank as giving porridge or cheese for the common man's ordinary fare about 1250, he relies upon a misreading which is exposed in Sandross's edition, pp. 228–9.

[5] Pirenne, *Soulèvement*, pp. xx, xxiv.

advantage of the exceptional conditions created by the Black Death; who know that labour is scarce, and disdain cold cabbage and bacon with penny-ale; they must have "fresh flesh or fish, fried or y-baken," and that piping hot. But, under more normal circumstances, even the ploughman must be content with far less than this in a year of scarcity, until the next harvest brings relief. Chickens, geese and pork or bacon are beyond him; he has "two green [fresh] cheeses, a few curds and cream, and a

BONT COTTAGE, ABERAERON.

cake of oats, and bread for my bairns of beans and of peases," with leeks, onions, parsley and cherries. Lower in the scale come "the most needy" of the villagers;

poor folk in cottages, charged with children and chief lord's rent: that they with spinning may spare, spend they it in house-hire, both in milk and in meal, to make therewith pap, to glut therewith their children that cry after food. Also themselves suffer much hunger.... There is bread and penny-ale taken for a pittance [*luxury*]; cold flesh and cold fish is to them as baked venison; on Fridays and fasting-days, a farthing's worth of mussels were a feast for such folk, or so many cockles[1].

Christine de Pisan, about 1420, describes the fare of the labourer's wife as "black bread, milk, and water"[2]. About the same time, we have the casual evidence of one who was perhaps the greatest churchman of that century, Jean Gerson, who

---

[1] C. IX, 331 and 304; X, 71. [2] Hentsch, p. 160.

speaks in the same breath of the peasant's and the Carthusian's abstinence from flesh-foods[1]. We come next to two legists, who base themselves, it is true, on Roman civil law, but whose testimony agrees with what we have already seen. Bonus de Curtili, of Brescia, insists that the proper food of peasants is "beans and onions," as the Gloss says. Troilus Malvitius, the canon of Bologna, in his *De Sanctorum Canonizatione*, points out that "peasants must not eat fowls, but onions and cheese, nor rolls or white bread, but coarse bread; for base and coarse foods are to be given to base persons, and delicate foods to noble folk"[2].

These generalizations are in fair accord with concrete instances. The monastic compiler of the St-Père chartulary reckons a serf's dinner in about 1050 as equivalent to 1 denier in money—roughly $4\frac{1}{2}d$. in pre-war English currency. When working for this abbey, the serf had a ration of three eggs[3]. For English serfs three herrings a day, and sometimes cheese also, with bread and beer, are ordinary allowances; sometimes less; in harvest-time, generally a little more[4]. This was at a time

---

[1] *Opp.* vol. ii, col. 529 a (ed. 1606, 637 a). Therefore, he says, both classes live beyond the average of mankind.

[2] *Tract. Jur.* vol. xii, f. 18, § 76; vol. xv, f. 422, n. 74. The distinction is marked in practice by a provision of 1262 for a yearly feast given to the dependents of the chapter of Passau (*Pataviensis*: *Mon Boica*, xii, 349). Fowls and wine were to be on the table; but "the serfs shall be fed without fowls and wine." There is a thirteenth-century story which anticipates the famous French princess of the Ancien Régime: "I have heard that a certain lady, seeing the poor in time of famine picking grass in the fields to eat, said, 'Can they not eat bacon and peas'? One man replied, 'They could if they had it'" (Abp Peckham's *Letters*, R.S. iii, introd. p. xcii).

[3] *Cart. St-Père*, pp. cxcv, 444, 711, 712. At Glastonbury, in the twelfth century, one servant gets a daily loaf with two gallons of beer, and has been receiving a penny a week for all his farther food; it is a promotion for him to get, instead of this penny, a daily ration from the monks' kitchen, "like the other servants, by reason of his good service" (*Lib. H. Soliac*, p. 15). This would seem to work out at something very similar to the St-Père rate.

[4] *E.g.* taking the entries in the Ramsey chartulary as they come, "one loaf of second-rate bread, and beer," for carting (1, 290); for the first day of harvest-work "bread, beer, pottage [of peas or beans] flesh and cheese, and three loaves for every two men...of wheat and rye, with more wheat than rye"; for the second day "bread, pottage, water, herrings and cheese"; on the third day "as on the first, if my lord [abbot] be willing" (p. 300); for carrying a load on his back to the abbey, "one second-rate loaf" (p. 304); for harvesters, again "on the first day, sufficient bread, beer, fresh flesh, pottage and cheese; on the other days, fish; and, if the bread be bought, there shall be a three-

when, even in monasteries that were never specially wealthy, a monk might claim as his allowance, for a single course of a single meal, from four to six eggs, or herrings, or other fish of that size[1]. When we find a specification of quality, it is nearly always provided that the bread and beer given to the working peasants shall not be of the monks' loaf and tap, but of the qualities made for the abbey servants[2]. At Butley priory, in 1532, the monks complained to their visitor that "the brethren go on foot to be ordained [by the bishop], to the scandal of the monastery." Their beer, again, was criticized as no better than peasants' beer; therefore the visitor takes serious measures to provide horses and better beer[3].

It was only at rare times and places that the monk really humbled himself to the position of the peasant. Certainly the small Order of Monte Oliveto began thus, in their food and in their clothing: "pannus ille rusticus et grossus, fusco colore, illius similitudinis quo rustici utuntur"[4]. The early Cistercians, apparently, did the same, and they ate the same brown bread as the lay brethren; but they, like the Olivetans, gradually changed their cloth to pure white. The early Franciscans began with coarse undyed wool, but gradually changed to a dyed brown-grey.

Poetically true, therefore, if not exact in antiquarian detail, is William Morris's unforgettable picture of the dinner in the

farthing loaf for every two" (p. 347: a very similar custom on p. 358; similarly p. 368, except that each pair have one portion of flesh between them, or three herrings each; so again p. 394). A specially favoured group feed, at harvest time "once a day at my lord's cost, and for supper two billings [*small loaves*] and cheese, or two herrings" (p. 401). An interesting account of expenditure on harvesters' wages and food at Creake abbey may be found in *Norf. Archaeol.* vi (1864), 356.

[1] At Westminster it was six; so also at Spalding, quite in the second or third rank of wealth. I am dealing fully with this in *Five Centuries of Religion*, vol. ii.

[2] *E.g.* at Ramsey *panis militis*, which, like the *panis armigeri* of Peterborough and other abbeys, took its name not from knights and squires in the later medieval sense, but from the lower military retainers of early days.

[3] *Vis. Norwich*, C.S. pp. 286–9. Instances of food-allowances are given by Anton, iii, 152 ff., but without indication whether they are for ordinary days or for the special work at harvest-time. Delisle, pp. 189–191, gives others; but in one case, at least, he has mistaken the allowance of a well-to-do corrodian for that of a labourer (Beaumont-le-Roger, 1268).

[4] *Chron. M.-O.* p. 18.

harvest field, where Michael, on his ride to the Castle of the Rose, sees

> The masters of that ripening realm,
> Cast down beneath an ancient elm
> Upon a little strip of grass,
> From hand to hand the pitcher pass;
> While on the turf beside them lay
> The ashen-handled sickles grey,
> The matters of their cheer between:
> Slices of white cheese, specked with green,
> And green striped onions and rye bread,
> And summer apples faintly red,
> Even beneath the crimson skin;
> And yellow grapes well ripe and thin,
> Plucked from the cottage gable-end[1].

Incidentally, we have already seen a little evidence as to the peasant's dress; just enough to dispel to a very small extent the impenetrable mist in which we are left by one of the greatest archivists of the last generation[2]. To a very small extent; for the inventories, which are sometimes so significant, help us but little here. In the nature of the case, no inventories could come down to us but from exceptionally well-to-do serfs; again, we may be sure that the family did a good deal to minimize his possessions; yet, even so, such a list as we find in the Hales Rolls seems scanty enough[3]. We have already seen evidence for linen shirts or sheets among the English peasantry; and Luce gives a good deal more for the countryfolk of Normandy and Brittany[4]. Clothes must often have been home-made from beginning to end, spun, woven, cut and fashioned. I have only once met with any allusion to the professional tailor in the village[5], and *Piers Plowman* implies that some peasants would turn to this job as a relief from their ordinary field-work[6]. The same passage includes foot-wear: "Canst thou...shape shoes or clothes?" In medieval Germany, at any rate, there were men who cut

---

[1] *Earthly Paradise*; "The Man Born to be King." The "green cheeses" of *Piers Plowman*, however, mean not what we nowadays call ripe cheeses, but fresh and new, just as our ancestors spoke of a "green wound."

[2] Delisle, p. 189: "Nous avouons humblement ne rien nous rappeler sur l'habillement de nos paysans au moyen âge, qui mérite d'être signalé."

[3] See above, ch. IX, p. 101.　　　　　　　　　[4] pp. 61–2.

[5] I have, unfortunately, mislaid the reference.

[6] C. VI, 18.

and shaped sabots in the forests[1]. The distinctive peasant-costumes, which still survive, *e.g.* in parts of Switzerland and the Black Forest, are post-medieval[2]. The general evidence on all points seems to lead to the conclusion that the peasantry of the Middle Ages, as of every other age, lived ordinarily very much from hand to mouth. In Hesse, a series of seven exceptionally good harvests, from 1241 to 1247, had the result "that people could get no servants, so that nobles and clergy must needs work at their own harvests, and the villages could get no girls to herd the flocks"[3].

This chapter may close with brief pictures from two sides of village life which have already appeared to us in casual and occasional glimpses.

The rougher side, in some cases, was very rough indeed. Geiler v. Kaysersberg, quoting from Poggio Bracciolini, in the first years of the fifteenth century, shows us the shepherds of southern Italy habitually practising as amateur banditti[4]. Nearly three centuries earlier, we get almost as gloomy a picture of Hungarian manners, not from a mission-preacher and a satirist, but from a friar who is seriously recording his own life-experiences and those of his elder companions. Jordan of Giano thus describes the sufferings of the Franciscan mission to that country in 1219:

The Hungarian mission was brought by sea [from Italy] to that country by a certain bishop of Hungary; and, when they began to scatter and go through the land, the shepherds set their dogs upon them and, speaking no word, beat them incessantly with the butts of their spears. When, therefore, the brethren disputed among themselves why they should be thus handled, one said: "Perchance these men would fain have our frocks"; which, therefore, they gave up; yet, even so, the shepherds ceased not to smite them. Then said he: "Perchance they would have our inner tunics also"; so they gave these up; yet even so they ceased not from smiting them. So he said: "Perchance they will have our breeches also"; which at last they gave up; whereupon the shepherds ceased to beat them and suffered them to depart naked. And one of these same brethren told me that he himself had thus lost his breeches fifteen times. And seeing that he, overcome with shame and modesty, grieved more for his breeches than for the rest of his garments, he himself befouled them with

---

[1] Anton, III, 445. [2] Bartels, p. 45. [3] Anton, III, 209.
[4] *Navicula Fatuorum*, turba XCVII, xxxi N. Cf. app. 40 here below.

cow-dung and other filth, so that the shepherds' gorge rose at the sight thereof, and they suffered him to keep his breeches. These friars, then, after suffering many other outrages, came back to Italy[1].

The Hungarian shepherd, then, was a child of nature; but doubtless he had also that happier side of the child's nature which my final extract will show. It tells the story of the growth of an important medieval town from what we may almost call a medieval football-club.

In those days [early in the eleventh century], in the place where the market of Ardres now stands, there was a certain ale-brewer or taverner in the midst of the meadow by the highway, whither the rustic folk were wont to resort in their rough fashion, to play at football or at hockey, by reason of this long and wide expanse of level grass.....*Pasture*, in the vulgar tongue, was called *arda*. Wherefore these shepherds would say one to the other—and others who haunted that spot, not knowing the taverner's name, and knowing no better name for that uninhabited land, would say the same, each pricking and challenging the other to play—"let us go, let us go" (said they) "and meet on Arda, to wit, The Pasture." In process of time men came from other districts and began to dwell there—

and thus grew up the town of Ardres[2].

Here we see the pastoral folk in a far happier light. But this, again, is a mere casual reference, from an author who was not really concerned to tell us about the peasant in himself; no more concerned than the rest of them, in days when even Chaucer has so little to say about the Ploughman. If in any sense we may truly say "Happy is the people that has no history," yet certainly we cannot safely apply that beatitude to a people whose history has come down to us only in half-unwilling driblets, and who would doubtless have anticipated the words which Beaumarchais puts into the mouth of his son of the people. Figaro has no complaint against the mere ingratitude of the privileged classes towards the common man: "Je me crus trop heureux d'en être oublié; persuadé qu'un grand nous fait assez de bien quand il ne nous fait pas de mal."

---

[1] Jordanus de Giano, *Chronica*, c. 6 (*Analecta Franciscana*, I, 1885, 3).
[2] A. Duchesne, *Hist. des Maisons de Guînes*, etc. (1631); *Preuves*, p. 142.

CHAPTER XXIII

LABOUR AND CONSIDERATION

UNDER these conditions the peasant laboured ordinarily from dawn to dark, from Morrowmass to Evensong, with a short interval for the midday meal. So, at least, he must needs work in early days for his lord, and so to the end he worked for himself or for the employer who hired him. In the later Middle Ages, a full day's work at hedging or ditching or ploughing counted as two "day-works" in England; but this modification grew up slowly, and was evidently resisted by conservative landlords. "Let him work with his hands from dawn to vespers"; so runs a capitulary of 800 A.D.[1] On two Ramsey manors the monks were making similar demands even at the end of the twelfth century: "Whatsoever kind of work he have to do, except in the wood, he shall work the whole year through from sunrise unto sunset": "He shall hoe from dawn to evensong, with a brief eating-space between"—*parvo spatio comestionis mediante*[2]. Nearly two centuries later, under the monks of Münster in Georgenthal, "the serfs shall be at work by Morrowmass-time, and shall quit their labours when men ring for Evensong"[3]. So, again, the statute of Henry VII in 1495 (ch. 22). The king and parliament there enact

that every artificer and labourer be at his work, between the midst of the month of March and the midst of the month of September, before 5 o'clock in the morning, and that he have but half an hour for his breakfast and an hour and a half for his dinner at such time as he hath season for sleep to him appointed by this statute, and at such time as is herein appointed that he shall not sleep, then he to have but an hour for his dinner and half an hour for his noon-meat; and that he depart not from his work, between the midst of the said months of March and September, till between 7 and 8 of the clock in the evening....And that from the midst of September to the midst of March every artificer and labourer be at their work in the springing

---

[1] Caggese, I, 125. [2] *Cart. Rames.* I, 398, 288; cf. p. 297.
[3] Anton, III, 155, 1330 A.D.

of the day and depart not till night of the same day; and that the said artificers and labourers sleep not by day[1].

For holidays he had nominally all the red-letter saints' days; a ninth-century abbey counted 24 of these per annum[2]; but, although saints' days increased in the later Middle Ages, (to the regret, as we have seen, of some ecclesiastical disciplinarians), it is evident that a large number of these were not allowed by the masters, and were kept, if at all, at the workman's expense[3]. The children worked too, at everything for which they could be utilized[4]. At harvest-time, the whole family must come and work except the wife[5]; or, with the farther exception, quoted in one case by Vinogradoff, of one "marriageable daughter"[6]. In so far as he works for himself, he has a painful struggle with the elements; winter-time is the peasant's hell[7]. For winter

[1] For this dinner-time compare the prescription for the York Cathedral masons (*York Fabric Rolls*, Surtees Soc. 1858, p. 181, 1370 A.D.). The men are to work for the winter half year from as early till as late as they can see; there are elaborate prescriptions for the avoidance of excess in mid-day meal and rest. See also the Eton cases printed by Willis and Clark, I, 382; these masons were apparently restricted to half an hour for their noon-meal, while they claimed an hour. I have summarized and commented on all this evidence in *Social Life in Britain*, pp. 470, 489. For hours of work under the régime of Church and Squirearchy in Sardinia, see appendix 39.

[2] Adalhard, p. 30; on the other hand, Walter of Henley reckons only 56 days in the whole year "for holy-days and other disturbances [of work]" (p. 9). For masons and similar workmen see Thorold Rogers, *Six Centuries*, etc. 1901, p. 181; he takes a bare five holidays in the year as a normal number, noting that the men sometimes worked on Sundays as well. Mr H. S. Bennett has collected evidence which shows that the peasant did not always get the nominal holidays.   [3] See, for instance, the above-cited act of 1495.

[4] Lamprecht, *Wirth.* I, 463.

[5] *Cart. Rames.* I, 339, 358, 367, 385, 395; III, 250, 278, etc. On one manor, however, the children are excused for the *first* day of harvest: "every soul in the village that can work shall come, save only the children" (I, 367).

[6] Vinogradoff, *Villainage*, p. 284.

[7] Benvenuto da Imola, *Comentum*, ed. Lacaita, II, 190–1. Benvenuto is there extolling the insight which Dante shows into real peasant life (*Inf.* XXIV, 1–15). The poet has hit the exact thing with his word *pecorelle*, since the villager has "few sheep, and those small and ill-fed." Compare Lamprecht, *Wirth.* I, 1237, for the struggles of the rural proletariat. Prof. T. H. Okey has supplied me with a sidelight upon the misery of the later Italian peasantry. Canon Pietro Casola passed through Venice on his way to Jerusalem in 1494. He describes the Venetian ladies and their fashions in minute detail, and remarks incidentally: "The greater part is false hair; and this I know for certain because I saw quantities of it on poles, sold by peasants in the Piazza San Marco. Further, I enquired about it, pretending to wish to buy some, although I had a beard both long and white" (*Canon Pietro Casola's Pilgrimage to Jerusalem*, Manchester Univ. Press, 1907, p. 144). For a peasant-woman to sell her hair is a very evident token of distress.

intensifies all his other hardships; in winter he must herd in confined space with his family and his cattle, and sickness will be the too frequent consequence. Abbot Ekkehard of Aurach, while implying that the peasants of his own land were far better off, assigns a definitely economic cause for the multitudes who joined the First Crusade in 1095 from France[1].

"It was easy," he writes, "to persuade the western Franks to leave their lands, since Gaul had now for some years past been sorely afflicted, at one time by civil wars, at another by famine, at another by plague; and, lastly, the terror of that plague which arose around Ste-Gertrude de Nivelle had driven them to despair of their lives."

This was St Anthony's fire, which raged especially all through the eleventh century, and most of all, naturally, among the poor. Many of these conditions have not yet been stamped out by civilization; yet Ekkehard's first cause, that of war, pressed upon the Middle Ages as it has not pressed upon Europe even during the worst years of this present century. It is difficult to say which of the great countries suffered most in this respect. Among the worst, certainly, were those bitter and protracted civil wars which made all medieval Italy into what Dante calls "a hostelry of pain." I have printed elsewhere Salimbene's description of the devastation wrought under his own eyes in the thirteenth century by the papal and imperial soldiery, and the civil conflicts which were kindled or fanned by emperor and pope[2]. Villages were deserted; "nevertheless, hard by the town walls, men tilled the fields under guard of the city militia." Even in the later days of medieval Italy, in the fifteenth century, nearly all the villages were fortified, and the peasants tilled their fields with one ear open to the alarm-bell which would call them and their cattle to immediate refuge within the walls[3]. The fortifications which surround quite ordinary villages in the Rhine and Neckar and Main valleys (to quote only one district of Germany) bear eloquent testimony to a similar state of things. Thomas Basin, in the fifteenth century, describes the desolation of all the rich country between Loire, Seine and Somme; it

[1] P.L. vol. 154, col. 968.
[2] *From St Francis to Dante*, ch. VI *ad fin*; 2nd. ed. pp. 59 ff.
[3] Sismondi, *Rep. It.* ch. 91.

was overgrown with thorns and brambles except within a brief radius from some castle or fortress; and, even there, men and beasts were so accustomed to the alarm-bell that the plough-horses, loosed from the plough, fled of their own accord, from force of habit, towards the warning signal; the very sheep and swine did the same[1]. Moreover, the peasants' sufferings far outlasted the Hundred Years' War, and even the civil wars which followed; since the Ordinance of Charles VII riveted upon the people a mercenary army and a system of irresponsible royal taxation. Commines, therefore, says no more than truth about the French kings:

Their subjects they poll in such sort that they leave them nothing; for, notwithstanding that they pay them tasks and subsidies above their ability; yet seek they not to redress the disorder of their men of arms, which live continually upon their people without payment, doing besides infinite mischiefs and injuries, as all the world knoweth. For they are not contented with such cheer as they find in the husbandman's house and is set before them, but beat also the poor man and constrain them to go forth to buy wine, bread and victuals; and, if the good man have a fair wife or a daughter, he shall do wisely to keep her out of their sight[2].

What did all this mean for the ordinary peasant? We have already seen pretty plain answers to this question[3]; we must remember, too, that civil conflicts were even more frequent in the Middle Ages than international campaigns. Van Houtte, who is far from exaggerating the weaknesses of Flemish civilization in the past, writes of "that open sore of society in the Middle Ages proper, private war." He continues:

It was certainly the peasants who suffered most from this calamity. When the lords attacked each other, they always took care to lay waste each other's lands, and especially the "mansiones proprias"— i.e. the holdings exploited by the serfs to the almost exclusive profit of the lords. We even find Count William Clito carrying off the peasants from the manor of the "magnus preco" of Oostcamp and taking them by force to Winendale and Oudenbourg[4].

[1] I have translated this description, with much similar evidence, on pp. 246–253 of *Chaucer and his England*.
[2] *Mémoires*, bk v, ed. Michand et Poujoulat, p. 132; Danett's translation, p. 196.   [3] *E.g.* pp. 104–114.
[4] *Essai sur la civilisation flamande* (Louvain, 1898), p. 106. Van Houtte notes how the growth of the great towns of Flanders in the later Middle Ages made the citizens "the irreconcilable enemies of the countryfolk."

St Peter Damian, writing at a time when Italy was less distressed than in her later centuries, tells the same story in a single sentence; directly two nobles quarrel, "the poor man's thatch goes up in flame"[1]. The États Généraux of Tours, in 1483, drew a heartrending picture of the peasants' sufferings at the hands of their own soldiery (*Recueil*, pp. 88 ff.):

The poor labourer must needs pay the wages of men who beat him and cast him forth from his own cottage....In truth, were it not for God who giveth counsel and patience to the poor folk, they would fall into despair[2]...and, but for the people's hope that things would go better at the joyous accession of the king, they would have abandoned their labour....They are of worse condition than serfs; for the serf is fed...some have fled to England, Brittany and elsewhere, and a great number of the rest, beyond all count, are dead of hunger; others in despair have killed their wives, their children, and themselves, seeing that they had no livelihood. And many men, women, and children, for want of beasts, are constrained to plough with the yoke on their own shoulders; others ploughed by night, for fear lest, in the daytime, they should be taken and apprehended for the said tallage.

The Estates pleaded with the king that at least a peasant's working beasts and necessary tools should be free from seizure for debt by royal or seignorial officers (p. 117). It was the French here who did most harm to the French: *Gallus Gallo lupus*. Thomas Basin, good Frenchman as he is, points out that lower Normandy, under the heel of the English conqueror, enjoyed a comparative prosperity which was denied to those other parts that were disputed between France and England; and Denifle, with all his just sympathy for France, brings other evidence to the same effect[3]. In 1365, the English free-companies ravaged as far as Alsace; and a concrete instance from the petty wars of the fifteenth century may serve to conclude this subject here:

On Wednesday after the Nativity of our Lady [Sept. 8] the Dauphin came down with 12,000 horse into the land. Then the city of Strassburg warned the whole countryside to bear away their corn; but the peasants said that this was only done in order that, when they

---

[1] P.L. vol. 144, col. 228.
[2] Compare Michelet's words which I have already quoted: "Cet homme [the peasant] aurait crevé, s'il n'espérait dans le démon."
[3] *La désolation des églises*, etc. 1, 497 ff. and 514 ff.

brought it into the city, they might have to sell it at such price as the magistrate would. They said they would rather give it to the enemy; and so indeed it came to pass; wherefore many peasants thenceforward must take to the beggar's staff[1].

England was the one important country of Europe in which, during the last four medieval centuries, the peasant suffered least from the horrors of war. Commines's contrast between ordinary continental conditions and ours is well-known: " But (as before I said) the realm of England hath this special grace above all other realms and dominions, that in civil wars the [common] people is not destroyed, the towns be not burned nor razed, but the lot of fortune falleth upon the soldiers, especially the gentlemen "[2].

Another curse, that of famine, needs only the briefest mention. Man was then at the mercy of the elements; and, with those imperfect methods of communication, one district might starve even when there was plenty within a hundred miles or so. Delisle, on pp. 628 ff., gives a list of famines and plagues for which he can show documentary evidence in Normandy: Alwin Schultz gives a similar list for Germany in his *Deutsches Leben*[3]; chroniclers like Ralph Glaber tell us of countryfolk driven to cannibalism[4]; and folk-tales of the *Hänsel und Gretel* type, drifted down from those ancient days, contain only too much truth on both sides; the children cast forth by sheer parental famine, and their possible fate in the forest.

But is there not one poor man's plague, at least, from which the medieval peasant was free? True, the Church commonly bade him keep to his own place in society[5]; true, papal mercenaries might ravage his fields alternately with imperial soldiers; but did not the Church at least save him individually from the bloodsucking moneylender, and collectively from the curse of modern capitalism? This has been asserted, and is now being

---

[1] Chronicle printed in J. v. Königshofen (ed. 1698), p. 1003; cf. pp. 137, 333; also Vogt, p. 30; and, for other ravage of war, Joubert, pp. 33–4; Commines, *Mémoires*, bk III, ch. 11; bk IV, chs. 3–5; E. Lavisse, *Hist. de France*, IV, ii, 390, 394.

[2] *Mémoires*, bk v, ch. 20; trans. T. Danett, 1596, p. 201.

[3] Vol. II, 1892, pp. 451 ff.   [4] P.L. vol. 142, col. 676.

[5] Unless, indeed, he could buy himself free, or in rare cases get gratuitous emancipation, and study for the priesthood. But this movement, though so frequent at times in the Dark Ages as to provoke authoritative repression, touched comparatively few villeins in the later Middle Ages.

repeated with increasing boldness and frequency from year to year, by writers who seem to draw the historical bow at a mere venture, and who would certainly disdain to treat their fellows in money-matters with that reckless irresponsibility which they display wherever the Christian religion is concerned. I hope to deal with this subject much more fully elsewhere[1]; meanwhile, a few quotations and examples may suffice to transfer this question from those regions where journalists play at haphazard with church affairs, to the field of legitimate history. Let us judge here, as elsewhere, by what trustworthy medieval witnesses tell us of their own times.

Capitalism grew up much earlier than most historians have yet recognized; Prof. Pirenne brought this out clearly in his remarkable lecture before the International Congress of Historical Studies in 1913[2]. And, with the growth of capitalism, the old prohibitions of usury broke down even more completely than before. We have seen (Chapter XX) that even the clerical or monastic usurer was a fairly familiar figure. Petrus Cantor in Paris at the end of the twelfth century, and Benvenuto da Imola at Bologna 250 years later, note that the merchant has little choice between going to hell for usury, or falling into beggary by respecting the Church's prohibition[3]. So, also, St Bernardino of Siena, about 1420, finds it necessary to argue formally against the feeling that society cannot be organized on an advanced economic scale without public usury[4]. A capitalist at Douai, in about 1300, was leading poor men and women, through the gate of usury and insolvency, into actual serfdom[5]. In 1365, the ravages of war had driven the peasants of Cologne and Liège dioceses into the usurers' hands[6]. About the same time, we have two witnesses from England. In the dialogue of *Dives and Pauper*, written about 1400, we read[7]:

D. I dread me that nigh all our nation hath so drunken of this well of Sardinia [which blinds men's eyes with covetousness] that they

---

[1] In an appendix to a volume which Mr H. G. Richardson is preparing for the series of *Cambridge Studies in English Legal History*.

[2] Translated in the *American Hist. Reviews* for Ap. 1914. Long before this, Eden pointed out that capitalism began earlier than his contemporaries generally realized (1, 74).

[3] P.L. vol. 205, col. 263; cf. cols. 145–6, 149, 157–8; *Comentum*, 1, 579.

[4] *Opera*, 1, 158 b. [5] Pirenne, *l.c.* p. 511.

[6] Fierens, *Suppliques d'Urbain V*, p. 599. [7] *Com.* VII. ch. 28.

be ghostly blind. For if I take heed what theft of simony reigneth in the clergy, what theft of usury reigneth principally among merchants and rich folk, what theft of ravine and extortion reigneth among the lords and great men, what michery and robbery among the poor commons that be alway inclined to slay and to rob, methinketh that much of our nation is guilty in theft and overdon [*sic*] much blinded with false covetise.

P. Therefore God saith thus: "From the least to the most, all they followen avarice and false covetise, from the prophet to the priest all they make lyings and do guile and falsehood; and therefore they shall fall and I shall give their women to strangers and their lands and their fields to other heirs" (Jerem. viii, 10). And by the prophet Isaiah God undernameth [rebukes] the governors of the people both in temporality, and in spirituality, and saith thus: "Thy princes be false, and fellows of thieves. All they love gifts, and follow meeds and yielding again, for they deemed not after the right but after that men might pay" (Is. i, 23). "If thou sawest a thief thou rannest with him to help him," as false judges in temporality do these days, "and with lechers and adulterers thou puttedst thy part," as judges in spirituality do these days (Ps. l, 18).

And the contemporary Langland tells us that the usurer pities the poor as the pedlar pities the cat, whom he entices into his hands and then flays for the sake of his skin[1]. At the same time, Pierre Berchoire writes in a similar vein from France; the usurer "catches the peasant by the nose"[2]. Princes, both lay and ecclesiastical, often kept their own tame usurers; usury in later medieval France was not so much forbidden as licensed, under certain restrictions which probably benefited the princes rather than the people: so also in Flanders and Italy[3]. The German peasants, says Werner Rolewink in about 1480, sometimes sell themselves into servitude; even the Carthusian ascetic does not lead so hard a life as the labourer[4]. A generation later, Wimpheling writes of them that they are eaten up with usury[5]. Whole districts of Germany were gradually sucked dry by the usurers of the later Middle Ages; the townsfolk dealt no less hardly with the peasants than other landlords had done[6]. Indeed, the

[1] B. v, 257.   [2] *Opera*, I, 597, 12; cf. III, 129 d.
[3] *Tract. Juris*, vol. XVI (Lyons, 1549), f. 83 b; cf. ff. 80 ff. See also my appendix 40.   [4] Leibnitz, *Scriptt. Rer. Brun.* III (1711), 632, 635, 639.
[5] J. A. Riegger, *Amoenitates*, p. 453; cf. Bert. v. Regensburg in appendix 1 (pp. 398–9).
[6] Bartels, p. 87; cf. Vogt, p. 26. Brandt's *Narrenschiff* complains of this; see paraphrase in Barclay's *Ship of Fools*, 1874, II, 168, and Scheible, pp. 719–

German peasant's helplessness in face of the moneylender was one of the causes of the great revolt of 1525 and of its forerunners; more than once these insurgents put forward a formal claim for the total suppression of usury. There were townsfolk who, though they lent to the peasant at only 5 per cent., did so on the excellent chance of being able to foreclose, and thus to swallow up a holding that was worth many times more than the sum actually lent. Other unimpeachable evidence gives point to Luther's complaint that "the man who had 100 gulden to lend could eat up one peasant or small citizen per annum"[1]. That is why Luther, as Dr O'Brien puts it, "harked back to the harsh and unbending standards of the Middle Ages"[2]. The existing state of things seemed to him so bad, that he would gladly have abolished the indulgences introduced by Aquinas and other schoolmen, as a compromise which had shown itself unworkable. In other words, Luther took the position which had been orthodox in Catholicism before Aquinas, and which is actually maintained in a papal ruling embodied in canon law, the curious decretal *Naviganti*[3]. We must give great credit to the Church for her attempts to solve this difficult question, but it cannot be asserted that she did in fact solve it, or that the poor man enjoyed more practical protection under her than he does in modern society. Moreover, Caggese is driven by his researches into Italian rural and civic labour to the conclusion that the attempt to fix a just price in all matters of trade often operated to the advantage only of the landlord, and to the detriment of the consumer; so that "a policy whose main aim was democratic resulted, more often than not, in rendering the landlords masters of the situation"[4].

Nor was there more true dignity and self-respect in the life

724, where Geiler uses the same word as Langland; the usurer gets the poor man's skin. Caggese is most emphatic for Italy; the great towns of the later Middle Ages ground down their rural tenants as steadily as the nobles had done (II, 218 ff., 373, 379).

[1] Bezold, pp. 452, 460. Janssen admits the growing prevalence of usury in the generations before the Reformation (bk III, ch. iii).

[2] *Econom. Effects of the Reformation*, 1923, p. 17.

[3] *Decret. Greg.* lib. v, tit. xix, c. 19. I have brought out the significance of this for economic history in *History*, July 1921, p. 67.

[4] Vol. II, p. 225. For similar examples of the breakdown in practice of the medieval "just price" theories, see Mr A. S. Walker's article in *History*, Oct. 1921, p. 163.

of these real poor, so far as we can follow the documentary evidence, than in that of their descendants in our own day. It is difficult to assert that any larger proportion rose then in soul above their material disabilities. Certainly the very status of serfdom was in ill repute; this we have already noted in passing; but it will be well to clinch the matter here.

From the earliest date we find not only that the serf pities himself, but that the disinterested third party looks upon his state as pitiable. The serf bears a stigma which may even frustrate the Sacrament of Matrimony, permitting man to put asunder those whom God seemed to have joined together. An eighth-century conciliar decree, incorporated in the *Corpus Juris Canonici*, runs: "If a freeman take to wife another man's bond-woman, in the belief that she is a freewoman, and if the woman be afterwards convicted of servitude, if he be able to buy her free from her servitude, let him do so; if he cannot, let him take another wife if he will"[1]. Peter Lombard and Albertus Magnus (and probably all the other commentators) accept the full consequences of this principle. Concealed servitude is an impediment to marriage, and destroys the contract; it renders the union so heavy a burden that the free party cannot be justly bound to shoulder it: "it is of viler condition in the goods" of this world. This matrimonial impediment, argues Albert, rests not upon natural law but "has its force from positive law, to wit, from a statute of the Church, which has God's authority and inspiration to correct sin by means of penalties"[2]. Allusions to servile misery meet us sometimes in the most formal documents. When, in 1250, the citizens of Ivrea transferred the inhabitants of a neighbouring village to a better-fortified site, they rewarded this obedience by making the peasants thenceforward "frank and free, seeing that (as the law testifieth) liberty is a priceless thing, 'nor can we profitably sell it for all

---

[1] Gratian, *Decret*. pars II, c. xxix, q. 2, can. 4. The semi-official gloss to *if he cannot* runs: "That is, *if he will not*, as explained in the next sentence; but, on the other hand, the lord is not bound to sell the woman." The principle holds equally if a free woman have unknowingly married a serf. Serfdom is here worse than leprosy; see appendix 40.

[2] Alb. Magnus, *Sup. Sent.* lib. IV, dist. xxxvi, artt. 1, 3. I have already had occasion, in Chapter X, to note other matrimonial disabilities of bondage.

the gold in the world'"[1]. Barbour's apostrophe to freedom is fairly well known:

> Ah, freedom is a noble thing!...
> A noble heart may have none ease,
> Nor ellës naught that may him please
> If freedom faileth; for free liking
> Is yearnëd over all other thing,
> Nor he that aye has livëd free
> May not know well the property,
> The anger, nor the wretched doom
> That is coupled to foul thraldom.
> But, if he had assayëd it,
> Then all *par coeur* he should it wit,
> And should think freedom more to prize
> Than all the gold in world that is[2].

The Cistercian revival, with its quickened sense of religion, forbade it as incongruous that the monks should accept serfs as part of their endowments. This prohibition was not long effective[3]; but it shows very clearly that the institution of bondage was beginning to shock the higher moral sense. Again, we cannot rule out altogether, as a merely economic question, that complaint of the House of Commons to the king in 1344, that prelates suffer bondmen and bondwomen nowadays to make wills and dispose of their property like other people, "which is against reason"[4]. It is evident that these knights of the shire and burgesses felt that there ought to be a gulf between the serf and the rest of society, and that it was dangerous to bridge that gulf. So also the author of *Piers Plowman*, with all his democratic sympathies, rehearses it as one clear sign of social decay at the end of the fourteenth century that "bondmen's bairns have been made bishops"; an indulgence of which very few concrete cases could be quoted from the whole Middle

---

[1] "Nec bene libertas pro toto venditur auro" (Salvioli, p. 193). Prof. E. Bensley informs me that this verse is from the 14th *Fable* of Walter, archbishop of Palermo, *De Lupo et Cane*. The next verse runs: "Hoc caeleste donum praeterit orbis opes."

[2] *Bruce*, bk 1, ll. 225 ff.

[3] The Kirkstall Coucher Book, for instance, is full of cases where these early Cistercians accept, or even purchase, serfs singly or in batches, perhaps even more frequently than the older Benedictines.

[4] *Rot. Parl.* II, 149 b, 150 a. The royal reply is oracular: "The King wills that law and reason be done."

Ages, but which Langland takes as a *reductio ad absurdum*[1]. Again, we cannot ignore the contemporary words of Froissart:

There was an usage in England, and yet is in divers countries, that the noblemen hath great franchise over the commons and keepeth them in servage, that is to say their tenants ought by custom to labour the lord's lands, to gather and bring home their corns and some to thresh and to fan, and by servage to make their hay and to hew their wood and bring it home. All these things they ought to do by servage, and there be more of these people in England than in any other realm. Thus the noblemen and prelates are served by them and especially in the county of Kent, Essex, Sussex and Bedford. These unhappy people of these said counties began to stir, because they said they were kept in great servage, and in the beginning of the world, they said, there were no bondmen, wherefore they maintained that none ought to be bond, without he did treason to his lord, as Lucifer did to God....Why should they then be kept so under like beasts; the which they said they would no longer suffer, for they would be all one, and if they laboured or did anything for their lords, they would have wages therefor as well as other[2].

The grievance is here not only financial, but definitely moral also; and this feeling naturally grew with time. Mr Leadam, quoting a late fifteenth-century record, writes: "Even comfortable circumstances, which he apparently enjoyed, created in the Malmesbury bondman no satisfaction with his lot. There is a pathetic ring in the words which, in his old age, he is recorded to have used, that, 'if he might bring that [his freedom] aboute, it wold be more joifull to him than any worlie goode'"[3]. In Germany, as we have seen, this feeling of the indignity of servitude was recorded in the two great collections of customary law, the *Sachsenspiegel* and *Schwabenspiegel*. Verriest prints the

[1] C. VII, 70. While believing personally in the single authorship of *Piers Plowman*, I try to avoid all arguments which assume that authorship. Whoever wrote the C. text was, so far as we can see, a man who sympathized in general with the poor.

[2] Globe ed. p. 250. Froissart's native Flanders was far beyond the average of Europe in peasant freedom.

[3] I. Leadam, *The Star Chamber* (Selden Soc.), p. cxxviii. Cf. G. M. Trevelyan, *England in the Age of Wycliffe*, 1st ed. p. 185. For the serf's gradual awakening to the painful contrast between his own conditions and the freeman's, see Imbart de la Tour, I, 467. According to Baumann (II, 630), "from the fifteenth century onward, it was usual [in Bavaria] to compel malefactors who had been freed from prison to join the ranks of the bondmen." Knapp gives farther evidence for the low estimation of the serf in the eighteenth and nineteenth centuries (p. 369).

pathetic plea of a serf who "is in desire and affection to marry, and ally himself with a poor young girl of these same parts, the which refuseth to take him by reason of the servitude whereunto he is subject from the womb of his mother a bondwoman, whereby his prosperity and honour and advancement are delayed and retarded; wherefore he hath presented this humble supplication" to Duke Philip of Burgundy, who graciously sells him his freedom for 40 livres in cash. Another, two years later, buys his freedom for the same reason: no girl in Mons will marry him, "to his great reproach and damage." A third pleads "the great reproach and reviling which he suffers by reason of his serfdom"[1].

"If we are to believe the petitioners," so wrote the monks of la Ferté-sur-Grosne in a charter of freedom in 1446, "by reason of the heriot which we have over the inhabitants and peasants of St-Ambreuil, the greater part of the aforesaid inhabitants, especially the young folk, are leaving this domain, because their neighbours despise them and will not give them their children in marriage"[2]. Savine quotes a similar case from the first year of Elizabeth's reign: "A bondman of the manor of Shapwike begs the Queen to manumit him. 'Froward' persons object to him the name of bondman, and nobody desires to marry his children"[3]. Similarly, we find the seventeenth century peasants of the Heilbronn district offering to pay heavier dues, if only they may be no longer counted as bondmen; they complained of the scorn which their status entailed among the free peasants around; in the Catholic district of Paderborn, again, certain villages where the peasants were unfree found it almost impossible to induce men or women from the free villages around to contract matrimonial alliances with them[4]. Erasmus thought it a scandal that serfdom had not been long since

---

[1] *L.c.* pp. 596–603. The dates are 1435 and 1437. On p. 70 Verriest certainly minimizes the social disadvantage of serfdom.

[2] Lavisse, *Hist. de France*, IV, ii, 128.

[3] *Bondmen*, p. 267. Savine rightly emphasizes the fact that, in proportion as the serfs decreased in numbers, the more invidious their social position would become; but in his remarks on p. 268 he very much postdates the moral stigma of bondage; in the face of the evidence which I have given in Chapter IX, we cannot possibly say that "under Edward I...it was a hard lot, but it was no shame to be a villein." As early as 1180, men presumed that a villein was always the descendant of the conquered Saxons (*Dial. of Exchequer*, bk I, ch. x).

[4] Knapp, pp. 17, 369.

abolished in all Christian lands[1]. Hansen, dealing with post-Reformation conditions, shows how essentially bad serfdom was in principle, both for the man and for his master[2].

In the face of all this evidence—and I feel convinced that much more might be produced by any student who could devote full time to the subject—it is difficult to gauge the mentality of those who, with Janssen, cast about for all sorts of far-fetched causes to explain how the happy German peasant could have risen in revolt when a blunderer like Luther began to proclaim his gospel of freedom, however limited. It is like the duke of Northumberland's naïve astonishment that the peasants of France should have risen sometimes against their medieval lords, and should finally have welcomed the Revolution; facts which he attempts to explain by some virus of original sin in the common working-man—nay, to some extent, in the common middle classes also—which has hitherto escaped the notice of serious historical students[3]. The condition of the medieval peasantry as a whole, even when we reckon those numerous cases where the worker had become a freeman and perhaps a fairly prosperous yeoman, is quite sufficient to account for a great agrarian revolt[4]. And, by the analogy of all history, that revolt was most likely to come in some district where, and at some time when, the growing prosperity of the villager had given him an appetite for more. If such lords as the abbot of Kempten were already exceptional in Luther's day, then all the more reason why an indignant multitude should rise to shake off the whole system which defended and supported such indefensible exceptions, and which afforded the tyrants a legal excuse for all but their worst injustices.

[1] *Opera*, v, 1704, 670 a.

[2] pp. 28, 29, 33, 44, 46; they finally "became, through oppression and need, too dull and lethargic to feel the need of personal freedom." Hansen notes (what Savine suspects for Tudor England) that servile marriages were less fruitful than others, and infant mortality was higher (*Bondmen*, p. 247).

[3] *National Review*, May 1924. The duke, it is true, takes the modest line that he has written mainly to "stimulate inquiry and discussion"; but the editor, though twice requested to permit discussion, turned a deaf ear; and his readers, in so far as they take this journal seriously, will form a very curious conception of Labour in the past.

[4] In the mid-fifteenth century, we find a bondman able to buy his freedom from the abbot of Malmesbury at the price of £26. 13s. 4d., riding a horse and keeping a servant of his own (*Star Chamber*, S.S. 1, cxxix; cf. Savine, *Bondmen*, pp. 276 ff.).

It will be seen that I have often made considerable use of preachers and moralists, as witnesses who supply us not only with details but also with ready-made generalizations with regard to their own age. We must, of course, be cautious here; we must make great allowance for the words of indignant churchmen, especially in a society of imperfect self-control. But fortunately, in this field, we have corroboration of the most valuable sort, supplied by cold-blooded official documents, in the shape of reports from ecclesiastical and royal officials from very varied groups of parishes in France, Germany and England. Although these, in their turn, must be used with the same caution with which we argue from modern police reports, yet preacher and policeman differ so widely in their outlook that, wherever their evidence coincides, we may feel ourselves on fairly safe ground in social history. And here the agreement is very striking; these business reports, never intended for the public eye, tell practically the same story which saints and orthodox reformers were proclaiming from the housetops. I have already dealt briefly with this evidence elsewhere, especially for the middle of the thirteenth century[1]. Two generations later, we find similar evidence for these sides of village life in the Cerisy register[2]. This deals with four parishes in full, and incidentally with about sixteen more, from 1314 to 1346 almost continuously, and thenceforward, with very considerable gaps, to 1457. Taking the first period only, before the ravages of the Black Death and the English wars, we are first struck by the enormous number of villagers excommunicated for not paying their fines in this church court. The lists grow longer from year to year, in spite of special measures to which the official is driven (p. 306); to judge from those of 1336–1339, which fill more than 26 quarto pages, this score of villages must have possessed at least one excommunicate household in every ten[3]. The presentments for incontinence in these 33 years, among a total population

---

[1] *From St Francis to Dante*, 2nd ed. pp. 292–302 and *Medieval Studies*, No. 8; see also L. Delisle in *Bib. Ec. Chartes* for 1846, pp. 479 ff.

[2] *Mém. Soc. Antiq. de Normandie*, vol. 30, 1878, pp. 271 ff.

[3] This was recognized as one of the worst abuses in the later Middle Ages. It was complained at the Council of Constance that "excommunicated folk are almost infinite in number"; we hear again of "the innumerable multitude of excommunicates."

which was probably nearer 4000 than 5000, amount to 395 for layfolk and 42 for clerics; and it is noticeable that, whereas the courts were held in four only of these twenty villages, the majority of presentments come from those four: not that these were likely to be the most indisciplined, but they would be those in which the offenders could be more easily brought to book[1]. Seven of the clerical incontinents are priests; another is an ex-prior; one of the priests is connected with three different women (p. 374); another is accused of breaking into a woman's house with his accomplices and attempting to violate her daughter (p. 428). Clerical assaults are extraordinarily frequent; in ten cases clerics assaulted each other (one priest was killed); in ten, clerics assaulted lay folk; in eighteen, layfolk assaulted clerics[2]. Usury, witchcraft, "leprosy" are frequent presentments, especially the last. Parishioners absent themselves from Church; some evidently for years; Thomas le Conte, a usurer, has been excommunicated for more than seven years and "never cared to take the Body of Christ" (pp. 294, 309). Samson Vautier is worse; "asked wherefore, excommunicated these seven years, he had never taken Christ's Body, and had said that the *pain bénit* was just as good, he answered that this was one and the same, and that *pain bénit* is as good as Christ's Body, provided it be taken with good intention; and this in the presence of [five monks and two other witnesses named]. *Item*, he says that he fears not excommunication. *Item*, he says that his labour will save him" (p. 308). Another heretic is noted on p. 293. But why, after all, should these men care much, when their spiritual masters cared so little? The official visited only these four church-fabrics; yet two at least were neglected. At Deux-Jumeaux, which belonged to the monks, and which the scribe calls *monasterium*, the priest, Ralph Ravengnier, is incontinent in 1314, he neglects to celebrate one of the weekly Masses for which he receives an endowment; his church is in a bad state and "swine often dig and strive to disinter the dead bodies,

---

[1] *E.g.* in the three cases where we can identify the peccant priest's parish, two are from these four villages, and only one from the other sixteen. At Littry, one of the four, the priest is presented six times between 1332 and 1346; he keeps Thomassia as if she were his wife.

[2] It is difficult to be sure that one or two of these cases are not repetitions of other entries, the offender not having yet paid his fine.

which is a thing abhorrent" (pp. 306–7). In 1315 "nothing has been amended," and fresh defects are noted (p. 314). In 1319 the priest still retains his concubine "as he was wont" (p. 335). In 1325 "Ralph Cauvin found Ralph Ravengnier the priest with his wife, and the said Ralph Cauvin had come back from [the town of] Trévières [about eight miles distant], and they fought together; yet he does not believe that they were suspected, for report doth not hold"[1] (p. 373). The Church books are not yet in a fit state for divine service, and the windows are so broken that the lights will not burn before the altars (p. 378). Seven years later, "rain drips into the church, and such a wind sweeps down that the lights cannot burn; moreover, the books are defective" (p. 385). Two years later, 1333, the same report is repeated (p. 391). The church of Littry also is neglected, but not so grossly. When the register was resumed after the Black Death, and especially after the wars, things were naturally far worse; the editor summarizes this briefly and benevolently on pp. 277–8.

There are other entries of neglected church rites; but by far the most painful is in 1315 (p. 316):

John le Franceis is of ill report—*diffamatur*—together with his wife, because he hath had seven children who have not been christened, and the said [Richard] Piog, [one of the jurors], deposed that he saw how a certain sow carried one of them away, and (as he believes) by fault of the pair themselves. They are present and deny their fault; the rest they confess, and say that they were never at fault; concerning the sow they know not what befel; when they were still-born she herself knew not what became of them. We have assigned Monday to do what shall be just.

This may be partly matched with two cases from the records of St Louis's *Enquêteurs*[2]. A boy of ten found, in the fields, a jar full of "enchantments"; his mother warned him to leave it alone, but he secretly took it. The royal officer accused her of concealment of treasure-trove; she was cast into prison for five

---

[1] The Latin is corrupt, but the official plainly gives his clerical colleague the benefit of the doubt: "Sed tamen non *credit* quod *esset suspecte*, quia fama non tenet." Should we not read *creditur, essent, suspecti*, all easy variations? *Fama*, in canon law, means of course the deliberate opinion of trustworthy neighbours.

[2] Summarized by Ch.-V. Langlois in *Rev. Hist.* vol. XCII (1906); these two cases are on pp. 12, 25. I translate the former fully in appendix 40.

weeks; there "she was brought to bed, and had no help, but the dogs came and ate her child." Again, there was a quarrel between two monasteries for possession of a certain meadow; each enlisted its own peasants in the fray; a lay-brother was killed; enormous fines, apart from necessary bribes, were inflicted on the offending village; meanwhile sixty undisciplined men were quartered on the peasants, "whence it befel that several women of the township, for fear of the coming of these men, were brought to bed shamefully before their time in the fields and woods, and the children died unbaptized, and some of so shameful a death as that they were eaten of swine." Langlois truly notes the former story as "characteristic"; by far the most frequent type of animal-trial in the Middle Ages is that of swine for devouring children[1], and characteristic also is the incident with which we may quit this subject. Child-murder, like other murders[2], might be treated with modern compassionate leniency; but, if the culprit must bear the full penalties of the law, these were atrocious. In 1531, near Angers,

a poor creature called Julienne Rabeau killed her child, after a very painful delivery. Condemned to be burned alive, she showed an intention of appealing to Angers, and if necessary to Paris. But a pious relative made her understand that she would do better simply to accept the sentence of the judges at Craon as a just punishment for her crime, and to spend on prayers the hundred sols which it was reckoned would be spent on an appeal. Julienne prepared for death. She was led to the ordinary place for executions, "la justice." She was strongly bound to the fatal stake by an iron chain which held her up under the arms. When all the preparations were completed, the executioner set fire to the pile and "six quarterons of faggots" sufficed to reduce the miserable creature to ashes[3].

These are characteristic, of course, only in the sense in which "Wragg is in custody" is characteristic of nineteenth century England; but of this, as of that, we may say with Matthew Arnold: "There is profit for the spirit in such contrasts as this;

[1] See E. Agnel, *Curiosités judiciaires*, etc. Paris, Dumoulin, 1858, where twenty cases are recorded on pp. 8–13.

[2] In Northumberland, taking two years of the thirteenth century, we find 145 murderers recorded; six were hanged; two abjured the realm; the remaining 137 escaped with outlawry (*North. Assize Rolls*, Surtees Soc. 1891, p. xviii). But this was one of the wildest parts of England.

[3] Joubert, p. 229; see also pp. 353–5 for the original documents.

criticism serves the cause of perfection by establishing them"[1].
For we must bear in mind first, how highly the generality of
those days valued baptism and the last rites of the Church, and,
secondly, the fact that ecclesiastical usage refused to Julienne
Rabeau the full dying consolation of an honest woman; confession and absolution would not be refused her; but, otherwise,
she must go into eternity "unhousell'd, disappointed, un-
aneal'd," since it was the regular practice, in France especially,
to refuse the Eucharist to condemned criminals[2].

Passing on from the Cerisy neighbourhood to that of Josas,
we find a society which has suffered severely from plague and
war, yet has begun to recover. The district here concerned
was, like that of Cerisy, rather above the average of Western
Europe in culture and prosperity; the visitational records run
from 1458 (seven years after the final expulsion of the English)
to 1470[3]. "The serfs and villeins had been decimated by
massacre and famine," and the landlords had been compelled
to grant them better terms than of old, in order to keep their
lands in cultivation at all[4]. The Church had suffered heavily
from the general impoverishment (p. 305); absenteeism and
pluralism had naturally increased (pp. 307, 316); priests were
more than ever tempted to illegal extortions from their parishioners for rites or sacraments (pp. 309–310). There are only
about ten clerical incontinents noted in more than 150 parishes;
but these are somewhat mildly treated (p. 313). Concord between parson and parishioners is the exception rather than the
rule (p. 309). As to the general religious and moral condition,
Petit-Dutaillis summarizes in words which it would be difficult
for any reader of these visitations to contradict:

So great are the rudeness and indifference of a part of this rural
clergy that the visitor is compelled, at every page of his register, to
denounce the shameful squalor of some church or some churchyard.
A good quarter of the parishes visited earn his vehement reproaches;

[1] *Essays in Criticism*, No. 1 (ed. 1875, p. 27).
[2] See *Five Centuries of Religion*, i, 115 ff., in correction of a misconception
of Cardinal Newman on this subject.
[3] *Visites archidiaconales de Josas*, ed. J.-M. Alliot (Picard, 1902). A few years
ago, and perhaps still, this important document was obtainable at a very
moderate price.
[4] Ch. Petit-Dutaillis in *Rev. Hist.* LXXXVIII (1905), 304. I quote mainly
from this admirable summary, as being far more accessible than the original.

the consecrated ground is left open, the Hosts are eaten by maggots, the service-books are in pieces, the altar-linen rotten, and spiders and snails are found in the font. At Asnières, in 1470, the visitor notes that the side-door has been out of order for three years, and that swine trot freely about the church. Nor are the parsons' sins always sins of omission. Many see no harm in keeping chests in the church, or casks, or stores of corn. The parson of Magny-les-Hameaux, for instance, has carted his corn into the church and threshed it and winnowed it there. The church of Ver-le-Petit, for the same reason, is littered with straw and has not been cleaned for 2 years. The parishioners have no more scruples than the parson; it is not only during the *Guerre du Bien-Public* and for fear of the soldiers that they install themselves in the churches with their furniture and their provisions. In 1459 Nicholas le Roux, having the keys of the church in the parson's absence, brought thither and threshed the tithe-sheaves which he had purchased. In 1460, at Asnières, Jeanne la Mulote is fined by the visitor for storing her barrels and household goods in the church. In 1461, arriving at St-Yon, the visitor found an inhabitant of St-Sulpice-les-Ferrières, Jean Mansel, threshing his barley there. In 1462, at Viry-Châtillon, Alison la Chevallière has established herself in the church, and her hens are sitting on the altar. When Jean Monchard, [visitor], came to the church of Pecq, in May, 1461, he found a dung-heap left there since Christmas by Jean du Tillay.... Many churchyards, at different times, are covered with bushes or dung-heaps and unfenced; beasts enter them freely and disinter the corpses. At Chesnay, the parson has set up his hogsty in the churchyard[1].

Although (as Petit-Dutaillis points out), even these visits show a real moral improvement in village life since the earliest surviving visitations (1248–1269), he continues:

In fact, our visitor's register depicts a rural society scarcely delivered from the terrors of the great war, very thinly scattered, and still decimated by violent epidemics; more avaricious and greedy for gain than ever; rent by furious village feuds; brutal and often licentious. The priests seem to be little loved and little respected; they are spied on and denounced to the visitor; they are calumniated at a pinch, and get little help; good churchwardens are rare. Religious practices are observed, but without much fervour; and the coarseness of the faithful is reflected in the naïve account of an attempt made by the parson of St-Vrain, in 1469, to give a performance of the miracle-play on St Sebastian; he assembled the seven performers in a chapel; and, during the rehearsal, they denied God and fought with each other [*denegando Deum, pugnando ad invicem*].

[1] p. 310.

Scarcely less sordid is the visitation of 1496 in the Worms district, among those Rhenish villages which were very decidedly above the average of Europe in well-being[1]. If we take the first three deaneries here—and these are quite typical—we find sixty-seven parishes and chapelries, mostly in the presentation of monks or canons. In one the pyx was broken; in five others the Host was neglected (in one place swarming with maggots); eight had dirty altar-furniture. Fifteen churches were out of repair, some no longer rain-proof; one was utilized for storing corn and wine. Nine churchyards were unenclosed, and pigs were rooting up the bones; in eleven cases the parson was either omitting the Masses for which he was specially endowed, or otherwise embezzling parish moneys.

English parish life was decidedly more regular than this, but far from ideal. The *Liber Archidiaconi Eliensis* (Camb. Antiq. Soc.) suggests a diocese in which bad neglect is exceptional; but the *Visitation of Totnes Archdeaconry* in 1342[2] is scarcely more satisfactory than the Worms record, especially when we remember that this was before the Black Death.

Nor do we get a more favourable impression if we turn from ecclesiastical to lay reports. We may note, in some modern writers, a strong tendency to defend the social and legal irregularities of our less-developed forefathers on the ground that these conditions spelt freedom, and therefore happiness. But the records of St Louis's *Enquêteurs* seem to exclude this optimistic assumption even more hopelessly than it is excluded by other converging lines of evidence. The summary published by Ch.-V. Langlois[3] shows us essentially the same society which we should infer from our ecclesiastical reports. In the latter, we have seen a population struggling slowly out of a still rougher past of heathenism; in the former, we may trace a similar halfway stage between modern legislation and the backwoodsman's customary law; a stage in which men were far more cruelly fettered by the uncertainties of arbitrary discipline than the modern man is fettered by his multitude of more definite, more

---

[1] I have analyzed this at some length for the 3rd volume of *Five Centuries of Religion*. The original is printed in *Zeitschrift f. d. Gesch. d. Oberrheins*, XXVII, 1875, 227 ff., 385 ff.

[2] *E.H.R.* 1911, pp. 108 ff.

[3] *Rev. Hist.* XCII, 1906, 1–41; cf. c, 63–92.

logical, and more generally-known enactments[1]. We see all
this in the comparatively happy France of St Louis, during
those years when Dante was growing out of infancy, and
Aquinas was writing his *Summa* at Paris, and Brunetto Latini
was choosing the French tongue as "more delightful, and of
more common use than all other tongues," for his encyclopaedia,
even as Gibbon once dreamed of doing for his *Decline and Fall*.
In the England of that day, and in a few other districts, men were
perhaps living a little more easily than in France; otherwise,
the whole of Northern Europe must have had reason to envy
St Louis's subjects.

But need our modern villager envy them? It is difficult to
anticipate an affirmative from any open-minded reader who runs
through Langlois's summaries and dips here and there into the
originals. The discipline was that of the sergeant-major. When
the inhabitants of three villages in the south maintained, quite
justly, that they would not pay for substitutes but come in
person at the royal call for a levy of defence against the Spaniards, the *viguier* of Béziers settled the dispute with one level
volley: "March to the bridge of Vidorle or don't march, just
as you please: I intend to have £12. 10s.... You bloody peasants!
whether you will or whether you won't, you shall pay all the
same"[2]! The royal officer at Nîmes arrested Pierre Reboul
"on the false charge of having removed a landmark; he put him
under deadly torture until he had extracted a confession, and
confiscated all his goods. Pierre spent nine months in prison,
under occasional torture; he was thus compelled to pay £60 of
local currency, and, when he regained his liberty, his patrimony
was reduced to nothing"[3]. "The common folk were ordinarily
too poor to find ready money for the fines which rained upon
them; therefore the police officers regularly recouped them-

---

[1] The word *arbitrary* is here, naturally, only relative. On a well-ordered
manor the purely local customs might be thoroughly understood; but, on the
other hand, not only peasants, but even lords, might be hopelessly mistaken
as to their rights with regard to their overlords; cf. Langlois, pp. 11, 15, 23 n.,
28, 30; but especially p. 22: "non secundum jus, sed proprio arbitrio."

[2] p. 29: *O rustici sanguinolenti, vos dabitis, velitis vel non.* This is the earliest
instance I have met of this oath; the next earliest occurs two centuries later,
where the *Ménagier de Paris* advises his wife not to retain maidservants who
"curse at 'bloody bad fevers,' 'this bloody bad week,' 'this bloody bad day'"
(II, 1846, 59).

[3] p. 25.

selves by going to their houses and confiscating 'pledges'. . .
which were ordinarily either put into the hands of Jews, who
thereupon advanced the amount of the fine to the court, or else
sold by auction. The man who was a little better off suffered
the visit of a detachment of soldiers, who enjoyed themselves
at his expense—*cum meretricibus*—until he had paid up"[1].
"Not infrequently, the most humble supplications were met
with coarse language or threats; *e.g.* 'Say no more, or I will
have you thrown into the cesspool'; or 'Go and browse [on
grass].'" To another remonstrant: "It would serve you right,
you and your brother, to stop your mouths with dung"; and,
in fact, "the bailiff picked up mud and filth from the road,
wherewith he filled the mouth of the said Durand even to
suffocation. Meanwhile the village had flocked together to see
all this. Durand indicated his sad state by gestures; the bailiff
said, 'Do you want more?' Durand, poor simple fellow, kneeled
down and said again, 'You may do it, as bailiff and lord.' Then
the bailiff, catching sight of the poor wretch's brother, continued, 'Do you wish me to do the same to you'"[2]? Blackmail
was regularly paid (as the manor accounts show it paid in
England) to divert the royal "purveyors" from one village to
another, or from one man's field to another; "nothing was more
frequent than these secret extortions, which indeed were scarcely
secret"[3]. The officials imposed illegal forced labour even on
Sundays and feast-days[4]. They cared little for excommunication; "the bailiff of Aunis, excommunicated by the parson of
Esnandes, seized his parsonage and quartered sixty soldiers
upon him"[5]. Forced marriages, of course, were often possible[6].

Moreover, the ubiquity and continuity of this pressure on the
common people is almost as noticeable as its arbitrary nature.
"To begin with, it transpires [from these documents] that the
police discipline was very regularly exercised in royal hands during
the thirteenth century, and that it was still more restrictive of
individual liberty than ours is, in spite of the fact that manners
were even rougher then"[7]. "To sum up: the *enquêtes* of 1247
give the impression of a country very closely administered by
a bureaucracy which enjoys very extensive authority; there is

---

[1] p. 24.   [2] pp. 19, 20.   [3] p. 26.   [4] p. 27.
[5] p. 21.   [6] p. 32.   [7] p. 10.

no indication anywhere of the least resistance [to the king]. Therefore abuses are sure to be committed; the ordinary abuses engendered by the power of committing them with impunity; venality, arbitrary acts, bribery"[1]. We have seen enough already of the connexion between medieval justice and money to anticipate that the officials who buy their offices will administer them somewhat after the fashion of the Roman *publicani*: "Isabel, widow of Guillaume Dolé of La Flèche, reports that the *prévôt* Mocart said to her husband: 'You must help me to pay what I had to give for my *prévôté*.' So was it also with Raoul de St-Quentin, *viguier* of Beaucaire: 'My friend, my office cost me a round sum, and I want something from you.' The *maire* and commune of Crépy say that Robert de Paregin, who had been *prévôt* of Laon since 1229, told them one day [in 1247] that he had given too much for his *prévôté* and needed their help; fearing to be molested in case of refusal, they consented to give him tribute for the next six years[2]." There is strong indirect evidence that the officers found it very profitable to protect Jewish usurers in contravention to the king's strict laws[3]. Langlois sums up with moderation; the higher officials were not, as a rule, either tyrants or rascals; but "as to the lower officers, they doubtless resembled those village *stanovoï* and *ispravniks*, coarse, dissolute, and formidable to the poor, who have been painted in concordant colours by three generations of Russian novelists"[4].

Here, then, is something very different from that imaginary picture which is too often presented to us, of a simple, happy world where the peasant's healthy and spontaneous religion forbade his taking too seriously the official puritanism of his Church, while the priest, for his part, was too tactfully Christian to enforce in practice what he preached from the pulpit; of a village where all lived together in a free-and-easy communion, spiritually united even while they cut each other's throats, eating and drinking and dancing their fill, and reasonably secure all the time of making some sufficient final peace with their Creator. Many of us do not even desiderate such a society; for those who do, no employment could be pleasanter and more profitable than the collection of real evidence for its existence in the past.

[1] p. 21.
[2] p. 26; cf. pp. 22 and 25: "He was much feared, for he was a royal sergeant."   [3] p. 30 and note.   [4] p. 40.

CHAPTER XXIV

THE REBELLION OF THE POOR

IF, as Michelet says, the earlier medieval peasant was kept alive by his hope in the devil even under the worst injustices, we now approach an age in which he is sustained by hope in God. The gradual emancipation of the peasant in material things, which had gone on sporadically and irregularly since the thirteenth century, was accompanied by something like a correspondent spiritual emancipation. Although each separate county, and even each separate district, had followed its own line of development, there was unquestionably a great advance in freedom along the whole front. The few fairly exhaustive studies which have as yet been published show, with all their differences, a solid foundation of common ground. Almost everywhere, by 1500, the peasant was far better off than in 1200; and the few exceptions were due to the conscious and violent struggles of some reactionary lord. If the Kempten tenants suffered so severely during the last two generations before the Reformation, this was because their progress had alarmed the prince-abbots, who deliberately set themselves to rivet the old chains afresh, but were met with the resistance natural to men who had not only begun to taste freedom themselves, but were surrounded also by comparatively free neighbours. And they were no less free in mind, as compared with their ancestors of distant centuries. The peasant, driven to sullen or active protest against his own unchristian place in a society where the most Christian king was supported by a very imperfectly Christian hierarchy, needed less and less to turn back towards his ancient pagan gods; he could look forward now, to something like the world of the present day. We cannot separate the last peasant's revolts of the Middle Ages—thus far all parties are agreed—from that radical religious revolt which is commonly called the Reformation. The sincere rebels pleaded God's will and God's word; the insincere hoped to plunder in the name of God. From one point of view, there is but little exaggeration in the insistence of modern apologists that this meant death to the society of the Middle Ages. That society had its living and elastic side, as testified by the survival of many medieval ideas to the present day. But the prevailing conception of it was inelastic. "Everywhere [in the thirteenth century] a sort of stable equilibrium prevails. Men are proud of the way in which they have organized human existence.... The thirteenth century believed that it had reached a state of stable equilibrium, and...their extraordinary optimism led them to believe that they had arrived at a state close to perfection"[1]. Those are the words of a writer whose theological position tempts him somewhat to magnify medieval solidarity; but no one will be likely to deny his main contention, that Aquinas and his contemporaries are extraordinarily optimistic, not to say self-satisfied, on these points. A daring thinker here and there, like Roger Bacon, might contend that all this rested upon insecure foundations; but these were voices crying in the wilderness; and even the gradual disillusionment of the succeeding centuries left the world of 1500 still convinced, in the main, that any deliberate change of direction would be even worse than slow decay. As in the later Roman Empire, men felt the dislocation of the machine, but had an almost hysterical fear of reconstruction[2]. From that point of view, therefore, the birth of the new did indeed mean the death of the old, as the birth of a vigorous child may spell death to an ailing mother; Mr Chesterton and the duke of Northumberland are so far right. The ideas rapidly growing up in 1500 were subversive of complacent conservatism; almost as subversive as Christianity itself had been in its infancy. We may say of them, *mutatis mutandis*, what Auguste Sabatier says concerning the words of Jesus: "His method is that of the sower, to whom he loves to compare himself. In the furrow ploughed by his word through the old soil of Judaism, he dropped quietly and noiselessly a new seed. ...Nothing was less violent, but nothing could be more fundamentally revolutionary, because nothing could be more fertile

---

[1] Prof. M. de Wulf of Louvain, *Philosophy and Civilization in the Middle Ages* (Princeton Univ. Press, 1922), pp. 18, 268.

[2] This comes out very strongly in Sir Thomas More's *Dialogue* and similar controversial writings; he was inclined to believe that the end of the world might be at hand.

than this"[1]. The violence of the extremists on both sides in the sixteenth century must not blind us to the fact that an almost impassable gulf was growing up even within the comparatively moderate mass; reasonable conservative and reasonable radical were drifting more and more apart. The impatience of Luther was, in a sense, the explosion of the pent-up long-suffering of generations and even of centuries, during which thousands of quiet folk had thought these things over in their own minds, and talked them over quietly each in his own narrow circle, and waited with Simeon's patience for the Consolation of Israel. Such people are not of the sort that echo down the centuries, even though there had been no Inquisition to stifle their voice; but we may infer their existence from many scattered hints, and not least from the comparatively innocent sayings and deeds which bishops and inquisitors have recorded against otherwise very ordinary people. Such were a good many of the English villagers who got into trouble for Lollardy. Such, again, in Italy, were the descendants of quiet folk who had believed in St Francis more simply and more literally than the official Church believed in him; who gradually formed whole populations of peasant-Nonconformists; and whom the Blessed James of the March dislodged in 1449, by the effective argument of burning recalcitrants alive, from four large mountain villages[2]. Nobody can understand the Middle Ages who has not clearly realized the fact (and, however we may interpret it, this must remain a fact) that men might be burned alive for contesting publicly and impenitently any papal decretal—even, for instance, that decretal *Naviganti* which flatly contradicts the teaching of St Thomas Aquinas and all the orthodox of the later Middle Ages on the subject of usury[3]. To plead that, as a matter

[1] *Esquisse d'une philosophie de la religion*, 1903, pp. 223 ff.

[2] Jacobus de Marchia in Baluze-Mansi, *Misc.* ii, 609. This really saintly mission-preacher tells us elsewhere certain reasons which helped to reconcile him to the burning of heretics (pp. 600, 610). (1) In the earlier days of the Catholic Church, the more martyrs were burnt the more the Church increased; yet now when we burn a few heretics the rest can be got to recant. (2) It was an orthodox commonplace that the flesh of real martyrs emits an odour of sanctity: yet these heretics "when they are burned, stink like rotten flesh. As for instance, at Fabriano, when Pope Nicholas V was there, certain of the heretics were burnt, and for three days the whole city stank therewith, as I know myself, for I smelt the stench those three days even unto the monastery [wherein I lodged]." [3] See *History* for July, 1921, pp. 67 ff.

of fact, nobody was ever hereticated for opposition to that particular decretal, and that only a small minority of all the unorthodox were actually burned is, in effect, to add insult to injury; for that minority of victims was naturally chosen, as a rule, from among the more defenceless majority of the population; and it would have been a poor consolation to the peasant to know that the fire which was kindled for him would probably spare the lord of his manor, so long as the great man gave the authorities an excuse for ignoring him. A society in which manslaughter for religious differences is made into an integral part of the Christian creed is one which must either survive in virtue of its continued and incontestable superiority to all other forms of society, or be overthrown sooner or later by the living forces which it has repressed[1]. I ask my readers, therefore, to bear this in mind while weighing the undoubted excesses of these sixteenth century revolutionaries against their claims for redress. The fundamental question is: Had this existing Church and State of 1500 deserved so well of the peasant that they were justified in proclaiming an Eleventh Commandment?—"Thou shalt not strive to better thyself, since that would be the ruin of Us"[2]. Men disagree now in their answer to that question; but there is no dispute as to the premises on which it rests. All are agreed that the orthodox religious theories and social theories were so much of one piece, and that the hierarchy was so closely modelled on the State, so inextricably intertwined with the State, as to render religious and social radicalism practically inseparable, at least, in the large majority of cases[3]. Therefore it was in Germany, alive now with the printing press and with universal discussion, that the new ideas found their first and most emphatic expression,

---

[1] See, for instance, p. 42 of my *Medieval Studies*, No. 18.

[2] See appendix 40.

[3] It is often objected against the Anglican catechism that it prescribes this immobility of classes: "In that state of life unto which *it hath pleased* God to call me," the actual words thus misquoted run *it shall please*; a very different thing. Yet, just before the Reformation, so liberal a theologian as Geiler preached the narrower doctrine; he reckoned as one of the great sores of society in 1510 "that no man is content with the class and rank which is given him by God, but every man strives to climb higher. The peasant would fain be a citizen, the citizen a squire, the squire a baron, the baron a count," and so on (Scheible, p. 672).

both theoretically and practically, in this social-religious field[1]. Fourteen editions of the vernacular Bible were printed in Germany before Luther's; and, although these publications were contrary to imperial decree and to ecclesiastical policy, yet no man was actually burned for them, nor even, so far as I know, any volume. Books of devotion, with fragments of the Bible embedded in them, were more numerous still; and the press began to swarm with religious or political tracts. Presently, therefore, a mystic-socialistic spirit showed· itself not among the clerical authorities, but among lower social strata. According to this view, the peasant and the workman are the highest Christian types; their merits are those of the martyr; the poor man's sweat quenches hell-fire and washes the soul clean[2]. But (as Bezold remarks) such doctrines did not merely shade off easily into heresy; in a sense, they were heretical at their very foundation, as contrasting sharply with the whole spirit of past medieval centuries. No man could take such words seriously without thinking of a new social order altogether; thus to conceive the peasant, was to conceive revolution. In 1508 Joseph Grünbeck, himself a cleric, published a prophetic booklet. More than ever before (such was his text) men and women are speaking now of a world in which the Church shall be turned upside down and the laity shall take their revenge upon the clergy; the peasant, with his wife and daughter, shall not labour in the fields but stand at the altar, while priest and monk drive the plough[3]. Far more important, however, is the so-called "Reformation of Kaiser Sigismund." Written as early as 1438, printed in 1476 and in many editions between that date and 1525, it gained almost universal credence as a genuine and authoritative expression of a good emperor's hopes for social reform[4]. This general acquiescence of the orthodox,

[1] Any student who attempts to take a general measure of thought and life in the principal European countries during the last generations of the Middle Ages must be struck by the mass of valuable evidence derivable from printed and MS. sources in Germany as compared with England, or even Italy and France. Men seem not only to have printed and read much more, but to have written much more.

[2] Bezold, pp. 142 ff.

[3] *Ibid.* p. 147; see the facsimile of Grünbeck's title-page here reproduced.

[4] *Ibid.* pp. 70 ff. and Janssen, vol. I of German 17th ed. pp. 736–7 (this is not in the English ed.); again, vol. IV of English ed. pp. 132 ff. It will be

for long after the pamphlet's first appearance, reduces the question of its actual authorship to a secondary place. The writer was in fact a Waldensian who, after a long missionary

CHURL AT THE ALTAR, PRIEST AT THE PLOUGH

career, was burned in 1457 for heresy; but the success of the book shows how many men shared his ideas; and the acceptance of its supposed authorship proves that the sentiments which he attributes to the emperor can have been vitiated by no inherent

seen that I quote liberally from Janssen in this chapter, as an authority who cannot be suspected of exaggeration in my favour. Vogt's brief summary of this pamphlet may be compared with those similar conditions among the French peasants before 1789 from which I give selections in appendix 39. Readers will note how closely the conditions resembled each other in both cases, on the brink of a great revolt. The attempt to throw the main blame of 1525 upon Luther may be compared with the similar attempt to fix upon Philosophy and Freemasonry the main responsibility for the French Revolution.

improbability. The book is inspired by that dream of centuries earlier, that a Good Emperor should some day come to bring peace between nations, and harmony between class and class. That was Roger Bacon's dream in the thirteenth century; it took body again, towards the end of the fifteenth century, in the legend of a "Reformation of Frederick the Third," which should give the daughters of the rich to the sons of the poor and poor girls to rich men; which should marry monks and nuns, indemnify the helpless who had suffered violence, help all men to their rights, and depress the clergy. Sigismund's or Frederick's "Reformation" was now to accomplish, at one stroke, what the Church Councils had vainly striven to bring about; and, while thus amending ecclesiastical shortcomings, it must brush ecclesiastical protests aside. Freedom is man's birthright;

it is an unheard-of thing that we should have to mark this great injustice in holy Christendom, that one man can find it in his heart before God and can dare to say to another: "Thou art my chattel!" For think that our Lord God was willing to suffer so sore in wounds and death for our sake, in order that he should free us and loose us from all our bonds; and herein is no man exalted above another; for we are all of one state in His redemption and liberty, whether nobles or commons, rich or poor, great or small. Whosoever is baptized and believeth, he is counted a member of Jesus Christ. Wherefore let every man know, whosoever he may be, who calleth an even-Christian his own chattel, that he is not with Christ but against Him, and all God's behests are lost upon him.

It is intolerable that monasteries should possess bondmen. If a lay noble will not free his serf, the man "shall be taken and altogether removed from that lord; but if it be a monastery that will not wholly renounce [such claims], then let it be razed even with the ground; that is God's work."

To this may be added the first printed manifestoes of different leaders on the verge of, or during the first days of, the great revolt of 1525[1]. But we really need go no farther than this Reformation of Kaiser Sigismund, which has been called a

---

[1] They are summarized by Janssen, IV, 185–206. For that which was falsely attributed to the Emperor Frederick III, see Bezold, p. 463.

"trumpet of the Peasants' War"[1]. When words of this kind could be attributed to the highest civil authorities, and when the peasants had before them the constant example of their free and prosperous brethren in Switzerland, then theory and practice alike, religion and common-sense, seemed to promise them final success[2]. *It is God's work*; here we have a second *Deus Vult*, the motto of a new crusade which, through all its crimes and follies, will be at least as fruitful as those papal crusades of centuries before. The best of the revolutionaries had the faith of mystics; a contemporary chronicler tells us how, when the two ringleaders of the Schlettstadt revolt of 1493 were led out to be drawn and quartered, "men say that their last words were: 'The Bundschuh must go forward, be it soon or late'"[3]. And, even in their anti-clericalism, the insurgents often kept to theological orthodoxy. In a great revolt of the year 1502 "the country-folk about Speyer gathered together against the lords and the parsons, that they might cast off their tyranny and have all else free and common. In order to come to good fruit, they bound themselves to say the Paternoster and the Ave five times daily. Their watchword was the question 'How goeth it?' and the answer 'It is because of the parsons that we get no good'"[4].

The great Hussite war in Bohemia had been almost as truly social as religious; peasants formed the backbone of those insurgent forces which for twenty years defied crusading armies sent against them by pope and emperor[5]. In spite of its final failure, it evidently brought more encouragement than discouragement to the German country-folk; it showed how

[1] Janssen, IV, 133 n. His contention, however, that the pamphlet did not gain "full appreciation" until "the second decade of the sixteenth century" is another attempt to fix the blame upon Luther which is contradicted even by the facts acknowledged in his own text. The book was printed *five times* before 1500; and Janssen supplies no evidence for growing frequency of editions after that date.

[2] For the rebels' frequent appeals to the Swiss example, see Janssen, IV, 130, 137, 204, and the words of the insurgents at Speyer: "We will be Switzers" (Vogt, p. 81).

[3] Vogt, p. 115.

[4] "Was ist das für ein Wesen?" "Wir mögen vor den Pfaffen nicht genesen" (Hottinger, Theil II, p. 545).

[5] It is significant that the spokesman of the Kempten peasants before the Council of the Swabian League was stigmatized by the prince-abbot as "the Hus of Unterasried" (Zimmermann, I, 16).

formidable peasant forces might be, if only they could unite, against even professional armies. In 1431 there was a great revolt of peasants in the Worms district; these, among other levelling claims, demanded the heads of the Jewish usurers in the city; they marched 3000 strong, under the banner of the Bundschuh[1]. Their defeat did not prevent a number of similar risings; there were at least eleven very serious revolts in Germany during the thirty years before Luther's appearance in 1517[2]. It seems to be agreed by general consent that similar disturbances would have gone on beyond 1517, even if Luther had never existed[3]; and it is difficult to see how these troubles could have failed to coalesce more and more with the ecclesiastical discontent which (for here again we have general consent) had been gathering for a long time. There must have been thousands of villagers like those insurgents of Speyer; content with tradition in religion, but demanding reform in the existing religious establishment as definitely as they demanded reform in the economic field. The very emphasis which Janssen lays upon the follies and vices of some among these popular leaders (whom we know mostly from the records of their adversaries) might have suggested to him that these folk could not have found so swift and so widespread answers to their appeals if the ground had not been prepared by a correspondingly deep and widespread discontent. One army (he tells us) followed a mad bagpiper; another, a ruined innkeeper; others were led by a murderer, a flute-player, a drunkard, a thief, a broken nobleman, a knightly robber, a cobbler[4]. But such men we have always with us; it is only when such men can command thousands ready to risk their lives with them, that we suspect something rotten in the State. Again, that very well-being which he attributes to a great many of the peasants, rehearsing the actual inventories of their goods in certain cases, should suggest some solid ground of reason underlying the demands for which these men were willing to stake their all. "We will be like Switzers"!

---

[1] The peasant's clog, bound with thongs up the calf, as distinguished from the riding-boot or the open shoe of the richer classes. Many of the later risings adopted this ensign and name.

[2] Maury, pp. 360–1; Janssen, IV, 128–142; Bartels, pp. 99 ff.

[3] *Ibid.* p. 143; see my appendix 39.

[4] pp. 130, 177–8.

well, after all, why not? With a little better fortune, why should not these men have become as free and as prosperous as their neighbours among the Alps?

The clergy of the day saw this more clearly than their apologists see it in our day. The Zürich Canon Hemmerlin, who hated the rebellious Hussite peasants of his day even worse than the rebellious Swiss, confesses their great provocation. He writes: "Undoubtedly this was the root cause of the ruin of the realm of Bohemia, that the layfolk were sorely impatient to see how their little holdings—*terrarum particulas*—were overburdened with pensions and tributes to the clergy. For there was scarce one foot's pace throughout that whole realm wherefrom the clergy did not draw some fruit of tribute or pension." The result is (he continues), that churches and monasteries are pillaged and destroyed in Bohemia, and that the same process is beginning now (1450) in Switzerland[1]. He goes on to speak of these exactions in general; the clergy, with their demands for dues and their excommunications for non-payment and their invocation of the secular arm to help them, are doing their best to afflict the people as Pharaoh did the Israelites. "And this is the worse that, as Bede saith, these peasants and cottars see the clergy not living spiritually, as they should, but fighting according to the flesh, making that House of Prayer, built of living stones, into a den of thieves by their actions, supposing gain to be godliness." And he has started from the old text of canon law utilized by Boniface VIII: "Our forefathers have told us how the laity are always inimical to the clergy"[2]. It was not from any class of the clergy that, by this time, the peasant hoped for salvation. What he had already won had been mainly through his own slow struggles against landlords lay and ecclesiastical; he can scarcely be said to have had any downright declared ally in that fight; but, in so far as other personal forces fought for him, he owed almost, if not quite, as much to public opinion as to the later medieval church. Erasmus, when he so plainly stigmatized bondage as an abuse which ought long ago to have been ended, spoke not for the priestly class but against it, and in unison with the heretic Wyclif. Mr Leadam writes very truly of England: "Notwithstanding the absolute powers over a bondman in

[1] Reber, p. 313: *Tract*. f. 51 b.   [2] *Ibid*. f. 44 a.

blood and tenure, and the all but absolute power over his person theoretically possessed by the lord, there is evidence that by the fifteenth century public opinion exercised, as a rule, some check upon oppression"[1]. And the same may be traced elsewhere: reactionaries might misuse Roman law in Germany, but the Kempten case, to which we shall presently come, shows the peasants relying on a public feeling that was setting in favour of liberty, until their own excesses set the clock back again.

The claims of the insurgents, when analyzed, will always be found essentially reasonable in the main[2]; usury to be put down in reality and not merely in hollow theory; equitable game-laws; their fields to be protected from ravaging soldiery; their own persons not to be conscripted for unjust war; justice to be dealt impartially and bondage to be abolished altogether[3]. The tithes, they pleaded, should really go to the support of the needy and other proper parochial purposes; the "small tithes," which extended to the pettiest and most vexatious details, should be abolished[4]. And it should not be forgotten that they made that appeal, so characteristic of the later Middle Ages, to "natural law"[5].

If, with all this, they were in every case anti-clerical, that was because their experience, and this appeal to natural law, brought them into necessary conflict with an enormously wealthy corporation which had its ramifications in every corner. It was, if not almost inevitable, yet a very easy corollary to other far less controversial claims, that "all the monks must be made to hoe and till like other country people"[6]. The labourer himself could not be expected to see these things from the exact academic standpoint of Cochlaeus, in his pamphlet on the revolt of 1525: "Who is there who will not grieve for all these hundreds of monks and nuns whom these proceedings have reduced from an honourable, God-fearing meritorious calling to every species of infamy, calamity and dishonour, so that they are compelled

---

[1] *Star Chamber* (S.S.), I, cxxv.

[2] They should be read as presented by Janssen's not too favourable pen, pp. 131, 135, 139, *187–8*, 190 ff., 202, 204 (note especially pp. 187–8); cf. Ranke, pp. 220, 236.

[3] Ranke, pp. 219, 237–8; Maury, p. 360; Janssen, IV, 127–9, 137–9, 170, 187, 199, 252.

[4] Janssen, pp. 187, 190, 196–7; Ranke, p. 219.

[5] *Ibid.* pp. 125, 191–2; see appendix 38.   [6] *Ibid.* p. 267.

either to die of starvation or to earn their living in disreputable ways, for these poor victims have never been taught any handicraft or agricultural work?"[1] In all these revolts, the insurgents turned at once against both regular and secular clergy[2], except in so far as poor clerics led the rising themselves[3].

If farther facts were needed to emphasize the serious grounds underlying these revolts, they would be found in an analysis of the evidence which Janssen brings to prejudice that revolt. When he adduces Wimpheling and Murner as witnesses to peasant excesses (pp. 148-9), he ignores the fact that Wimpheling probably, and Murner certainly, wrote those words long before even Luther had come forward; Murner's were in print before 1512. So far, therefore, are these evidences from prejudicing the rioters' case, that they tend to make the riot itself more explicable; we see it still more clearly as the breaking-point after generations of growing disorder; as early as 1512, the measure was already heaped full and running over. When Lord Acton had to characterize the causes of the Bauernkrieg in a single sentence, he attributed it to "the demoralizing servitude and lawless oppression which the peasants endured"[4].

---

[1] Janssen, p. 346.

[2] *Ibid*. pp. 209, 234-5; Ranke, pp. 221, 224, 229, 231.

[3] *Ibid*. pp. 179-180; compare the priests Ball and Wrawe in 1381, and that earlier case in 1327, when the "10,000" villeins and townsfolk who marched against the monks of St Edmundsbury were led by two clerks bearing the rebel banners (*Mem. St Edm.* R.S. II, 1892, 335).

[4] *Hist. of Freedom and other Essays*, 1907, p. 156.

CHAPTER XXV

THE REBELLION OF THE POOR (*cont.*)

THE uprising, then, was natural and almost inevitable; no less naturally or inevitably, again, the rebels struck at the Church landlord as at the squire[1]. Many parsons were too rich, many others too poor, to allow the parishioners what everybody knew to be, in theory, their share of the parish revenues. So, again, with the monasteries. Peter of Blois had expressed the feelings of the best churchmen of the twelfth century when he wrote: "It is detestable in a monk that, under any custom of colour, or honour, or title of power, he should possess feudal rights and bondmen and bondwomen, or homages and fealties and allegiances, or that he should lay forced labour upon them, and extra-services and other burdens of public works," and that, on the strength of these revenues, he should lead an easy life[2]. Luchaire shows how, in that same century, when monasticism was at its strongest, the monk suffered almost more than any other from any outbreak of lawlessness, since his wealth was always a temptation to the spoiler, and here, for the moment, was a spoiler restrained by no religious considerations[3]. Great and well-ordered abbeys, it is true, were centres of charity to the country round; but even here their influence is very commonly exaggerated by modern authors, as I hope to show in the second volume of my *Five Centuries of Religion*. And nobody, so far as I am aware, has yet pointed out the effect upon the popular mind of the numerous smaller monastic houses which, even before the end of the thirteenth century, were scattered about the countryside in decay or even in ruin. These were sometimes inhabited by two or three monks who kept up

[1] Commines, in one of the most remarkable of all his reflections on the society of the later fifteenth century, draws no distinction between lay and Church landlord in this respect. He is speaking of the fundamental infidelity often betrayed by men's actions; if they really believed in God and heaven and hell they would not so rob their fellows or so oppress the poor; and among these faithless offenders he specifies "Churchmen, prelates, bishops, archbishops, abbots and abbesses, priors and parish parsons" (bk v, ch. 19).

[2] Ep. 102, to the abbot of Reading.

[3] See the remarkable series of incidents which he prints on pp. 227–8.

no choir-services, but often they were farmed out as though they had never been built for the service of God. The visitations of the archbishop of Rouen, in one of the best dioceses in Europe during the mid-thirteenth century, show already a large proportion of small derelict monasteries; this proportion steadily increased in the three succeeding centuries; there was probably not a county in which you could not see what Abbot Tritheim describes in a smaller house dependent upon his own, reformed and restored in past generations but now fallen again into decay. "By reason of these evil times [1512 A.D.] and the negligence of the church rulers it hath gradually come to such misery and desolation that it hath today neither abbot nor a single monk...all the buildings are ruinous, and a great part of them fallen to the ground"[1]. We must remember that, to our ancestors, the Devil was at least as real and as personal as God, and the demons as the angels. We know that here and there, in the early history of a great and beneficent abbey, heavenly radiances were seen playing by night over the buildings, and angelic voices heard; we know how princes and nobles, in moments of danger, took heart again from the thought that, at this moment, hundreds of monks of their own foundation were raising their voices to the Lord. But (to give one of many instances on the contrary side) did not the Kentish countryfolk hasten onwards and cross themselves, when they passed by the spot where the nunnery of Newington had once stood, until the prioress was strangled in her bed and buried in "the pit called Nunpit"? and where, among the seven secular canons substituted by Henry II as a community for these nuns, four were presently found guilty of murdering a fifth, and their house was dissolved and given to St Augustine's, Canterbury[2]?

Moreover, if the monk's hand had never pressed quite so heavily as some lay lords', yet it clung with more provoking conservatism. Revolution comes when men have tasted enough to want more; the peasant was resolved to advance, and here

[1] *Chron. Hirsaug*, ed. 1690, II, 682.
[2] Turner-Salter, p. 283; cf. Dugdale-Caley, VI, 620. The medieval authorities agree in all particulars but one, which is doubtless due to a misreading on one side or the other. The strangling was done, according to the chronicler Thorn, by her cook (*cocus*); according to Sprott and the compiler of St Augustine's chartulary by her cat—*de cato suo*.

was an obstacle the more serious because it was not one of frowning menace; just as earthworks may check an army for longer than stone walls, or swamps for longer than a precipice. No abbess, so far as we know, ever wasted the bondfolk's time with gathering snail-shells and winding her yarn upon them, like the countess of Lupfen in 1524[1]. No prelate required, as the countess of Saarbrücken did, that "when my lady comes to

SEAL OF THE PRINCE-ABBOT'S COURT AT KEMPTEN

lie at her manor of Folkelingen, then the serfs shall keep the frogs quiet so that they trouble not her sleep"[2]. Nor, again, did any monastic tenants complain of overwork so bitterly as those of Kisslegg: "When a man has driven the lord's game all day long, often foodless and drinkless so that he can scarce go—

[1] Ranke, II, 210, from the *Villinger Chronik*, etc. Ranke adds: "If it be true, as contemporaries affirm...it is certain that never did a more trifling and fantastic cause produce more serious and violent effects." For the 62 articles of complaint against the count of Lupfen see Bezold, p. 465; the peasants' grievances, writes the Villingen chronicler, had driven them "as wild as foxes."

[2] Schultz, p. 117, 1422 A.D.; *Weisthümer*, II, 10. This service lingered on some French manors till 1789 (Champion, p. 140).

and yet must he still run on—then his thank and wages are paid in reviling, cursing and swearing, or he is even beaten and smitten about the head; moreover, the hawkers ride over our crops and waste our fields, which should not justly be done"[1]. But the abbot of Kempten, as late as 1491, was still enforcing a right which, even if it could have pleaded its hoary antiquity, connoted almost equal oppression on one side and exasperation on the other. "The men of Kempten complained that free tenants, when they married serfs of the abbot, were kept away from divine service in church until the free party had accepted servitude under the abbot, whereby 'his freedom and right was taken from him, and he was unlawfully brought to a hard state and case'"[2]. Therefore, though the rising began first on the Lupfen estates, it was Kempten that turned a revolt into a revolution.

The abbots of this great South German monastery had long been at feud with their tenants[3]. They were princes of the Allgäu, a fertile district lying between Tyrol and the Lake of Constance. The generality of their subjects, closely akin to the Swiss, claimed to have been free in past times from bondage in the strict sense; about half of them had been free tenants, and half *Freizinser*, *i.e.* personally free, but paying certain yearly dues in money or kind. The only servile due to which the Freizinser was liable was a comparatively small heriot; he and his wife at their death, owed their best garment to the abbey. There was, of course, a third class also, viz. a minority of abbey bondfolk. Gradually—so claimed the peasants, and other evidence makes this claim most probable—the monks had encroached, from generation to generation, by treating as serfs those Freizinser who took land under them upon servile tenure. We have here,

---

[1] Vogt, p. 12. A picture of a lord hawking through a cornfield is reproduced in *Medieval Garner*, p. 378.

[2] Miss Levett has noted cases of this kind in England, in her review of the 4th volume of the Calendar of Close Rolls (*History*, Oct. 1924, p. 237). We cannot decide, at this distance of time, which party had the legal right; we can only see the very serious discontent which prompted villagers to risk their money in royal courts.

[3] The story is told by Zimmermann, vol. I, chs. 2, 3, p. 278 and, with very striking omissions, by Janssen, IV, 227, 233. The clearest and most impartial summary is in Ranke, II, 213 ff.; a good brief account in Bartels, pp. 82 ff.; cf. Bezold, pp. 45, 468, 509. Zimmermann has worked from the numerous original documents of the lawsuits between the abbot and his people.

then, on a larger and more systematic scale, what we know to
have happened elsewhere; the lord used his power to convert
servile tenure illegally into servile status. Every Freizinser who
was not watchful or strong enough to resist found himself
gradually on the same list as the acknowledged serfs. Presently
the monks began to forbid free marriage to these Freizinser.
Then, even the freemen were deprived of their immemorial
right to choose their own feudal lord; many, under this right,
had commended themselves to the abbey; and now, after some
generations, the abbey began to ignore these men's free choice,
assimilating them to others who had been given to the monastery
by their masters. This was done methodically, with a consistency of policy against which these unlettered and scattered
villagers were almost helpless. The breaking point came, however, when the abbot forged a charter of Charles the Great
which gave him the same rights over the freemen and the
Freizinser as over his bondfolk. This was early in the fifteenth
century; the peasants were now driven to combination and
resistance; they claimed to exercise their right of choosing
another feudal lord, and threw themselves under the protection
of Count von Montfort-Tettnang. The case was brought before
an assembly of nobles and burghers, who decided against the
peasants[1]. They then chose for protector the knight-advocate
of the abbey; here, the abbot procured a papal prohibition,
fortified with all the pains of excommunication. In 1423, the
peasants brought their claims before official arbitrators. These
offered the frequent medieval facilities of "compurgation; if the
abbot would swear on the Gospels that he and his predecessors
had exacted these unfree services from the Freizinser, and if
two of the senior monks would swear by his side, then they
should have the verdict." The abbot asked for a respite; the
peasants pleaded for immediate oath, then and there. The
arbitrators granted a respite of some weeks; the abbot and his

---

[1] Janssen has emphasized very strongly the power which was given to the
upper classes at this time by the introduction of Roman Law, and the extent
to which this law was misused for the suppression of immemorial customary
rights. This is quite true; Bezold puts it almost as strongly (pp. 45, 452);
the false perspective only comes in when we attempt thus to explain all the
troubles of the sixteenth century, ignoring other more ancient and deeper
causes.

friends then swore, and their case was won in that court. The peasants then appealed to Rome, and demonstrated the falsehood of the forged charter. The abbot, on his side, procured a papal absolution for this and for his perjury before the arbitrators, which he had acknowledged under seal of confession to his neighbour-abbot of Zwiefalten. He procured an imperial decree that no peasant should appeal from him to any other protector. Thenceforward he, and his nephew who succeeded him as prince-abbot, had a free hand. An attempt of the peasants to prove their freedom by a charter of 1114 was only partially successful; the abbot contested (and probably he was here right) its applicability to any but freemen. Then it was that he systematically forced servitude upon the free party in all mixed marriages, under pain of repulse from the Church services. For a time, these measures commanded success in proportion to their calculated and remorseless application.

Those who would not submit to this were brought for weeks and weeks before the spiritual courts, or manacled in prison, or compelled to give pledges or driven from their possessions; the length and multiplicity of these persecutions broke the spirit even of the stronger and more obstinate tenants, so that they solemnly promised to take no outside protector and to render obediently their dues of tribute, cartage, services, Lententide hens, heriot and fines for relief. The freeborn wives and children of the tributary peasants were, without exception, brought in dependence under the monastery[1].

In this case, admittedly the worst of all that have come down fully to us from those last pre-revolutionary generations, nothing was left undone to exasperate the countryfolk. The year 1489 was one of severe famine; corn stood at a fabulous price, and the two following years were very dear. Yet the abbot chose those years for an increase of taxation; the peasants appealed to the Council of the Swabian League, before which they pleaded literally upon their knees: "if we are in the wrong, we are willing to amend; yea, if it be found that our demands are unjust, we will lay our heads on the block"[2]. One of the peasants' envoys to the imperial court was probably murdered by the prince-abbot's men; he disappeared on the way and was never seen again. Hundreds of the peasants emigrated into Switzer-

---

[1] Bartels, p. 83.   [2] Zimmermann, I, 16.

land; twenty-two parishes had been concerned in the general rebellion; only with difficulty had they been persuaded by the Swabian League to lay down their arms without actual civil war; yet, in the heat of the quarrel of 1481, the abbot had defended himself on the plea that "he was only doing what other landlords did also"[1].

There was only too much truth in this. The Council of the League represented the capitalists; it never gave the peasants a fair chance. From the beginning of the open quarrel, in or soon after 1423, "all the monasteries and ecclesiastical chapters saw their own interests concerned in the struggle between the free Zins-folk and the abbot of Kempten. Forty prelates leagued together and pledged themselves, for twelve years or more, to fight the peasants in partnership, to bear the expenses in common, and to support each other in every way"[2]. For the people had similar grievances, if not quite so serious, against other Church lords. The whole province of Allgäu rose against their bishop of Augsburg, and formed a strict alliance with the Kempten rebels; thence the revolt spread all along the Lake of Constance. The separate complaints of these folk swelled into a common fund. The villagers of Attenweiler felt it intolerable that, "when a man dies, the abbot of Weingarten comes and takes a share of the man's or the woman's goods. We hold that this is against God's justice, that he should take our children's heritage; God have mercy on it in His everlasting Kingdom." In some districts these mortuaries amounted to only 5 per cent. of the goods, in other to 10, 14, 15, or even 30 per cent.[3] The abbot of Kempten had even illegally revived an ancient impost on his free tenants; if they wished to migrate to any other manor, they must fine with him by paying one-third of their whole property, real and personal[4]. The monks of Ochsen-

---

[1] Zimmermann, pp. 15, 16, 17.   [2] *Ibid.* p. 12.

[3] Vogt, pp. 8–10. He points out that Janssen omits all mention of the tithe system, and tries to excuse the mortuaries by urging that they were still higher in towns, often as high as 25 per cent. This, though it goes far to explain to us why the town proletariat so often joined in with the peasants (Ranke, II, 230–1), cannot have brought much comfort to the peasant of 1525; nor, again, can Janssen's other excuse, that in Tyrol the lord took only one cow. As Vogt points out, the land is poor there, and thus one cow may often have been the only beast the family possessed.

[4] *Ibid.* p. 13.

hausen were still "collecting rents and taxes in full for fields
and meadows which the river Iller had swept away"[1]; and the
peasants complain of similar injustices on the part of lay lords.
The peasants of Rottenacker "used to give four pounds rent
for each holding; then [the abbot of Blaubeuren] added thirty
shillings to our rent, that we need neither do military service
nor forced labour; yet now we must pay the thirty shillings,
and serve and do our labour into the bargain"[2]. The abbot of
Kempten, again, was enforcing a custom which the archbishop
of Prag, more than a century before, had condemned as heathenish, though it was common on ecclesiastical estates. Even the
free tenants, if childless, were not allowed to leave their property
by will; so that the clerical landlord inherited all that they had
possessed. The abbot did not deny that he was enforcing this
custom; he took his stand on his "immemorial and uncontested
exercise thereof"[3]. Even though we had no more evidence than
what has come down to us from these years and this district, we
should yet understand something of that pessimism which distils
from the pen of an orthodox German Catholic of the present day,
who owns that one of Napoleon's most beneficent achievements
in Westphalia was his dissolution of the monasteries[4].

But there was no Napoleon in 1524; and the Kempten
peasants were soon driven to follow the example of their
brethren of Lupfen. "They determined to pursue the matter
legally before the judges and councillors of the [Swabian]
League, and if they could get no redress, to sound the tocsin,
and repel force by force. Already they beheld allies rising
around them on every side. Similar, if not equal, wrongs, the
force of example, and the hope of success, set the peasantry
all over Swabia in motion"[5].

The first agitation developed in the space of a few weeks to a general
outbreak, and from July 1524 the socialist insurrection spread like

[1] Vogt, p. 16.
[2] *Ibid.* p. 17; this is only a fragment of a long complaint.
[3] *Ibid.* p. 18. The "heathenish" side of this was, that it treated the serf
as an animal; if he produced no brood, the master recouped himself at death.
We have seen how landlords sometimes claimed the right of compelling
marriage for similar economic reasons.
[4] Gladbach-Stratner, p. 31; I quote the full passage in Chapter XXVI.
[5] Ranke, II, 214.

wildfire from town to town, from village to village. Confined at first within the space running along the Swiss border, from the Black Forest to the Lake of Constance, it very soon covered the whole district between the Danube, the Lech, and the Lake of Constance, and stretched over Alsatia, the Palatinate, the Rheingau, Franconia, Thuringia, Hesse, Saxony, and Brunswick; over the Tyrol, the archbishopric of Salzburg, and the duchies of Styria, Carinthia, and Krain; in South Germany, Bavaria, where no quarter was given to the demagogue agitators and where the Government acted with firmness and wisdom, was the only district which remained free from disturbances[1].

This is true only of *South* Germany; in the north, Hanover and Brunswick and other wide districts escaped for a far better reason than Bavaria; the worst disabilities of the peasants had long been removed from those lands, mainly through the initiative of the dukes and the acquiescence of the nobles. Southern Germany, then, was aflame; for now the two lines of social and doctrinal revolt coalesced: "the political excitement was not produced by the preaching, but the religious enthusiasts caught the political fever"[2]. "This revolution [of 1524–5] had from the first assumed the character of a religious war"[3]. Significant is the impression of a contemporary treasurer and councillor of Nuremberg: "Large bodies of peasants were mustered (and their numbers increased day after day) in order to defend the Word of God with their swords, and to stand up for the holy evangel."

This revolt of 1524–5 resembled, on a larger scale, many before and many after. The original aim of the peasants was not to destroy the existing order, but to find a place for themselves within the more comfortable order from which multitudes were practically excluded; they wanted "to be no longer the pariahs of society"[4]. But a revolt necessarily attracts all the looser elements of society. The landlords were unconciliatory, except under intimidation; and to yield under fear is to invite farther attack. The League demanded that the peasants should lay down their arms as a preliminary to all negociations; the League routed small detached bodies; but the mass stood firm. The peasants published their *Twelve Articles*; they "were determined

[1] Janssen, IV, 171.   [2] Ranke, II, 208.   [3] Janssen, IV, 207.
[4] Bartels, p. 99; cf. Bezold, pp. 453, 471.

no longer to be serfs, for Christ had redeemed them with His precious blood"; but, though religious are thus mingled with social demands, the general tone of their manifesto "is far removed from all schemes of general convulsion, and not at variance with common sense and humanity"[1]. They found powerful allies among the poorer classes in the towns[2]. The extremists gained more and more the upper hand; shady political motives and political leaders came in; while in some parts no quarter was given to the insurgents, in others the insurgents were in a position to refuse quarter to their foes. Many soldiers refused to serve against the peasants; the League was obliged to temporize by hollow negociations; meanwhile "in Swabia only, nearly 300,000 men are said to have been enrolled in the rebel confederacy"[3]. Georg v. Waldburg, the able and unscrupulous general of the League, at last gathered an army which enabled him to rout the peasants at Leipheim (April 4, 1525); but he did not venture to press this success at the moment. The peasants had got support from the banished and politically disreputable duke of Württemberg and from the scarcely more responsible freelance Götz v. Berlichingen, whose autobiography is one of the most interesting documents of that time. They took the town and castle of Weinsberg, and committed atrocities which very justly prejudiced their cause (April 16). They found, the farther they went in their projects of reform, increasing political difficulties; some of the things they demanded would have needed radical constitutional reforms. Luther hastened to dissociate himself from their doings, and condemned them with that extreme vehemence of language which he always used when he felt deeply. Georg v. Waldburg beat them over and over again in detail; Götz deserted them;

---

[1] Ranke, II, 220; compare summaries in Janssen, IV, 186–9 and Bartels, p. 106. Compare also the earlier fourteen articles of the 1512 rising, for which see Zimmermann, I, 48; Janssen, pp. 138–9; Bartels, p. 100. One of the most revolutionary of these is No. 9: "A lasting peace shall be made throughout Christendom; he who opposes this shall be slain; or, if he be fully bent upon war, let him be given his wages to go fight against Turks and unbelievers." Some others were within the strictest common-sense: that clerical courts should try only clerical cases; that no cleric should have more than one benefice; that monasteries should be reduced in numbers and in wealth; that effective measures should be taken against excessive usury, etc.

[2] *Ibid.* pp. 230–2; Janssen, IV, 236.   [3] Janssen, pp. 236–7.

by the middle of June they were driven out of the more important towns which they had occupied, and the general cause was lost. In the mountains, the peasants held out for a whole year longer; in Tyrol and Salzburg they finally surrendered on singularly advantageous terms. Elsewhere, Germany saw a series of bloody assizes which have fortunately no exact parallel in British history. The peasants are said to have destroyed about a thousand castles; monasteries also had been plundered wholesale; here and there, as at Weinsberg, they had committed bestial excesses; and the reaction was now correspondingly violent[1]. In most districts, the peasants were worse off than before, and their best step forward came with the French Revolution[2]. They had risen in revolt under a sense of compelling necessity: if they failed to take this chance, one of their orators told them, "Your children, after you, would have to draw the plough themselves"[3]. But they failed under that weakness defined long before by Berthold of Regensburg; they had not learnt cohesion; the cohesion which comes only with wisdom and experience, since no large body can be held long together on principles which contain too great an alloy of disputable assumptions. It was not enough for these insurgents that their demands were workable in the main; existing society was also workable in the main, badly as it stood in need of certain almost fundamental changes. If the new is to succeed, it must be so much better than the old as to counterbalance that vast weight of passive resistance which favours the old; evangelical righteousness must exceed the righteousness of the Scribes and Pharisees. It is possible to sympathize far more with these peasants than with their masters, and yet to admit that they overreached themselves, and that overreaching must always spell failure.

[1] For these reprisals see Janssen, IV, 316, 326, 347–8.
[2] Bartels, pp. 111–2.
[3] Janssen, IV, 205; so, as we have seen, it was complained at the États Généraux of 1484 that there were peasants, "faute de bestes, labourant la charrue au cou."

CHAPTER XXVI

THE DISSOLUTION OF THE MONASTERIES

THESE German occurrences of 1431 to 1525 point a different moral from that which is very commonly drawn from the events of 1536 to 1540 in England. The Dissolution is often described by popular writers as an unmixed calamity for the poor. But Professors Pollard and Savine, Mr R. H. Tawney and Mr H. A. L. Fisher have done much to put this event in its true proportions; and, serious as the question is in itself, it need not detain us here beyond this single chapter[1].

We have seen how many lines of evidence tend to suggest that the monk was not essentially different from other landlords; that he was capitalist first, and churchman afterwards. Let me here add the testimony of that friar who wrote *Dives and Pauper* in Chaucer's day, one of our most valuable witnesses on social questions (Com. IV, c. 7):

They [the monks] show well that all their business is to spare, to purchase, to beg of lords and ladies and of other men lands and rents, gold and silver; not for help of the poor but to maintain their pride and their lust fare [*sic*].... By such hypocrisy, under the colour of poverty, they maintain their pride and their avarice and occupy greater lordships than do many dukes, earls and barons, to great hindering of the land and great disease of the poor people.... For the goods of religious should be more common than other men's goods, to help the land and the poor people.... It is a shame and an over-great abusion that a man of Religion shall ride with his tenth sum or with his twenty sum [*i.e.* with a train of 10 or 20 people] on an horse of ten pound, in a saddle all gold-begone, and for poverty that he bindeth him to in his profession, as they say, he may not give an halfpenny for God's love, nor help his father and mother at need, without asking leave of his sovereign.... And therefore God may say to such folk of Religion that withholden alms from father and mother and from the poor people to make their house and

---

[1] We must, however, take account of Prof. Gay's criticisms on Prof. Pollard in *Trans. Roy. Hist. Soc.* 1904, pp. 195 ff. The present volume was already in the printer's hands when I learned of the existence of Dr Liljegren's *Fall of the Monasteries and Social Changes in England*, etc.; but, in so far as I can gather from Mr Tawney's review in *E.H.R.* Jan. 1925, p. 132, Dr Liljegren's conclusions would not substantially modify what is written here.

their convent rich, that He said to the masters of the law and to the Pharisees, that were men of religion that time: "Why break ye God's commandment for your statutes and your lore?"

Bromyard, about the same time, writes: "In many monasteries ...they do not feed the Lord by hospitality to the poor, but rather deceive the poor by a sophism"[1]. This is what two very earnest and orthodox friars could find it in their heart to write about 1400 A.D., and their words would apply equally well to 1536. The monasteries were not then, perhaps, at their very worst; but it has never been argued, so far as I know, that they had gained more in early Tudor times than they had lost between Henry IV and Henry VII. Even the anti-Lollard apologists of that period write in a significantly low key on some most important points. In so far as there is truth in the contention that the Lincolnshire Rising and the Pilgrimage of Grace were essentially revolts of poor folk not against the monasteries, but in their favour, those events are not normal but highly exceptional in medieval history. We have seen how wide-spread were the anti-monastic mutinies of the year 1326[2]; how commonly the monk regarded the peasant as his natural enemy, and how general is the rule that, whenever or wherever the labourers rise in revolt, they turn as instinctively against the monastery as against the castle. There can be no doubt, of course, that both the Lincolnshire and the Yorkshire rebels rose mainly

Ipse morietur. Quia non habuit disciplinam, & in multitudine stultitiae suae decipietur. Prover. V

Il mourra, Car il n'a receu
En soy aulcune discipline,
Et au nombre sera deceu
De folie qui le domine.

THE ABBOT
From Holbein's *Dance of Death*

---

[1] Tract. Jur. Civ. et Can. s.v. *Religio*, e.
[2] *Mem. St Edmund's Abbey*, R.S. II, 329, quoted above in Ch. XI.

in protest against Thomas Cromwell's policy, and especially against his ecclesiastical measures, which included the Dissolution; but, though they were unanimously anti-Cromwellian, they were far from a homogeneous body of rural malcontents[1]; and, in case of victory, some would inevitably have turned their arms against their fellows. Apart from those extremists who boasted "that they would not leave one gentleman alive in Lincolnshire," at the time when the movement was still being engineered to a great extent by gentlefolk, there were elements in the demands of both rebellions which would soon have arrayed the peasant classes against the capitalists in general; against the monks no less than against the lay lords. The claim that all "gersomes" should be abolished struck equally at both. In fighting against enclosures, these rebels fought the abbot almost as directly as the squire. The natural dislike of absentee landlordism certainly did not spare the monk[2]. Their formal articles contain one explicit demand for redress of the tenants' grievances on "the abbey lands" in some Northern districts[3]. "Cobbett, and those who follow Cobbett in representing the economic evils of the sixteenth century as the fruit of the religious changes, err in linking as parent and child movements which were rather brother and sister, twin aspects of the individualism which seems inseparable from any swift increase in riches"[4]. Capitalism had long been growing in the agricultural world; Mr R. C. Dudding, in his *History of Saleby*, notes that, between 1291 and 1425, though the rents were stable, the number of tenants had decreased by half, "showing the gradual absorption of the small holding by the larger farm" (p. 169). The change of religion was not directly responsible for the evils which developed in that century—the fall in wages and the rise in cost of living. Neither, again, was it directly responsible for the good—the abolition of

[1] Cf. Tawney, pp. 318, 323 ff.: "The incompatibility of the allies was obvious." This is brought out also by Prof. Gay, *l.c.* pp. 196–7.

[2] "The estates of the larger houses were often scattered over several different counties, and before the Dissolution they were quite frequently managed by laymen. In such cases the monks were simply rentiers, who needed to know no more about their tenants than the fellows of an Oxford college know about theirs at the present day" (Tawney, p. 383).

[3] *Ibid.* p. 334, from Gairdner, *L. and P. of Henry VIII*, xi, 1246.

[4] *Ibid.* p. 382. Compare p. 339 for a contrast between the German and English agrarian revolts.

bondage. But it had considerable effect on both, as different scholars have shown from different points of view.

The downward progress of the labourer had begun, as even Janssen practically confesses, before Luther had appeared. And this may be brought out far more strongly here by the reminder of matters which we have already noted in preceding chapters; the gradual growth of enclosures and absentee landlordism and rackrenting and capitalism; the confessed defeats in the fight against usury and trade-injustices; the heavy taxation involved by grandiose schemes of popes and princes under the Renaissance and the New Monarchy. Indeed, one measure of Henry VIII may possibly have done more economic harm than the Dissolution; his war-taxation of the years 1524–5. An extreme example of the distress which this caused may be found in Miss M'Clenaghan's *Springs of Lavenham*[1]. No less than £35,000 was taken in 1524 from the single county of Suffolk; it was rather a capital levy than a mere tax; its effect on the cloth-making industry was, for the moment at least, disastrous. Multitudes were thrown out of work, since the great men "sought to ease themselves by abatin the poore workemens wages. And when that did not prevaile, they turned away many of their people....Many a poore man (for want of worke) was hereby undone, with his wife and children; and it made many a poore widow to sit with a hungry belly. This bred great woe in most places in England." For, side by side with this, the debasement of the coinage struck the poor with terrible severity; and it is idle to contrast the conditions of 1600 with those of 1500 as though the Dissolution had been the only operative factor, or as though the change had begun first with the year 1536[2].

Moreover, we must bear in mind that bondage still subsisted; and, though it had lost much of its severity, yet the less merciful landlords and the lawyers were struggling with some success to revive ancient conditions here and there. Even though we had had no Reformation, the same process was beginning to show itself here which Janssen and others have

[1] Ipswich, 1924, pp. 48–59, a very valuable monograph.
[2] For the blow struck at English peasant prosperity by this debasement of the coinage see J. E. T. Rogers, *Six Centuries of Work and Wages*, p. 325.

emphasized so strongly in Germany; that a strong executive, under cover of Roman Civil Law, broke down the customary safeguards of the later Middle Ages, and applied more and more pitilessly to the serf of 1500 those disabilities which imperial Rome had inflicted upon the *servus* of antiquity. Prof. Savine's conclusions are very interesting, in his article on *Bondmen under the Tudors*[1]. As to their numbers,

Though no real statistics of the Tudor population and its division into classes are available at the present time, it is probable that, even in the beginning of the period, bondmen formed hardly more than one per cent. of the whole population. It is very little, but it is much more than some people believe, and it is a strong testimony of the great vitality of the manorial system. When we consider that late in the reign of Elizabeth there were still thousands, if not tens of thousands, of people paying merchet and chevage, and with very precarious rights over their real and personal property, we may feel amazed at the vitality and force of medieval serfdom.

As to their status, he justly notes the still-surviving possibilities of oppression.

The fact that the common-law courts were always inclined to decide in favour of manumission when they found the least cause for it does not rest solely on humanitarian and religious grounds; on the contrary, it was partly due to the harshness of the legal theory of villeinage. This theory would have become impossible in strict practice; therefore the courts of 1500 interpreted cases of disputed serfdom in favour of the villein, just as those of 1800 (though Prof. Savine does not apply this analogy) strove by acquittals to evade certain impossible severities of the death-penalty. As to strict theory, "the statutes and the rolls contain but few entries relating to the villeins, but of these few hardly one is favourable to them" (p. 258). The law was such that even a gentleman might be claimed as a villein by a rascally debtor who sought thereby to avoid payment. "Then the reaction set in. I have little doubt myself that to a considerable extent the 'favour of liberty' was a matter of self-preservation for the propertied classes themselves" (p. 261). "From the tragic story of Whithorne's wrongs we observe that when the lord of the manor, in the middle of the

[1] *Trans. Roy. Hist. Soc.* XIX (1905), 248, 256 ff.

fifteenth century, was a prince of the blood it was difficult for the supposed villein to prove his free estate, even when he was a gentleman and a large landowner. Such stories help us to understand why the burgesses and the gentlemen addressed their petitions to the king for the 'favour of liberty.'" So late as 1481, an abbot lends a villein as he would lend out a horse; and again, while a lord claims that he could, if he had chosen, have taken a bondman's whole property, the injured party

does not deny at law [the lord's] right to treat his villeins thus, he replies only that he is of free estate.... Mr Page (who is too optimistic in his estimate of the bondmen's condition) remarks that in the Ramsey Abbey Court Rolls the old formula "seisire in manum domini omnia bona et catalla omnium nativorum istius manerii" ["to seize into the abbot's hands all the goods and chattels of all the bondmen of this manor"], occurs until the very Dissolution (p. 264)[1].... The last bondmen did no week-work and very little boon-work or *averagia*. Often they went into towns and became artisans or merchants. But the heavy hand of the lord weighed upon them everywhere. They would have been astonished if anybody had told them that their serfdom was a mere shadow of the past and a mere antiquarian survival. They would have pointed out that they must apply to the lord for licence to leave or to marry; that they must pay heriots and fines of admission; that the steward could in many ways interfere with their lives. They would have reminded us that for their charter of freedom they had to sacrifice one quarter or one third of their lands and goods and that many a neighbour would not give his daughter to a villein's son until he had bought his freedom. Their serfdom was indeed keenly felt by the last bondmen, and this must be taken into serious consideration by anybody who desires to understand their condition (pp. 280–1).

Elizabeth inherited a considerable number of bondfolk, mainly from the abbey estates; and her dealings with them exemplify Montesquieu's bitter words, that the slave owes his freedom more to his own exertions and to economic circumstances than to the favour either of Church or of State. Just as the worst injustices of Tudor courts like the Star Chamber were inherited from the medieval Inquisition, so we find Elizabeth parodying the words and imitating the deeds of

[1] "The return made in 1539 to Henry VIII of his newly-acquired estates 'of the late attainted abbey' [of Glastonbury] is careful to show the number of bondmen on each manor, 'whose bodyes and goodes are always subject to the king's pleasure'" (*Rentalia*, p. xxii).

medieval churchmen. Nothing could be more unexceptionable than her preambles to her deeds of manumission; her words are as pious as those of Gregory the Great[1]:

The Queen, etc., to all whom etc., Greeting. Whereas from the beginning God created all men free by nature, and afterwards the law of man placed some under the yoke of servitude, we believe it to be a pious thing, and acceptable to God and consonant with christian charity, to make wholly free certain who have been thrown into villainage to us, our heirs and successors, and bound in servitude. Know ye therefore that we, moved by piety, and at the humble petition and special request of our beloved servant Sir Henry Lee, otherwise Lea, knight...have manumitted and made free, and by these presents do manumit and make free, Margaret Cawston, etc., etc.

At the back of these pious words lay the fact which we have had so frequent occasion to note already, that the bondfolk were paying heavily for their freedom; and, in Elizabeth's reign, more heavily than they were likely to have paid before, in proportion as the central government had a stronger hold upon them than any local lord had possessed since the days of real feudal anarchy. She did not indeed rob her bondfolk of all their possessions, as the lord had a right to do and as many lords had done in the distant past; but she demanded and exacted, as ransom-money, a very considerable proportion of the serf's possessions. To Sir Henry Lee, the courtier named in this preamble, she granted the lucrative privilege of liberating 300 of her bondfolk in the Duchy of Lancaster, and doubtless the queen took a considerable share of the spoils. "It was further enacted that, if the bondmen failed to agree with the queen's agent as to the terms of manumission, they were liable to complete and entire forfeiture."

Here was a great legal injustice; yet it was not more unjust than what was being done by Catholic princes on the Continent under shelter of Roman Law, or than what had been done in Henry VIII's days by the prince-abbot of Kempten. We have no reason to assume that, if Philip II had ruled England at that time, he would not have made exactly the same grant, in equally pious language, to some time-server at his own court.

[1] See Chapter XIII above. For Elizabeth, I quote from Miss Davenport's valuable article in *Norfolk Archaeology*, vol. XIX (1917).

Nor, in arguing thus, are we merely speculating in the air; for we have the post-Reformation history of Roman Catholic countries to guide us. A most instructive object-lesson may be found here in the story of the great abbey of St-Gall, which kept its religion and its state long after the Reformation had flooded neighbouring lands, and until the French Revolution swept it away with thousands of its fellows. No other case, perhaps, could show us more clearly the actual working of Catholicism and Protestantism side by side. The actual facts will not be found to justify extremists on either side. The little world of St-Gall did not rush straight from barbarism to culture; from degrading superstition to pure Gospel morality. Nor, on the other hand, did these loyal adherents of an infallibly-guided moral and religious system show any marked moral and social superiority, even after many generations, over the welter of heresy around them; such difference as can be marked was slightly the other way. The whole story has been told by the learned and patient archivist von Arx, a monk of the abbey who, at the dissolution, was retained by the new government as archivist in charge of a library and muniment-room which are among the richest in Europe. His *History of the Canton and Monastery of St-Gall* is one of the most learned and dispassionate works of its kind; and his generalizations on the actual effect of the Reformation upon peasant life will be found more enlightening than any mere speculation can possibly be. He writes (III, 280 ff.): "Serfdom, which had gradually lost its first severity during the course of centuries, was almost altogether abolished by the Reformation and the advent of the humanistic spirit. The landlords especially favoured those serfs who belonged to a lord outside their own district." The abbot first reduced the services of his bondmen settled in fifteen other cantons or lordships, and then sold to them, upon easy terms, a complete freedom from the remaining dues, so small that they were now hardly worth collecting.

This came about first in the Canton of Zürich, where, in 1562, by decree of the courts at Grüningen and Kiburg, 500 persons of Griffensee and Andelfingen redeemed themselves from this serfdom at the rate of 3 gulden apiece. But this favour was refused to native serfs on economic grounds; nay, even strangers who allowed themselves to become monastic copyholders [*Gotteshausleute*] must submit to the payment of heriot and shrovetide-hens. Yet, with this exception, they were treated everywhere as freemen; and in 1602 the monastery declared to the papal legate that it neither considered these as bondmen, nor knew that others did so.

The fine for merchet, which the neighbouring monastery of Pfäfers found too lucrative to give up, fell into desuetude at St-Gall; and Arx concludes with the reflexion that serfdom, under those later conditions, was not so onerous that the age of modern enlightenment can claim much gain from its final abolition (p. 284).

Arx, though a cloisterer by profession, wrote as a free man after 1792, and his study confines itself to one great monastery; so let me next quote from a Catholic monograph on the monks and their tenantry in another great abbey, this time in Westphalia[1]. Speaking of the tithes which the monks, after appropriating the churches, naturally took from the tenants, the author writes:

It may be imagined with what hate the peasants regarded such behaviour [as became traditional among the middlemen to whom the abbey farmed out the right of collecting these tithes]; and how they loathed this tribute, which was doubtless the most oppressive of all burdens on the subjects of the manor.... Even today, in this Gladbach district, an antipathy to the rule of the monks may be traced among old folk who have heard of abbey-days from their fathers or grandfathers. They would call Napoleon a great man for the sole reason that he freed the population from such a plague by the dissolution of the monasteries, even though he had done nothing else.

In the later Middle Ages, while other burdens on the peasant were growing lighter, "the right of heriot, on the contrary, had been maintained in all its severity" on these Gladbach abbey lands. Again,

It will be seen from my detailed exposition that the position of the serfs was by no means enviable, even though it had considerably improved in the last centuries of the Middle Ages, as compared with

---

[1] For full German title, see my List of Authorities under *Gladbach*; I translate it here: "History of the Economy and Government of the Abbey of München Gladbach in the Middle Ages"; a doctoral dissertation by Joseph Stratner (M. Gladbach, 1911). The brief autobiography on the last page specifies the author's religious confession. My quotations here are from pp. 31, 21, 39.

earlier times. This heriot was, above all, an oppressive burden upon the bondmen. True, the best beast itself was generally no longer claimed; it was commuted for a money payment. But this fine was by no means light; so that the bondmen, under their usually impoverished circumstances, which themselves were an inevitable consequence of restrictions on economic life, were pretty sure to be driven into debt for a long time by the payment of this due.

Compare this judgement with that of a scholar who has done similar work in France. The archivist B. Prost, in his brief but valuable monograph on the Cistercian abbey of Rosières, which was one of the most considerable in Burgundy[1], speaks of the sufferings of the monks during the troubles of the Hundred Years' War. He continues:

If to this we add innumerable difficulties and contests with the neighbouring lords; continual vexations from these men; frequent revolts of serfs; refusal to pay tithes and dues; daily manifestations of the keen and implacable hatred which all the neighbouring villages nourished against the abbey; incessant and interminable lawsuits which the monks were forced to sustain in defence of their rights, to resist usurpations and trespasses, then we shall have a fairly faithful picture of the history of this abbey of Rosières during the fourteenth and fifteenth centuries.

Similar evidence emerges from the English documents. Mr Archbold, in his unequal but often original and valuable *Somerset Religious Houses*, discusses the question in detail and sums up very fairly:

It is no doubt a simple way of solving a difficulty to assume that the decline in the prosperity of the working classes, which went on in the sixteenth century, was a direct result of the Dissolution; but there is every reason to suppose that such was not the case.... The effect of the Dissolution on the position and life of the agricultural labourer must in the end have been largely beneficial, though attended in the immediate results with much misery[2].

A full study of the evidence, therefore, will warn us against exaggerations on either side. Landlords, doubtless, were often individually generous and beneficent in the Middle Ages, as they were in South Carolina and as they had been under

---

[1] Poligny, 1870, p. 6.
[2] pp. 300–301. Compare Miss Davenport: "The claims of the individual emphasized by the Reformation did much to complete the process of enfranchisement" (*Norf. Archaeol.* XIX, 9).

imperial Rome. Ecclesiastical landlords, I believe, lived on the whole, in pleasanter personal relatìons with their tenants than the lay nobles did. Christianity contributed something real to the gradual improvement of the peasant; but, too often, the Christian was first of all a churchman, and the churchman was first of all a landlord, hampered by rigid institutionalism and by a network of feudal customs and ideas. The common judgement is perfectly just, that feudalism was an orderly system compared with the anarchy of the Dark Ages, but disorderly in comparison with modern civilization. What Guizot truly said of France may be applied to all European countries, though to England with rather less emphasis than to some others.

No time, no system has remained so hateful to the public instinct. ...You may go backwards in French history, and stop where you will; everywhere you will find the feudal *régime* looked upon by the mass of the population as an enemy which must be fought and exterminated at any cost. In every age, whoever has struck a blow at feudalism has been popular in France....From its birth to its death, in the days of its glory as in its decay, the feudal *régime* was never accepted by the peoples [of Europe]. I defy you to show me any epoch in which it appears to be rooted in their prejudices and protected by their sentiments. They have always suffered it in hatred, and attacked it with ardour[1].

If, again, in the face of the actual records, it is patently absurd to speak of the medieval peasant as leading a life of Arcadian simplicity, yet on the other hand we must recognize that his roughness was mainly the roughness of his time and place, and that the monks did at least as much for him as the average lay lord would have done; probably, indeed, a little more, partly because a corporation is generally a slightly easier landlord than a keen business man, and partly because the monk seldom altogether forgot his profession. The amount of Christian feeling imported into monastic financial relations was so small as to stir bitter indignation in men like Hugues de St-Cher; but, on the other hand, it was enough to make some real difference to the peasant. The cases where the monk proved a more merciless landlord than the layman were mainly due to economic pressure, or to the crushing weight of a conservative

---

[1] *Essais sur l'hist. de France*, 4th ed. 1836, p. 341.

tradition against which the individual monk was powerless, kindly as his own nature may have been. But that conservative tradition, in the rapidly-changing world of the sixteenth century, was becoming more and more intolerably mischievous. The barriers burst suddenly; much was swept away which a wiser policy on either side might have kept for the profit of humanity; but the monks themselves must bear a heavy share of the guilt in all this. The modern contention, based mainly on the well-meaning but ignorant Cobbett, that "viewed merely in its social aspect, the English Reformation was in reality the rising of the rich against the poor"[1], will not bear even a moment's comparison with the facts of medieval history. Nor will the social history of Roman Catholic countries since the Reformation support this theory; never, perhaps, has there been a more miserable rural population, even from the moral and spiritual point of view, than that which can still be found in the Campagna, within a few miles of Rome; a population which seems almost as miserable as that of the worst city slums[2].

For here is another interested mis-statement to be faced; the assertion that not only English poor-laws, but also the poverty which called for them, begin with the Dissolution. *Piers Plowman*, to go no farther, might enlighten us on the latter point; his world is full of workless beggars, and this constitutes one of his hero's hardest problems, "how I might amaistrien [teach] them, and make them to work." He knows these men for his "brethren in blood, since God bought us all"; but he knows also that many of them "work full ill," and will not work at all but under peril of starvation; it is only Sir Hunger that can help this saviour of society to compel these folk to "labour for their livelihood"[3]. The common-sense of the Poor-Law question would seem to be put in a few sentences by a writer in *The Westminster Review* for May 1888, p. 591:

The nuisance [of idle beggars] was particularly bad just before the Dissolution. We might conclude as much from the extraordinary congregation of "wayfaring bold beggers" at the funeral "of a man

[1] W. Cobbett's *History of the Protestant Reformation*. A new edition. (London, Washbourne.) Preface, p. vi. See appendix 4.
[2] See appendix 39.
[3] A. VII, 191 ff.; B. VI, 205 ff.; C. IX, 209 ff.; cf. D. Chadwick, *Social Life in the Days of Piers Plowman*, 1922, pp. 75 ff.

of much worshype in Kent," in the year 1521, of which a vivid account is given by Harman. An eye-witness had described to him "the great fat ox sod (boiled) out in furmenty," with "bread and drinke abundantly to furnesh out the premisses," and the dole of twopence each to the crowd. The "wayfaring bold beggers," to the number of "seven score persons of men, every of them having his woman," were allowed to spend the night in a barn. But more direct proof of the height to which professional vagrancy had risen before the Dissolution of the monasteries is afforded by the elaborate statute passed in 1530–1. It recites that: "In all places throughe out this Realme of England, vacabundes and beggers have of long tyme increased and dayly do increase in great and excessyve nombres," etc.; and this in spite of the "many and sondry goode lawes and streyte statutes before this time devysed and made," etc.; and then it enacts that aged and impotent persons may be licensed to beg within certain districts, but if caught begging outside these limits, or without a license, they are to be set in the stocks or stripped from the middle upwards and whipped; and all able-bodied beggars are to be taken to the nearest market town, and there tied to the end of a cart, naked, and beaten with whips throughout the town till their bodies are bloody, after which they are to return to the place where they were born[1].

Eden, in fact, pointed out long ago that the English Poor-Law dates really not from Elizabeth but from 1391 (1, 63). Prof. Imbart de la Tour, an orthodox Roman Catholic, describes the insufficiency of French palliatives for pauperism, the low wages, and the growth of an urban proletariat between 1483 and 1514[2]. The German, Johann Geiler, preaching at Strassburg in 1510, complained of the social harm wrought by the absence of poor-laws: "this cometh from no other cause, but only from the negligence of the authorities, who pay no heed to this matter but let every man beg who hath lust to beg. Hence springeth in due course all manner of idleness, and every man betaketh himself to beggary"[3]. Bishop Guillaume Durand had already said the same, more briefly, to the pope and Ecumenical Council

[1] The pre-Dissolution poor-laws are well summarized by Archbold, pp. 252–4. For the comparative inefficacy of monastic almsgiving see Prof. C. H. Pearson's *Historical Maps of England*, 1883, pp. 50 ff.: "It was impossible" (he concludes) "that institutions thus scattered should be any efficient substitute for a poor-law system."

[2] Vol. i, p. 509.

[3] *Narrenschiff*, in J. Scheible, *Das Kloster weltlich u. geistlich*, Stuttgart, 1845, i, 567.

in 1311[1]. A strong caveat must be entered here against the treatment of this subject by Bishop Hobhouse, who is frequently quoted as an authority, but who evidently knew very little of medieval Church life beyond the text of those actual Somersetshire parish accounts which he edited with a diligence which has earned public gratitude. Noting that these documents are absolutely silent as to "the care of the poor and disabled," he adds, "I can only suppose that the brotherhood tie was so strongly realized by the community, that the weaker ones were succoured by the stronger, as out of a family store"[2]. Contemporary witnesses forbid this assumption; there was doubtless much private almsgiving then, but not enough to make the present poor regret those days.

To trace the growth and progress of the poor-law is altogether beyond my competence; but I have seen enough of the original authorities to warn my readers emphatically against the fantastic assertions which are often made as to the beauty and efficacy of almsgiving under the pre-Reformation régime, and the losses entailed upon the poor by the breach with Rome. The evidence of Dr Ébrard's monograph on Bourg-en-Bresse is, so far as my experience goes, not exceptional but typical. Here, under Roman Catholicism, there was no efficacious system of relief in 1531; it was only in 1573 that the rich were taxed in relief of the poor

like the poor-rate of Scotland and England, but with this very important difference, that it was only temporary....At this time, not only did the clergy of Bourg not set an example of charity, but even the friars' convents solicited alms to the detriment of the poor. Thus, during this famine [of 1531], we find the ecclesiastics claiming exemption from the poor-rate, and the nuns of St Clare demanding food from the town council; they pleaded that the plague prevented them from begging as usual through the town. The answer was, that they must apply to their own families[3].

This was nothing new; long before the end of the Middle Ages, the friar had begun to prey upon the poor after the fashion which Branche describes in France under the Ancien Régime (p. 419): "A la fin du dernier siècle, et malgré les oppositions que nous

[1] *Tractatus*, etc. pt iii, tit. 18, p. 264.
[2] *Churchwardens' Accounts*, Somerset Record Soc. 1890, pp. xxiii ff.
[3] Ébrard, pp. 85–7.

avons racontées, ils s'étaient propagés en tout lieu. Or, pas de jour ne s'écoulait qu'ils ne vinssent demander, comme une redevance et comme un véritable impôt ecclésiastique, la pitance et l'aumône à ces pauvres gens qui bien souvent avaient peine à nourrir leurs enfants." At a parish in Normandy, in 1425 and 1426, there were eighty households paying taxes, with thirty-four clergy and four beggars from whom no taxes were demanded[1]. At Paris, in 1536, it was calculated that there were more than 5000 beggars[2]. It is unlikely that the total population was then more than 100,000. The poverty of French peasants and artisans in the next century has often been described; it has formed the subject of a solid and most valuable monograph by A. Feillet: "La misère au temps de la Fronde &c." The great French satirist's description of the peasant under Louis XIV is well known:

L'on voit certains animaux farouches, des mâles et des femelles, répandus par la campagne, noirs, livides et tout brûlés du soleil, attachés à la terre qu'ils fouillent et qu'ils remuent avec une opiniâtreté invincible: ils ont comme une voix articulée; et quand ils se lèvent sur leurs pieds, ils montrent une face humaine, et en effet ils sont des hommes. Ils se retirent la nuit dans des tanières où ils vivent de pain noir, d'eau et de racines: ils épargnent aux autres hommes la peine de semer, de labourer et de recueillir pour vivre, et méritent ainsi de ne pas manquer de ce pain qu'ils ont semé[3].

Abbé Bernier quotes a letter of 1774 from a Norman parish priest to his bishop, which describes a state of things worse than in any English country district, and worse even than among the Lancashire cotton-mills[4]. There were villages in which 60 per cent. of the population were on the parish, or even 75 per cent. A charitable farmer sometimes cut bread for 350 poor folk in a day, "chacun sa bouchée," a phrase which is of terrible significance. While there were many priests receiving less than 100 francs a year, and the whole hospitality of a great abbey was reckoned at only 200 francs, a monk estimated his own single cost of living at 350 francs a year[5].

In Germany, again, as Below says very truly, "The Peasants' war brought no essential change into the state of the peasants,

---

[1] Delisle, p. 173.   [2] Desmaze, p. 133.
[3] La Bruyère, *Caractères*, "Les paysans et les laboureurs."
[4] pp. 64 ff.; cf. p. 70.   [5] *Ibid*. pp. 83, 86, 102.

on the whole; their condition in Protestant districts became in no way different from that of the Catholic districts...the revolt was a rising not of Protestant but of Catholic peasants"[1].

The economic causes of the Reformation have been enormously exaggerated, as G. v. Below points out[2], by materialistic socialists like Kautsky. Its economic effects, again, need no paradoxical exposition. Every change in society must operate to the disadvantage of those who have least power of coherence and least self-control. Peasants and the poorer artisans, as Berthold v. Regensburg saw as early as 1250, had less cohesion and self-control than the average of well-to-do folk. The task of modern society is to ensure equal opportunities for all; to give the peasant power and education together, but (if need be) power even beyond his education—power, indeed, as a means of education for him. We give him a personal freedom unknown to the Middle Ages; and, even if he never learns to use that freedom well; even if he uses it to strike not only against employers but against economic law, yet it will be well to have tried an experiment unknown to earlier history. A newspaper has recently quoted aptly from Wordsworth in this connexion:

> The discipline of slavery is unknown
> Amongst us; hence the more do we require
> The discipline of virtue.

[1] p. 60.   [2] p. 40, n. 2.

CHAPTER XXVII

CONCLUSION

THIS book has become far longer than I had intended; we have travelled north and south and east and west, up-hill and down-dale, in pursuit of a trail that is perhaps clearer to myself than it can be to my readers. My aim has been to emphasize those features of medieval village life which have disappeared, or to a great extent disappeared, from modern society. More than once, however, it has been necessary to recall the essential unity underlying all human life, and the danger of separating these men's experiences too sharply from our own. But there remain certain elements that are really characteristic of medieval society; elements which, in varying degrees and combinations, are common to all civilized Europe during all the centuries with which this book deals. If, in tracing these elements, I pass from age to age and from land to land in apparent caprice, this is not because I am not following certain fairly definite clues in my own mind. But it would be wearisome to pause and justify these transitions at every turn; and the reader will probably prefer to do a good deal of the thinking for himself. For, while making no secret of my own personal conclusions, I do attempt to give such clear indications of time, place and character, in the case of all my principal witnesses, as may enable others to check my results.

In spite of all the uncertainties which beset the enquiry at this stage, it is generally agreed that the labourer's progress was neither simultaneous in all countries, nor uniform in any. There were even great variations from district to district within the same country; Kent, apparently, scarcely ever knew anything of serfdom; the causes which kindled the North to the Pilgrimage of Grace left the South cold; Brunswick and Hanover, in the thirteenth century, had already reached the goal for which all South Germany fought madly in 1525; there was probably a smaller proportion of actual bondfolk in the France than in the England of 1500, yet the English peasant was the more pros-

perous of the two. But, amid all these variations, there seems to
have been one general law of development. The early medieval
serf was distinctly above the slave, yet no less distinctly below
the freeman. He did not always gain, immediately at least, from
strong government either in Church or in State; the strong
Norman rule in England protected him to some extent from petty
tyrannies, but increased that weight of central authority which
pressed upon a class deprived of any voice whatever in the
government; again, where the Church was strongest, serfdom
was often most literally enforced. It was mainly by his own
efforts, and with the help of economic changes, that the serf
struggled into freedom. In England, he gradually commuted
his services for money rents, which became fixed; the depreciation of money values then brought him a considerable unearned
increment; the catastrophe of the Black Death helped him to
break down antiquated disabilities; there grew up a yeoman class
in the village. We cannot apply indiscriminately to these yeomen what Latimer tells us concerning his father; it is one of the
first rules of evidence in the Middle Ages, and even in far more
recent times, that those witnesses who are most trustworthy
in matters of immediate experience cannot be followed with
equal confidence when they describe a supposedly happier past.
But a yeoman class certainly did grow up; and this apparently
separated itself almost as widely from the lower peasant, as the
modern prosperous mechanic is separated from the unskilled
worker[1]. In France, bondage disappeared from many districts
far earlier than with us, because the peasants became rich
enough to buy their freedom *en masse*; whole villages paid a
heavy lump sum, and secured general emancipation. In Flanders and Northern Germany, the pioneer-peasant had great
influence; draining marshes and clearing forests under some
great lay or ecclesiastical lord, he received land for himself on
terms which practically made a yeoman of him; and his prosperity naturally reacted upon others; the lords found less and
less profit in enforcing feudal dues, more and more profit in

[1] "It is quite likely that at the very moment when one great section of the
daily labourers and small holders of villein allotments was developing into
prosperous tenant farmers, another was rapidly sinking, until at last there
grew up that great mass of pauperism which so burdened the country in
Tudor times" (W. J. Corbett, in *Social England*, II, 1902, 533).

selling them; then princes passed laws definitely in favour of
the peasant, and at last the little that remained of bondage was
not worth the lord's while to enforce. In Italy, the same
pioneer system had often the same results; here, as in Flanders,
the enormous growth of the cities brought not only example to
the peasant, but many chances of exchanging village for municipal life; here, therefore, the countryfolk were early freed from
bondage, but were abandoned (as again in Flanders) to many
of the struggles and incertitudes which beset an independent
labouring class. These seem to be the main currents in a somewhat complicated stream of progress; but nowhere, I think, did
this stream really reach the level of the modern French or
Italian peasant proprietors, or of the British hired labourer;
there are real differences between medieval and modern peasant
life, and it must be the task of history to seize and mark those
differences for the instruction of social students.

It is very difficult to compare human lives at different times
and in different places. Yet without such comparisons, explicit
or implicit, social history can teach us nothing; and, after all,
we may eliminate the worst chances of error by bearing in mind
the tentative nature of our study. Human character and endeavour do remain sufficiently constant from age to age and from
land to land, and the same words do stand sufficiently for the
same things, to serve us in this quest, provided only that we
conduct it under a constant sense of relativity. Thus forewarned, we shall not often reverse the true points of the compass. Here and there we may mistakenly pity what is enviable,
or blame that which a wider view would teach us to commend;
but, on the whole, the careful calculator's errors are likely to
be less serious than this; moreover, so long as he is honest with
himself, some of those errors may cancel each other out, and
the worst will be neutralized by becoming obvious to critical
readers. Our essential loneliness is proverbial: "The heart
knoweth his own bitterness, and a stranger doth not inter-
meddle with his joy." Yet it is equally true that man may draw
nearer to man, and class to class, by trying to understand and to
make ourselves understood. I have, therefore, accepted the
difficulty of this task as some measure of its importance, and
have rushed in where angels have feared to tread.

For certainly the hesitation of the angels affords no general guarantee against trespass; otherwise there would be less excuse for the first intruder. We may almost say, with the Psalmist, that the hedges of this vineyard have long since been broken down, and the boar out of the wood doth waste it. In the language of more modern metaphor, the social history of the Middle Ages is often hailed as a happy hunting-ground for the imagination of writers whose very occupation almost precludes any careful study of the original documents. Theories which, a generation ago, were stimulating even in their inaccuracy of detail, are now handed on as commonplaces from mouth to mouth, and as clichés from leader to leaderette. Meanwhile, the falser element grows in proportion as the original piquancy evaporates; and the public now drinks from a cup in which fresh spoonfuls of sugar are constantly added to quicken its flatness into some sort of effervescence. Ruskin and William Morris did splendid work; but they would have had scant sympathy with followers who, even at this distance of time, cannot rise above the hasty generalizations and the frequent blunders which are unavoidable in every pioneer movement[1]. History is still encumbered with masses of Strawberry-Hill Gothic; the plaster is peeling away from the laths and the brick-work; let us at least strive for something more solid, were it no more than A. H. Clough's "stumpy-columnar, which to a reverent taste is perhaps the most moving of any."

Three very different causes have conspired to disparage facts and encourage fancies in this field. Religious conservatism, naturally, has been the most potent of all. But many political Conservatives also, remembering the smock-frocked peasants of their childhood, and forgetting how much of this patriarchal content was either superficial in itself or due to the static character of social and economic conditions, resent the disturbance of this ancient equilibrium, and are willing to believe that the serf, whose movements at this distance of time are almost invisible, was essentially happier than the too stirring modern labourer. Lastly, in quite the opposite camp, there are Radicals and Socialists impatient of our tardy progress, and convinced

[1] Moreover, Ruskin had no illusions as to the lower strata of Swiss peasants; cf. *Modern Painters*, pt v, ch. xix, "The Mountain Gloom."

that there must be some shorter royal road; these men often listen as eagerly as the others to any empiric who can produce a plausible nostrum from far-off times. We have, therefore, a whole class of authors who give this public what this public wants. No human ingenuity, to be sure, can reconcile their facile generalizations with recorded medieval facts; but these writers, who earn their livelihood by being lively, exercise a cruel tyranny over thousands of readers to whom all naked records of the past seem dull. For the average busy man, however intelligent, is greatly at the mercy of any publicist bold enough to spin facts out of his imagination, and persistently impenitent enough to bore people into believing him, even though he lacked the charm of style which some of these popular authors certainly command. Therefore it is a laborious race, though in the long run it must be a successful race, to overtake a host of misrepresentations which have been rolling so long, and acquiring meanwhile a momentum which we might call reckless, if we did not mark that it has also something of that subconscious and natural eccentricity which makes a butterfly's flight as protective as it is picturesque.

Much, however, is gained to begin with if the public will accustom itself to require real documentary evidence throughout this necessarily contentious stage of social history. Those who substitute fancy for facts will thus become a separate and clearly-marked class, just as, fifty years ago, the country banks which published no yearly balance-sheets began to form a marked category, and gradually disappeared. This will be pure gain; for why should documentary accuracy drive us into regrettable extremes? When we have collected all the details we can, there will still be imagination, whether active or latent, in our present-ment of those details. We know that Milton had great business qualities, and we have reason to suspect the same of Shake-speare. To weigh carefully every pertinent fact is not an occupa-tion which need blind us to imponderable values; on the con-trary, we are not likely to get the imponderables even approxi-mately right unless we are scrupulously just to the ponderables. Therefore, in proportion as we pursue history by those accurate and common-sense methods by which children of this world have done so much to secure clearness and harmony in money-matters, in that same proportion are we likely to avoid the subtle temptation of assuming all the imponderables to be in favour of our own party. Bossuet said it of theology, Pasteur quoted it concerning science, and we may apply it no less truly to history, that "the worst intellectual vice is the vice of believing that things are, simply because we wish them to be." Even in the Middle Ages, no really great man ever wilfully divorced imagination from fact. Those men did not really prefer tradition to the written word, or set vagueness on a higher plane than accuracy. Tradition and vagueness were accepted only where nothing better could be had; and one of the commonest types of preambles to papal and monastic documents recites how, for the sake of avoiding uncertainties and lapses of memory and disputes, some merely verbal promise or gift is now being fixed in clear and enduring black and white[1].

Not, of course, that the most explicit record can prove one man to be, or to have been, happier than another. Yet human curiosity is never tired of asking; speculative comparisons are unavoidable; and, since the men who refuse to argue this question do not on that account abstain from begging it, we shall all do well to test current theories by recorded facts. In these preceding chapters, I have tried to supply such a factual conspectus as may serve for a stepping-stone to higher imaginative planes; let us now try, within the limitations imposed by these and similar records, to think ourselves back for one moment into that peasant life of the past. Even those who would shrink most from actually going back may look sympathetically into these more primitive minds and simple lives. It is a sort of mental holiday to glimpse new things which, however insignificant intrinsically, may by their very novelty take us out of ourselves, and feed the luxurious and fleeting desire to be that which we are not, and which we would not permanently be—"Dort wo du nicht bist, dort ist das Glück"—"How happy the peasant, if he but knew his own bliss!" Distant times, like distant lands, have this appeal to many minds. Others, again, may wish to go farther, and to examine this medieval village, this cluster of thatched huts nestling under the white church

[1] To give the first instances to hand: Innocent III, *Epp.* l. x, No. 145 (P.L. vol. 215, col. 1243); Winchcombe charter in Dugdale-Caley, II, 305.

tower on the edge of common and woodland and open field, in something more than the tourist spirit, asking themselves as they gaze: "What sort of man inhabits these hovels? How can we so enter into these men's lives as to see what they really were, and thence to infer what they reasonably might have been, and thus finally to help in making them what some day they shall be?" If it be true to confess that not one of the nineteen Christian centuries can show a clean record of justice and consideration towards the village, how then can we so formulate this problem of rich and poor as to arrive now at some better solution? How can we frame the question clearly enough to indicate the one satisfactory answer?

The medieval peasant was, essentially, the kind of man who still meets us by the thousand in outlying districts of the Continent, and by handfuls even in Great Britain. He lacked some very important things which his descendants now enjoy even in the remotest corners of Europe; yet, in the main, his existence was what may still be found here and there. Looking closely at him and his village, we see the rough life of labouring folk hardened by their constant fight against land and weather; we see taskmasters whose interests necessarily conflicted with the needs of those elementary breadwinners; yet who, to their credit be it said, did not always enforce every advantage that the strict law might have given them. Our general impression will be that of a society very engaging in its old-world simplicity, but with much to learn before it can struggle through into modern civilization, whether we take that word in Richard Cobden's sense or in the sense of those romantics who picture an ideal society enjoying all modern material gains, yet purged from the dross of Reformation and Capitalism. No thoughtful and unprejudiced reader, however unfamiliar with special medieval conditions, is likely to go far wrong in his judgement on what we find (for instance) in the Durham and Halesowen Rolls. He will probably conclude, as Berthold concluded nearly seven centuries ago, that it will need the experience of many generations to teach these men an efficient sense of social solidarity. And the real tragedy is that so much truth should be in Berthold's words, and that so much of the peasant's degradation should be accountable to all rich folk, from that day to our own. As the operative Higgins says to Margaret Hale in *North and South*: "If I'm going wrong when I think I'm going right, it's their sin who ha' left me in my ignorance. I ha' thought till my brains ached." The medieval peasant was what he was, and the modern is what he is, partly because the sifting process of civilization has left him at the bottom, but partly also because luckier folk have pushed him down. His annals are short and simple; the ploughman does not wade through slaughter to a throne, but all the cruellest elements of tragedy may be found in his village, as Turgenieff shows in his *King Lear of the Steppe*, and Gottfried Keller in *Romeo und Julia auf dem Dorfe*. There was much real neighbourly kindness; but there were also desperate jealousies and feuds, with crimes which seem all the more sordid when so little is at stake. The medieval peasant shows us mankind in the making, human nature in its elementary aspects. If we try to reckon up the things which he most truly enjoyed, we shall find that all, or nearly all, are common to all countries and ages—earth's bosom, the sun and clouds and rain, the inexhaustible love and endurance of the human heart:

> I said it in the meadow path,
>   I said it on the mountain stairs—
> The best things any mortal hath
>   Are those which every mortal shares[1].

Those simple things the peasant enjoyed as we do; and, if this simplicity shows his faults naked and unabashed, it is equally transparent of courage and moral beauty. That the life of the medieval village had a true dignity at its best, and even a true glory in the highest sense of that word, no man can doubt who reads Chaucer's brief description of the Ploughman. Here we have the least cultured stratum of society in that day, even though the Ploughman was, by his calling, near the top of that lowest stratum. We cannot escape from the significance of that public judgement, all the more damning because of its impersonal and unconscious character, which has transmuted *villanus* into *villain*, and *Bauer* into *boor*. Polite speech, as early

[1] Lucy Larcomb, in *Songs of Faith, Nature, and Comradeship*, No. 36. The writer is a manual worker, who in Chaucer's day would probably have been what the present writer and reader might also have been, a serf.

as the thirteenth century, used the word *village* to characterize coarseness of thought and deed[1]. Yet nobody who knows the modern peasant can doubt that, if we could travel back, we should find many comparisons humiliating to ourselves in the lives of these "poor folk in cottages, charged with children and chief lord's rent." This sort of family, in quite recent times, has begun to supply the universities with some of their best stuff; and this sort, in the Middle Ages, formed a village aristocracy not of rank but of merit. Here and there the medieval peasant bought his freedom and took to learning; it is possible, though far from certain, that this happened even more frequently than in the seventeenth century, when so many yeomen's sons did the like. But, in the vast majority of cases, these medieval peasants pursued the even tenor of their way, from cradle to grave, along their native fields and lanes. We may conclude— and to me no other conclusion seems possible—that the modern labourer is better off, even materially, than these men, and incomparably superior in social, political and religious liberty; but this should not make us forget how truly, in every age, the Kingdom of Heaven is within a man. We may keep our thoughts sweet by reading and re-reading what Chaucer tells us concerning the Poor Parson's brother:

> With him ther was a Plowman, was his brother,
> That hadde y-lad of dong ful many a fother,
> A trewë swinker and a good was he,
> Livinge in pees and parfit charitee.
> God loved he best with al his holë herte
> At allë tymes, thogh him gamëd or smerte,
> And thanne his neighëbour right as him-selve.
> He woldë thresshe, and therto dyke and delve,
> For Cristës sake, for every poorë wight,
> Withouten hyre, if it lay in his might.
> His tythës payëd he ful faire and wel,
> Bothe of his proprë swink and his catel.
> In a tabard he rood upon a mere.

For the land is eternally healthy, and we suffer when we feel the least divorce or estrangement from it. But, so long as urban life and village life exist, the peasant will always be a child com-

---

[1] Alwin Schultz, *Höfisches Leben*, 2nd ed. 1889, I, 156. *Dörperie* was used in the language of German chivalry as *villenie* in French.

pared with the city-dweller. The contrast was clearly marked even 600 years ago, in spite of what Maitland has taught us concerning the strong agricultural elements in the urban civilization of those days. This gulf has since widened, and it becomes enormous if we regard the medieval village solely through modern spectacles. It was W. H. Riehl, I think, who made exhaustive researches and found that the German peasant-farmer of about 100 years ago had a vocabulary of only 600 words, all told. Mr Tawney suggests that most medieval villagers saw no more than a hundred separate individuals in the course of their whole lives[1]. There is a deep abyss between these men and the modern villager with his bicycle and picture-palace, and perhaps with his memories of strange lands and folk in the Great War. As compared with him, we must repeat the word, medieval peasants were children. We should find even Chaucer's Ploughman a child in his serene unconscious con-servatism and dead-weight of inattention, concentrated on his own things in his own little corner, while we vainly dangle a crown of more complicated civilization over his head—yet child-like, again, in his divine receptivity at sudden moments, and in his resolve to take the kingdom of glory by force. We should find in him the child's April moods of sunshine and shower; a nature sometimes hidebound and selfish and narrow to the last degree, and sometimes generously impulsive; with the child's pathetic trust at one moment, and unreasonable distrust at another; and, above all, with a child's fear of the dark[2]. The modern peasant often retains a faith which is no longer the

---

[1] *L.c.* p. 264. The isolation may be exaggerated in this sentence, but not much.

[2] Compare what Sensier tells us of the peasant-painter, J. F. Millet, in his beloved forest of Fontainebleau: " Il revoyait toujours l'homme du passé dans ces antiques contrées, l'homme sauvage, heureux de vivre sous ces ramures paisibles. Puis, quand le soleil baissait, venaient et revenaient les légendes. Son imagination prenait la teinte décroissante du jour. Il expli-quait les terreurs populaires avec la lucidité du voyant. 'N'entendez-vouz pas le sabbat des sorcières, là-bas, au fond du Bas-Bréau, les cris des enfants qu'on étrangle, les rires des forcenés? Eh bien! ce n'est pourtant que le chant des oiseaux de nuit et le dernier cri des corbeaux. Tout jette l'effroi et la peur, quand la nuit, cette grande inconnue, succède à la lumière. Toutes les légen-des ont une source de vérité. Et si j'avais à peindre une forêt, je ne voudrais pas qu'on pensât aux émeraudes, aux topazes, à tout un écrin de couleurs précieuses, mais à ses verdures, à ses sombretés qui dilatent ou étreignent le cœur de l'homme'" (p. 219).

townsman's; so did the medieval peasant keep, in essence, much of his pre-Christian faith[1]. Simple, therefore, was his life as compared not only with ours but even with his own brother's in the little white-walled town; but simple it could not remain, since the way of human life runs from complexity to fresh complexities. Moreover, that which seems so simple to us often seemed complex to them, and was in fact very complicated in comparison with Stone Age conditions. In the sixteenth century, the whole balance of the western world changed, and nothing could have kept it entirely stationary. It was

a new order of things...an awakening of new life; the world revolved in a different orbit, determined by influences unknown before. After many ages persuaded of the headlong decline and impending dissolution of society and governed by usage and the will of masters who were in their graves, the sixteenth century went forth armed for untried experience, and ready to watch with hopefulness a prospect of incalculable change. That forward movement divides it broadly from the older world[2].

It went forth armed for untried experience, as every generation must, more or less definitely, go forth. Whether we like it or not, whether we allow or refuse the name of *progress* to what goes on, the world's story is that of a daily-repeated Paradise Lost and Paradise Regained: for even a paradise that never existed may yet be a true Paradise Lost to some most honourable minds. Here, therefore, we may look to Milton, and conclude with him on that note of naked realism, yet of hope that maketh not ashamed. Nothing is to be gained by looking back, except the eternal lesson of thanks to those who set us a glorious example of struggle for better things, and the lesson of bitterly-wholesome reflections upon their failures. It must now be a new Eden, and not the old; that gate, once passed, is now and henceforth "with dreadful faces throng'd and fiery arms." In front lies a world of hard work and repeated failure, or, at best, of successes for which we need to be consoled almost as truly as for failures. Nothing useful is to be got from this world of reality but what we wring from it in the sweat of our brow. It is no walled garden of innocent and sheltering ease; but it is a

---

[1] See App. 40. [2] Lord Acton, *Inaugural Lecture on the Study of History*.

forward land in which our path follows the sun: "What, are you stepping westward!" And, in every generation, stout and resolute hearts march forward here with the sober courage of our first parents, poetic in their naked need and simplicity:

> Some natural tears they dropt, but wiped them soon;
> The world was all before them, where to choose
> Their place of rest, and Providence their guide:
> They, hand in hand, with wandering steps and slow
> Through Eden took their solitary way.

APPENDIXES

I

(Chap. I, p. 11)

THE WORKER'S LOT

MANY readers will be glad to compare my text with the judgements of other scholars on the matters there treated. I have arranged these in two categories: (a) summaries by modern scholars of the evidence supplied on these points by medieval preachers or monastic records, and (b) summaries by first-rate specialists who take their evidence from all sources. Five at least of the writers are orthodox Roman Catholics—Bourgain, Lecoy, Schönbach, Arx and Robiou.

L. Bourgain, *La chaire française au xii* siècle. 1879. pp. 297–9.

Les seigneurs rencontraient une résistance vigoureuse dans les églises et dans les monastères: ils disposaient à leur gré des gens de la campagne. "Les paysans qui travaillent pour tous, qui se fatiguent dans tous les temps, par toutes les saisons, qui se livrent à des œuvres serviles dédaignées par leurs maîtres, sont incessamment accablés, et cela, pour suffire à la vie, aux vêtements, aux frivolités des autres!... On les poursuit par l'incendie, par la rapine, par le glaive; on les jette dans les prisons et dans les fers, puis on les contraint de se racheter, ou bien on les tue violemment par la faim, on les livre à tous les genres de supplices....Les pauvres crient, les veuves pleurent, les orphelins gémissent, les suppliciés repandent leur sang!"[1]
Les seigneurs prélèvent la taille (*exactio extraordinaria*) avec une exigence barbare. Nous avons comme une plainte de ces pauvres serfs courbés sous le poids de la servitude et trop longtemps restés à la merci de leurs maîtres: *talliabiles ad misericordiam et nutum!* "Ces hommes ont des griffes; ils s'étudient à tondre leurs sujets. Ils habitent avec des bêtes féroces, c'est-à-dire qu'ils s'associent des complices cruels et sauvages comme eux. Ils dévorent leurs sujets, gens simples comme des agneaux, par la taille et par les exactions"[2].
L'Église reconnaît leurs droits; elle prêche l'obéissance légitime: "Bone gens, rendés a vostre segnor terrien ço que vos li devés: vos devés croire et entendre que a vostre segnor terrien devés vos cens et tailles, forfais, servises, carrois, os, cevaucies. Rendés li tot en leu et

---

[1] Geoffroy de Troyes, MS. lat. 13586, fo. 86.

[2] "Hoc faciunt ut subditos, simplices, pullos, et agnos, per tallias et exactiones devorent." Anonyme, MS. lat. 16506, f. 133.

en tens salvement"[1]. Mais sa voix, protectrice des opprimés, s'élève et demande justice de pareilles oppressions; rien ne peut l'étouffer; elle declare qu'elle vengera toujours la veuve et l'orphelin. Elle accuse avec sévérité les prêtres qui demeurent insensibles à la vue des villages dépeuplés et de la dévastation générale[2]; qui ménagent le tyran parce qu'ils tiennent sans doute à le visiter dans ses châteaux, à se promener dans ses parcs, à labourer ses terres. "Non, je ne puis pas le dire sans verser des larmes, nous les chefs de l'Église, nous sommes plus timides que les disciples grossiers du Christ, à l'époque de l'Église naissante. Nous nions ou nous taisons la vérité par crainte des séculiers; nous nions le Christ, la Vérité même! Quand le ravisseur s'abat sur le pauvre, nous refusons de porter secours à ce pauvre. Quand un seigneur tourmente le pupille ou la veuve, nous n'allons pas à l'encontre: le Christ est sur la croix, et nous gardons le silence!"[3] "Quels sont ces loups? Des tyrans, des ravisseurs qui, entraînés par leurs convoitises, poussés par leurs passions, dévastent les bergeries du Seigneur, dépouillent les veuves et les orphelins, proscrivent les pauvres....Et le prêtre fuit comme un mercenaire, par amour de la flatterie, ou par crainte de la persécution! Qui abandonnent-ils donc ainsi? La droiture de la justice, la défense de l'Église, la liberté de la patrie, la vengeance du pupille et de la veuve!"[4]

Hélas! cette voix généreuse fut trop souvent impuissante à prévenir le crime....

A. Lecoy de la Marche, *La chaire française au moyen âge, spécialement au xiiie siècle*, 2me éd. 1886. pp. 424-5.

Au xiiie siècle comme toujours, on retrouve chez le villageois l'envie, la convoitise du bien de son voisin. Il manque rarement de tracer un petit sillon en dehors de son champ, de reculer à droite ou à gauche les bornes de son pré. Mais la grande plaie qui le ronge, plaie que la difficulté des communications rend parfois incurable, c'est l'ignorance. Quelques manants vivent tellement confinés au fond des bois, qu'ils ne savent même pas l'Oraison dominicale; d'autres sont assez étrangers au cours du temps pour n'avoir pas la première notion des jours où tombent les fêtes. Heureux encore ceux qui ont pour les reconnaître un signe matériel, comme les habitants de certain hameau, où demeurait un vieillard, un ancien, très au courant sur ce point, et servant à tout le pays de calendrier vivant. Quand il se chaussait autrement qu'à l'ordinaire, on se disait: "Il faut chômer aujourd'hui: maître Gosselin a mis ses chausses rouges (caligas suas rubeas)"[5]. C'est dans les régions de montagnes que le mal était le plus grave: car

---

[1] Maurice de Sully, MS. fr. 13314, Sermon du 23e dimanche après la Pentecôte.
[2] "Ubique exterminium," Anonyme, *Opp. S. Bernardi*, v, 1480.
[3] Raoul Ardent, 71^a h, in *Epist. et Evang.* 1^a pars.
[4] Anonyme, *Opp. S. Bernardi*, v, 1479.
[5] MS. lat. 15970, f. 425; 17509, f. 124.

il y avait là des hommes qui restaient des saisons entières privés de tout rapport avec leurs semblables....

L'ignorance enfante naturellement la superstition. Une foule de vieilles pratiques païennes s'étaient depuis longtemps réfugiées chez les paysans (*pagani*), et s'y conservaient plus ou moins défigurées. Elles étaient répandues dans la masse du peuple; mais leur principal asile était les campagnes, d'où les curés et les missionnaires s'efforçaient en vain de les extirper.

Oberlehrer Dr Gärtner, *Berthold v. Regensburg.* (Zittau 1890.) p. 23. (The notes refer to F. Pfeiffer's ed. of Berthold's sermons, 1880.)

Ein recht unerfreuliches Bild der gesellschaftlichen Zustände jener Zeit gibt auch das, was Berthold über das Verhältnis zwischen Arbeitern und Arbeitgebern sagt. Schlechte Arbeiter und Dienstboten hat es freilich immer gegeben: Dienstboten, welche ihre Herrschaft bestehlen, Wollespinnerinnen, welche einen Teil des Gesponnenen zurückbehalten, Schnitterinnen, welche sich Getreide aneignen, Arbeiter, welche " gar gut arbeiten, so lange es der Herr sieht, sobald er aber den Rücken kehrt, die halbe Zeit müssig stehen und plaudern," oder welche bei Akkordarbeit (wie sie damals besonders bei Zimmer- und Steinmetzarbeit gebräuchlich war) so schnell als möglich fertig zu werden suchen, so dass ihr Werk "in ein oder zwei Jahren einfällt"[1]—solche also hat man zu allen Zeiten gefunden, und die Klagen Bertholds geben uns noch kein Recht zu der Behauptung, dass es damals in dieser Beziehung besonders schlecht bestellt gewesen wäre. Dagegen waren in jener gewaltthätigen Zeit, welche dem Armen den nötigen Schutz versagte, die Dienstboten und Arbeiter der rücksichtslosen Ausbeutung und Bedrückung seitens ihrer Herren preisgegeben. Diese gaben ihnen nicht genug zu essen und setzten ihnen "eine Schüssel vor wie eine Katzenschüssel," sie liessen ihnen nicht genug Zeit zur Mahlzeit, und was noch schlimmer war, enthielten ihnen den erarbeiteten Lohn vor, oder benützten ihre Notlage, um ihnen einen Vorschuss zu geben, den sie dann doppelt abarbeiten mussten. Berthold wünscht deshalb, dass die in einigen Ländern herrschende Sitte, dass der, welcher zur Auszahlung des erarbeiteten Lohnes erst durch eine Klage genötigt werden muss, eine Busse von 6 Schillingen geben musste, auch in Süddeutschland eingeführt würde[2].

Die gegebenen Ausführungen zeigen, dass die Lage des Volks zu Bertholds Zeit eine recht traurige war. Schutzlos—denn die Rechtspflege versagte, wo sie hätte eingreifen sollen—stand es den Bedrückungen der Herren gegenüber, und diese steigerten nicht nur ihre rechtlich begründeten Forderungen ins Maasslose, sondern fügten noch ungerechte Auflagen hinzu; unter ihren Fehden gingen Hab und Gut des Landmannes zu Grunde, was ihm aber noch blieb, das fiel oft

[1] 1, 479, 5 ff.; 84, 25 ff.; 87, 3 ff.; 17, 6 ff.; 85, 2 ff.; 147, 15 ff.
[2] 1, 90, 7 ff.; 107, 33 ff.

genug in die Hände des Wucherers oder Betrügers[1]. Hierzu kamen schwere Krankheiten, welche ganze Volkskreise heimsuchten und um so drückender empfunden wurden, je seltner gute Ärzte waren und je kostspieliger ihre Hülfe zu erlangen war, wenn nicht einzelnen Krankheiten überhaupt, wie dem Aussatz und der Epilepsie, welche beide als ansteckend galten, die arztliche Kunst ratlos gegenüberstand[2].

Welcher Gegensatz, wenn wir von der Masse des Volks unsern Blick auf die vornehmen Herren in ihren Burgen und die Bürger in den aufblühenden Städten richten! Was der Landmann erarbeitet, das kommt zum grossen Teil seinem Herr zu gute oder fliesst als Gewinn aus Handel und Gewerbe in die Taschen des Städters.

Prof. E. Bernhardt, *Bruder Berthold v. Regensburg.* (Erfurt 1905.) pp. 54, 59–61.

Verwerflich ist einem bedrängten Landmann sein Korn abzukaufen, ehe es gesät ist, den Wein, ehe er geblüht hat (1, 418, 20) oder sich gegen ein dargeliehenes Malter Korn anderthalb nach der Ernte auszubedingen; kann der Bauer dann nicht zahlen, so werden ihm die Ochsen vom Pfluge genommen (1, 258, 3)....Da nun die die gesellschaftliche Ordnung auf Gottes Willen berecht, so soll der Niedere nicht murren und nicht höheren Stand wünschen (1, 14, 4; 15, 271, 14).

Daneben aber beklagt Berthold oft die gedrückte Lage der Armen. ...Betrug in Handel und Wandel schädigt gerade sie am meisten (1, 17, 13; II, 119, 33). Ihre Arbeit wird schlecht bezahlt (1, 58, 38), ihre Not wohl gar ausgebeutet, wie die der armen Spinnerin (1, 108, 4). Nach einem Leben voll mühseliger Arbeit, wie wenig haben sie oft zusammengebracht! Da hat einer dreissig Jahre gearbeitet und sollte hundert Pfund haben, hat aber kaum zehn und weniger (II, 236, 14); der Habgierige, der Richter, der Vogt, der Scherge haben es ihm *abgebrochen.* "Da sitzt mancher vor meinen Augen," heisst es (1, 58, 18), "der jetzt von seinen Arbeiten hundert Pfund haben sollte; der hat nicht so viel, dass er sich vor dem Froste schützen kann, und mancher ist in diesem kalten Winterwetter barfuss und in dünnem Gewande hergelaufen." Tragen die Armen ihr Los demütig und geduldig, so ist ihnen der himmlische Lohn gewiss, den "Abbrechern" die ewige Pein....

Den Dienstboten wird als erste Pflicht die Treue, d.h. Ehrlichkeit, empfohlen, und mancherlei Untreue wird gerügt (1, 84, 25). Der Knecht oder die Dirne entwendet und verkauft Butter, Korn, Fleisch u.s.w.; am Morgen, wo sie das Vaterunser beten sollten, begiessen sie das ihnen bestimmte Brot mit Fett. Vor den Augen des Herrn sind sie

[1] Man sieht, dass schon zu Bertholds Zeit die Keime zu jenen Zuständen vorhanden sind, welche später zu den Aufständen der Bauern führten. Eine gute Zusammenstellung dieser Verhältnisse gibt Wilh. Vogt, *Die Vorgesch. des Bauernkrieges,* Halle, 1887.

[2] Über die Ärzte der damaligen Zeit, über die Art ihrer Behandlung und über einzelne Krankheiten spricht Berthold, 1, 154, 8 ff.; 509, 26 ff.; 514, 38 f.; 517, 26 ff.; II, 49, 20 ff.

fleissig, wendet er den Rücken, so beginnt müssiges Geschwätz, und zwei oder drei vollbringen kaum die Arbeit, die einer hätte bewältigen können (1, 176). Ebenso steht es oft mit den Tagelöhnern: hinter der Schnitterin, der alten Diebin, geht ein junges Dieblein einher, dem sie eine Hand voll Ähren nach der andern in die Furche drückt. Die Drescher stehlen Korn, die Spinnerin einen Teil der Wolle, worauf sie, um das Gewicht voll zu machen, die übrige anfeuchtet (1, 84, 479).

Other sayings of Berthold, from A. Schönbach, *Stud. z. Gesch. d. altdeutschen Predigt*, achtes Stück. (Wien 1907.)

Capitalists, says Berthold, are often conscious of their community of interest (p. 49). It is almost impossible for them to live without fraud (p. 51):

for they themselves confess "if we will not lie or cheat, we can sell nothing"; this is the devil's mark, the Sign of the Beast, which his merchants commonly bear whithersoever they go upon earth.

As to the poor (p. 53):

When ye preach unto them, say "Ye countryfolk and artisans and servants, ye are in the true way of great saints, in hardship of life"; and here add much, describing the hard life they lead; and then say "Yet scarce one of you is sainted; I say not *saved*, but *sainted*, so that your holy-day is kept; whereas many from all other conditions have been sainted."

And he explains why:

They are simple and roughly-fed, and many perish and go from poverty to poverty; for they do divers evil deeds. For among them flourish the greatest lies, perjuries, revilings, curses, thefts, witch-crafts, frauds; nay, and even heresies. Wherefore? because they are anxious only for this present life, like brute beasts, and care not for God. On holy-days they would rather haunt the dance and so forth than the Mass or the true God; that, brief though it be, is too long for them.

And they are hardly treated (p. 56):

Do not as some do, who, when their servants fall sick, cast them forth after two or three days from their house and let them die; or, if they keep one, it is to thrust him under the stairs like a dog, and to use him no better than a dog....Some men [of the better classes] will not do any good deed whatsoever. Thou demandest of thy servant—to whom thou givest twenty shillings [a year]—and thou wilt that he should be ready, night and day, to serve thee at all points....Nay, some are so avaricious that they would be served as heartily as by brute beasts, yet cannot endure to see their servants eating heartily,...they love to see them work hard, before and after dinner, but not to see them eat hard.

Again, it is either Berthold or a contemporary who says to his audience "many folk, for a mere word, beat and strangle their servingmen and maidservants" (A. Schönbach, *Ueber eine Grazer Handschrift*. Graz, 1890. p. 130). Compare the praise which the contemporary Salimbene gives to his own mother: "Never was she seen to be wroth; never did she smite any of her maidservants with her hand" (*M.G.H.* xxxII, 55; I have quoted analogous evidence at the beginning of Chapter II of *From St Francis to Dante*).

Ildefons v. Arx, *St-Gallen*, I, 52 ff.

The second, and far most numerous, class of the population were the serfs, who were considered unfit for war, and were only kept steadily to field-work.... Their lord could exchange, give away, buy, or let them out on hire, in which case their stature was measured, and the [average] serf was valued at 25 acres of land. But usually they were conveyed with the little holding which they held and tilled. Many serfs earned possessions of their own on their holdings, and even bought serfs of their own. Yet, in spite of this, the lord inherited the greater part of their property at death, especially the cattle and the clothes. Since the serfs were thus very profitable to the lord, he who slew a serf must pay the master an equivalent sum; but to the magistrates he paid a smaller fine than if he had slain a freeman. As a freeman might come into servitude through poverty, especially if he could not pay the fine inflicted for some offence, so, on the other hand, might a serf buy his freedom; but emancipations by this or any other means were rare in these parts....

Serfdom was the fundamental basis on which the economy and prosperity of a monastery or a rich lord rested.... The abbey of St-Gall possessed several hundreds. [Some lived within the precincts as servants, artisans, herdsmen, etc.; others on the outlying farms, scattered not only over south-west Germany, but even as far as Alsace, France and Italy; in each district there was a monk and a bailiff deputed to rule over them]....(P. 161). Seldom was a serf given his freedom, as, for instance, when he was allowed to take priests' Orders[1]. Brunwart is an example of this; he had been a serf of the abbey, and became priest, bishop, and apostle to the Hungarians. When the serf was allowed to buy his liberty the price was very high; for instance, one gave a woman with her holding and ten other serfs; and then, even as a freedman, he must pay his former capitation-tax of two silver pennies[2]. Those who claimed freedom unjustly were prosecuted; we find one buying off a claim of this kind by paying four acres of land. When a freeman had unknowingly married a bondwoman, he bought his two children by her

[1] Author's note: "At St-Gall there is no instance of such a manumission during this period" [820–920 A.D.].

[2] This was in strict conformity to early Church law; it was prescribed that, even when a Church serf had been manumitted, he must still remain a tributary and dependent of that Church: see appendix 27. (G. G. C.)

at the price of two silver pennies, and four days' labour, per annum; otherwise, according to Swabian law, he must have divided them with the abbey, taking one as a freeman to himself while the other went to the monks as a serf. The freeman was distinguished by his long beard; the serf's was clipped. A noble would have thought himself humiliated if he had taken off his hat to a serf. But these men's lot was much softened by the fact that they need never feel anxiety at the growth of their families, nor were they tortured with cares for food, since the bondman's family had seldom less than a holding of forty acres for its sustenance[1].

In his second volume, reviewing the social conditions between 1300 and 1429, v. Arx returns to this subject (pp. 164 ff.):

The lords had, indeed, been compelled by the pressure of the spirit of their times to give up a good deal of the roughness of serfdom. They no longer claimed to be universal heirs of their men, but allowed children to inherit from their parents or the nearest relatives from their kinsfolk. They still took the whole property of such as died without wife or children; they still gave only one-third of the husband's belongings to his widow[2]; they still inherited the whole property, movable and immovable, of the unmarried[2], and from those dependent tenants who died outside the district they took all personal and a third of the real property[2]. In order to avoid dividing the children, they restricted marriages within the circle of their own lordship, and punished those who broke the law by marrying into outside manors by deprivation of holdings, withdrawal of inheritances, corporal punishment and fine[3]. This severity was not without its reasons; for such outside marriages might easily have involved the different lords in disputes and compelled them to divide the children, which some could not concede, since they, like the abbey of Pfäfers, regarded as their own all that were born on their land or from their own men and women. They laid no hindrance in the way of marriages within their lordship, except that the contracting parties must ask leave or pay a fine of five shillings. This law against outside marriages pressed very hard upon the serfs of lords who had but few subjects; but these softened it by easily allowing their women to buy themselves from their service into that of the

[1] This was true only so long as the population was kept fairly stationary by wars, plagues, etc.; and, even then, it makes no allowance for the too frequent famine-years recorded in the chronicles, of which the dim memory survives in many of Grimm's *Tales*. (G. G. C.)

[2] The author exemplifies all these three cases from the archives of the abbey of St-Gall. By not marrying, the serf deprived the monastery of so much potential live-stock in the shape of bondfolk in the next generation. (G. G. C.)

[3] From the Golden Book of the abbey of Pfäfers: "Whosoever of either sex shall marry outside his own lordship, or shall in any other way escape from our monastery, all his holdings and goods held from the abbey are forthwith forfeited to us, and the abbot may and ought to punish him, without any contradiction, in body, goods and possessions, according to his own will."

bridegroom's lord[1]; or again they concluded the covenant called Robbery and Exchange [*Raub und Wechsel*], whereby intermarriage between two lordships was unhindered, and the bride and children belonged to that of the bridegroom, so long as he had given to the bride's lord, before the marriage, three shillings and a pair of gloves for his "robbery" in thus removing her. The abbey of St-Gall, to the profit of its serfs, concluded this covenant with all its vassals and neighbours, and with many other monasteries. The abbey of Pfäfers had also done the same with many religious houses....

(P. 171.) Since lords found so much profit in their serfs, each tried to get as many as he could[2]. These were therefore among the most frequent articles of commerce; and fourteenth century documents are full of deeds whereby one lord bought[3], exchanged, leased or pledged[4] bondfolk.... For this reason men were seldom released from serfdom, not even clergy[5]. On the contrary, these were even worse off than others in testamentary matters. For their lords, who had the immemorial right of inheriting from them as bachelors, continued still to take all that they left, even after they had allowed collateral relations [in other cases] to inherit. But afterwards the abbots of St-Gallen and Pfäfers contented themselves with a small sum called technically *spolium*, and allowed the clergy to leave property by will[6].

On p. 176, v. Arx records other instances of the monks' tenacity of their legal rights; but he leaves the same general impression which may be gathered from other sources, that tenants were, on the whole, rather better off on monastic estates than on others.

In his third volume, dealing with the Reformation period, he deals briefly again with the serfs (pp. 280 ff.): "Serfdom, which from

[1] *E.g.* in 1441 Peter Häf gave Walther v. Münchwil two oxen in order that his bride might pass from Walther's lordship to that of the monastery of St Johann.

[2] *E.g.* Heinrich Göldli of Zürich bought 127 serfs, whom Hermann v. Laudenberg-Werdegg had received on lease from St-Gallen.

[3] Their values varied much. The abbey of St-Gall bought one for five pounds. In 1392, it gave Edel v. Altstädten 327 pounds for five households which had migrated from Lüchingen to Härdern.

[4] Abbot George pawned Morshuber's family in 1373 for 20 pounds. [A lay lord pledged 14 families, two years later, for only £13. 13*s*.]

[5] Johann Koch, parish priest of Wil, in 1359, gave 18 pounds to Bernard Schenk of Landegg, whose bondman he was, for permission to return to the lordship of the abbey of St-Gall.

[6] The author gives two cases in which the monks allowed children to inherit from their fathers, parish priests, reserving to themselves a considerable share in the second case. The priest, of course, counted as a bachelor for all legal purposes. Such cases could not have occurred in England, where the serf, once manumitted by benefit of clergy or otherwise, was really a freeman, no longer bound by the earlier canon law which made complete freedom impossible in most cases where the Church had once been interested. (G. G. C.)

century to century had lost something of its old severity, was almost altogether abolished by the Reformation and the humaner spirit of the time"[1].

H. Sée, *Classes rurales*, p. 637. Summary of conclusions which he has argued out on pp. 537–557.

Arguments in favour of the prosperity of the medieval peasant; the part played by the Church; the numbers of the population. Fragility of these arguments. Other more trustworthy sources of information as to the material condition of the country folk; methods of cultivation, dwellings, furniture, dress, and food. These tend to show that, in general, the peasant's life is wretched enough (*assez misérable*). The rich or well-to-do peasant is only exceptional. Insecurity, perhaps even more than the burdens of the manorial system, contribute to make the peasant's life painful. The peasant's moral character, according to literary sources; the serf is despised by the upper classes.

H. Sée, *Classes rurales*, pp. 538 ff.

If the statistical data are not very certain, if scientific conditions permit the historian only to formulate hypotheses, this does not mean that all hypotheses are equally legitimate. Some of them, for instance, are inspired by preoccupations with which science has evidently nothing to do. Thus certain writers who, in their dislike of the society which has sprung from the French Revolution, have found a false and imaginary ideal of the Middle Ages, spend much ingenuity in proving that the peasant was very happy in feudal times. M. Lecoy de la Marche declares that there has been no sensible progress in their condition since the Middle Ages; he almost seems to think that, because the Church was all-powerful then, therefore the peasant was happy. [Reference to an article by this author in *Le Correspondant*, 1884, Nouv. Série, t. 101, pp. 499 *sq.*] Such also is M. P. Allard's thesis [*Esclaves, Serfs, et Mainmortables*, 1884]: according to him, it was to the Church that the peasants owed all their progress; the disappearance of slavery and the suppression or softening of serfdom. In reality, as we have seen, the manorial system was essential to ecclesiastical landlords, and they exploited their peasants no less harshly than laymen. The fact that the medieval Church exercised an undisputed empire over men's souls is no proof that the economic condition of the country folk was satisfactory.

The study of the manorial system shows indisputably that the

---

[1] He has tried to hold the balance evenly between the two parties; see the long note, II, 511, beginning "There will never be a unanimous verdict on the question whether the Reformation was a fortunate or an unfortunate event, so long as there are Catholics and Protestants." In this third volume he traces the gradual extinction of the medieval ideas of serfdom. (G. G. C.)

innumerable dues and services imposed by the landlords absorbed the greater part of the tiller's revenues and reduced the profits of his labour to a minimum. When we study all the manifestations of seignorial exploitation, it seems that the peasants must have led a somewhat miserable life.... The yield of the land was not rich; it may be estimated at about half or one-third of a present-day crop.... The peasant's dwelling was scarcely more than a roughly-built hut...his furniture also was of great simplicity.... He was extremely dirty; his contemporaries, who themselves were not of the most refined cleanliness, constantly note this; indeed, living as he did, it was scarcely possible that he should have kept himself clean.... On a Norman manor, in 1312, the peasant who does a day's labour for his lord is to receive a loaf, peas for his pottage, either three eggs and a quarter of cheese, or six eggs; in Lententide, herrings and nuts instead; but the Norman peasants were particularly well-treated.

Sée notes that there were great differences at different times and places, and adds:

But, even admitting that at normal times the peasant enjoyed a tolerable existence, it cannot be denied that his condition was singularly aggravated by the insecurity to which he was condemned. In the Middle Ages, feudal wars were continual, and it was the country-folk who suffered worst.... This insecurity, which was one of the characteristics of medieval society, contributed perhaps even more than the burdens of the manorial system to render the peasant's life painful.

Finally,

M. Léopold Delisle notes very truly that it would be vain to seek moral purity among these peasant-folk; drunkenness was very common; marriages were treated simply as money-matters; adultery was frequent, and often it was the parson who seduced his parishioners. But it is evident that the morals of the upper classes were no better.... In general, the caste-spirit stifled all generous feelings [towards the peasant]. Medieval society was wholly military; it had nothing but scorn for the peasant, by whose hard work the clergy and nobility were fed. The Middle Ages honoured only the noble, who lived by exploiting the lower classes.

A. Luchaire, *Les communes françaises*. 1890. pp. 17–21. A fuller description of the French peasant's lot will be found in the same author's *Social France at the Time of Philip Augustus*. (Eng. trans. 1912.) pp. 392 ff.

On connaît l'obscur document qui, sous le nom généralement adopté de *poème satirique d'Adalbéron*[1], appartient aux premières années du

---

[1] *Historiens de la France*, t. x, et Migne, *Patrologie latine*, t. cxli. Traduit dans la collection Guizot, t. vi.

xie siècle. Ce dialogue curieux entre un roi de France et un de ses évêques nous apprend quelles idées avaient cours dans la société privilégiée, celle des nobles et des clercs, sur la "question sociale." L'évêque décrit les diverses conditions humaines et constate avec satisfaction que le monde est divisé en trois classes: ceux qui prient, ceux qui combattent, ceux qui travaillent. Mais cette répartition harmonieuse des hommes en trois castes bien définies, dont chacune avait sa fonction sociale, ne correspondait que très imparfaitement à la réalité. Au lieu de combattre pour protéger les autres, les nobles ne faisaient que se battre entre eux, piller les paysans, rançonner le marchand, pressurer odieusement l'ouvrier. Ils manquaient donc absolument à leur mission. Ceci est prouvé non seulement par les faits que rapportent les chroniqueurs, mais encore par les précautions que prenaient contre la féodalité ceux qui instituaient à la même époque la trêve de Dieu et les associations de paix.

Pendant que l'évêque Adalbéron préconisait, à son point de vue, en l'idéalisant, l'état de la société contemporaine, un autre évêque, Warin, de Beauvais, soumettait au roi Robert[1] le pacte de paix qu'il voulait faire jurer aux seigneurs. On y lisait les clauses suivantes: "Je n'enlèverai ni bœuf, ni vache, ni aucune autre bête de somme; je ne saisirai ni le paysan, ni la paysanne, ni les marchands; je ne prendrai point leurs deniers et je ne les obligerai point à se racheter. Je ne veux pas qu'ils perdent leur avoir à cause de la guerre de leur seigneur, et je ne les fouetterai point pour leur enlever leur subsistance. Depuis les calendes de mars jusqu'à la Toussaint, je ne saisirai ni cheval, ni jument, ni poulain dans les pâturages. Je ne démolirai ni n'incendierai les maisons; je ne détruirai pas les moulins et je ne ravirai pas la farine qui s'y trouve, à moins qu'ils ne soient situés dans ma terre ou que je ne sois à l'ost; je ne donnerai protection à aucun voleur."

On peut juger des habitudes de la classe seigneuriale par cette édifiante énumération de choses défendues. La phraséologie optimiste de l'évêque Adalbéron ne saurait nous faire illusion. En réalité, au début du xie siècle, l'opinion ne reconnaissait que deux classes d'hommes: celle des nobles et des clercs, qui dominait et exploitait les autres, et celle des serfs qui travaillaient pour nourrir et vêtir la noblesse et le clergé. Adalbéron ne fait point de distinction en parlant de cette dernière couche de la société; tous les travailleurs sont englobés sous le nom de serfs, parce qu'en effet le servage était encore à cette époque la condition de la grande majorité des populations urbaines et rurales. Quoi qu'en dise l'évêque, le sort de ces serfs était déplorable; autrement on ne pourrait s'expliquer les exclamations de commisération profonde que l'auteur du poème a placées dans la bouche du roi Robert. Mais il est certain aussi que, dès cette époque, la classe populaire avait manifesté quelques velléités de secouer le joug. Des tentatives d'affranchissement ont eu lieu, puisque l'évêque ajoute mélancoliquement: "Mais aujourd'hui les lois sont sans force, la tranquillité

---

[1] Pfister, *Études sur le règne de Robert le Pieux*, p. 170 et lx.

fuit de partout, les mœurs des hommes se corrompent, et tout ordre s'intervertit...."

L'insurrection normande fut générale et très étendue, puisque les assemblées des paysans eurent lieu dans plusieurs comtés de Normandie, sinon dans tous.... Ce soulèvement rural annonçait, par des analogies singulièrement étroites, les insurrections communalistes qui éclatèrent au xiie siècle parmi les paysans du Ponthieu et du Laonnais, et aboutirent à la formation de plusieurs communes collectives, fondées sur une fédération de villages et de hameaux....

Quoi qu'il en soit, l'explosion du mécontentement populaire se manifesta sur bien d'autres points : en Bretagne, où les paysans se concertèrent aussi pour une action commune ; dans la France du Nord, où la *Vie de saint Arnoul*, évêque de Soissons, nous fait connaître les meurtres et les pillages commis par la populace exaspérée.... Un des plus curieux documents qu'on puisse citer à cet égard est, sans contredit, le *Conte des Vilains de Verson*[1], récit en vers de l'insurrection d'un village du Calvados qui avait voulu s'affranchir des corvées et des redevances auxquelles il était assujetti envers l'abbaye du mont Saint-Michel.

L'auteur de ce petit poème est évidemment hostile à la cause populaire. Les détails qu'il donne au début de la pièce sur la révolte et sur le principal meneur sont obscurs et insuffisants. Ce qui fait l'intérêt du récit, c'est la liste détaillée des servitudes dont les malheureux villageois sont accablés. Il semblerait que l'énumération de ces iniquités et des souffrances qu'elles entraînaient dût émouvoir celui qui nous en fait le tableau. Au contraire, il redouble d'indignation contre les vilains insurgés : "Allez et faites-les payer.—Ils se doivent bien acquitter.— Allez et prenez leurs chevaux—prenez et vaches et veaux—car les vilains sont trop félons.—Sire, sachez que sous le firmament—je ne sais plus servile gent—que sont les vilains de Verson." La féodalité ne se contentait pas d'accabler le paysan : elle se vantait de ses propres excès et ne comprenait pas que la victime essayât de secouer le joug.

Le clergé, qui, en qualité de grand propriétaire féodal, bénéficiait aussi de la condition misérable faite à la classe populaire, fut de bonne heure obligé de prêcher l'obéissance à ces foules que l'esprit d'insubordination envahissait. "Bonnes gens," leur disait, du haut de la chaire, Maurice de Sulli, "rendez à votre seigneur terrien ce que vous lui devez. Vous devez croire et entendre qu'à votre seigneur terrien vous devez vos cens, tailles, forfaits, services, charrois et chevauchées. Rendez le tout, au lieu et au temps voulus, intégralement." Celui qui parle ainsi est, il est vrai, un évêque, un membre du clergé féodal. D'autres prédicateurs, au xiie et au xiiie siècle, songent moins à rappeler au peuple ses obligations, qu'à s'apitoyer sur ses souffrances, à dénoncer la cruauté des nobles et la lâcheté des clercs qui ne font rien pour protéger les opprimés. Ceux-là sont des moines. S'ils ne sortent

---

[1] *Musée des Arch. départ.* No. 97.

point tous du peuple, ils sont en contact journalier avec lui; ils ne craignent point de plaider sa cause auprès des puissants.

"Les paysans qui travaillent pour tous, dit Geoffroi de Troyes, qui se fatiguent dans tous les temps, par toutes les saisons, qui se livrent à des œuvres serviles dédaignées par leurs maîtres, sont incessamment accablés, et cela pour suffire à la vie, aux vêtements, aux frivolités des autres.... On les poursuit par l'incendie, par la rapine, par le glaive; on les jette dans les prisons et dans les fers, puis on les contraint de se racheter, ou bien on les tue violemment par la faim, on les livre à tous les genres de supplices.... Les pauvres crient, les veuves pleurent, les orphelins gémissent, les suppliciés répandent leur sang."

Voilà la féodalité jugée par le clergé monastique: il est vrai qu'elle finissait par porter sur elle-même un jugement tout aussi rigoureux. Les préambules des chartes que les rois ou les seigneurs accordent aux villes constituées en bourgeoisies privilégiées ou en communes contiennent, à cet égard, les aveux les plus significatifs. La charte de 1091 donnée par les comtes d'Amiens, Gui et Ive, débute comme il suit: "Considérant combien misérablement le peuple de Dieu, dans le comté d'Amiens, était affligé par les vicomtes de souffrances nouvelles et inouïes, semblables à celles du peuple d'Israël, opprimé en Égypte par les exacteurs de Pharaon, nous avons été émus du zèle de la charité; le cri des églises et le gémissement des fidèles nous ont touchés douloureusement." Louis VII confirme la commune de Mantes "à cause de l'oppression excessive sous laquelle les pauvres gémissaient." Il accorde une commune aux habitants de Compiègne "en raison des énormités commises par les clercs de cette ville." Les comtes de Ponthieu font de même pour les villes d'Abbeville et de Doullens, "afin de les soustraire aux dommages et aux exactions que les bourgeois ne cessaient d'éprouver de la part des seigneurs du pays."

On pourrait multiplier ces citations. Elles ne prouveraient pas toujours que les auteurs des chartes fussent réellement émus des souffrances du peuple. Ceux qui accordaient de tels privilèges n'oubliaient pas de se les faire payer chèrement par les mêmes bourgeois dont ils déploraient la condition misérable. Ces chartes n'en attestent pas moins l'oppression intolérable dont souffraient la classe urbaine et la population rurale.

Robiou, *Populations rurales*. p. 397.

Je serais désolé si aucun lecteur m'attribuait la pensée de vouloir faire considérer comme acceptable, à aucun degré, la condition civile des paysans du xiiie siècle, je ne dis pas dans le présent, ce qui serait de l'idiotisme pur et simple, mais même dans le passé. Toute restriction au droit de propriété est contraire au droit naturel, et au degré, quel qu'il soit, où elle existe, elle est un lamentable obstacle aux progrès économiques d'un pays. Le droit naturel était bien plus odieusement violé encore, même avec la servitude la plus douce et à d'autres égards presque nominale, par les restrictions apportées à la liberté des mariages. On l'explique avec toute vraisemblance, mais on ne la justifie en rien, quand on fait observer que l'on voulait retenir sur la terre sujette à redevance les enfants issus de ces unions et en garantir ainsi la culture. Ce qu'il est permis de retenir des précédentes observations, c'est que la propriété de la personne signifie souvent alors celle des redevances qu'elle est assujettie à payer. Mais si l'horreur que doit inspirer partout et toujours une atteinte portée par les lois ou par les mœurs à la liberté naturelle, doit nous rendre sévères pour le passé, elle ne doit pas nous rendre injustes ; et celui-là serait à plaindre qui ne trouverait pas un véritable soulagement à penser que, depuis longtemps déjà, quand le servage a cessé dans toute la France, le mal matériel et moral était en fait beaucoup moindre qu'on ne le croit communément, et que surtout il y avait un abîme entre le servage du moyen âge et l'esclavage antique, tel que l'ont pratiqué, pendant tant de siècles, les peuples de la Grèce et de Rome.

Seignobos, *Régime féodal*. pp. 58 ff.

§ III. *Rôle des vilains*.

Leur rôle est purement économique ; ils forment à peu près seuls la classe des agriculteurs. En Bourgogne, le cultivateur est rarement homme de commune, le noble ne touche jamais à la terre. Sauf la banlieue des villes fortes, tout le sol du duché est cultivé par les vilains. Ce sont eux qui labourent, travaillent la vigne, élèvent le bétail. Les listes dressées par les châtelains ou données dans les préambules des chartes d'affranchissement mentionnent parmi eux fort peu d'artisans. ...La classe des vilains nourrit donc les autres classes et c'est son unique fonction. Elle est l'assise sur laquelle est fondée la société active, elle n'est pas une partie de la société. Les paysans n'ont aucune place dans la société du moyen-âge ; ils ne paraissent ni dans ses assemblées, ni dans ses armées, ni dans ses tribunaux ; ils ne prennent part ni directement ni par délégués au gouvernement. Ils ne comptent pas pour elle ; et même quand le pouvoir voudra leur prendre de l'argent, ce n'est point eux qu'il consultera, il ne leur fera pas nommer de représentants, il s'adressera aux seigneurs pour obtenir la permission de taxer "leurs hommes." Dans les affaires de leur propre village ils n'ont aucun droit à intervenir. Ils n'ont "corps ni commune," ne peuvent s'assembler ni même nommer un procureur. "Tels personnes ne sont que propre chatelx au seigneur." Ce mot que la coutume applique aux serfs seulement, on peut l'étendre à tous les vilains. Tous sont la matière exploitée par les hommes des classes supérieures et rien de plus. C'est au-dessus de leurs têtes que fonctionne le gouvernement des hommes vraiment libres.

2

(Chap. II, p. 20 *note*)

THE FRENCH CUSTOM OF *DÉSAVEU*

In many parts of France, during the later Middle Ages, a serf might "disavow" his lord and march away, so long as he left his land and all his goods to the lord. He was thus, nominally, not tied to the soil; compare the German customs quoted on p. 48. But, for the practical working of this law, we must take account of what Seignobos writes (*Régime féodal*, pp. 50 ff.):

Le serf, en désavouant son seigneur renonce à la terre qu'il possédait dans son domaine.... Cette condition est le lien même qui attache le serf à son seigneur. En principe, il n'est pas esclave de la terre, puisqu'il a le droit de la quitter, ni du seigneur puisqu'il peut le désavouer. Mais le champ qu'il cultive de père en fils, son héritage, comme il l'appelle, est sa seule ressource. Que deviendrait cet homme avec sa famille, lui qui ne sait que cultiver, dans un pays où la terre est tout entière partagée en parcelles et où l'on n'a pas besoin d'ouvriers ruraux? Quand même les bourgeois l'admettraient à partager leurs privilèges, comment gagnerait-il sa vie? L'oppression est une calamité moins atroce que la faim; le paysan surtout aime mieux supporter l'une que de s'exposer à l'autre. Et puis le seigneur et le prévôt de son village sont moins à craindre que les juges criminels et leurs procédés sommaires. Dans une société qui traite l'homme sans feu ni lieu à l'égal du criminel, mieux vaut encore être serf que vagabond. Aussi faut-il des maux inouïs, que sa maison ait été détruite par les gens de guerre ou que les exactions le réduisent au désespoir, pour décider le vilain à abandonner sa terre....

Tant que ce gage reste au seigneur, il est fort à croire que l'homme reviendra de lui-même et reprendra sa servitude plutôt que de renoncer à son bien. S'il ne reparaît pas, la perte n'est pas grande; le seigneur a gardé la terre et trouve sans peine à la regarnir.... Le seigneur conserve donc un moyen efficace de retenir ses hommes. Mais ce qui était une garantie pour le maître était une protection pour le serf. Si précieuse que fût la terre aux yeux du paysan, il avait besoin qu'elle lui donnât de quoi vivre et nourrir sa famille, et quel que fût son amour pour son village, son horreur pour la vie errante, encore pouvait-il être poussé hors de son héritage par trop de dureté. Le seigneur est donc obligé à quelque modération, à n'exploiter et n'opprimer le serf que dans la mesure où la vie ne lui devient pas impossible ou intolérable.

The most favourable terms of *désaveu* in fourteenth and fifteenth century Burgundy are stated by J. Bertin, *Droit coutumier au M.-A.* Gray, 1898, pp. 5 ff. On the other hand, Chassin (*Serfs*, p. 36) shows how far this right had declined before the Revolution; "encore trois seulement des neuf Coutumes parlent-elles du désaveu, et elles en compliquent les formalités au point de le rendre à peu près impraticable."

3

(Chap. II, p. 17, cf. p. 44)

COMPLICATION OF SERVICES

It is sometimes argued that this grievance exists only in modern minds, and that the medieval peasant and landlord found no real difficulty here. Apart from innumerable other indications scattered about in medieval records, it is possible to meet this plea directly from the words of the Muri chronicler who wrote early in the twelfth century (*Origines Murensis Monasterii*, 1618, p. 44):

In the year of our Lord 1106 our predecessors, wishing to increase the possessions of this holy place, bought from this Rudolf [the heir of Guntran, a neighbouring tyrant] all that he had there, whether justly or unjustly, acquired, at the price of 200 pounds of silver. For this purpose they broke up here a golden chalice adorned with most precious stones and gems, and two silver crosses which the Countess Richilda of Lenzburg, sister to Count Wernher of Hapsburg, gave to this monastery, and they sold many very profitable farms and despoiled and stripped the monastery of almost all its substance, whether within or without. Here therefore let every man weigh in his own mind what happiness or profit may come to him, soul or body, from possessions so unrighteously gotten[1]; seeing that everyman ought to attend to the one question of so nourishing his body as not to lose his soul; and let him consider where is the profit if a robber steals and the monk eats [of his theft]. But let us leave these matters, whether righteously or unrighteously acquired, and let my little book set forth what substance we possess in this village.

There are, then, two courts[2], an upper and a lower. To the upper belongs so much field as can be rightly ploughed with two teams of oxen, and so also to the lower; in hay, the produce of 32 meadows. The peasants who have day-works are 22; some doing personal service, while others, paying rent, contribute all the rest that we have there as rent. Now this is the constitution of the above-named freemen. The rent is paid only by those who possess dwellings and tofts. For these may do what they will with their fields and meadows; they may sell or give to whomsoever they will as to their peers; yet none pays rent but those who have dwellings. Yet the disposition of the rent is so intricate that scarce any man can get himself clear[3]. So are all things

[1] The chronicler has told how this man had reduced groups of freemen on his estates to the condition of serfs: how these peasants had seized the occasion of a royal visit to Soleure: there "they began to cry aloud against this unjust oppression; but among such a multitude of princes, and by reason of the foolish words of some of the peasants, their cry came not unto the king, and they, who had come in evil case, returned home yet worse" (p. 43).

[2] *Curtes*, commonly used for a manorial farm.

[3] "Ita vero intricata est ratio census, ut vix aliquis possit se inde expedire," a memorable sentence, which might have been repeated on the majority of manors.

wont to be that arise from evil and from greed. A certain measure of spelt is imposed upon them [as rent], to wit, four bushels by the measure of Zürich and somewhat more. Some pay this rent in full, some the half, some the quarter, and others twofold or threefold or even sixfold, emptying the measure to the very bottom, in order to fulfil his due[1]. This diversity comes to pass whensoever some holding is left, and the heirs divide it among themselves; for each giveth so much for rent as he possesses öf the hereditament; and, in proportion as he gives rent, so also he ploughs and mows and reaps and works at the hedges, and gives hens and skeins of flax. When therefore they have to plough, it is measured for them with the rod wherewith the holdings[2] are measured; and this rod is marked according to each man's proportion; and, wheresoever the mark comes, there a peg of wood is fixed in the ground; and yet they [the peasants] plough at the first cutting and sowing. So also is it done in the meadows and the hedges. For he reaps the seed which he has sown; and oftentimes he has to spread out the hay which he mows. So, when he is told beforehand to mow the hay, if he do not cut it forthwith on the morrow, and if rain come, for that he suffers judgement. But if he cut it and the rain come, he suffers no judgement, but cuts the hay and prepares it all through and brings it to our stable with his own oxen. So also with the hens and the flax; the peasant brings all to the monastery. Those who live on this side of the torrent give two [pence?] for wood, and those who live beyond, one [penny?][3]. On the last day of December they pay a rent of oats, which also some give together, according to the aforesaid proportion of measure. All these dues were originally asked as a favour; now they are compulsory[4]. In early days there were freemen there, yea far more than now, because a certain pestilent man of that family [of Guntran], named Gerung, had sorely troubled them, and deceived them with fraud and power, and cast them forth from their hereditaments, and driven them from the district, wherefore also he himself was slain by them in after days.

The monastic chronicler comes again to these difficulties of labour and dues on p. 59, when he has to speak of the vineyards:

The constitution of vineyard labour has been often dropped and as often resumed; because, as often as we ourselves had to till them, we could not endure. But, whether we ourselves attend to the tillage, or the peasants, all things turn out toilsome—*laboriose proveniunt*—and need the greatest care and attention. For if we wish to cultivate them, we cannot endure; again, if the peasants take the care of the vines,

[1] The text is sometimes obscure and perhaps corrupt; here I have ventured to read *ut* for the *et* of my text, but without substantial change of sense.

[2] *Mansi*: corresponding to the English *yardland*, on a rough average, about 30 acres, enough to keep a peasant and his family well.

[3] The sum is omitted. At the end of the sentence, *citra* is an obvious misreading for *ultra*.

[4] "Ista omnia primitus fuerunt petibilia, modo sunt potentibilia," a sentence of deep import.

they do all things negligently and fraudulently, and defend them with lies; and all that they give by the constitution they themselves and their wives and children consume.

He then enters into the complicated services of the vinedressers, from which it is easy to see how much friction there must have been between two parties whose interests were so sharply opposed. We are doubtless to understand these words above, *cuncta quae constitutione dant*, in the sense of "all that they *ought to* give by the constitution."

Let us take, again, an extract from the Glastonbury customal exemplifying the very frequent complication of services (*Lib. H. de Soliaco*, Som. Rec. Soc. 1882, p. 16):

John Pese (of Lympsham, page 77) held a virgate for xxx pence in money and in work on the lord's demesne, from Michaelmas to Martinmas (Nov. 11) to plough one acre for winter corn, and half an acre for spring corn when called upon, and to harrow every Monday in the year one hand-work, except on annual solemnities. To carry loads three times to Glaston[bury], to mow and carry three boon-days, and to go to vineyard. If John Pese preferred to pay his xxx pence in work instead of in cash, his holding then ran as follows: From Michaelmas to Martinmas to plough one acre, besides another whenever called upon, every week. From Martinmas to Hock-day (second Tuesday after Easter) to plough and harrow half an acre every Monday. From Hock-day to Aug. 1st, three "hand-works" every week. After Aug. 1st, in harvest time, to cut half an acre every Monday, Tuesday, Wednesday and Friday. Three Bed-ripes on three Thursdays. To have every day, on leaving off work, his bundle of corn, and to find a sumpter or pack-horse whenever called upon. At Hock-day to subscribe a penny towards a sheep (?). At St Martin's to pay half a day's work as Church-set, and at Michaelmas 5d. land-tax. In some places vexatious services of this kind were already compounded for, as page 49 "pro omni servitio" etc.

For the litigation arising from complex feudal dues see Verriest, p. 289. For the uncertainty of measures of time see Abbot E. C. Butler, *Benedictine Monachism*, ch. XVII; and Fr. H. Thurston in *The Nineteenth Century* for July 1899, pp. 39–41. For the injustices that might arise from the dependence of both parties on custom and tradition, without clear evidence from documents, compare what the monk of Muri tells concerning his own abbey and its tenants, and the document printed by Fyot, *Preuves*, p. 49 (cf. text, pp. 72–3). Helgand, prior of St-Etienne-de-Dijon, somewhere about 900 A.D., imposed upon thirteen tenants of one of his manors an additional tax of a yearly *modius* of new wine—perhaps as much as fifty-two gallons—from each holding. After three years, the tenants complained to the bishop, and procured an inquisition which resulted in their favour; but, if the bishop had not thus taken their part, they would probably have been helpless.

4

(Chap. III, p. 25; XII, pp. 146, 150; XIII, p. 156; XIV, pp. 167, 176; XVII, pp. 224, 229)

INTERESTED MISSTATEMENTS

A distinguished critic has lately blamed me for assuming that the historical writings of earnest Roman Catholic medievalists need, as a rule, to be carefully checked from the actual documents of the Middle Ages (*History*, Jan. 1924, p. 264; April, pp. 9, 14). I confess myself quite unable to follow his reasoning; it is one of the first canons of historical evidence that we should carefully look into a witness's position and mentality. The late Lord Cromer and Lord Morley were exceptionally able and honest men; yet we should blame any serious writer who accepted the former on the Egyptian question, or the latter in favour of Mr Gladstone, without examining his vouchers more carefully than usual. And, if this is so with all men whose position makes them necessarily partisans, it is specially true of those who owe loyal allegiance to an institution which claims wider and more unquestioning obedience than any other, and which still plays, by the confession even of its enemies, one of the most conspicuous rôles in the Western world. There are certain historical points (*e.g.* the question whether St Peter was ever bishop of Rome) on which the orthodox Roman Catholic has no right even to enquire; he must admit here that Cardinal Manning was right in repudiating the appeal to history as "both a treason and a heresy"[1]. And, on every question which concerns the honour of European civilization during those centuries when his Church dominated society, the orthodox Roman Catholic has necessarily an even stronger bias than the Protestant ecclesiastic; since this latter can afford to admit the grossest errors of his Church in the past, so long as she is willing henceforth to correct them, whereas the former claims to have been infallibly guided, on all essentials of faith and morals, for nineteen centuries. If, therefore, we could appeal to an impartial observer from Mars, I feel convinced that he would scout the idea of accepting the statements of an orthodox Roman Catholic, wherever the honour of his Church is in any sense at stake, without very careful examination of the evidence alleged in favour of such statements. He would doubtless recognize that the best of these men have often written the truth even to their own disadvantage, and he would commend them morally in proportion to the strength of the temptation here trodden under foot. He would, as a personal matter, find proportionate moral condemnation for those who, without the Roman Catholic's special temptation,

---

[1] See *The Daily Telegraph* for Oct. 8, 1875, p. 5, col. 7, for the cardinal's arguments in justification of his pronouncement.

grossly distort the truth in favour of their own party. But I think
he would conclude on examination of the facts, what the consideration of human nature in itself would suggest, that, on the whole, the
party worst tempted had most frequently fallen. I have given startling examples of this, for other fields, in the appendix to the 2nd
edition of the 1st series of *Medieval Studies*, and in Nos. 14, 15 and 17
of the 2nd series. I must now give similar evidence for matters
directly concerning this present volume. So long as interested misstatements are made, and left uncorrected, in spite of exposure, in
books which still sell by the thousand, so long is it necessary to continue exposing them in detail. I have tried to state the truth in my
text; this brings me into flat contradiction with others who, in my
opinion, have not tried sufficiently to get at the actual facts. The
public, in the face of these flatly contradictory assertions, would
normally find it very difficult to decide between the two contra-
dictors; the present appendix is designed to help towards that
decision. I deal here with only seven of the authors upon whom most
reliance is placed by present-day writers who idealize the conditions
of the medieval village and the economic policy of the medieval
Church; but the evidence given in this appendix is only a small
fraction of what I could produce if necessary.

(a) WILLIAM COBBETT

For popularity and inaccuracy combined, it would be difficult to
find any book so conspicuous as Cobbett's *History of the Protestant
Reformation*. This blunt Hampshire farmer and Radical agitator,
towards the end of his life, came suddenly to the conclusion that the
Reformation had been a robbery of the poor, and expressed this in
a style which, for simple and direct combative force, has seldom been
equalled in our language. Not many years before, Cobbett had
published concerning the popes in his *Register* (vol. XXVI, 1814, pp.
370-3):

these inhuman Pontiffs immolated to their God a thousand times more
human victims than Paganism sacrificed to all its divinities....Even
Popish writers admit that no throne was ever filled with such monsters
of immorality as the chair of St Peter....The sketch which I have
attempted to give is but a faint one indeed of the atrocities committed
by these pious, or rather impious, Pontiffs[1].

This "observer"—in all probability Cobbett himself—went on to
complain that the Regent had actually allowed an abbey of Bene-

[1] C. H. Collette, *Reply to Cobbett's "Hist. of the Prot. Ref."* (London,
1869), pp. 4 ff. I am not aware that any attempt has ever been made to
answer this book. The quotations are from a letter signed "An Observer,"
which has every characteristic of Cobbett's style, and was almost certainly,
like most of the other letters, from his own pen.

dictines to be re-established on the Continent; in this he detected danger not only to the consciences, but finally even to the bodies, of men, the pope having just "published another edict, for the purpose of restoring all those ancient *Monastic Orders*, by which the Catholic cause was formerly so extensively promoted, and the popedom supported in its arrogant pretensions to dispose of crowns, and to release entire nations from their oaths of allegiance." For him, the monks are "a fraternity whose existence, in former ages, was so prejudicial to society, and who are again threatened to be let loose to ravage civilized Europe" (col. 374). Cobbett, moreover, in his earlier days of journalism, had called the Anglican Church "an ornament, an honour and a blessing to the nation." But these were the days in which he wrote of Tom Paine: "Hypocritical monster.... He merited death, or at least transportation.... No language can describe the wickedness of the man.... Like Judas, he will be remembered by posterity; men will learn to express all that is base, malignant, treacherous, unnatural and blasphemous by that single mono-syllable." In 1824, however, on his return from America, he had boxed the whole compass; he brought with him, as sacred relics, the reputed bones of Tom Paine, "the greatest enlightener of the human race." And in that same year he began publishing his *Protestant Reformation*. Here Anglicanism becomes "her [Elizabeth's] new-fangled Protestant Church"; Roman Catholicism is "the religion under which England had been so great and happy for ages so numerous; that religion of charity and hospitality; that religion which had made the name of pauper unknown"[1]. And, since Cobbett still claimed the name of Protestant for himself, the book has been assiduously advertised and disseminated by the Roman Hierarchy, as the verdict of an impartial student, from its publication to the present day. It has been published below cost price for distribution; it has been reprinted again and again; the latest edition (which still sells) was brought out in 1896 by the Abbot President of the English Benedictines, with a long commendatory preface. Here, while admitting that Cobbett is not always accurate, the editor not only refrains from correcting some of his falsest and most telling controversial statements, but distinctly implies that all statements of importance which are thus left unreproved are, in fact, substantially correct[2]. Thus Cobbett's influence, though often unacknowledged

---

[1] *Hist. Prot. Ref.* §§ 341–2.

[2] A new edition, revised with Notes and Preface by Francis Aidan Gasquet, D.D., O.S.B. (London, 1896, reprinted, since the editor's elevation to the Cardinalate, by Burns and Oates). On pp. iv–v of the Preface we find: "How far the verdict of Sir H. Lytton Bulwer that the work in question is 'not to be regarded as a serious history' is correct, must be left to the judge-ment of those who will take the trouble to examine into the authority of Cobbett's statements of fact. For the purpose of this edition I have been at

and untraced, has been immense. When Messrs Chesterton and Belloc discourse on social history, they are generally quoting consciously or unconsciously, directly or at second or third hand, from Cobbett. On popular platforms, men of the most opposite religious views may be heard preaching Cobbett's gospel, that the Reformation was a revolt of the rich against the poor. It is one of those things which has often been treated as a commonplace through sheer pertinacity of repetition; therefore we cannot altogether disregard it here.

If there is one important question of social history on which even the most orthodox Roman Catholic might be expected to acknowledge the truth, it is the question of population-statistics in the Middle Ages; for, however a professional journalist like Cobbett may attempt to make capital out of the figures, there is really no such necessary connexion between population and dogma as need compel even the extremest Ultramontane to reject this particular appeal to historical fact as a treason and a heresy. Yet, even in this field, Cardinal Gasquet does not hesitate to lend his authority to statements which are not only absurd, but which we know that he himself knew to be absurd; for he had flatly contradicted them in other places where no controversial advantage was to be gained by misrepresenting the truth. Not, indeed, by any means the falsest section in Cobbett's book, but the section which can most easily and briefly be convicted of falsehood, is No. 453. He has already written in § 452: "I will now show not only that the people were better off, better fed and clad, before the 'Reformation' than they have ever been since, but that the nation was more populous, wealthy, powerful and free before, than it ever has been since that event"[1]. Thence he proceeds (§ 453) to assert that, "in the three first Protestant reigns, thousands of parish churches were pulled down" (which is false); that the size of the existing churches proves the parishioners to have been "three, four, five or ten times the number of their present parishioners" (which is not only false in fact but logically absurd). Equally absurd, as even beginners in history know, is his assertion that there were

some pains to enquire into the truth of the assertions made and to set down the result in the shape of notes, either giving authorities which may be taken to bear out the writer's statements, or pointing out wherein, in my opinion, he was mistaken, or has somewhat misstated or exaggerated the bearing of some fact. I confess that I was surprized to find how few were the instances in which some satisfactory authority could not be found to bear out the picture presented in Cobbett's pages.... The fact that Cobbett has relied in the main upon so careful and, as is very generally allowed, so exact, calm and judicial a writer of history as Dr Lingard, will probably be sufficient to clear him in the opinion of most people from the reputation of being 'a reckless perverter of facts' and his general history from the charge of being 'a mere tissue of lies.'"

[1] The population of England and Wales, when Cobbett wrote these words, was a little over 12,000,000.

"frequently 100,000 pilgrims at a time assembled at Canterbury," and, again, his attempt to infer the population from the assertion "there was one parish church to every four miles, throughout the kingdom," which he brings forward as "the best criterion." Then he quotes Chalmers as estimating "the population of England and Wales, in 1377, at 2,092,978." Here his accusation is false; Chalmers distinctly rejects this lower estimate, and decides for 2,811,204, a figure which agrees almost exactly with that calculation which has been worked out by the best authorities of today, which was copied from them by Cardinal Gasquet himself only three years before he reprinted Cobbett[1], and which was again reprinted by him even while this edition of Cobbett was still running uncorrected[1]. And not only does the cardinal thus vouch, as editor, for Cobbett's wild delusion that the population of 1377 was greater than that of 1824, but he actually gives a sort of farther *imprimatur* to those pages by supplying the references to Hume according to the pagination of a cheap modern edition, and by allowing Cobbett to sum up, uncorrected: "well, then, if the father of lies himself were to come, and endeavour to persuade us, that England was not more populous before the 'Reformation' than it is now, he must fail with all but downright idiots." This, then, is what is still offered as social history, it may almost be said officially, by that Community which claims and exercises a far more stringent censorship over its authors than any other in the civilized world!

I have chosen this particular section as the easiest to expose; but there are scarcely a dozen pages of Cobbett's book without some error of equal importance. I say this deliberately, and am willing to prove it against any serious student of history, if such there be, who is prepared to stake his reputation on the substantial accuracy of Cobbett's work. A few generations hence, it will seem almost incredible that such a book can have enjoyed so great a vogue, even as the partisan handbook of a religious denomination, in any educated community; and one of the most curious tasks of the future literary historian will be to trace its acknowledged and unacknowledged influence during this last century.

Mr G. D. H. Cole's *William Cobbett*, which has appeared since the foregoing words were written, gives a fair account of the book, with an admirable analysis of the author's mind at the time, on pp. 287 ff.

(b) JOHANNES JANSSEN (WITH PASTOR'S CONTINUATION)

We have here a very different author from Cobbett, or in fact from any English-speaking Roman Catholic medievalist of modern times except Edmund Bishop, who wrote very little, and Lord Acton, who

---

[1] *The Great Pestilence*, 1893, pp. 194–5; reprinted without alteration in the 2nd edition (1908).

narrowly escaped excommunication for writing so little to please his Church. Janssen was the typical laborious German professor, with the typical German *Seminar* at his back for the collection of facts; and, though a verification of his references will suggest that he had often not seen the context of the quotations which he masses in his footnotes, yet these are generally of real value. His English translators, however, have nearly always omitted these footnotes altogether. This would have been unfair to the public in any case; and it is doubly unfair in view of Janssen's peculiar historical methods. For, on analysis, we find that a good many of these notes refer to local Roman Catholic periodicals or monographs which are practically inaccessible even to readers at the British Museum; and the English reader can form only a very faint conception of the extent to which Janssen's theories repose on such *ex parte* evidence. Again, many of the other notes are indispensable for a very different reason; they are more important to a reflective reader than the text itself. For Janssen has a habit of relegating to his footnotes a good many facts too well-known among specialists to be omitted altogether, yet too inconvenient to be displayed in the plain daylight of the text; the author has thus salved his conscience by burying the awkward admission in decent obscurity, amid references which, by their multiplicity and their general vagueness, have taught the average reader habitually to neglect them. Moreover, a startling proportion of Janssen's most important references in the footnotes will not bear serious investigation; and it is to this point that I come here. Pastor, again, when he had to revise Janssen for later editions in the light of intermediate criticism, often followed his master's methods. English readers, therefore, are defenceless against misstatements which, even in their original form, can be verified only by many hours of labour in a first-rate library, and which often escape verification altogether.

One of the most important questions in social history, and one of the most hotly-debated, is that of the extent to which monastic charities supplied the admitted absence of an efficient poor-law during the Middle Ages, and especially on the verge of the Reformation. Whole volumes have been written on less important subjects, and it deserved at least a page or two of first-hand evidence among the 650 pages which Janssen devotes to his description of German society before Luther's appearance. Yet he gives us only one line of text, and four lines of note, with reference to the charities of the main religious Orders—monks, friars and nuns. His text runs (vol. I, p. 595 in 7th, p. 679 in 17th edition; Eng. translation, vol. II, p. 290): "the doles at the gates of the monasteries were often superfluously abundant"—*überreich*, which the translator has exaggerated into "far in excess of what was required." And his footnote runs: "As to the conventual almsgiving, we need only refer to Hirschau, which gave yearly to the poor about 400 bushels of uncooked cereals, and fed 200 persons daily at the monastery gate (Cless, *Culturgesch. v. Württemberg*, II, 443)."

We are therefore given one single reference for this sweeping and highly controversial generalization; but the English reader, deprived of the footnote, has no reason to suspect the flimsiness of Janssen's documentary evidence. Moreover, he would see the whole matter in a very different light if he could refer to Cless's actual words. The book is very rare in England; neither the British Museum nor the Bodleian has a copy: at Cambridge, it is only in the special Acton collection. Directly we look at Cless's actual words, we find Janssen's quotation embedded in a section of four pages dealing specifically with this question of monastic charities; a section in which Cless concludes with a plain contemporary generalization which directly forbids our taking the Hirschau conditions as even approximately normal. This falsification of the evidence can be fully exposed only by printing Cless's whole section here in full, including that fragment which Janssen has chosen to quote, and with black type for that which his quotation conceals from his readers. It will thus be seen why I have no hesitation in repudiating Janssen, in spite of his reputation, wherever the contemporary evidence tells against him.

Translation of the whole section (§ 2) entitled "Charity," in D. F. Cless, *Landes- und Culturgeschichte v. Württemberg*, vol. II, ii (1807), pp. 442 ff.:

§ 2. CHARITY. At this point we naturally ask: What were the more especial contributions of the monasteries from their superfluity to relieve the poorer among their poor folk? It is already well-known that many of the pious founders of endowments directed that the poor also should have a share in their gifts. This is especially the case in most of the anniversaries which were founded. A countess of Helfenstein made an arrangement of this kind for the convent of Königsbronn which was kept up until quite modern times; and the common folk assert that she appears to warn men when her last will is not properly carried out. The alms which were yearly given at Hirschau before the Reformation amounted to some 400 bushels of uncooked cereals, apart from daily bread-making. Besides this, two other great doles were given out, one on Shrove Tuesday and another on Maundy Thursday. From 800 to 900 people came to these doles; on Shrove Tuesday each received a pound of bacon and two pounds of bread; on Maundy Thursday young folk received one kreutzer each, and grown folk three, together with a plate full of uncooked peas, and bread. Furthermore, some 200 folk came daily to the gate, none of whom was sent away without some money or food[1]. I have already shown,

[1] Cless's note. "This is from a report of Reformation-commissaries for Württemberg; in which the commissioners report also that a foundling child

when writing about Abbot William's Constitutions[1], how great had been the throng for which he had provided in his infirmary budget; and we may thence conclude how vast must have been the consumption of food at this monastery; but we shall also see what it was that bound the multitude to these convents, in spite of their steadily sinking respect for them. In other monasteries, there were similar arrangements in proportion to their income or their religious sense[2]. At Alpirsbach, in 1299, Abbot Albert bought an estate for the infirmary; and he, with his monks, arranged that a hundred beggars should be brought yearly to the Refectory on All Souls' Day; to each of whom a dish of meat and of pottage was to be given, with a beaker of wine for each two; and afterwards wheaten bread; all from the income of this estate[3]. But now, in order to understand how the growth of self-indulgence in the cloister led to neglect of the benevolent object of monastic foundations in general, and of charitable foundations in particular, let us hear a witness who was not, indeed, a monk himself, but who was called upon by an abbot to draw up a memorial upon the shortcomings and transgressions of the Benedictine Order, to be laid before the General Chapter which was to be held at Hirschau[1]. The writer tells how a mighty king whom Charles the Great had more than once conquered, finally decided to embrace Christianity, and came to Charles's court. At his table he found different classes of men— bishops, monks, canons and lastly poor folk, whom Charles honoured with the title of "God's Messengers." The princely stranger expressed his wonder that God's Messengers should be treated with so little respect, saying that this gave him no taste for Christianity. Yet Charles (continues Conrad) did not feed the poor with the crumbs from his table or the sweepings of his kitchen; he let them eat at his own table, and gave them food cooked in a caldron of their own which no other man had touched. If the heathen prince took so great offence at this from a worldly king, how great offence must we give when we give to the poor only the crusts that we have first gnawed and the rinsings of our kitchen-pots! In this matter we are shamed by the Saracens, who, as travellers write to us, have very rich hospitals wherein even

had been laid at the cloister-gate, and had perhaps met its own father among these its spiritual foster-fathers."

[1] Of about 1080 A.D.; Cless analyzes these carefully earlier in this volume, II, i, 39 ff. (G. G. C.)

[2] Hirschau was one of the richest in Germany, and, for a great abbey, one of the most orderly even in the fifteenth century. (G. G. C.)

[3] Cless notes that Reichenbach had a similar anniversary. (G. G. C.)

[4] Cless's note. "'A Hortative Tract concerning Ten Defects of Monastic Votaries, by Magister Conrad Sumenhardt of Calw, D.D. Written in the year 1492 at the University of Tübingen, at the request of a certain Abbot, and sent by that same Abbot's command to the convent of Hirschau at the time of the then impending General Chapter, to be read aloud by the reader in Refectory.' The tract bears no imprint of place or year, nor are the pages numbered. There was a current proverb, that Monks had two hands, one for taking and one for keeping; but no third hand for giving away."

Christians are excellently treated. Ought not we to be above them? we, who are not only Christians but Ecclesiastics, and who possess convents endowed with so great wealth? [*so vorzüglich reiche Klöster haben*]. Why, even the Mendicant Friars give their leavings to the poor. But, [ye monks], give ye not food alone but clothing also; give shoes to the poor from the hides of your oxen; that would be a better use for your cattle than to sell them for money which ye spend upon the silly daubing of your walls. Refresh the needy with milk from your cattle, give to the weary from your fair and sweet fruit-stores. Spare to lay yet heavier burdens upon the poor tenants of your convent, lest they be constrained to sell their paternal inheritance, their Naboth's vineyard, to the irremediable loss of their own heirs; nay, rather lend them money when they are in need, etc. [*sic* (G. G. C.)].

But Janssen was re-edited and amended by a professor of almost equal reputation, Ludwig Pastor, whose *History of the Popes* ranks as a classic in his communion. Pastor undertakes to justify, against many adverse critics, Janssen's rosy picture of German peasant life before Luther (17th ed. 1, 367 n.). He therefore quotes a few sentences suitable to his purpose from a valuable local history, Otto v. Heinemann's *History of Brunswick and Hanover*. Here, for clear comparison, I *italicize* the portions utilized by Pastor; and the reader can compare these with the equally important passages which he ignores.

On p. 341 of his first volume, Heinemann has spoken of the peasant's gradual loss of freedom during the twelfth and thirteenth centuries. He returns to the subject on p. 265 of his second volume, dealing now with the fifteenth century. He writes:

In contrast to this strict organization [of the towns in the fifteenth century] the social order and economic position of the country population certainly shows still a sorry picture of decay and distress; but the worst time for the German peasantry was now past, and for them also *a gradual change for the better began to show itself in this period*. In the preceding centuries the peasant's position had become worse and worse in these Guelfic territories, as in the rest of Germany.... The land came more and more into the hands of feudal landlords, ecclesiastical or lay—monasteries and Church corporations, country nobility and cities.... The frequent wars, in especial, wherein the adversaries did their best to strike at each other by cruel devastation of territory, not only tended to the decrease of the free peasantry but resulted in a retrogression of the country folk in general.... Here, the flourishing towns enticed the serf to flee from his master; there, the neighbouring Wendish territories offered the free and wandering peasant a more favourable position and a better wage for his labour. So, as time went on, the country population melted gradually away. Hence—and, sometimes, indeed, for other reasons—the landlords were often compelled, even from the early thirteenth century onwards, to let whole villages disappear. This was called "laying a village down" [*einen Ort legen*]¹. The extraordinary force which the German peasantry had developed even in the twelfth century was exhausted; the time of wholesale "Rodungen" [*i.e.* of clearings to found new villages] was past. A contrary current began to flow, and quickly gained the upper hand. As early as 1229 the abbess of Gandersheim decided to let the village of Meinholdeshusen go, in order to put the produce of the manor to the use of her canons and nuns. The fields of Othonrode, Kaunum and Marquarderode were enclosed by the Cistercians of Riddagshausen, to amplify the possessions which the monastery exploited directly. The monastery of Königslutter swallowed up the great village of Schickelsheim; that of Helmstedt swallowed the hamlets of Bassallo, Gross-Seedorf and Klein-Seedorf. The monks of Mariental "dropped" and rooted out the villages of Opperfelde, Königsdorf, and other places. These instances of vanished villages, whether in consequence of the general decay of rural population or of the arbitrary action of the landlords, might easily be multiplied. They are a symptom of the growing desolation of the countryside. In 1372 a document complains "that, with the decay of the peasant population, the cultivation of the land was also decreasing terribly, and that most of the fields lay waste and almost untilled"; and in the preamble to the decree of Duke Henry the Peaceful, to which we shall presently come, it is recorded how, by reason of the manifold oppressions to which the serfs and bondmen of the monasteries and the nobility and their heirs are exposed, many of them have fled into foreign lands, whereby the landlords are suffering great loss, and whereunto the devastation of the land is due.

But the excess of these evils was destined gradually to bring its own remedy. In the long run, ecclesiastical as well as lay landlords could not help seeing that it was to their own interest to lighten the peasant's burden and to treat him more humanely....*But the most sweeping measures for raising the peasant class and relieving it of its oppressive burdens came from the dukes. Duke Frederick recognized the necessity of helping the rustics. In some districts of his State he abolished the so-called "Baulebung" or "Besthaupt," whereby the best head of cattle or the best garment fell to the lord at the peasant's death. Duke Henry the Peaceful went much further. On the 17th of May 1433 he made a covenant with the country folk, abolishing the "Kurmede," which the heirs of a dead tenant had to pay for leave to take up his tenancy. This document provided also that the "Bedemund," or fine for the peasant's leave*

¹ This is fully borne out by F. Winter (*Cist. d. N.-O. D.* i, 180–1 and ii, 171: "They [the Cistercians] often let whole villages disappear." Compare the English government enquiry of 1518 concerning enclosures made since the 4th year of Henry VII (*Reg. Bothe*, p. 64): "Furst ye shall inquyre what towns, villagis, and hamlettis hath ben decayed and layde down by inclosures into pasturis within the shyre sythe the IIIIᵗʰ yere of the reigne of Henry the VIIᵗʰ. Item, how many plowes by reason of the same inclosure be layde down? Item, how many messuages, cotagis, and dwelling howses be fallen in decay and the inhabitants of the same departed from theyr habitacion by reason of the same inclosure?" (G. G. C.)

to marry, might not be increased; that at the peasant's death there should be no claim on the best beast, but only on the second best; that all immigrant strangers should have the rights of free settlers; and, lastly, that freemen should not be liable to the "Bedemund." This land-law was epoch-making for the social position of the peasant population in the principality of Wolfenbüttel. It is true that, even now, the landlords by no means ceased altogether from oppressing the workers; and they still did all they could to shift their own feudal services to the shoulders of the peasants, especially their services in the cavalry and at court; but this law did really bar the way to the worst abuses; and in its wider consequences it was inevitably destined to bring about the gradual abolition of serfdom. The promise of freedom to immigrants was bound, as time went on, to attract a multitude of strangers, who occupied the deserted holdings. Moreover, the landlord, through these provisions as to "Kurmede," "Bedemund" and "Baulebung" lost the greater part of the income which he had drawn from his serfs, so that it was now scarcely worth his while to keep the system up. Therefore serfdom gradually died out in Wolfenbüttel; in this principality, we get no documentary notice of it from this time forward. The bondmen became free farmers, with full rights of inheritance. As early as 1478, when Duke William persuaded the estates to grant him an aid, they appear in this light. In that document, the Duke promises his protection not only to the estates themselves, but also to the farmers.

It is obvious that, if Pastor had quoted both sides of Heinemann's judgement, this would have been most unfavourable to Janssen's main thesis, that the Church was the peasant's best friend in the Middle Ages, and the Reformation his worst enemy. Hanover and Brunswick became Protestant in 1534, and have steadily remained so. I shall have occasion to expose other equally strange distortions of documentary evidence by Janssen and Pastor in the third volume of *Five Centuries of Religion*.

(c) EMIL MICHAEL, S.J.

Though Prof. Michael is more straightforward, on the whole, than Janssen or Pastor, yet he draws a picture of rural prosperity which depends for most of its effect on the omission of notorious facts. His *Geschichte des Deutschen Volkes* is, of course, appealed to by Pastor as a valuable corroboration of Janssen's thesis that the sufferings of the modern peasantry are due to the Reformation (Janssen-Pastor, 1, 328, 2; 369, 5; 370, 1). But when we turn to these pages of Michael to which they refer us (1, 37–85), we find the same untrustworthy methods. Michael, like Janssen, makes a general statement which begs the whole question (p. 85): "there was as yet no proletariat among the [German] countryfolk"; but the arguments and quotations which he brings in support of this and similar generalizations are often childishly lacking in logic or in accuracy of quotation.

It was the Church (argues Michael) which lightened the peasant's lot (pp. 37–47). In spite of exceptions, the bondmen lived on the whole a truly patriarchal life (p. 53; the iniquities of the manorial marriage laws are mainly thrust into a long footnote on p. 54). "The mass of the population felt themselves at no disadvantage" through the medieval system (p. 55). "These work-duties during the week found a welcome interruption in the enjoyments on Sundays and the numerous holy-days. Dance formed the kernel of all their recreations" (p. 64). This last statement is vouched by a footnote: "Brother Berthold, say what thou wilt, we [peasants] cannot be undanced!" It will be sufficient to illustrate Prof. Michael's methods if I give here the whole context of the sermon from which he has picked out this single line as his one support for the idyllic picture of Sunday dance in the village.

Berthold is expounding the Ten Commandments; they are (he says) ten half-pence which we must render as tribute to God, who will give a rich return to the faithful tributary—no less than the Ten Joys of Heaven.

The third halfpenny is the third commandment; *Thou shalt hallow thy Day of Rest*. This halfpenny hath two parts. The first is, thou shalt not work on the day of rest, as those heretics do who are gladder to work on Sunday than on Monday.... Those who work more [than is strictly necessary] have broken our Lord's third commandment. Thus they go now on holy Sunday and on the days of the holy Apostles, with waggons and carts and horses and asses, over field and over land, to the town markets and to the villages. Thou hind, thy master doth thee wrong, in that he constraineth thee to any sort of work on thy day of rest, except to drive the cattle to and from the pasture, or to give them fodder and water at home; that, indeed, thou canst not defer to another day. Thou maidservant, thy master doth thee wrong, or thy lord or thy lady, when they bid thee do on the day of rest any other work but to cook a meal and to heed the child or to care for one of the beasts; such works we may not escape.... Ye hinds, manservants and maid-servants, man or woman, young or old, poor or rich, whosoever doth more labour than I say here, hath broken this commandment.

Moreover, for this same cause, ye shall not dance on the day of rest, nor play nor cast the dice, because ye have naught to do.—Now, brother Berthold? thou wilt make our path strait indeed![1] Shall we have no business, nor ride anywhither, nor do anything else, neither dance nor play? Lo! how then shall we pass the time?—Behold, ye shall pass the time even as God hath there spoken and commanded to us all, that we should hallow the day of rest. A man shall pass the time of rest only in holy works; churchgoing and praying busily to God, and saying your prayers with true devotion in church, and bearing yourself there as well-mannered folk. For a great part of you—and

---

[1] Berthold often carries on such dialogues with objectors in his sermons.

the uplandish folk one and all, though they are very few in number—
can never once come to church in the whole week; wherefore there is
great need that ye should fulfil on the holy-day that which ye have left
undone all the week long. Then, when church service is done, ye should
go to dinner; and after dinner rest in sleep or in some other well-
mannered fashion. When ye have worked and laboured all the week long,
then have ye much need of rest and repose. Then, when ye have rested,
ye should go again to church, or say your prayers faithfully at home or
in the field; in what place soever thou callest upon God with quiet
heart, that place is holy. Thus should ye pass the time on holy-days,
with prayer and almsgiving and churchgoing and obeisance and going
to sermons wheresoever ye can seek such preaching, and earn indulgences and other graces thereby. And ye should visit the sick that lie
bedridden, when they are in need and when ye can; or, if ye cannot,
then have true pity upon them and pray God that He give them respite
for amendment, and a good end. Ye shall also go where folk lie in
prison, and comfort them. Lo, there are many ways wherein ye may
pass your day of rest in God's love and to God's honour, if ye would
follow my counsel.—"*Brother Berthold, say what thou wilt, we cannot
be undanced*"[1].—Hear St Augustine of that matter: "It is better that
a man go to his field-work on a holy-day than that he should dance";
I make exception for the bridal feast; there, a man may dance without
mortal sin. Therefore, thou mayest so dance as to commit mortal sin.
He who on Sunday goeth to field-work, doth mortal sin; he who
danceth doth the same. But there is profit in field-work; in dance is no
profit to any man.

Berthold, in short, great-hearted man and wonderful preacher as
he was, took the ordinary Church attitude of his day towards the
dance. He is, indeed, practically repeating here the words of Aquinas's
master, Albert the Great (in *Lib. IV Sent.* dist. 16) which again are
adopted in substance by Aquinas (*Expos. in Isaiam*, cap. III). In
Albert, it is essential to morality that dance should be "at due time
of rejoicing, as at weddings, or in time of victory, or of a man's personal liberation or that of his country, or the home-coming of a
friend from some far-off land." Neither Aquinas nor Albert think
of suggesting the ordinary Sunday or holy-day as a time for lawful
dances, and, indeed, later Church decrees explicitly excluded such
occasions: "They who dance on Church holidays commit mortal
sin," writes Luther's adversary and Aquinas's fellow-Dominican,
Guillaume Pépin (*Destruct. Ninive*, Serm. 17); and again: "It is not
permitted to any of the faithful to dance publicly on holidays or
Sundays" (Richard et Giraud, *Bib. Sacrée*, s.v. *danse*). Again, with
regard to the "respectable songs," Albert is quite explicit: "That
the songs and music which excite [the dancers] on such occasions
should not be of the unlawful kind, but songs of moral matters or

[1] "Bruoder Berhtolt, rede waz dû wellest, wir mügen ungetanzet niht sîn."

concerning God." It will be seen that there is nothing here which puritans like Milton and Baxter would not have freely allowed, and that we have no right to put the medieval dance to the credit side of that society, without facing the fact that most churchmen condemned it altogether, while the most indulgent would have restricted it very considerably. See my text in Chapter XIX, which would have rendered it unnecessary to dwell on the matter here, but for the irresponsible levity with which men of the highest reputation have caught at a single sentence from the Middle Ages and neglected the masses of contrary evidence staring them in the face.

(d) DR GEORGE O'BRIEN

This writer confessedly bases his conclusions on medieval *theories*, and professes no direct acquaintance with medieval *practice*. The absurdity of this method in ordinary affairs would be at once apparent; who, for instance, would dream of describing the British army merely in terms of the King's Regulations? or the Church of England in terms of the Thirty-nine Articles? Moreover, it is as impossible as it is absurd; for not only the public but Dr O'Brien himself is more interested in practice than in professions; and, in fact, Dr O'Brien does constantly lapse into statements about practice, begging the questions as they suit him, without pretence of actual proof. I pointed out, some time since, two important points on which he thus committed himself to the exact opposite of the actual facts (*History*, July 1921, pp. 69, 75): I am not aware that he has made any attempt to defend those misstatements.

His recent *Economic Effects of the Reformation* is, if possible, more wildly inaccurate than his earlier volume. In reliance upon such apologists as Janssen and Pastor and Michael, he writes:

The Middle Ages did, in fact, witness the building up of a beautiful and harmonious civilization....Anything resembling the modern notion that religion should be confined to Sundays, and should not be allowed to interfere with a man's business or pleasure on other days of the week, was utterly foreign to the medieval mind....The oppressor of the poor might succeed in evading the keenest regulations of the civil power, but, sooner or later, he was driven to disclose his wrong-doing to a tribunal which had the power to order restitution under pressure of the most terrible sanctions....Throughout the Middle Ages, poverty, far from being regarded as a disgrace, was regarded as a badge of holiness....The Reformation has given us [misery and beggary, wrangling and spite] in exchange for the ease and happiness and harmony and Christian charity enjoyed so abundantly and for so many ages by our Catholic forefathers[1].

---

[1] *Economic Effects of the Reformation* (1923), pp. 34, 42, 47, 55, 59.

Here we have a flagrant example of the unabashed nonsense which can be written by an enthusiast who has freed himself from any sense of moral responsibility towards the evidence of recorded facts in the past. Under cover of this self-imposed limitation, the writer is able to contrast the highest ideals of the Middle Ages with the most sordid facts of his own day. The natural result of this truly medieval indifference to history is an equally medieval standard of inaccuracy; and books of this kind are mischievous in strict proportion to the writer's general honesty and good intentions. Few volumes can have done more to breed strife and misunderstandings in Europe than that medieval compilation which is now, by general consent of all parties, called the False Decretals; a book which owed most of its success to the skill with which tendencious falsehoods were engrafted upon commonplace, and therefore generally accepted, truths[1]. All this jumble was presented together in the same matter-of-fact and confident style; the public had no means of distinguishing between that which everybody knew to be true and that which any well-placed and impartial critic would have seen to be false. Thus, also, in our own day, the mischief of books like Dr O'Brien's is increased by the author's evident enthusiasm and general good intentions. There can be no great advance in social history so long as a large and influential public demands from its historians party enthusiasm in the first place, and facts only so far as the facts happen to be acceptable.

(e) MONTALEMBERT AND HURTER

Montalembert commits himself on this subject, as on most others, to the most reckless generalizations (bk XVIII, ch. 6; I quote from ed. 1882, vol. VI). When he writes (p. 28): "among the abbots placed at the head of monasteries after the barbarian invasions, it may be asserted that there is not one whose biographer has not recorded his participation in tillage, in ploughing, harvesting, reaping, etc." this is a gross exaggeration even for those times of first missionary fervour to which his words, taken strictly, are confined. Still more random and false is this other generalization (p. 283): "It is certain that, in general, the lands granted to the monasteries were quite worthless, and that the givers did not think them worth keeping for themselves"[2]. Again, in proof of monastic kindness to tenants, he cites

[1] Pope Nicholas I, on being consulted as to the genuineness of this book, formally decided for it in a letter which was afterwards embodied in canon law (*Decret. Gratian*, pars I, dist. xix, c. 1). One of the reasons he gives is, that the unquestioned portions of this compilation give authority to the otherwise doubtful passages.

[2] If it be pleaded that the context means this to be understood only of *original* foundations, it is still contradicted by that very case of Micy which Montalembert, it will presently be seen, has tried to utilize for his own theories a few pages earlier.

"only a single example" (p. 290), in which an abbot of 960 A.D. grants lands for pioneers to clear, taking for himself only one-seventh of the grain and one-third of the wine thus produced. Yet this is a very exceptional case; *e.g.* the single instance adduced by his own chosen authority, Hurter, is far less favourable than this; the monks of Prüm took two-thirds clear, and left less than a third to the tiller (Bd III, p. 536: French translation, II, 124). It is pretty plain, even from the context, that this more lenient contract of 960 was imposed upon the abbot by circumstances; as a business man, he was ready to pay any terms which would persuade the decimated peasantry to work again upon his ravaged lands after the Saracen invasions. Where scholars like Caggese and Lamprecht collect all the instances they can find of such contracts with pioneers, it will be found that there is no evidence in favour of the monastic as compared with the lay landlord. The abbot of St Matheis took half of the produce to himself; so did the canons of St Simeon in two separate cases, and again the monastery of Münstermaifeld; the nuns of St Rupprecht took a quarter; the canons of Chur two-thirds, etc. Only in one of the many cases quoted by Lamprecht does the lord take one-seventh, and in one case even as little as one-tenth; it is not plain whether these are lay or ecclesiastical estates (*Wirth*. I, 906–910; III, 6–7). Not only does Montalembert constantly permit himself to generalize thus from one or two exceptional instances, even on subjects of capital importance for social history, but his references themselves are constantly so incorrect that he can scarcely have seen the actual texts. He writes, for instance (p. 277): "If we would get a clear idea of the care which monks gave to agriculture, from the very first, we must read a very important text from the life of St Mesnin, abbot of Micy, taken from the *Acta Sanctorum O.S.B.* and quoted by M. Aurélien de Courson in his work on ancient forests." Here we are referred, without the least indication of page or volume, to one work which runs to nine folio volumes, and another of which there are probably not half-a-dozen copies available to the British reader. When we have discovered that St Mesnin is the St Maximinus of the *Acta*, and run him down in vol. I, we find that there are two separate lives of him, and must read on as best we can in the hope of finding our text. When we have found it, we discover that it is far from bearing out Montalembert's emphatic appeal; a discovery which will surprise nobody who has tested Montalembert in this way; in a later volume I shall have occasion to show how, out of more than fifty consecutive references, less than a quarter are to the purpose, and a good many tell the exact opposite of what Montalembert claims for them. In the Micy case, the *Life* tells us no more than that Clovis gave to St Maximin for his monastery a delightfully-situated island in the Loire, of unusual fertility, which, at the later and uncertain time at which the author wrote, presented a paradise of cornfields and vineyards, garden and woods (pp. 584, 593). There is not a word to show that a single monk did a single day's work in this paradise; the results here described are simply such as we should expect from any capable landlord whose means permitted him to employ a good bailiff and sufficient labour. We need not for a moment contest the probability that, in this sixth century, the monks of Micy did a certain amount of work with their own hands; but the author who has appealed to the *Vita S. Maximini* as a capital proof of this fact has either never read it himself or is taking a cruel advantage of his readers.

Hurter, again, though far more scholarly and trustworthy, often breaks down under serious analysis; and there is much loose writing in the page in which he develops his text that "no man has yet contested the fact that the serf was better treated [by the monk] than by lay lords as a rule, and even by other ecclesiastical lords"[1]. He classes these advantages under heads: (1) easy rents; (2) allowances made for child-bearing women; (3) remission of arrears, especially in hard times; (4) milder contracts as time went on; (5) permission to buy freedom; and (6) popularity of the abbeys. In support of all these six counts he produces only seven documentary references, all told, and the first, as he confesses in his note, will not be found strictly to the point. When we verify it, we find it is a case where the bishop of Bamberg is the remitter of strict rent, and the persons to whom it is remitted are not the poor peasants but a rich monastery; yet this is given in proof of *monastic* indulgence to *the serf*[2]! The only other proof offered is scarcely more pertinent: in this case, the chapter does indeed pledge itself to remit part of a peasant's rent in bad years, but without personal sacrifice of a single penny: the chapter themselves are to take their full rent; it is only the rent due to their "advocate," (*i.e.* their Vogt), of which 50 per cent. is to be remitted to the peasant[3]. Only the third and last reference on this count has a real, though limited, pertinence; the monks of Prüm, at one time, were landlords of "12 peasants' holdings (*mansi*) which for their extreme poverty (*pro nimia paupertate*) render neither service nor payment." How many equally large landholders are there today, in any civilized country, of whom the same could not be said?

Yet, even so, Hurter is too balanced to please his French translator, upon whom Montalembert relies. This pious *traditore* takes the liberty of omitting that "*as a rule*" which softens Hurter's judgement

---

[1] Ed. 1838, p. 541; ed. 1843, p. 587.

[2] *Monumenta Boica*, XII, 404. Similarly Montalembert, among his too few proofs for *monastic* charity to the poor labourers, quotes a case which concerns not a monastery but a collegiate church (p. 289, n. 2).

[3] *Ibid.* IV, 350.

on the lay lords, and of inserting an unauthorized word to soften Hurter's comparison with other churchmen: "par *quelques* seigneurs ecclésiastiques" (ed. 1843, II, 129). Comparing the rest of the paragraph, we find that this is his habit. Where Hurter says that "*perhaps no rent was demanded*," this becomes "*souvent même* on n'cn cxigcait aucun." Hurter writes: "A good many (*manches*) contracts were rather softened than made stricter"; this becomes "les concessions furent *toujours* plutôt augmentées que diminuées." When we note also that more than four-fifths of Hurter's footnotes are altogether omitted—there is not one, for instance, for all this most important page, and the reader is practically obliged to take it all on the author's, or rather the translator's, word—we see here a typical instance of the way in which this system debases the historical currency. Each writer is concerned not to verify his predecessor's statements, but to outvie him in "edification." Thus, under the strict system of Roman censorship, really great Church historians like Döllinger and Monsignor Duchesne are actually put upon the Index, while the hierarchy exerts itself to puff and disseminate the clumsy fictions of farmer Cobbett. In this artificially-confined atmosphere men breathe and re-breathe each other's air; the intellectual bacilli which are apt to infest every atmosphere find here a hotbed for survival and propagation and infection; and the individual writer, under these unhealthy conditions, can scarcely be blamed if he catches a sort of sectarian gaol-fever. The same causes are as strong today as they were when the two greatest Roman Catholic writers in the English language complained in words which must not be allowed to pass into oblivion until they cease to be true[1]. Newman, in 1864, wrote to a friend who wanted to start a Catholic Historical Review:

Nothing would be better than an historical review—but who would bear it? Unless one doctored all one's facts, one should [*sic*] be thought a bad Catholic. The truth is, there is a keen conflict going on just now between two parties, one in the Church, one out of it —and at such seasons extreme views alone are in favour, and a man who is not extravagant is thought treacherous[2].

Attempts have recently been made to confine these words to that particular year, and to argue that, though the Catholic could not be trusted to write real history in 1864, yet the distorting circumstances press now no longer. But Newman's words plainly forbid this distinction. The main conflict then was between one party *in*, and one *outside*, Catholicism; so is it now; again, the main bone of contention was Papal Infallibility; so is it now; what Newman in 1864 spoke of as an extreme view (for he was then opposed to the Definition) is the

---

[1] I have dealt more fully with these in *The Modern Churchman* for March, 1925, reprinted as a pamphlet on *Roman Catholic History* (Simpkin Marshall & Co. 6d.). [2] *The Month*, Jan. 1903, p. 3.

view which every orthodox Catholic is now pledged to defend, a
pledge by which he is even more definitely committed to be "extravagant" than when Newman wrote. Moreover, Lord Acton wrote
even more strongly in 1876, and in words which imply no limitation
of time. He was speaking then of Ultramontanism; *i.e.* the party
committed to Papal Infallibility; and he wrote: "It not only promotes,
it inculcates distinct mendacity and deceitfulness. In certain cases it
is made a duty to lie. But those who teach this doctrine do not
become habitual liars in other things"[1]. It is true, both of these were
private letters to friends, and there we must make some allowance;
but Acton evidently wrote deliberately, since he kept a copy of what
he had written; and, discount the strong language as we may, it will
go far to explain these faulty references and strange reticences which
we find even in the most accredited Ultramontane historians when
they are dealing with their Church's rôle in the history of human progress. Of Montalembert, Janssen and Pastor I am prepared to assert
deliberately that to cite these writers, unverified, *as authorities* is to
make a proof of historical ignorance, though their citations and re-
flexions are often very valuable. Among those who may very probably
blame me for this strong general condemnation, I am convinced that
not one would dare to assert publicly that he has verified their
references adequately, and found them even up to ordinary standards
of historical accuracy.

5

(Chap. III, p. 30)

CHRISTMAS AT TYNEMOUTH

Dugdale-Caley, III, 319 a.

Here is a scene from the priory of Tynemouth; the Christmas
festivities at the manor of Whitley. It was prescribed by charter that
all the men of the priory, all the horses and dogs of the priory aforesaid, and all the prior's servants at the manor of Preston, and the hayward our servant and the carter with one horse from the manor of
Seaton, and all the servants in the barge, who are called *keelers*, and
four threshers, and a winnower or winnowing-woman, shall come
yearly at Christmas, on Innocents' Day, to Whitley on this side of the
village. And there the lord of that village[2] shall meet them, and receive
them decently and honourably, and on the aforesaid Innocents' Day
and the morrow he shall find, for those two days and nights, all necessaries for their proper lodging and food; to wit, that all the men afore-

---

[1] *Letters*, ed. Figgis and Lawrence, 1917, p. 43; *Letters to Mary Gladstone*,
introd. p. lv.

[2] There was a peel-tower at Whitley, in which the monks probably kept a
sort of soldier-steward.

said be served at noon with two proper and sufficient courses and cheese, and the whole company of freemen servants for supper likewise with two courses and cheese. And also that the squires and their peers be served on the meat-days with whole hens for the second course at supper, to wit, one hen between each two; and those of lesser rank shall be served with half a hen between two, with fresh roast flesh, for their second course at supper. And all the cowherds and their peers shall be served at supper with gross flesh and cheese; so, however, that all, both freemen and herdsmen, have good and proper ale; and that each two shall have one sufficient bed, and competent to their rank[1].

Compare the following particulars from a customal of the abbey of Savigny, written by the claustral prior of that monastery about 1500 A.D. (Guigne, p. 425). At Savigny, the monks had a mid-Lent bonfire outside the abbey gate—"ignem gaudii, id est, *les joanes.*" The abbey servants fetched faggots from the forest, and every inhabitant of Savigny had to provide "unum fasciculum lignorum competentem"; for *il y a fagots et fagots.* If any inhabitant refused, "the servants may remove the door of the recusant's house and bring it away to the abbey until the faggot have been paid. But at this monks' bonfire neither they nor their servants ought to make any hubbub, nor sing any ballad nor dance any dances, but speak honestly and in a low voice without shouting, by our laudable use and custom; and thus I have seen it used and done; but the aforesaid hath ceased now for nearly twenty years, and wrongly."

6

(Chap. IV, p. 40)

YOUNGER SONS

(*a*) Vinogradoff, *Villainage*, p. 246.

[Borough English] is certainly a custom of great importance, and probably it depended on the fact that the elder brothers left the land at the earliest opportunity, and during their father's life. Where did they go? It is easy to guess that they sought work out of the manor, as craftsmen or labourers; that they served the lord as servants, ploughmen, and the like; that they were provided with holdings, which for some reason did not descend to male heirs; that they were endowed with some demesne land, or fitted out to reclaim land from the waste. We may find for all these suppositions some supporting quotation in the records. And still it would be hard to believe that the entire increase of population found an exit by these by-paths. If no exit was found, the brothers had to remain on their father's plot, and the fact that they did so can be proved, if it needs proof, from documents.

---

[1] Dugdale-Caley, III, 319 a.

(b) Tawney, *Agrarian Problem*, p. 104, n. 3.

When a large number of agricultural and industrial workers (in the sixteenth century probably a majority) were small landholders or small masters, did the fact that they had to wait for the death of a parent to succeed to their holding, or (in towns) for the permission of a guild to set up shop (*i.e.* to reach their maximum earning powers) tend to defer the age of marriage? If the possibility of this being the case is conceded, ought we to connect the slow growth of population between 1377 and 1500 (on which all historians seem to be agreed) with the wide distribution of property, and ought we to think of the considerable increase in the landless proletariate which took place in the sixteenth and seventeenth centuries as tending in the opposite direction? In the absence of statistics we cannot answer these questions. But I am inclined to argue that they are at any rate worth investigation. (1) Contemporary opinion shows that in the eyes of sixteenth century writers the problem of population was a problem of underpopulation. The prevalent fear is "lack of men" for military purposes....There are some complaints as to excess of population in 1620 (see below, pp. 278–279), but these do not become general till the very end of the seventeenth century (see Defoe, *Giving alms no charity*). (2) The position of a son who acquires a holding when his parent dies is analogous to that of an apprentice who cannot set up as a master till given permission by the proper authorities. It is quite plain that in the eyes of the ordinary man in the sixteenth century one of the advantages of a system of compulsory apprenticeship was that it prevented youths marrying at a very early age....One may contrast the extraordinary reduction in the age of marriage of the people of Lancashire brought about by the early factory system, with its armies of operatives who had nothing to look forward to but the wages earned immediately on reaching maturity (Gaskell, *Artisans and Machinery*, 1836, and *The Manufacturing Population of Great Britain*, 1833), and compare the results usually ascribed to the wide distribution of landed property in France.... Young ascribed "a great multiplication of births" to the fact that "the labourer has no advancement to hope" (*Suffolk*, 1797, p. 260); Duncombe, "The practice of consolidating farms...tends to licentiousness of manners" (*Herefordshire*, p. 33). A witness before a Select Committee on Emigration, 1827, stated, "The labourers no longer live in farm houses as they used to do, where they were better fed and had more comforts than they now get in a cottage, in consequence there was not the same inducement to early marriage" (qu. 3882). In the absence of direct statistical evidence all we can say is (1) that when persons look forward to entering on property or setting up as small masters their point of maximum earning power is later than it is when they can earn the standard rate of the trade at twenty-two or twenty-three; therefore (2) that the average age of marriage is likely to be higher in a society composed largely of small property owners than in one composed largely of a propertyless proletariate.

Some light is thrown on this question in Germany by a document from which Brons has quoted. In about 1220, under the nunnery of Vreden, the sons of an unfree man, even though he were a bailiff, were under a definite prescription: "When the parents are dead and the eldest son takes over the holding, then the younger brothers must serve the eldest as hinds on the land; and, if they receive wages, they must pay a tax to the convent, which takes all that they leave at their death"[1].

7

(Chap. IV, p. 43; XVII, p. 214)

BACKWARD TILLAGE

Very interesting details are quoted in *The Quarterly Review*, CLVII, 118, from Mr Harriss-Gaskell's report on the district of Wetzlar, near Frankfort, published in the Parliamentary Blue-book on Foreign Land Tenures:

No better department could probably be found for seeing in the present day the united results of equal division on inheritance of land and of the old system of agriculture. It is in all essential points unchanged.... The peasants were always freemen.

The population is "stationary at 43,000." Out of 20,000 properties less than one hundred are over 200 acres.

The three field system flourishes here in all its pristine sterility. The field compulsion accompanies the system as a necessary part of it. The head of the village fixes the days on which all must begin and cease to plough, and on which all must sow and reap. This system causes deficiency of fodder, and consequently a diminishing produce. It prevents a practical alternation of grain and green crops, the introduction of hoed crops, the restoring effects of several courses of clover, and the intelligent use of each part of a property for the most suitable cropping. Neighbouring properties often differ as to the right time and right weather for certain operations and as to the quality of the soil, but all are obliged to cultivate the same crop, at the same time, and with the same weather.... Agriculture also suffers from the widespread habit of underfeeding the cattle.... Manuring is little understood, and the state of the open farmyard is pitiable to see.... The plough is primitive, and the ploughing is usually scratching.... The soil is by no means poor, but the average corn yield is about $11\frac{1}{4}$ bushels to the acre.

For the simplicity of Italian agriculture see Lina Duff-Gordon, *Home Life in Italy* (1908), pp. 126, 265, 296, 305, 317–319; and Janet Ross, *Old Florence and Modern Tuscany* (1904), pp. 141 ff.

[1] *Vreden*, p. 40, n. 1.

Robiou brings out certain minor disabilities of the medieval peasant which would be looked upon as grave disadvantages in our own day; the hindrances to agriculture consequent upon bad roads and tolls or customs duties at frequent intervals (pp. 417, 437); regulations against carriage of grain from one district to another, which were far from answering in many cases to the good intentions of the authorities (pp. 423, 436), and the custom of *purveyance* (p. 424). The insufficient tillage of those days in England is brought out by Cullum, p. 197. Moke discusses the question at some length, and with evident efforts to hold the balance; he concludes that the French provinces in which the feudal system lasted longest were the poorest (p. 26); that the superior cultivation of the central provinces was due to the comparative absence of serfdom (p. 27); that the freeman "must have wrung far more abundant crops from the soil" than the villein (p. 33). He shows also that great lords, both lay and ecclesiastical, recognized the fact that these free peasants could till more profitably than they themselves could (p. 32). This was the case especially in Languedoc, where

in 1340, the nobility represented to the king that they could not avoid parting with some of their lands, since, but for the help of rich commoners, they would have been constrained to leave them untilled, or to farm them themselves. The *vile race of peasants* being unable to offer its lords the resources and the help which they needed, it was only *the citizens* who could undertake the exploitation of their estates and the direction of their affairs. Not only nobles, but prelates also sold their lands thus to commoners. An ordinance of 1328 shows us that the inhabitants of Carcassonne had long made acquisitions of this kind. The holdings which they had bought from lords and bishops were at first barren or half-tilled; but the labour and the money of the purchasers had improved them. This increase in value from properties thus transferred was so great that the sovereigns sought in vain to oppose this subdivision, even of fiefs. The nobles alleged that their lordships were thus improved; and this may be observed also in several documents concerned with central France. (p. 56; italics his.)

In 1487, the prior of Romainmotier, finding that "the greater part of the land [at Vallorbe] remained untilled by reason of the servitude" of the peasants, commuted the feudal dues for fixed money rents, thus abolishing a system which "discouraged the tiller by absorbing the fruit of his labour" (Charrière, p. 68). For the crass ignorance of the modern French peasant on many of the simplest questions of agriculture see Noël, pp. 87 ff.: "He has begun to realize that his educators in past centuries have generally misled him; and this, unfortunately, impels him to throw overboard, without examination, both ancient beliefs and modern science."

8

(Chap. V, p. 52)

KILLING OF SERFS

Those modern authors who recognize the probability of a great deal of illegal oppression on the part of medieval landlords—by no means universal, no doubt, but enough to weigh very considerably in the historical balance—would seem to have practically the unanimous support of contemporary documents. A great deal of allowance, of course, must be made for the normal medieval view of human life, which was much the same as that of the modern Russian peasantry as described by Gorki: "Men are now cheap"[1]. But, cheap as life was in general, the serf's was cheaper than other men's.

The actual defencelessness of the ordinary unprivileged man comes out strongly in a letter of Archbishop Peckham in 1284, where he taxes the archdeacon of Oxford with protecting the rector of St Ebbe's, who had begotten two children in adultery with the wife of his parishioner William le Bolter:

And, when the said William rebuked this rector aforesaid, by name, for this baseness, then the rector, detesting these hindrances to his lechery, uttered fierce threats against his rebuker, and proceeded to still more execrable deeds; for he accused him of detaining certain tithes (falsely, as is believed), and pronounced him *de facto* excommunicate, and by this suggestion of falsehood procured his imprisonment, that he might the more freely exercise his lechery aforesaid. But, while the said William languished in prison and was now at death's door, and besought his mercy, he then procured his liberation; and, when the liberated man reproached the adulterer with his wicked contumacity, this lecher, enraged again at the thwarting of his lust, procured that William should again be cast into bonds, and kept so long in this cruel prison that he there gave up the ghost, even though he confessed humbly and instantly, through William of Woodstone, that he was always ready to stand by the commands of the Church[2].

Such incidents have come down to us, in the nature of the case, only where the scandal was great and some really great prelate like Peckham was ready to interfere.

We need not linger over such early examples as Caggese supplies (I, 47–8), from the days when the serf was scarcely yet developed from the slave. But a German manorial document of 1172 prescribes that, if a serf kills his fellow-serf, he must produce in his stead another man, at least seven *gemundas* long, whom the bondfolk judge a fit

---

[1] *The Times*, Oct. 7, 1922; article headed "Gorki's Grim Picture."
[2] *Epp.* R.S. p. 856.

substitute; in addition, he pays the bishop a fine of five pounds, of which the bailiff takes one-third. If the bishop's serf is killed by a stranger, the penalty is the same, but the bishop gets only one-third[1].

About the year 1200, the abbot of Evesham "cast into prison a layman, our [*i.e.* the monks'] reeve, a serf, one Austin of Salford, and caused him to be scourged almost to the last gasp in order to extort money from him; and, when he saw that the man must die, he took him from prison and had him taken home, where he presently gave up the ghost." Nobody, apparently, would have reported this if the monks had not had many other grievances against their abbot; nor did it, even so, prevent the murderer's being pensioned off with a priory (*Chron. Evesh.* R.S. p. 242). At Meaux in Holderness, about 1240, the monks tried to drive Sir Sayer of Sutton by armed force from a certain meadow which he held; one of the knight's serfs was killed in the quarrel. The monastic chronicler, who frankly confesses that the meadow was really Sir Sayer's, treats the death as it was evidently treated by the judges at the time; it raised rather an economic than a moral problem, and the only question was as to the exact pecuniary indemnity (*Chron. Mels.* R.S. II, 6–7: cf. preface, p. ix).

I give a few more cases in chronological order. Fra Filippo da Lecceto, writing about 1400, speaks of a lord who, returning from the chase, set a savage hound upon a poor peasant in mere wantonness[2]. Here, again, is an extract from the Vatican archives:

The recent petition of Thomas Micgillavanach, archdeacon of Kilmacduagh, contained that formerly between him and Philip Ohaill, layman, his serf (*mancipium suum*) words of contumely arose, that Philip over much excited Thomas to wrath, that Thomas, full of fury, without reflecting, threw after Philip a knife which he was wearing and so wounded him with it that he died within three days, and that he had no intent to kill him. At the said petition and that of bishop John (asserting that Thomas has ceaselessly and intrepidly helped him, since he became a bishop, in the defence of the rights of the said church, and can still be useful to it) the pope hereby orders the above bishop to absolve Thomas, who is a priest and of noble race, from the fault of homicide, enjoining a salutary penance, dispense him on account of irregularity, and dispense him to minister in minor orders only and to receive any benefices and retain them and all others which he at present holds, and rehabilitate him[3].

"In 1444, Ulrich v. Heimenhofen, who had killed a bondman belonging to the bishop of Augsburg, gave the bishop a serf of his

---

[1] Anton. III, 175, from *Mon. Boica*, V, 133. The exact measure denoted by *gemunda* is not known. This is characteristic of the early law; it is the serf's master who must be indemnified for his death; cf. v. Arx, II, 614.

[2] W. Heywood, *The Ensamples of Fra Filippo*, Siena, 1901, p. 204.

[3] C.P.L. IX, 116 (1440).

own in compensation"[1]. In 1443 it was represented to the pope that John, abbot of Kinloss, "had not shrunk from causing a certain woman to be branded with a hot iron on the face, from which she afterwards died." This, probably, was in the way of formal justice, so that the only blame incurred by the abbot was that of ecclesiastical irregularity, from which he could have obtained dispensation at the regular tariff-rate[2]. It was one of the counts against the prior of Walsingham, in 1514, that he had struck one of his serfs, so that the man died within a month; this again, as in the Evesham case, comes in only as a minor matter; and, though the prior was forced by the bishop to resign for other misdeeds, it was only on condition of a good pension[3].

It is only by accident that we hear of such cases; but their frequency may be inferred from medieval moralists. "The servant that is not chastised with words must be chastised with wounds"; so writes even the merciful Bartholomaeus Anglicus in 1250[4]; and it is very natural that the wounds should sometimes prove as serious as in the Walsingham case. St Bernardino of Siena, two centuries later, inveighs against

certain foolish confessors who easily absolve manslayers, not considering the restitution necessarily incumbent on such transgressors, as though an impious homicide could pass more easily than (so to speak) a canicide or a bovicide. For, if any man killed his neighbour's ox or dog, he would not be absolved without restitution; yet he is lightly absolved of the impious homicide he has done....Moreover, a serf who has been slain should be restored to his lord by the gift or purchase of an equivalent serf, or by a price competent to buy such[5].

A generation later, we get similar complaints from a great French preacher:

"Every beast," saith the Wise Man, "loveth its like" (Ecclus. xiii, 19). Those therefore whom we find lovers of men, and fearing to kill men, are themselves men. Those whom we see loving wild beasts and their dens and their preservation, they are themselves beasts; and perchance it is to be feared that they so love this dwelling of wild beasts that God will send such indwelling into our realm, as He did of old. For thou shalt see that a man [nowadays] would get easier pardon for slaying a man than for a deer or a boar; and men are not cast into prison for devouring a man, as the good peasant's beasts [are put into the pound for eating crops][6].

---

[1] Baumann, II, 630.   [2] C.P.L. IX, 353.
[3] *Vis. Norwich*, C.S. pp. 116, 121, 146. I give long extracts from this visitation, which occurred within a few months of Erasmus's celebrated visit to Walsingham, on pp. 33–39 of *Medieval Studies*, No. 11.
[4] Tr. Trevisa, lib. VI, c. 17.
[5] *Opera*, I, 163 a.   [6] Raulin, f. 359, 2 h.

We always discount a preacher's or moralist's complaints to some extent; but here are the words of a Tudor judge expounding the law with regard to the maiming of a villein:

Moreover, the king hath an interest in his person; for the villein is bound by law to attend on the king for the safeguard of the kingdom in time of war, just as much as any other liege man of the realm; moreover, a villein will be compelled to serve in husbandry if the lord have not labourers enough; and thus this proves that every man may have an interest in the villein; and when he is maimed he can render service to no man; and so, if the lord cannot give him meat and drink he is not able to work for his livelihood[1].

So long as these were the fundamental principles of social legislation, and so long as the old feudal traditions endured, it was natural that evil opportunities should often breed evil-doing. We may fairly conclude with an illustration from France in 1789: "A seigneur in the neighbourhood of Tinténiac," says the *cahier* of that parish, "wished, a short time ago, to compel his vassals to turn hay on Sunday; one of them replied that he wanted to go to Mass, when the seigneur flew into a rage, covered him with blows, knocked him down and struck out his eye" (Sydney Herbert, *Fall of Feudalism in France*, 1921, p. 16).

9

(Chap. VII, p. 65)

MEDIEVAL POPULATION

I know of no approach to a complete synthesis of the details worked out as yet by different students; the following detached notes are given in the hope that they may be of some use to others.

(1) GERMANY

Lamprecht (*Wirth*. 1, 163) makes the following calculation for the Moselle basin, which he has specially studied. The top line (*A*) denotes the years A.D., the second (*B*), the number of villages and hamlets, and the third (*C*), the population, in thousands:

(A)	800	900	1000	1050	1100	1150	1200	1237	1800
(B)	100	250	350	470	590	810	990	1180	2000
(C)	20	60	80	100	140	180	220	250	450

For the villages round Frankfort a/M., see K. Bücher, *Die Bevölkerung von Frankfurt a/M.*, Tübingen, 1886, pp. 659 ff. He makes it plain that in the fifteenth century, from which the earliest statistics come, the population was scanty compared with modern times.

[1] R. Keilway, *Reports*, London, 1688, f. 134 a, § 116. The judge's name, Keble, shows that we are in the reign of Henry VII.

(2) FRANCE

Prof. Pirenne allows me to quote him as agreeing with me that Luce exaggerates greatly when he writes that "the population of France, during the first half of the fourteenth century,...at least equalled, if it did not even somewhat exceed, that of present France, *if we take only those parts of the country which were then inhabited, and except the great urban agglomerations [of to-day]*"[1].

This rests, apparently, to a considerable extent upon the researches of Dureau de la Malle, which are summarized in the *Bibliothèque de l'École des Chartes* for 1841, pp. 173–188. Taking as his basis the tax-rolls of 1328, which cover less than one-third of the territory, he estimates that the total population of what we now call the land of France was about 34 million souls. Prof. Coville, working upon these same rolls in 1902, deduces from them "from 20 to 22 millions, at the most moderate calculation" (Lavisse, *Hist. de France*, IV, 2, 20). This agrees with the calculations of an economist who has studied and discounted de la Malle's calculations (Moke, p. 14). Yet, when Moke infers from this that the agricultural population was then about 14 per cent. higher then than in 1856, it is difficult to reconcile this with the *pouillés*. It is true, these give us details, so far as I know, only for Northern districts, and Moke insists on the greater relative prosperity of the Centre and the South; but one of these Northern districts is Normandy, and it is difficult to put Normandy below the average before the Hundred Years' War. These diocesan directories (as the *pouillés* may be called) give us sometimes, among other statistics, rough totals of the *parochiani*, who doubtless answer to the "housling folk" of the English chantry certificates; *i.e.* parishioners old enough to be admitted to Easter communion. The *pouillé* of Chartres diocese, in the latter half of the thirteenth century, gives these statistics for 935 out of the 963 parishes (*St-Père*, pp. cccvi ff.). The average number of *parochiani* per parish is 97·13. For the city of Chartres we have no statistics. By far the largest parish is St-Pierre-de-Dreux, with 2000; next comes St-Martin-de-Vincennes, with 600; there are ten others with more than 300. The smallest range from 1, 3, 4 upwards; twelve have less than 20 *parochiani* each. Taking the deanery of Épernon as a sample, we find that the thirty-six parishes had then a total of 4329 *parochiani*. Multiplying these by $2\frac{1}{2}$, to make generous allowance for children under housling age, these 4329 yield a probable population of 10,805 at most. The present population of these parishes is 27,596.

[1] *Hist. de B. du Guesclin*, 1882, p. 47. Later apologists, borrowing these words at second-hand, commonly neglect the two important qualifications which I have here italicized, and thus credit Luce with a still more exaggerated conclusion which his scholarship would certainly have repudiated.

Langlois, again, gives very valuable comparisons, parish by parish, for five rural deaneries; he concludes that "the population of the districts round Paris, even at the most prosperous times of the Middle Ages, can never have been comparable to what it is today." In 1467 it was scarcely more than one-eighth of the present figure; but the country had not then fully recovered from the ravages of plague and war (*Revue historique*, vol. LXXXVIII (1905), pp. 299 ff.).

Take, again, the *pouillé* of Rouen diocese (ed. L. Delisle, 1876, *Receuil des hist. de la France*, tom. 23). The first rural deanery gives the following results, (if we omit Elbeuf as coming under Luce's exception of *agglomérations urbaines*, and six other parishes which I cannot identify with any modern names). In the remaining thirty-three villages there were 3364 *parochiani* in 1240; this makes 8395 souls at most; the population in 1900 was 15,886. Very similar is the evidence drawn by Imbart de la Tour from the *Irminon polyptyque* (*Rev. hist.* vol. LXIII, 1897, p. 12).

Lastly, we can get a comparison from Longnon's *Pouillés de la prov. de Trèves*, 1915, though this is much later, in the eighteenth century, and the terms are more uncertain. The deanery of Boppart is recorded to have 13,926 communicants, and 4892 non-communicants. This would seem, *à priori*, more probable than that higher proportion of children which I have suggested above in order to be sure of not doing injustice to the medieval population. But, on the other hand, in this district and at this date it may represent a distinction, not of elders and children but of Catholics and non-Catholics. Useful for inference are the statistics given by Leadam in his introduction to the *Domesday of Inclosures*; in 1517 the families averaged 5 in Berks. and 5.52 in Bucks.

The French population fell off terribly during the Hundred Years' War and after the Black Death. For a typical province like Burgundy, in 1375, "rarement le nombre des feux [dans un village] descend au-dessous de 10, il oscille d'ordinaire entre 20 et 40 (de 100 à 200 âmes, en admettant qu'une famille ait en moyenne 5 membres). Un petit nombre s'élèvent jusqu'à 60, très peu au-dessus de 80." During the later years of the war, things were still worse: "Dans toutes [les paroisses], le nombre des feux a baissé de près du tiers, et les répartiteurs sont obligés, outre les insolvables, d'admettre encore une catégorie 'de misérables et mendiants' plus nombreuse que les deux autres"[1].

---

[1] Seignobos, pp. 35–6. These passages refer directly only to Burgundy; but some parts suffered even worse. The taxable property at Alais sank from 40,000 livres in 1338 to 19,000 in 1440 (Lavisse, *Hist. de France*, tom. IV, ii, p. 115).

(3) Switzerland

In St-Gallen canton there were 2493 houses in 1460, 7069 in 1811 (v. Arx, II, 622 ff.).

(4) Flanders

H. Pirenne (*Soulèvement*, p. lxviii) recognizes the impossibility of exact calculations for the early fourteenth century, but is convinced that the villages of Western Flanders were far more populous then than "those around Frankfort, which had an average of less than 200 souls in the fifteenth century, and those of the Neckar valley, which seldom exceeded 400." Other helpful details may be found in his *Histoire de Belgique*, I, 259, 264–5, 286–7; II, 48, 66, 73, 388, 403, 410.

(5) England

Here the poll-tax returns are of great assistance. For the later Middle Ages there is general agreement; the population from the end of the fourteenth century to the end of the fifteenth was fairly stationary at about $2\frac{1}{2}$ millions (W. Cunningham, *Growth of Eng. Industry and Commerce*, 5th ed. pp. 331–2; J. E. T. Rogers, *Six Centuries of Work and Wages*, pp. 120–1; see also appendix 4 of this present volume). The real dispute is as to the figures before the Black Death. Seebohm thought they might be put as high as 5 millions, while Rogers contended (1) that the land, under then methods of cultivation, could not have fed so many, and (2) that we have no reason to treat as impossible a rapid recovery after these fourteenth-century pestilences, so that the population of 1400 might have been much the same as that of 1300 (*Fortnightly Review*, vols. II, III, IV). Cunningham sums up here very impartially, and is inclined to believe that Rogers allows too little. But we must bear in mind (1) the rapid increase of population wherever it has real room to spread, and (2) the high infant mortality under the ordinary medieval fight for existence. In the single year 1429, with no special plague to account for it, so far as can be traced, there died in three contiguous Yorkshire hamlets 26 adults and 111 children (Blashill, pp. 125–6). I cannot help thinking that Rogers was far nearer the truth than Seebohm, and that the population of England never rose higher than about 4 millions, at most, before the Reformation. An excellent summary of the evidence for the city of Norwich, by Mr W. Hudson, is printed in *Hist. Teach. Misc.* II, 171 ff.

In any case, the general European evidence tends to prove what we might have expected *à priori*. Quite apart from the urban agglomerations, even the purely village population was decidedly smaller in the Middle Ages than at present.

10

(Chap. VII, p. 67)

THE DURHAM HALMOTE ROLLS

Cardinal Gasquet has twice appealed to this book as proving the happiness of rural life in pre-Reformation England. First, in the preface to his edition of Cobbett's *Protestant Reformation* (1896), where he writes:

Viewed merely in its social aspect, the English Reformation was really the rising of the rich against the poor.... His [Cobbett's] pages help us to realize the fact that the reformation effected, besides a change in religious beliefs and practices, a wide and permanent division in the great body politic. The supposed purification of doctrine and practice was brought about only at the cost of, as it were, driving a wedge well into the heart of the nation, which at once and for all divided the rich from the poor, and established the distinction which still exists between the classes and the masses.

After which the cardinal proceeds (p. xiii) to quote a part of Mr Booth's preface to the *Halmote Rolls* in a context which implies that these words support his thesis, though in fact they have no such force in their own context, with the exception of this one concluding sentence: "He [the prior of Durham], appears always to have dealt with his tenants, either in person or through his officers, with much consideration; and in the imposition of fines we find them invariably tempering justice with mercy." I have already shown in my text that this generalization is very hasty. The fines remitted by the prior are very considerably less than in some lay courts; for instance, the first four pages record thirty-four different fines, totalling £16. 19s. 6d.; yet of these there is only one doubtful case of remission, 2s., and that is not to a bondman but to a priest. The Norwich Leet Court would have remitted at least £5 or £6 under similar conditions. The rents (contrary to Mr Booth's assertion), are far more frequently raised than lowered; I have shown this in my text.

Cardinal Gasquet then continues, speaking for himself:

In fact as the picture of medieval village life among the tenants of the Durham monastery is displayed in the pages of this interesting volume, it would seem almost as if one was reading of some Utopia of dreamland. Many of the things that in these days advanced politicians would desire to see introduced into the village communities of modern England[1], to relieve the deadly dulness of country life, were seen in

---

[1] This quotation from Mr Booth's preface and the cardinal's own continuing words, are reproduced almost word for word in his *English Monastic Life* (1904), p. 199; the only variation worth noting is that the cardinal

Durham and Cumberland in full working order in pre-Reformation days. Local provisions for public health and general convenience are evidenced by the watchful vigilance of the village officials over the water supplies, the care taken to prevent the fouling of useful streams, and stringent by-laws as to the common place for clothes washing and the times for emptying and cleansing ponds and mill-dams. Labour was lightened and the burdens of life eased by cooperation on an extensive scale. A common mill ground the corn, and the flour was baked into bread at a common oven. A common smith worked at a common forge, and common shepherds and herdsmen watched the sheep and cattle of various tenants when pastured on the fields common to the whole village community. The pages of the volume contain numerous instances of the kindly consideration for their tenants which characterized the monastic proprietors, and the relation between them was rather that of rent-charges than of absolute ownership.

In these additional words of his own, in which the cardinal claims implicitly to speak from full knowledge of the text of this volume, it would be difficult to find a single accurate statement of any importance. It will be noted that the lord's monopoly of mill and oven, which represented one of the most galling village disabilities, which led to actual revolt at St Albans and on other manors, and which was among the feudal oppressions most bitterly resented by the French peasantry of 1789, are actually boasted of here as "easing the burdens of life" for them! The whole description might have been written by a man who had not only not looked at one word of the actual text, but who had not even found time to read the whole of the editor's preface; for in the later pages of that preface Mr Booth does speak plainly about the readiness of these peasants to quarrel and draw knives or arrows, the necessity of cucking-stools to control the women's tongues, the chastisement of servants by their masters, the prohibition of ball-play, the burdensome fee paid for marriage, and, finally, the fact that "incontinence was common in the vills; [the fines for marriage] are considerably less in number than fines for leyrwite" (pp. xxvii–xxx). The cardinal can scarcely have read those four introductory pages when he claimed that the book takes us back "to some Utopia of dreamland"; and that the benevolent rule of the prior of Durham had anticipated what advanced politicians are still vainly desiring "in the way of improved sanitary conditions, and to relieve the deadly dulness of country life." If I am so often compelled to overload my text, and even my appendixes, with documentary matter, it is because widely-read authors, who profess to have studied these documents, have so misled the public with regard to their real contents, that we must charitably suppose them never

specifies more closely these pre-Reformation improvements for which post-Reformation society is still vainly striving; after *England*, he adds "in the way of improved sanitary and social conditions, and to relieve," etc.

to have read the authorities to which they so confidently appeal. For, as I have shown elsewhere, well-known French and German apologists, though seldom quite so unconscientious, are often culpably inaccurate in their most important references.

With regard to the question of rents raised or lowered, and to other natural economic relations between monks and their tenants, much valuable evidence will be found in the Eynsham Cartulary. In the court-rolls before the Black Death, we find bondmen purchasing their freedom; but, after 1349, Mr Salter points out how many simply ran away from the manors, and were known to be living hard by, yet the abbot shrank from the appeal to law, since even success might cost him more than the villein was worth (II, xxvi, xlv). And in those days the abbot found it necessary to put the whole economy on a new basis; he held a series of inquisitions about 1360, in which the old services and rents were brought into conformity with new economic conditions. The Woodeaton inquisition is most interesting, since here the compiler has definitely expressed what we could only have inferred from the other manors (I, 19). After describing in detail the pre-plague conditions of a typical holding, he continues:

In the days of that mortality or pestilence which was in the year of our Lord 1349, there scarce remained two tenants on this manor, and these would have departed unless brother Nicholas of Upton, who was then abbot of the said manor, had made a new composition with them and with other tenants who came in. He agreed with them in the following form; namely that the said Walter and other tenants [should be subject to certain dues; relief, heriot, merchet, and a certain amount of forced labour] and that he should [also] pay a yearly rent of 13s. 4d. so long as it may please my lord [abbot]; and may it please my lord to perpetuity, for the aforesaid services [from which he is now released] were not worth so much [as this 13s. 4d.]; yet, let the lords at any other time do as they think to be most profitable [in their then circumstances].

II

(Chap. VII, p. 73)

JUSTICE AND MONEY

This connexion is well marked by Lipson, pp. 19 ff., 524 ff.; Seignobos, pp. 243, 247 ff.; and Sée, *Bretagne*, pp. 73–8. Guérard's verdict carries great weight here in view of his learning and balance of mind. He writes (*Cart. St-Père*, pp. cclxvi–cclxvii):

Les droits de justice possédés par les religieux de S.-P. étaient fort considérables....Ces institutions, qui mettaient les biens et la vie de nos pères à la discrétion d'un officier institué par des moines, et dont les lumières et l'équité même n'offraient pas plus de garanties que l'indépendance, étaient sans doute bien imparfaites, et sont assurément bien peu regrettables; trop souvent, sous leur empire, la justice ne semblait pas moins une ferme qu'une magistrature, et trop rarement les vertus de l'homme venaient compenser les vices de la chose.

Verriest supplies, from the archives of the counts of Hainaut, a very interesting list of offences and fines (pp. 134 ff.). He notes expressly how preponderantly financial was the lord's interest in justice (pp. 19, 133). One very characteristic item is the interest which the lord had in the chattels of felons, or in the deodand which became due when any animal or possession had been the direct cause of a man's death. Thus, in the reign of Edward II, John, servant of William de Brickhulle, was drowned by mischance by falling into the river Weaver from a cart. This was on the lands of Vale Royal; and the monks took as deodand "one cart bound with iron, with two horses and other chattels to the value of £4" (*Vale Royal*, p. 81). The bailiff regularly enters such perquisites to his lord's account; they often form a very regular and considerable item of manorial incomes. At Florence, about 1320, the fines in the lawcourts brought in 20,000 gold florins a year, even though the actual amounts paid amounted to only from one-twentieth to one-eightieth of the legal tariff to be inflicted. "Buying oneself free, under the cloak of kindly forgiveness, became a glaring abuse...with what profit to morality and public safety, we need not discuss" (Davidsohn, pp. 116, 322). Such bribery, under these conditions, was almost inevitable; and everywhere we meet with evidence for its prevalence in fact. Jocelin of Brakelond reports the indignation of suitors when they found what an exceptional man Abbot Samson was: "cursed be the court of this abbot, where neither gold nor silver profiteth me to confound mine adversary!" (C.S. p. 25, Clark, p. 43). The bribery rampant in the lawcourts, said St Edmund of Canterbury, is the ruin of Christendom; and, a century later, Bishop Guillaume le Maire repeated his words, adding that the worst bribery was in the Church (*Lib. Guil. Major*, p. 487). Gower speaks equally plainly in his poem on the vices of his age (*Political Poems and Songs*, R.S. 1, 356). Elsewhere, in his *Vox Clamantis* and *Mirour de l'Omme*, he brands the venality of the church courts in especial; and, generations before this, reforming churchmen had insisted that the current system of fines lent itself to abuses of this kind (*e.g.* Grosseteste, *Epp.* R.S. p. 160). Things went still worse where, as in France and other countries, the State offices were publicly sold. Even under St Louis, we have seen royal officers telling the peasants or citizens that they must have more money, or they would never make up the capital laid out in the purchase of their posts. As time wore on, this became worse and worse; Nicholas de Clémanges complains of the public sale of offices involving justiciary powers (*l.c.* f. 52 b) and the États Généraux of the later Middle Ages concerned themselves with the same abuse. Among the "Hundred Grievances" put before the emperor at the Diet of Nürnberg in 1522, the 1st and 55th deal with the legal oppression of the poor and the venality of the courts (Browne, *Fasc.* I, 354, 366). Justice, therefore, was everywhere unpopular; it is quite typical that one of the first acts of the revolting peasants in 1381 was to "cut off the heads of all the jurors in their district whom they could catch, asserting that the land would never enjoy its freeborn liberty until these men had been slain" (Walsingham, *Hist. Ang.* R.S. I, 455). Bishop Pecock, cataloguing the classes whose operations were most widespread and mischievous in the fifteenth century, specifies "forsworn jurors" (*Repressor*, R.S. p. 516).

12

(Chap. VIII, p. 75)

HERIOT AND MORTUARY

(*a*) ENGLAND

The author of *Fleta* seems to have a vague sense of the essential injustice of the heriot, "a due which is rendered rather of grace than by law" (bk III, ch. 18). But Maitland thought poorly of *Fleta* as a law-book, and it would be difficult to find documentary evidence for this judgement. Sometimes, indeed, the tenant paid a separate heriot to every landlord from whom he held; it was on this plea that Dunstable priory secured the second best beast of Thomas the Painter in 1291 (*An. Dunst.* R.S. p. 371). So also in Flanders, where he might even have to pay two heriots to the same lord in two different capacities (Verriest, p. 150). We have seen that this was practically so in England, though the Church and the lord called the due by different names. In 1356, Bishop Grandisson as arbiter settled a quarrel between the parson of Moreton Hampstead and his parishioners with regard to certain dues; the bishop decided that the rector must no longer charge money for the Sacraments (which, of course, was definitely illegal) but that, in all cases where a tenant owed a heriot to the lord, he must pay a mortuary also to the priest[1]. Thus it was that the monks often got a double death-due, as lords of the manor and as rectors of the parish. Under Gloucester Abbey, for example, "when [this tenant] shall come to die, the lord [abbot] shall have his best beast as lord, and another as rector" (*Gloucs. Cart.* R.S. III, 159; cf. pp. 138, 170, 172, 182). The abbot of Cirencester,

[1] *Reg. Grand.* p. 1177.

again, got both (*Bristol and Gloucs. Arch. Soc.* IX, 304). Similarly
with the serfs at Otterton; the prior took the best beast in his secular,
and the second best in his spiritual capacity. With regard to the
"relief," or fine for change of tenancy, the sum is "at the lord's will;
yet in case of poverty less should be taken, and the tenant should be
spared." On the other hand, it is provided that "if poor or weakly
serfs fail in payment of rent, so that they pay not competently, then
the lord [prior] may assign that land to more able folk, as he shall
judge expedient" (Oliver, *Monast. Dioc. Exon.* pp. 254–5). We need
not be surprised, therefore, at incidents like that which is related in
Noakes's *Monastery and Cathedral of Worcester* (p. 90): "A great
riot broke out at Shipston in the sixth year of Henry IV with reference
to heriots, and the question was ultimately referred to the abbot of
Winchcomb, who determined that the prior and convent [of Wor-
cester] had from early times received at the death of every tenant the
best animal, while the parson of Tredington received the second
best." In 1350, the royal justices admitted the claim of the abbot of
Vale Royal "that, if any one's villein shall have fled to the said abbot's
land and wish to remain there, he shall give to the abbot and convent
yearly 4*d*., or more or less according as he can make an agreement;
and if he dies in the said land without an heir, the aforesaid abbot
shall have all his goods; and, if he have an heir, a heriot" (*Vale
Royal*, p. 134). As to the friction produced by the system, see the
8th of my *Medieval Studies*, and compare this petition to the Star
Chamber:

"To my Lord Cardinalles good grace. Humbly complayneth John
Cokeson of Werrington, co. Lancaster, that oone Sir Edward Mole-
neux, clerk, about 5 Henry VIII. [1513/4] with force of armys entered
into a certen mere and land in Littel Crosby, which the complaynant
hath in leese of one Nicholas Blundell, squyer; and caused his servants
to kylle a fat oxe of the complaynantes, value 53*s*. 4*d*."...The defendant says he is parson of Sefton, and the complainant occupied in
farm a certain messuage and land there, to which his wife and family
then had resort. About seven years since the complainant's wife died,
and the ox in question was peaceably delivered by some of the family
to the defendant's deputy as her mortuary....The complainant
replies that Molyneux claims a mortuary for the occupation of certain
land in Sefton, without alleging that she died in that parish; nor is
there any custom there that a woman covert should pay any mortuary,
especially one that died not in Sefton, but in Werryngton, a distance of
16 miles [etc.].   *Star-Chamb. Lanc.* I, 75.

How often difficulties of this kind must have occurred, we may infer
not only from the act of 21 Hen. VIII (1529), ch. 6, which regulated
mortuaries and abolished them altogether for people dying with less
than £6. 13*s*. 4*d*. in movable goods, but also from the lawyer

St-Germain's complaints written shortly after this act (*A Treatise concerning the Division between the Spiritualty and Temporalty*, ff. 24 ff.). He writes:

And as for mortuaries, they are annulled already by statute, but yet beginneth to rise one thing to maintain the first division concerning such mortuaries, if it be suffered to continue; and that is that many curates, not regarding the king's statute in that behalf, persuade their parishioners when they be sick to believe that they cannot be saved but they restore them as much as the old mortuary would have amounted to.... The cause why they were taken away was forasmuch as there were few things within this realm that caused more variance among the people than they did when they were suffered; for they were taken so far against the order of the king's laws and against justice and right as shall hereafter appear. First, they were taken not only after the death of the husband but also after the death of the wife, which after the laws of the realm had no goods, but that it was taken of the husband's goods; and they were taken also of servants and children, as well infants as other. And if a man died by the way, and had an household in another place, he should pay in both places[1]. And sometimes when the parson and vicar of a church appropred varied for the mortuaries, the people, as it hath been reported, have been enforced, ere they could sit in rest, to pay in some places mortuaries to them both. And some time the curate would prohibit poor men to sell their goods in time of sickness, if they were such goods as were like to be their mortuaries, for they would say it was done in defraud of the Church. And if the quick goods were better than the dead goods, they would in some places take the quick. And if the dead goods were better than the quick, they would take the dead. And the mortuaries must be delivered forthwith, or else the body should not be buried. And they prescribed to have right to mortuaries only by prescription of the spiritual law. And under that manner mortuaries increased daily in many places, and of likelihood would have gone farther if they had not been stopped in time. And they were in many places taken in such manner as made men to think that the curates loved their mortuaries better than their lives. And thereupon rose in many places great division and grudge between them [clergy and laity].... For these causes the said mortuaries be annulled by parliament, as well in conscience as in the law. And yet it is said that some curates bore great extremities concerning the said mortuaries, another way, and that is this: if the executor at the first request pay not the money that

[1] Records show mortuaries thus taken from travellers. A Yarmouth witness, testifying to the wreck of a Breton ship there in about 1500, remembers that he helped to bring three drowned sailors "from thens to Yermouth ch. yerde upon a slede, and ther buryed them in their cloths in one pitt; and further seith, that one of the seid thre persons hadd a sylver whystle abought his nekk of the value of xxvis viiid or thereabought, and that the prior of Yermouth at that tyme being, hadd the seid whystle for a mortuary" (H. Swinden's *Yarmouth*, 1772, p. 365).

is appointed by the statute, they will anon have a citation against him, and then shall he be so handled that, as is said, it had been most commonly much better to him to have paid his old mortuary than the costs and expenses that he shall pay there.

I have warned readers later (p. 459, n. 3) against the slip in *The Political History of England*, v, 293, where the significance of this passage is greatly affected by representing the parson as *compelling* those sales which in fact he *prohibited*. The law being what it was, prospective beneficiaries naturally provided against evasion; and in England it seems that all transfers made during the last illness were invalidated (Lyndwood, *Provinciale*, 1679, pp. 19 ff., esp. note c, *sine dolo*). But here and there, in what is now Switzerland, the sick owner was allowed a sporting chance, so long as he cared to risk surviving his gift by months or years and finding himself in King Lear's case. At Altdorf, near the Greifensee, under the monks of Zürich, in 1439,

If a man or woman, boy or girl, come to the deathbed, if they are then strong enough that they can walk without staff, crutches, or help for seven feet beyond the house, in their clothes, then they may give their movables to whomsoever they will, in order that it may not come to the aforesaid lord; and if they have two honest folk who see this and hear it and can also assert it before the lord according to the law of the court, then the lord must allow this. (*Weisthümer*, I, 13.)

At Stäfa on the Lake of Zürich, about the same date, the prescription speaks of the man alone; he must first "clothe himself without help, even as he goes to church and to market" (*ibid*. p. 46). Under the counts of Kyburg, at about the same date again, the man need go only 3 feet (*ibid*. p. 21). Similar provisions, more or less strict, may be found on p. 106; II, 22; III, 127, 150, 151, 154, 191; VI, 298.

The ordinary man, therefore, had no affection for the mortuary system; but, on the other hand, many well-to-do and pious parishioners met the Church half-way here, and comforted their last moments with the assurance that their body would be borne to its last home under convoy of a substantial sin-offering, in the shape of a "foredrove." Of this custom the Rev. E. Gepp writes:

Its existence in Essex is abundantly plain. In every one of some fifteen wills, quoted by Mr King, it is specifically mentioned. The wills, which date from 1493 to 1534, show that the usual offering was one or more sheep, sometimes a bullock, a cow, or a horse: not pigs, presumably because they, unlike the staider animals, would probably behave themselves unseemly on the march.

Thomas Swete, a wealthy yeoman of Prittlewell, in a will (1493) of queer Latin, directs "Item lego summo altari pro decimis meis negligenter oblitis vi^s viii^d., et tres boves ad fugandos corpori meo in die sepulture mee." Compunction for tithe unpaid appears in two other wills. Others provide for the offering of "a schepe," "a shepe called a weder," "oon of my best shepe," "a shepe price xx^d.," another price "ii^s.," "a bullock of twoo yeres age," "a cowe," "a horsse," "a trotting grey colt of ii yeres age and the vauntage." Three extracts direct that the offering be for the use of the priest. For instance, John Kyngesman (1522) declares "I give to the vicar of the same Church (Althorne) for my foredrove ii moder ewes." (*Essex Review*, Jan. 1921, p. 16.)

(b) FRANCE

Luchaire touches on this subject on p. 394 of his *Social France at the Time of Philip Augustus* (Eng. trans.). A suggestion of natural heart-burnings comes from such a casual notice as this, that the abbot of St-Germain, in about 1240, gave the heriot of a tenant as a dowry to the sister of one of the abbey servants; from another heriot he himself gained ten livres, and the prior three (Guilhiermoz, pp. 297, 302). Even as late as 1789, we find a lord in Berry taking by custom half the possessions of each of his tenants who was subject to heriot, leaving only half for the wife and children (Bruneau, p. 58. Compare p. 57 for the invidious nature of this due in general; and, for the frequency of the practice in medieval Berry, des Méloizes, pp. 196, 202, 214, 219).

One custom, however, which was bitterly complained of in Tudor England, seems to have been even more general in France; that of seizing the dead man's or woman's bed as a perquisite. The first notice I know is in a very significant letter of Innocent III, in 1204, to his legates in Southern France; but it seems evident that the custom was then already of great antiquity. The great pope writes:

You have reported also, that in some churches a custom has grown up that the bedding wherein the bodies of the dead are carried to church should become the property of the ministers; but now[1], since the charity of the people grows cold, and devotion is decaying, scandal is oftentimes generated between the clergy and the people by reason of these beds.... Warn the clergy with more diligence that they use no burdensome exaction or dishonourable importunity with regard to the bedding which is brought with the corpses to their churches; on the other hand, take care to induce the laity, by diligent warnings, to maintain in these matters that laudable custom which hath hitherto been observed by the devotion of the faithful; and compel them thereunto, if necessary, by ecclesiastical pressure, admitting no appeal. (*Epp.* bk VII, ep. 165; Migne, P.L. vol. 215, col. 472.)

---

[1] Reading *nunc* for the *nec* which, as the editor remarks, is an obvious error.

The pope's attitude here contrasts with that of Ferdinand V, who, in 1486, solemnly forbade certain abuses, among which was that of seizing as lord's perquisite the dead peasant's best blanket, and refusing burial to the corpse until the blanket had been rendered (Brutails, p. 192). Under papal protection, this seizure of beds went on in France. But resistance grew with growing civilization; and an unprinted manuscript in the Bibliothèque Nationale supplies evidence so valuable that I must dwell upon it here[1].

Pierre Albert, grand-prior of Cluny, wrote during the sitting of the Council of Bâle (1431–43). His treatise is in defence of monastic rights, and, as we might expect, of Cluniac rights in especial. In Book II, ch. 20 (to quote from the list of contents) "the author deals with the excesses of layfolk who refuse to pay corpse-bedding." He takes a position which, in canon law, is inexpugnable (f. 156 a):

The laity cannot deny that the bedding is due, since this has been the custom from time immemorial; and the observance thereof hath the force of constitution and nature and observance which no man can contravene; therefore it must be kept, and the heirs and executors of such folk must be compelled to keep it.... And if, in condemnation of this custom, it be objected that this bedding-due is contrary to good manners or God's command, or Canon or Civil Law or the Law of Nations, or that it contains a base cause or the guilt of simony, this objection cannot stand, since these flaws do not exist in our case, but the custom was introduced from just cause, as I shall say later; nor does the burden of proving its justice lie upon the Church.

The proximate cause of this due is "the labour of the ministers, the favour of the Church, and the remission of sins"; and what better can there be? Moreover, these objectors are blind to fine legal distinctions; they confuse *occasion* with *cause*:

for I note that a harlot, although she does evil in that she does harlotry, yet she may accept money, since it is not base to receive....It would indeed be a base cause, if [the bedding] were taken for divine service, especially by a bargain, or by retention, or by cessation from sacraments until the bed were rendered; for such a custom would be base, and the bed would not be paid, and there would be no ground for an action at law; for such a custom would not be laudable, but base and even detestable....It would be simony, if the clergy refused to bury the body unless they first received surety for the payment of such dues; but in these cases let the corpse first be buried, and then let an action be brought against the heirs and detainers [of the bedding].

[1] It is briefly described by L. Delisle, *Inventaire des MSS—fonds de Cluni*, Paris, 1884, pp. 322–3. But Delisle omits to note that nearly all the first part of the treatise is missing: and this, to judge from the contemporary list of contents, should have been the most interesting.

The objectors prove too much; according to their arguments, the priest would not be allowed to charge fees for marriages. This bedding-due may be defended by analogy; at Venice, the Church takes a death-duty of 10 per cent. on a man's personal property, and in Brittany a third. The mere fact that the due has so long been paid is a presumption in favour of its justice; otherwise protests would have been raised from the beginning. It is specified by Hostiensis, in his great commentary, as one of those laudable customs to which we must give the force of law, side by side with the similar custom by which, elsewhere, the priest sometimes took the dead man's garments (f. 158 a). There is no real simony in this, since "this temporal payment is not demanded for a spiritual thing, in the sense that the spiritual thing is not the mediate [immediate?] cause of demanding the temporal payment, but the custom [is the cause]; therefore, because the custom is such, let the man who strives to infringe it be constrained by ecclesiastical censure." For, even though there were no ground at law for an action against recalcitrants, "yet the people may be compelled to keep an honest custom"; and, in fact, good authorities grant the priest an action at law. The priest is not simoniacal when he takes such things "for his labour and for his livelihood, and not for a sacrament." He is demanding "*in* spiritual things, but not *for* spiritual things." In short, the argument is mainly based upon the painful but notorious fact that parochial revenues were so greatly absorbed by monasteries and other appropriators as to leave the parson little choice between starvation and exacting casual dues of this kind. As the unimpeachably orthodox Prof. Imbart de la Tour puts it,

ce sont d'abord l'administration des sacrements, le baptême, la sépulture et surtout la messe pour les défunts qui sont taxés par le prêtre. L'Église luttait en vain pour maintenir le principe de la gratuité. Hincmar rappelle dans les lettres canoniques données aux nouveaux évêques qu'ils ne doivent pas permettre à leurs prêtres de tirer profit du baptême, des choses saintes, de la sépulture; mais cette règle restait morte. Les faits économiques étaient plus forts que le droit. Les prêtres de paroisse, dépouillés souvent par les exactions mêmes de leurs supérieurs et par les usurpations des grands, privés des dîmes ou des revenus de leur domaine, tenus de payer à leur évêque des droits énormes, étaient obligés de tirer parti à leur tour de leur ministère spirituel. Ils vivaient du sacerdoce, sans qu'à l'origine ces usages aient blessé la conscience des populations. Les fidèles, depuis longtemps, aimaient à offrir quelque souvenir à leur église au moment des fiançailles, des funérailles ou à la suite d'une pénitence. Ces dons volontaires se transformèrent peu à peu en un véritable impôt. À l'époque féodale, la vente des sacrements fut un des revenus réguliers des paroisses[1].

[1] *Revue historique*, LXIII (1897), 31.

Complaints of the sale of sacraments are universal in the later Middle Ages; the Diet of Nürnberg pressed this subject on the emperor's consideration in 1522[1]; and in 1515 our Commons reported to the king that priests "daily refuse to fetch and receive the corpse of such deceased person...but if such best jewel, garment, cloth, or other best thing as is aforesaid be given them." Therefore they pray for an enactment "that no parish priest refuse to bury in their church [on account of unpaid mortuary, and] that every curate shall administer the sacrament of holy church, where required, to every sick person in his parish, and shall receive into his church or churchyard the corpse of every person dying in his parish, under a penalty of forty pounds"[2].

But to return to our grand-prior of Cluny. He applies himself, from f. 159 b onwards, to demolish the arguments of objectors in detail. (1) "Perchance our lay adversaries, very unfriendly to the clergy[3], argue that this custom is unjust, and an unjust custom does not gain full prescription by time." To this he opposes a flat denial; the custom is laudable. (2) They argue that canon law prohibits exactions for spiritual services: "but you may answer, as I have already said, that this is not given for spiritual things, but for another cause, by settled custom and settled Church constitution." (3) Again, they allege that many parsons, on the strength of this custom, make a composition with the heirs concerning the bedding, or have kept it or something similar as a pledge; and yet this is forbidden [in canon law]. (4) Again, they argue that "the said custom was introduced for fear of the priests, on account of the preambles which priests make." But in fact the custom was brought in without any sort of compulsion; and, "even though there had been compulsion [at first] yet through patience and paying of the beds and frequent consent" that plea is annulled.

We cannot presume that the priests struck fear, since their office is to benefit all men and to harm none....Moreover, seeing that the parochial place is commonly a public place, wherein many parishioners dwell, and wherein they assemble for divine service and the sacraments, the priest could not have struck fear into them, since no violence could be inflicted in a public place, by one little man, such as a simple vicar or rector is with respect to his people.

(5) Again, if they plead poverty, alleging

the poor dead man who had nothing in his possession but only this bed which the priest demands, then this objection is thus solved. Seeing

---

[1] Browne, *Fasc.* vol. I, p. 372, § 82.

[2] *Letters and Papers, Hen. VIII*, vol. II, No. 1315, p. 354.

[3] *Oppido clericis infesti*; the words from Gratian's *Decretum* which Boniface took as his text in the bull *Clericis Laicos*.

that the debt of this bed[1], and the payment thereof, take their rise from the piety and devotion of the faithful, as has been shown above, it follows that this bedding-due should be more benignly and humanely moderated [reference to a law book]; and in this case a broad and kindly interpretation should be made on the poor man's behalf, lest the devotion and munificence of the laity themselves towards the churches should be retarded [another reference]. Nay, in this case it seems that the due should be remitted, as with him who had but one single sheep, who did not pay it for tithe or first-fruits, as we read in the 12th chapter of the second book of Kings[2] [farther law-references]. Otherwise, the poor man might implore the service of the episcopal judge, which is founded upon equity[3] [reference], or the payment of the bedding might sleep until his children or heirs came to better fortune.

(6) Finally, the laity object

that the priest ought to minister the Church sacraments gratis; both according to the text "Freely ye have received, freely give," and because stipends are assigned for these and like duties [reference]; therefore he who doeth the contrary is acting basely. The solution of this is apparent from what has already been said; for the priest does confer the sacraments freely and for nothing[4]; but he does not abandon these alms and this gift, spontaneously bestowed on him, and customary, and justly initiated and continued by the consent of the people to a good end; from which good it is not right to depart, since that which is good must be kept. Moreover, the bed is due not to the priest but to the church in whose name the priest demands the bed, for the church never dies [reference]; and this due is owing to custom, not to the priest's ministration of the sacraments; and the priest could not with a safe conscience abandon the bed, for this would be to the prejudice of the church, which he has no right to prejudice or deteriorate.

All through, however, our author is conscious of one weak point, the history of the due. He knows that, however the custom may be immemorial, this prescription cannot hold good at law unless it be a good and wholesome custom; and he sees that the laity are more and more vehemently contesting this essential point. To this, therefore,

---

[1] Reading *debitum* for *debiti*, which seems an obvious slip.

[2] *I.e.* the "one little ewe lamb" of 2 Sam. xii, 3.

[3] This is the same cold comfort which the English canonist, John of Ayton, gives (Lyndwood, *Provinciale*, 1679, pt ii, p. 127). If the priest does not save the poor of his parish from starvation, have these a case at law against him? Not *directly*, says John, "but they may denounce the affair to the ecclesiastical judge, who will compel [the priests and rich folk] thereunto." It would be interesting to find a single recorded case in which the poor ventured on this course.

[4] Peter is here taking the liberty of alleging Church theory as if it were Church practice. There is overwhelming evidence for Imbart de la Tour's censure, that the illegal sale of sacraments was a constant abuse.

he constantly recurs; and on this note he ends, with an appeal to the Bestiary which could scarcely have convinced the awakening intelligence of the French laity in 1430, even if it had been more correct. The bear-whelp, according to medieval natural history, is born a shapeless mass, and licked into shape by his mother; the lion-cub is still-born, but the father's roaring awakens him to life. A confused recollection of these two facts supplies Peter with his final illustration:

And so this custom [of the beds] began as a lion-cub, which cometh forth at first as an abortion, and is afterwards quickened by his mother's licking. Thus this, though at first it might not seem to be valid, for it was dead and deformed, yet it is quickened by the unbroken course of time, and by consent, whether tacit or by the mere rendering and payment of the thing.

And it is a custom "of public utility, viz. the soul's health of dead folk; for almsgiving covereth a multitude of sins." Peter, it will be observed, takes the liberty here of reading *elemosina* for the *charitas* of 1 Pet. iv, 8; and it is characteristic of him and his brethren that he counts this compulsory due to the priest as almsgiving, just as the Romainmotier monks gave the same name to the tribute exacted from tenants.

In some parts of France, this heriot system, under the name of *mainmorte*, lasted down to the Revolution. The hardened lawyer Dunod, whose *Traité de la Mainmorte* coldly describes and implicitly upholds the whole system as it subsisted still in his native Franche-Comté (1760) is yet betrayed into the confession of its unpopularity: "It is said that *mainmorte* is odious, and that it ought to be restricted as far as possible.... In short, we see that the general spirit of the nation tends to weaken *mainmorte*, and even to banish it from the kingdom; and that, in the provinces where it survives, it has been much softened by legal judgements and by the reformation of the Coutumes" (p. 15). How far this last sentence is true, may be judged from the details which I give in appendixes 14 and 16, and from Dunod's own comments on this subject in Chapter III of his book. It may be judged also from the following law which held good until the Revolution (Chassin, p. 49):

According to art. 3 [of Coutumes, tit. xv] the freeman who marries a serf's daughter and lives with his wife in a place subject to *mainmorte* does not himself become a serf if, during his wife's lifetime or within a year of her death, he abandons his house and land to the lord. Only, if he dies there, his children born there are subject to *mainmorte*. [The memorial to the Etats Généraux complains:] "The wretched father has but one resource to save his children from this stigma; when he falls ill, he must get himself carried, over rocks and precipices, into some free district, and there breathe his last.... More than one father's death has been thus caused." As to the woman under similar conditions, can she save her heirs from the consequences of *mainmorte* by getting herself carried to die in a free district? A judgement of the Parlement of Besançon (Aug. 4, 1645)[1] decided in favour of the monks of La Charité who pleaded against the brothers of a woman named Verdoz who died thus.

Dom Grappin, who pleads all that can without absurdity be pleaded in favour of *mainmorte*, gives his case away by his apology for the state of the French peasantry of his time (p. 72), and by the story for which he claims our special admiration on p. 139:

Le vrai mérite a des droits sur tous les cœurs. Mais on ne se rappelle qu'avec sensibilité l'impression qu'il fit sur un homme dont la bien-faisance est égale à la noblesse de son origine. De deux frères nés main-mortables de l'Abbaye de Baume, l'un avait mérité la Croix de St-Louis [dans les guerres], et l'autre s'était distingué dans les Missions étrangères. Il y a peu d'années que M. de la Fare, alors Abbé de Baume, les affranchit et refusa généreusement le prix de leur liberté. *On ne me doit rien*, répondit-il à ceux qui le lui offraient; *on n'est point esclave quand on a aussi bien servi le Roi et la Religion.*

(c) FLANDERS

Here, nearly all my evidence is from Verriest, pp. 34, 44, 124, 334.

In Hainaut, the heriot amounted originally to half the dead man's movables, or more. In 1327, it is complained of as the main cause of depopulation in one village; men fled elsewhere to live under a less burdensome tax. Even in its greatly modified form, it remained the most unpopular, on the whole, of all feudal dues. On the verge of its final abolition in Belgium, the Chambre des Comptes reported: "It is notorious with what horror men regard this, since the head of a family is no sooner dead than men come and take this tax even before the corpse has left the house; an officer comes while the whole family, and even the small children, are often in tears; he carries off their best possession, and often the only one which could help to pay for the expenses of the dead man's illness and burial, etc. and which would often help the family to buy bread for some time." What these distinguished government officials were privileged to write in 1789 must have been murmured during the past centuries by millions whose voices have never come down to us. Verriest writes: "We have a few examples of its abandonment from motives of pity"; but he quotes only one; the count of Hainaut, in 1415, took as his due half the price of the bondman's house, "but for his movables we account not here; for his widow was a very poor woman with six small children

---

[1] Chassin, by an obvious misprint, has 1845.

living on alms." He quotes an extreme case of subdivision of the right of heriot in one village. When a tenant died, his heriot was divided among five landlords in the proportion of eleven-twenty-eighths, one-fourth, one-fifth, four-thirty-fifths and three-seventieths. But, in a good many other parts of Flanders, serfdom disappeared early, and with it the mortuary dues: see Pirenne, *Hist. Belg.* I, 275, 281.

(d) GERMANY

A long passage in Cless is so valuable that we may take it here for our starting-point. I quote from vol. II, i, pp. 424-5, 428 ff.

It marked a considerable mitigation of the earlier conditions when Bruno, abbot of Hirschau

decreed that the serfs of his monastery should no longer be given in exchange to any other lord, ecclesiastical or secular, and that, by way of heriot, the man should pay only his weapons and one head of cattle, and the woman her best garment[1]....The usual heriot for a man is his best head of cattle, together with a whole suit of clothes and his weapons (which, however, if there is a son, are passed on to him), and often a part of his movable property also[2]. The woman gave her best suit of clothes, which she was wont to wear at Church on Sundays or feast-days. In the village of Lombach, it was the best gown that she had been able to spin. The customal of Leidringen records the earlier custom of claiming the bed also; but this was left in the husband's possession until he should marry again, when it fell in to the monastery, unless he had a daughter by his first wife, to whom the bed then went: the same rule held at [the monastery of] Nellingen. At Leidringen, the heirs had to bring all their cattle before the monks' bailiff, who then chose the best. If it were found that the best had not been shown to him, then he had a right to a second heriot, and so on for nine times. It might happen that the front of a house was on the monks' land, and therefore liable to these servile dues, while the hinder part was on some other domain and free from such services. If the owner was so ill that his death was looked forward to, they would move him to the back room, thus giving him plainly to understand his hopeless case, but saving the heriot. At Alpirsbach, if a man sold his best beast before his death, and it could be shown that this had been to defraud the [monastic] lord of his heriot, then the beast was taken back from the purchaser, who was left to indemnify himself from the rest[3]....

[1] "Her best garment, that she was wont to wear at church," says a customal of the village of Tettingen, whose lords were the monks of St Blasien (J. Grimm, *Weisthümer*, 1840, I, 303).

[2] *I.e.* one-third of his movables and his best head of cattle; or, two-thirds without the cattle; this was the rule of the monastery of St Georgen.

[3] Compare Bishop Quivil's prohibition of death-bed sales (Wilkins, II, 158) and the complaints of Christopher St-Germain in his "Treatise concerning the Division between the Spiritualtie and the Temporaltie," 1530,

In some places, when a holding was sold, the lord took also a third part of the movable goods....The most startling operation of this right of ownership over the serf's property is in the so-called *Bachelor-right* [Hagestolzen-Recht]....The customal of Nellingen says: "When a serf of our monastery dies leaving neither wife nor children, then the monastery inherits his possessions in preference to all his kin"; and this seems to have been a pretty general principle, in a greater or less degree[1]....It is counted as a special benefit conferred upon all the tenants of St Georgen in 1435, when Abbot Heinrich decrees: "Whereas, in former times, certain of our predecessors have taken the heritage of poor folk as bachelors, according to the bachelor-custom, seeing that the poor folk of our domain have ever thought this unjust, We therefore have recognized this, and have abandoned this right of inheritance, as is here written, so that the poor folk of our domain may pass their inheritance to their fathers, mothers, and kinsfolk even to the fourth degree; but, beyond this degree, shall and may We, Abbot Heinrich, or our successors or our monastery inherit, with the help and will of our poor folk, and without let or hindrance."...The customal of Leidringen, however, never excluded the parents from such inheritance. By this custom, the monastery inherited all the chattels of bondmen who died in their twelfth year [or upwards] and from bondwomen who died in their fourteenth, leaving no parents; even when there are several brothers and sisters who have property in common or in severalty, the monks inherit the dead child's chattels. ...At St Georgen, freemen were not subject to this bachelor-due. On the other hand, in the domains of the convent of Alpirsbach, where in most villages the air made bondmen[2], even the freeman was subject to this due, and the monks inherited the bachelor's chattels....In this district, bachelors are men or women who die unmarried after their fiftieth year, or have remained widowers or widows for thirty years, and die in that state. The author of the dissertation which I have often quoted [*i.e.* Harprecht] sees in this a punishment for the neglect of the sacrament of matrimony; and, in cases where the right is exercised in this form, the supposition seems not improbable; but the matter is most easily explained by the desire of seeing one's bondfolk

f. 24 v⁰. In Mr H. A. L. Fisher's volume of *The Political History of England* (p. 293) this evidence is curiously distorted, and St-Germain is represented as saying the exact opposite of what he really says. On some German manors, there was a relaxation which must have led sometimes to a lamentable struggle on the sick man's part. He might escape some of the death-dues by sale of the property, even "when he had come to his death-bed," if he could manage to clothe himself "in such array as he goeth to church and to market"; and to hobble seven (sometimes even three) steps, with or without crutches, but without other help, in the presence of trustworthy witnesses (*Weisthümer*, I, 13, 46, 131, 245, 290, 805; four of these are monastic estates).

[1] Cf. v. Arx, II, 165, 194. The origin of the custom is obvious; it was to the lord's interest to discourage barren serfs; he needed a brood. (G. G. C.)

[2] *I.e.* the very fact of holding land in such a village rendered the holder liable to servile dues.

increase in numbers, which, under certain circumstances, was just as natural as the desire of multiplying one's cattle.... In the other monasteries of Württemberg either there is no mention of the bachelor-due, or there were agreements which expressly forbade it.

Cless's researches are confined almost altogether to Württemberg; but in most parts of Germany the mortuary dues seem to have been exacted with great severity. At Udern, under the monks of Metloch,

if a man die in the district or village, when his body is taken to church his widow must lock the door and take the key and follow his corpse to the grave; nor may she come into the house again until she have received admittance from the abbey steward. The said steward shall take the seven jurors and lift [*heben*] the best heriot which the jurors point out; and if the woman afterwards dies then they take a like heriot as they took before for the husband. If it be that they are so poor that no goods are found in the house, then they must take a three-legged stool from it in recognition of their right [to a heriot].

The abbots of Weissenburg took heriots even from youths and maidens, if they lived outside their parents houses; and one of the most formidable lists in all the *Weisthümer* is that of the heriots due from Zürich folk to the bishop and his officials[1]. The monks of St Michael in Bavaria took the best beast, and, in addition "the best garment which the dead man or woman had been wont to wear in church on feast-days." Those of Ottobeuren, in the same district, took half the dead man's belongings; the peasants struggled against this with varying fortunes, from 1298 until 1356, when the emperor finally decided that they need give only their best beast and their Sunday garment. In the fifteenth century, the abbot of Kempten not only took half the dead man's goods but claimed a heriot from the other half also; this the peasants successfully resisted (Baumann, II, 624, 634). Here, again, is the law from a German customal of the fifteenth century. At Schontra (apparently under the canons of Würzburg) it was required that "If, on any of these sixteen holdings, the man die, then shall the woman give fifteen pence for a mortuary. If she be so poor that she have not the pence, and is distrained with a pledge, the bailiff shall stay his hand until the woman has been round to her neighbours and found the pence and redeemed her pledge; if she cannot do this, then he must proceed." The same village had a custom far more iniquitous, for it was directly contrary

---

[1] *Weisthümer*, II, 65; I, 106, 765. The three-legged stool was a common symbol in customary law for a minimum of furniture. At Schwanheim, the abbot could claim a heriot "from any who had only so much land on his domain as he could set a three-legged stool upon"; another monastery claimed as its serfs "all who had enough land to hold a stool with three legs" (Grimm, *Rechtsalt.* I, 112–3). In another case, if a man had no other possessions than a little wine, a quart of this was to be taken as heriot.

to canon law. "*Item*, if a man, woman or other person die, having received the last sacrament, that person shall give seventeen groschen, of three pence to the groschen, for the health of his soul" (*Weisthümer*, III, 888). The so-called *Reformation Kaiser Sigmunds*, written in 1438, complains that not only the nobles, but "what is more, we mourn to say that it has come to such a pass that monasteries also take folk into bondage. They do not only say: 'This man is our own [possession]'; they make widows and orphans; when the father dies, the monks inherit his goods and rob the true members [of his family]. ...They take money in fines from the men by whose labour they live" (Bezold, p. 46). For farther evidence see Bartels, p. 106.

As a set-off to these, we may note a case recorded by Caesarius of Heisterbach, of individual renunciation worthy to be set side by side with those in my text. He is writing of a model prelate, Ulrich, prior of Steinfeld, who, he says,

left also another sign of his liberality, a most profitable example against the avarice of Religious. One day, before the aforesaid lay brother [a businesslike but hard man] had been removed from his stewardship, the prior came to one of his granges wherein he saw a very fair foal, whereof he asked the aforesaid brother whose it was or whence it came. The other made answer: "So and so, our good and faithful friend, left it to us at his death." Then said the prior: "Did he leave it from devotion to us, or by some law?" The brother answered: "It came from his decease; for his wife, since he was a serf of ours, offered it as heriot." Then the prior shook his head and made this pious answer: "Was it because he was a good man and our faithful friend that thou hast despoiled his wife? Restore therefore to this widowed woman her horse; for it is robbery to seize or take other men's goods; for it was not yours before his death." (*Dial. Mirac.* dist. IV, c. 72; II, 231.)

13
(Chap. VIII, p. 76)

SKELTON, "WARE THE HAUKE"[1]

Skelton assures us (ll. 145 ff.) that he brought the case before the archdeacon, but the offender gave a bribe and escaped. His poem is here necessarily much abbreviated; it should be read in full. It complains how one of Skelton's neighbour-priests,

—a lewde curate,
A parson benyfyced,
But nothing well aduysed:
He shall be as now nameles,

[1] *Poetical Works*, ed. Dyce, 1843, I, 156 ff.

But he shall not be blameles,
Nor he shal not be shameles;
For sure he wrought amys,
To hawke in my church of Dis.
This fond franktyte fauconer,
With his polutid pawtenar,
As priest unreverent,
Streyght to the sacrament
He made his hawke to fly,
With hogeous showte and cry.
The hye auter he strypt naked;
There on he strode, and craked;
He shoke down all the clothis,
And sware horrible othes
Before the face of God,
By Moyses and Arons rod,
Or that he thens yede,
His hawke shoulde pray and fede
Upon a pigeons maw.
The bloude ran downe raw
Upon the auter stone;
The hawke tyrid on a bonne;
And in the holy place
She mutid there a chase
Upon my corporas face....
The church dores were sparred,
Fast boltyd and barryd,
Yet wyth a prety gyn
I fortuned to come in,
This rebell to beholde,
Wherof I hym controlde;
But he sayde that he woulde,
Agaynst my mynde and wyll,
In my churche hawke styll.

CONSIDERATE

On Sainct John decollacion
He hawked on this facion,
Tempore vesperarum
Sed non secundum Sarum,
But lyke a Marche harum,
His braynes were so *parum*...
The church is thus abused,
Reproched and pollutyd;
Correccion hath no place,
And all for lacke of grace.

DEPLORATE

Say to me, Jacke Harys,
Quare aucuparis
Ad sacramentum altaris?
For no reverens thou sparys
To shake my pygeons federis
Super arcam foederis:

. . . .

Apostata Julianus,
Nor yet Nestorianus,
Thou shalt no where rede
That they dyd suche a dede
To let theyr hawkys fly
Ad ostium tabernaculi,
In quo est corpus Domini.

At the abbey church of St-Pierre-sur-Dives, "le clocher sud (St-Michel) servait de colombier aux Bénédictins" (*Ann. Normand.* 31e année, 1865, p. 47). For other English examples of church towers as dovecotes see S. O. Abdy, *Church and Manor*, 1913, pp. 407–9.

14
(Chap. VIII, p. 80)

JUS PRIMAE NOCTIS

The best discussion of this subject from the point of view of an orthodox Roman Catholic is, so far as I know, the article by A. de Barthélemy in the *Revue des questions historiques* (1, 1866, 95 ff.).

The author does not deny that, on certain manors, custom demanded a fine from newly-married peasant couples as an alternative to the lord's right of passing the first night with the bride. The most explicit account is in a Béarn customal of 1538. It runs:

Art. 38. Item, in the village of Aas, there are 9 houses with their appurtenances belonging to the said lordship [of Louvie] and affieffed to the same. These houses, their inhabitants and their owners are and were serfs, of such servitude that they cannot and may not quit the said houses, but are bound and constrained to live and dwell there to do their service and pay their dues. If any stranger marries into one of the said houses, he falls into the same servitude as if he had dwelt there since his birth. If an inhabitant of these houses were to quit them, the lord of Louvie might cause him to be pursued, arrested, cast into chains and brought back to the house which he has left. The inhabitants of these houses are called and named, in an ancient term of the vulgar tongue, "the Bragaris of Louvie." *Art.* 39. Item, when the inhabitants of these houses marry, before they know their wives they are bound to present them the first night to the lord of Louvie, to do with them according to his pleasure, or else to pay him a certain tribute. *Art.* 40. Item, they are bound to pay him a certain sum of money for each child that is born to them; and, if the firstborn be a male, he is free provided that it can be proved that he was begotten in the work of the said lord of Louvie in the said first night of his pleasures aforesaid.

In the same year and province, the lord of Brizanos exacted a similar tribute by way of redemption from a similar right. In 1419, we find a Norman lord exacting the same, and another equally plain instance comes from Drucat in 1507; finally, examples might be given from Germany. These are irrecusable business documents, which both sides admit to be genuine. Beyond this, we have the testimony of a poet not otherwise favourable to the peasants, who accuses the monks of Mont-St-Michel of taxing their serfs in redemption of this immoral right at the end of the twelfth century; Nicolas Boyer makes similar assertions about "certain nobles of Gascony" in the sixteenth; Hector Boyce, about the same time, says the same about twelfth-century Scotland, and Montaigne, in his 22nd *Essay*, alludes to it as a notorious fact. We know, however, that Montaigne must be discounted; and certainly Boyce is not a good authority for the conditions of four centuries before his own time.

We must remember that only a small proportion of the thousands of medieval customaries have come down to us, and that a complete collection would probably have provided many more instances than those which can now be quoted. But, even so, there can be no doubt that the *droit du seigneur* has been grossly exaggerated by a good many antiquaries and historians from the seventeenth century onwards, in Roman Catholic as in Protestant countries. Even Ducange is here among the exaggerators, and de Barthélemy's article has rendered a real service to the public. He points out justly that our most irrecusable witnesses testify to the abuse only as alternative; the serf has always, at least from about 1170 onwards, the power of redemption. His farther arguments are less convincing; but it is only fair to state them here. He doubts whether the lord had ever a real customary right of dishonour, redemption or no redemption. In his opinion, the whole story may be explained by a canon of the 4th Council of Carthage, confirmed by a capitulary of Charles the Great: "Let the husband and wife, when they have received benediction from the priest, remain in virginity that night by way of reverence for the said benediction." This prohibition, like others of the kind, soon passed into a stage of redemption by payment in money or in kind to the Church, and presently a similar right of blackmail was "usurped by layfolk, after the analogy of tithes, which had originally had a purely ecclesiastical character." Apart from this, the lord naturally exacted a fine when the couple had omitted to get his permission. From the later fifteenth century onwards, individual lords were inclined to exaggerate their feudal rights, and claimed to enforce these marriage-fines by the most brutal sanctions. Such sanctions, however, were simply a legal device to ensure payment of the fine; as when, in 1337, a gambler at Orthez was compelled to sign a formal abjuration before his lord, a notary, and a priest: "if he broke his oath, he swore to pay a considerable sum of money or to plunge from the bridge of Orthez into the river." Thus far Barthélemy; but, from what we know of early serfdom, and of the slavery from which in some cases it had developed, it seems far more probable that these customs were survivals of an abuse once literally enforced. Yet there seems no doubt that, within the five centuries with which we are concerned, no national or provincial code of laws enforced it, and that, even in this form of a legal threat, it existed only sporadically on certain manors. But, so far, its existence is admitted by all who have troubled to look at the actual evidence; and we cannot leave it altogether out of account in any true survey of medieval peasant life.

I know of no authentic evidence for the *jus primae noctis* in England; but such a case as I have printed in Chapter XI (p. 123) shows how easily an unscrupulous lord might have taken advantage of his unquestioned constitutional rights, and refused marriage-licence to a serf-girl whom he coveted for himself. Such possibilities must have contributed to the result that "of all manorial exactions, the most odious was incontestably the *merchetum*" (Vinogradoff, *Villainage*, p. 153).

I subjoin farther evidence which has come to hand in the course of preparing this volume for the press. The peasants of the Persen valley in the Trentino entered a protest against certain new exactions on the part of their lord; they complained of forced labour and of the "fruictiones primae noctis de sponsalibus." This was apparently in the twelfth century[1]. In Normandy, at Bourdet, in 1419, the lord's customal makes this formal claim:

I have a right to take from my men and others, when they marry on my lands, 10 sols tournois and a joint of pork of the whole length from the chine to the ear, and the tail frankly comprised in the said joint, with a gallon of whatsoever drink is drunk at the wedding; and

[1] F. Schneider, *Die Entstehung v. Burg und Landgemeinde in Italien*, Berlin, 1924, p. 194; cf. p. 195, n. 1. I owe this reference to Mr C. W. Previté Orton, who tells me that he has met with a similar case in Sardinia.

I may and ought, if it please me, go and lie with the bride, in case her husband or some person on his account fail to pay to me or at my command one of the things above rehearsed. (Delisle, p. 72.)

On the manor of Maur or Mure, under the abbess of Zürich, the customal of 1543 prescribes that, "whosoever here comes to holy matrimony, he shall invite a bailiff and his wife also . . . and, when the wedding-feast is over, then the bridegroom shall let the bailiff lie with his wife the first night, or shall redeem her with five *batzen* and fourpence." A similar custom obtained in 1538 on the manors of Hirslanden and Stadelhofen, dependent upon some abbey in Zürich and apparently upon the same as Maur (*Weisthümer*, I, 43; IV, 321). On a Burgundian manor, if a man in complete serfdom chose a wife outside the manor, "il perd tout ce qu'il a, à moins qu'il ne 'la mène gésir le premier soir dessous son seigneur'" (Scignobos, p. 43). A judicial sentence of Ferdinand V, dealing with the lords of Catalonia in 1486 has, among other articles: "We declare that the said lords may not take as foster-nurses for their sons or other children the wives of the said peasants, with or without indemnity, against the will of the said women; again, they may not, on the first night after the peasant had taken a wife, sleep with her, or, as a sign of lordship, when the woman is laid in her bed, pass over the bed and over the said woman." Brutails (p. 193), while maintaining with great probability that this marks a dying and exceptional abuse, rightly rejects Schmidt's attempts to explain it away altogether. Montalembert recognized the realities which underlay even the anti-clerical exaggerations of his day: he speaks of "ces abus révoltants du droit seigneurial qui, conservés et développés à travers les siècles, ont si cruellement affaibli et dépopularisé la féodalité" (*Moines d'Occident*, livre VII, ch. I). Finally, Bishop Fléchier had no doubt as to its sporadic survival even in the seventeenth century. He writes (*Grands Jours d'Auvergne*, p. 157):

Il y a un droit qui est assez commun en Auvergne, qu'on appelle le droit des noces. Autrefois on ne l'appeloit pas si honnêtement; mais la langue se purifie dans les pays même les plus barbares. Ce droit, dans son origine, donnoit pouvoir au seigneur d'assister à tous les mariages qui se faisoient entre ses sujets; d'être au *coucher* de l'épousée; de faire les cérémonies que font ceux qui vont épouser par procuration les reines de la part des rois. Cet usage ne se pratique plus aujourd'hui, soit parce qu'il seroit incompatible aux seigneurs d'être de toutes les noces le leur village et d'emporter leurs jambes dans les lits de tant de bonnes gens qui se marient, que parce que cette coutume étoit un peu contraire à l'honnêteté, et qu'elle exposoit les gentilshommes qui avoient l'autorité et qui n'avoient pas toujours la modération, à des tentations assez dangereuses, lorsqu'ils en trouvoient quelques beaux sujets. Cette honteuse cérémonie a été changée en reconnoissance pécuniaire, et, par un accord mutuel, les seigneurs ont demandé des droits plus solides, et les sujets ont été bien aises de se rédimer de cette loi si dangereuse à leur honneur. M. de Montvallat trouvoit que les anciennes coutumes étoient les meilleures, lorsque quelque belle villageoise alloit épouser, et ne vouloit pas laisser perdre ses droits; et, comme on le tenoit assez redoutable sur ce sujet, et qu'on craignoit que la chose passât la cérémonie, on trouvoit encore plus à propos de capituler, et de lui faire quelque présent considérable selon leurs forces. Quoi qu'il en soit, il faisoit valoir ce tribut, et il en coûtoit bien souvent la moitié de la dot de la mariée.

Chassin gives farther evidence, some of which seems valuable in spite of his evident exaggerations (*Serfs*, pp. 50 ff.). And certainly the marriage-restrictions suffered by the serfs under the abbey of St-Claude, down to the very Revolution, are sufficiently scandalous to corroborate the worse scandals of earlier times. The Coutume de Franche-Comté, ratified by the duke of Burgundy in 1459 and thenceforward authoritative as to the relations of serf and lord, prescribed that no bondwoman could claim her parents' inheritance unless she had slept her bridal-night in her father's house (Tit. xv, art. 10). Here, then, are the words in which the countryfolk of 1789 branded this custom in their appeal to the Assemblée Nationale; words which may be historically incorrect in their speculations as to the origin of the custom, but which are conclusive as to the custom itself as it subsisted until 1790:

Cet usage ne paraît aujourd'hui que ridicule, mais il en rappelle un autre qui prouve combien la force a toujours abusé de la faiblesse. Dans les terres mainmortables, le seigneur obligeait anciennement les jeunes épouses à venir dans son donjon lui faire hommage de leur virginité. Ce n'est qu'après lui en avoir fait le sacrifice qu'elles pouvaient aller habiter avec leurs maris. C'est pourquoi il leur était défendu de s'absenter de la seigneurie la première nuit de leurs noces sous peine d'être déclarées incapables de succéder à leurs pères et mères. Cette défense devait disparaître avec les indignes sacrifices pour lesquelles elle avait été établie. Cependant elle subsiste encore avec la peine que la barbarie y avait attachée, et chaque jour elle donne lieu à des procès. Qu'après la mort de son père une femme introduise une action en délivrance de sa légitime, ses frères ou son seigneur ne manquent jamais de lui opposer qu'elle est non recevable, à moins qu'elle ne prouve qu'elle ait couché la première nuit de ses noces dans la maison paternelle. Pour prouver ce fait, il faut procéder à des enquêtes. Souvent plusieurs années se sont écoulées depuis le mariage de la fille jusqu'à la mort du père: souvent ceux qui auraient pu porter témoignage sont morts dans l'intervalle, ou se sont retirés dans quelque contrée inconnue. Dans ce cas, la preuve devient impossible, et la malheureuse est renvoyée de sa légitime et condamnée aux dépens. Si quelquefois elle trouve des témoins, la partie adverse cherche des prétextes pour les récuser, en séduit d'autres et oppose ainsi témoins aux témoins. Nous avons vu, en 1771, le Chapitre de Saint-Claude obtenir et faire publier un monitoire qui lançait *les foudres de l'Eglise contre tous ceux qui, sachant qu'une pauvre femme avait passé chez son mari la première nuit de ses noces, ne viendraient pas le révéler*: c'était pour balancer l'enquête de cette femme qui avait prouvé, par six témoins irrécusables, qu'elle avait passé cette première nuit dans la maison de son père. Le mari qui a la facilité de trouver un notaire et les moyens de le payer l'appelle le soir des noces dans la maison de son beau-père, et lui fait dresser un acte portant *qu'il y a vu l'épouse et que cette épouse a déclaré qu'elle y est venue pour y coucher*. Mais, si cette maison est éloignée de la résidence du notaire, si le mari est pauvre, il n'a pas cette ressource, et sa femme court le risque de perdre ses droits à la succession de son père.

See also Vinogradoff, *Villainage*, p. 155; St-Aiglan, pp. 126 ff. and Bonnemère, II, 64.

15
(Chap. VIII, p. 80)

NOTES ON MARRIAGE

At first, serfs inherited the disabilities of slaves; they could not contract a legal marriage without their masters' consent. Gradually this was made easier; it was only when a serf married a bondwoman from some other manor that the contract needed the lord's consent for its legality; and, at last, by a decree of Pope Hadrian IV [1150] the serf's marriage was made legally binding under all conditions[1], the ancient disabilities surviving only in the fine which was paid generally in all cases, and always when he married off the manor. A freeman, on many manors, fell into servitude by his marriage with a bondwoman; did he therefore recover his freedom at her death? This was an open question: Ducange, under the word *capitale*, quotes a case where it was disputed between the monks of Marmoutier and one of their tenants, and left to wager of battle. When it came to that point, the tenant repented, came before the high altar with four pennies on his head, and gave himself up as a serf to the monks[2].

For compulsory marriages see *Weisthümer*, I, 169, 311; on the other hand, they were forbidden on St-Gallen manors in 1428 (*ibid.* V, 210) and on one in Westphalia (*ibid.* III, 152). The terms of these prohibitions seem to imply that compulsion was a common, if

[1] With the exception which I mention on p. 330.
[2] Cf. *Irminon*, I, 395 ff., where other interesting cases are quoted. "In the fifth century, Pope Leo the Great seems to have permitted masters to repudiate bondwomen from their beds in order to marry freewomen their equals."

not usual, seignorial right. Very interesting is the custom under the nuns of Frauenchiemsee (*Weisthümer*, III, 674, redaction of 1562, from an older customal of fourteenth or fifteenth century):

He who has a child (be it son or daughter), so long as he promises for the child, his warranty is sufficient; but, when the children grow too heavy for him, so that he can no longer rule them, then he shall set them [here] and answer that they may pledge themselves to my lady [abbess] never to marry without her will and knowledge. Whosoever transgresses this, must pay a fine to my lady and the convent, for a son, of fifteen pounds in coin, and he must get her grace as he finds means to do so; and for a daughter he must pay as much as he gives her for dowry, and must also get afterwards my lady's grace.

The division of children among different lords lasted as late as 1390 on the St-Gallen manors (Arx, II, 166). For other instances of partition see Potgiesser, pp. 368 ff., and Marquiset, p. 53, where its essentially unchristian character is emphasized.

In some German instances abbeys or chapters seized the whole property of an out-married serf, *e.g.* "If they take foreign wives, then let their whole heritage, and all that they possess, go to the monastery of St Nicholas, and let none of their heirs have anything therein" (Potgiesser, pp. 367–8). Nor does there seem to have been the least sense here of anything inconsistent with Christian brotherhood; on the contrary, God Almighty would find personal satisfaction in the arrangement, when He received His share of the profits. Potgiesser (p. 365) quotes from a document in which a donor, while granting a number of serfs to the abbey of St Maximin at Trèves, adds: "But if any of them marry outside, or dwell outside, or otherwise wander abroad, let each of them on St Maximin's day pay one pennyworth of wax for the remedy of my soul."

Nor did religion necessarily step in even after the Reformation. Bishop Fléchier, in his *Grands Jours d'Auvergne*, recounts what he saw and heard in a single province to which Louis XIV had sent commissioners for hearing appeals against local injustices (1665). He found an Augustinian monastery rebutting the pleas of the serfs of Combrailles: the good bishop thought these canons wrong in Christian charity, however right in customary law; and he approved the serf's plea that a man ought not to inherit servitude from a bondwoman mother; indeed, he found good theological reasons for this, since "if Adam had not sinned, Eve might have eaten as many apples as she chose, and we ourselves would have felt no ill effects." The canons, however, relied not only on the indisputable custom of the district but also on the Roman law of slavery; they contended that the serfs' marriages, like those of the ancient slaves, "were no true marriages but mere cohabitations," *non matrimonia sed sodalitia.*

Even the royal judges found the question so complicated that they adjourned the case, probably *sine die*. It is significant as showing how easily powerful churchmen might ignore not only ordinary human sentiments but even the public pronouncement of Hadrian IV, and that earlier judgement of Charles the Great, that the marriage of serfs was a "conjugium legale," consecrated like other marriages by Christ's words: "What God hath joined together, let not man put asunder" (*Capitula*, ed. Boretus, 1, 218).

16

(Chap. VIII, p. 80)

MARRIAGE AND KINSHIP[1]

The great stress laid on restriction of marriage within the limits of the manor seems, to the modern mind, unjustifiable enough in natural ethics; but there was a far stronger case against them in medieval Church law, if the abbot's relations to his tenant had been primarily those of a pastor set over souls whom Christ had died to save. Between 1065 and 1215 at least, canon law strictly forbade all marriages between kinsfolk to the seventh degree; that is, between all who had a common great-great-great-great-great-grandfather. Innocent III, in the great Lateran Council, reduced these prohibitions, "because they cannot now be kept without grievous harm"; thenceforward, the prohibition extended only to the fourth degree: but this must be kept with inviolable strictness[2]. A modern Roman Catholic commentator of great authority, Santi, insists that the earlier prohibition of seven degrees "had been very wise, since in those ages of continual war between neighbouring cities it practically compelled large numbers to marry outside their own community, and thus to establish more peaceable political relations indirectly through the matrimonial tie"[3]. This might have been so, if the prohibition had been really kept; but the towns were very small in proportion to the rural populations, whom this law must have compelled to live normally in a state of incest; scarcely any peasant, in those small communities, can have been so unrelated to the rest as to keep within the

---

[1] Let me call attention to the great value of Mr Tawney's note (*Agrarian Problem*, pp. 104–6), which bears indirectly upon this present subject.

[2] Ch. 50. St Antonino echoes these same words (*Chronica*, Lyons, 1586, II, 98 a).

[3] *Praelectiones Juris Canonici* (Ratisbon, New York and Cincinnati, 2nd ed. 1892), IV, 139. Benoît, similarly, defends the marriage restrictions within the domains of the monks of St-Claude, as tending to turn the whole manor into one happy family under the easy yoke and the light burden of Jesus Christ! (II, 775, 835).

code[1]. Even when Innocent had softened the law, at least half the bondmen in a normal village had probably some common great-great-grandfather with any prospective bridegroom or bride; and where, as it often happened, the bondmen of a particular lord formed quite a small group of the community, then any serf who was particular about his soul must have paid the enhanced fine for marriage outside, or have condemned himself to celibacy. In France and Germany, even in this latter case, the lord often took care to indemnify himself; we have seen how he took the whole property of all dead celibates, even though they might leave numbers of near kinsfolk. As churchmen, the monks had every reason to protest against such iniquities; yet it was precisely the monks who most frequently and most successfully asserted this right of seizure on the dead bachelor's estate. Marriage, said St Jerome, fills the earth, while virginity fills heaven. The landlord-monk will never be found discouraging marriages which tend to populate his own manor.

Let us see how the peasant lay between the upper and the nether millstone; between landlordism and the Church. The first and most obvious disadvantage was the encouragement of illegitimate connexions, in spite of the fines for leyrwite. Modern apologists allege similar restrictions on marriage as a reason for the enormous proportion of illegitimates in Bavaria[2]. No doubt, when the consanguinity prohibition was at seven degrees, there was very little serious pretence of observing it. As the *Catholic Encyclopaedia* puts it: "while, in the twelfth century, the theory of the remote degrees was strictly maintained by canonists, councils and popes, in practice marriages ignorantly contracted within them were healed by dispensation or dissimulation" (IV, 265). This is doubtless true of the upper classes, who paid heavily for such unions. William the Conqueror and Matilda, for instance, though only remotely connected, were not suffered "to riot in the bed of consanguinity"; each, in expiation, built a great abbey at Caen, and William laid his infant daughter as an offering to God upon the altar of Matilda's convent (Will. Malmesbury, *De Gestis Regum*, an. 1085). Here, again, is a typical papal indult of the year 1451:

To the same [papal legate in England]. Faculty to grant to thirty men and as many women, provided that they be noble or grave persons,

---

[1] Perhaps it is with special reference to the village-folk that the author of *Dives and Pauper* speaks of the frequency of incest in Chaucer's England. He writes (Com. VI, c. 3) that people "are so mad in lechery that the brother is not ashamed to hold openly his own sister."

[2] *The Statesman's Year-book* figures for 1892, which are quite normal, give 28,500 illegitimates among a total of 206,000 births, or 13·2 per cent., as compared with 4·6 for England and Wales, 7·5 for Scotland, and 2·8 for Ireland. Bavaria is, of course, a Roman Catholic country, and the marriage laws were such as the Church and the government had chosen to impose upon that community.

related in the third or the third and fourth degree[s] of kindred or affinity, and to any persons, of whatsoever condition, related in the fourth degree of kindred or affinity, who desire to marry, or who, ignorant or aware of such relationship, have contracted marriage and had offspring (i) dispensation to marry, (ii) in the case of those ignorant, dispensation to remain in the marriage contracted, and (iii) in the case of those not ignorant, absolution from excommunication incurred and, after temporary separation, dispensation to contract marriage anew and remain therein; decreeing offspring born and to be born legitimate. Those who knowingly contracted marriage are to send a sum of money for the fabric of the churches of Rome. (*Cal. Papal Letters*, x, 225; 1451.)

But nobody has pretended that a serf could have enjoyed the licence granted to these *noble or grave persons*, and that he could have procured a dispensation for marriage within the prohibited degrees.

Even Innocent's decree shows how little the medieval Church had grasped the full sociological import of marriage; she was far more concerned to vindicate it for her own exclusive province as a specifically Christian sacrament, and to reconcile this theory with the obvious objections (1) that marriage is a sacred reality even among pagans; (2) that, even in the Church, the priest is not the minister of this sacrament, which depends only on mutual consent and cohabitation; and (3) that Scripture gives no excuse for denying the name of marriage to Mary's unconsummated union with Joseph. Innocent does, indeed, relax the stricter prohibition for the express reason that it has worked so badly in practice; so far he recognizes plain facts. But the reasons he gives for choosing four degrees now, instead of the former seven, are embarrassing to a modern scholar like Santi, who painfully strives to shift this responsibility from the great pope to the Fathers of the Council (*l.c.* tit. xiv, § 10):

"This number of four," so runs the 50th chapter of Innocent's Lateran decrees, "is most proper for the prohibition of bodily union, whereof St Paul saith 'the husband hath not power of his own body, but the wife, and the wife hath not power of her own body, but the husband'; for the human body hath four humours, being composed of the four elements. Since, therefore, the prohibition of marital union is now restricted to the fourth degree, we will that this be so perpetual—notwithstanding any constitutions formerly published on this matter by others or by Ourselves—that whosoever presume to be joined together in contravention to this prohibition may be protected by no length of time, since the lapse of years does not diminish but increase their sin, and crimes become more grievous, the longer they hold an unhappy soul in bondage."

Yet a large proportion of peasants must have lived on in a bondage to this sin which was as hopeless and ineluctable as the bondage to their lay or ecclesiastical landlords. Many villages in the Middle

Ages must have come near to this tale of consanguinity told by an English traveller who traversed Switzerland in 1776:

This little vale [of the Lac de Joux] is very populous, containing about 3000 inhabitants.... In the small village of Pont, where we lodged, most of the inhabitants bear the name of Rochat; a name which also runs through the village of Charbonière, with the exception of only 2 or 3 families, and is prevalent likewise in that of Abbaye: the whole number of these Rochats amounts to above a thousand; they are supposed to be descendants of the same family, and their ancestors came originally from France. (W. Coxe, *Travels in Switzerland*, 4th ed. 1801; II, 108.)

Mr Hudson's microscopic researches into the Martham records have convinced him that "most of the old residents were more or less [connected by marriage]" (*Hist. Teach. Misc.* I, 195). And Lamprecht, relying upon original documents of the twelfth century, gives some illuminating details. In his text he writes (*Beiträge*, p. 92): "Thus, in this age, the local restriction of the right of marriage constituted a very deeply-felt abuse. Kinship within a manorial population rose to an extreme degree. At last matters came to open, though useless, opposition of the bondfolk to this unnatural circumscription, and to the [consequent] limitation of the law of inheritance." To this Lamprecht adds in a note:

The abbey of St-Marcel had in one manor 10 families of serfs; one serf was their tithing-man; if we number them from 1 to 10, their pedigree is as follows (Nos. 9 and 10 are unrelated):

See especially *Polyptyque d'Irminon*, II, 370–1 (about 1102 A.D.): "We desire to make it known that certain serfs and bondwomen of [the abbey of] St-Arnoul have...come to contradiction and revolt, and that their numbers and the popular tumult have waxed so strong that they utterly refuse to give a tax for marriage or that share of their goods which is commonly called *heriot*. They assert that they will marry free wives without regard to our monastery, and that they will give their free daughters to other men; yet they granted to do homage to our monastery without other conditions." The revolt failed. Among the rebels were two men who had lost their liberty by marrying [bondwomen]...this is the kinship between them

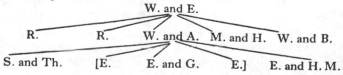

These have the following "kinsfolk":

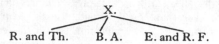

R. and Th.　　B. A.　　E. and R. F.

There is another independent family among the rebels:

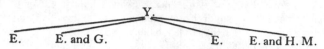

E.　　E. and G.　　　　　　E.　　E. and H. M.

I must note that, among the descendants of W. and E. in the 2nd degree, those whom I have put 2nd, 3rd and 4th are uncertain. Even among the unfree witnesses named later in this case a good part...perhaps all but 2, were kinsfolk of the rebels.

If the Church had seriously troubled herself about this problem, it would have been easy to insist, as ecclesiastics sometimes did where questions of servile pedigree were financially important, on the oath of eight persons of the kindred as to the relationship of the two contracting parties[1]. That monks had often plenty of written records from which they could have ascertained most kinships, is shown not only by the case I have noted in my text, where the St Albans authorities trace with exactitude the ancestry of one of their serfs, but also by the two rival pedigrees supplied by the abbot of Meaux and Richard Cellerer in the long suit as to Richard's villeinage (*Chron. Melsa*, R.S. III, 130–140). But here, as in many other matters, monks and prelates showed themselves landlords in the first place, and soul-shepherds scarcely even in the second or third.

Mr H. S. Bennett informs me that interesting statistics as to village breeding in-and-in may be found in an article by Mr B. S. Bramwell in *Eugenics Review*, Oct. 1923, pp. 480–1. Hansen emphasizes the evil effects of these restricted marriages among the unfree populations of German villages in the eighteenth century (p. 29). I have lately, by the courtesy of the vicar, seen an index to the parish registers of Hawes in Wensleydale, extending from 1695 to 1747. Under the letter M. there are 281 names, of which 271 are Metcalfes! Out of the 211 names under D., 161 are Dinsdales. And this was under ordinary conditions, with no feudal compulsion to marry within a certain group, the only operative factor being the remoteness, though not extreme remoteness, of the parish.

And other feudal customs operated sometimes, though less directly, to violate the natural freedom and harmony of family life,

---

[1] Verriest, p. 180. The chapter of St-Vincent-de-Soignies refused certain responsibilities to the tenants except under this oath, thus securing themselves against litigation by third parties.

and to encourage promiscuous connexions. The famous abbey of St-Claude, in the Jura, affords a strong instance of this preference of economic to moral or social considerations. Our most definite evidence comes from the last generation of the Ancien Régime; but the two customs to which I come here date from at least as early as 1459, when the Coutume de Franche-Comté was for the first time committed formally to writing and approved by the Duke of Burgundy, who was then sovereign of that district. One of the customs, that which forbade the bride to leave her father's house, I have already dealt with more fully in appendix 14. The second was still more mischievous in its operation. According to the Coutume de Franche-Comté (tit. xv, art. 16, 17): "If serfs wish to be and to remain capable of inheriting from each other, they are bound to live together under the same roof, at the same fireside, and at the same table. And if this 'community' be dissolved, if they separate for any motive whatsoever, they may never come together again (according to art. 15) without the lord's consent." This restriction was branded as intolerable in the inhabitants' petition to the États Généraux: "Each house seems to be a mere prison, in which captives are obliged to shut themselves up together, under pain of losing their share in the few roods of ground which they have so often watered with the sweat of their brow." The petitioners describe how, when several of the sons are married and the wives are not sympathetic, it becomes the interest of each pair to wear out the other's patience, since the departure of one will so far increase the heritage of those who stay:

The little which we earn by our sobriety and daily work is not our own; stranger hands await our death to seize upon it, to take it from our kinsfolk and even from our children. True, we can keep these people away for ever by subjecting ourselves to live our whole lives in the same house with our children, our brothers, our nephews, our cousins to the tenth degree.... Why impose upon us a restriction which brings no advantage to the lord so long as we submit to it? a restriction which, by concentrating a numerous family within the narrow limits of its holding, prevents its extension and multiplication, and thus damages population and agriculture?

If we discount this as the plea of an interested party, we shall find an equally strong moral condemnation in the words of the contemporary priest of Ornans, abbé Clerget, who alone among the clergy was inspired by Christian indignation to publish a powerful pamphlet on this subject. He speaks of this forced "community" as "an outrage against nature, a perpetual source of crimes and plagues." And, apostrophizing the great Italian legist of his day: "Worthy and generous Beccaria, when your profound wisdom weighed in the balance the justice of Crimes and Punishments, could you have heard without a shudder that, in the midst of a civilized people, to have one's dish and one's bread apart, or to consummate a marriage in the husband's bed, are crimes punishable with the cruel penalty of disinheritance?" (Chassin, *Serfs*, pp. 38–40, 59).

17
(Chap. VIII, p. 81)

LEYRWITE

The legal foundation for this fine seems to have been twofold. The lord had cognizance of all transgressions on his manor, and unchastity might be reckoned directly or indirectly as a breach of the peace; the temptation was obviously to a stricter interpretation here, since the fines were a regular source of profit. Secondly, the rural dean or archdeacon had cognizance of all immoralities; the unchaste serf was therefore subject to a fine in the ecclesiastical court; and, on the principle that he had nothing which was not his master's, his unchastity thus involved waste of the landlord's property. This is clearly set forth in two entries which Maitland has printed from the manor rolls of Ramsey[1]:

[A.D. 1290] Richard Dyer, a married man, was convicted in the [ruridecanal] chapter of adultery with a certain woman...and so lost the chattels of the lord [abbot of Ramsey]. Therefore he is in mercy. The amercement is forgiven.

[about 1320] They [the jury] say that John Monk still continues his lechery [*luxuriam*] with Sarah Hewen wife of Simon Hewen and is constantly attending divers chapter courts, where frequently he loses the lord's goods by reason of his adultery with Sarah, as has often been presented before now; nor will he be chastened. Therefore be he in the stocks. And afterwards he made fine with one mark on the security of [6 pledges named, who] undertake that if the said John at any time hereafter be again convicted of adultery with the said Sarah, they will bring him back and restore him to the stocks, there to remain until they have some other command from the lord or his steward.

These should be compared with the articles of enquiry printed on p. 102 of *The Court Baron*, from the year 1342. The lord's steward is to make enquiry in the court "whether any bondman's unmarried daughter hath committed fornication and been convened in chapter, and what she hath given to the [rural] dean for her correction."

If, therefore, I am not mistaken in supposing—I must confess, from very incomplete generalizations—that leyrwite-fines are more frequent on monastic manors than on others, the difference can easily be explained by the fact that on many such estates there would be

[1] *Select Pleas in Manorial Courts*, 1888, pp. 97–8.

no conflict of jurisdiction on this subject. The lay lord would have to dispute or divide the fine with the rural dean or archdeacon; but the monks, in many cases, had themselves full and acknowledged archidiaconal or ruridecanal rights; *e.g.* the monk-archdeacon at Westminster and St Albans, and the dean of Christianity at Evesham. Even where there was no such important and definite official as this, the monastery could easily keep these matters in its own hands; the cathedral priory of Norwich had its own "dean of the manors," and thus kept its tenants out of the ruridecanal court (W. Hudson in *Norf. and Norwich Arch.* xx, 205, n. 54). Therefore, whereas the lay lord might well find it scarcely worth his while to glean for fines after the church courts had fleeced the offenders, yet on the manors of large monasteries there would be no such conflict, but the fines would represent every case reported in court; that is, probably every case where a child had been born, and the township must therefore report, or risk a fine for concealment. The abbots of Ramsey evidently attached great importance to these fines; their right is very frequently asserted in the customal; far more frequently than the index would lead the reader to suppose. On St Albans manors, as Miss Levett points out, the collection of leyrwite seems to have been particularly strict, at least in the thirteenth century. The abbot of Glastonbury claims a fine "whenever one of the bond-girls is unchaste of her body, whereby my lord loseth the sale of her"[1], *i.e.* the marriage-fine which he would otherwise gain; the ordinary legal phrase was that the serf thus "bought his own blood." Similarly, under the cathedral chapter of Münster in Westphalia, the peasant who let his daughter come to marriageable age and let her run wild, so that she lost her honour, was to "be fined for as much money as the lord of the manor would have enjoyed from her if she had been honourably married"— *i.e.* to pay the same for leyrwite as for merchet (*Weisthümer*, IV, 128; for other notices of leyrwite see *ibid.* I, 97, 504, 846; also a curious provision at Ossingen near Zürich, *ibid.* I, 96).

Thus, then, the lord is the damaged party; the abbot of St Albans claims 12*d.* from Hugh the Clerk "for that his daughter was impregnated, to the damage [or disgrace] of his lord—*ad huntagium domini sui*" (Reg. *Halimote Roll of Abbot's Langley*, MS. Sidney Sussex Δ, I, i, 47 Hen. III, kindly communicated to me by Miss Levett). In Wales, leyrwite was called *ammolrag*: under this term, the abbot of Bardsey "claims to have two shillings from every bondwoman of his that is convicted of fornication" (Dugdale-Caley, IV, 660). Further references may be found in the Burton Chronicle, R.S. p. 246 (rights of Westminster Abbey and its cells), Neilson, *Fleet.* pp. lxxxvii, 107; Muratori, *Antiquitates Medii Aevi*, Milan, 1742, VI, 290 e.

---

[1] Vinogradoff, *Villainage*, p. 154.

18

(Chap. IX, p. 90)

GLEANING

Even this most natural of charities, permission to glean in the fields at harvest, was not granted indiscriminately by monks to the poor. To the rich Praemonstratensian house of Ninove, in Flanders, a married couple gave a plot of land in 1270, only reserving the use to themselves for the rest of their lives. In return for this, *inter alia*, the convent granted them the privilege "that Christina, wife of the said Walter, may glean corn-ears yearly at harvest-tide, in our fields of Pamèle, between the sheaves and the corn-shocks, wheresoever it may seem best to her" (De Smet. *Corpus Chronicorum Flandriae*, II, 1841, 934). There were evidently small privileged groups of this kind on the Glastonbury manors (*Rentalia*, pp. 135, 140, etc.). There is the same implication in *Piers Plowman*, B. VI, 67, where Piers says:

Ac whoso helpeth me to erie [*plough*] or sowen here ere I wende,
Shall have leave, by our lord, to lese [*glean*] here in harvest.

"The right of gleaning," writes Delisle, "was doubtless not recognized as an unrestricted right of the poor: for, on some of the domains of St-Ouen [de Rouen], it was a privilege reserved for certain vassals of the abbey." And again:

St Louis seems to have issued an ordinance on gleaning which we cannot pass in silence, even though it was probably applicable only to his own domains. It is a fresh proof of this good king's solicitude for the unfortunate. He had forbidden the driving of cattle into the fields during the two first days following upon the gathering of the sheaves; "Which ordinance," says J. Bouteiller, "was made by my lord St Louis, King of France, in order that the poor, who are members of God, should be able to glean there" (pp. 310, 736).

P. Degrully, in his *Droit de Glanage* (Paris and Montpellier, 1912, pp. 36 ff.) quotes this ordinance, and other cases where there were similar customs, though sometimes the privilege lasted only one full day. And he quotes, from Martene's *Thesaurus*, vol. II, col. 461, a letter of Clement IV addressed in 1267 "*To the Bishop and Chapter of Maguelone, that they exact no tithes from the gleanings of the poor....* In the township of Montpellier, as we hear, it cometh oftentimes to pass that the rectors and clergy of the churches there do notably out-stretch their greedy hands to extort from the poor, at certain times, tithes of their gleanings." Such tithes, writes the pope, ought to be "Christ's portion"—*i.e.* sacred to the poor; and he altogether reprobates the practice as savouring of filthy lucre. Yet the archives of St-Juste-de-Lyon contain a deed of 1493 showing that the tenants had to pay tithes from their gleanings as well as from their chickens; and in other districts gleaners had to give to the local hospital one-third of what they had picked. Degrully adds: "The laity, for their part, were scarcely more tender; and, in spite of the exhortations of the Christian religion to brotherly love and the practice of charity, certain tenants did not always show themselves tolerant, or even very humane, towards the gleaners" (p. 46).

19

(Chap. IX, pp. 93, 95)

GAMES

The French name for this tumultuous football was *soule*, and Émile Souvestre has immortalized the tragic side of it in his tale of *François le Souleur* (*Les Derniers Bretons*, vol. 1). For England, see J. Strutt, *Sports and Pastimes*, bk II, ch. III, § 13, and especially Sir M. Shearman's *Football*, 1904, pp. 3–15, from which I borrow the following four extracts:

By the reign of Edward II we find that not only football was popular in London, but that so many people joined in the game when it was being played in the streets that peaceable merchants had to request the king to put down its practice. Accordingly, in 1314, Edward II, on April 13, issued a proclamation forbidding the game as leading to a breach of the peace: "Forasmuch as there is great noise in the city caused by hustling over large balls (*rageries de grosses pelotes*)...from which many evils might arise, which God forbid: we command and forbid on behalf of the king, on pain of imprisonment, such game to be used in the city in future."...In 1349 football is mentioned by its present name in the statute of Edward III; who objected to the game not so much for itself, but as tending to discourage the practice of shooting, upon which the military strength of England largely depended. The King, writing in that year to the Sheriffs of London, says that "the skill at shooting with arrows was almost totally laid aside for the purpose of various useless and unlawful games," and the Sheriffs are there-upon commanded to suppress "such idle practices." The injunction can hardly have been of much avail, however, for forty years after-wards Richard II passed a similar statute (12 Rich. II, c. 6, 1389 A.D.) forbidding throughout the kingdom "all playing at tennise, football and other games called corts, dice, casting of the stone, kailes, and other such importune games." The same statute had to be re-enacted by Henry IV in 1401, so that it is tolerably obvious that, like some other statutes still in force and relating to sporting matters, it was more honoured in the breach than in the observance....In 1457 James III decreed that four times every year reviews and displays of weapons were to be held, and "footballe and golfe be utterly cryed down and not to be used"; but as in 1491 his successor had again to prohibit golf and football by a fresh statute providing that "in na place of this realme ther be used futeball, golfe or other sik unprofitable sportes," it appears that in Scotland as well as in England football was strong enough to defy the law....

That Elizabethan football was dangerous to life and limb and property, is made plain by many records. The Middlesex County Records contain several entries which are of interest to the historian of football, and show how rough was the game. In the eighteenth year of the reign of good Queen Bess the grand jury of the county found a true bill:

"That, on the said Day at Ruyslippe, Co. Midd., Arthur Reynolds, husbandman, [with five others], all of Ruyslippe afsd, Thomas Darcye, of Woxbridge, yeoman [with seven others, four of whom were 'husbandmen,' one a 'taylor,' one a 'harnis-maker,' one a 'yoman'], all seven of Woxbridge afsd, with unknown malefactors to the number of one hundred assembled themselves unlawfully and played a certain unlawful game called foote-ball, by means of which unlawful game there was amongst them a great affray likely to result in homicides and serious accidents."

Mr G. R. Pateman informs me that

The ancient game of Football is still played on Shrove Tuesday in several parts of the country. On February 13, 1923, a game was played on the north demesne of Alnwick Castle when the opposing sides were the two ecclesiastical parishes of St Michael's and St Paul's (*The Star*, Feb. 13, 1923). At Ashbourne, Derbyshire, the game was played between the "Up-Towners" and "Down-Towners." The goals were three miles apart and the course included the negotiating of a river. The whole town took part (*The Daily Herald*, Feb. 14, 1923).

The dangers of medieval village sports, including the risks run or the frays initiated by spectators, are brought out by Mr Walter Rye in his *Crime and Accident in Norfolk temp. Ed. I* (*Archaeol. Review*, Nov. 1888, pp. 201 ff.). He specially emphasizes the extent to which the clergy are found sharing in the excesses of their parishioners (pp. 212–14). A very picturesque account of a fatal affray at a wrestling-match may be found in the Dunstable Annals under the year 1283 (R.S. 1866, pp. 298, 306 ff.), and such matches in London sometimes caused very serious riots. Compare Noël, p. 135, for the roughness of peasant sports. Petrus Cantor speaks of it as a usual sport to set old women running for a pig; and the grave Mussulman Ousâma was much scandalized to find the crusading knights thus amusing themselves at Tiberias at the expense of two decrepit hags (*Vie*, ed.

Derenbourg, 1889, p. 479). A thirteenth century moralist, speaking
of rich and greedy folk, alludes to a similar sport:

> The devil doth marvellously delude such folk; they are like the blind
> folk at the Feast of Fools; men give these blind a pig to lacerate [with
> their knives], and when one believes he is cutting the pig he cuts his
> fellow's hand, and the fellow his, and he gets little fruit therefrom,
> but hath bought that at the great price of his hand. So are these rich
> who get a small worldly gain by swearing and lying, but contract great
> wounds of sins which they heed not. (*Dictionarius Pauperum*, s.v.
> *divitie*, ff 27, 28.)

A similar rough practical jest underlies the fabliau of *Les Aveugles
de Compiègne*.

20

(Chap. X, pp. 111, 112)

ILLEGAL OPPRESSIONS

Let us begin with an extract which has almost the value of a direct
generalization. Richard Middleton (or de Media Villa) was an
English Franciscan who became professor of Divinity at Paris about
1285, and is reckoned among the masters of Duns Scotus. In the
27th question of his third quodlibet he discusses the question whether
subjects are morally bound to obey a lord who imposes tallages which
are justified neither by custom nor by public utility:

> I answer, that these subjects are either serfs [*servi*] or free. If they
> be serfs, I say that they are bound to pay the tallages newly imposed
> upon them, even though these tend to the profit of their lords alone;
> for serfs and their possessions are the property of their lords; where-
> fore Aristotle saith in the first book of his Politics that a slave [*servus*]
> is a chattel; wherefore again, if the serf flee he must be restored to his
> lord, as it is written in Canon Law (*Decret. Greg.* lib. I, tit. xviii, c. 2)
> where it is said that, if any serf fleeing from his master shall reach
> ecclesiastical orders by any cunning or fraud, it is decreed that he be
> deposed and that his master take him back.... [In the case of freemen],
> if those tallages be in no way to the profit of the community, then I say
> that neither king nor prince can impose such new tallages upon his
> free subjects. And the reason here is, that the possessions of free
> subjects are not the property of their lords.

Here is a member of the most democratic ecclesiastical order of
his day, the Franciscans, writing as a theologian and moralist, un-
trammelled by the respect which writers like Bracton constantly
paid to Roman Civil Law. When a doctor of this kind can thus decide
against the moral right of the serf to resist new and arbitrary taxation,

it is more significant even than the complaints of his fellow-moralists that the lords and their bailiffs commonly oppressed the poor.

Yet these complaints are universal. Innocent III writes, in the 17th chapter of his *De Contemptu Mundi*:

The serf serves; he is terrified with threats, wearied with corvées, afflicted with blows, despoiled of his possessions; for, if he possess nought, he is compelled to earn; and, if he possess anything, he is compelled to have it not; the lord's fault is the serf's punishment; the serf's fault is the lord's excuse for preying on him.... O extreme condition of bondage! nature brought freemen to birth, but fortune hath made bondmen. The serf must needs suffer, and no man is suffered to feel for him; he is compelled to mourn, and no man is permitted to mourn with him. He is not his own man, yet no man is his!

The great pope was an accomplished rhetorician; but few will be found to deny that real feeling underlies these words. They are repeated with approval by St Bernardino of Siena (ed. De la Haye, III, 391 b):

The third state is that of bondfolk and underlings, who are never free from labour. Bondfolk are always subject to fear, to the threats and tyranny of their lords; every fault of the lord is the servant's penalty; whensoever the lord is angry, the servant is punished and uneasy: wherefore Innocent [III] writing *On the Misery of Man's Condition*, saith, "O extreme condition of bondage! [*etc.* as above]."

St Antony of Padua is almost equally explicit (*Opp.* p. 256). Knights and rich citizens, prelates and clerics of our time and false Religious, are thieves: "from the poor, whom they call their villeins —though they themselves are the devil's villeins—they take their substance and their blood by every possible means."

The thirteenth century poem of Meier Helmbrecht is too definitely satirical to be used without great caution; but its picture of the sufferings of the peasantry at the hands of robber-knights and their retainers is substantiated, in the main, by unexceptionable independent evidence. Robert of Brunne wrote in the early fourteenth century:

> For wellnigh every a steward
> The doom that they give, is over hard;
> And namely to the poorë man;
> They grieve him allë that they can.
> E.E.T.S. 1901, ll. 5, 423; cf. ll. 6, 777 ff.

The contemporary canonist John of Ayton says the same; Justice is in a bad way throughout England; knights and squires "oppress, now by purveyances, now by [forced] cartages, now by taxes or amercements, and by other forced burdens [*angariando*], treading underfoot in divers manners the pursuit of justice.... Nay, when they cannot themselves do these things, they protect and harbour abominable robbers in these and other such things, as it is said" (Lyndwood, *Provinciale*, 1679, app. p. 78). The États Généraux, in their assembly at Tours in 1483, complained of the oppressions of nobles who enforced illegal corvées upon their vassals (*Recueil*, p. 58). Jakob Wimpheling (1450–1528) was one of the most learned and saintly churchmen of his age. He wrote to a friend in 1508: "I am inclined to believe that, if Christ were to come down to earth in these days of ours, preaching poverty and rebuking covetousness, he would again be crucified by certain men who grudge at virtue and who foster quarrels and filthy lucre" (Riegger, *Amoenitates*, p. 78; for Wimpheling, see Erasmus's letter of Jan. 24, 1529, to Johann Vlatten). His contemporary, Felix Hemmerlin, the canon of Zürich, wrote that princes and nobles of old time were a bulwark to the poor; "but now they are a fear and marvel and horror and terror and luke-warmness and pallor and gnashing of teeth and trembling to all and every who are within their reach, and more especially to all whom they meet and see to be lowlier or weaker or more powerless than themselves" (*Nob.* c. 31, f. 123 b). Instances of the illegalities which could pass long unpunished in France, even under the strong government of Louis XIV, may be found in *Grands Jours*, pp. 210–15; cf. pp. 262–3. Moreover, although the king tried to make an example of the worst offenders in 1665, Fléchier doubts whether this will put a real end to the tyrannies (p. 293).

Here and there, the documents enable us to trace concrete instances where the lord used his power to break down customary law, and where even customary law gave him a power which, if exerted to the full, was intolerable. Count Baldwin of Flanders, in 1202, fixed the tallage of one manor at a lump sum of £20 a year, confessing in this charter that "We had hitherto been wont to tallage our tenants in a very disorderly fashion [*satis inordinate*]" (Verriest, p. 33). Tallage at the lord's mercy was very common abroad, *e.g.*

I, Pierrot, called Norret, of La Planée, give all men to know that, of mine own will and without constraint, I have given myself and my heirs and my goods, wheresoever they may be, to the noble lady Laura ...and I recognize that I am under taxation and exploitation [*taillable et explectable*] high and low, by the said lady and her folk, to do their will. In witness whereof I have caused to be set upon these present letters the seal of my lord Vaucher, lord of Chastelvilain, and the seal of my lord the prior of Mèges. (*Cart. Chalon*, p. 223, 1275 A.D.)

This "high and low" [*aut et bas*] refers to the full power of taxation at her own discretion which the lady possessed over the "hommes taillables."

Maitland prints a significant breach of custom:

The Castellans of Gloucester used, on the first day for the sale of beer, to take 28 gallons (*lagenas*) from every brew, paying two pence for them: they either paid the money down, or gave a tally (*tallia, dica*) for it, and so long as the tally remained in the hands of the woman (for of course the person who brews is a woman) they could take no more beer from her. But Rochford introduced the practices of taking two-pence when he took no beer, of taking beer on the last day as well as on the first day of sale, and of taking beer of those who still held outstanding tallies. (*Select Pleas of the Crown for the county of Gloucs.* p. 153, 1221 A.D.)

Similarly, a passage in Grandisson's register (p. 574) shows how the fourteenth century bailiff might violate an agreement made between the tenants and the dean and chapter, by exacting twice the yearly sum agreed upon. Again, there is much to be learned from Abbot Burton's long account of the lawsuit between his abbey of Meaux and its rebellious serfs in 1367. Though we see here only one side of the dispute, it seems pretty clear that the serfs were wrong in law. But the length, difficulty and expense of this litigation in the king's courts, assuming the monks to have had as good a case as the chronicler claims, speaks volumes as to the difficulties a serf would have had against a powerful lord in the manorial court, however strong his claims may have been in strict justice. And the rival genealogies pleaded by the litigants afford an interesting illustration of the fact that we do not know whether Sir John Paston's grandfather was a bondman or not (*Chron. de Melsa*, R.S. III, 127–42).

Another testimony to the advantage which the landlord had over the peasants, in spite of custom and the manor court, was the enclosure movement. This began long before the Reformation, and was still proceeding when the Reformation broke out. As early as 1346, we learn almost by chance that "the lord William Montague, earl of Salisbury, hath enclosed and emparked [at Hampstead Marshal, Oxon.], three hundred acres and more which were wont there to be ploughed and tilled, and the rest of the land of the aforesaid village is stony and very poor" (*Inq. Nonarum*, p. 8 a). The enclosure movement was retarded, in so far as it was retarded, not by help given to the peasants on the part of the Church, but by the action of the Crown. Among all the decrees of provincial or diocesan synods, I do not think that any touch this evil. When an orthodox layman like Sir Thomas More inveighs against it, he brands abbots among the chief offenders. But the parliaments of the early Tudor period, and the king's commission to Wolsey in 1517, did provide some real remedy, if only by taking public evidence as to the extent of the mischief and the personality of the offenders. The fact that the Reformation was followed by worse enclosures does not annul the fact that enclosures were among the abuses which provoked the Reformation.

In earlier times, again, and in Rome and Italy even beyond the Reformation, there comes the question of actual slavery. Cardinal Jacques de Vitry, describing to Ste Marie d'Oignies the abominations of the city of Acre in 1216, writes:

Who could number the crimes of this second Babylon? among which Christians denied baptism to their Saracen slaves, even though they besought it instantly and with tears; "for," (said these masters; Lord, leave me not to their counsel!) "if these slaves become Christians, we shall not be able to lay the same burdens upon them at our own good pleasure"[1].

For the recognition of slavery even in Aquinas's day, and the reluctance of the Church to interfere decisively, see *Sum. Theol.* 2^a 2^{ae} Q. X, art. 10, *conclusio*. If a Jew's *personal* slave becomes a Christian, he is to be freed; but, if the Jew bought him for traffic, he is only compelled to put this newly-converted Christian up for sale within three months: "nor doth the Church herein do any injustice; for, seeing that the Jews themselves are the slaves of the Church, she may dispose of their possessions."

Further evidence as to oppression by lords or bailiffs may be found in Luchaire, *Social Life*, etc. pp. 249-62; Sée, *Bretagne*, p. 55; Verriest, p. 39. On the other hand, for a favourable judgement on the treatment of serfs under a particular monastery, see Belbuck, p. 30.

21

(Chap. XI, p. 122)

FREEMEN REDUCED TO BONDAGE

The want of anything like complete legal protection for the serf, even at the end of the Middle Ages, is illustrated by Mr Leadam in the preface to his *Star Chamber* (I, 1902, cxxiii ff., cxxvi ff., 118 ff.). He prints the plea of Carter *v.* the abbot of Malmesbury in 1500 A.D. This house, like the neighbouring abbey of Bath, was in great financial and moral disorder; the abbot had put his natural son upon a farm on the abbey estates. Carter's grandfather had paid the high price of £26. 13s. 4d. for manumission, double the price paid for freedom by a contemporary bondman of Bath abbey; yet now in 1500

---

[1] *Sur des lettres inédites de J. de Vitry* (Acad. Royale de Bruxelles, séance du 8 nov. 1847, tom. XXIII, p. 38).

it was attempted to bring the grandson back to bondage. Passing on from this case, Mr Leadam continues (p. cxxvi):

The two cases of bondage in the volume of Select Cases in the Court of Requests, published by the Selden Society in 1898, exhibit the enforcement of an extreme degree of extortion by a lay peer, and a case of minor gravity on the part of a knight. In the second case the plaintiff declared his apprehension "that the seyd Sir Edward (Gorge) wolde take or imprison him for a bondman." Some such threat appears to have been made, but not to have been carried into effect. But Olveston, Abbot of Malmesbury, had fewer scruples. If we are to believe the plaintiff, he not only robbed but tortured. Imprisoning his alleged bondman in the monastery, he "put hym both handes and fete in strayte stockes and ponderous irrons and tied hym to a great new cheyn to a great stocke and so yet kepyth hym in that intollerable duresse." The conservative instincts of the clergy had in this case apparently maintained methods of oppression familiar, it may be, to the thirteenth century, but repugnant to the lay conscience and practice of that age. That the abbey maintained its grip upon its bond-men till the Dissolution appears from a letter to Cromwell in 1537 of Sir John Bryggys and Giles Pole, commissioners appointed to enquire into a claim by Abbot Frampton, the last abbot of Malmesbury, to one William Lane as his bondman. "We hear the abbot," they write, "claims Lane as his bondman, and if he be not so the abbot does the man great wrong." The reason for this tenacity on the part of the Abbots is disclosed in a chance sentence of a letter to Cromwell from Dr William Petre on January 17, 1539. "The demesnes [are] all in their [the monks of Malmesbury] own hands." Demesne lands in the hands of the lord were cultivated by bondmen, tenants at will at common law. It is clear that the monks of Malmesbury exercised a practical supervision of the cultivation of their estates, and for this purpose used their bondmen as their labourers. In his answer to the plaintiff's petition the abbot for the most part contents himself with a formal traverse of the counts[1].

Upon all this Mr Leadam comments:

Philosophic historians sometimes suggest that medieval bondage was, after all, not a more degraded condition than that of the modern free labourer tied by necessity to an employment which he dares not abandon. To the sentiment there is all the difference between economic compulsion, apparently the outcome of inevitable conditions, and a legal dependence upon personal caprice. Even comfortable circum-stances, which he apparently enjoyed, created in the Malmesbury

---

[1] Compare p. cxxiv, n. 8: "A gross case, if we are to credit the allegations of the plaintiff Thomas Paunfeld, of Chesterton, Cambs., occurred in the reign of Henry 5, when the prior and canons of Barnwell claimed the free tenants holding in villainage as their bondmen, imprisoned the complainant for seven years, and after his release by judicial authority again imprisoned him for more than a year. *Rot. Parl.* IV, 566–616."

bondman no satisfaction with his lot. There is a pathetic ring in the words which, in his old age, he is recorded to have used that "if he might bring that [his freedom] aboute it wold be more joifull to him then any worlelie goode."

Compare with this Bishop Hobhouse's note in the appendix to *Rentalia*, p. 243:

Here we have one of those remarkable cases mentioned by Littleton, in which a man undertook the base obligations which marked the condition of a serf. "If a free man," says Littleton, "will take lands to hold of his lord by such villein-service as to pay a fine for the marriage of his sons or daughters, then he shall pay such fine for the marriage notwithstanding, though it be the folly of such free man to take in such form to hold by such bondage, yet this maketh not the free man a villein." There had been in fact a great legal contest in the very reign in which our entry was made, on the question whether the acceptance of a servile condition reduced a man to the status of a serf. One Aluric de Bestenovre had taken 100 acres of land in Sussex on the terms of doing the usual rustic work, and of being taxed with the other men when the lord pleased, and of not being allowed to give his daughter in marriage till he had paid a fine. The lord claimed Martin, son and heir of this Aluric, as his serf; but after much litigation it was decided that there might be free men on bond land, and that such a tenant might go away if he did not wish to perform the conditions of the tenure. The person who made the entry in the rental of Wrington evidently thought that one of the regular tenants might have insisted upon retaining his land, so long as he performed the service. But it was not until generations had passed that this rule was established; and at the date with which we are dealing the movement was rather in the direction of ignoring the mutual tie between lord and tenant, and of treating the latter as if he were no better than one of the "chattel-slaves" described in the books of the civilians. When the manor of Dicheat was surveyed in the first year of Abbot Michael, the customary tenants were actually described as slaves: "These are the rents customs and servitudes of the slaves (*servitutes de hominibus servis*), holding full virgates of land."

Bezold points out how, though the large majority of Bohemian peasants were nominally free by the beginning of the fifteenth century, yet the lords were struggling, and with some success, to bring them back to servitude (*Zur Gesch. d. Husitentums*, Munich, 1874, p. 56). This policy was followed sometimes even by Church lords; Albert Ranconis, a university teacher of the second half of the fourteenth century openly opposed a decree of the archbishop of Prag which was designed to defend the rustics against such exactions. He, in turn, was opposed by another master, Kunesch, whose thesis has come down to us in full (printed by Höfler, p. 48). Kunesch laments the conduct of a minority of churchmen who, "blinded by greed, impertinently allege Holy Scripture and Canon Law against pity, justice and mercy, and, under pretext of evil custom, presume to usurp the possessions of the poor. Under colour of *devolutions* (to use their own words) they are now striving to suck up the poor man's goods." If their tenant has no children they claim to inherit all at his death; and, to secure the full spoils, they do not allow him in his lifetime to make a will or even to give any of his property away. The archbishop's decree had recognized the existence of this custom, but had reprobated it as contrary to Catholic justice; Albert had written "in railing words" against it, "maintaining that the peasants are ribalds and serfs who have only the bare life-use of their goods, and that none but the Church should succeed to their rights and possessions." It is notorious, argues Kunesch, "that the peasants of Church and other landlords in the realm of Bohemia are free and not bondmen . . . therefore it is a very rash and audacious thing to impoverish the poor in this impudent fashion." To this Bezold adds in comment:

Serfdom and villeinage, moreover, had existed in Bohemia from of old; and Palacky's assertion that no trace of it was left among the Bohemian peasants at the beginning of the fifteenth century goes much too far. Even the will of Markgraf Johann (1366 A.D.) enumerates not only independent tenants but also customary tenants and men "bound to the soil." The landlords' aim was to bring the whole country population into the sad condition of these men whom they treated so barbarously. It is most significant that the Emperor Charles IV [*d.* 1378] forbade his nobles to put out their bondmen's eyes, or cut off their noses, hands, or feet.

And he points out how the main strength of the Hussite rebellion, which shook Bohemia for 66 years, "rested definitely at first upon the peasant class" (p. 55).

Pavini, at the end of the Middle Ages, speaks of it as a common thing for marquises in Italy to reduce freemen to servitude (*Tract. Jur.* vol. XIV, f. 140, § 86).

22
(Chap. XI, p. 131; XIV, p. 175)

THE CUSTOMS OF DARNELL AND OVER

(*Vale Royal Ledger Book*, pp. 117 ff.)

Concerning the customs [*fo.* 39 (276)] *of the manor of Dernale.*

Here begin the customs of the bond-tenants of the manor of Dernale. . . . They all owe suit to the mill under pain of forfeiture of their grain, if they at any time withdraw suit; and every year they owe pannage for their pigs.

Also they ought to make redemption of their daughters, if they wish to marry out of the manor, at the will of the lord.

They will also give *leyrwithe* for their daughters if they fall into carnal sin.

Also, when any one of them dieth, the lord shall have all the pigs of the deceased, all his goats, all his mares at grass, and his horse also, if he had one for his personal use (*si habuerit domesticum*), all his bees, all his bacon-pigs (*bacones integras*), all his cloth of wool and flax, and whatsoever can be found of gold and silver. The lord also shall have all his brass pots or pot, if he have one (but who of these bond-tenants will have a brass pot for cooking his food in?), because at their death the lord ought to have all things of metal. Abbot John granted them in full court that these metal goods should be divided equally between the lord and the wife of the deceased on the death of every one of them, but on condition that they should buy themselves brass pots.

Also the lord shall have the best ox for a "hereghett" and Holy Church another. After this the rest of the animals ought to be divided thus, if the deceased has children, to wit, into three parts—one for the lord, one for the wife, one for the children; and if he leaves no children, they shall be divided into two parts—one for the lord and one for the wife of the deceased equally. Also if they have corn, in grange or in field, then the wife of the deceased ought to choose her part, to wit, half the corn in the grange or the field, as she chooses... always provided that, wheresoever the wife shall choose her part, whether in grange or in field, the lord shall have his moiety and part,... and if he has children, or a child, the division shall be made in the same way into three parts, to wit, among the lord, the wife of the deceased and his children....

Also it is not lawful for a bond-tenant to make a will, or bequeath anything, without licence of the lord of the manor.

The lord shall choose the best ox by his bailiffs, before the "hereghett" be given to the church....

And as to the sheep, let them be divided like all the other goods of the deceased which ought to be divided. But this is inserted in this place by itself, because, when the convent first came to Darnhale, the bond-tenants said that no division ought to be made of the sheep, but that all the sheep ought to remain wholly to the wife of the deceased. Which is quite false, because they always used to divide them without gainsaying it at all, until Warin le Grantuenour was bailiff of Darnhale; and while he was bailiff he was corrupted with presents, and did not exact the lord's share of all things in his time; and afterwards the bond-tenants endeavoured to make this a precedent and custom, which they by no means ought to do, because they have been accustomed so to do according to the customs of this manor in the times of former lords....

Also be it remembered that, if there is war in the neighbourhood and watches are kept at night at Chester, then they ought to keep armed watch at night round the court of Dernhale by turns, or in order, six, eight, ten, twelve, or more at a time as may be necessary, as they shall be ordered, or to redeem their watches from the lord....

Also, if the lord wishes to buy corn or oats, or anything else, and they have such things to sell, it shall not be lawful to them to sell anything elsewhere, except with the lord's licence, if the lord is willing to pay them a reasonable price....

They ought also to keep the lord's pigs and mares and horses of the woods (silvestres), and to be bee-keepers and parkers, and to feed the abbot's puppies (catulos).

Ibid. p. 121.

These are the conditions by reason of which the abbot of Vale Royal and the convent say that the people of Ouere are their bondsmen (neiffez).

And to prove that they are truly bondsmen, in the beginning, when our lord the King Edward, who is dead (whom God assoil), enfeoffed the aforesaid abbot and convent with the manor of Darnahale, the bond-tenants aforesaid, on account of certain grievances which they were told the abbot made them suffer, went to complain to the king aforesaid, carrying with them their iron ploughshares; and the king said to them: "As villeins you have come, and as villeins you shall return." And after this the abbot threw them out of their houses, and took their goods and kept them in his hands [fo. 40 (277)] until they had made acknowledgement of their bondage, and done his will in all things. And touching their bond condition, Abbot Walter was impleaded concerning the same in the time of Sir William de Ormesby, justiciar of Chester [c. 1307], and they were so adjudged by inquest and by recognizance of their neighbours, and for the seisin thereof Richard de Foulushurst, then sheriff of Chester, took five [? *sint*] oxen to their (lour) grange of Moresbarwe.

23
(Chap. XIII, pp. 150, 153)

SLAVERY IN THE ROMAN CHURCH

It may be well to give here a very brief analysis of Brecht's monograph, which is difficult to procure; *e.g.* there is no copy in the Cambridge University Library. It was published at Barmen in 1890. It is a frankly polemical work; but I have verified the most important statements in this summary: and I believe that no attempt has been made to confute him.

The New Testament preaches kindness on the master's part and obedience on the slave's. The early fathers express themselves, as we should expect, in the slave's favour, but without definitely reprobating the system (p. 24). When, under Constantine, the Church got not only freedom but domination, there was never any official reprobation of the slave-system (p. 25). The pious phrases with which Gregory I prefaces an act of manumission about 600 A.D., (though they are always cited by apologists, down to Pope Leo XIII, as the main proof of their thesis,) are quite exceptional; Gregory made no effort to abolish slavery in general, though as pope he owned thousands of his own (p. 26). The task would have been far easier than many which the Church took in hand; Imperial Rome became Papal Rome; popes undertook to make peace and war, to make and unmake emperors and princes; but no pope dreamed of laying his axe to the root of slavery (p. 28). When monasticism began—that is, the reaction of a fraction of Christianity towards original Christian poverty—these ascetics forbade themselves all property in slaves, as in every other worldly possession (p. 35). Archbishop Theodore of Canterbury, in the seventh century, contrasted the slave-owning Western monks with the slaveless Easterns; in the middle of the eighth century we find an Eastern rule forbidding monastic slavery; in the ninth, an exceptional reformer like St Benedict of Aniane freed all slaves on the lands that were given to him; but canon law, as codified by successive popes, definitely consecrated the system, and made it very difficult even for the willing monk or cleric to free his bondmen (p. 36). Monks became the greatest of serf-owners (for the slave was gradually passing into the serf); more than one abbey possessed as many as 15,000 peasant-holdings (p. 38; the majority of these, in the Dark Ages, were unfree). The Russian clergy, in 1760, possessed nearly a million serfs (p. 39). Brecht next sums up the formal teaching of canon law on this subject. From Gratian (1150) to John XXII (1334) this official Church legislation went on; no apologist has dared to deal with it, for the laws are all against the bondman (p. 47). Church incomes are sometimes estimated not in coin, but in slaves; the slave can have no free choice of a husband for his daughter (p. 49); he cannot make a will, for his whole *peculium* belongs to the Church his mistress; the traffic in slaves is legalized (p. 50). The Church slave is a chattel which may no more be disposed of than any other chattel (pp. 51–2); only here and there come stray allusions to the ethical merit of freeing a slave. Even the manumitted Church slave must still remain in a state of dependence; complete and absolute manumission is nowhere provided for (pp. 53–4). The slave is a *vilis persona* (p. 55). Leo XIII proclaimed to the world the exact contrary of the historical facts when he wrote, in his Encyclical of 1888, that the medieval Church had ordered bishops to confer freedom upon all slaves who had earned it by years of praiseworthy conduct, or at least that she had made it easy for bishops to free them by their last will and testament (p. 58)[1].

[1] Compare the following sentence from another page of Leo's solemn pronouncement to the world: "It is sufficient to recall the fact that slavery,

Brecht passes on to analyse the teaching of St Thomas Aquinas, to whose authority six popes have testified with an emphasis which it would be difficult to exaggerate. Innocent VI wrote, in words which were repeated with approval by Leo XIII under circumstances of special solemnity, "His doctrine above all other doctrine, with the one exception of the Holy Scriptures, has such a propriety of words, such a method of explanation, such a truth of opinions, that no one who holds it will ever be found to have strayed from the path of truth, whereas any one who has attacked it has always been suspected as to the truth"[1]. Aquinas does not only follow the orthodox medieval view that all Jews are by nature "slaves to the Church, who may dispose of their property as she chooses" (*Sum. Theol.* 2ª 2ᵘᵉ, q. x, art. 10). Wherever he deals with the general subject of slavery, apart from this more specially theological question, he bases himself mainly upon Aristotle, and practically adopts the heathen philosopher's point of view. To him, as to Aristotle, slavery is a natural state of things; it is true, Aquinas adds "since Adam's fall"; but the limitation is meaningless in this context, seeing that the Earthly Paradise can have no place in practical politics (p. 60). Aquinas's pupil, Egidio Colonna, "declared slavery to be a Christian institution" (p. 63). St Alfonso Liguori, whose influence as a teacher in the Roman Catholic Church has been almost as great as that of Aquinas, treats slavery also as a natural institution (p. 64). So does the most authoritative of their modern followers, Gury, who teaches that "slavery is in itself not unpermissible, though it is rightly forbidden in most places by Civil Law"; he cannot quote any existing Church law against it (p. 65).

It was not until the twelfth century that the Church ventured to declare the binding force of marriages between two slaves, even against the will of their lord or lords (p. 66). Many of the decrees of Church councils most favourable to slaves were borrowed from civil legislation (p. 67). It is difficult to say that medieval slaves—even Church slaves—were appreciably better treated than in the Germany which Tacitus describes (p. 69).

Pp. 74 ff. show how little the churchmen were willing, or able, to emancipate their bondfolk. Pp. 76 ff. describes the "patron-rights" which they still kept over so-called "freedmen." Pp. 96 ff.

that old reproach of the heathen nations, was mainly abolished by the beneficent efforts of the Church" (*The Pope and the People*, Select Letters and Addresses on Social Questions by his Holiness Pope Leo XIII, edited by the Rev. W. H. Eyre, S.J., London 1895, p. 150).

[1] Encyclical letter of our Holy Father by Divine Providence Pope Leo XIII, on the restoration of Christian philosophy in Catholic Universities, according to the mind of St Thomas Aquinas the Angelic Doctor. Translated by Father Rawes, D.D. with a Preface by his Eminence the Cardinal Archbishop of Westminster (London, Burns and Oates, 1879), p. 30.

deal with the serf of the later Middle Ages; pp. 100–102 ff. with the so-called *jus primae noctis*, a custom which is still in dispute, but which, even by the admissions of apologists, testifies to a state of things which would not be tolerated in any modern community[1]. On pp. 103 ff. Brecht meets Janssen's attempt to deny the connexion between serfdom and the Bauernkrieg; pp. 112 ff. deal with the development of serfdom in other European countries; the example of Spain alone would be sufficient to confute the arguments of Roman Catholic apologists[2]. The Papal States were perhaps the most miserable and troubled in all Europe; under Clement VIII (1592–1605) it was reckoned that they contained 15,000 bandits (p. 121); the population and the production of corn decreased in proportion as the clergy increased in numbers (p. 122). The main agricultural and stock-breeding improvements in modern Europe have come from England, Holland and Switzerland (p. 129); (Brecht should also have added Belgium). Pp. 139 ff. deal with the effects of the French Revolution.

Slavery proper died out so soon in England that few readers in this country realize how long and how briskly the slave-trade lasted in other European lands. Not only the princes, but the Church, formally protected the Jews in this traffic (p. 151; cf. p. 58, and Gratian, pars 1, dist. 54, c. 15: "ne forsitan [the Jewish slave-dealers] utilitates suas irrationabiliter aestiment impediri"; from a letter of St Gregory to the bishop of Naples). Christian sovereigns protected this traffic without any papal protest; even as late as the fourteenth century, the Teutonic knights dealt in slaves (p. 153). Most of these were probably sent to supply the galleys of Mediterranean ports; but it is likely that the women were sold to the municipal brothels[3].

[1] See *e.g.* Michael's explanations in the long footnote to p. 54 of his first volume.

[2] Lord Acton, also, has marked for special attention a series of passages in which S. Sugenheim describes the reaction against peasant emancipation which marked the reign of Charles V (*Gesch. d. Aufhebung d. Leibeigenschaft*, St Petersburg, 1861, pp. 36–9). The last of these passages runs: "As the rights of the Cortes and the constitutions of the towns were trodden under foot by the kings [*i.e.* Charles V and his successors], so also the nobility were allowed to treat the customary rights of their peasants as scraps of paper [*bedeutungslose Pergamente*]."

[3] A good many towns had the acknowledged right of keeping these institutions; see especially W. Rudeck, *Gesch. d. Oeffent. Sittlichkeit in Deutschland* (Jena, 1897), pp. 26 ff. At Nürnberg and Nördlingen, in the fifteenth century, it is expressly recorded that this was with the consent of the clergy. The popes derived a regular income from the brothels of Rome; here, for instance, is a passage marked by Lord Acton's watchful pencil: "Of the *alma mater* Rome, it is thus reported by Jacob Heerbrand, who died in 1600 as rector of the University of Tübingen: 'When I was at the Council of Trent in 1552, I heard from the master of the horse of the lord Erasmus Bishop of Strassburg (who had then returned with his episcopal master from Rome),

In Italy, and the capital of the popes, the trade flourished most of all; Brecht gives startling examples on p. 154; slaves were common as household servants even in the eighteenth century.

Pp. 155 ff. deal directly with the papal attitude towards this question. We have already seen how Benedict VIII, in the early eleventh century, condemned the children of priests to be made slaves of the Church. Boniface VIII, in 1303, threatened the adherents of his political enemies with slavery. Clement V condemned the whole rebellious population of Venice to slavery in 1309; two pages are filled with the rehearsal of similar incidents; Paul III decreed slavery for all Englishmen who presumed to support Henry VIII against the orthodox princes upon whom he called to invade England in 1535[1]. In the later fifteenth century, three popes had already granted licence to the kings of Portugal to invade and conquer heathen countries and reduce the inhabitants "to everlasting slavery" (pp. 158–9). It was Catholic nations which began the negro slave-trade (p. 160); "the majority of Spanish ecclesiastics, from the highest bishop to the lowest monk, was either directly concerned in slave-holding or publicly defended it" (p. 166). Paul III, in 1537, did forbid the enslaving of Indians in the New World; but men knew that the prohibition came from a pontiff who had done nothing to put down slavery in his own Italy (p. 170). Individual Catholics, and even whole Orders like the Jesuits, sometimes fought against Indian slavery (p.171); but nobody, apparently, reprobated the traffic in negroes (p. 174).

Pp. 174 ff. deal with ecclesiastical apologists on this subject; pp. 178 ff. with the attitude of Roman Catholic missionaries to the African slave-hunters; pp. 184 ff. with "slavery in Rome from the sixteenth to the nineteenth century." Not having verified the statements of this latter part, which seem to rest upon a monograph by Bertolotti, archivist of Mantua, I give them very briefly. Paul III, the friend of the Indian slaves, expressly permitted slave-dealing and slave-holding in his own city of Rome (p. 185). Innocent X bought slaves to use in his army; Alexander VII is found dealing in slaves (pp. 199–201); and this in the middle of the seventeenth century. Before 1800, much had been done against slavery by worldly rulers; the Papal States were not in the van here, but quite in the rear

that there were at Rome more than 24,000 public prostitutes, who paid a monthly tribute to the Roman Pontiff in proportion to their professional gains'" (S. Sugenheim, *Baierns Kirchen- und Volks-Zustände im 16ten Jhdt.* Giessen, 1842, p. 448 n.). A surprise search for suspicious characters made throughout the London wards one night, by government commissioners, made a far greater haul "at the stewhouses within the liberty of the Bishop of Winchester [at Southwark]" than in any other London district (*Letters and Papers of Henry VIII*, vol. III, pt i, p. 127).

[1] The bull is printed in full by Burnet (*Hist. Ref., Records*, Pt. I, Bk. III, document No. 9, § 17).

(p. 210). The first organized body to fight against slavery on definitely Christian grounds was the Quakers, at the impulse of three German Protestant emigrants (pp. 213–19); and the real world-leader of emancipation was Wilberforce, from 1785 onwards. The first pope who committed himself to the doctrine which Wilberforce had printed as a boy of 15 was Gregory XVI, who in 1839 declared slavery to be unchristian (p. 222).

I have already noted how little Kröss ventures to come to hand-grips with these facts; I must now turn to Allard; for, as long as these apologies are taken seriously, and quoted from journalist to journalist, the average intelligent reader can only wonder on which side the real truth can lie.

To begin with, Allard ventures even less to grapple directly with Fournier's arguments, than Kröss does with Brecht's.

And, in so far as he is compelled to take account of the same documents which Fourner uses, his methods are, throughout, those of a special pleader. He first attempts to put a purely humanitarian construction on the decree of the council of Reims in 625, "that no bishop shall sell either the slaves *or the property* of the Church"[1], by ignoring not only the words here italicized, but also § 11 of the same council, which has already dealt with slave-sales from the moral and religious point of view. He then distorts the decree of the 4th Council of Orléans (p. 541) by breaking off in the middle of the sentence, where the emancipation is distinctly defined as only partial; "ita ut ab officio ecclesiae non recedant"; the man is no longer a slave pure and simple, but he is still a bondman of the Church. Then, though forced to admit that the councils of Toledo (p. 633) and Mérida (p. 666) "se montrent un peu moins généreux," yet here again he tampers seriously with the text. To begin with, he gives no full references; and we find that while appealing to § 67 of the Toledo council of 533, he is ignoring §§ 70–1, which are destructive of his thesis; for these demand that, even after what is called manumission, the so-called *liberti* must remain under control of the Church, "which never dies," and which therefore has a right to maintain them in perpetual dependence[2]. And, secondly, the summaries by which Allard tries to fit even the decree of 555 into his argument is extraordinarily misleading, as may be seen from the translations which I print here side by side:

Allard, p. 202	4th Council of Toledo, cap. 67 (Labbé, vol. v, col. 1721)
En Espagne, le quatrième concile de Tolède (633) et celui de Mérida (666) se montrent un peu	If those who distribute nothing of their possessions to the poor shall be condemned in future by

[1] Labbé, vol. v, col. 1691, § 13; Allard, p. 202.
[2] Labbé, vol. v, col. 1722.

moins généreux : ils ne permettent à un évêque d'affranchir les esclaves de son église qu'autant qu'il aura laissé à celle-ci quelque chose de son bien propre. La condition est encore facile à remplir.

the voice of the Everlasting Judge, how much more [shall they be condemned] who take from the poor that which they have not given? Therefore let those bishops, who have given nothing of their own in compensation to the Church of Christ, fear this divine sentence; and let them not presume to make freemen of the serfs of the Church, to their own condemnation. For it is impious that he who hath not given his own possessions to the Church of Christ should do her harm and strive to alienate that which is hers by right. Wherefore the succeeding bishop shall recall such freedmen, without any opposition, to the rightful possession of the Church; for it was not equity but improbity which alienated them.

It is evident here that the bishop is required to give to the Church not only "something of his own goods, a condition easy to fulfil," but something at least roughly equivalent to the value of the bondmen whom he frees; in other words, that his charity must be at his own expense. This is made still more plain by the much longer canon of Mérida, which Allard professes to be summarizing also. This grants liberty only to those whose liberating bishop is found to have given, by legal deed in due form, *very much* of his own possessions to the Church[1]. And the assembled fathers of Mérida are even more emphatic than their predecessors of Toledo in providing that such "freedmen," even if they intermarry with freeborn folk (*personis ingenuis*), shall never shake off their original dependence upon the Church; if they are caught in the attempt, they must be reduced again *ad servitium ecclesiae*.

He is equally inaccurate in his next assertion:

Mais, en Angleterre, les conciles font plus que permettre, ils commandent, en certaines circonstances, l'affranchissement des esclaves anglais. Le concile de Celchyte, tenu en 816, ordonne qu'à la mort d'un évêque tous ses esclaves seront affranchis, et de plus oblige chaque évêque et chaque abbé à libérer lui-même, pour le repos de l'âme du mort, trois esclaves, en leur remettant une certaine somme d'argent.

The canon thus appealed to is No. 10 of the Council of Celchyth, which was held in 816 (Wilkins, I, 170; Haddan and Stubbs, III, 583). Earlier canons of this council (7 and 8) are distinctly unfavourable to alienations of Church property; this No. 10 prescribes the distribution of the *personal* property of bishops at their death:

For the good of his soul, we ordain that the tenth of his substance be divided among the poor, whether in flocks or herds, sheep or swine,

---

[1] Labbé, vol. VI, col. 507, § 20: "qui de suo *bona plurima* sanctae ecclesiae, in qua praesident, per suae scripturae textum cognoscuntur contulisse."

or in cellar-stores [*in cellariis*]; also that every Englishman be freed who was brought into servitude in his days; that by this means he may earn the due fruit of his labour and remission of his sins.

It will be noted that not all of his slaves are to be freed, but only those of recent servitude, which must have been a very small minority; nor is the whole decree in any sense representative of *les conciles* in England; on the contrary, it is quite unique, and there is no evidence, I believe, that these prescriptions were ever carried out. The greatest obscurity hangs over this council, which at best spoke only for the southern province; on the other hand, Archbishop Egbert of York, in about 750, compiled a collection of Church canons which enjoyed considerable authority; and these include that decree, afterwards fixed finally by Gratian in canon law, "that no abbot nor monk shall liberate a serf of his monastery; for he who has nought of his own cannot free another man's chattel" (Gratian, *Decret*. dist. LIV, c. 22).

Allard admits that "un seul texte paraît, au premier abord, en contradiction avec ceux-ci." This is the decree at St-Romain-d'Albou in 517: "Let no abbot manumit any slave given to the monks; for we deem it unjust that, while monks work daily in the fields, their slaves should gain the leisure of liberty"[1]. He has nothing to oppose to this but three pages of vague and most misleading rhetoric about the monks as cultivators of the soil. From this point onwards, he ceases to struggle against the evidence of canon law that the bondman was, with very rare exceptions, treated as a chattel by ecclesiastical no less than by civil law.

24

(Chap. XIII, p. 158)

RECORDS OF BONDAGE

The following St Albans document, from *Reg. Whethamstede*, R.S. II, 333, is of exceptional interest, as illustrating three points—the chances a serf had of shirking some of his legal dues through official favouritism or oversight; the pains taken to counteract this by keeping full written records; and the natural tendency of landlords on monastic, as on other estates, to strive for the increase of these dues as time went on. There may have been less rack-renting on monastic estates than on others, but certainly there was a good deal. While

---

[1] "Libertatis otio potiantur." There is no real warrant for Allard's invidious translation, "vivraient dans l'oisiveté." The earlier part of this canon, which he omits, lays stress on the illegal sales of Church property which abbots presumed to make (Labbé, vol. IV, col. 1577).

Knapp, in the districts which he has studied, finds a striking uniformity of rents and dues from the sixteenth century onwards, he notes frequent instances of rack-renting before that date (pp. 296 ff.). This St Albans document, written apparently in 1302, has unfortunately been much damaged by fire towards the end. It may be compared with the extraordinarily interesting depositions of a large number of local witnesses as to the status of a peasant family which Muratori printed in his *Ant. Ital. Medii Aevi* (1738), vol. I, cols. 811 ff.

There was a serf of the lord abbot, in the days of King John, Aylmer by name, who did servile works all his life for the land of Agate which he held. He was succeeded by his son Alger, who gave [only] one woodcock [as a fine] for marrying his daughter without licence; and he was a friend of the cellarer's. He was succeeded by one of his sons, called Robert the Clerk, who gave my lord a pair of spurs for licence to take a wife. He was succeeded by a son named John, who in 1225 took up the land of his father Robert and gave one mark for fine. This same John, for licence to marry his daughter Mabel to one Gerard son of Geoffrey, gave 6s. in 1249. For licence to marry another daughter, in 1269, he gave 5s. He was succeeded by a son Robert who in 1273 took up his father's land at a fine of 5 marks. Item, for licence to take to wife...when he was long hindered, and he made [fine]....He was succeeded by a son John, who in 1288 took up [the land and made fine for?] 3s....

25
(Chap. XIV, p. 168)

MANUMISSION AND MONEY

(a) JUDGEMENTS OF MODERN SCHOLARS

Seignobos writes (pp. 63–4):

Les maîtres n'ont été amenés à ces concessions ni par la religion ni par l'humanité. Les considérations philosophiques ne paraissent dans les préambules de chartes qu'au xvie siècle et l'on peut douter qu'elles soient sincères. Les seigneurs du moyen-âge déclarent plus naïvement que lorsqu'ils affranchissent ou abonnent leurs serfs, c'est qu'ils ont besoin d'argent comptant ou craignent de voir déserter leur domaine[1].

And he sums up for Burgundy (p. 79):

Rien ne montre qu'il [le haut clergé] ait songé à améliorer le sort des paysans, ou cherché à supprimer le servage. C'est sur terres d'Église

---

[1] "Considerata magna utilitate dicti monasterii" (Saint-Seine)—Garnier *Chartes*, II, 449. "Regardant le profit de nous" (Grancey)—Garnier, *ibid* II, 479.

qu'il est resté, jusqu'après le xve siècle, le plus de serfs; c'est le clergé qui affranchit le plus rarement ses hommes et leur impose les conditions les plus rudes. Sur 61 chartes d'affranchissement ou de commune accordées jusqu'en 1350, 8 seulement, et les moins favorables, sont l'œuvre de seigneurs ecclésiastiques. Non pas que les nobles d'Église eussent le cœur plus dur que les nobles laïques. Mais leurs domaines étaient plus grands, ils n'avaient ni famille à pourvoir ni frais d'expéditions à supporter. Ils avaient donc moins besoin d'argent comptant et n'étaient que rarement forcés de vendre à leurs hommes leurs droits d'exploitation.

With regard to England, Savine writes:

The charters of manumission spoke *always* of Word of God and law of nature, of charity and piety, of natural equality of all human beings, and unnatural character of serfdom. The manorial accounts and surveys when dealing with manumission waste little space in grand words, but they *often* mention that the grant of freedom was made *in consideracionem summe legalis monete Anglie*[1].

Dom Grappin (p. 131) quotes with approval from Linguet:

Les Rois rendirent des libertés; leur marchandise se trouvant décriée, ils furent réduits à faire des lois pour contraindre les hommes à s'en charger. Louis Hutin ordonna à ses Baillis d'affranchir de force ceux même qui le refuseraient, et de leur faire payer de grosses amendes.

Des Méloizes, whose sympathies are almost as definitely on the side of medieval institutions, notes that in Berry the lords "conféraient assez souvent la franchise à titre purement gratuit," but "fréquemment aussi, la liberté qu'ils accordaient n'était donnée qu'à prix d'argent"; again: "L'idée chrétienne a eu sa part dans la concession des chartes d'affranchissement, mais beaucoup de couvents et de monastères ont donné tardivement la liberté à leurs serfs" (pp. 76, 85). Compare v. Arx, I, 161–2, for St-Gallen, and Muratori's confession that, while lay lords often freed their serfs, yet, for pecuniary reasons, this was very seldom done [*perquam raro*] by religious corporations (*Ant. Ital. Medii Aevi*, 1738, vol. I, col. 841). Dunod, the learned lawyer who wrote his *Traité de la mainmorte* in a district and at a time when monastic serfs were still numerous (1760), and who was a staunch upholder of the feudal customs, is severe on the absurdity of supposing that non-economic causes can account for the gradual extinction of serfdom: "What can have become of that prodigious quantity of serfs which filled the whole world? Are we to believe that they were freely manumitted, in those days when they might have been turned into *mainmortables* [tenants subject to heriot], from whom some profit could be drawn?" (p. 12).

---

[1] *Bondmen*, p. 269. In the interests of strict accuracy, we ought to substitute *not infrequently* for the two words I have italicized.

An excellent example of the danger of arguing vaguely from a few indeterminate cases, without reference to the far wider generalizations available, is supplied by Bishop Hobhouse on pp. 252–3 of his *Churchwardens' Accounts*. All his surmises in favour of the ecclesiastical lords are natural enough from his pen, and they are not actually contradicted by the scanty documentary evidence which he produces; but all his conclusions rest upon mere guesswork; he produces no evidence in favour of *gratuitous* manumission, and, when dealing with purchased manumissions, he takes the liberty of assuming without evidence that the price was such as an average serf could well afford to pay.

(b) FARTHER MEDIEVAL EVIDENCE

Capgrave, in his life of St John of Bridlington, mentions among his many beneficent activities that he "gave health to the sick, and liberty to serfs." Capgrave was not a contemporary, and his book is very rhetorical, and he gives no farther evidence; but it is quite possible that St John did free enough to distinguish him honourably from the large majority of Church landlords.

The classical canonist Hostiensis decides (I omit his corroborative references):

A bishop may manumit bondfolk if they have deserved well of the Church; he can also manumit others who have not so deserved, provided that he give to the Church, in compensation for each one, two of the same efficiency and *peculium*. Also he may do so for mercy's sake; or perhaps we must understand this of those who have deserved well. Again, an abbot may manumit a bondman of his monastery (but not fully, since he has no compensation to give,) but there we must understand "with the consent of the bishop and of his monks," unless there be a custom to the contrary. (*Summa Aurea*, lib. 1, *De servis non ordinandis*, f. 62 b, §§ 9, 10).

Guérard quotes eleven cases in which the monks freed whole villages at a time; in ten of those cases we have direct evidence that this was done for money, and in the eleventh (St-Denis) the probability is on this side (*Irminon*, 1, 392). At Vale Royal, wherever we have definite evidence for the manumissions in either direction, we find them to have been bought by the bondmen (*Ledger*, pp. 28–9). Another suggestive instance, of the year 1322, is given by Potgiesser, p. 922 (*Prioress of St Walburga*). Another still more significant is recorded in Grandisson's *Register* (p. 1159, an. 1355):

John [bishop of Exeter] to our beloved son in Christ, Thomas Knollynge, son of William Knollynge, Our serf in Our episcopal manor of Ashburton, greeting etc. Whereas thou, being now come to thy fifty years[1], hast no longer any wife or offspring lawfully begotten of thy body, and art so insufficient in worldly goods that thou must needs live from thine own labour, and knowest no art but that of a boatman, having learned none other from thy youth upward, therefore we cannot hold it unprofitable to Us or to Our Church of Exeter to restore thee to thy natural liberty. Wherefore, in order that thou mayest be able to labour more freely and seek thy daily food and clothing by boatmanship, in consideration of the aforesaid facts and moved by pity, We do hereby, in so far as pertaineth to Ourselves, manumit thee and restore to natural liberty both thyself and all goods and chattels whatsoever, occupied or possessed by thee in any manner, specially reserving for Ourselves and Our successors and Our Church aforesaid the patronage of thyself and of all thine offspring if perchance thou do beget any such[2].

In 1374, Boniface IX directed a bull to the abbot of Neath against those who had despoiled Margam Abbey of "sheep, swine, *serfs purchasable*, and other goods" (W. de Gray Birch, *Margam Abbey*, 1897, p. 322). In 1397, the pope grants indults to St Mary's, York, to violate canon law by farming out churches, etc. to laymen, and "to sell and alienate serfs [*servos*] and born bondmen [*nativos*] of the monastery who have not acknowledged their serfdom [*servitutem*] or have without leave taken themselves off from the demesne of the monastery to other places beyond its liberty and district." In other words, to make the best of a bad business bargain and sell the remnants of a servitude from which these bondmen have nearly escaped (C.P.L. v, 8). In 1405, the patron of Castleacre priory exacted from the monastery "an oath not to alienate its woods, corrodies or other possessions, nor to manumit its serfs without licence or consent" (C.P.L. vi, 78). In 1410, the monastery of Mottisfont complains that it has lost heavily in income through the deaths of serfs by pestilence; for this and other reasons it obtains leave to appropriate the revenues of another parish church (*Ibid.* p. 200; cf. iv, 396). In 2 Hen. V, a man complains in the royal courts that "the abbot of Hide, with other persons, made an assault upon him, and by various threatenings compelled him to apply for manumission, for which, according to the award of the arbitrators, he paid £10 to the abbot." It is significant in this connexion that "the preponderant majority of the last bondmen [in England] were either (a) well off, or (b) paupers." (a) The former were too profitable to the lord to buy their freedom except at exorbitant prices; in less than thirty years of the mid-fifteenth century the lord of Castle Combe squeezed at least £264 in marriage-fines, etc. out of a single family

[1] "In aetate quinquagenaria constitutus," a phrase which may cover anything between 50 and 60.

[2] The most important feature of this reservation would probably be the heriot and other rights of succession. See appendix 27, *Incomplete Manumissions*.

of bondmen. (*b*) The latter had no money for buying their freedom; therefore they remained in bondage (Savine, *Bondmen*, pp. 276–8). The Paston Letters show us a prior mortgaging a serf to another farmer, certainly not for charitable reasons (ed. 1901, Introd. p. xxxv).

Similarly strict economic considerations led not only to the keeping of serfs but even sometimes to the making of serfs. A freeman of Gladbach, who had been "insolent both in word and in deed" to the abbot, redeemed his transgressions by making himself a bondman of the abbey in 1323 (*Gladbach*, p. 291). In default of money to pay the full fine, he must pay with his person: earlier documents contain more frequent instances of this.

It may not be out of place to quote here the story of a serf from the Rougham court-rolls; Dr Jessopp is not always accurate, but there is no reason to distrust the facts here given, which are quite typical (*Nineteenth Century*, February, 1883, p. 253, *Village Life Six Hundred Years Ago*):

At Rougham there was a certain Ralph Red, who was one of these villeins under the lord of the Manor, a certain William le Butler. Ralph Red had a son Ralph, who I suppose was an intelligent youth, and made the most of his brains. He managed to get ordained, about six hundred years ago, and he became a chaplain, perhaps to the very chapel of ease I mentioned before. His father, however, was still a villein, liable to all the villein services, and belonging to the manor and the lord, he and all his offspring. Young Ralph did not like it; and at last, getting the money together somehow, he bought his father's freedom, and observe, with his freedom the freedom of all his father's children too, and the price he paid was twenty marks. Of the younger Ralph, who bought his father's freedom, I know little more; but less than one hundred and fifty years after the elder man received his liberty, a lineal descendant of his became lord of the manor of Rougham; and though he had no son to carry on his name, he had a daughter who married a learned judge, Sir William Yelverton, Knight of the Bath, whose monument you may still see at Rougham Church, and from whom were descended the Yelvertons, Earls of Sussex, and the present Lord Avonmore, who is a scion of the same stock.

<h1 style="text-align:center">26</h1>

(Chap. XIII, p. 160)

LAY AND ECCLESIASTICAL MANUMISSIONS

J. Yanoski's *Abolition de l'esclavage ancien* (1860) is written from a strongly orthodox point of view; but the author admits that we have no adequate vouchers for the theory of predominant Church influence in manumission (pp. 44 ff.). He writes on p. 51: "À partir de la fin du viie siècle (et ici nous nous appuyons sur le témoignage des légendes) les saints n'interviennent que rarement dans le rachat des captifs." Compare Sommerlad, II, 89. The monks of Monte Cassino, in all cases where they claimed possession of a serf, had an imperial privilege to hold him until the imperial court had adjudged him otherwise (Tosti, I, 250, diploma of Henry II in 1002). So that, whereas in England civil law did all it could to throw upon the lord the onus of proving his lordship, under St Benedict's own monastery the serf had the onus of proving his own freedom. Houdayer, while he brings out all that can be said for the benevolence of the monks of Cluny, adds: "Cependant, les Clunisiens ont maintenu ces tenanciers sur leurs terres assez étroitement, et les affranchissements sont peu nombreux" (*Mill. Cluny*, I, 238). So, again, with the nunnery of Prâlon in Burgundy, founded under St Bernard's auspices. Garnier is inclined to think that these nuns, at first, tilled their own lands; but, presently,

Quoi qu'il en soit, des colons ne tardèrent pas à s'établir autour du monastère; ils en prirent les terres à cens et se soumirent aux corvées pour l'exploitation du domain seigneurial. Rien d'ailleurs ne fut changé quant à leur condition première: serfs ils étaient venus, serfs et mainmortables ils demeurèrent, sans que les religieuses adoucissent une servitude qui devenait chaque jour une exception. Ce fut seulement en 1722 que, déjà réduites aux expédients par les dettes qu'elles avaient imprudemment contractées, l'abbesse et les religieuses accueillirent la demande de trente et un chefs de famille de Prâlon, et leur concédèrent, aux conditions les plus onéreuses, la liberté de disposer de leurs personnnes et de leurs biens. Le demeurant, par des raisons qu'on n'expliqua pas, resta mainmortable jusqu'en 1770. (Garnier, III, 365.)

On the other hand, I may add here another small indication that monastic servitude, though longer lived, was slightly easier. A serf of Romainmotier, in the twelfth century, married a bondwoman from a neighbouring manor. In order to keep his family intact, he was obliged to buy the forfeited half of his own children for sixty shillings; and it is probably a testimonial to the monks that, instead of buying the monks' half, he bought the knight's half, thus putting the whole family under serfage to the priory (Charrière, p. 175).

As for general manumissions, without pretty plain indications of an equivalent price paid, the nearest approach I have found is at Schwarzrheindorf in 1172, when the abbess "freed" the serfs on her home manor; but this left them still subject to heriot, and there is nothing to indicate clearly that the manumission was gratuitous (Gladbach, p. 26).

Nor (as has already been pointed out) were the lay manumissions generally gratuitous, though sometimes they certainly were, especially on the lord's death-bed. And it is equally plain that wholesale lay manumissions were far more frequent than ecclesiastical. In Languedoc, the countess freed all her own serfs by will in 975; the count of Besalu did the same with a great many of his own. Count Alphonso and his wife enfranchised most of theirs in their lifetime, as against a yearly payment; and the former by his will in 1270 freed the rest. Servitude was abolished generally through Languedoc by Philippe-le-Bel in the early fourteenth century (*Hist. Gén. de Languedoc*, II [1872], 179, 257; [1879], 919, 943. But the king had not, apparently, been able to free the monastic serfs; for there were still many such in 1667; *ibid.* XIV [1876], col. 961). Then, "cet exemple fut suivi par les seigneurs, dont un grand nombre émancipèrent en masse leurs serfs; les affranchissements individuels ne furent pas moins fréquents" (Robiou, p. 400). In the wide district of Allgäu (Bavaria) by far the most generous landlords were not abbots or bishops but a municipality, Wangen; here, in the fifteenth century, the tenants were being levelled up, while all others of the district were being levelled down (Baumann, II, 626). It would be difficult to find any spiritual lord of whom it could be said, as of the dukes of Austria in the fifteenth century, that "as soon as bondfolk came into their possession, whether by purchase or by other ways, they became freemen at once without farther formality" (*ibid.* p. 631).

27

(Chap. XIII, p. 160)

INCOMPLETE MANUMISSIONS

The partial character of these manumissions is brought out by A. Blondel, on pp. 24–28 of his *Institutions municipales de Chartres* (Chartres, 1903), and by Sommerlad, II, 89. It may be seen most clearly, perhaps, in the numerous early cases in which a person surrenders him or herself in bondage to a monastery. Even though this practice had been far commoner than is often implied, it had for both parties an economic advantage quite separable from religious or charitable motives. By far the greatest number of instances which I have found are recorded in the chartulary of St-Trond, near Liège; the index gives only a faint idea of their frequency[1]. The earliest is dated 956 A.D., and the latest clear instance 1243; the document shows that the monks were already taking special measures to encourage it;

[1] Ed. C. Piot (Brussels, 1870–4). The practice is recorded in documents No. 5 [8?], 14, 17, 20, 21, 23, 26, 30, 32, 60, 65, 68, 69, 86, 91, 109, 111, 115, 119, 124, [129?, 130?], 135, 136, 138, 141, 152, 154, 172, 176, [256?, 277?]. Sidelights are thrown on these by Nos. 13, 27 59, 66, 76, 101, 117, 131, 137.

and the last document which can even vaguely suggest the continuance of the practice dates from 1270. It is noticeable that the inhabitants of St-Trond had already a certain vague communal organization before 1108; that this gained consistency as time went on; and that, in 1288, the two lords of the place, the bishop of Liège and the abbot, endowed this community with municipal rights, revocable at any moment, but never in fact revoked. In the light of these events, we can read between the lines of these earlier deeds of surrender, of which the first is the mildest specimen: "A certain woman named Guodrada, coming to the monastery...there lost her freeborn liberty and devoted herself to serve God and St-Trond under the yoke of serfdom, on these conditions here following": that she and her offspring shall pay a yearly head-tax of 1d. each, and that they may deal with their own *peculium* as they please. In the second (between 1006 and 1023), Ruzo pays 25 shillings to redeem his wife, a serf, and his child; the woman's owners handed her over to the monastery, on condition that she and her posterity should pay a head-tax of 2d., and that, when each came to die, the abbot should take their "best possession" (*i.e.* heriot) "for the good of their souls." It is probable that the monks who have drawn up these documents are correct in describing this as "a yoke of freer servitude," even as compared with the nominal liberty of a struggling freewoman in the Dark Ages; but there is certainly exaggeration in the formula which they afterwards adopt. When a serf has lost his charter, and has to apply to the monks for a renewal, it is drawn up under the title of "charter of liberty," though these servile dues are still retained[1]. Nearly all these cases of surrender to the abbey are those of women; the one or two cases of men have exceptional circumstances which imply that there was no such normal practice. This word "liberty" has sometimes been taken too literally by editors, *e.g.* Fyot (*Preuves*, p. 60), where the "liberation" described evidently only means transference from lay to monastic servitude, the monastic writer employing this common euphemism.

For a discussion of the extent to which these semi-manumissions really benefited the serf, see Verriest, pp. 146 ff. He seems slightly to exaggerate the actual gain; but he is doubtless right in insisting that they did efface personal servitude, though they left the tenant still subject to servile burdens, sometimes heavy.

A few more concrete instances may serve as illustrations. In 1240,

---

[1] *E.g.* 1, 149, an. 1186. Piot misrepresents the facts in saying "placés sous la sauvegarde de l'abbaye ils étaient, pour ainsi dire, libres: *quasi ingenua et libera*, est-il dit dans un acte de 1088" (introd. p. xxv). He has here omitted the crucial words *preter supradicta*—viz. head-tax, heriot, marriage forbidden without licence of lord and payment to him, male descendants also to be under similar marriage-restrictions (1, 27).

the monks of St-Germain manumitted the whole population of three villages but still reserved a certain number of servile dues from these "freemen," and took £1400 *parisis* for the price of that which had been remitted. In 1250, they dealt similarly with three more villages, but took £2000 for this bargain[1]. We may calculate this £3400 at about the purchasing price of £15,000 sterling pre-war. Even at the end of the fourteenth century, the *Summa Angelica* insists that the Church has a longer hold on its serfs than a lay lord. Ecclesiastical manumissions, in certain cases, may be revoked; the children of a freedman still owe a certain subservience; the Church, in freeing a bondman, may stipulate to take all his goods at his death (*Manumissio*, § 7). So also the almost contemporary *Pupilla Oculi*, composed for the guidance of parish priests in England as the *Summa* was for their Continental brethren (VII, 4 q.). A bishop of Augsburg, in 1479, sold freedom to a serf who wished to become a citizen of Wangen, but on the condition that, if the man came back to the land, he should return *ipso facto* to his bondage under the bishop (Baumann, II, 630). For other similar cases see Caggese, I, 38 and Charrière, pp. 64, 81.

28

(Chap. XIV, p. 167)

GRATIAN'S AUTHORITY

In the strictest sense, Gratian's *Decretum* was never of final authority in canon law; it did not rank with the papal Decretals which were formally embodied in the *Corpus Juris Canonici*, and concerning which Archbishop Arundel proclaimed that to dispute or misinterpret them was flat heresy.

But, in practice, it was of enormous weight. In the very century in which it was compiled, two glossators appeal to it as a *Corpus Juris*. Popes quoted its authority from the first; and none (I believe) ever repudiated it. When the Decretals were compiled at the formal bidding of Gregory IX, this was by way of appendix to the *Decretum*; and this act amounted, therefore, to something like a formal acceptance of the book to which these Decretals were to form an appendix. Then, gradually, the title of *Corpus Juris Canonici* was applied to Gratian and the Decretals, answering to the *Corpus Juris Civilis* of Justinian. Further authority was given to the book by the papal commission of 1582, which edited the whole *Corpus* without drawing any distinction between Gratian and the Decretals, and in which Gregory XIII's brief specially forbids any changes in this text of

[1] *Irminon*, II, 383, 388.

Gratian[1]. Therefore, although Joannes Andreae [d. 1348] points out that there is no definite papal authority for the book, yet in practice it would be difficult to find legists drawing any clear distinction, in their frequent citations, between *Decretum* and *Decretales*; and certainly the party which could claim definite support from Gratian would, in default of rebutting quotations, have been pretty sure to win his case.

Sir Thomas More, somewhere in his English works, protests justly against the attribution of the same force to Gratian's *Decretum* as to the papal Decretals; yet, on the other hand, it was possible for a really educated friar like the author of *Dives and Pauper* to write (Com. VII, c. 14): "For the great clerk Gracian, in the *Decrees*, that is chief book of law canon, saith that the clerk notorious lecher should have no part in the goods of Holy Church (dist. LXXXI, *Si quis amodo*, with the other following chapters)." All this is typical of the ambiguities and contradictions which meet us everywhere under the surface in the Middle Ages, even under the formal and apparently clear definitions of lawyers and theologians. We may apply here, with a great deal of truth, what Prof. Imbart de la Tour says of the Dark Ages: "Un des traits de cette société est que les mœurs y sont plus fortes que les lois et que la façade des institutions cache mal l'anarchie intérieure qui les menace" (*Rev. hist.* LXIII, 1897, 23).

29

(Chap. XVII, pp. 216, 217)

MONKS AND HUNTING

The prohibitions of canon law were little regarded here. The general subject has been treated in a popular and fragmentary fashion by H. Gourdon de Genouillac, *L'Église et la chasse*, Paris, Jouaust 1886; but there is not much evidence here about monks in particular. In ecclesiastical records, on the other hand, scattered notices are significantly frequent. Implicit condemnation may be found in Gratian's *Decretum* (dist. LXXXVI, cc. 8–12; from hence it was that Chaucer took his "text...that hunters be not holy men"), and explicit in the Decretals (*Dec. Greg.* C. V, tit. xxiv and *Clement*, C. III, tit. X, c. 1). Innocent III decreed, in the Ecumenical Council of 1215: "We forbid hunting to the whole clergy; wherefore let them not presume to keep hounds or hawks" (Can. 15). Other conciliar prohibitions, down to the Council of Trent, may be found in Van Espen's *Opuscula Varia*, Cologne, 1715, pp. 179–180.

[1] For all this, see the articles on *Corpus Juris Canonici* in the Protestant Herzog-Hauck's *Realencyclopädie*, and the Roman Catholic Herder's *Kirchenlexikon*.

The medieval commentators on these texts may be recommended to the notice of those who believe that Puritanism began with the Reformation. Some do all they can to explain the prohibitions away; others take exactly the line which Macaulay satirized in our reformed Puritans, that bull-baiting was sinful not because it gave pain to the bull but because it gave pleasure to the public. One semi-official gloss asks why Gratian's texts forbid hunting, yet allow fishing with a line (in dist. LXXXVI, c. 11; I quote from the Venice edition of 1572, "now freshly purged of errors, and especially of those thorns and thistles which had been sown in this most sacred field of canon law by heretics, in the leaven of malice and wickedness"). The answer is, "Perchance because fishing is done without noise, while hunting is noisy; or, because there is greater pleasure in hunting; for, while a man is busy with the hunt, he can have no thought of divine things." Even more explicit is the English Canonist John of Ayton (Lyndwood, *Provinciale*, appendix, p. 147). Religious, he says, are bound to the narrow way of salvation; therefore they are

more narrowly restricted from hunting and hawking of their own free will, as is plainly to be read and noted in *Dec. Greg.* v, xxiv and *Clement*, III, x. For which matter I say briefly that to hunt for pleasure's sake [*causa voluptatis*] is a mortal sin, even in a layman; but to hunt for the sake of necessity or of health or of bodily need is not a mortal sin even in a cleric; for what is prohibited in the chase is rather the enjoyment [*delectatio*] than the act of hunting.

This for the law; let us now look at the practice. The Clementines forbid monks even to be spectators of the chase; yet, a few generations earlier, it was one of Abbot Samson's exceptional virtues that he enjoyed the sport only indirectly: "He made several parks, which he stocked with beasts of the chase, keeping a huntsman with dogs; and upon the visit of any person of quality, sat with his monks in some walk of the wood, and sometimes saw the coursing of the dogs; but I never saw him take part in the sport"[1]. Prior Moore of Worcester, just before the Reformation, was a keen hunter and falconer:

Great care was taken to ensure a variety of sporting on the various manors for the prior and his friends. Conigree, Coneygree, or Coningry, in St John's, was charged with the payment of eighty couple of "conings" (rabbits), to be delivered at the priory, and to the convent six couples, at certain times specified, the said prior and convent to have liberty "to kill and carry away coneys as well with bowes as with graunds (greyhounds?) ferrets, nets, and other engines, so that the said

---

[1] C.S. p. 21, Clark, p. 36. It is just possible, however, that by *de venatione nunquam vidi eum gustare* Jocelin means, "I never saw him taste venison." To take the example of a great non-monastic churchman, the archbishop of Cologne's hounds consumed two sacks of oatmeal daily; but this would be an extreme case (Anton. II, 355).

prior or his successors be there in their proper persons, and to permit the prior and convent, or such as they shall bring with them, to walk, shoot, and take their pastime there at all times." In all their leases was reserved a liberty to hawk, hunt, fish, and fowl[1].

Abbot Litlington of Westminster kept greyhounds, and offered a waxen image of a falcon at the altar in 1368 for the recovery of his own sick hawk (J. A. Robinson, *Abbot's House at Westminster*, p. 10; see Westlake, *Last Days*, p. 44, for other monastic hunting at Westminster). Bromyard writes in his *Tractatus Juris* that monks, wishing to live like knights, are oppressive to the poor; just as the worldly aristocracy sometimes flesh their weapons on "those wretched peasants whose defence they have undertaken, so also are those Spiritual Knights, of whom some turn to trade, others to hunting, others worse still, to fights and seditions" (*Incipit Opus Trivium*, B. Museum, 1, B. 2986 and MS. Roy. 10, c. x, s.v. *religio*).

Abbot Tritheim, writing in 1493 at the command of the Abbot-President to the other heads of German monasteries, said: "Lo! how many are found among us (pardon my saying this) who spend their substance on light folk, on hawks and hounds and feasts"; and again, as speaking to one of the offenders: "Lo! thou sportest with the fowls of the air in violation of the Rule; lo! thou chasest with unclean hounds, contrary to the law of the clergy" (*De Statu et Ruina*, chs. VII, VIII, ed. 1898, pp. 257, 260). A few years later, the Dominican Guillaume Pépin bears similar testimony (*Ninive*, serm. XIX, f. 134 a). In 1503, the Benedictine Gui Jouennaux wrote:

Some monks also join in noisy hunting-parties, and chase headlong after wild beasts, so as almost to outrun the hounds themselves; and they are not ashamed to feed their packs from the possessions of the poor; so that dogs and slender greyhounds batten on that which should have gone to feed the poor.... Do not such things cry for reformation? Answer that, O monk, whosoever thou mayest be, who carest to defend these abominations. (*Reformationis Monastice Vindicie*, Paris, Demarnet, f. 9 a and b.)

About the same time, the canon lawyer who wrote the *Baculus Pastoralis* complained that monastic visitors themselves were sometimes among the worst violators of this monastic prohibition: "They bring falcons and hawks and hounds with them; and, if their will be not satisfied, the doors of the monasteries and churches are often violently broken and the ornaments carried away" (ed. Rembolt, 1503, f. 27 a). The German satirist Thomas Murner, Franciscan friar and professor at Paris, wrote in 1512 his *Schelmenzunft* or *Gild*

---

[1] Noake, *Monastery and Cathedral of Worcester*, 1866, p. 501; cf. p. 499.

of Rogues. There he speaks of *The Devil as Abbot* (§ 46; Scheible, p. 884):

How deem you this a strange tale, even though the Devil himself were abbot? You may well find such evil prelates, who do far more devilish deeds than the devils in hell. Spiritual prelates will hunt and blow their horns and howl and kill great game; they will gallop madly, and chase and drive through the poor man's wheat, with twenty or thirty or forty horses; are those fit doings for spiritual prelates? When bishops become hunters, and the hounds sing mattins, and perform God's service with their howling, then abbots also in their cloisters do the same; I know well what sort of life is lived there. Cloisters were founded to keep up a spiritual Order; but ye must now live like princes; if ye were out of the cloister, men would give you a scant pennyworth of food; the Devil hath indeed possessed you, that ye have used these spiritual gifts to feed a pack of hounds.

The Spanish canonist Azpilcueta, in the seventeenth century, wrote: "I know many not only canons but also monks, pious men in other ways and of considerable learning," who keep hawks and hounds and hunt with them. He speaks also of clergy who "bring the aforesaid hounds and hawks to church and choir, to the scandal of the more pious folk, and to the hindrance of due attention to psalmody and the singing of God's service" (*Comment. in 2 Part. Decret.*, Venice, 1688, vol. 1, col. 80). In 1790, when the États Généraux were discussing the abolition of feudal dues, "the bishop of Chartres described the ravages caused by the hunting-rights which were reserved to the nobility [including, of course, bishops and abbots] and declared that he renounced those which were enjoyed by his own bishopric, in spite of the Church laws forbidding the clergy to hunt" (Chassin, *Serfs*, p. 92). Story's admirable *Roba di Roma* will supply interesting illustrative evidence from modern times (1864, p. 340).

Medieval visitations and similar formal documents corroborate the satirists; see Archbishop Peckham's letters, R.S. pp. 162–3, 225, 343; Dugdale-Caley, III, 319 a; *Reg. Giffard, Worcs.* p. 392; *Reg. Romeyn*, I, 160; *Vis. Dioc. Norwich*, C.S. pp. 121, 147; *Norf. Arch.* XVII, 320; Rad. de Salopia, *Register*, p. 604; *Collectanea Anglo-Premonstratensia*, C.S. II, 77, 98, 180; III, 22, 59, 181, 187, 218; Flemyng's and Gray's *Vis.* pp. 27, 47, 78, 97; Alnwick's *Vis.* p. 62; Finchhale Priory (Surtees Soc.), p. 28; Duckett, *Vis. and Chap. Gen. of Cluni*, p. 241; H. E. Salter, *Aug. Chap.* p. 263; F. A. Hibbert, *Dissol. Monast.* p. 110; Baildon, pp. 103, 177, 232; *Sussex Arch. Coll.* IX, 64 (archery); *Archiv. Hist. Poitou*, VII, 187; Depoin, pp. 155–9.

There are frequent references also to clerical hunting in general; *e.g.* in Eudes Rigaud's *Registrum*, pp. 29, 34, in the Lollard poem I print in appendix 36, and especially the long and lively description of the hunting rector in Gower's *Vox Clamantis*, bk III, ll. 1493 ff. In this connexion G. C. Macaulay refers aptly to a story in Froissart which gives so vivid a picture of one corner of country life that the reader may care to see it in full. The Bastard of Mauléon, a soldier of fortune, is telling how he took the little town of Terry in Albigeois (Globe ed., p. 338; Buchon, II, 411):

Without the town there is a fair fountain, and of usage every morning the women of the town would come thither with pots and other vessels on their heads, to fetch of the clear water there. Then I took fifty companions of the garrison of Culier, and we rode all a day through woods and bushes, and the next night about midnight I set a bushment near to Terry, and I and a six other all only did on us women's array and with pots in our hands, and so we came to a meadow right near to the town and hid ourselves behind great cocks of hay that were there standing, for it was about the feast of St John, when they make hay. And when the hour came that the gate was opened to let the women go out for water, we seven took our pots and filled them at the fountain and went toward the town, our faces wrapped in kerchers so that we could not be known. The women that we met going for water said to us: "Ah, St Mary, gossips, ye were up betimes." We answered in their language with a feigned voice, "That is true"; and so passed by them and came to the gate, and we found nobody there but a cobbler dressing forth of his baggage. Then one of us blew a horn to draw thither our company out of the bushment. The cobbler took no heed, but when he heard the horn blow, he demanded of them: "What is this? who was that blew the horn?" One answered and said: "It was a priest went into the fields." "Ah, that is true," quoth the cobbler, "it was sir Francis our priest: gladly he goeth a mornings to seek for an hare." Then our company came and we entered into the town, where we found no man to draw his sword to make any defence.

30
(Chap. XVII, p. 222)

LAY AND MONASTIC CLEARINGS

Mr H. G. Richardson writes to me:

As regards the drainage of marshes the following particulars may afford ground for an opinion.

The earliest reference I have to an agreement to drain a marsh is in 1260 (referring to some time previously). The marsh was in Sussex on the coast, and the owners agreed to enclose it with walls and dikes. One of their number met the cost (about 600 marks) and then had to sue some of the other owners for their share of cost. All are laymen. (P.R.O. Assize Roll, No. 911, m. 7 d.) About 1300 one John de

Courceray undertook to drain Whitefleet [Hwyteflet] Marsh (Rye) on the terms that the owners should give him half the land. This arrangement was subsequently modified by a separate agreement of 29 June 1302 with one of the parties (P.R.O. Add. Charters, No. 959). Parties mentioned are laymen. You will observe that these agreements are exactly parallel to those of the seventeenth century. Documents of this kind would obviously be scarce at an earlier period, but I think there is some evidence that the draining of marshes had been undertaken extensively by laymen. There are many references in the thirteenth century to *leges marisci* or *de mariscis*. The earliest I know relate to Essex: and of these the earliest (1201) refers to a *lex de mariscis* made in the time of Henry II: it was clearly not committed to writing, for a jury who know the law of the marsh is summoned. These facts appear in an action (novel disseisin) brought by Wm Tovell against the abbot of Stratford (Curia Regis Roll No. 25, m. 9 d). There is a similar case a few years later between the prior of Hosp. of St John of Jerusalem and Roger de Cramaville (Feet of Fines, 52/13, No. 250; Curia Regis Roll No. 112, m. 6 d): in this case the two parties have come to an agreement regarding the making and repair of walls, gutters and dikes. There is nothing to show that in these cases the churchmen took any more prominent part in draining than laymen. There is a reference about this time however (Rotuli de Oblatis et Finibus [Rec. comm.], p. 365—1206 A.D.) which shows that the monks of Revesby (Lincs.) had made dikes and walls within and without a marsh belonging to William of Raumare, earl of Lincoln, presumably to drain their own property: the earl granted them the dikes and walls (clausura) and 14 acres of marsh land.

For the twelfth and earlier centuries my information is at present sadly to seek: but I have not worked diligently at the earlier material as I have at the later. My first object was to get information about the administration of marshlands, and the thirteenth century is the best starting-point for that. In the later centuries churchmen are certainly no more prominent than laymen, although both participated in the work of reclamation and drainage as landowners.

The evidence cited by Moke from Languedoc in 1328, which I have quoted in appendix 7, shows how much that country owed to the layman in the way of improving cultivation. In the later Middle Ages, monasteries were frequently sued for neglecting even their own share of the dikes, and thus letting floods into the whole district (*e.g.* Baildon, pp. 9, 40, 136, 171, 193; all Yorkshire cases between 1295 and 1439). In 1457 the monks of St Mary's, York, representing to the pope that one of their manors costs great sums to keep from floods by constant repair of the embankments, obtained leave to appropriate the revenues of two churches for that purpose—in other words, to improve their own lands by robbing two parishes of the greater part of their endowments (C.P.L. XI, 62). Story points out how little the Church ever did to drain the Roman Campagna, which gradually sank into worse barrenness and barbarism from the Dark Ages until modern times (*Roba di Roma*, 1864, pp. 284–5).

With regard to the work of individual pioneers, there is more evidence than that given in the text; and my impression is that a systematic search would reveal far more again. The references to Malicorne which I give on p. 220, suggest the pioneer; so also do the following: Winter, *Cistersienser*, II, 177–182; Lamprecht, *Wirth*. pp. 107, 109 n. 2, 117, 123; Hales, pp. 413, 416 (see also the *essarta* in *Domesday of St Paul's*, pp. 8, 12, 23); Sée, *Bretagne*, pp. 42, 91, 93. This author supplies a very interesting and independent analogy to Prof. Stenton's theory; he suggests that Brittany owes her comparative freedom from serfdom to the invasions of the Northmen; when these were past, fresh cultivators had to be attracted to come and till the desolate lands, and they could not be attracted by the ordinary conditions of villeinage. Couppey, independently, makes a similar suggestion for Normandy itself (pp. 53, 61) and Delisle, without searching for reasons, emphasizes repeatedly the freedom of the Norman peasant as compared with his fellows in other provinces. In twelfth-century Germany, many lords invited strangers to come and till their waste lands:

The new-comer is welcome; he need only go to the bailiff, who takes him behind on his horse and brings him to the land. "And, so soon as the stranger is on the land, in that place where it pleases him and he springs from the horse, and is willing to do tillage, there shall the bailiff measure him 15 Morgen in width and breadth, and grant him this in fee, and offer him fellowship on the manor."

Large numbers were thus attracted from Flanders and Holland, who drained swamps and cleared woods, primarily for themselves and secondarily for the manor[1]. The first to undertake such clearings on a great scale was Count Adolf II of Holstein (1131–64); his example was followed by Albert the Bear of Brandenburg (1144–70) and Henry the Lion of Brunswick (1145–80); at the same time, of course, the new Orders of Cistercians and Praemonstratensians were following a like policy. The Worcester Register seems distinctly to imply that numbers of the clearings on the monks' estates had been done by individual pioneers (*Registrum Prioratus Wigornensis*, C.S. 1865, p. 12 a; cf. p. xlvi). The abbot of Leno regularly took tithes of the lands which his tenants cleared (Zaccaria, pp. 171, 173). The case of the Belgian abbey of Liessies is very interesting. It was founded in 1095; but at some date between 1153 and 1191

---

[1] Bartels, pp. 31, 80. Fifteen Morgen, taken strictly as a square measure, would amount only to about 12 acres; the text seems to suggest a square measuring 15 plough-strips each way, which would make more than 100 acres, and seems more probable for this waste land.

the reclaiming of forest-land had ceased, and the woods were even gaining ground again upon the arable[1]. The peasants, writes the chronicler, being thus prevented from extending their holdings, "began for that reason to marl their lands, and those which before were barren became abundantly fruitful." He distinctly implies that the progress here came not from the monastic landlords, but from the peasant's own diligence in intensive cultivation (*Jacquin*, pp. 351, 394). A similar deduction seems natural from the words of the Muri chronicler in the early twelfth century: "Alchusen was originally woodland; but it was cleared by the men called Wends, and under Godfrey our prior it was made into a grange" (p. 47; he goes on to enumerate the services which the peasants owed to the monks). Anton supplies a good deal of evidence as to these pioneer-clearings, as they may be called. Vast tracts of marsh in North Germany were drained by Dutchmen and Flemings, before the rise of the Cistercians; and the promoters were not only bishops but lay lords also. The pioneers received their share of the reclaimed land on tenure which, in its freedom, contrasted so strongly with the servile tenures of the older peasants that it was called "Dutch" or "Flemish" law, and that Archbishop Adalbero of Bremen (1123–48) was obliged to apologize for the liberties thus granted: "It is better, after all, that we should bring in colonists to till our lands, and draw profit from their tillage, than that we should let the ground lie waste"[2]. And it must be remembered that the villagers did a great deal in this way on their own account: in 1152 it is complained on a German manor that the tenants have cut down so much as to cause a serious shortage of wood[3]. In Switzerland, though the monks did even more, perhaps, than elsewhere, yet some lay lords contributed to the clearing of land for cultivation (L. F. A. Maury, *Hist. des grandes forêts, etc.* Paris, 1850, p. 265). I subjoin a few miscellaneous references which might be useful to anyone who pursues the subject further: Sackur, *Die Cluniacenser*, I, 382; Winter, *Cistercienser*, I, 94, 119, 133, 146, 150–1; Boissonnade, pp. 125, 152, 174, 183, 278–285, 301, 393, 399; Borderie, pp. 51–4; *Rev. Hist.* LXI (1896), 35–6.

For enclosures, I have already quoted an early example from *Inq. Nonarum*, p. 8 a, where these jurors of 1347 report that the earl of Salisbury has "enclosed and imparked" more than 300 acres of the best land in an Oxfordshire village. The abbot of Eynsham was enclosing perhaps almost as early as this, and certainly before 1442 (*Eynsham Cartulary*, II, xlvii). But these are only scattered indications.

[1] For similar relapses to desert in the Middle Ages see Lamprecht, *Wirth*. pp. 128–31.　　　　　　　　　　[2] Anton, II, 21; cf. II, 14 ff.
[3] *Ibid*. II, 327; cf. pp. 248–50 for instances of individual clearings; also III, 161, 178, 439.

31

(Chap. XVIII, pp. 234, 239, 247, 250)

PEASANT CIVILIZATION

I reserve the further evidence for this appendix in order not to overload my text, hoping that all thoughtful readers will agree that it should not be omitted altogether. A great deal of current writing on medieval society has become so conventional, that even historical specialists are sometimes startled and suspicious in face of the actual documentary evidence; and I have more than once been accused of choosing those citations alone which favour my own preconceptions. I must repeat here, therefore, that I shall be very glad to print the supposed rebutting evidence, if only my critics will show me where it is to be found. So far as I know, no favourable generalization as to *contemporary* peasant life has survived from the Middle Ages, with such slight exceptions as I have printed; therefore, if I am to draw a true picture, I must show how enormous the preponderance of un-favourable evidence is. Readers, of course, must discount it by the usual considerations; zealous churchmen exaggerate, as satirists do; and we must allow for the comparative want of balance and self-control in even great writers of the Middle Ages; but, after these allowances have been made, it is difficult to see on what principle we are asked to neglect this evidence altogether, by critics who claim to speak in the name of high academic impartiality. I have received no answer to the question which I put lately, in public print, to one of my ablest and most benevolent reviewers: "If, like previous critics, you have no references to supply, but are only expressing a general sense of discontent, how then can you justly blame me for not printing that which, so far as you and I know, does not exist at all?" We do not want to read quotations from people who said that things were happy in their grandfathers' days, or, in the still more distant past; such evidence from a medieval writer is even more worthless than from a modern; Roger Bacon, with all his philosophic breadth of view, looked back regretfully to paganism in Aristotle's day as to a far more moral society than that of his own thirteenth-century Christendom. We want to know what people said about their own day, concerning which they were competent witnesses: and I will begin here with Rodrigo, bishop of Zamorra, who dedicated his *Speculum Vitae Humanae* to Pope Paul II in about 1465: the most convenient edition is Goldast's of 1613. In Chapter XXI of his first book (p. 60), Rodrigo makes the friends and relatives commend agriculture to the boy, who is about to choose a life-occupation, just as they had previously set forth the happier side of other walks of life, each in its turn. They begin on a very high note: "no man, save he who knows not how to live, doubts that agriculture is the best kind of life." This would be more impressive, if we had not already heard them commend other lives with the same exaggerated enthusiasm—the courtier's, the soldier's, the married man's—only to be confuted, in each case, by the mother's counterpleas. But we read on; agriculture is the happiest life because God decreed it for the first man, because it is most useful to the community, because Cato Major did not disdain it, because it is so simple and innocent, far from the temptations of the great city.

"For who among those who labour in the field usurps that which belongeth to another? who perjures himself, or blasphemes, or is proud, or angry, or envious, since he cannot wish a blessing on himself alone without its falling upon others also? Who, in short, of those who labour at agriculture, hath enemies? What doth he hate but hail-storms, what doth he curse but the tempests? What, in fine, doth he greedily covet but things which belong to no other man? Who, again, committeth fornication, among those whom no delicacies of food await, but hunger and a scanty table, and whose weary limbs and long daily labour compels to sleep rather than to wantonness? Again...in this manner of life more is rendered to God than in all others; and, so to speak, a man often offers to God more than he possesses. For sometimes, when the tithes have been given to God, and when expenses have been deducted, nothing is left [to the peasant] but his labour; so that very many years, even of the most fertile, are barren to the very men who till the earth. Just and true, therefore, is that old Spanish proverb, that the peasant is counted for a martyr; for he does not shed his blood once for all to make the earth fatter for men's uses, but he daily bedews it with sweat and blood, that we may be able to live, and that we may thrive upon his torments and continual agonies."

With such words as these would my kinsfolk have persuaded me to give myself to agriculture, even though not in my own person, yet through my serfs and husbandmen, as many illustrious men are wont to do. But they had scarce ended, when lo! my mother answered, earnestly dissuading this fashion of life by the following reasons.

Ch. XXII. "We have said enough in praise of the practice of agriculture, which no man doubts to be necessary and delectable, but which hath its own thorns. For (as Pliny saith in his book of Natural History), agriculture, in times of old, was the beginning of most innocent and blessed life; but now it is exposed to far greater labours and to new shortcomings. For (as Virgil saith in his *Georgics*, and as we learned first from Holy Scripture), man was not destined to serve the earth and the fields, but earth was destined to serve man. Therefore it is by man's fault that earth answereth not to her possessors without toil, and oftentimes the toil itself hath no fruit of sweetness; so that man's indigence and necessity compelled him to vex the earth with iron, and to soften her with far-fetched blandishments. What bodily labours do men

suffer in tilling the soil, and what anxiety of mind? no man knoweth
but the tiller himself, so that Petrarch saith true: He who soweth wheat,
soweth cares therewith. And again the poet saith that the grain is
enjoyed by many, but the sower hath anxiety for his pains, so that, to
speak truly, the field is his mind, the culture his intention, the seed his
care and the harvest his toil.... In short, this is most certain, though
to many it will be incredible, that in tilling the fields and laying out
vineyards the harvest scarce equals the outlay. Moreover, as St Gregory
said, it is good to till the fields if nothing better can be found to be
done. Therefore, in this age of ours, it is not the part of an excellent
man or of an eminent mind to busy oneself with agriculture, either as
an art or as a calling or as a trade, but it is praiseworthy only for the
sake of leisure and alternation of cares, or when necessity itself compels.
For this art improves the earth, but not the intellect; it profiteth not
for intellectual power, but it exercises the external powers,"

for which reason Aristotle definitely subordinates peasants, artisans,
traders and journeymen to the more educated classes.

"Again, I think that the peasant's occupations would be most truly
innocent, if indeed the peasants were such as they were of old (for
these were most innocent and simple), and such as we read that they
ought to be, not such as we find them to be. For those bore their toils
with patience and longsuffering, praising God when the fruits were
plentiful and never murmuring when they were scanty, but saying with
the patriarch Job: The Lord gave, and the Lord hath taken away:
blessed be the name of the Lord. Moreover the first tillers were such
as (to speak with the prophet) beat their swords into ploughshares and
their spears into hoes; but the peasants of our day turn their plough-
share and handle and pruning-hook into weapons, not defensive only
but offensive. They defraud God of His tithes, and the king of his taxes;
they confound the boundaries of the fields, or steal for themselves;
they have no reverence for the Church; they wax proud against their
lords; they haunt fairs; they till the fields through their bondmen and
hired labourers, but appear in person to litigate in the lawcourts; and,
while they desert their own duty, they usurp the perilous duties of
others. These, alas! outdo all traders in greed, pride, pomp, varied
adornment, plenty of furniture, fraud, deceit, litigation and quibbles.
I see not how such peasants can be called martyrs; for martyrdom
depends upon a man's cause, rather than upon his sufferings: therefore
I should call the countryfolk of our day martyrs rather of earthly greed
than of Christ. And, to be brief, they so till the earth, they are so utterly
earthly, that we may truly say of them: They shall lick the earth and
eat it. Nor do they think of heavenly things; for they are ever speaking
and meditating of earthly things. They envy each other; they abhor
other classes [of men]. But God oftentimes chastiseth them in that
sort of fault wherein they offend; for it is just that those who sin in
pride and greed in the earth (which is the humblest and most fruitful
of all the elements) should be deprived of the goodness of that same

earth. Therefore God turneth their fruitful land into barrenness for the wickedness of them that dwell therein; whence it cometh to pass that, though the earth be fruitful of her own nature, yet their iniquity maketh her barren."

Our next witness shall be Felix Hemmerlin, canon and precentor of Zürich, in his dialogue on Nobility (ch. xxxii, f. 124 a; Reber, p. 248). He writes:

Now know I of a truth that the peasant pricks the man who flatters him, and flatters him who pricks; wherefore a certain wise man said: "Wash a hound and comb him; hound he is and hound he remaineth"; and another speaketh most certainly concerning the peasant class in these words: "Rustic folk are best when they weep, worst when they rejoice."

After quoting Deut. xxxii, and Gregory (*Moralia*, l. vi, c. 3) he goes on:

Whence those who have most learned from experience argue reasonably—nay, judge this to be the saving health of the State and of human well-being, and even the living remedy which will best and most justly befit the peasantry themselves, and rural life and the countryside—that the peasants' abodes and homes and barns and sheds and hovels and farms and sheepfolds, with their houses and cottages, should be laid waste or burned with fire every year of jubilee[1], and stripped and spoiled and laid bare; whereby, even as a too luxuriant tree, they are pruned with hook or hoe from their superabundant branches, boughs, twigs and suckers, and are thus brought back to rich and fecund health; and, from their natural arrogance and pride and consequent ingrained wickedness, and from their deadly envy, they are more effectually trained to the discipline of obedience, humility, subjection and servitude and self-knowledge.... But, that we may more clearly analyze the properties of peasants, let us go to the gloss on Gratian's *Decretum*. First, he saith that they are (as they are nowadays) intemperate in their manners, that is, coarse and blubbery, gluttonous, rough-skinned, dirty, rarely well-proportioned in body, and that their crooked manners are a consequence of their crooked bodies.... Secondly, the Gloss saith that peasants are commonly flatterers.... Thirdly, it calls them traitors, and blabbers of all sorts of secrets.... Fourthly, that they are most bitter backbiters.... Fifthly, that they are cursers against God and certain of His saints, and especially the Blessed Virgin, presuming publicly to let loose their tongues in blasphemy more than any other men in the world...this may often be evidently noted; when they see their carts stuck in the wheel-furrowed fields owing to the impotence of their beasts, then they set themselves to remove these impediments with execrable curses and horrible blasphemy and loud gnashing of teeth, so that we may properly say of them (Ps. ix, 7), "their mouth is full of cursing and of bitterness and of deceit; under their tongue are labour and sorrow." Sixthly, that they are envious. Seventhly, he saith that they are scurrilous and wordy,

---

[1] He probably means, every fiftieth year.

expressing themselves waywardly in the foulest of words. Eighthly, they are prone to avenge injuries, nor do they leave vengeance to their superior or to God's judgement.

Hemmerlin then enumerates the peasant's seven nicknames in a doggerel rhyme, evidently traditional. He is *Rusticus* as *rudis in rure*, *Rustinard* as emitting an odour very different from spikenard, *Rustibald* as a ribald; and so on through *Rustibold*, *Rustincus*, *Rustoicus* to *Rusticellus*, which rhymes with *ass* [*asellus*] and may remind us that he lives, eats and is buried like a beast[1]. The common proverb speaks truth; it is equally safe to leave one's flock with a wolf in the field, or to trust in that which has been left to a monk's conscience, or to the bond of a peasant's oath. The same man who is wont to leave no limb of Christ uncursed—head, brain, hair, ears, teeth, heart, spleen, kidneys, lungs, bowels, belly, nerves, veins, eyes, mouth, bones and marrow—he recks as little of an oath in the way of perjury. And it is the peasants who practise witchcraft and bring hail and thunder upon the land.

I know well that your wives are wont to mingle most venomous and unclean materials, and certain herbs, with smoky roots; these they cook over the fire for a sufficient space in a carefully-closed caldron, and then set the pot open under the clearest rays of sunlight. First a smoke comes up naturally; then, presently, clouds collect in this most serene sky, and by the devil's assistance, as aforesaid, unaccustomed tempests arise. And wonder not that I say "your wives"; for I say this not without cause, seeing that one of the chief materials is procured only by the cooperation of women.

The Valais especially, "the county and bishopric of Sion," is infested by such witches, of whom "innumerable numbers have been burned, men and women, and all peasants or common folk." Again, "Let us now return to the peasants, who have for many centuries been full of these sorceries; nay, so accustomed to them that, even when they are taken with some natural disease, they fancy themselves bewitched." They believe in the tying of love-knots by witches, to the hindrance of true matrimony; and so also, it transpires, does Hemmerlin himself: "I have seen it in experience, in both sexes." "But let us return to our purpose, lest thou be moved with weariness. By reason of these and other acts and operations of the said peasants, I bid thee note that, by legal authority[2], peasants ought not to ride on horse-

[1] Hinc rusticellus, Ut asellus Nascitur, et pecus ad arandum. Sicut bufalus exoritur Ad jugiter triturandum. Ut hericius volvitur, Nec aliud scit colendum; Et, sicut miser pascitur, Sic se novit sepeliendum.

[2] The following prescriptions are from Roman Civil Law, which in Germany was beginning to take the place of the old customary law. They are applied by other jurists of the time to the German and Italian peasantry; this was part of a general movement on the side of the landed classes to repress the growing prosperity and independence of the peasants.

back, but only on carts or on asses; nor ought they to eat white bread, but coarse; nor should a peasant's household eat fowls or other delicate foods, but garlic, cheese, onions and beans." They are forbidden to bear arms, and even cudgels; but this they openly or covertly disregard. Witness the story of a certain village wake:

The peasants visited the dedication-feast of a certain church in crowds, according to the fashion of the country, on foot and on horseback, in carts with two or three or four horses; and, as the lord [Emperor Frederick I] had commanded, without arms. But lo! they wore great belts, reinforced and weighted with wrought-iron knobs or balls like the knob of a sword-hilt, strung together as on that instrument of prayer for the unlearned which is called *paternoster*. Then, seizing their opportunity, they violently smote each other to their hearts' content, bruising and wounding with these instruments as with the most deadly weapons, and left many dead or half-alive at that dedication-feast[1]. From these, and other notable things collected in this chapter, thou mayest fitly infer that, whensoever princes or nobles, in reward for the malice and contumacy and disobedience and many demerits of the peasants, have wreaked upon them terrible ravin and robbery and spoil and other kinds of plagues and stripes, then, I say to thee, they have thereby hallowed their own hands, as Moses saith to the Levites in Exodus xxxii, when they slew some 23,000 of the people for their rebellion and disobedience.

The peasant is a domestic bird, like a goose or a capon; the lord is a noble bird like a hawk or falcon; but with this difference, that the hawk does not call in "rustic" birds to help him to his prey, whereas the lords find their most ready tools among the peasants themselves, who, when thus perverted, are more fierce and merciless than the lord himself.

And here is a true story. When I, Felix, the writer of this book, was travelling lately with a party of friends through the land of the marquis of Baden, at the time of the Hussite terror, I rested for refection at a public inn in a certain great town, which was mainly supported by the custom of the peasants. And lo! here were hosts of rustics feasting after their usual crazy fashion [*solita dementia*] in the same parlour as myself by reason of the holy-day; and (perchance for the sake of irritating me and my clerk) they fell all together, the whole crowd as one man, with contumelious words against clerics and the clergy, concluding as cruelly as they could that these were worse than any other men in the world for their fornications and their sins of concubinage. I meanwhile was struggling to refresh my body amid the claims of hunger, yet I heard none the less how, with many arguments, they so arrogantly constructed

[1] Grosseteste of Lincoln, and several other English bishops, legislated against the fights at cathedral dedication-feasts. Each parish was led by the flag of its own patron saint; there was much jostling for precedence; the flag-poles supplied formidable weapons, and bloodshed was not uncommon.

their case and commonly alleged this single stain of crime against the clergy. At length, when my belly was comforted and my mind strengthened, I asked for silence, which they granted. Then I said (in words to this effect): "Yesterday, as I came up the Rhine from Mainz, I passed by the city of Oppenheim, and there, in a level field, I found twenty-four wheels set up on high in a single group, and twenty-four peasants bound singly limb by limb, each to a wheel; all of these were thieves, and all came from one township. There was no noble or clerk among them; all were pure countryfolk, yet, if there had been a single noble or cleric among them, this company of yours would have gone on for everlasting (and, to your own mind, reasonably) denouncing the ill-fame of us nobles and clerics. Wherefore I have listened to your cruel and reviling words which ye have so irreverently dinned into mine ears, by reason of one or a few clerics; and them you abuse for a natural thing, which began two thousand years before the Flood, and then went on for five thousand more unto Christ's day, and was then continued for nearly a thousand years without reproach to our Creator; since which time it has been restricted by man's prohibition and turned into a sin; yet none the less is it natural, and it is common to you with them." Wherefore, as against these and their like, we turned aside altogether from the matter of their rude reviling of the clergy, and bitterly proclaimed their thefts, which are a thing against nature[1]; and all were disturbed by my words. Then said I to my clerk, "Now let us depart"; and so we did; else would these men have risen up against us and swallowed us up quick; and perchance, in their wrath, would have drowned us in the river.

Nature, proceeds Hemmerlin, balances one rough force against another, as poison and counter-poison; for instance,

against the bite of a mad dog she gives its own hairs as a healing balm... so also, against the clergy's vain and fastidious glitter of worldly pomp, and their presumption of ineffable pride, God hath ordained, or at least permitted, the corrosive and unceasing jealousy and latent envy of the laity...as Pope Eusebius knew well when he said that the laity are very inimical to the clergy (Gratian, *Decret.* II, c. ii, q. 6, c. 5, *laicos*)[2]. That is why St Augustine said that the miserable calamity of bondage hath reasonably been brought into the world because of the demerits of the peoples, so that bondage is now fitly rooted among peasants and common folk[3].

---

[1] The text of this sentence seems corrupt; but I have tried to make sense of it.

[2] It was this sentence, ascribed to his predecessor Eusebius (d. 310), which Boniface VIII took for the text of his famous bull *Clericis Laicos*.

[3] It was from this text of Augustine that Aquinas and the other schoolmen set out to justify serfdom. Bondage was a result of sin, of the fall; it could therefore be justified on moral as well as on economic grounds. But they do not sufficiently explain why Adam's fall should weigh upon one class alone.

Even the tyranny of unjust lords, from this orthodox point of view, is part of God's providence; "they are one of His instruments, as demons also are, for the punishment of sinners." Chastisement makes men think, and gives them more chance of turning to God; therefore even these tyrants are among those servants of the parable "Compel them to come in"; "the noble landlords compel the peasants to enter in to a house and a habitation which are salutary both for this life and for the next." It is true that this servitude is not only burdensome but invidious, so much so that a fierce tribe in Spain is recorded in the chronicles to have chosen death before servitude. But this curse has rightly fallen upon the peasantry; for Hemmerlin has read very widely and had extraordinary opportunities of wide and close observation:

and at length, on mature and serious deliberation, I think I must firmly assert that no creatures are found more abominable, deadly, cunning, unreasonable, prevaricating, execrable, impudent and audacious than peasants and countryfolk. And especially, by universal report of all time until now, when any event, whether fortuitous or of purposeful intention, sets a peasant in authority over the peasants, or grants him a magistracy among them. For thenceforward, having altogether broken the snare of servitude and escaped[1], as he claims, he becomes as it were an apostate and persecutor of his former order; he rages more cruelly and increasingly than the nobles against his fellow-peasants, as against members of a profession which he has renounced...wherefore a poet hath written:

> Rusticus et porcus, ignis et fluminis ortus,
> Nulli salvantur ubi talia [nunc] dominantur.

Let us now pass to briefer notices. Gower, again, dwells on the evil nature of the peasant in that poem which Wright printed in *Political Songs*, R.S. 1, 359; the whole of English society is out of joint, and there is no hope in the villages for any immediate amendment. The peasants of our day, writes the banker-saint Rulman Merswin in 1352, live like beasts without fear of God or sense of justice; God still bears with them as best He may, but some day He must strike (Merswin, p. 42: *Susonis Opera*, p. 378). Bishop Grandisson of Exeter, writing in 1352 to the king's chancellor, described the remote Cornish peasants as wallowing in a state of sin from which none but the pope could absolve them.

I will not repeat, for shame, the things that are reported: yet I may speak of those which are manifest to all. Living as they do, like brute beasts, in the very tail of the world, they contract marriages in all the prohibited degrees, and are divorced [when married] in all lawful degrees. They fall under the sentence of Canon Law, and never rise again (*Reg. Grand.* p. 74).

---

[1] The words here used are those of Ps. cxxiii, 7, Vulg.

There is a very significant document of 1350 in the register of Ralph of Shrewsbury, bishop of Bath and Wells, condemning "the blind covetousness and damnable dishonesty of the workfolk and serving-folk who are called 'laborers' in the vulgar tongue." These men, he thinks, have "a thirst for gain which cometh from the pit of insatiable greed"; and he bids his rectors warn their parishioners against breaking their agreements as to wages (*Reg. R. Salop*, 1896, p. 640, § 2475). The rustics suffer much oppression, says Meffret, a century later, but this is partly God's punishment for their sins:

If you consider the state of country-folk, you will find it much degraded; for in old days rusticity was looked upon as holy, as St Jerome saith in his prologue to the Bible and in that text [of canon law, Gratian, c. II, q. vii, § 56]. But nowadays they are fallen from that holiness, for they pay not their tithes and firstfruits [Gratian again]. And, even if they pay them, it is only under compulsion; again, they give [for tithes] the worst corn that they have. Moreover, they are prone to manslaughter and perjury, fornication and hatred, and to the damage which they do in other men's fields [see *Decretales Gregorii*, lib. v, tit. xxxvi, c. I]; wherefore, as saith St John, the whole world is seated in wickedness (*Temp.* p. 28, 2).

For the attitude of the fifteenth-century chronicler Chastellain towards the working classes, see Huizinga, *The Waning of the Middle Ages*, pp. 48–50.

The wife-lending referred to on p. 250 is thus prescribed in the customal of the Sieben Freie Hagen (*Weisthümer*, III, 311): "If a man have no child, he shall carry his wife on his back over at least nine hedges from his own house, and there find some other man to raise up an heir for him; or, in the last resort, bring her to market for that purpose." The accusation of bestiality on p. 244, article 12, is to some extent corroborated by a judicial register of 1540–1692 quoted by Desmaze, p. 123. Nobody, I think, who has really gone into the facts can fail to agree in the main with Léopold Delisle, one of the greatest archivists of all Europe in our time, who has never been accused of anti-clericalism. He writes on p. 187:

MORALITÉ.—Nous ne nous étendrons pas sur cette question, à laquelle nous consacrerons bientôt une étude spéciale. Bornons-nous à indiquer les faits principaux qui ressortent du registre des visites de l'official de Cerisi, dans les paroisses rurales soumises à sa juridiction au xive siècle. En lisant ces procès-verbaux, dont l'authenticité ne saurait être contestée, on reste confondu à la vue des désordres qui régnaient dans la plupart des ménages. A chaque instant, notre official doit enregistrer les plus scandaleux débordements. De tous côtés le concubinage et l'adultère appellent une répression, qui presque toujours reste impuissante.—Le mariage ne conserve plus la moindre dignité: nos malheureux paysans n'y voient guère qu'un marché, peu différent de ceux qu'ils concluent journellement entre eux....En parcourant les lettres de rémission dont sont remplis les registres du Trésor des chartes, on n'arrive pas à des résultats plus consolants. Seulement, dans les documents de cette espèce, ce sont d'autres vices qui se manifestent au lecteur: le principal est l'ivrognerie, dont au moyen âge les suites étaient probablement encore plus terribles qu'au xixᵉ siècle. En effet, les excès de boisson étaient fréquemment suivis de rixes dans lesquelles un ou plusieurs des combattants perdait la vie. Ce dénouement paraissait alors un accident très-ordinaire, et, il faut l'avouer, la facilité avec laquelle, dans ces circonstances, les coupables obtenaient des lettres de rémission, dut puissamment contribuer à pervertir la conscience publique. Ainsi, en lisant le registre de l'official et les registres de la chancellerie, on ne peut se défendre d'assez tristes pensées; mais du moins, on se rendra le témoignage que, pour la régularité et la douceur des mœurs, nous sommes loin d'avoir quelque chose à envier à nos pères.

This may be compared with Maxim Gorki's judgement on the Russian peasant, who a few years ago was commonly put before us as a model by writers who had evidently never realized the stages which must intervene before simple civilization can pass into complicated civilization. *The Times* of Oct. 7, 1922, quotes from Gorki's new book:

The Russian people's outstanding quality is a sense of special cruelty....I believe that women are nowhere else so pitilessly and terribly beaten as in the Russian village....Children are also thoroughly beaten; Russians like beating generally, and it is all the same whom they beat.

Again,

Gorki relates that a scientific expedition in the Urals was met in 1921 by a peasant with these words: "You are scholars; tell me what to do. A Bashkir killed my cow; I, of course, killed the Bashkir. But now I have stolen a cow from the Bashkir's family; will anything be done to me?" He was asked whether he did not expect to be punished for killing the man, but he quietly answered, "Oh, that is nothing; men are now cheap."

The peasantry, Gorki says, has become very ill-disposed towards the towns, regarding the townspeople as parasites, living on the labour and products of the country, and producing only unnecessary things with which they impose on the simplicity of the country-people. "Sometimes," he says, "you hear such sentiments as these: 'We must wipe out all the educated people from the face of the earth; then it will be easier for us fools to live.'" "But the Russian peasant," continues Gorki, "is not malicious; he forgets the evil he himself commits, and at the same time he does not remember the good anyone else does him." ..."Now," he says, "we may with conviction affirm that at the price of the intellectual and working classes, the Russian peasantry has come to life. As with the Jews whom Moses led out of Egyptian bondage, the semi-savage, foolish, apathetic inhabitants of the Russian villages, including the monsters described above, will die out, and their place will be taken by a new race, literate, intelligent, courageously healthy. I do not think this will be a very gentle or kind people; but it will be an active people, suspicious, and indifferent to everything for which it can have no direct need."

32

(Chap. XVIII, p. 241)

PEASANT SAINTS

Here is the result of a summary survey from Alban Butler's *Lives of the Saints*. I chose at random the first and last months in vol. I— *i.e.* January and June. In 46 of the 321 lives given in those two months, Butler supplies no indication of the saint's parentage or status. The remaining 275 may be classed as follows:

Humble birth is clearly specified in	16 cases
Noble birth equally clearly in	130 ,,
Prelates and dignitaries (*i.e.* cases where the probabilities point against humble birth) in	82 ,,
Implication of good education and means	47 ,,
	275 ,,

Another worker might, of course, slightly modify these figures, and a search undertaken over the whole twelve months might conceivably even double this proportion of humble saints, though it would be just as likely, on the other hand, to halve it. But I am convinced that no reader who looks through the first dozen notices in this book, with their emphasis on the worldly nobility of these men whose prayers are to profit us in heaven, will fail to understand why Berthold of Regensburg, who knew both the Church calendar and the living rustic better than most men, emphasized the paucity of peasant saints. There was perhaps only one medieval saint who was both fairly popular and famous for her humble birth among her worshippers—St Zita, the thirteenth-century servant-maid of Lucca, who appears in England as St Sithe, and has often been confused with St Osyth. In saying this I do not forget St Peter; for the average medieval worshipper would probably have been as much astounded to hear that St Peter was a fisherman, as the London citizen's wife (Sir Thomas More tells us) was to realize the Virgin Mary's Jewish parentage.

It may be of interest to subjoin the names and days of the sixteen humble saints:

Jan. 3. Geneviève. Tradition says, daughter of a poor shepherd; but B. gives strong reasons for doubting this.

  „   5. Simeon Stylites. Son of a poor shepherd.

  „ 13. Veronica, daughter of poor peasants in village near Milan.

  „ 16. Macarius, who was brought up in the country and tended his father's cattle.

  „ 19. Lomer, who kept his father's sheep, studied under the priest and took Orders.

  „ 22. Anastasius, who was a soldier in the Persian troops and son of a magician.

June 2. Blandina, an inconsiderable slave.

  „ 10. Henry of France, of mean extraction and to the end a day-labourer.

  „ 12. Basilides, Quirinus, Nabor and Nazarius, four soldiers in the Roman army.

  „ 15. Crescentia and Modestius, a Christian nurse and her husband, martyred with her lady and the child.

  „ 28. Potamiana, a slave.

  „ 28. Basilides, a soldier who led Potamiana to execution.

Even those strict articles of reform which the University of Paris drew up for the coming Council of Constance made allowance for privilege as against spiritual efficiency in the Church. The memorialists urged "that none be admitted to cathedral churches except graduates or nobles of high birth [*nobiles magna nobilitate*]" (Finke, p. 136, § 14). And nobody can read the Calendars of Papal Letters or Petitions with any care, without noticing how constantly the petitioner's noble birth is pleaded in support of his plea for some moral or religious relaxation.

33

(Chap. VII, p. 68; XVIII, p. 249)

PUNISHMENTS

For the barbarity of punishments in Flanders see Van Houtte, *Essai sur la civil. flamande*, pp. 131–4. Siméon Luce, who is in one sense an apologist for the Middle Ages, prefaces his list of punishments with the confession that "la honte de cette époque, c'est la barbarie et, il faut bien le dire, l'immoralité de la justice" (*B. du Guesclin*, p. 65). Some medieval penalties, it is true, are strange, not so much for their barbarous severity as for their old-world form. For instance, in the villages on the Benker Heide in Westphalia, "if a wife beat her husband, so that he must quit his house, then shall he set a ladder to that house and make a hole through the roof, and thus enter his home, and take with him a pledge of the worth of a gold-gulden, and fetch two of his neighbours and drink this pledge away [at the inn]; and they shall be so exact with each other in drinking out the pot, that a louse might creep with ears erect under the peg" (*Weisthümer*, III, 42; Bartels, p. 58; they drank, that is, from a "prick-pot," in which a peg marked the exact measure). At a group of villages in Lower Saxony, the Sieben Freie Hagen, if a householder finds a burglar in his house "he shall strike him dead, and dig a hole under the sill, and drag the evildoer through it, and cut off the house-cock's head and lay it on the dead man's breast, or else a shilling; that shall be his fine." By the same laws, if a good dog be killed, it shall be hung up by the tail and the offender shall heap red wheat until he covers it; if a goose still ravage a neighbour's lands after two plain warnings, the sufferer shall catch him, thrust his neck between the two top rods of the fence-hurdle, and throw his body over: "if the goose can get free, then he has saved his life" (*ibid.* III, 308; the actual written document dates from about 1720). But in others, the barbarity of fact is as terrible as the barbarous form. As with forest-fires, so the community was pitiless also to the man who wilfully spoiled fruit-trees or, in marshland, the willows which held the dikes together. In the Sieben Freie Hagen, when a man barks a willow, "his belly shall be ripped up and his bowels taken out and wound round the harm he has done; if he can get over that, the willow also can get over it" (*Weisthümer*, III, 309). The same punishment is more brutally expressed in a manorial custom of Wetterau in 1461 (Bezold, p. 48). By the statutes of the city of Augsburg, a cutter-down of fruit-trees must lose his hand and pay damages, or be banished for life; but few codes were so severe as this (Anton, III, 427). The officers of the nunnery of Manbuisson, in the early fifteenth century, burned one Quentin Dubris "for thefts and robberies by him committed" (Dutilleux-Depoin, p. 36; cf. p. 37). Next to war, hail and fire were looked upon as the peasant's worst enemies (Anton, III, 209). Incendiaries were sometimes burned to death; in one Rhenish village of the eighteenth century, the incendiary and the man who stole from his neighbour's crops were denied sanctuary even in the Church (Anton, III, 214). At Corbach in Westphalia, in 1454, when a man has criminally removed his neighbour's landmark

he shall be buried in the earth, with his head standing out, in the place where that landmark stood; and men shall take a new plough wherewith no man hath yet ploughed, and harness thereunto four [oxen] which have never yet been used, and new harness to the plough, and a plough-

holder and driver who have never before holden or driven a plough;
and these shall plough the field, and the buried man may help himself
as best he can. (*Weisthümer*, III, 80; see also I, 794; II, 122, 124, 739;
IV, 802; VI, 466.)

Bartels (p. 52) quotes a grislier custom; the sinner is buried only
to the waist, and the plougher is to plough his heart out. The civic
authorities of Laon, when banished malefactors of either sex fell
again into their hands, "bury them, three Saturdays running, for the
half of a day, from opening of market to before vespers, upright on
their feet, enclosed even to their paps in earth...after which we warn
them that they never come to this city again, under pain of burial
alive" (Desmaze, p. 44, document of the late thirteenth century). In
1449, a woman-thief was hanged in Paris. "Never before had a
woman been hanged in France; they had always been buried alive.
This gipsy-woman who was hanged in April 1449 had herself demanded this form of execution, 'this being the custom of her country
in such cases'" (Joubert, p. 4). When a prostitute became trouble-
some to the community, her nose might be cut off (Ugolini, II, 529),
or her upper lip[1]; for other barbarous punishments see Heywood,
Assempri, p. 229 and Lavisse, *Hist. de France*, vol. IV, ii, p. 122.

On the other hand, nothing was commoner than to compound for
a murder with a fine. Not only was this an integral principle of law
in earlier times, each code having its own tariff of fines graduated
according to the importance of the victim or the heinousness of the
deed, but it survived in practice long after it had died out from formal
law. A rather cold-blooded murder was committed in 1533 near
Craon in Anjou. The victim was Étienne Viel; his widow, giving
evidence before a court of enquiry, concludes: "in answer to a
question, that she will not take part against the said Lucas [who had
abetted the murderer], because the said Lucas has appointed with her
for the sum of 6 livres tournois, which she has received from the said
Lucas's wife." The victim's daughter ends her evidence with a
similar phrase: she and her mother have settled with Lucas for these
6 livres (Joubert, pp. 342–3).

This may be compared with the spirit which sometimes granted the
culprit a chance of escape. On the manors of the abbey of Rot in
Bavaria (fifteenth century)

if any harmful man or woman come within the bounds, the abbey
bailiff [*Richter*] may seize his body and goods, and keep them and let
the Landrichter know that he has such a man...and after three days
he shall take the offender to the Landrichter or his official, bound with
a girdle, and tie him to the outer doorpost with a thread of silk or twine;
and the goods that he has brought shall not go outside the [abbey]
manor bounds, and no man is responsible for [delivering] them [up

[1] I have mislaid my reference, but feel sure of the fact.

to any authority who may claim them]. And when this has been done, if the Landrichter, or anyone on his behalf, comes and takes the harmful man, he may do so; if no man comes to take him, then the abbey Richter may and shall leave him by the post, and take his troth that he will do no harm to the abbey, its land and its people, and be no man's enemy on this account; and after this neither the abbey nor its Richter bears any farther responsibility. (*Weisthümer*, III, 670.)

At Chiemsee in Bavaria, by the customals of 1393 and 1462, if a thief were caught on the manor, the abbot's bailiff was to bring him over the lake to Gstad, where there was a gallows under a lay lord. The lord's bailiff was to ride into the lake up to his saddle to receive the thief: "but, if so be that neither he nor his authorized deputy come, then shall our bailiff set the thief, bound as he is, in an empty boat; if he escape, we and our abbey shall bear no blame, but be free from all claim upon us; and the same shall be done to a manslayer" (*Weisthümer*, III, 671). Sometimes, again, the person buried alive was allowed a reed to breathe through (compare the case I quote on p. 249 n. 1), or (as in *Monte Cristo*) he was given a hand free, and a knife worth 1d. in that hand (*Oest. Weisthümer*, VI, 70; VIII, 1094; XI, 22; cf. VII, 74 and VIII, 1091). Karl v. Amira has a couple of very interesting pages on such *Zufallsstrafen* (*Die germanischen Todesstrafen*, Abh. d. Bayer. Akad. d. Wiss., Philosoph-philolog. Klasse, Bd XXXI, 1922, pp. 222–3). This very valuable study is mainly confined to the earlier ages; it came into my hands too late for full use. Amira gives references to the following other sources: Ackerman in *Archaeologia*, vol. XXXVIII (1860); Ducange, s.v. "sepeliri, fossa, interrare, defossus, subterratio"; W. Andrews, *Old-time Punishments*; A. Schulz, *Höf. Leben*, II, 183 n. 2; Shakespeare, *Tit. Andron.* Act V, sc. 3; and J. v. Gierke, *Gesch. d. deut. Deichrechts*, II, 679, 685. On p. 223 he alludes to the old-world belief that the relics of executed criminals bring luck—skull, fingers, toes, etc.

34

(Chap. XIX, p. 255)

SABBATARIANISM

Guérard, writing of the Dark Ages, says: "Chez les Allemands et chez les Bavarois la même peine [de servitude] était prononcée contre l'homme libre qui, ayant été repris trois fois d'avoir travaillé le dimanche, persévérait dans la même conduite." Persistent sabbath-breaking was thus punished with the same penalty as adultery, abortion, forgery, poisoning, etc. The Laws of Ine, about 692 A.D. prescribe the same penalty within his kingdom of Wessex (*Irminon*,

I, 289). Medieval miracles very often turn on the extreme necessity of avoiding Sunday work, *e.g.* fishes show their respect for God by refusing crumbs from a Sunday-baked loaf (Heywood, *Assempri*, p. 255; cf. p. 228). St Bernardino of Siena has a special sermon, *De Observantia Sabbati, et celebratione Festorum* (*Opp.* II, 52). He bases it on Exod. xx, 8: "Remember that thou keep holy the Sabbath day," and has no hesitation in applying Jewish sabbath precepts to the Christian Sunday. At the same time, he is very indignant with a practice which is much commended by his co-religionists of to-day, in unison with the modern world in general—the Saturday half-holiday. Abbot Eustache de Flay, in 1201, had preached Sabbatarianism through England on the text of a miraculous letter sent down from Christ, which in fact can be traced back to the sixth century. This letter insists that the holiday must be kept from Saturday noon to Monday dawn; and, thinks Father Thurston (p. 41), "it is likely enough that he really did contribute in some measure to the institution of the Saturday half-holiday." This possibility must be discounted by the fact that, in Eustache's own France, there has for centuries been scarcely any trace of any such holiday, while in England it is mainly a product of modern times; moreover, Roger de Hoveden, in the same breath in which he describes Eustache's wonderful success for a time, emphasizes the destructive jealousy of his fellow-churchmen who resented this inconvenient zeal, and the fickle folly of the general public which, "fearing more to lose earthly and transitory than heavenly and eternal things, returned (shameful to relate) like a dog to his vomit, and to the holding of markets on the Lord's day"[1]. In fact, complaints of sabbath-breaking are not less frequent in the later than in the earlier Middle Ages. And St Bernardino, if he had lived in those days, would evidently have been among these opponents of Eustache's doctrine, since he looks upon the Saturday half-holiday as a heretical innovation. He writes:

Devotees of the Blessed Virgin are indeed wont to fast on Saturday from reverence for her, because on the Saturday after our Lord's passion the whole faith of the mysteries of Christ remained in her; and such fasting is laudable, if they do not on that account relinquish the fasts instituted by Holy Church. Many [*plerique*] also cease from labour or servile works at the hour of noon on Saturday, wherein they are deluded by many folk over whom the devil reigned of old, and by some over whom he now reigneth, and hath made them messengers of Antichrist [ref. to Coloss. ii, and to Gregory the Great's prohibition of the

---

[1] *Chron.* R.S. IV, 172. It is curious to contrast St Bernardino's sentiments with the miracle which Hoveden recounts in corroboration of Eustache's mission, that a miller of Wakefield who presumed to work after noon on Saturday was punished by a sudden rush of blood which almost filled the meal-barrel set under the hopper (p. 171).

Saturday holiday in Gratian's *Decretum, de consecratione*, dist. III, c. 11, as partaking of Jewish superstition]. But in our own days many are deceived on this point, and deceive others by means of a certain letter which they affirm to have been brought by an angel in Jerusalem and laid upon St Peter's altar, whereas in truth it is brought from the chancery of hell, and containeth many things false, foolish and full of lies; wherefore they cannot be pleasing to God and the Blessed Virgin[1]. Moreover, Hostiensis saith (in his gloss on *Decretales Gregorii*, lib. II, tit. ix, c. 3) that we ought to work harder on Saturdays than on other days, lest we should seem Judaizers....Yet this should not be preached in places where the Sabbath is ill kept.

That the Sabbath was still ill kept, we are assured in the early years of the sixteenth century by Sebastian Brandt and his commentator Geiler v. Kaysersberg (Scheible, pp. 728–30). The short-comings of Christendom in this respect, says Brandt, expose us to the scorn of the Jews, and justly.

35

(Chap. XIX, p. 260)

PEASANT AND PRIEST IN ITALY

The remarkably unanimous testimony of medieval disciplinarians, and the scattered indications which may be gleaned from other sources, indicate that the medieval peasant's relations to his parish priest were very much what they are in the remote country districts of modern France and Italy. The evidence of a very observant and well-informed modern writer[2] may be printed here as complementing, without materially altering, the picture of the peasant which has been painted from medieval documents.

Considering the sacred character of their office, this aversion [of the Italian peasant] to the company of priests while going on any particular business is one of the first curious facts to strike the Northerner. In his delightful books about the Abruzzi, Signor Antonio de Nino describes a group of girls going to a neighbouring sanctuary to pray for a sick relation. If they pass a yoke of oxen they rejoice, but if they meet a priest they hurry to the sanctuary with aching hearts, for they feel that the sick person is doomed. Italians have always separated the man from his sacred office, and besides this you must remember that the parish priest is closely linked in the minds of the people with Death, of which the Southerner has more than the usual horror. With the exception of the Easter blessing, practically the only time that a priest

---

[1] Hoveden (*l.c.* p. 167) gives the letter in full; it certainly deserves St Bernardino's characterization.

[2] Lina Duff-Gordon, *Home Life in Italy* (Methuen, 1908), p. 231.

enters a house is when he comes to administer the last sacraments. "È venuto il prete" sounds like a death-knell to the family[1].

On pp. 200–201, again:

I tried to give them [the peasants] an idea of the life of a hard-working Roman Catholic priest in England, too busy from morning to night among the schools, and visiting prisons and poor people, to get into mischief. "It is very wonderful all this," they said, very politely, but I saw that they had difficulty in believing me.... The spirit of severe criticism against the clergy is so widespread in Italy that I do not feel it to be unfair to record these impressions.

36
(Chap. xxi, p. 304)

PRIESTS AND PEOPLE

(a) Perhaps the fullest of all pictures of the relations between ecclesiastic and peasant, is to be found in that course of sermons *On the Destruction of Nineveh* which the Dominican Guillaume Pépin, Doctor of Theology, preached in the convent of his Order at Evreux in 1524, and dedicated to the Bishop of Lisieux. He is bitter against the new Lutherans; but on almost every page he warns his hearers that society cannot go on indefinitely on its present lines; he takes as his text Jonah iii, 4: "Yet forty days, and Nineveh shall be destroyed." There is little to choose morally between the tyrannous rich and the oppressed poor. The Jews were forbidden to eat certain unclean birds of prey;

these typify men who live by rapine, and such are almost all knights and squires [nowadays]; for they are not content with their own revenues but rob the poor peasants. Not only do they seize victuals in sufficiency, but after excessive gluttony they despoil the peasants of all that they can get in garments or in money, so that the poor say they would not be worse treated by our enemies, if these were among us. Nor are these mad dogs restrained by the princes or their lieutenants or captains.... Such tyrants give the poor man's crops as pasture for their horses[2].

---

[1] Compare the evidence of Cardinal Jaques de Vitry in the early thirteenth century: "In some districts I have seen that men crossed themselves at once on meeting a priest, saying that it is an ill omen to meet one. Nay, I know for certain that in a certain village of France, when many folk were dying all round, men said to each other: 'This deadly plague cannot cease unless, before we lay a corpse in the grave, we cast our priest into the same pit.' Wherefore it came to pass that, when the priest drew near the grave to bury his dead parishioner, the peasants and their women folk rushed together upon their priest, clad as he was in his holy garments, and cast him into the grave. These are diabolical inventions and illusions of demons" (*Exempla*, ed. F. Crane, 1890, p. 112).

[2] Serm. 23, f. 180, col. 1.

Yet the poor also are cruel to each other. That confusion of tongues which fell upon Babel in the Bible is a type signifying the confusion of our own times; not only the cruelty and tyranny of princes and nobles, but also the envy and hatred and domestic strife among their peoples. The "contradictions" spoken of by the Psalmist (lv, 10, Vulg.) "may be referred to the artisans and workmen [of our day], among whom there is scarce one who doth not strive to tread down the others of his own calling, and specially any newcomer or stranger." Wage-earners shirk their work or, again, desecrate Sundays and holy-days by labour; employers hold back wages justly earned. Crime is commonly unpunished; few are confederate with God; the majority are bound together by bonds of conspiracy in sin[1]. And not only is this fratricidal strife carried on among workers under cover of the gild system, but the peasant on the land is even more backward in social progress[2]. Pépin repeats his text: "Yet forty days, etc." and goes on to prophesy the destruction of Peasant-Street in Nineveh, as he has already done with Luther-Street, Judas-Street, Manslayer Lane, etc. He is a preacher after the people's own heart, as racy as Bunyan, and frequently he studs the Latin in which he printed his sermons with the actual phrases of colloquial French in which they were preached.

Now we must treat of the destruction of Peasant-Street in Nineveh, by reason of the multitude of faults in which that sort of men are wont to be emmeshed. For the peasants are commonly indevout, and ignorant even of the things which they are bound to know, such as the Ten Commandments, the Church's decrees, the Creed, and so forth. Again, they are most irreverent to God and the Church, mocking at ecclesiastics, despising their curates and pastors, making nought of lies and false witness; double-tongued, backbiters, perjurers, false, detainers of other men's goods; and, (what is most grievous of all,) they are unjust moderators and distributors of tithes and Church dues. Therefore we need not wonder if the Lord is oftentimes angry against them, scourging them in many ways, now with wars and men of arms, now with pest and fever, now with most grievous taxes and tallages, now by the devastation of their fields and vineyards, now with frost, now with excessive heat, now with hail, now with water-floods, or again in divers other ways. For these and such-like reasons, therefore, this Peasant-Street in Nineveh ought deservedly to be destroyed; but most specially by reason of the lack of good and lawful payment of tithes, whether of crops or of other things; wherefore I shall treat of this cause above all others in this present sermon.

He goes on, therefore, with more than twenty pages of arguments against bad tithe-payers, from the Bible and the Fathers, canon law and common sense.

---

[1] Serm. 1, f. 2, col. 2 to f. 3, col. 2. [2] Serm. 39, ff. 319 ff.

"The nobles and rich of this world commit their possessions to poor peasants under heavy rents or tributes"; they are like Pharaoh, who took one-fifth of all the Israelites' crops; "but our most merciful God hath retained only one-tenth part of all worldly possessions." Again: "the spiritual goods which we minister unto you are infinitely more precious than the carnal or worldly things which we receive from you." Therefore it is right for the priests in their sermons to excommunicate all who neglect tithe-paying.

There are some who ask: "Wherefore should we give our tithes to these monks or canons or parsons who have abundance of bread? Is it not better to give them as alms, or give them to our poor tumbledown churches all about?" [*pauperibus ecclesiis nostris, quae ex omni parte minantur minam*]. For it seemeth unreasonable that some should be immensely enriched from Church goods, when they have a wealthy patrimony to boot. Some, again, excuse themselves by the reason of poverty; they allege their own need and penury, saying that tithes are the tribute of needy souls, as in that text of Augustine [quoted in Gratian, *Decret.*] whereof the sense is, that tithes are due to those who are in want. "Therefore, this being so," say these poor folk, "we do no sin if we keep for ourselves the tithes of our own goods, which are but small; for the tithes which the clergy take, beyond what is required for their sufficient sustenance, belong to us." Thirdly, some excuse themselves from tithe-paying by alleging the reason of wickedness, and saying, "Our priests are notorious concubinaries, keeping mistresses, (as men say in the vulgar tongue) at their bread and their pot; they have a multitude of children, wherein they seem in no wise to differ from married folk; such men as these seem unworthy to take tithes, which are intended for good and devout clergy. Moreover, many of them do not reside, but get their parishes served by simple and ignorant curates. Since, therefore, the benefice is conferred for service, it seems that such men ought not to take the tithes." This is how many worldly folk excuse themselves in their sins; and these excuses we must meet.

In all his long reply, Pépin makes no attempt to deny these accusations against the clergy; he tacitly dismisses them as irrelevant. The priest who has abundance is morally bound to give thereof to the poor: you must make this possible for him; otherwise you are guilty: "as many poor as die of hunger, so many manslaughters are on the heads of those who detain tithes." Your own need may be great; but your duty is plain:

First and foremost, the poor peasants must pay tithes of their scanty crops, or compound for the same with the tithe-gatherers. Then, if need compel, they must beg from door to door, or find some more honourable way of succouring their own necessity. And if their poverty can be met in neither of these ways, then let them take of these tithes where they can, as from other goods also, to succour their extremity of need, protesting the while that they will make it good if they come to some better fortune. For men who do thus sin not, especially since the aforesaid necessity renders all things common, as hath been said.

As to the third excuse, you do not give to the cleric for himself, but for God. If a prince demands taxes from you through his official, and this official turns traitor and runs off with his spoils to England, you have nothing to do with that man's treachery. Those, therefore, who give tithes only under compulsion, and try even then to choose the worst sheaves for the parson, are ungrateful to God, from whom, as St James tells us, "every good gift and every perfect gift cometh."

And they cut their own throat; for good tithe-payers are commonly prosperous on their farms; tithe-falsehood brings misfortune:

nowadays, when devotion to God is departed, the collector's oppression has come in....None need wonder, therefore, that the peasants of today are distressed in many ways, now by unbearable tallages and taxes, now by soldiers and robbers that waste the whole land, now by hailstones that shatter their crops. For these evils are fallen upon them by reason of God's wrath against a people that payeth its tithes ill.... It is by His just judgement that, in penalty for this, kings and princes are suffered to make divers levies and a multitude of exactions, and soldiers and other robbers to despoil the peasants' possessions in many ways.

Let the reluctant villager ponder the miracle by which one of his class was once punished; the man went by candle-light to winnow his ill-detained tithe-corn; the candle fell into the wheat; barn and corn and man were burned together. Finally: "Such ill-tithers shall come at last to hell, and stay there to all eternity."

Other dues have, by custom, become almost as obligatory as tithes; especially the custom of offering something in church at Christmas, Easter and Whitsunday. This is now a precept of the Church, and the peasant will do well to obey it. Only towards the end does this Dominican preacher try to redress the balance somewhat by insisting on the corresponding clerical obligations (f. 325 b):

With regard to this matter, we must note that many incumbents, led by covetousness, importune their parishioners more to pay their tithes than to keep God's commandments—tithes even of the smallest things, and even of fruits which they have never tithed before—declaring them excommunicated and outside the way of salvation, breeding many scruples in their hearts and oftentimes even bringing various lawsuits against them. These are the men who are wont to ask of preachers who come into their parishes, "Cry out manfully against tithe-defaulters," when perchance they would be loth to hear the preacher bark against men who live uncleanly. Woe therefore to such priests and rectors or vicars, who are so zealous and clamorous to exact tithes or other altar-dues, while they care little or nothing for the souls of their flocks.

As the scribes and Pharisees tithed small herbs, but neglected the Law,

so also, even nowadays, do many prelates and priests of the Church, who are solicitous to rebuke, or get and procure others to rebuke, their subjects in the matter of tithe-paying and suchlike dues, and who care little if the same subjects are entangled in worse crimes; to wit, lecherous, usurers, blasphemous, perjurers, liars and so forth.

And again (f. 328): "But, on this point, we must note that many ecclesiastics render themselves unworthy of the fruits of tithes, in God's sight." They will not fight against heresy, they neglect their Church services, and

lastly, they "eat the milk of their sheep" [Ezek. xxxiv, 3]; for they are nourished with the substance of their people, and feast splendidly every day, and yet they feed not the flock, either with the bread of salutary doctrine (perchance by reason of ignorance) or with that of the Sacrament of the Altar at the right place and time (perchance by reason of non-residence), or with the bread of bodily sustenance (perchance by reason of their own covetousness).

He applies to them the accusations and the curses of Ezekiel xxxiv.

A careful perusal of this sermon throws a flood of light on the real relation of the classes to each other at the moment when Luther came forward; especially f. 329. We see here how keen-witted and well-informed the advocates of the villagers were; fairly often, no doubt, some cool-headed peasant had heard and pondered and discussed the questions which citizens were busily discussing in the towns, with the printing-press at their back. Pépin shows the objectors pleading against the abuses of the tithe-system on grounds of natural and divine law alike. In natural law, they plead, how can poor starvelings be justly required to contribute to the superfluities of men who fare sumptuously every day? In divine law, neither Christ nor His apostles preach the payment of tithes; as to the Old Testament, why should this particular precept of tithes bind us when the rest of the ceremonial law has been abrogated? Pépin, as a good Dominican, has all his rejoinders pat from Aquinas; but these scholastic subtleties are feeble and unconvincing in face of the plain and straightforward objections which they profess to remove. The old order is here visibly breaking down. Pépin's real trump-card is that of custom and physical force: you have paid from time immemorial, and pay you shall until the end of time! On the ground of biblical history and common-sense, the village advocates were already more advanced than St Thomas Aquinas.

(b) Some two generations later, we get a most valuable complementary picture of the priest in his parish, this time from the

country parson's own point of view. It comes out incidentally from
the "Complaints and Grievances of the Priests in the three Cantons
of Uri, Schwyz and Unterwalden, to the Deputies of the said Cantons
assembled at Brunnen in 1579" (*Nuntiaturberichte*, pp. 495 ff.;
cf. pp. 481, 525). The bishop of Vercelli, sent as papal nuncio to
reform Switzerland, had complained frequently to St Carlo Borromeo,
his immediate superior, that he found concubinage not the exception,
but the rule, among the priests; he therefore held a synod at which
he decreed that they should keep no women-servants under fifty,
and that any priest found drinking in a tavern should pay a fine of
ten crowns. Against this the clergy protest:

We must not put the cart before the horse, or we shall go backwards
like the crab; and if a bow is too far stretched it will break; if we would
fain set all things straight at once, either nothing will be done or things
will be worse than before.... If all we priests are to live after the commands of this bishop of Vercelli, then our benefices must be otherwise
ordered than they have been hitherto; else it would be impossible for
us to find a livelihood. If priests, who have neither mothers nor aunts
nor grandmothers, may not have other women in their houses, even
of their own kinsfolk, then ye will soon have few priests in your cantons; for no priest can himself collect the tithes of hemp and fruits of
the earth (which are generally our principal tithes) and also till his
garden and mend his hedge and cook and keep his stove alight. But
that we [priests] should dwell with boys, as the Italians do, Heaven
guard us therefrom for ever! But if we must needs live with women
of fifty, and a man must make himself an eunuch for the Kingdom of
Heaven, this will be as ill as if he lived with a young one; for the old
will just as soon wish to be wanton, or she will have a young one with
her: but whither has our pen run? what need of farther words? Other
means should first be sought, which pertain mainly to a diligent bishop
and faithful pastor of our see[1], that such scandals and sins may be
removed. For we can all recognize that concubinage is a sin and
scandal, and that it would be well, as aforesaid, to remove it and that
all priests should live chastely; but it is not given to all men to receive
this, and he who maketh not himself an eunuch for the sake of the
Kingdom of Heaven can never live chastely; for, whether he keep a
concubine or no, worse things are to be feared. And a main cause of
this is, that there is no seminary wherein the young may be brought up
to learning[2]. In our cantons none becomes a priest who has wealth

---

[1] The priests had already pointed out (p. 500) that these parochial reforms
had been "often tried, but never rightly succeeded," because the prelates
and higher clergy set no such example; their own bishop, they pointed out,
was non-resident and wasteful, and was himself a concubinary: one of his
sons was later legitimated and raised to a dukedom through his influence at
the Roman court.

[2] The Council of Trent had decreed the erection of a seminary in every
bishopric: but (write the priests, p. 501), "our bishop not only erects no

of his own, but only poor folk who must seek their livelihood by begging; they beg hither and thither, and often come to places where they learn lechery; and what else can they do afterwards, when they emerge from mendicancy and have a better livelihood than before?... Secondly, the bishop of Vercelli hath forbidden any priest to enter a tavern under pain of ten crowns. This, again, would be much to our profit if we kept it; but, if we may keep no woman or maidservant, who is to cook for us, and where are we to eat? Pray, must we light our stove, cook, pray, study, fetch pot-herbs, celebrate, and preach all together? Will any man permit us to eat and dwell with his own family? "Out of the house with this priest!" some man will cry, "for he will seduce my wife and my daughter." Perchance this good Italian bishop dreams that we can live in Germany as he lives in Italy? Our climate is too cold, and our winter too sharp and long, nor does wine grow here, and our benefices are commonly too poor for us to buy wine, and so we must drink cold water. Therefore, to warm ourselves again, we light our stove and eat warm pottage and other warm foods. The Italians, on the contrary, have a hot climate and need no stove; they have wine to drink and care little for hot food, and need to fight harder against the heat than we Germans against the cold. Wherefore no Italian is easily suited with German manners, as no German with Italian; and therefore we priests shall go to the taverns, when honest men bid us thither for honest causes, and the bishop of Vercelli may say what he will, whether we have ten crowns or not. But if any priest is drunken and immodest, whether in the tavern or elsewhere, then the venerable Chapter [of Constance] spares no man, as we think has happened even before now.

The papal nuncio has annotated this document with his own hand; to this particular claim he notes (p. 511): "Nay, but the priests are wont to be drunken promiscuously [*passim*] nor is any penalty inflicted upon them, but they have not usually been even rebuked."

These three forest cantons of Switzerland naturally presented difficult conditions; the people were poor, simple, and ignorant; but, on the other hand, they have never accepted the Reformation, and are in many ways typical of medieval parish life in the poorer districts. Morals may have deteriorated under the solvent influence of religious revolution in other places, but the poorer parson's domestic helplessness can scarcely have been affected. It would certainly be easy to choose other more unfavourable districts; and, when all is taken into account, we may well doubt whether the average village in Western Christendom would have presented a much more favourable picture than this.

seminary in Germany and in his see, but he sends to Italy the great revenues which come in to his treasury, nor does he care for learned scholars or for educating the priests." Already, however, Borromeo and the Jesuits were beginning to supply this long-felt want.

(c) From the Lollard's point of view (*Political Poems*, R.S. 1, 330):

> For the tithing of a ducke
>> Or of an apple, or an aie,   [egg
> They make man swere upon a boke;
>> Thus they foulen Christës faie.   [faith
>> Soche bearen evill heaven kaie;   [keys
> They mowen assoile, they mowe shrive   [may
>> With mennes wives strongly plaie
> With true tillers sturte and strive   [quarrel
>
> At the wrastling, and at the wake,
>> And chiefë chauntours at the nale;   [ale-drinking
> Market-beaters, and meddling make,
>> Hoppen and houten with heve and-hale.
>> At fairë fresh, and at winë stale;
> Dine and drinke, and make debate:
>> The seven sacraments set a saile;   [to sale
> How kepe soche the kaies of heaven gate?
>
> Mennës wives they wollen hold,
>> And, though that they been right sorye,
> To speake they shull not be so bold,
>> For sompning to the consistorye;   [summoning
>> And make hem saië mouth I lie,   [I may lie.
> Though they it sawë with her iye;
>> His lemmen holden openly,
> No man so hardy to askë why.
>
> He woll have tithing and offring,
>> Maugrë who so ever it grutch;
> And twise on the day he woll sing[1];
>> Goddës priestes nere none soche.   [were not
>> He mote on hunting with dogge and bich,
> And blowen his horne, and crien, hey!
>> And sorcerie usen as a witch.
> Soche kepen evill Peters key.

37
(Chap. XXIV, p. 353)

JANSSEN ON THE PEASANTS' REVOLT

While confessing that there would have been a good deal of sedition even apart from Luther, Janssen is compelled by his thesis to ascribe all the excesses of this revolt to Luther's influence; and his English translator, as usual, forces the note and removes

[1] He sings two Masses a day, for the sake of extra profit, in spite of canon law.

the story one degree farther from true history. Here (IV, 143) Riezler is quoted as saying:

In consequence of the enforcement there of the religious edicts there was an absence in Bavaria of those inflammatory elements which elsewhere incited preachers and demagogues to clamour, in the same breath, for religious and for social freedom, and which added fuel to the fire in other parts of the Empire. But even in the districts where the apostles of the "new gospel" confined themselves to religion, they prepared the way for the rising of the peasants by awakening the spirit of liberty and inculcating contempt for existing authorities. It is time that controversy should cease around a fact, the intrinsic verisimilitude of which is backed up by overpowering evidence, and which if rightly appreciated *leaves the Protestant cause no peg to hang on.*

The words which I have here italicized should really run "cannot cast any blemish upon the Protestant cause [*der protestantischen Sache keinen Makel anzuhängen vermag*]." And Riezler, a few lines lower in this same paragraph, shows how little we are justified in making religious disputes, rather than centuries of social injustice, responsible for this cruel revolt. There he balances the different factors against each other, and writes:

False as it is to place the foundation of the Peasants' War elsewhere than in that economic and social oppression of the peasant-class which had gone on increasing for centuries and had reached its zenith in the fifteenth century, yet on the other hand it is vain to deny the close connexion between the Reformation and the Bauernkrieg. That connexion is not disproved by the fact that isolated outbreaks in anticipation of the Bauernkrieg occurred long before Luther's appearance. The most significant and effectual program of this revolt, the Twelve Articles, originated in the circle of reformers at Memmingen. It was through the preaching of the New Doctrine that the people in general was awakened to that spirit of freedom, without which neither the consciousness of bondage, nor the courage to throw it off, could come to their full growth. Specially coloured with religion was the peasants' most weighty, most universal, and justest demand, that of the abolition of serfdom; the cry now echoed from all sides, that we are Christ's men, but no human lord possesses us for his own. (*Sitzungsberichte d. phil.-hist. Classe d. Akad. zu München*, 1891, p. 709.)

And Riezler exposes the falsehood of an assertion which is implied, if not expressed, in Janssen's book, that serfdom was practically dead in Bavaria at this time. That italicized misstatement about the Reformation is, no doubt, attributable only to the translator's ignorance and prejudice; but it cannot be too often repeated that many thousands of German-speaking people are dependent upon Janssen for all they think they know about social life on the verge of the Reformation, and thousands more in Great Britain and America depend upon his still more untrustworthy translator.

What chance the peasantry of Europe would have had, but for a religious revolt which implied some measure of social revolution also, may be judged from the attitude towards Russian serfdom of one of the ablest and most influential Roman Catholic thinkers of last century. Count Joseph de Maistre, in his *Quatre chapitres inédits sur la Russie* (Paris, 1859) concludes with a few pages of emphatic warning to the Russian government as to its immediate and future policy. In the translation here subjoined, I italicize the words which Lord Acton has marked as specially noteworthy:

I. Restrict enfranchisement [of the serfs,] far from favouring it by any law; *for any law in that direction would be fatal; and suppress at the same time, by every possible means*, the abuses which might make the people too desirous of enfranchisement. II. Never reward enfranchisement as an action morally good and politically expedient on the nobles' part....IV. *In the same way, restrict learning [la science] in several ways*; viz. (1) by not declaring it necessary, *in general*[1], for any civil or military employment; (2) by demanding only the knowledge essentially necessary for certain occupations, as mathematics are for engineering, etc.; (3) *by suppressing all public teaching of the knowledge which might be left to the taste and means of each individual*; as history, geography, metaphysics, ethics, politics, commerce, etc.; (4) by not favouring, in any way, the propagation of knowledge towards the lowest classes of the population; and even by hampering (without betraying oneself) any enterprise of that kind which an ignorant or pernicious zeal might imagine.

Romanism and the Greek Church must, of course, be favoured; but VIII:

Keep an unremitting watch, on the other hand, over Protestant teaching; keep it in its place and hinder it with silent prudence, to the utmost possible extent, from filtering into the domain of the two Churches; for it is the universal solvent....X. Submit to the most rigorous inspection all strangers (especially Germans and Protestants) who come to Russia to teach anything whatever to the young folk; and be quite sure that, among a hundred of this kind who come to Russia, the State makes at least ninety-nine fatal acquisitions; for the man who has property, family, morals and reputation stays in his own country.

To which he adds:

In these ten articles, there would seem nothing ideal or paradoxical, and especially not a single atom of party-spirit; for if, under pretext of impartiality, it were forbidden to point out evil and give it a name, then we should not even be allowed to speak ill of fevers. All that has been [here] said is founded on experience, on an intimate knowledge of men, of this age, and of circumstances; and of Russia in particular —where de Maistre had been ambassador fourteen years.

---

[1] De Maistre himself italicizes these two words.

38
(Chap. XXIV, p. 355)

NATURAL LAW

There seems to be a tendency to exaggerate the practical value of this theory which the Middle Ages borrowed from antiquity, and to which canon law gave a more definitely religious and humanitarian tinge. It is assumed that modern society runs the risk of being crushed under the omnipotence of the State, and that we have cast off the more liberal rule of the Church in order to submit to the cold despotism of Hobbes.

It is true that "natural law" does play a great part in medieval legal, and therefore in political, writing. But it may be doubted whether it did more to modify tyranny, in practice, than the similar words "justice" and "equity" do nowadays, or even so much. My point will be best understood by any reader who, not having yet approached the subject, refers to R. W. and A. J. Carlyle, *Medieval Political Theory in the West*, vol. II, pt i, ch. 3 and pt ii, ch. 3.

To begin with, there was much uncertainty in definition of "natural law." Then, the more clearly it is defined, the more difficult it is to reconcile it with actual facts, or with theories which must face those facts.

Natural Law represents the immutable principles by which the world is governed (p. 32). It commands men to do what is useful, as for example: "Thou shalt love the Lord thy God"; it forbids that which is hurtful, as for example: "Thou shalt not kill"; and it points out what is expedient, as for example, that all things should be held in common, that there should be liberty for all mankind (p. 103, from an early commentator on Gratian). The *jus naturale* is contained in the law and the Gospel, and commands us to do to others as we would that they should do to us (p. 106). Natural Law, therefore, is superior to all other law—it is primitive and unchangeable; all customs and laws contrary to the *jus naturale* are void (p. 105).

If there ever had existed an age in which these assertions represented general realities, as apart from the pious aspirations of a few and the cheap lip-homage of the official world, then we might indeed be tempted to return to the principles of that age. But what are the historical facts?

First, how did men deal even with the general theory? If this had been part of their rooted principles, behind the mere words of their mouth, then it would have created a world in which naked despotism would have been impossible. Yet not only were the later medieval States models of despotism, and often of the cruellest kind; not only did despotism flourish most, down to the French Revolution, in the

States which clung most faithfully to the medieval tradition; but the unrestricted legislative power of the pope, of the man in whose person and office that tradition is most completely represented, is categorically asserted by himself, and proclaimed to the whole world in canon law; the pope "is considered to have all laws within the casket of his own breast" (decree of Boniface VIII, in *Sext. Decret.* lib. i, tit. ii, c. i). What force could the frequent, but vague and conventional, reference to natural law have against this naked principle of absolutism? Imperialists, for their part, applied to the emperor the sentence of ancient Roman law, that "the prince's pleasure has the force of law." Moreover, the unreality of this appeal will become more apparent if we descend to details. Fortunately, the canonists who most clearly define natural law give concrete instances in illustration of their general theory. Natural law (as we have seen) teaches "Thou shalt not kill"; it proclaims man's personal freedom; it is communistic; property is contrary to natural law. And "ignorance of the civil law may sometimes be condoned, but ignorance of the natural law is always to be condemned in those of mature years" (p. 106).

Yet almost before Gratian and his early glossators had put this clear principle into words, the medieval Church and State agreed in deciding that religious Nonconformists must be killed, by the thousand if necessary. Gregory IX and St Thomas Aquinas are, in effect, excused by many modern authors on the plea of their ignorance of this natural law; for we do in effect ignore a law when we abrogate it in favour of considerations which our descendants are more and more ashamed to bring forward. It was this which aroused in Lord Acton an indignation which most people think excessive; he held: "Thou shalt not kill" to be so plain and universally understood, long before the days of the Inquisition, that the Inquisitors were unpardonable for finding the excuses they found to break it. No civilized society has ever erected manslaughter for religious differences into so strict a written law, as this medieval world which professedly subordinated all written laws to: "Do to others as we would they should do to us."

Again, natural law prescribes "liberty for all mankind." We have seen how Aquinas, and all schoolmen except the heretic Wyclif, begin by admitting this, yet end by justifying slavery and serfdom on pleas which no respectable ethical writer of today would dare to put forward. We have seen how serfdom lasted longest on Church estates, and how popes, even after the Reformation, were among the most conspicuous supporters of slavery pure and simple.

Thirdly, natural law prescribes communism. This was whittled away by the legists and theologians exactly as the principle of personal liberty was; and, even to the present day, especially after certain modern papal pronouncements, Roman Catholics seriously discuss in public whether it is possible to be a Socialist, and yet theologically orthodox. In France and Belgium, at any rate before 1914 when I made personal enquiries, the fusion of Socialism and Orthodoxy was almost impossible.

Therefore the task which confronts those who preach this conception of natural law as a saving force in society is clear. There never has been a civilization in which men have not appealed from the written law to some higher principle—in modern terms, to Religion or Justice or Equity. There never has been a society in which, when this appeal had sufficient reason behind it (and, especially, a sufficient number of people who might be provoked into fighting for it), it would not have had some real effect in tempering, or perhaps even nullifying, written law. By their fruits ye shall know them. If the medieval conception of natural law was in fact more humane and more directly operative than this, let somebody prove it by recognized historical methods. Let him adduce cases, and as many as possible, in which the plea did more for humanity then than the wronged man's plea for ordinary Justice does for him now. Let him show the judge in court admitting (where he himself was free from temptation to partiality) that X had indeed no case in civil or canon law, but that natural law was on his side, and therefore the statute or the papal decree must be disregarded in this one case. Or let them show us the political philosopher, tempted to make the most of his inexpugnable case in constitutional law or custom, yet granting that these must be swept away, even to the disadvantage of his own party, because they cannot be squared with "Do to others as we would they should do to us." It is difficult to see how anything short of this can really differentiate the medieval doctrine of natural law from other merciful generalities which have everywhere had a certain weight in civilized society. The thing does, it is true, stand out more conspicuously; it was enunciated in imposing academic formalities. Yet here, as in so many other places, the apparently clear doctrine lacks strict definition; or, if one writer is precise and detailed, he conflicts with others almost equally precise. And, at the back of all, we need to bear in mind that one of the most fatal misconceptions in medieval history is the belief that we may judge that society by the simple test of its academic theories, and neglect the far more difficult task of comparing theory with practice. We may say even of Aquinas's doctrines what an orthodox churchman said of the Bible shortly before Luther's appearance. This book was so definitely emphasized by the Church wherever it suited her policy, and ignored in its less convenient texts, that Geiler wrote:

There are many folk who say: "Dear fellow, why dost thou quote so much to me from Holy Scriptures? They are even as a wax-nose; a man can fit them or shape them to anything, first to this and then to that; and, after all, they name no [living] man by name. Why dost thou so often cite them? The parsons have easy work to talk of the Bible; they get from it all that they desire; it fills their chests and their cellars." (Scheible, p. 282.)

Janssen, taken off his guard, exemplifies this very clearly. He summarizes the Twelve Articles and other manifestoes of the revolting peasants, which in essence rest upon this appeal from oppressive human law and custom to natural law; yet for the peasants' folly in thus appealing from realities to ideals Janssen shows nothing but contempt. And here he is only following the example of Church and State authorities in 1525. The "Twelve Articles" began with an appeal to God's will: "Who will fight against the Divine Majesty? He who heard the children of Israel crying unto Him, and delivered them from Pharaoh's hand, can He not save His own people even today?" Yet, as, Bezold says (p. 472):

The actual core of this remarkable manifesto, whose attitude is most honourable to the political sense of its authors, is formed by the idea of "God's Justice," as it had long been rooted in the peasant's brain. Abolition of serfdom (that is, the grant of leave to quit the manor) is the central point of the peasant's desires; if this had been granted, it would have resulted in a complete emancipation of the villagers, and perhaps also a certain participation of these freed communities in political life, at least in that of their own district. But two things stood in the way of a peaceful solution of the agricultural problem; first and foremost, the lack of good will on the part of the majority of the lords; secondly, that very evangelization of "God's Justice," which was certainly favourable to revolutionary propaganda, but which at the same time made any peaceful agreement difficult, by reason of its very elastic and epigrammatic character, and of the [general] desire for a clear determination in writing. It was not without mockery that the town-councillors of Memmingen answered the peasants' delegates: "Considering that God once came in human form among us, He will not again come in person and judge between us."

Compare these facts with the theory blandly enunciated by Prof. De Wulf in his Princeton lectures (p. 56):

Roman Civil Law and Canon Law and Feudal Law...in the name of [natural] right, based on human nature...had proclaimed the equality of all men [in the Middle Ages]. With this beginning, they came to regard all differences of rank as conventional; and slavery and serfdom were declared to be contrary to natural law.

39
(Chap. XXVI, p. 379)

POST-REFORMATION PEASANTRY

We have seen how the attempt to make a definitely religious question out of village history rests, in England, mainly on the absurd exaggerations of Cobbett, and in Germany on the scarcely less un-historical, though far more subtly delusive, presentations of Janssen. It seems quite true that the German peasant's condition became definitely worse in the fifteenth, seventeenth and eighteenth centuries, and that the Junkers of some of the Protestant States bear here a heavy load of guilt. Janssen emphasizes this by avoiding all serious comparison (I think we must say, *intentionally*, since he can scarcely have been entirely ignorant of some of the best-known documents in history), first with the unfavourable evidence for the status of the pre-Reformation peasant, and, secondly with village life in many purely Roman Catholic districts since the Reformation.

At the present moment, there is perhaps no such miserable peasantry in any civilized country as exists, and has existed for centuries past, in the Campagna within a day's journey of St Peter's and the Vatican. Moreover, a great deal of the injustice there has thriven under ecclesiastical landlords.

This was briefly brought out by Story in 1864 (*Roba di Roma*, pp. 265 ff.). The author's conclusion is that "it is only directly under the influence of the Church that agriculture languishes and dies." But a more detailed and terrible indictment may be found in a far more recent book, A. Cervesato's *The Roman Campagna* (Fisher Unwin, 1913, pp. 176 ff.). Cervesato writes:

Another category of workers that also live in isolated huts or hamlets are the "guitti," looked upon as the lowest class of peasants, for the literal translation of their name means "dirty ones," and their huts are perhaps the most primitive in the world. They form about four-fifths of the population of the Agro, where they toil for nine or ten months of the year, returning to the healthy hills of Latium or the Abruzzi, for a month or two each autumn. It is not lust of gain but hunger that drives them from their own sterile soil to these murderous plains to obtain food even at the cost of a yoke that is practically slavery, riveted by the "caporali" who enroll them, a yoke that even death does not break, for their sons have to go on after them, paying the iniquitous debt bequeathed them by their fathers. They are looked upon as human goods and chattels, as active and submissive machines, known and cared for by none except the "caporale" who feeds them—after a fashion— and profits by their helplessness, for they rank in the eyes of the owner or tenant as mere implements and tools necessary for the cultivation of the land. They have no individuality, no citizenship, no defence; they are spoken of as "gangs" of nine, ten or eleven pence, not as human beings entitled to the most elementary rights of life.... To stand in the midst of these hovels and look across the plain to where the cupola of S. Peter's rises on the horizon, is to doubt the evidence of one's senses; it seems impossible that the city, rich in marble and gilding, full of art treasures, and whose imperial pomp has astonished the world for centuries, should be so near cabins that resemble those of the Fiji Islands and Tierra del Fuego.... I will not endeavour to describe my visit to these hamlets, the picture I should draw might appear to the reader exaggerated, but instead I will give the impressions of a well-known member of parliament, who spent many years in Africa far from civilization, and was therefore able to compare the condition of the poor workers of these two continents. "On a plain nestling under a low hill, hidden from the deserted Via Tiburtina, we found the hamlet of Salone. It is composed of about twenty-five huts erected regardless of order, huddled close together in the small space which was all that the avaricious overseer could spare these poor people out of the immense estate. They represent the rudimental form of habitation, such as man lived in after the days of cavern dwellings; they are rectangular, with sloping roofs, and a frame made of sticks, to which are bound grasses, dry branches, and maize canes. In every one dwells a whole family, which, given the singularly prolific tendencies of our agricultural classes, rarely numbers less than eight or ten. The interior of these huts is a miserable picture; the entrance, which is low and narrow, leads into an airless space in the centre of which is the primitive hearth composed of two stones and a heap of ashes.".... There are several thousands of these poor peasants who do not even possess the small sum necessary to buy the wood frame wherewith to build a hut, and who settle down in caves dug out of the tufa hills. One comes across these quite unexpectedly throughout the Campagna, and the casual passer-by would never guess that they sheltered whole families of workers, who live there not for one night but for months and whole seasons. The nearest of these to Rome are on the Prima Porta Road, at the Grotto Rosso, and on the Via Flaminia only a short distance from the Villa Borghese and the beautiful church of Santa Maria del Popolo, one of the glories of the Renaissance, in which Sansovino and Nino da Fiesole, in the spring of Italian art, gave to marble and bronze the breath of immortality. There is great need of missionaries as pioneers in introducing civilization into the Roman Campagna. The work has already been started by the Women's Union, which has taken the initiative in carrying moral and material assistance to the poor people both in the Campagna proper and in the Pontine Marshes; and the Italian Red Cross Society, in order to come to their aid, has organized a branch exactly as in time of war.... Such is the life today of those pariahs, the same as it was yesterday and as it will be tomorrow; they live and die in the dumb, impassive silence of the plain, patient and uncomplaining like the cattle they tend. Little has been done for them, though attention has often been called to their miserable state since the time of Garibaldi, who denounced their existence as a national shame. Parliamentary committees have made reports upon the intolerable life of the poor people in this territory and the miserable sweating system to which they are subjected, but up to now no steps have been taken to really improve their condition.

Nor is peasant misery confined to the immediate neighbourhood of Rome. Sismondi, in the 91st chapter of his *Histoire des républiques italiennes*, draws a contrast between the peasant of 1450 and his successor of 1800:

The country [in 1450] was still covered with villages and harvesters, in provinces which now are changed into deserts. Desolation has spread over a considerable part of Italy, which was formerly of very great fertility; from the banks of the Serchio to the Volturno. The rich lands of Pisa were, it is true, ravaged by floods and rendered unhealthy by stagnant waters as early as the fifteenth century; yet, even then, the whole coast from Livorno to the Ombrone was animated by flourishing villages; yet now it is desolate.... In the Roman Campagna the Colonna family alone possessed more populous villages in the fifteenth century, than there are farmers nowadays in the whole province.

Gibbon, travelling through South Italy in 1765, noted "the wretched state of this fine country, and the misery of its idle and oppressed inhabitants" among the fields which, in the thirteenth century, the Emperor Frederick II had boasted as unrivalled in the world for fertility and for climate (Gibbon's *Letters*, 1896, I, 73). And a modern Italian scholar tells us what Sardinia was like on the eve of the French Revolution (*Cong. Intern*. IX, 1904, 195 ff.). A few were direct owners of their holdings, "but these were rare and very exceptional, and their possessions stood like islands in the midst of the vast and monotonous expanse of feudal lands." The next class, the *fittaioli*, or "hirers," were small tenant farmers, few of whom made really enough for themselves and their families; a contemporary commission reports that "the sweat of their brow, and their yearlong toil, does not suffice to save them from suffering and misery." Below these came the hired labourers, "dispossessed of the soil, and farther deprived of the political rights which are bound up with economic power." These numbered 12,034 in 1767, as against 39,477 of the two upper classes, out of a total population of about 400,000 persons, which would mean about 160,000 adults. In 1788, the proportion was 29,430 hirelings as against 63,459 of the other classes.

The work of these hirelings was regulated down to the smallest details. In the midst of a crystallized, mummified society, where every energy and impulse was regulated by a dense and most rigid network of customs and laws, this labouring class certainly could not escape from the common lot.... All political and social power was in the hands of the wealthy classes, that is, the aristocracy and the clergy.... The working day began at sunrise and lasted to sunset. There was no break beyond two hours at noon in summer, or an hour and a half in winter, for dinner.

A humane pamphleteer pleaded that labourers were treated worse here than the galley-slaves. For lack of proper housing, many spent two or three hours trudging from home to work, or slept in the fields, or in huts of branches, between their working hours. "Their wages were not sufficient to supply the most pressing needs of life, and to keep their families from starvation." "At Orzoli, about 1780, an epidemic broke out; the parish priest and the mayor asked the Government to send a doctor from Cagliari. He came, but nobody would receive his visits; they 'feared the expense of paying him, and the added cost of the medicine.'" Salaries were fixed by the Government; in other words, by the privileged classes, as by our Statutes of Labourers in the fourteenth century; the result was that, "if a land-owner was satisfied with a peasant's work, he was unable to give him an adequate and honourable reward; at the very most, he could offer him a sort of alms when the work was done. Charity was allowed, but not the recognition of just claims." The generous pamphleteer, Gemelli, "tried to touch men's hearts, and invoked feelings of justice, religion, and Christian charity. But theoretical principles avail nothing; they foam themselves away when they dash against concrete material interests." It was indeed an advance upon primitive feudalism, but definitely behind modern conditions; "the peasants, when asked to work, were not permitted [by law] to refuse. All was at the will of the landlords. Thence it followed, as a necessary consequence, that wages were low and unequal to the main needs of life. A sense of distrust, prostration, and discouragement was diffused through all souls." Then came the French Revolution, and the fetters were broken.

From Catholic Italy let us pass to Catholic France. The wretchedness of the hovels, even in modern times, is brought out by Bogros, p. 112, and Noel, p. 138.

The seventeenth century French royalty, devoted to the Church and preparing for the final suppression of Protestantism when occasion should serve, had no idea of creating a village paradise; the most favourable king to the poor was the semi-Protestant Henry IV. In 1609, the English ambassador in France advised his employers as to the then state of that country:

Concerning common people, they hold it for a true principle of state in France, that they must be kept low and out of heart by exactions and oppressions; for otherwise they would be apt to mutinies and rebellions: and accordingly they have at this day so many burdens on them, as keep them from all fancy of skipping or running; for they are scarce able to go or wag under them.... Touching food, God hath blessed that people with a plentiful region, and fruitful soil. And for making it yield all possible increases, the industry of the inhabitants is very great; as it is also in all handicrafts, as before I partly related: but the disorder consisteth in the unequal distribution of the soil, some having more than enough, for riot and excess; and others not sufficient for their necessary use. The subjects of France are also, as it is in other kingdoms, composed of three sorts of persons: The ecclesiastical, who have first rank, as those who are dedicated to the service of God. The nobles, who are selected for the service of the king and state; and those have the fees and jurisdiction of the realm. And lastly, the people, under which are comprised the inhabitants of the country towns; as merchants, artificers and such like. The two first degrees have more than enough; but the latter is so infinitely opprest, as they have their mouths filled with imprecations and bitter complaints; exclaiming, that their king seeketh not to be *Roy des François*, but *des Gueux*. And indeed both this king, and some of his predecessors, use over them an oppressing servitude, more after the manner of the petty pilling tyrants of Italy, than according to the greatness and magnanimity of their ancient princes, who governed their subjects in a mixt temperature betwixt fathers and lords. Hereof, at my first coming, I heard a tragical example happened in a village near unto Paris. The rigour of the king's officers, for levying of the king's taille, is so great, as, if they find no other stuff, in default of payment, they sell the doors, windows, and tiles of the houses. The fear whereof made a poor man, having wife and children, for payment of the king's duty, to sell one only cow, which served for their sustenance; intending out of the price thereof to have bought them food and paid the king's duty. At his return to his house he found his money to be all counterfeit; so he was like to go to prison. His children call on him for food, which he had no means to give them; which made him enter into that desperateness, as he first killed his own children, and then destroyed himself.... Out of this disorder there ariseth this danger, that the husbandman, and the citizen or artificer, finding that they have no interest in the conservation of a government, whereby they are oppressed, and that they receive of the monarchy nothing but *le fournir et le servir*, must needs be desirous of a change.... Hence it comes, that in a country so populous, yet have their kings few soldiers, and in their need they are driven to use mercenaries; not daring to put arms into their subjects' hands, whom they have so ill used. So that out of this immoderate exaction there ariseth a chain of disorders, consisting of many links to wantonness and riot in the commanding persons; discontentment and repining in the commanded; a great weakness in matters of force to resist invasions or repress rebellions.... Another disorder is noted in this overmuch couragiousness of gentlemen, that they are apt to duels and combats, which the king pretendeth he is desirous to repress, though others think he is contented to have the most dangerous and boiling heads weeded out in that sort. Besides, they never raise soldiers, but they oppress the husbandman: with us it is otherwise. And the oppressed people are like to make proof of their discontentments, when they shall have leaders able to make them know their own strength. (Sir George Carew, *Relation of the State of France in 1609*, printed on pp. 461 ff. of T. Birch, *Hist. View of the Negociations*, etc. 1749.)

Hanotaux, quoting this in his *La France en 1614*, adds: "this comparison with brute beasts is frequently repeated in the writings of those who speak of the people" (ed. Nelson, p. 394). As he has said two pages higher, French literature of the seventeenth century, "sous des apparences de bonhomie, est presque toujours hostile [aux paysans]."

Bishop Fléchier thus describes the relations between a body of monastic landlords and the peasantry under Louis XIV:

Voici le sujet du procès; les chanoines réguliers de Saint-Augustin, qui ont plusieurs maisons en ce pays, ont un droit de domination fort particulière dans un certain endroit du pays de Combrailles, par lequel ils ont des sujets esclaves et dépendant d'eux en toutes manières. Les coutumes écrites de ces provinces, l'usage et la longue possession les autorisent; mais il semble que la charité chrétienne et les règles de la douceur évangélique sont fort contraires à cette servitude personnelle, qui consiste à ne pouvoir point sortir du lieu de leur habitation, sans la permission des seigneurs, à n'être pas libres dans la disposition de leurs biens, les seigneurs étant leurs héritiers au préjudice de tous les parents collatéraux, et à mille autres redevances fort onéreuses. Quelques-uns voulurent s'exempter de cette sujétion, et demandèrent la liberté avec instance....Les autres crioient au contraire contre des esclaves qui vouloient rompre leurs chaînes et briser leurs fers, et soutenoient que la mère doit faire la condition des enfants, parce que, quoi qu'elle ne soit pas le principal principe de notre naissance, elle en est le plus assuré. Ils alléguaient les diverses coutumes de la province qui sont expresses sur ce fait....M. Talon dit les plus belles choses du monde sur l'esclavage et sur la liberté, et quelque apparence qu'il y eût de maintenir ce droit d'usage et de coutume, il trouva que ces droits étant odieux et contraires aux lois du christianisme, il falloit les réformer, et conclut à la rédemption de ces captifs sans chaînes; mais il ne fut pas suivi, et la cour appointa l'affaire;

—*i.e.* it was adjourned, and very likely *sine die* (*Grands Jours d'Auvergne*, ed. Ste-Beuve, pp. 100–1).

As late as 1790, within a few weeks of the final abolition of feudalism in France, Lanjuinais complained before the Assemblée Nationale: "four hundred lawsuits have been begun [since last August, in Brittany], on the single subject of mills....The handmills, which form the poor man's only means of subsistence, have been violently broken" (Chassin, *Serfs*, p. 105).

The case of St-Claude was in many ways exceptional; serfdom had lasted so long there that the patchwork of old and new customs was almost inconceivable in its disorder. Many of the serfs had become rich enough to have serfs of their own; another might have wandered to Paris and there become a successful professional man, yet his family would be under degrading legal restrictions; and, at his death, the monks might under certain circumstances seize the whole of his property. The scandal was vehemently combated by Voltaire, in concert with a young local lawyer called Christin. The most that can be said in defence of the system may be found in dom Benoît's *Hist. de l'abbaye et de la terre de St-Claude* (Montreuil, 1890), II, 774 ff. A strong exposure of its defects, not altogether impartial but very fully documented, is given by C. L. Chassin, *Les Derniers Serfs de France* (*Journal des économistes*, Nov. 1879 to Feb. 1880). I have already made use of this book in appendixes 12, 14 and 16; here I will only briefly summarize his evidence as to the condition of the serfs of St-Claude until the famous night when the Ltats Généraux abolished all feudal dues on the threshold of the Revolution.

Heriot subsisted in a specially odious form (pp. 17 ff.); there were odious marriage-restrictions (pp. 17, 39, 40, 50, 60, 77, 79) and the tenant's improvements continually turned to the landlord's profit. The system, therefore, was thoroughly uneconomic (pp. 22, 31, 49, 60, 75, 78, 79). The inhabitants themselves, for instance, pleaded as follows in their petition to the États Généraux:

The Jura [in which we live], has so little cultivable soil that, in the most favourable years, this does not produce enough to feed a quarter of the inhabitants. Our industry might atone for the barrenness of the soil. With Switzerland and Italy at our gates, we should see commerce flourishing in our land, if our condition could inspire some confidence, instead of depriving us of all credit. The man who can offer no securities can contract no loans; the man whose destined heir is his tyrant is tempted neither to improve his field nor to better his fortune. Hence comes general discouragement, and that multitude of beggars who are to be met at every step in this unhappy part of the province. The lord, who seizes the rich serf's heritage, is not bound to feed the poor serf.... Your Majesty has in his army more than thirty thousand serfs from Franche-Comté[1]. When some of these men rise by their merit to be officers, and are pensioned off, if, instead of coming back with their fathers and their nephews to the hut in which they were born, they choose some more convenient house in their village for a habitation, then at their death they cannot dispose of their furniture or of the little savings they have made from their pension; all their belongings will be the lord's when they are gone.

[1] They are here speaking of the whole province. The abbey of St-Claude, by far the largest single serf-holder, had only 20,000 altogether; and the figures here are probably exaggerated.

Of all these lords, the most tenacious were the monks (from 1742 onwards, the bishop and chapter) of St-Claude. How entirely responsible they were, and how unyielding, may be gathered from pp. 8, 10, 14, *20*, 21, *32–3*, *42*, 48, *59*, *61*, *63 ff.*, *66*, 67, 68, 80, *85*, *94*, 97 (italics for the more important references).

The lord-bishop, several times solicited by Necker [to follow the king's recommendation and allow his serfs to purchase their freedom], continued to take refuge behind the opposition of his noble chapter.

The Marquis de la Villette wrote in 1779:

The lay noble, whose *mainmortable* lands are a hereditary patrimony, spares his vassals, since he aims at improving his children's heritage. ...The noble churchman, who has only a life interest in his lordship, sees nothing in his benefice but the temporal usufruct....He abandons his flock to the voracity of middlemen and the immorality of pettifogging lawyers; he prays to God for them and never sees their faces.

Moreover, it is practically certain that some of the St-Claude rights had been obtained by unjust encroachment; certainly some of the documents upon which the canons relied were exposed as gross forgeries, and they accepted the exposure in silence. When, in the Provincial Assembly of 1789, a lay noble rose and proclaimed the gratuitous enfranchisement of all his vassals, he was followed by the bishop of St-Claude, who hoped "that it may please His Majesty to enfranchise gratuitously the persons and the goods [of my serfs], hoping from the justice and the loving-kindness of this best of Kings that He will deign to indemnify my see and my chapter by allowing us to appropriate a few ecclesiastical benefices." And it was the same elsewhere: the *cahiers* of 1789 are there to prove it:

In general, the clerical assemblies in which the parish priests have a majority make short work of servile dues, which are profitable only to the wealthy holders of benefices. But, when the majority are swayed by a bishop or a powerful abbey, if the *cahier* is not silent on the subject of *mainmorte*, its redemption is hedged round with all sorts of precautions drawn from the principle of the inviolability of ecclesiastical property. (p. 85.)

Voltaire might well reproach the French royalty and the French Church with the example of contemporary England (p. 17).

Although St-Claude is the worst example, the same abuses prevailed in many other parts of France (pp. 27, 74 ff., 83, 84). Voltaire could write:

It is a mortal sin for a Carthusian to eat half an ounce of mutton; but he may eat the substance of a whole family with a safe conscience. I have seen the Carthusians of my neighbourhood inherit 100,000 crowns from one of their *mainmortable* slaves, who had made this fortune in trade at Frankfort. It is true that the family thus robbed (let us tell the whole truth) is free to come and beg alms at the monastery gate. (p. 13.)

The fact that the misery of the French peasant in 1789 has often been exaggerated for party purposes does not affect the admitted truth that he was worse off than his English contemporary. This comes out quite clearly from Taine's *Ancien Régime*, though this is sometimes quoted as a reactionary book, unjust to the Revolution.

It is true that much of what has been said in this appendix might be said also of the Irish peasantry and the Scottish crofters. It is true that no government and no age has been beyond reproach. But it is not true that there is a clear line of cleavage here on the lines of the great religious cleavage; and indeed, if a comparison must needs be instituted, this will be found to tell, on the whole, rather against the Roman Church.

40

FARTHER CORROBORATIVE EVIDENCE

(ARRANGED ACCORDING TO THE PAGES OF THE TEXT)

p. 13 (cf. pp. 80, 172). *That the children should be divided.*
Chassin (*Serfs*, pp. 81, 83) gives curious evidence on this point from the *cahiers* of 1789, when the tenants of the abbey of St-Pierre-le-Moustier pleaded to the Assemblée Nationale:

Let the servile *mainmorte* be abolished everywhere, seeing that this abuse...exposes folk in this unhappy condition to be shared like common beasts, when their father owes *mainmorte* to one lord and their mother to another.

p. 38 n. *The plough-team of eight.*
Four seems very plainly implied as the ordinary number for a working plough-team in *Piers Plowman*, B. xix, 256, 262.

p. 40. *A serf's younger sons.*
"Ninety-five men who are juniors" are to be sent up every year at harvest-time from the manor of Alverstoke to reap in the prior of Winchester's fields (Pontissara, introd. p. lv). This seems a valuable indication of a floating population of young landless serfs.

p. 55 (cf. p. 78). *To grind at their lord's mill.*
One of Baildon's documents throws valuable light on the capacity of what seems an ordinary water-mill. In 1369, the prior of Monk Bretton complains that whereas his mill at Derfield, in former times, "could and was wont to grind in a day and a night four quarters of

any kind of corn," it is now hindered by the building of another mill higher up, with such diminution of the water-current that "the mill cannot now grind in a day and a night more than one quarter of corn" (p. 142).

p. 78 (cf. p. 90). *Rabbits.*

The documents printed by Baildon contain frequent notices of rabbits and their careful preservation by the landlords; see pp. 14, 36, 114, 143, 180, 201. On some pages there are more notices than one. Compare also Pontissara, pp. 674–5, 742, and introd. p. liv.

p. 81 n. 2. *To a sort of temporary slavery.*

The bishop's secretary is recording the fines and other occasional sources of revenue upon the manor of Swainston in 1284. He writes:

If any bondwoman of my lord [bishop] be pregnant, unless she be married, she shall go forthwith after her purification to the lord's fold and help in the cheese-making, unless she can pay a fine for her freedom. In that servitude she shall remain from year to year, until she be dispensed by my lord's will; these dues are worth, at a low computation, £1. 6s. 8d. [a year]; for, if they had to be kept at my lord's livery, much more would be paid [*quia si deberent sustineri ad liberacionem domini multo plus expenderetur*].

p. 99. *A peasant's cottage in 1281.*

A very interesting sidelight is thrown upon the medieval cottage by certain details printed by Baildon (pp. 21, 43, 90, 161, 224). In 1295, at Askham in Yorkshire, a farmer is sued for pulling down three cottages belonging to the priory of Bridlington; the prior values the three at £1; in modern pre-war currency, this would come to about £7 each. The twenty apple-trees which were cut down at the same time are valued at 10s.[1] At various times and places between this date and 1372, certain manorial buildings are similarly destroyed and sued for by the landlords; sheephouses are priced at £3. 6s. 4d., £2 and £1 respectively; a kitchen at £20; a dovecote at £6. 13s. 4d.; a brewhouse at £5; a bakehouse and brewhouse together at 13s. 4d.

p. 147. *Transfer of serfs from Romainmotier to Chalon.*

A somewhat similar case may be quoted from the year 1265. The monks of Corneux exchanged certain lands with a lay lord. A serf who, in the ordinary business way, found himself thus transferred without his consent, left his holding and migrated to the abbey lands. While this testifies on one side to the tenant's preference for a monastic lord, on the other hand, it shows that the monks had no objection on principle to throwing their serfs upon the mercy of outsiders (J. Bertin, *Droit Coutumier au M.-Â.*, Gray, 1898, p. 7).

---

[1] Here, as in other places, Baildon mistakenly translates *pomeria* (Fr. *pommiers*) as "orchards."

p. 165 n. *Transference to an easier landlord.*

Here are two more precisely similar cases: "In 1203, Eudes III, duke of Burgundy, at the request of the abbot of St-Seine, promised not to allow the abbot's tenants to take refuge with him" (J. Bertin, *ibid.* Gray, 1898, p. 5). In 1342, the inhabitants of Val-Saugeois in Burgundy attempted to escape *en masse* to the sway of a neighbouring lord, Gui de Montfaucon; but the abbot, relying upon his legal rights, forced the majority back to his allegiance, and confiscated the holdings of the rest (Grappin, p. 136).

p. 191. *Monasteries claim this right of hanging as a far from negligible item of revenue.*

It was not that the monks were thirsty for the blood of a sinner; all these rights of justice were treated from an almost exclusively economic point of view. For instance, the long-standing quarrel between the monks of St-Germain and the lords of Pogy with regard to the gallows at St-Germain-Laval was terminated in 1176 by an arbitral sentence of the archbishop of Sens, who decided that the monks should strip the thief of all he possessed and hand him over to be hanged by the lord, who might claim no part in the chattels unless the monks had let the criminal escape from their prison (*Archives de la France monastique*, III, 1906, 278).

p. 191. *Trial by battle.*

The monks of St Augustine's, Canterbury, had their professional champion in 1212. Symon Tyrel held twenty acres, at a rent of 3s. 4d.

for all service except duel, if such must sometimes be done for the monastery of St Augustine; which service the said Symon shall do his whole life long, either in person or through another proper man, on these terms: viz. that if he offer wager of battle for the monastery and need to go no farther in that business, then we give him 50 shillings; if, again, he offer the wager and come armed to fight before the justices, yet be not compelled to fight the duel, then he shall have 100 shillings and no more; if he fight the battle, he shall have 10 marks and no more (Turner and Salter, p. 456).

In 1295, the English clergy petitioned the king that clerks, and especially priests, be neither compelled to fight in judicial duels, nor allowed to offer themselves without episcopal request (Pontissara, p. 776).

p. 201. *Loss by bad weather.*

The bishop of Winchester here took every advantage of his serfs:

Item, if they be hindered by rain, or in any other way, from doing their day's work, they shall come on the morrow; and if they be hindered on that day also, they shall come on the day following, and so from day to day until they have fully completed one day's work. (Pontissara, p. 659, A.D. 1270.)

p. 204. *Harshness and severity*.

Mr Baildon's monastic gleanings in Yorkshire supply valuable evidence for the relations between monastic landlords and tenants. For instance (p. 95):

A.D. 1290. Adam de Haskerugg *v.* the Abbot of Jerevall, Bro. Thomas de Mildeby, Bro. William de Broxerton, Bro. John de Benigton, monks of the same house, Bro. William de Bentham, Bro. William Skot, John de Bellerby, and others, for assaulting the plaintiff at Helsehall on the Sunday after the feast of St Bartholomew, 17 Edw. I, and taking him to Elnouhall, and there keeping him in fetters and in prison for 7 days, and for taking his goods and chattels to the value of £10, to wit, a horse worth 20s. and corn worth £9. The Abbot says that Adam is his villein. Adam says he is a free man. Jury.

In this case, as in so many others, we know nothing of the jury's decision. Compare the cases on pp. 75, 109, 202, 232. Again, Mr Baildon's collections are full of cases where monks distrain upon their tenants; see pp. 23-4, 39, 91, 122, 124, 129, 130, 199, 201, 212. Compare *Belbuck*, p. 30.

A clear case of monastic rack-renting comes from the *cahiers* of 1789. The villagers of Donnain in Belgium, dependent on the abbey of Marchiennes, demand "that, henceforth, none may deprive the tiller of the soil of his possessions so long as he pays punctually" (Chassin, *Serfs*, p. 76). Under the abbey of St-Claude, the conditions were even worse. Anyone who had the ill-luck to be descended from a serf is thus described in the petition of the inhabitants to the États Généraux of 1789:

If, through extraordinary industry and a luck which is rare in these parts, a serf makes a fortune; if, on a piece of ground worth 50 francs, he builds a house worth 50,000 francs; and if, afterwards, some misfortune compels him to sell it, then the lord[1], who has contributed nothing to the building, will yet secure from this sale a third or a half of the price through his right of *lods*; and if, finally, the buyer dies *without any relation living in his house*, the house itself will fall in to the lord.

The words which I have here italicized are explained by that title xv of the Coutumes, articles 16, 17, which I have summarized at the end of appendix 16.

p. 215. *The hunting monk*.

To the references already given, we may add from Pontissara's *Register*, pp. 393, 659, 675, 715, 717, 761 and introd. pp. l, lv.

pp. 255, 275 (cf. also p. 425). *The Village Dance*.

There is a vague belief, natural enough among those who have not studied contemporary documents, that we can best realize medieval

---

[1] Formerly the abbot; by this time, the bishop and his chapter.

English society by picturing something diametrically opposite to that seventeenth century society which took its place. Yet the Puritans, in both their extremes, were true sons of the Middle Ages; they had inherited formalism on one hand, hysteria on the other. Nearly all the restrictions that we associate with Puritanism had been steadily taught for centuries in the medieval Church; again, it can scarcely be said that any Anabaptist or Leveller ever outdid the wild things that were done under the Popes. Let us take these two points briefly in order.

(1) In the first connexion, the question of the village dance is most important. Dancing was frequently done, of course, on Sundays and holy-days in the Middle Ages; and it is equally certain that the Puritans fought hard against this. But we shall jump to very false conclusions if we ignore two equally relevant facts—first, that people did dance even under the Puritans, and, secondly, that the dance had found a determined enemy, long before, in the medieval Church. If we should set ourselves to collect all Puritan utterances on this subject, from moderates like Milton and Baxter down to the extremists, it is doubtful whether these would be found more violent and consistent than a similar catena of medieval passages, from canon law and St Thomas Aquinas down to the ordinary sermon-writers and moralists. We mistake the medieval village until we realize that Chaucer's Poor Parson was probably as loth to sanction the village dance as he was to curse for his tithes.

On this subject, I printed what seemed sufficient evidence in the first volume of *Five Centuries of Religion*, appendix 23. But this has not sufficed for some critics; and Mr Chesterton in especial has attacked it in *The Dublin Review* for Jan. 1925. I have, therefore, printed a mass of farther evidence in *The History Teachers' Miscellany* for March and April, 1925, and in *The Review of the Churches* for July, 1925.

From English manor customals, I have found no evidence either way. For German prohibitions or regulations see (in addition to references in my text), *Weisthümer*, I, 353; II, 412; III, 370 n.; V, 52, 137, 154; for general approval, III, 636; for approval at harvest-time, IV, 576. At Merzig, in 1529, it is recorded that the peasants have now got free from the earlier restrictions upon their dances (VI, 429).

But the really important question is that of Church theory. To summarize here what I have proved by documents elsewhere, a sentence attributed to St Augustine, and constantly quoted by moralists, proclaims that even ploughing on a holy-day is less sinful than dancing. The only allusion in canon law is decidedly unfavourable. The great schoolmen, including even Thomas Aquinas, exonerate the dancer from sin only on condition that he observes four limitations, one of which is that he should dance only on certain occasions of public rejoicing which would, in the nature of the case, be few and far between. Still more unfavourable is the standard moralist of the later Middle Ages, St Antonino of Florence, who insists that dancers commonly commit all seven mortal sins in the dance. Yet even he is outdone by another Dominican, Pépin, whose sermons were delivered shortly after Luther's appearance, and who devotes one whole sermon to the iniquities of the dance as he devotes another to the wickedness of Lutheranism. Here, again, is an extract from another sermon of about the same time, which I have not printed elsewhere (*Luculentissimi Sermones parati de tempore et de sanctis*, Paris, 1536, serm. 132, dom. xiii post Trin.):

The third Commandment is: "Keep holy the Sabbath Day" [*Sabbata sanctifices*]. This is expounded in two ways. The first, thus: Commit no mortal sin on holy-days, for then the sin is greater, as fornication, drunkenness, dancing, than on another day. Augustine saith: "It is better to plough on holy-days than to dance."....Here again is an example concerning the dance. A certain girl would make exception for no holy-day, but would haunt the dances. One holy-day, when she came back wearied from the dance, she cast herself upon her couch and fell asleep; and it seemed to her that black horsemen came and bore her off into a gloomy valley for judgement. Then said the Judge: "She is a good dancer; purge her neck, that she may be able to sing songs." Then one caught up a flaming torch and thrust it through her mouth into her throat, so that she awoke with a cry and found herself all burnt; and the flesh fell in gobbets from her body, and her parents, unable to suffer the stench of her, bore her to an hospital, where she vowed to God and the Blessed Mary that she would keep her chastity and flee from all worldly delights; and then she was made whole.

One of the least unfavourable passages I have met with anywhere is this following from the great chancellor of Paris University, Jean Gerson (*Opp.* Paris, 1606, vol. iv, c. 333, *Sermon against Lechery*):

Is it always sinful to dance? I say that, in many cases, it is not wrong in itself [*in pluribus casibus quantum est de se*], but human frailty is such that dances are hardly practised without divers sins. It is certain that he who, for dancing's sake, omits to do what he ought to do, or knowingly makes another to sin, sins grievously. Also when dances are disorderly, altogether public, and without reasonable moderation [*sine rationis mensura*], or when pregnant women lose their fruit, as happens. Note that all the sins dance in the dance, etc.

[*sic*; he is doubtless referring here to St Antonino's elaborate proof that the dance combines in itself all seven mortal sins]. The persistence of this orthodox Catholic tradition may be gathered from the article on *Dance* in the modern *Catholic Encyclopaedia*.

The medieval ecclesiastic was prejudiced also, as a rule, against all forms of sport. Here and there, very seldom, we find sport in general not only permitted, but even commended, generally with a back-reference to Aristotle, as by St Thomas Aquinas in his commentary on Isaiah (iii, 16). On the other hand, I have frequently met with disparaging allusions such as these two with which Dr Owst supplies me, and which I give here because they are from MS. sources scarcely otherwise accessible. Bishop Brumpton, in the fourteenth century, says: "Such folk go willingly to a long day's occupation, to wrestlings and fairs and spectacles, and vain bodily recreations, while they will scarce trouble to go one mile to hear a sermon" (MS. Harl. 3760, f. 176). And Master Robert Rypon, subprior of Durham, about 1401 speaks of

wrestlers, stone-smiters, lifters of weights, and fellows of this kind, wherein some vainly glory in their bodily strength and exercise themselves in such like things. For what have they in the end, save weariness and labour? For their bodies are wearied, and sometimes much enfeebled, and they carry off nothing in the end save the wind of vainglory; and they are like unto a burning candle, which shines before the beholders and continually consumes itself (MS. Harl. 4894, f. 176).

(2) Again, we are told that the result of revolt from the authority of the medieval Church has been irregularity and licence in society. Mr Chesterton, catching at a hint from Mr Bernard Shaw, instanced "going about without clothes" (*The Superstitions of the Sceptic*, p. 2; *St Joan*, p. 76). Though he has written a life of St Francis, he has evidently forgotten that this was precisely one of his hero's most conspicuous achievements in his earliest days of enthusiasm. One day, Francis went through the streets and into the church pulpit "naked as he was born, save for his drawers only," and compelled one of his chief disciples to do the same (*Little Flowers*, ch. xxx; Celano, *Vita Prima*, c. vi, § 15; cf. a similar case in *Mirror of Perfection*, ch. lxi). I quote a parallel in *St Francis to Dante*, ch. xxiv, and others might be given; here it may suffice to print three more in chronological order.

(a) Luchaire writes on p. 397 of his *Social Life* (Eng. translation):

There is an interesting passage in the [twelfth century] treatise of the abbot of Aumône, Philip of Harvengt, on the continence of clerics, in which he states the following facts: "Last year several of our brothers were sent to certain parts of Flanders to attend to some of the business of our church. It was in summer. They saw most of the peasants walking about in the streets and on the squares of the villages without a bit of clothing, not even trousers, in order to keep cool; thus naked they attended to their business not in the least disturbed at the glances of passers-by nor by the prohibition of their mayors. When our brothers indignantly asked them why they went thus naked like animals they answered: 'What business is it of yours? You do not make laws for us.'" And the abbot adds by way of moral: "What astonishes me is not the bestial impudence of these peasants, it is the absolutely reprehensible tolerance of those who see them and do not prevent their going about in this way."

(*b*) From *Cronache Fermane* (*Doc. di storia italiana—Toscana, Umbria e Marche*, 1870), IV, 38:

In the year 1412, and on the 11th day of October, a certain brother Antonio da [*blank*], who wore the habit of the Brethren of Poor Life [*qui habebat habitum istorum de paupera vita*] seduced many men and women of the county of Fermo, in number about a thousand, and especially from the fortified villages of the midst of the county; and he said that he himself was God the Father, and he said among all men that he had been Christ and that he had wrought many miracles. When these things had been done, on this day aforesaid he got together certain men and women, of the number of twenty or thereabout, and brought them with him towards Fermo, saying unto them that he would go to Jerusalem and would cross the sea, and that the sea should be opened before him, and he would cross dry-shod; and, when they were come nigh unto the river Tenna, he made all that were with him strip themselves of all clothing, whether woollen or linen, both men and women; and at length he baptized them in the river; and thus he with all the rest, men and women alike, came into the city of Fermo naked of any woollen or linen cloth, and even without drawers[1]. And many men and women of that city rebuked them for this simplicity: but they were silent and made no answer; and when they were on the Piazza San Martino they took a turn along the head of the Piazza[2]; and when the bishop's vicar, who was then my lord Ascario, saw this, he had them taken and cast into prison.

(*c*) From a paper read at the International Historical Congress of 1903:

In seventeenth century Rome, during the first day of the carnival, the populace had the diversion of seeing the Jews run a race, naked as they were born, from the Porta de Popolo to the church of San Marco (*Att. cong. intern.* 1903, III, 183).

The fact is, that all parties are tempted, in the neglect of recorded facts, to charge upon some hostile party certain failings which are really common to all, being inherent in ordinary human nature. The wilfully blind are like the fatally blind; they strike indiscriminately at fancies and realities; and it would be a cruel practical jest if Mr Chesterton could be confronted in the flesh with some equally

---

[1] *Etiam sine tarabolis.* Ducange suggests "tabard" (s.v. *taraber*); but the quotation he gives seems, like our present text, rather to suggest "drawers." Both passages are evidently intended to emphasize nudity.

[2] *Fecerunt voltam per caput platee.*

boisterous and orthodox body resuscitated from the real Middle Ages. The two champions might be armed with knives against the Protestant pig; but the gashes would mostly be exchanged between one man necessarily ignorant of the future, and another complacently ignorant of the past.

p. 285. *Priestly usurers.*
See also Pontissara's *Register*, p. 227.

p. 290. *This matter of medieval tithing.*
It will be apposite to add here a quotation from L. Lamborelle, *Le bon vieux temps* (3rd ed. Brussels, 1875, p. 100; italics his):

En 1750, [les curés] de la province de Hainaut adressèrent dans un mémoire leur réclamation au gouvernement. Ils n'y épargnèrent pas les reproches à *l'avidité insatiable* des gros décimateurs, à ces asiles de *pieux fainéants*, aux monastères et aux chapitres que *l'avarice* et *l'ambition dominaient*, qui ne *rendaient aucun service aux églises dont ils tiraient tous les fruits*. (*Exposition des Droits des curés*, 1 vol. in-12, Bruxelles, 1751. Cité par Defacqz, *Ancien droit belgique*, II, 143.)

p. 319. *Poggio Bracciolini.*
The satirist is here corroborated by a cold legal document recording a piteous complaint from the twelfth century peasants of a valley in the Trentino: "Let us no longer be compelled [by the lord of the castle] to keep watch and ward in the roads and public ways and to rob the passers-by, as the lord Gundibaldo has established" (F. Schneider, *Die Entstehung v. Burg und Landgemeinde in Italien*, Berlin, 1924, p. 195 n.). If more documentary evidence had come down to us, we should probably find similar echoes from the wilder districts of France and Germany.

p. 328. *Usury...in Flanders and Italy.*
For Flanders, this is proved in an essay to which Sir William Ashley has kindly drawn my attention: J. Lameere, *Un chapitre de l'histoire du prêt à intérêt dans le droit belgique*, in *Bulletin de l'acad. royale de Belgique, classe des lettres*, 1920, pp. 77 ff.

p. 330. *The Sacrament of Matrimony.*
Even as late as 1320, the Dominican canonist Durand de St-Pourçain, bishop of Le Puy, repeats this doctrine, as indeed there was no legal possibility of repudiating it. In this respect, adds Durand, serfdom is worse than leprosy; for leprosy is no sufficient ground for divorce (*In Sententias Comment.* lib. IV, dist. xxxvi, q. 1; ed. 1586, f. 281 a, b).

p. 331. *Bondmen's bairns have been made bishops.*
Early in the ninth century, Bishop Thegan had complained of one

fault which stained the virtues of Louis the Pious (*Rec. des hist. des Gaules*, tom. VI, p. 78):

For that abominable custom had long reigned, whereby the noblest pontiffs were raised from the lowest ranks of serfdom [*ut ex vilissimis servis summi Pontifices fierent*] and the king did not forbid this; yet this is a very great evil among Christian folk, as the Book of Kings testifieth concerning Jeroboam son of Nebat [ref. to 1 Kings, xiii, 33]. After such men as this are raised to honour, they are never so mild and affable as before, without beginning at once to be wrathful, quarrelsome, backbiters, stubborn, insulting, dealing in threats to all their subjects, through which conduct they begin to be feared and praised by men. They strive to raise their basest kinsfolk from that yoke of servitude which is their due, and to give them liberty. Then they instruct some of these in liberal studies; others they wed to noble women, and compel the sons of nobles to take their kinswomen to wives. No man can live quietly with them, but such as have entered into such ties; the rest spend their days in the utmost sadness, groaning and weeping....Moreover, these prelates' kinsfolk, when they have come somewhat to years of discretion, are dragged into Holy Orders, which is a most perilous thing both to givers and to receivers. And, although some are learned, yet the multitude of their transgressions surpasses their learning, so that oftentimes the Pastor of the Church does not dare to bring to canonical justice certain negligent criminals by reason of the crimes of his [or their?] kinsfolk; thus that sacred ministry is oftentimes greatly despised by some folk, because it is thus exhibited by some folk. Wherefore, may it please Almighty God, with His kings and princes, from this time forward to root out and choke this abominable custom, that it may reign no more among Christian folk. Amen.

Yet it would be difficult, as I have remarked, to name many of servile origin among all the thousands of medieval prelates.

p. 337. *A jar full of enchantment.*

Here is the full story (Langlois, *l.c.* p. 12; *Rec. des Historiens*, tom. 24, ann. 1248):

Pierre Ag...s of Vieilleville deposeth that, in the days when Sire Pierre de Naiencort was seneschal [*i.e.* in 1240], and Gregory was vicar of Sommière, he had a son of the age of 10 years who, as he was keeping his sheep on the pasture of Vieilleville, found a certain jar, not so as to touch it, but he said to all whom he met that he had found a jar full of witchcrafts [*fachuris*]. But, two days afterwards, he told his mother that he had found a jar full of witchcrafts. When his mother heard this, she told him by no means to go back thither nor to touch the afore-said jar. He did not believe her, but went thither and took the jar and hid it. And, when this had been done, the court learned all that had been done, and took the boy. When the boy was asked if he knew the jar, he denied it. His mother likewise, asked whether she knew aught of the deed, denied it; but afterwards, being asked for the second time upon oath whether she knew aught of the deed, she said *Yes*, and confessed how the boy had told her that he had found a jar full of witchcrafts, and she had forbidden him on any account to take it. She said also more, that she did not remember this[1]. When she had been examined on oath, they kept her and set her in irons. Now she was big with child, and nigh unto her time; and she remained there five weeks; but, being nigh upon her time, she was brought to bed there, and had no help, but dogs came and devoured the child. And when the said woman was within [*intus*], her husband found bail for her, and yet they set her not free. Now, when the said woman was examined, the chaplain said that he should not have her, and that he should think of something else. But her husband came before the seneschal and said that he should hear him of right. And he, when he heard his reasons, bade the baily clear him at once of the whole affair; but he would not; nay, he assigned him a day of trial; and that deed cost the aforesaid Pierre, contrary to justice, a good 50 sols of Vienne, which he begs may be given over and restored unto him.

p. 348. *That would be the ruin of Us.*

Alphonse Feillet's exhaustive study may enable us to realize how heavy was the price which the French peasant paid for retaining his medieval institutions until 1789 (*La misère en France au temps de la Fronde*, 1862, pp. 52 ff.; italics are mine):

"The history of the ancient monarchy," writes M. Louandre, "may be summed up in three words: War, Plague, and Famine. The populations kill each other or die of starvation and disease; and when, through these old-world stories, we follow this list of bloody quarrels and disasters, we wonder that any people could survive so many miseries, and that any men are left." The most precise official documents attest the veracity of historians whom, but for the multiplicity and importance of these testimonies, we should be inclined to suspect; *and, since we cannot accuse Nature, which has not sensibly varied, we must needs seek the cause of the evil in the institutions. The organization of the Ancien Régime presented a prodigious assemblage of mistaken measures, which could not be altered without changing the very base of society.* What needed amendment was the constitution of the government; the mass of laws which governed property, production and consumption; the system of taxation which pressed upon the country; the method of collection and the way in which these taxes were spent; the regulation of industry, the state of the roads and markets; the indiscipline of the soldiery, who were mostly strangers with no scruples to restrain them from treading upon a population from which they themselves had not sprung; in brief, we needed a complete change of administration and a radical reconstitution; no mere change piece by piece, since *every wheel of the machine was an active agent of pauperism.*

[1] Or possibly, "that she remembered no more than this" [*dixit etiam plus quod de hoc non erat memor*].

The point of view from which pauperism was then regarded was itself an obstacle to improvement; misery, in the seventeenth century, was regarded as a punishment for original sin; the desire to interfere with it became almost an impiety, a rebellious pride; that belief stopped men's ears against all serious efforts for improvement, which, thus, were often condemned to sterility. The proper remedy (men said) was in rich men's charity and poor men's resignation; and that resignation, preached by one party and almost accepted by the other, has even deceived a good many historians, who have doubted whether pauperism existed under the Ancien Régime.

If this word "pauperism" means what most economists take it to mean, the permanent status of a class of citizens who would starve without the help they receive, when was it ever more obvious than in the days when crowds of beggars came to feed at the gates of convents, hospitals, or great houses, constituting a serious menace to society, which the latter met from time to time by the severest and sometimes even the most cruel measures? Every historian reports ordinances of this kind; let me be permitted to quote one that is little known. What barbarous age was it which gave birth to the decree "that, at the least symptom of contagion, beggars and vagabonds must come and report their sickness, under pain of being shot down with bullets [*arque-busés*]"? That bloody law dates from 1633; and the Draco who invented it was named Isaac Laffemas, a sort of seneschal of Champagne. In these days we reserve such treatment for the mad dogs that terrorize a district; even formidable criminals find more consideration than the tramps of the past....

The nobility had no idea of those works which change the whole face of a country, which improve average soils or fertilize waste lands; their manner of life exhausted the soil, demanding all from it and giving nothing. The monastery cast over the neighbourhood a shadow scarcely less baleful than that of the château. Far in the past lay those days when monks, with tireless hand, cleared forests and heaths or drained marshes; in the seventeenth century, their one superiority over the nobility lay in a wiser administration of their immense domains; but, if the monk preserved his landed estates better than the noble, he had no better idea of improving its yield. It is true that the dole at the convent gate restored a part of these riches to the otherwise destitute poor; but even this habit of doles was an obstacle to work, by creating among the country-folk a mendicant population who "lived on alms as a man lives on the income of a benefice." Hence followed, in agriculture, that torpor and sterile immobility which [my] statistics will show in their sad reality.

A judge and antiquary at Sens (continues Feillet) has worked out the produce of six different holdings, leased from the Hôtel-Dieu of that city, at four different times; about 1550, 1650, 1750 and 1857. Calculating for the different values of money, he finds the following movement; the average yield per hectare was worth 37 fr. 50 in 1550,

13.40 a century later; in 1660, the Fronde had brought it down to 10.72; in 1750 it was 14.12 and in 1857 49.86.

p. 394. *Much of his pre-Christian faith.*

There is a certain pathos in the list of Swabian practices, loudly condemned as pagan by the Church, but maintained with dumb tenacity in the villages, which Baumann rehearses (1, 406). Even priests drank to the Saints at their meals, as their fathers had drunk to the heathen gods. The dead were buried with weapons for use in the next world, children with their toys; "women who died in child-birth (a custom not yet quite extinct in Upper Swabia) were buried with a pan and a spoon, that they might cook pap and feed their dead children." The funeral feast was a time of intemperance; and the villagers sang heathen charms [*carmina diabolica*] over the graves.

The essential sameness, in all ages, of this backward glance upon religion, is exemplified by the old-fashioned farmer's complaint of modern agricultural weather in Petronius's *Supper of Trimalchio*, about 90 A.D.:

Nobody keeps the fasts nowadays; nobody cares a straw for Jupiter; everybody just shuts his eyes and counts his money! In old days, the women marched up the slopes of the Capitol white-robed and bare-footed, with loose hair and pure minds, and prayed Jupiter for rain; and so the rain came straight down by the bucket-full, hit or miss, and we all came home like drowned rats [*udi tanquam mures*].

The Latin is printed on p. 9 of S. Gaselee's *Anthology of Medieval Latin*.

p. 446. *To be most profitable.*

The Eynsham bailiff assures his monks that they had made a good bargain by their readjustment after the Black Death, and had secured more in rent from the peasants than the earlier dues had been worth. The monks of Romainmotier had similar success at the end of the sixteenth century; their readjusted rents and fines brought them in more than the old dues[1]. This does not, of course, negative the chance that the peasants also may have gained by any stable and reasonable readjustment.

[1] Charrière, p. 43; cf. p. 64.

POSTSCRIPTS

I. PARISH LIFE

WHILE the last sheets are still in the press, I have come across very valuable evidence on this subject, which strongly corroborates that already given on pp. 335–341. It is a Visitation of the Churches in the Diocese of Lausanne in 1416–17, printed as tom. XI of the second series of *Mémoires et documents pub. soc. hist. de la Suisse Romande*, 1921.

A. Population (cf. p. 65 of my text).

The bishop's commissaries visited 273 parishes and chapelries, urban and rural[1]. They nearly always record the number of households [*foci*]. In five cases, these amounted to less than ten; in the teens were 37 parishes, in the twenties 28, thirties 27, forties 20, fifties 23, sixties 27, seventies 9, eighties 13, nineties 6. Between 100 and 120 came 14; thence to 150 came 15; thence to 199 came 5. Then came Lutry, La Vilette, Montreux and Aeschi with 200 each; Estavayer and Anet, 220; Tavel, Köniz and Erlenbach, 300; Yverdon 320; Payerne 340; Gsteig 350; Vevey, Romont and Frutigen 400; Zweisimmen 500. Three were too large to be counted, viz. Neuchâtel, Fribourg (where the visitation was not completed "by reason of the multitude of the people there") and Berne, which had "focos innumerabiles." The average number of households for the 255 localities recorded is 63·69. If, however, we omit the urban agglomerations, this brings the average down to about 50; we may reckon, therefore, that the average village in this large district contained 250 inhabitants, since it is generally agreed that we must multiply the households by five to get the total population of all ages. The Berne villages and small towns were evidently more populous than those in Suisse Romande.

B. Easter Communion.

In 220 cases, the visitors record not only the numbers of households, but also the numbers of folk of age to communicate, who were excommunicated for not having fulfilled their duty of communicating once a year. These records are evidently incomplete; scarcely any of the clergy in the Berne district seem to have kept a register; but, even as they stand, they agree remarkably with the French evidence

---

[1] I have not gone over these figures a second time, but am confident that they may be taken as substantially correct.

given on p. 335 of my text. The first 100 pages of this Lausanne visitation give statistics for 69 parishes; these contained 2,979 households and 293 excommunicates, almost exactly 10 per cent. The remaining 133 pages are less unfavourable in this respect (though in some other important respects they are more gloomy): the figures are often left blank. When we count these pages in with the rest, we have 123 parishes, 11,513 households, and 692 excommunicates; this gives 6·01 per cent. But it takes no account of three cases where the sinners are recorded vaguely as "multi" (pp. 15, 112, 171), nor of Payerne, where they are "infiniti." The households here numbered 340; if the excommunicates were in this unrecordable proportion, they would seem to have outdone even Orbe, Lutry, Berchier, Siviriez, Vuisternens, Écharlens, Tours-Montagny, Estavayer, Dompierre and St-Aubin, where there were 242 excommunicates to an aggregate of 1,072 households; and, if we had full figures, the above-mentioned percentage of 6 would have to be considerably raised.

C. General Condition.

There is scarcely one of these 273 communities, now among the most prosperous and regular in the world, where serious defects are not found in the church buildings and furniture, and especially in the keeping of the consecrated Host. This was constantly found unprotected and dirty, even putrid (pp. 8, 10, 137); one parson had allowed "more than 120 Bodies [of the Lord]" to collect; two others "more than 60"; in the priory church of Lutry "they found the Holy Eucharist behind the high altar in a certain great chest, and in such quantities that there were more than 300 Consecrated Persons therein"; at Montagny, there were "many Consecrated Hosts broken and ill-placed" (pp. 3, 56, 63, 65, 120). Forty-eight of the churches were more or less ruinous; in 83 parishes the parson was non-resident, and in one or two there was not even a curate; 64 of the priests were concubinary, and 15 of the canons in the collegiate churches, not reckoning "many" others who are recorded without names or details (pp. 206, 222, 226). Yet the enormous majority of these livings belonged to (in the sense that they were in the gift of and probably a large proportion altogether appropriated to) ecclesiastical patrons—136 to monastic bodies, 46 to the Bishop, 27 to the Chapter of Lausanne, and 21 to other churchmen.

I give the first of these visitations as a specimen of what we should have found if we could have been transported bodily back to these medieval villages. It is as nearly typical, I think, as any other which could be chosen; the church and its furniture were in a similar state almost everywhere; while the parson's past condition was the present condition of more than eighty others in the diocese.

Préverenges. On Monday, Oct. 18, the commissaries visited this parish church, which has 23[1] households. It is in the gift of the lord prior of St-Sulpice; here, as rector in charge of souls, is Sir Peter Cornier, aged 40 years, of good life and knowledge, having good parishioners except eight who did not receive the Holy Eucharist on Easter Day, and who have held out under the sentence [of excommunication] beyond the year[2]. In this parish church the Eucharist, the consecrated chrism and oil, are not locked up in an aumbry [= cupboard], nor is there any written slip to mark the difference between the chrism and the oil. The books are not competent; viz. the missal is imperfect, nor is there a manual of the Sacraments. There is no glass in the window over the altar; the graveyard is not enclosed; there are no Lententide curtains. The rector, as the parishioners told us, was formerly concubinary and had and still has children; but now he is of good life. There is no vessel for carrying the Eucharist to the sick.

For the repair of which defects, viz. the enclosure of the graveyard within eight days, the making of an aumbry wherein the holy chrism and oil and Eucharist may be kept, the writing of a sacramentary and the making of a vessel for carrying the Body of Christ, the glass window, and the curtains, and the repair of the other defects, the said commissaries enjoined the parishioners to fulfil these things aforesaid within a year, under pain of excommunication; they themselves being present and hearing and consenting[3].

II. RABBITS (p. 556)

ANOTHER indication that rabbits were by no means so scarce as Thorold Rogers imagined may be found in P.R.O. Lists and Indexes, XII (*Early Chancery Proc.* vol. I), p. 25. There, early in the fifteenth century, we find two Englishmen and a German or Fleming, probably the consignee, suing the searcher at the London Custom House for "detention of coney and lamb skins, etc. freighted for Antwerp market."

---

[1] Or possibly, the editor warns us, 43; this first leaf is less legible than the rest.

[2] In a certain number of other cases, it is recorded that some or all of the excommunicates have procured absolution; but these are decidedly exceptional. In the majority of cases, they are entered as still holding out.

[3] In two other cases a later hand has added that the repairs thus ordered have not been done; but there is no hint of actual excommunication for the omission.

INDEX

passim, 361–8; absentee, 228, 370 n.; dancing forbidden by, 276; easy, 35, 146, 173, 181–5, 230, 378, 556; hard, 76, 105 n., 207, 556, 558
Money, definition of, in Canon Law, 302; depreciation of, 385; power of, 30, 301–2; scarcity of, 30, 51; value of, 44, 58, 145. *And see* Coinage
Monheim, 221
Monk Bretton, prior of, 555
Monks, acquiring bondfolk, 170; agriculture under, 146 n., ch. XVII *passim*; alms of, 297, 368, (inefficient), 380, 382; charity neglected by, 197; Church services neglected by, 357; commons enclosed by, 200, 223 (*and see* Clearings, Enclosures, Pioneers); cost of living of, 382; dancing forbidden to, 216; debts of, 297; decay of poverty among, 211, 280, 285; duel-rights of, 190 ff., 557; embezzlement by, 297 n.; few priests among early monks, 211; fines demanded by, 200; food-rations of, 317; Greek and Roman, 168; horses for, 317, 368; hospitality of, 296, (neglected), 301, 368–9; hunting by, 215, app. 29; hunting forbidden to, 216; and labour, 355; as landlords, *see* Monastic; lawsuits of, 377, *and see* Meaux; as lawyers, 206; literary culture among, 210 n.; manor-dues inherited by, 198; monopolies enforced by, 84; and mortuaries, ch. XIV *passim*; oppression of peasants by, 360, 364; as pioneers, 218, 224 n., app. 30, *and see* Clearings, Enclosures, Monastic, Pioneers; and poor-rate, 381; protection of woods by, 223; privileges of, 66, 196; quarrels of, 338; and rents, 181 n., 199, 285; and serfs, 14, 17, chs. XI, XII *passim*, 351, app. 23, (dues), ch. XVI *passim*, 377, (emancipation), 147, (sale of), 147; and tithes, 200; trading by, 285 n.; unpopular, 280, 377; voluntary bondage under, 142 n.; wandering abroad, ch. XVII *passim*; and wine-selling, 61
Monopolies, ch. VI *passim*; of breeding-animals, 196, 198; of cider-press, 176 n.; of doves, 77; of fords and waterways, 17; in France, 58; of mill, 17, 55 n., 78 n., 84, 130; and monks, 84, 196; of

oven, 17, 55 ff., 84; of smithy, 85 n.; of wine, 59, 130
Mons, 333
Monsteretum, Cluniac monastery of, 199 n.
Montague, *see* Salisbury
Montaigne, 465
Montalembert, 149; his misstatements, 197, 218, app. 4; *Moines d'Occident*, 63, 467
Montbertoud, 197
Monte Cassino, Aligerno, abbot of, 210; and serfs, 504
Montesquieu, 170, 373
Montfaucon, Gui de, 557
Montfort-Tettnang, Count von, 361
Montgomery, Roger de, 73
Montigny, Lady Agnes of, 157 n.
Montpellier, 479
Montréal, 64
Mont-Ronault, 193
Mont-St-Michel, 57, 193, 220, 465
Montvallat, M. de, 468
Moore, Dr John, 121
Moots, moot-halls, 70
Morals, of peasants, ch. XVIII *passim*, 265, 319, 335
More, Sir Thomas, 526; *Dialogues*, 346 n.; on enclosures, 200, 228, 485; on Gratian's *Decretum*, 508; on judicial bribery, 225; on priests' work, 282 n., 295; on sheep-rearing, 225; *Utopia*, 200, 228
Moreton Hampstead, 448
Morimond, 217
Morlaix, Bernard of, 192–3; *On the Contempt of this World*, 242
Morley, Lord, 414
Morris, William, 6, 7, 317, 387
Mörse, 249 n.
Morteau, 197
Mortmain, *see* Heriot, Mortuary, Statute
Morton's Dyke, 219 n.
Mortuary, 17, 75–7, 120, 172, 288–90, 300, app. 12; customs relating to, 76; exacted by monks, ch. XIV *passim*, 363; not exacted, 173; ordered by Canon Law, 173; percentages of, 365; values of, 75. *And see* Heriot
Mosbach, 107
Moselle, R., 182, 440
Moses, 233, 463, 521, 526
Motcombe Lane, 70
Mottisfont, monastery of, 502
Moyes, Mgr., 257 n.
Muisis, *see* Gilles
Mulberries, 218 n.
multura [*multa, moulte*], 56